Computational Advancements in End-User Technologies:
Emerging Models and Frameworks

Steve Clarke
University of Hull, UK

INFORMATION SCIENCE REFERENCE
Hershey · New York

Director of Editorial Content:	Kristin Klinger
Senior Managing Editor:	Jamie Snavely
Assistant Managing Editor:	Michael Brehm
Publishing Assistant:	Sean Woznicki
Typesetter:	Sean Woznicki
Cover Design:	Lisa Tosheff
Printed at:	Yurchak Printing Inc.

Published in the United States of America by
Information Science Reference (an imprint of IGI Global)
701 E. Chocolate Avenue
Hershey PA 17033
Tel: 717-533-8845
Fax: 717-533-8661
E-mail: cust@igi-global.com
Web site: http://www.igi-global.com/reference

Library of Congress Cataloging-in-Publication Data

Computational advancements in end-user technologies : emerging models and frameworks / Steve Clarke, editor.
p. cm.
Includes bibliographical references and index.
Summary: "This book contains leading research and practices into the advancement, significance, and comprehensive nature of end-user computing"-- Provided by publisher.

ISBN 978-1-60566-687-7 (hbk.) -- ISBN 978-1-60566-688-4 (ebook) 1. End-user computing. 2. Information management. 3. Information technology. 4. Management information systems. I. Clarke, Steve, 1950- II. Clarke, Steve.

QA76.9.E53C66 2010
004.01'9--dc22

2009032968

British Cataloguing in Publication Data
A Cataloguing in Publication record for this book is available from the British Library.

All work contributed to this book is new, previously-unpublished material. The views expressed in this book are those of the authors, but not necessarily of the publisher.

Editorial Advisory Board

Table of Contents

Detailed Table of Contents

To solve complicated problems, people often seek input from others. Knowledge management systems (KMSs) provide help in this activity by offering a computer-mediated approach to information sharing. However, if the KMS contains content that is obsolete or incomplete, those using the system may expend greater amounts of effort to detect what content is worthwhile or they risk relying on poor inputs, which may lead to less accurate solutions to their problems. As a result, most KMSs include rating schemes as part of the user interface designed to help those using the system identify high-quality content. Rating schemes depend on current users rating the quality of the existing content, guiding subsequent users in future content searches. If specific ratings are low in validity, then they may not reflect the true content quality (unintentionally or intentionally). This chapter provides a robust summary of the KMS literature and draws on the effort-accuracy trade-off framework to offer the results of a research study. The research study examines how rating validity influences how KMS users employ their limited cognitive resources to search and evaluate KMS content, with the goal of finding and using the highest-quality content. Through an experimental design, the study described herein manipulates rating validity and content quality in a replicated KMS setting and examines how users trade off search and evaluation effort. The results of the study demonstrate that rating validity differentially influences how KMS search and evaluation effort relates to decision accuracy. The chapter concludes with a discussion of the study findings and ideas for future research.

Knowledge management (KM) is a critical practice by which a firm's intellectual capital is created, stored and shared. This has lead to a rich research agenda within which knowledge management systems (KMS) have been a key focus. Our research reveals that an important element of KM practice--knowledge appraisal—is considered in only a fragmentary and incomplete way in research. Knowledge appraisal reflects the multi-level process by which a firm's knowledge is evaluated by the organization or individual for its value. The processes are highly intertwined with the use of the KMS. It therefore requires consideration of KA across multiple levels and types of knowledge across the entire KM cycle. To achieve this goal, the authors develop and present a taxonomy of knowledge appraisal practices and discuss their role in the KM lifecycle emphasizing implications for research and practice.

Organizations position their formal knowledge management (KM) initiatives as a continuous process of deriving strategic benefits from the knowledge resources dispersed in the various internal constituencies. While most organizations implement a rewards program attached to their KM initiative, the influence exerted by such programs on employees' responses to organizational KM is less well understood. In this context, this article focuses on the KM initiative of Rexon,1 a leading Indian software services and products company recognised globally as a successful KM exponent. Adopting the case study methodology, the authors conducted intensive fieldwork for 6 months over a 2 year period at Rexon. Evidence from the case highlights how a KM-related rewards program was used to build awareness about organizational KMS and how employees responded to the rewards program. The theoretical and managerial contributions of the study are discussed.

This article discusses system use as a measure of knowledge management success. It is proposed that for knowledge management systems (KMS) it is not the amount of use that is important, but rather the quality of that use and the intention to use the KMS when appropriate. Evidence is provided to support this proposition and a knowledge management system success model incorporating this proposition is discussed. Additionally, findings are provided that show that new users to an organization use the KMS differently than experienced users and implications of this difference are discussed.

Collaboration is fundamental to the goals and success of knowledge management (KM) initiatives aimed at supporting decision making and problem solving. Yet many KM approaches and systems do not provide explicit mechanisms which allow knowledge to be collaboratively built up, validated and

Contemporary end users are more knowledgeable about computing technologies than the end users of the early '80s. However, many researchers still use the end user classification scheme proposed by Rockart and Flannery (1983) more than two decades ago. This scheme is inadequate to classify contemporary end users since it is based mainly on their knowledge and ignores other crucial dimensions such as control. Cotterman and Kumar (1989) proposed a user cube to classify end users based on the development, operation, and control dimensions of end user computing (EUC). Using this cube, users can be classified into eight distinct groups. In this research, a 10-item instrument is proposed to operationalize the user cube. Such an instrument would help managers to identify the status of EUC in their firms and to take appropriate action. Based on the data collected from 292 end users, the instrument was tested for construct, convergent, and discriminant validities. Researchers can use this instrument to study the interaction between constructs such as development and control with end user computing satisfaction (EUCS).

Chapter 9
Social and Usage-Process Motivations for Consumer Internet Access 159
Thomas F. Stafford, University of Memphis, USA

Differences between light and heavy users of America Online are investigated using theoretical expectations derived from recent research on uses and gratifications theory. Measures of Internet-usage-process gratifications and Internet socialization gratifications were utilized to test for differences between light and heavy Internet users in the consumer market, and it was expected that heavy users would be more socially motivated in their Internet use while light users would be more motivated by gratifications related to usage processes. However, results indicate that both heavy and light users are more motivated by usage factors, although the difference between usage and social motivation was more pronounced for heavy users. Heavy users are more socially motivated than light users, but both heavy and light users show a significant preference for process uses and gratifications as compared to social uses and gratifications for Internet use.

Chapter 10
General and Specific Computer Self-Efficacy: An Empirical Comparison of their Strength in Predicting General and Specific Outcomes.. 176
James P. Downey, University of Central Arkansas, USA
R. Kelly Rainer Jr., Auburn University, USA
Summer E. Bartczak, University of Central Arkansas, USA

Computer self-efficacy is known to operate at multiple levels, from application-specific sub-domains like spreadsheets to a judgment of ability for the entire computing domain (general computer self-efficacy-GCSE). Conventional wisdom and many recent studies contend that the level of self-efficacy (specific to general) should match the level of its related constructs to maximize predictive power (Bandura, 1997; Chen, et al., 2001; Pajares, 1996). This thinking claims, for example, that GCSE should be used with a general attitude like computer anxiety (and vice versa). This study examines whether such a limitation is theoretically and empirically sound, given that SE judgments generalize across domains. Results indicate any self-efficacy judgment (specific or general) significantly relates to both general and domain-specific

constructs. These results suggest that an individual's cognitive processing of ability level is multi-faceted; that is, every SE judgment consists of general and specific components. The implication is that CSE is simultaneously generalizable and formative in nature. The results also suggest that the relationship between general and specific CSE is mediated by one's ability level in the specific domain.

Augmented-reality technologies as a new way of human-computer interaction make possible real-time modification of our perception of reality without active user interference. This article introduces the prototype of an augmented-reality shopping-assistant device, the PromoPad, based on a handheld tablet PC allowing see-through vision with augmentations. While this new interaction utilizing augmented reality that places products into contextual settings can enhance shopping experience and suggest complementary products, it also has challenges and issues when used in a public environment such as a store setting. This article discusses the design and implementation of the PromoPad, and addresses the issues and possible solutions. The concept of dynamic contextualization is further investigated in this setting with a list of possible context modifications and their relation to advertising and the psychology of consumer purchasing.

Electronic voting, or e-voting, is a relatively closed process that contains inherent risks associated with the potential for voting irregularities, translation errors, and inappropriate manipulation (Oravec, 2005). To develop a greater understanding of trust issues surrounding the use of e-voting, an investigation into the public trust and the relationship between trust and electronic voting technology were assessed. Men and women of various ethnicities, ages, educational backgrounds, technological experiences, political affiliations, and prior experience with e-voting participated in this study. Rogers' (1995) taxonomy of adopters—innovators, early adopters, early majority, late majority, and laggards—was used to classify individuals based on their willingness to participate in e-voting. A principle-components factor analysis (PCFA) with separate tests for discriminant validity and multiple-regression analyses were used to confirm the hypotheses. The findings suggest that innovators and early adopters are more likely to trust technology and express an intention to use an e-voting system.

While there has been research on the diffusion of a particular type of innovation, few if any studies have examined the acceptance of a set of innovations (behavioral innovativeness) over time. This study using the Rasch methodology found evidence that computer hardware innovations are adopted in a particular order.

This study looks at face to face (FTF) and virtual teams, the personality trait of agreeability and the impact of specific communication technology on cohesion and performance. We use the media richness theory to facilitate our literature review and to guide the development of our hypotheses.

Evidence has been growing that suggests Internet-based opinion systems influence users' purchase decisions. One of the most popular systems are the rating schemes found on Web sites such as eBay.com, expertcentral.com, bizrate.com, epinions.com, slashdot.net, moviefone.com, citysearch.com, etc. Rating schemes affect user productivity by changing their ability to search and find products and services on the Internet. Regrettably, ratings schemes can provide misleading information because those inputting ratings have personal subjective opinions, or they want to manipulate other users' behaviors. For example, an author of a book may ask family and friends to rate his or her book highly and his or her competitors' books poorly. This chapter provides a robust summary of the rating scheme literature and delineates the sources of rating scheme bias and the potential effects of this bias on how users utilize ratings. In a research study, data were gathered from 73 upper-division undergraduates completing a preliminary survey with open- and closed-ended questions and 164 additional students completing an exploratory survey to support the preliminary survey results. Based on the research findings, the chapter discusses preliminary insights and develops a set of propositions to encourage a more rigorous and in-depth examination of rating scheme bias by both practitioners and academicians.

End-user satisfaction has always been an important component of Information Systems (IS) success. This is also true for online applications, including online shopping systems, where in addition to being a customer, the shoppers play the role of end-users. Shoppers may not come back to or make a purchase on a Web site if they have an unsatisfactory experience. In this research, the authors focus on this aspect of online shopping by examining shoppers' experiences as end-users.

Preface

Welcome to the latest annual volume of Advances in End-User Computing (EUC). The wide range of subjects embraced by EUC research and practice is evidenced by the spread of topics in this volume. The internet and knowledge management continue to dominate, but other issues covered include common domains such as decision modelling, end-user classification, call centres, compliance, and innovation. In addition, more recently developing areas such as e-voting and media richness are also represented. These chapters continue to provide new insights into EUC, representing some of the most current investigations into a wide range of End-User Computing issues.

As always, we hope that you, as researchers, educators, and professionals in the domain, find something to enhance your understanding within these recent developments, and, more particularly, that you enjoy reading about them. A summary of the contents of the text is given below.

In **Chapter 1**, Robin S. Poston and Cheri Speier look at how knowledge management systems (KMSs) support us by providing a computer-mediated approach to information sharing as we seek help when solving complex problems. Clearly, however, if the content provided by the KMS is obsolete or incomplete, time will be wasted detecting and correcting this. The solution to this problem in many KMSs is to provide a rating scheme as part of the user interface, enabling users to assess the quality of the content. Unfortunately these ratings may be inaccurate, and fail to reflect the true content quality. This chapter undertakes the important task of examining how rating scheme validity influences how users trade-off search and evaluation effort for decision-making accuracy. The findings provide valuable insight into KMS user interface design, and help us to understand how end-users utilise the knowledge in KMSs to make decisions.

Hannah Standing Rasmussen and Nicole Haggerty consider knowledge appraisal to be an important element of knowledge management (KM) practice which is addressed poorly in KM research. In **Chapter 2** it is argued that knowledge appraisal should be seen as a multi-level process by which a firm's knowledge is evaluated by the organization or individuals within that organization for its value. Knowledge appraisal processes are highly intertwined with the use of the KM system, such that an understanding of how they work requires consideration of knowledge appraisal across multiple levels, and of types of knowledge across the entire KM cycle. Hannah and Nicole have developed a taxonomy of knowledge appraisal practices to address these issues, and this taxonomy is discussed within the chapter.

Most organizations implement a rewards program attached to knowledge management (KM) initiatives, but, argues Mayasandra N. Ravishankar, the influence exerted by such programs on employees' responses to organizational KM is poorly understood. **Chapter 3** looks at a longitudinal (over a two year period) case study of Rexon, a leading Indian software services and products company recognised globally as a successful KM exponent. The outcomes of the research demonstrate how employees responded to the rewards program, and highlight how a KM-related rewards program can be used to build awareness about organizational KM systems.

Chapter 4 looks at system use as a measure of knowledge management success. The problem, from Murray E. Jennex's perspective, is that all too often success is seen to be determined by the amount of use, whilst in fact it is the quality and appropriateness of that use that really matters. Evidence is provided to support this proposition and a knowledge management system success model incorporating this is discussed. Additionally, findings are provided showing how the approach to using a KMS differs between new and experienced users, and implications of this difference are discussed.

The starting point for Debbie Richards in **Chapter 5** is the concept of knowledge management as being concerned with assisting the decision and problem solving process. Call centers use and reuse knowledge about problem issues, possible solutions, and, importantly, the link between certain problems and potential solutions. The extent to which knowledge which is "systematized" in a KM system frequently fails to provide the "answer", is evidenced by the frequency with which *implicit* "know-how" is brought into play. Acquiring, accessing, maintaining, sharing, reconciling, and reusing knowledge in its various forms are particular challenges in the call center domain where the knowledge needed is complex and constantly changing. This problem is exacerbated by the frequently short-term nature of call center employees, resulting in implicit knowledge being lost. The research suggests an approach which allows knowledge, in the form of rules, to be incrementally acquired as a problem arises, in the form of cases, as part of the daily routine. Using this approach, knowledge workers are able to collaboratively and incrementally capture and maintain the information they use daily for troubleshooting.

Ashley Braganza and Ray Hackney look at the Sarbanes Oxley Act in **Chapter 6**, which was passed in response to financial misstatements and high-profile corporate frauds such as Enron and WorldCom, and aims to reduce the level and scale of financial fraud due to an organization's misrepresentation of its financial condition. They argue that, whilst information systems are vital to successful compliance with Section 404 of the Act, there is little published academic literature that explains how IS organizations might implement 404. From an in-depth case study analysis, they see the key to successful implementation as being directives from senior authorities, financial and resource subsidies, standards being set and adhered to, and knowledge being deployed. The findings deliver a real insight into this complex area of compliance.

In **Chapter 7**, Akhilesh Bajaj investigates the decision models of IS managers when evaluating computing architectures for use in an organization. The research uses a methodology which, by constructing individual decision models for each expert and novice in the study, examines and compares both experts and novices undertaking this task. Through this approach they are able to evaluate the growing consensus in the management literature that while experts may follow different processes, very often their performance does not differ significantly from novices in the business domain.

Chittibabu Govindarajulu and Bay Arinze contends in **Chapter 8** that, whilst many researchers still use the end user classification scheme proposed by Rockart and Flannery more than two decades ago, this scheme is inadequate to classify *contemporary* end users since it is based mainly on their knowledge and ignores other crucial dimensions such as control. As an alternative, the user cube has been proposed to classify end users based on the development, operation, and control dimensions of end user computing (EUC). In this research, a 10-item instrument is tested and proposed to operationalize the user cube, application of which, it is argued, would help managers to identify the status of EUC in their firms and to take appropriate action.

In **Chapter 9**, Thomas F. Stafford looks at the differences between light and heavy users of America Online using theoretical expectations derived from recent research on uses and gratifications theory. Measures of Internet-usage-process gratifications and Internet socialization gratifications were utilized to test for differences between light and heavy Internet users in the consumer market. The expectation of the research was that heavy users would be more socially motivated in their Internet use while light users would be more motivated by gratifications related to usage processes. However, results indicate that both heavy and light users are more motivated by usage factors, although the difference between usage and social motivation was more pronounced for heavy users. Heavy users are more socially motivated than light users, but both heavy and light users show a significant preference for process uses and gratifications as compared to social uses and gratifications for Internet use.

In **Chapter 10**, the authors look at the important area of computer self-efficacy, and most particularly at how it might be addressed and understood at different levels, varying from application-specific sub domains like spreadsheets at one end of the scale, to a judgment of ability for the entire computing domain (so-called general computer self-efficacy, or GCSE) at the other. Conventional wisdom and many recent studies contend that the level of self-efficacy (specific to general) should match the level of its related constructs to maximize predictive power. So, for example, GCSE should be used with a general attitude like computer anxiety. This study examines whether such a view is theoretically and empirically sound.

The authors of **Chapter 11** introduce the prototype of an augmented-reality shopping-assistant device, the PromoPad, based on a handheld tablet PC allowing see-through vision with augmentations. The idea is to provide an experience as close as possible to the reality of the "live" shopping experience, and from this to judge whether such an approach has the ability to enhance the shopping experience. The design and implementation of the PromoPad are discussed, and issues and possible solutions which arise from this are addressed. The concept of dynamic contextualization is further investigated in this setting with a list of possible context modifications and their relation to advertising and the psychology of consumer purchasing.

Susan K. Lippert and Ekundayo B. Ojumu have conducted research into electronic voting for **Chapter 12**, which they characterize as a relatively closed process that contains inherent risks associated with the potential for voting irregularities, translation errors, and inappropriate manipulation. To understand these problems, they have investigated the relationship between trust and electronic voting, using Rogers' taxonomy of adopters—innovators, early adopters, early majority, late majority, and laggards, to classify individuals based on their willingness to participate in e-voting. The findings suggest that innovators and early adopters are more likely to trust technology and express an intention to use an e-voting system.

In **Chapter 13**, Geoffrey N. Soutar and Steven Ward have examined the acceptance of a set of computer-based innovations (behavioral innovativeness), finding evidence that computer hardware innovations are adopted in a particular order, whilst computer software acceptance may be application-based. The results obtained suggest a unidimensional order for the purchase of computer hardware, but that the computer software decision appears to be more complex and a multidimensional innovation pattern may exist for such products.

The authors of **Chapter 14** argue that communications that are dependent on media richness are affected by individual user characteristics. Media richness theory suggests that a group's cohesion and performance are impacted by the technological modes of communication used; a situation exacerbated by the nature of groups, which often experience varying levels of individual member agreeability, further affecting cohesion and performance. This study identifies significant differences between groups, using specific media to communicate cohesion, the change in cohesion, agreeability, and performance.

By looking into the rating schemes found on Web sites such as eBay.com, Robin S. Poston and Marla B. Royne provide us with an insight into the extent to which end-users are influenced by Internet-based opinion mechanisms before making a purchase. End users clearly use rating schemes to find products and services on the Internet, but these can offer misleading information, either because the submitted ratings are simply subjective opinions, or because ratings may even be submitted to try to manipulate other users' behaviors. **Chapter 15** examines the sources of rating scheme bias and the potential effects of this bias on how users utilize ratings, and offers preliminary insights aimed at encouraging a more rigorous and in-depth examination of rating scheme bias by both practitioners and academicians.

In **Chapter 16**, Chung-Tzer Liu and Yi Maggie Guo look at end-user satisfaction, with a particular focus on online applications, including online shopping systems. They argue that it is important for online shopping that end-users have a satisfactory experience, since they will not return to the supplier or even to internet shopping generally if this is not the case. They focus on this aspect of online shopping by examining shoppers experiences as end-users.

CONCLUSION: CONTRIBUTION TO THE FIELD

End User Computing continues to be a major computing domain in which change and advancement shows no sign of easing. Advances in EUC aims to reflect this, and we hope that you will agree that the current issue has succeeded in this aim and has offered a valuable contemporary insight into EUC.

As always, enjoy reading.

Steve Clarke
Editor-in-Chief
Advances in End User Computing, Volume 2009

Chapter 1
Effort-Accuracy Trade-Off in Using Knowledge Management Systems

Robin S. Poston
University of Memphis, USA

Cheri Speier
Michigan State University, USA

ABSTRACT

To solve complicated problems, people often seek input from others. Knowledge management systems (KMSs) provide help in this activity by offering a computer-mediated approach to information sharing. However, if the KMS contains content that is obsolete or incomplete, those using the system may expend greater amounts of effort to detect what content is worthwhile or they risk relying on poor inputs, which may lead to less accurate solutions to their problems. As a result, most KMSs include rating schemes as part of the user interface designed to help those using the system identify high-quality content. Rating schemes depend on current users rating the quality of the existing content, guiding subsequent users in future content searches. If specific ratings are low in validity, then they may not reflect the true content quality (unintentionally or intentionally). This chapter provides a robust summary of the KMS literature and draws on the effort-accuracy trade-off framework to offer the results of a research study. The research study examines how rating validity influences how KMS users employ their limited cognitive resources to search and evaluate KMS content, with the goal of finding and using the highest-quality content. Through an experimental design, the study described herein manipulates rating validity and content quality in a replicated KMS setting and examines how users trade off search and evaluation effort. The results of the study demonstrate that rating validity differentially influences how KMS search and evaluation effort relates to decision accuracy. The chapter concludes with a discussion of the study findings and ideas for future research.

DOI: 10.4018/978-1-60566-687-7.ch001

INTRODUCTION

Like other information systems, knowledge management systems (KMSs) support the efficient and effective processing of information by facilitating the location of high-quality content from the mass of knowledge they contain (Fang, 2000; Kim & Compton, 2004; Nevo et al., 2003; Orlikowski, 2000). KMSs are shared repositories of potentially useful knowledge to support end users within the same work group or organization (Davenport & Hansen, 1999; Jones & Kochtanek, 2004). KMSs are designed with interfaces that incorporate rating schemes to help users screen out irrelevant, low-quality content (i.e., knowledge). Rating schemes allow KMS users to provide feedback about the quality of content through ratings, potentially improving subsequent content search and evaluation efforts (Shon & Musen, 1999; Standifird, 2001; Wathen & Burkell, 2002). However, future users may be misled if the ratings do not accurately reflect the content quality (Dellarocas, 2003; Resnick et al., 2000). Ratings can be misleading because those supplying the ratings may manipulate ratings intentionally or may rate the content based on a context very different from the users' current context (Cosley et al., 2003; Cramton, 2001). Consequently, users relying on misleading ratings may select high-rated, low-quality content that is obsolete and incomplete to use in their particular task (Cosley et al., 2003; Melnik & Alm, 2002).

Decision-making theory suggests decision–makers are constrained by their limited cognitive resources when performing knowledge tasks (Miller, 1956). Because of this constraint, decision-makers are motivated to use as little effort as necessary to solve a problem yet they want to maximize their chances of making the most accurate decisions (Payne et al., 1993). This chapter draws on the effort-accuracy trade-off framework to examine how rating validity influences how KMS users employ their limited cognitive resources to search and evaluate KMS content, with the goal of finding and using the highest-quality content in their task. KMSs are complex systems with the potential to deliver substantial competitive advantage though the efficient and effective sharing of unique, non-imitable firm resources (i.e., employees' knowledge) (Alavi & Tiwana, 2002). Therefore, it is important to better understand how user interface designs, such as rating schemes, affect how users use the knowledge in KMSs in order to improve KMS content search and retrieval. Developing insight into these issues will inform KMS designers and managers of the importance of ratings and ultimately how to develop more useful KMSs (Zhang & Dillon, 2003).

Prior research suggests KMS users use ratings in making decisions about KMS content usage (Poston & Speier, 2005). However, this research fails to adequately explain how ratings schemes influence how users trade off their efforts to search and evaluate content for accuracy in decision-making. Through an experiment, this study manipulates rating validity and content quality in a replicated KMS setting and examines how users trade off search and evaluation effort.

KNOWLEDGE MANAGEMENT SYSTEM USAGE

KMSs are technology-based systems that help employees make future use of the tacit and explicit knowledge of others (Alavi & Leidner, 2001). This chapter focuses on the "repository" type of KMS which emphasizes the documentation and storage of knowledge (i.e., KMS content) to facilitate its reuse through access to the codified expertise (Grover & Davenport, 2001; Jones & Price, 2004). Research has discussed social and technical limitations of KMS usage; however this chapter specifically examines how end users interact with KMSs to locate content to use in knowledge tasks (Alavi & Leidner, 2001). KMSs often include design features such as search algorithms and rating schemes to help users find relevant and reliable content (Fisher et al., 2003). A research stream examining search algorithms exists (Fang, 2000; Park & Kim, 2000); yet little is known about how users use rating schemes, especially in the KMS environment.

The complex conversion of information to knowledge suggests that knowledge is a multi-dimensional construct with more multifaceted characteristics than those of information. One viewpoint defines knowledge as an object to be stored and manipulated, another emphasizes the organization of knowledge to help workers access it, and a third views knowledge as a process of concurrently knowing and performing by applying expertise to solve novel problems (Kulkarni et al. 2006/2007). Another viewpoint states that knowledge does not exist without the knower because it is "shaped by one's initial stock of knowledge and the inflow of new stimuli" (Fahey & Prusak, 1998). Further along this direction, knowledge is defined as an "understanding gained through experience or study; the sum or range of what has been perceived, discovered, and learned" (Schubert et al., 1998). Regardless of the definition of knowledge, this chapter treats knowledge as the content of knowledge repositories or KMS and is concerned with how users search and evaluate the KMS knowledge content.

Thus the issue is one of knowledge search and evaluation in KMS. While people create knowledge, they also do not remember it or lose track of it. Organizational and individual memory is required in order to store, organize and retrieve knowledge (Palanisamy 2007). Organizational memory is the collection of individuals' memory and it is defined as "the means by which knowledge from the past experience, and events influence present organizational activities" (Stein and Zwass, 1995). Organizational memory includes knowledge residing as written documents, structured databases, expert systems, and organizational procedures and processes. Individual memory is based on each individual's observations, experiences, and actions (Stein and Zwass, 1995). Knowledge storage refers to the tacit and explicit knowledge that is captured and documented. Storing knowledge, as in a KMS, is essential for use in future decisions. Storing knowledge is helpful where there is high employee-turnover where highly valued employees retire or leave taking with them the knowledge and expertise they developed over the years. Through a KMS, the knowledge is retained and employees access it using tools such as databases and query languages in order to search and evaluate the knowledge content.

The process for locating knowledge content is iterative, beginning when KMS users enter keywords into a search engine to access relevant content. A KMS keyword search typically results in a lengthy list of content that users must evaluate to identify high-quality content (Brajnik et al., 2002). Finding high-quality content is difficult because of the sheer amount of information available and the potential for user disorientation given the existence of irrelevant, obsolete and incomplete content (Davenport & Beck, 2001; Farhoomand & Drury, 2002). Users reduce disorientation by evaluating a subset of items instead of every item from the search results (Resnick & Montania, 2003). Ratings (e.g., 1 = worthless through 5 = highly useful) offered by the KMS interface provide key information to guide users in selecting which content to evaluate[1]. Prior research has demonstrated that users rely on ratings to make decisions about KMS content usage (Poston & Speier, 2005).

While rating schemes can appear to be an effective design feature to identify high-quality content, relying on ratings can also create problems. Ratings may not reflect the actual quality of the content (i.e., have low validity) for a variety of reasons (Constant et al., 1994; Hansen & Haas, 2001). First, many ratings are 'taste-dependent' and can be inherently subjective and voluntarily provided. These ratings can be unintentionally biased and inherently noisy (i.e., have a random component in addition to the rater's true feeling about the object), meaning deriving a rating perfectly may never be possible (Jadad & Gagliardi, 1998; Melnik & Alm, 2002). Second, raters may use content in inappropriate contexts, and the effects result in poor perceptions and ratings low in validity (Dellarocas 2003; Resnick et al., 2000). Also, computing contexts describe the physical and social situation in which a system is embedded and these contexts may not be linked to specific content (Moran, 1994). KMSs typically de-emphasize much of the context surrounding its content, making it difficult for KMS users to fully understand the application or boundaries associated with re-using such content (Fisher et al., 2003; Park & Kim, 2000). Finally, ratings may lack validity because those submitting ratings may manipulate the rating value in an attempt to influence others to use content they have contributed (Nielsen, 1999) or to enhance their reputation and standing among their peers (Cosley et al., 2003).

While rating validity issues create difficulties for users, it is often junior employees using the KMS who may lack the experience needed to accurately identifying high-quality content. Senior employees often assign the time-consuming task of finding information to junior employees (Orlikowski, 2000). Junior employees typically understand the task and the context, but have greater uncertainty about judging content quality (Brajnik et al., 2002). A summary of the current research literature addressing knowledge management systems (KMS) is provided in Table 1. This list of current research has been grouped by how each paper informs Improving KMS Technology and Improving KMS Usage Outcomes.

In addition to the KMS research literature, a summary of the current research literature addressing effort-accuracy and search is provided in Table 2.

Given the research performed and challenges of KMS usage, the next section discusses the theoretical background of how users may interact with KMSs to search and evaluate content.

RESEARCH MODEL AND HYPOTHESIS DEVELOPMENT

Ultimately, KMS end users will search and evaluate content until they find the content they want for their task. One view in decision-making theory suggests rational users will perform a complete search and evaluation of all the information available as well as combine the best pieces together (Gigerenzer & Todd, 1999, p. 83). Alternatively, decision-making theory suggests users will search for and evaluate content in ways that minimize effort and maximize accuracy of finding high-quality content. Decision-makers trade off effort for accuracy, often reducing effort (i.e., search and evaluation activities) resulting in less accurate decisions particularly when addressing complex and/or ambiguous decisions (Payne, 1982). The nature of this effort-accuracy trade-off is not fully understood (Chu & Spires, 2000), especially in the KMS context (Mao & Benbasat, 2000). We expect KMS users to follow an effort-accuracy trade-off where they continue expending effort to search and evaluate more content until they believe they have reached the goal of using the highest-quality content in their task. The research model is illustrated in Figure 1.

As part of the effort-accuracy trade-off, decision-makers use simplifying strategies such as heuristics to minimize effort with the goal of maintaining adequate accuracy (Cook, 1993; Svenson, 1979). Research in heuristic usage suggests decision heuristics can provide decision-makers considerable savings of effort and come close to the decision accuracy of performing a complete search and evaluation of alternatives (Payne et al., 1993). Also, the selection of a heuristic is influenced by: (1) the emphasis placed on maximizing accuracy versus saving effort, (2) the constraints which cause decision-makers to choose among heuristics rather than choose between using a heuristic and performing a complete search and evaluation, and (3) certain facets of the decision task (Jarvenpaa, 1989; Payne et al., 1993).

Table 1. Summary of knowledge management (KM) current literature

Study	Area	Research Method	Searching and Evaluating KMS Content	Theory
Improving KMS Technology				
Li et al. 2006	Finding people with similar interests for knowledge sharing	Offers a collaborative filtering technology as a tool for finding people with similar interests	Collaborative filtering recommendation using a centralized knowledge base to retain the knowledge of its users. I.e., www.firefly.com uses the opinion of others to share knowledge about products such as music, books, Web pages, and restaurants.	Agent paradigm and Multi-agent systems
Iyer et al. 2006	Set of coordination requirements for the design of a KMS to support knowledge networks	Analyze 4 cases that capture KM practices representing different KM methods, to understand and identify the coordination requirements	*Create reusable knowledge object* creates knowledge before needed, saving knowledge objects and storing in a repository along with keywords to permit searching. A key issue is to anticipate users' needs. *Generate and select* creates knowledge when needed by presenting a problem and generating alternatives. A key issue is to communicate the details of the problem and to manage the flow of information. *Trial and error* creates knowledge iteratively as potential solutions are tried out and modified based on experience. A key issue is to manage the cost of and to learn from the iterations.	Coordination theory and Text-based process analysis
Kulkarni et al. 2006/ 2007	Organizational factors that complement the technology	Survey administered to managers	*Knowledge content quality* is its relevance, accuracy, timeliness, applicability, comprehensibility, presentation formats, extent of insight, availability of expertise and advice; and *KM system quality* is accessibility, ease of use for retrieval and input, output flexibility to meet needs, search capability, documentation.	DeLone and McLean 1992 and Seddon 1997 models
Nissen 2005/ 2006	Dynamics of knowledge	Field research to build a framework for dynamic knowledge	Techniques for modeling knowledge flows and stocks. Offers model of a KMS for information and data flows to work and knowledge flows to performance.	IS Design Theory and Kernel theory
Nevo and Chan 2007	Integrated view among technologies intended to support knowledge	Delphi method obtains expert group consensus using questionnaires and feedback	KM capabilities: *Enables knowledge sharing* with an expertise locator; *Includes sophisticated search and retrieval mechanisms* using intelligent search, quick response to queries, fast and easy retrieval of stored knowledge; *Includes a mechanism to assure the quality* and integrity of the knowledge with links to the creators of the knowledge for accountability, feedback for users to evaluate the content used, standardized templates and protocols for updating the knowledge.	Knowledge-based view of the firm
Hsu 2006	Exploiting KMS to effectively manage intellectual property	Case study on a leading bioscience firm	Organizations create knowledge, but they also forget it. Advanced technology and query languages enhance knowledge storage and efficiency of data retrieval, so that access occurs at any time and any place.	Organizational climate and structure, Management style, and Rewards systems
Palanisamy 2007	Organizational culture and KM in ERP implementation	Survey of ERP project managers, project team, IT professionals, CIOs, users, top managers, vendors, and consultants	Advanced tools such as databases, query languages etc. are used as tools in enriching organizational memory and data retrieval. It allows for ERP users to connect and communicate over great distances enabling the creation of new knowledge that might not otherwise occur.	Organizational culture

continued on the following page

Table 1. continued

Study	Area	Research Method	Searching and Evaluating KMS Content	Theory
Gottschalk 2006	Propositions for KM systems supporting outsourcing relationships	Model building	KMS provide tools such as Word, Excel and e-mail at stage 1. At stage 2, an address book is needed, to find updated information or vendor experts with appropriate knowledge. At stage 3, clients need access to the vendor's technical database. KMS should use all methods to facilitate expertise from the vendor flowing to client.	Resource-based theory
Datta 2007	Agent-mediated knowledge-in-motion model for knowledge creation and reuse	Model employing human and software agents to enhance the creation, transfer, application, and dissemination of knowledge	Software information agents are scouts in the transformation of data to information and are capable of using modularity for querying heterogeneous data sources and standardization of data by syntax and structure, which will contribute to higher levels of information acquisition and assimilation than human information agents alone.	Social network perspective
Improving KMS Usage Outcomes				
Cho et al. 2008	Peer-based versus expert-centric knowledge refinement	Experimental study verified with data collected from a consulting firm	Peer-based versus expert-centric knowledge refinement--to determine which knowledge submissions to be included and refined to make them efficacious. Examined impact of experts vs. peers on the quality of codified knowledge used by non-experts. Knowledge "distance" between experts and non-experts impaired expert-based knowledge-refinement, while the close knowledge distance among peers facilitated knowledge refinement.	Cognitive psychology
Wu and Wang 2006	KMS success model	Survey of firms using KMS	Perceived KMS benefits--Most KMS benefits are intangible, indirect, and long term. KMS benefits measured by those using it: helps me acquire new knowledge and innovative ideas, helps me effectively manage and store knowledge that I need, enables me to accomplish tasks more efficiently, My performance on the job is enhanced by KMS, KMS improves the quality of my work life.	DeLone and McLean's model
Prieto and Easterby-Smith 2006	Knowledge transmitted via social interactions a source of dynamic capabilities	Case study of the evolution of a new international business	Need to integrate the 'technology' side and the 'social' side of KM usage.	Dynamic capabilities and Knowledge management
Li and Kettinger 2006	Knowledge creation	Develop a theory of knowledge creation, using the decomposition and solution of a problem hierarchy	New knowledge is the combination of knowledge elements in the sub-problems. Tentative knowledge is generated through local search (i.e., exploitation and refinement of existing solutions) and distant search (i.e., exploration and experimentation). Information indicates whether existing knowledge, from within and outside the company, can solve the problem, but not how that knowledge is improved to produce a better solution.	Evolutionary information-processing theory
Olivera et al. 2008	Why people make KMS contributions in geographically distributed organizations	Provide model of contribution behaviors with mediating mechanisms: awareness; searching and matching; and formulation and delivery	Knowledge sharing involves matching personal knowledge and the situation described by the requester. The matching process requires an individual to search internal memory and external memory aids, such as KMS and may result in an exact, an approximate, or no match. Individuals take first acceptable solution rather than engaging in optimal search behavior. If matches are not initially found, search costs increase, and without motivation, the search will end with no contribution.	Human problem solving and Cognitive motivation theories

continued on the following page

Table 1. continued

Study	Area	Research Method	Searching and Evaluating KMS Content	Theory
Paul 2006	Collaborative activities in virtual settings enable parties to achieve their objectives	Case studies in the context of 10 telemedicine projects	Highlights the knowledge aspects involved in collaboration, provides insights into how collaboration enables parties to achieve outcomes that would be difficult to realize by working alone. Emphasizes the communication of relevant specialized knowledge to the situation at hand. Focuses on 3 aspects of KM—knowledge transfer, discovery, and creation—that represent collaboration in virtual settings.	Knowledge management perspective
Deng 2008	Market-based approach for a sharing-enabled KM model	Case study for a KM initiative implemented in a consulting firm	A knowledge market-based analysis identifies knowledge buyers, sellers, and brokers involved in the KM project (Who), understands their motives for participating in the knowledge market (Why), analyzes what they need and what they can offer (What), facilitates knowledge transactions (How).	Knowledge market analogy
Gray and Durcikova 2005/2006	Role of knowledge repositories in speed versus learning in user performance	Interviews and survey of technical support workers	Focuses on demand for—not supply of—knowledge, looks at analysts' learning orientation, perceived work demands, and risk aversion in predicting their knowledge sourcing behavior. Not much learning when using technical support repositories. Analysts focused on finding solutions not building a better understanding of the products they support.	Knowledge sourcing theory
Wang et al. 2007	Firms align KMS support to strategic needs to get dynamic capability link to performance	Survey of manufacturing firms	Examine KM processes (gather, store, communicate, synthesize, disseminate) along with corresponding KMS functions. Key KM activities lead to better outcomes for KMS usage.	Knowledge-based dynamic capabilities theory
Zimmer et al. 2007/2008	Individual perceptions of KM sources available and how this affects use of different types of sources	Survey of professionals	Examine the effects of accessibility and quality, and comparisons and trade-offs between relational and non-relational sources. Source accessibility and quality affect usage of a source and this is moderated by the type of source with accessibility having less effect on the use of relational sources. Use of each source type was affected by the accessibility and quality of alternative sources types.	Learning behavior
Huang et al. 2007/2008	Knowledge repository pricing	Experiment to study users' price and knowledge preferences for access to knowledge repository content	Single price of repository access or knowledge items sold individually. Consider price, knowledge, and user characteristics. Single price repository pricing attracts users and is essential to initiate the transfer process, yet individual pricing encourages knowledge preferences and is thus an effective approach for learning.	Mental accounting and Transaction decoupling
Nordheim and Paivarinta 2006	Implementation of enterprise KMS	Case study at a large oil company	Goals: 1. establish a best practice for information sharing across organizational and geographical boundaries, 2. establish information traceability and easy, accurate and secure access to information throughout the information life cycle, 3. improve search and retrieval functions for information sharing and reuse, and 4. limit duplication of data showing where all information is.	Motors of development and change: teleological, evolution, life-cycle, and dialectical
Lee and Ahn 2007	Reward systems for intra-organizational knowledge sharing	Analytical model building	*Group based* reward inferior to *Individual based* reward for firm's net payoff from knowledge sharing. Workers with more productive knowledge may not share under a group based reward, this is mitigated by organizational ownership norms.	Organizational citizenship behavior and Individual motivational drivers

continued on the following page

Table 1. continued

Study	Area	Research Method	Searching and Evaluating KMS Content	Theory
Haas 2006	Value of knowledge gathering	Multi-method field study using quality ratings of project outcomes and survey data from project-team members	Value of knowledge gathering is greater when enhance team processing, sense-making, and buffering capabilities. Capability enhancing moderated relationship between knowledge gathering and project quality as measured by slack time, organizational experience, and decision-making autonomy. More knowledge gathering helped teams to perform effectively but hurt performance under conditions that limited their capabilities to utilize knowledge.	Organizational design
Ghosh and Scott 2007	KM processes and organizational enablers	Interview and survey about designing and deploying a KMS in a hospital	Assessed structure, culture, and technology of KM processes: acquisition, application, conversion, and protection. KM effectiveness is based on KM infrastructure capability and KM process capability.	Organizational enablers
Ravishankar 2008	KM-related rewards program	Case study of the KM initiative of a software services and products company with a successful KM system	Organizational rewards program generates interest and awareness about KM initiatives among users. Rewards program leads to focus on rewards and ignoring the main reasons for the initiative. A rewards program used in the initial post-implementation phase to build awareness and then removed in a phased manner.	Organizational socio-cultural theory
Lin and Huang 2008	Antecedents to KMS usage	Survey of KMS users on task inter-dependence, perceived task technology fit, KMS self-efficacy, and personal outcome expectation	*Personal outcome expectation*: associated with using KMSs related to expectations of change in image or status or to expectations of rewards, such as promotions, raises, or praise; *Performance outcome expectation*: associated with improvements in job performance (efficiency and effectiveness) associated with using KMSs; *KMS usage*: The degree of use of KMSs in searching and contributing knowledge.	Task technology fit and Social cognitive theory
Espinosa et al. 2007	Knowledge helping coordinate geographically distributed software development teams	Field study	Software teams coordination needs, how team knowledge affects coordination, and how this effect is influenced by geographic dispersion. Teams have 3 types of coordination needs—technical, temporal, and process—which vary with the members' role. Geographic distance has a negative effect on coordination, but is mitigated by shared knowledge of the team and presence awareness. Shared task knowledge is more important for coordination among collocated members.	Team cognition research

Decision-makers will rely more on heuristics and reduce their information search and evaluation effort as the amount of information increases or the amount of time to complete a task decreases (Zuckerman & Chaiken, 1998).

Heuristics for making decisions about the quality of information affect the effort-accuracy trade-off. Examples of these heuristic include source credibility (e.g., experts provide high-quality information), consensus (e.g., information is high-quality when many users agree on quality) and attractiveness (e.g., sources whose physical features are pleasing to us provide high-quality information) (Chaiken et al., 1989). Heuristics for making decisions about what search and evaluation strategy to follow affect the effort-accuracy trade-off. Examples of these heuristics include the minimalist (e.g., look up information in a random order until an alternative is recognized as high quality), the take-the-last (e.g., use the same strategy that worked the last time in similar situations), and the take-the-best

Table 2. Summary of effort-accuracy and search current literature

Study	Area	Research Method	Searching and Evaluating	Theory
White at al. 2006	Difficulty devising queries to express information needs	Experimentally evaluate technique which estimates information needs, how well it estimates changes in needs and its appropriateness	Propose unobtrusive monitoring of system interaction to proactively support searchers, and it chooses terms by monitoring searcher interaction with different representations of top-ranked documents. Information needs are dynamic and change as a searcher views information. The approach gathers evidence on potential changes in these needs and uses this evidence to choose new retrieval strategies.	Heuristic-based implicit feedback model
Dennis and Taylor 2006	Effects of an acceptable time delay on information search behavior	Experiment	Increased time and effort caused by acceptable delays (7 seconds) provoked increased information search. When faced with acceptable delays, users tend to act as satisficing information foragers; they increase search within pages and reduce breadth of search by examining fewer pages to minimize time.	Information foraging
Yang and Hu 2007	Finding expert profiles	Design science prototype	Intelligent search framework to provide search capabilities for experts who not only match search conditions but belong to similar subject fields based on the user's needs.	Fuzzy abstraction hierarchy and Vector space model
Kamis and Stohr 2006	Parametric search engines, i.e., attribute-based	Experimental	Effects of search effort and domain knowledge are mediated through decision quality and decision confidence to impact perceived ease of use and perceived usefulness.	Behavioral decision
Kamis 2006	Shopping engines	Experiment	Users want maximal accuracy with minimal effort using shopping engines which work in one stage to quickly maximize accuracy with multiple stages by involving the user, to satisfy decision making. The best-performing shopping engine used two stages, QuickSearch first, then AdaptiveSearch. The 2 stages have different impacts on shopping. Shopping engines should be designed to first save the shopper effort and then provide attribute-focused support for examining the resulting set of items.	Effort-accuracy decision strategies
Song et al. 2007	Effects of Web-based consumer DSS	Experiment to compare Web-based DSS that support different decision strategies	DSS supporting compensatory strategies (weighted additive or equally weighted), over DSS supporting non-compensatory strategies (elimination-by-aspects), were perceived to be more accurate, less effortful, more effective, more satisfactory, and had superior consistency with stated preferences.	Decision making and User satisfaction
Sacchi and Burigo 2008	Information search strategies of individuals in pre-decisional stage	Experiment	To assess the influence of the individual's knowledge and information sources, participants selected from a list of relevant and irrelevant data. *Exper. 1* manipulated information source reliability, finding subjects used a sequential strategy with data from a reliable source. *Exper. 2* analyzed information source and individuals' knowledge. When subjects believed the source reliable, experts adopted strategy as sequential as novices. *Exper. 3* search strategy affects final judgment, illustrating the role of individual, task, and context.	Constructivist framework

approach (e.g., order alternatives on perceived quality and take the best one) (Gigerenzer & Goldstein, 1996).

Since KMS users are usually faced with a lengthy list of content, they likely apply effort-reducing and quality-judgment heuristics such as

Figure 1. Effort vs. accuracy research model

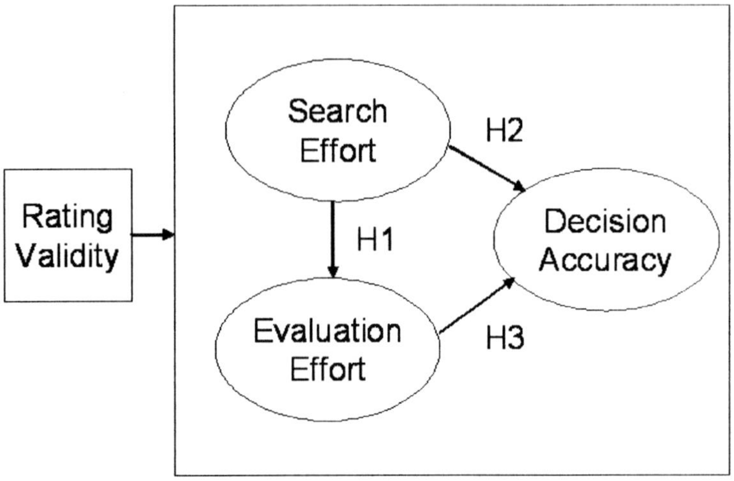

to use high-rated content because "high ratings should be associated with high-quality content". This is similar to the take-the-best search and evaluation strategy and consensus quality-judgment heuristics when ratings are valid. Valid ratings guide users to the high-quality content and reinforce users' evaluations and decisions to select that content for their task. Invalid ratings, however, may guide users to lower-quality content and may cause cognitive dissonance where the ratings do not entirely agree with novices' uncertain judgment of content quality. The task then becomes more complicated and increased effort may be needed. The next section discusses the effort-accuracy trade-off in KMS usage.

Searching and Evaluating KMS Content

One characteristic of search and evaluation effort is the amount of information accessed and evaluated. Search effort reflects how many of the available options are selected for subsequent evaluation. Evaluation effort reflects how much attention is spent on the options selected in order to determine what is appropriate for using in the task. Rationally, decision-makers should only need to evaluate information once and decide on its usefulness to the task. Yet decision-makers re-evaluate information because they forget what they have reviewed due to limits in working memory (Miller, 1956) or they may want to confirm their choices to be more confident in their actions (Svenson, 1979).

Another characteristic of search and evaluation effort is the amount of time taken for information acquisition. If time is limited people tend to reduce both search and evaluation effort (Gigerenzer & Todd, 1999; Payne et al., 1993). In the KMS usage context, as more content is searched, more evaluation is needed. Greater search and evaluation effort means end users select more content which is highly likely to lead to greater personal scrutiny of that content. Meanwhile, lower search and evaluation effort means users make decisions based on fewer alternatives and as such do not spend as much time evaluating a lot of content. Thus, regardless of whether ratings have high or low validity, users who increase (decrease) their search effort will need to evaluate more (fewer) options expending greater (less) evaluation effort. The first hypotheses are:

H1: The search effort expended on KMS content will have a positive effect on the evaluation effort expended (a) when ratings have high validity and (b) when ratings have low validity.

As noted above, decision-makers use simplifying strategies such as heuristics to minimize effort with the goal of making accurate decisions (Cook, 1993; Svenson, 1979). When searching through KMS content, users are likely to use the heuristic that "high ratings should be associated with high-quality content". In this case, when ratings are high in validity, users will select high-quality content. By using valid ratings to guide content selections for evaluation, users will focus on evaluating high-rated, high-quality content. The consistency between ratings and content quality eliminate the need for further search effort. Users are less likely to be distracted or influenced by low-quality content when they limit their search effort to only reviewing high-rated, high-quality content. Users reduce search effort and make more accurate decisions.

However, users who decide not to use valid ratings but to search and personally scrutinize content themselves will expend greater search effort and be exposed to lower-quality content. By ignoring ratings, these KMS users will likely be using the minimalist heuristic of looking up content in a random fashion until high-quality options are recognized (Gigerenzer & Goldstein, 1996). Because valid ratings are being ignored, users must rely solely on their own uncertain judgments of content quality making users more likely to be influenced by low-quality content. Research demonstrates that decision-makers are not able to fully detect low-quality information (Maier & Thurber, 1968; Wang & Strong, 1996). By not using valid ratings, users will increase their search efforts and make less accurate decisions. The next hypothesis is:

H2a: The search effort expended on KMS content will have a negative effect on decision accuracy when ratings have high validity.

In addition, some users will attempt to reduce their search effort by using ratings when ratings have low validity. In this case, users will select high-rated, low-quality content to evaluate. The inconsistency between ratings and content may trigger the need to increase search effort and ignore the ratings. Prior research has demonstrated that information incongruity can increase the amount of effort expended to solve a problem (Alden et al., 1994; Ruthven et al., 2003). By adapting to the information environment, users can change their search strategy to perform a more complete search of the information available (Gigerenzer & Todd, 1999; Payne et al., 1993). In the KMS environment, users who are aware of the inconsistency between ratings and content increase their search effort which broadens the amount of content reviewed and enhances the saliency of quality differences between options. Being aware of quality differences, users will increase their search effort and are likely to seek out and find high-quality content leading to greater decision accuracy.

Alternatively, some users may not detect the inconsistency between ratings and content because they may be overly focused on minimizing effort or they may choose to override their own beliefs with the ratings provided. Research has found decision-makers are not entirely sensitive to problems with information and tend to accept information as valid without questioning it (Biros et al., 2002). In this case, KMS users who decide to continue using invalid ratings will not expand their search efforts and will likely be influenced by high-rated, low-quality content. Limiting search effort to only review high-rated, low-quality content means users do not get the benefit of evaluating a broader amount of content which would expose them to higher-quality content. By using invalid ratings, users will decrease their search efforts and make less accurate decisions. The next hypothesis is:

H2b: The search effort expended on KMS content will have a positive effect on decision accuracy when ratings have low validity.

Many KMS users will minimize not only their search effort but also their evaluation effort by using the heuristic that "high ratings should be associated with high-quality content". In this case, when ratings are high in validity, users will be evaluating high-quality content. The consistency between ratings and content efficiently reinforces evaluation judgments to use that content in the decision task. With valid ratings, the heuristic to use ratings as an effort minimizing strategy is optimal and leads to accurate decisions of using the highest-quality content in the task. By reducing evaluation effort and relying on the heuristic to use ratings to guide content judgments, users will make more accurate decisions while minimizing their efforts.

However, users who decide to personally scrutinize content themselves will increase their search and evaluation effort and be exposed to lower-quality content. Because valid ratings are being ignored, users miss out on having their evaluation decisions reinforced by the ratings and are more likely to be influence by the low-quality content. Consistent with above, some decision-makers are not able to fully detect low-quality information (DePaulo & DePaulo, 1989; Wang & Strong, 1996), suggesting low-quality KMS content may get used in the task. Being junior employees, KMS users will be less certain about which content is high vs. low quality. By personally scrutinizing content and not using valid ratings, users will increase evaluation efforts but make less accurate decisions. The next hypothesis is:

H3a: The evaluation effort expended on KMS content will have a negative effect on decision accuracy when ratings have high validity.

Additionally, some users will attempt to reduce their search and evaluation effort by using ratings when ratings have low validity. In this case, users will evaluate high-rated, low-quality content. Some users will become aware of the inconsistency between ratings and content quality, which may trigger the need to increase evaluation effort and ignore the ratings. The inconsistency between ratings and content quality may also create cognitive conflict and motivate users to resolve the inconsistency by more closely scrutinizing more content (Festinger, 1957; Harmon-Jones and Mills, 1999). Consistent with above, users can change their evaluation strategy to perform a more complete evaluation of the information available leading to greater awareness of content quality differences (Gigerenzer & Todd, 1999; Payne et al., 1993). By increasing their evaluation effort, users will be more likely to evaluate high-quality content leading to greater decision accuracy.

Alternatively, users who do not detect the inconsistency between ratings and content may decide to continue using invalid ratings to make evaluation decisions. Because some users are not able to fully detect invalid information (DePaulo & DePaulo, 1989; Wang & Strong, 1996), low-quality KMS content gets used in the task. In this case, users who decide to continue using invalid ratings are likely to be influenced by high-rated, low-quality content. By using invalid ratings, users decrease their evaluation efforts but make less accurate decisions. The last hypothesis is:

H3b: The evaluation effort expended on KMS content will positively affect decision accuracy when ratings have low validity.

METHODOLOGY

A between-subjects single-factor experiment was conducted to test the research model and hypotheses. Rating validity (high and low) was manipulated.

Subjects and Task

Two hundred nine junior and senior undergraduates enrolled in a business information systems course at a large Midwestern university participated in this study. Subjects received course extra credit (1.5%) for their participation and were awarded incentive pay based on decision performance with an option to perform an equivalent task in lieu of the experiment. Subjects completed a pretest assessing demographics and knowledge prior to attending an experimental session. Subjects were randomly assigned to an experimental manipulation prior to attending their session by a pre-assigned login id, and each session began with a 10-minute tutorial on the task and the KMS. Sessions were held outside regular class periods with large breaks in-between sessions providing seemingly unlimited time to compete the task. The experimental task took place in a simulated online setting of a professional services firm created by the authors, where subjects completed a typical consulting task (Falconer, 1999; Orlikowski, 2000). Subjects were asked by their "manager" to determine what steps to include in a work plan for a data-modeling and database-design project by reviewing existing work plans focused on data-modeling and database-design projects in the KMS. All experimental sessions were run following an identical protocol by one of the authors. The task was designed to have an optimal answer, and as such, better and worse solutions could be assessed objectively. Participants did not have time restrictions and the average time taken was 30.5 minutes (s.d. = 10.6 minutes).

The work plans in the KMS were created based on work plans provided by practicing consultants. All work plans listed:

- data-modeling or database-design project steps based on the steps identified in an undergraduate information systems textbook (Whitten et al., 2000); and
- consultant ranks for each project step, with the appropriate rank being established based on feedback from practicing consultants.

Work plans varied in quality with the highest-quality work plans including (1) supervisors assigned to all important tasks, (2) consultant level(s) for all project steps, and (3) informative, nonvague project steps. Work plans with objectively lower quality were created by (1) deleting supervisors for important tasks, (2) not assigning consultant levels to project steps, and (3) describing project steps in uninformative, vague terms (see Murch, 2001 and Rosenau, 1998). Fourteen data-modeling and fourteen database-design project work plans were produced and listed in each subject's KMS search results. A screen snapshot is shown for the work plan contents in Figure 2. These work plans varied in quality such that one plan met all three quality criteria, six plans met two of the quality criteria, six plans met one of the quality criteria, and one plan did not meet any of the quality criteria.

We designed the experimental task to be one that first-year consultants might perform (i.e., one that the subjects might expect to perform as new employees). While subjects had limited prior experience with the task, pilot tests demonstrated that the subject pool had sufficient understanding and were able to distinguish work plan quality based on the criteria given. Also, ANOVA tests confirmed the significance of the work plan quality manipulation check ($t = 50.05$, $p < .001$)—for each experiment subjects perceived differences in work plan quality as anticipated. We used HTML, ASP, and MS Office products to program the experimental materials.

Experimental Measures

Manipulated variable: Rating validity was manipulated in this study. Each work plan was associated with a rating that was either high in

Figure 2. Screen snapshot of work plan contents

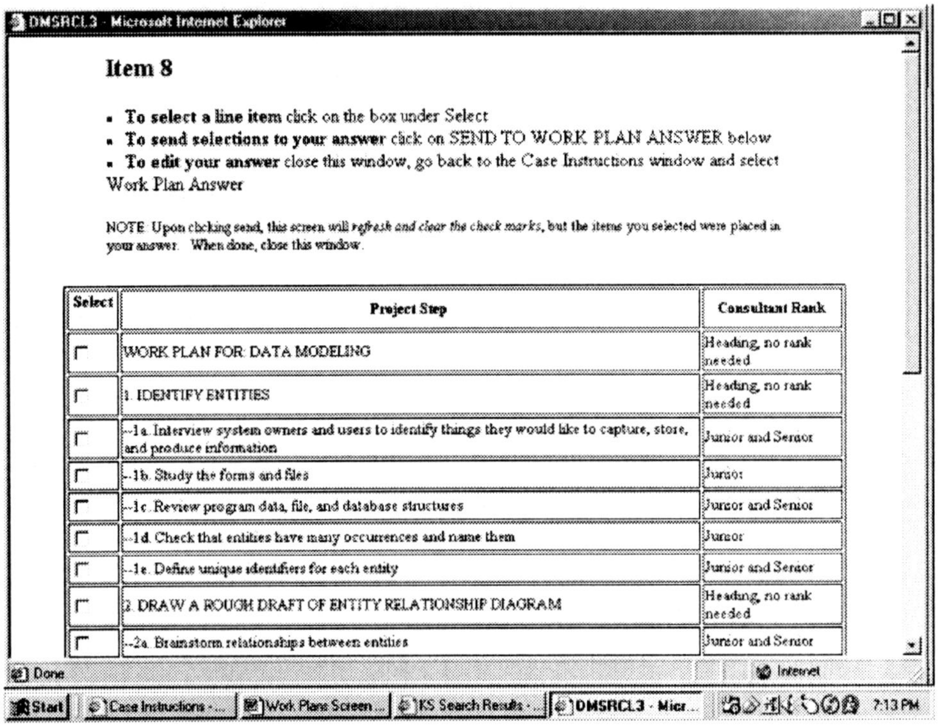

validity (if the rating accurately described the content quality) or low in validity (if it did not). Subjects were not explicitly told about the differences in rating validity. The rating scheme values were: 5 = highly valuable, 4 = somewhat valuable, 2 = somewhat worthless or 1 = worthless. To strengthen the rating validity manipulation we excluded the neutral rating of 3. Work plan orders were randomized; however the highest and lowest rated work plans were always located somewhere in the middle section of all the work plans listed. Thus, if a subject used the "rely on rating" heuristic they could not simply select the first work plan listed but they would have to scroll down to find the highest-rated work plans.

Independent variables: Search and evaluation effort measures were adopted from those previously implemented (Kim, 2001; Lazar & Norcio, 2003; Van der Linden et al., 2003). Search effort was operationalized as the number of different work plans opened to gauge how much of the KMS content a subject selected for subsequent evaluation. Evaluation effort was operationalized as the total time spent evaluating selected work plan options.

Dependent variables: Decision accuracy was measured as the number of line items in the subject's submitted work plan matching the 36 line items in the highest quality work plan. Each subject's score was calculated as the number of line items in the subject's answer matching the line items in the "best" answer, resulting in a maximum of decision quality score of 36 and a minimum of 0.

Control variables: In the experiment we attempted to control for individual differences between subjects by their random assignment to treatment conditions. However, some individual differences were deemed important to control. First, one's expertise in KMS usage can influence decision making and thus prior experience of KMS usage was captured (Newell & Simon, 1972).

Table 3. Descriptive statistics: Mean, standard deviation and correlation

Item	Mean	Standard Deviation	Correlations	
			Search Effort	Evaluation Effort
Both High and Low Rating Validity (N=209)				
Search Effort	15.68	7.00		
Evaluation Effort	30.00	10.41	.426**	
Decision Accuracy	17.37	11.43	-.080	-.122
High Rating Validity (N=111)				
Search Effort	13.72	6.44		
Evaluation Effort	29.05	11.21	.479**	
Decision Accuracy	24.65	8.70	-.154	-.256**
Low Rating Validity (N=98)				
Search Effort	17.64	7.00		
Evaluation Effort	31.00	9.37	.345**	
Decision Accuracy	9.13	8.05	-.500**	.179

** Correlation is significant at the .01 level.

Secondly, gender has been shown to influence the use of various technologies as such gender was captured (Agarwal & Prasad, 1999; Gefen & Straub, 1997; Venkatesh & Morris, 2000).

RESULTS

The data from two hundred nine subjects were analyzed using Partial Least Square (PLS), as implemented in PLS graph, to examine the structural relationship proposed earlier in Figure 1. We chose PLS due to its minimal demands on sample size and residual distribution (Barclay et al., 1995; Chin 1998; Fornell & Bookstein 1982). Chi-square tests indicated the subject pool was homogenous as no significant differences for year in school, age, gender or experience were found across treatments. Also, the control variables (prior experience with KMS usage and gender) were not significant and therefore not included in discussions below. Means, standard deviations and item inter-correlations for the constructs are presented in Table 3.

The results of the structural model from PLS, including path coefficients, explained variances and significance levels are illustrated in Figure 3 for high and low rating validity. Paths are interpreted as standardized beta weights in a regression analysis. Each construct comprises a single-item task-based behavioral indicator (Chin, 1998).

Hypothesis Testing

As stated in Hypotheses 1a and 1b, those who increased their search effort increased their evaluation effort when ratings were high in validity (path = .481, t = 5.498, $p < .05$) as well as when ratings were low in validity (.345, t = 3.767, $p < .05$). Contrary to the prediction in Hypothesis 2a, those who decreased their search effort did not significantly increase their decision accuracy when ratings were high in validity (-.041, t = 0.406, n.s.). As predicted in Hypothesis 2b, those who increased their search effort did significantly increase their decision accuracy when ratings were low in validity (.496, t = 5.421, $p < .05$). As predicted in Hypothesis 3a, those who decreased

Figure 3. PLS results for research model for high and low rating validity

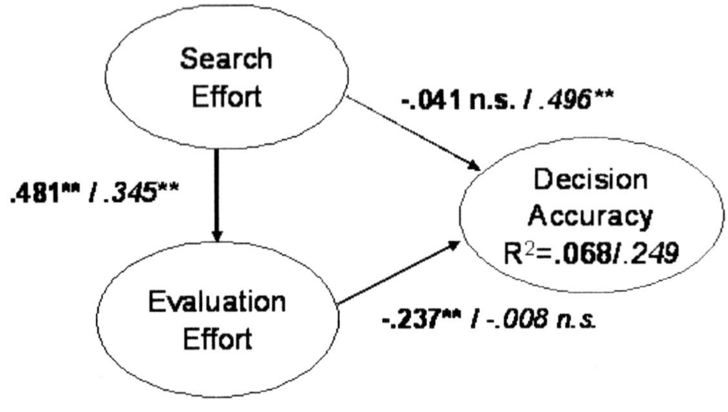

Bold High Rating Validity / *Italics Low Rating Validity*
** Path is significant at the .05 level

their evaluation effort did significantly increase their decision accuracy when ratings were high in validity (-.237, $t = 2.303$, $p < .05$). Contrary to the prediction in Hypothesis 3b, those who increased their evaluation effort did not significantly increase their decision accuracy when ratings were low in validity (.008, $t = 0.068$, n.s.). Thus, hypotheses 1a, 1b, 2b, and 3a are all supported, but hypotheses 2a and 3b were not supported. Table 4 provides a summary of all the hypotheses tested.

DISCUSSION

This study has examined how rating schemes influence how KMS end users trade off search and evaluation effort for decision accuracy. Based on the theoretical and empirical work described in the literature, we explored how rating validity and search and evaluation effort influence decision accuracy in the KMS environment. Overall the results provide support for the research model, supporting four of the six hypothesized relationships. Consistent with Hypotheses 1a and 1b, search effort expended on KMS content demonstrated a significant positive effect on evaluation effort expended in both cases of high and low rating validity. This finding is consistent with the literature suggesting that effort comprises both search and evaluation activities (Gigerenzer & Todd, 1999; Payne et al., 1993). When using KMS content, greater effort means users select more content (i.e., increase search) leading to more personal scrutiny of that content (i.e., increase evaluation). The positive relationship between search and evaluation effort occurs regardless of rating validity.

An important contribution of this study is the finding that rating validity influences the outcomes of user behaviors in different ways. Specifically, as Hypothesis 2b suggested, when ratings are low in validity, search effort expended on KMS content had a significant positive effect on decision accuracy. This finding suggests that additional search of the content exposed users to higher-quality content and that some of that content made its way into final task solutions. Meanwhile, contrary to Hypothesis 2a, when ratings are high in validity, search effort expended had no influence on decision accuracy. This suggests that the decision accuracy of users with helpful (i.e., valid) ratings was not hurt nor was it helped significantly by the level of KMS

Table 4. Summary of results for structural model and hypotheses

Hypothesis	Standardized Path Coefficient (direct effect)	t-value for Path	Indirect Effect	Total Effect [a]	Finding
H1a: Search effort positively affect evaluation effort, high validity	.481	5.498	--	.481	*Supported*
H1b: Search effort positively affect evaluation effort, low validity	.345	--	--	.345	*Supported*
H2a: Search effort negatively affect decision accuracy, high validity	-.041	.406	-.114	-.155	Not Supported
H2b: Search effort positively affect decision accuracy, low validity	.496	5.421	.003	.499	*Supported*
H3a: Evaluation effort negatively affect decision accuracy, high validity	-.237	2.303	--	-.237	*Supported*
H3b: Evaluation effort positively affect decision accuracy, low validity	.008	.068	--	.008	Not Supported

content search performed. Interestingly and not hypothesized, ANOVA tests indicate that the search effort for those with ratings low in validity (mean = 17.64) was significantly higher than for those with ratings high in validity (13.72) ($F(1, 207) = 16.31$, $p < .001$). Thus, those with ratings low in validity did search the KMS content more extensively as those with ratings high in validity. This is consistent with prior literature that information incongruity can cause people to change their search strategies and increase the amount of effort expended (Alden et al., 1994; Gigerenzer & Todd, 1999; Payne et al., 1993; Ruthven et al., 2003). Also, this lends support for the notion that some of those with unhelpful (i.e., invalid) ratings wanted to resolve their uncertain judgments of an inconsistency between ratings and content through additional search of the content. The additional search of the KMS content broadened the amount of content reviewed and enabled users to incorporate high-quality content in their decision task increasing decision accuracy.

In addition to the differential influence of rating validity on the outcomes of search efforts, rating validity also differentially influenced the outcomes of evaluation efforts. Specifically, as Hypothesis 3a suggested, when ratings are high in validity, evaluation effort expended on KMS content had a significant negative effect on decision accuracy. This finding suggests that additional evaluation of the content exposed the users to lower-quality content and that some of that content made its way into final task solutions. Users were better off relying on the heuristic that "high ratings should be associated with high-quality content" and minimizing their evaluation efforts. Meanwhile, contrary to Hypothesis 3b, when ratings are low in validity, evaluation effort expended had no influence on decision accuracy. This suggests that the decision accuracy of users with unhelpful (i.e., invalid) ratings was not hurt nor was it helped significantly by the amount of KMS content evaluation performed. Interestingly and also not hypothesized, ANOVA tests indicate that the evaluation effort for those with ratings low in validity (mean = 31.00) was not significantly higher than for those with ratings high in validity (29.08) ($F(1, 207) = 1.83$, n.s.). Thus, KMS users appear to exert the same level of evaluation effort. This is consistent with prior literature that some decision-makers are not able to fully detect low-quality information which could trigger the need to continue expending effort (DePaulo & DePaulo, 1989; Maier & Thurber, 1968; Wang & Strong, 1996). Also, it lends support for the notion that the users, being novices, are less equipped to evaluate and identify high-quality content on their own without the help of valid ratings.

In summary, valid ratings did not necessarily guide users to search efficiently for high-quality content, but these ratings did confirm or guide evaluation judgments of what was high-quality content to use in the task. Invalid ratings did appear to prompt users to increase their search efforts in order to achieve greater decision accuracy, but users were not able to sufficiently increase their evaluation efforts of the content on their own to achieve greater decision accuracy. In the trade-off between effort and accuracy, complexities of a particular decision problem may exceed the capabilities of decision-makers regardless of the amount of effort expended (Payne et al., 1993). Not hypothesized, ANOVA tests indicate that the decision accuracy for those with ratings high in validity (mean = 24.65) was significantly higher than for those with ratings low in validity (9.13) ($F(1, 207) = 177.58$, $p < .001$). Thus, exposure to ratings with low validity may create a more complex decision problem which some users may not be able to overcome by sufficiently increasing their search and evaluation efforts.

LIMITATIONS

The meaningfulness of the findings from any study must be assessed in light of the study's limitations. For this study, the increased control afforded by a laboratory experiment must be traded-off against the inherent limitations of the approach, primarily that of generalizability. Limitations in generalizability in this study involve the use of student subjects, the nature of the tasks, and the operationalization of how ratings reflect content quality.

Student subjects typically differ from business professionals in two ways: 1) they generally have less experience with the problem domain; and 2) they have less motivation to perform a task successfully. In this study, two steps were taken to offset the use of students as subjects. First, subjects had experience using web-based applications to accomplish tasks and had conceptual and hands-on experiences in the task domain used in the study. Second, subjects were offered course extra credit and financial incentives to increase their motivation to perform well on the task.

The task involved selecting line items from work plan examples provided to build a new work plan answer. The generalizabiltiy of these findings may be limited to comparable tasks. However, in general, when selecting from search results, end users are free to use entire items or parts of items when creating new documents of any kind. The information processing required by this task is comparable to many KMS tasks across a range of domains where old documents are re-used to create new ones.

IMPLICATIONS AND FUTURE RESEARCH

From a research perspective, this study extends prior research on the effort-accuracy trade-off framework. This study shows that the validity of information inputs to a task may vary causing complexities in a particular decision problem that decision-makers may not be able to adequately deal with regardless of the amount of effort expended or level of accuracy sought. Without valid ratings, greater search effort increased the amount of higher-quality content included in task solutions; however, contrary to expectations, greater evaluation effort did not make a difference. In this study, the optimal solution to the task was provided in the list of KMS search results, yet invalid information (i.e., ratings) mislead end users to incorporate non-optimal content in their task. Thus, the validity of information inputs is an influential factor in the effort-accuracy trade-off framework in the efficient and effective usage of knowledge in KMSs.

From a practical and managerial perspective, users may find it advantageous to rely on ratings as a simplifying heuristic strategy for handling KMS content. The findings of this study suggest the heuristic strategy for minimizing evaluation effort can be beneficial when ratings are high in validity and, at worst, have no effect when ratings are low in validity. However, the findings suggest the heuristic strategy for minimizing search effort can be beneficial when ratings are low in validity even though this strategy has no effect when ratings are high in validity. To achieve optimal results from using the heuristic strategy of relying on ratings, the findings suggest users should be provided with tools for properly assessing rating validity either in the KMS design or through better KMS training (Shouhong, 2005). KMS interface designs and end user training methods must help users accurately detect rating validity and when ratings have low validity help users build confidence in increasing search and evaluation effort enough to find high-quality content. Finally, managers who assign KMS retrieval tasks to junior employees should specifically incorporate the definition of high-quality content into their task assignments.

Our findings also suggest several guidelines for KMS interface designers. Rating schemes are an important interface design feature and influence how end users use KMS content. Care and attention is needed in how these rating schemes are implemented including finding ways to ensure valid ratings and high-quality content are entered into the KMS in the first place. KMSs may provide a setting where users are novices who find it difficult to accurately assess the context, content, and the effort needed to fully complete the task in a high-quality manner (Hockheiser & Schneiderman, 2000). KMS designers need to develop robust processes both to evaluate the content quality in a KMS and to ensure that ratings of that content are high in validity (Dellarocas, 2003; Resnick et al., 2000). One possibility is to allow only experts to contribute content and rate KMS content, or experts could verify submitted content and ratings before they are published on the system. Alternatively, expert-system or collaborative-filtering algorithms could scan KMS content and ratings to identify problems for review by experts.

An important finding of this research is that many of our subjects with ratings low in validity were still not able to achieve decision accuracy levels as high as those with ratings high in validity. Thus, we continue to wonder why some KMS users were unable to personally scrutinize content (i.e., increase evaluation effort) enough to achieve higher decision accuracy. The inability to increase evaluation effort enough is consistent with prior research showing decision-makers sometimes fail to fully detect low-quality information (DePaulo & DePaulo, 1989; Maier & Thurber, 1968; Wang & Strong, 1996), they fail to adopt new search strategies even when the environment warrants it (Payne et al., 1993), or the complexities of the task exceed the decision-makers' capabilities (Payne et al., 1993). One explanation is that end users want to minimize their effort (Chu & Spires, 2000; Payne, 1982), and therefore they focus on achieving an adequate but not optimal solution. This behavior is consistent with the idea that effort is weighted more heavily than accuracy because feedback on effort expenditure is more immediate, while feedback on accuracy is delayed and often times ambiguous (Einhorn & Hogarth, 1981; Kleinmuntz & Schkade, 1993). Thus, when ratings have low validity, minimizing effort may be easier than maximizing accuracy in the context of KMS usage. Additional research should examine how to help end users with ratings low in validity to increase effort levels enough to achieve higher decision accuracy.

We examined additional individual-differences characteristics measured as part of this study (gender, domain experience, computer experience, and broad information systems experience) to provide insight into why some subjects did not increase evaluation effort enough to achieve high decision accuracy. None of the characteristics was significantly more pronounced among either subjects who increased their evaluation effort or among those who did not. Additional research should investigate individual factors such as cognitive flexibility and field dependent/ independent characteristics to ascertain the degree to which end users tend to analyze content more fully and achieve higher decision accuracy.

Based on the results of this study, one way to improve the KMS interface design is by incorporating more useful metrics into search result feedback and rating schemes (Fang, 2000; Hockheiser & Shneiderman, 2000; Kim & Compton, 2004). This study highlights the influence that rating schemes have and informs KMS designers to use the limited space on search results screens to display information that helps KMS users to overcome low validity in information (Fogg & Tseng, 1999; Stiff & Mongeau, 2003). While prior studies found certain information about rating validity (i.e., number of raters and rater expertise) was not helpful (Poston & Speier, 2005), a more comprehensive examination of factors influencing how end users detect low-validity information is warranted. Future studies should examine characteristics that could be built into system features such as other rating validity indicators or content quality measures.

Given the impact of rating schemes on KMS usage, it is important for future research to examine how various characteristics of the rating values themselves influence content quality-judgments and KMS usage (Nielsen, 1999; 1998; Resnick & Montania, 2003). Research is needed to determine how the strength and scale of ratings, the usefulness of text explanations of ratings, and/or the role of rating consistency affects how end users use the KMS interface and content. Designers need to incorporate the influences of these factors into their interface designs in order to improve how end users efficiently and effectively use the knowledge in KMSs to make decisions.

CONCLUSION

The results of this research suggest the interface has an important impact on how end users use Knowledge Management Systems (KMSs). More specifically, the rating schemes designed into KMS interfaces influence how end users use the content. Ratings are important information to KMS users because ratings influence the outcomes of usage behaviors. Valid ratings did not necessarily guide users to search efficiently for high-quality content, but these ratings did confirm or guide evaluation judgments of what was high-quality content to use in the task. Invalid ratings did appear to prompt users to increase their search efforts in order to achieve greater decision accuracy, but users were not able to sufficiently increase their evaluation efforts to achieve greater decision accuracy. High rating validity leads to optimal KMS usage outcomes while low rating validity does not. The research findings provide an initial understanding of the relationship between rating validity, search and evaluation effort, and decision accuracy in KMS content usage. Informing end users and designers on how rating validity influences the outcomes of KMS usage is an important issue. This and future studies will help system designers and end users to learn how to develop and use KMSs more efficiently and effectively.

REFERENCES

Agarwal, R., & Prasad, J. (1999). Are individual differences germane to the acceptance of new information technologies? *Decision Sciences*, *30*, 361–391. doi:10.1111/j.1540-5915.1999.tb01614.x

Alavi, M., & Leidner, D. E. (2001). Review: Knowledge management and knowledge management systems: Conceptual foundations and research issues. *MIS Quarterly*, *25*, 107–136. doi:10.2307/3250961

Alavi, M., & Tiwana, A. (2002). Knowledge integration in virtual teams: The potential role of KMS. *Journal of the American Society for Information Science and Technology*, *53*, 1029–1037. doi:10.1002/asi.10107

Alden, D. L., Stayman, D. M., & Hoyer, W. D. (1994). Evaluation strategies of American and Thai consumers. *Psychology and Marketing*, *11*, 145–161. doi:10.1002/mar.4220110205

Barclay, D., Thompson, R., & Higgins, C. (1995). The partial least squares (PLS) approach to causal modeling: Personal computer adoption and use as an illustration. *Technology Studies*, *2*, 285–309.

Biros, D. P., George, J. F., & Zmud, R. W. (2002). Inducing sensitivity to deception in order to improve decision making performance: A field study. *MIS Quarterly*, *26*, 119–144. doi:10.2307/4132323

Brajnik, G., Mizzaro, S., Tasso, C., & Venuti, F. (2002). Strategic help in user interfaces for information retrieval. *Journal of the American Society for Information Science and Technology*, *53*, 343–358. doi:10.1002/asi.10035

Chaiken, S., Liberman, A., & Eagly, A. H. (1989). Heuristic and systematic processing within and beyond the persuasion context. In J.S. Uleman & J.A. Bargh (Eds.), *Unintended thought* (pp. 212-252). New York: Guildford Press.

Chin, W. (1998). Issues and opinion on structural equation modeling. *MIS Quarterly*, *22*, vii–xvi.

Cho, K., Chung, T. R., King, W. R., & Shunn, C. (2008). Peer-based computer-supported knowledge refinement: An empirical investigation. *Communications of the ACM*, *51*, 83–88. doi:10.1145/1325555.1325571

Chu, P. C., & Spires, E. E. (2000). The joint effects of effort and quality on decision strategy choice with computerized decision aids. *Decision Sciences*, *31*, 259–292. doi:10.1111/j.1540-5915.2000.tb01624.x

Constant, D., Kiesler, S., & Sproull, L. (1994). What's mine is ours, or is it? A study of attitudes about information sharing. *Information Systems Research*, *5*, 400–421. doi:10.1287/isre.5.4.400

Cook, G. (1993). An empirical investigation of information search strategies with implications for decision support system design. *Decision Sciences*, *24*, 683–697. doi:10.1111/j.1540-5915.1993.tb01298.x

Cosley, D., Lam, S. K., Albert, I., Konstan, J. A., & Riedl, J. (2003). Is seeing believing? How recommender interfaces affect users' opinions. In *Proceedings for CHI 2003, 5, April 5-10, 2003* (pp. 585-592).

Cramton, C. D. (2001). The mutual knowledge problem and the consequences for dispersed collaboration. *Organization Science*, *12*, 346–371. doi:10.1287/orsc.12.3.346.10098

Datta, P. (2007). An agent-mediated knowledge-in-motion model. *Journal of the Association for Information Systems*, *8*, 287–311.

Davenport, T., & Beck, J. (2001). *The attention economy: Understanding the new currency of business*. Boston, MA: Harvard Business School Publishing.

Davenport, T.H., & Hansen, M.T. (1999). Knowledge management at Andersen Consulting. Harvard Business School Case (9-499-032), July 7, 1999.

Dellarocas, C. (2003). The digitization of word of mouth: Promise and challenges of online feedback mechanisms. *Management Science, 49*, 1407–1425. doi:10.1287/mnsc.49.10.1407.17308

Deng, P. (2008). Applying a market-based approach to the development of a sharing-enabled KM model for knowledge-intensive small firms. *Information Systems Management, 25*, 174–187. doi:10.1080/10580530801941389

Dennis, A. R., & Taylor, N. J. (2006). Information foraging on the web: The effects of "Acceptable" Internet delays on multi-page information search behavior. *Decision Support Systems, 42*, 810–824. doi:10.1016/j.dss.2005.05.032

DePaulo, P. J., & DePaulo, B. M. (1989). Can deception by salespersons and customers be detected through nonverbal behavioral cues? *Journal of Applied Social Psychology, 19*, 1552–1577. doi:10.1111/j.1559-1816.1989.tb01463.x

Einhorn, H., & Hogarth, R. (1981). Behavioral decision theory: Processes of judgment and choice. *Annual Review of Psychology, 32*, 53–88. doi:10.1146/annurev.ps.32.020181.000413

Espinosa, J. A., Slaughter, S. A., Kraut, R. E., & Et, A. (2007). Team knowledge and coordination in geographically distributed software development. *Journal of Management Information Systems, 24*, 135–169. doi:10.2753/MIS0742-1222240104

Fahey, L., & Prusak, L. (1998). The eleven deadliest sins of knowledge management. *California Management Review, 40*, 265–270.

Falconer, J. (1999). Implementing a dynamic corpus management system within a global consulting practice. *International Journal of Technology Management, 18*, 520–534. doi:10.1504/IJTM.1999.002784

Fang, X. (2000). A hierarchical search history for web searching. *International Journal of Human-Computer Interaction, 12*, 73–88. doi:10.1207/S15327590IJHC1201_3

Farhoomand, A. F., & Drury, D. H. (2002). Managerial information overload. *Communications of the ACM, 45*, 127–131. doi:10.1145/570907.570909

Festinger, L. (1957). *A theory of cognitive dissonance*. Stanford, CA: Stanford University Press.

Fisher, C. W., Chengalur-Smith, I., & Ballou, D. P. (2003). The impact of experience and time on the use of data quality information in decision making. *Information Systems Research, 14*, 170–188. doi:10.1287/isre.14.2.170.16017

Fogg, B. J., & Tseng, H. (1999). The elements of computer credibility. In *Proceedings of the CHI 1999, May 15-20, 1999* (pp. 80-87).

Fornell, C., & Bookstein, F. (1982). Two structural equation models: LISREL and PLS applied to consumer exit-voice theory. *JMR, Journal of Marketing Research, 19*, 440–452. doi:10.2307/3151718

Gefen, D., & Straub, D. W. (1997). Gender difference in the perception and use of e-mail: An extension to the technology acceptance model. *MIS Quarterly, 21*, 389–400. doi:10.2307/249720

Ghosh, B., & Scott, J. E. (2007). Effective knowledge management systems for a clinical nursing setting. *Information Systems Management, 24*, 73–84. doi:10.1080/10580530601038188

Gigerenzer, G., & Goldstein, D. G. (1996). Reasoning the fast and frugal way: Models of bounded rationality. *Psychological Review*, *103*, 650–669. doi:10.1037/0033-295X.103.4.650

Gigerenzer, G., & Todd, P. M. (1999). Simple heuristics that make us smart. New York: Oxford University Press.

Gottschalk, P. (2006). Research propositions for knowledge management systems supporting it outsourcing relationships. *Journal of Computer Information Systems*, *46*, 110–116.

Gray, P. H., & Durcikova, A. (2005/2006). The role of knowledge repositories in technical support environments: Speed versus learning in user performance. *Journal of Management Information Systems*, *22*, 159–190. doi:10.2753/MIS0742-1222220306

Grover, V., & Davenport, T. H. (2001). General perspectives on knowledge management: Fostering a research agenda. *Journal of Management Information Systems*, *18*, 5–21. doi:10.1201/1078/43196.18.3.20010601/31284.1

Haas, M. R. (2006). Knowledge gathering, team capabilities, and project performance in challenging work environments. *Management Science*, *52*, 1170–1184. doi:10.1287/mnsc.1060.0530

Hansen, M., & Haas, M. (2001). Competing for attention in knowledge markets: Electronic document dissemination in a management consulting company. *Administrative Science Quarterly*, *46*, 1–28. doi:10.2307/2667123

Harmon-Jones, E., & Mills, J. (1999). *Cognitive dissonance: Progress on a pivotal theory in social psychology*. Washington, DC: American Psychological Association.

Hockheiser, H., & Shneiderman, B. (2000). Performance benefits of simultaneous over sequential menus as task complexity increases. *International Journal of Human-Computer Interaction*, *12*, 173–192. doi:10.1207/S15327590IJHC1202_2

Hsu, L. L. (2006). The impact of industrial characteristics and organizational climate on KMS and BIP-Taiwan bioscience industry. *Journal of Computer Information Systems*, *46*, 8–17.

Huang, M. J., Chen, M. Y., & Yieh, K. (2007). Comparing with your main competitor: The single most important task of knowledge management performance measurement. *Journal of Information Science*, *33*, 416–434. doi:10.1177/0165551506076217

Iyer, B., Shankaranarayanan, G., & Vvyner, G. (2006). Process coordination requirements: Implications for the design of knowledge management systems. *Journal of Computer Information Systems*, *46*, 1–13.

Jadad, A. R., & Gagliardi, A. (1998). Rating health information on the Internet: Navigating to knowledge or to Babel? *Journal of the American Medical Association*, *279*, 611–614. doi:10.1001/jama.279.8.611

Jarvenpaa, S. (1989). The effect of task and graphical format congruence on information processing strategies and decision making performance. *Management Science*, *35*, 285–303. doi:10.1287/mnsc.35.3.285

Jones, M. C., & Price, R. L. (2004). Organizational knowledge sharing in ERP implementation: Lessons from industry. *Journal of Organizational and End User Computing*, *16*(1), 21–40.

Jones, N. B., & Kochtanek, T. R. (2004). Success factors in the implementation of a collaborative technology and resulting productivity improvements in a small business: An exploratory study. *Journal of Organizational and End User Computing*, *16*(1), 1–20.

Kamis, A. (2006). Search strategies in shopping engines: An experimental investigation. *International Journal of Electronic Commerce, 11*, 63–84. doi:10.2753/JEC1086-4415110103

Kamis, A. A., & Stohr, E. A. (2006). Parametric search engines: What makes them effective when shopping online for differentiated products? *Information & Management, 43*, 904–918. doi:10.1016/j.im.2006.08.006

Kim, K. (2001). Implications of user characteristics in information seeking on the World Wide Web. *International Journal of Human-Computer Interaction, 13*, 323–340. doi:10.1207/S15327590IJHC1303_3

Kim, M., & Compton, P. (2004). Evolutionary document management and retrieval for specialized domains on the web. *International Journal of Human-Computer Studies, 60*, 201–241. doi:10.1016/j.ijhcs.2003.10.004

Kleinmuntz, D. N., & Schkade, D. A. (1993). Knowledge displays and decision processes. *Psychological Science, 4*, 221–227. doi:10.1111/j.1467-9280.1993.tb00265.x

Kulkarni, U. R., Ravindran, S., & Freeze, R. (2006/2007). A knowledge management success model: Theoretical development and empirical validation. *Journal of Management Information Systems*, Winter.

Lazar, J., & Norcio, A. (2003). Training novice users in developing strategies for responding to errors when browsing the web. *International Journal of Human-Computer Interaction, 15*, 361–377. doi:10.1207/S15327590IJHC1503_03

Lee, D., & Ahn, J. (2007). Reward systems for intra-organizational knowledge sharing. *European Journal of Operational Research, 180*, 938–956. doi:10.1016/j.ejor.2006.03.052

Li, Y., & Kettinger, W. J. (2006). An evolutionary information-processing theory of knowledge creation. *Journal of the Association for Information Systems, 7*, 593–617.

Maier, N. R. F., & Thurber, J. A. (1968). Accuracy of judgments of deception when an interview is watched, heard, and read. *Personnel Psychology, 21*, 23–30. doi:10.1111/j.1744-6570.1968.tb02283.x

Mao, J., & Benbasat, I. (2000). The use of explanations in knowledge-based systems: Cognitive perspective and a process-tracing analysis. *Journal of Management Information Systems, 17*, 153–180.

Melnik, M. I., & Alm, J. (2002). Does a seller's e-commerce reputation matter? Evidence from eBay auctions. *The Journal of Industrial Economics*, (September): 337–349.

Miller, G. A. (1956). The magical number seven, plus or minus two: Some limits on our capacity of processing information. *Psychological Review, 63*, 81–97. doi:10.1037/h0043158

Moran, T. P. (1994). Special issue on context in design. *Human-Computer Interaction, 9*, 1–149. doi:10.1207/s15327051hci0901_1

Murch, R. (2001). *Project management: Best practice for IT professionals*. Upper Saddle River, NJ: Prentice Hall.

Nevo, D., Benbasat, I., & Wand, Y. (2003). Exploring meta-knowledge for knowledge management systems: A Delphi study. In *Proceedings of the International Conference on Information Systems (Seattle, Washington)* (pp. 439-449).

Nevo, D., & Chan, Y. E. (2007). A Delphi study of knowledge management systems: Scope and requirements. *Information & Management, 44*, 583–597. doi:10.1016/j.im.2007.06.001

Newell, A., & Simon, H. A. (1972). Human problem solving. Englewood Cliffs, NJ: Prentice Hall.

Nielsen, J. (1998). The reputation manager. Alertbox. Retrieved from http://www.useit.com/alertbox/980208.html.

Nielsen, J. (1999). Reputation managers are happening. Alertbox. Retrieved from http://www.useit.com/alertbox/990905.html.

Nissen, M. E. (2005/2006). Dynamic knowledge patterns to inform design: A field study of knowledge stocks and flows in an extreme organization. *Journal of Management Information Systems, 22*, 225–263. doi:10.2753/MIS0742-1222220308

Nordheim, S., & Paivarinta, T. (2006). Implementing enterprise content management: From evolution through strategy to contradictions out-of-the-box. *European Journal of Information Systems, 15*, 648–662. doi:10.1057/palgrave.ejis.3000647

Olivera, F., Goodman, P. S., & Tan, S. S. L. (2008). Contribution behaviors in distributed environments. *MIS Quarterly, 32*, 23–42.

Orlikowski, W. (2000). Using technology and constituting structures: A practice lens for studying technology in organizations. *Organization Science, 11*, 404–428. doi:10.1287/orsc.11.4.404.14600

Palanisamy, R. (2007). Organizational culture and knowledge management in ERP implementation: An empirical study. *Journal of Computer Information Systems, 48*, 100–120.

Park, J., & Kim, J. (2000). Contextual navigation aids for two World Wide Web systems. *International Journal of Human-Computer Interaction, 12*, 193–217. doi:10.1207/S15327590IJHC1202_3

Paul, D. L. (2006). Collaborative activities in virtual settings: A knowledge management perspective of telemedicine. *Journal of Management Information Systems, 22*, 143–176. doi:10.2753/MIS0742-1222220406

Payne, J. E., Bettman, J. R., & Johnson, E. J. (1993). The adaptive decision maker. New York: Cambridge University Press.

Payne, J. W. (1982). Contingent decision behavior. *Psychological Bulletin, 92*, 382–402. doi:10.1037/0033-2909.92.2.382

Poston, R. S., & Speier, C. (2005). Effective use of knowledge management systems: A process model of content ratings and credibility indicators. *MIS Quarterly, 29*, 221–244.

Prieto, I. M., & Easterby, S. M. (2006). Dynamic capabilities and the role of organizational knowledge: An exploration. *European Journal of Information Systems, 15*, 500–510. doi:10.1057/palgrave.ejis.3000642

Ravishankar, M. N. (2008). Rewarding end-users for participating in Organizational KM: A case study. *Journal of Organizational and End User Computing, 20*, 35–49.

Resnick, M. L., & Montania, R. (2003). Perceptions of customer service, information privacy, and product quality from semiotic design features in an online web store. *International Journal of Human-Computer Interaction, 16*, 211–234. doi:10.1207/S15327590IJHC1602_05

Resnick, P., Zeckhauser, R., Friedman, E., & Kuwabara, K. (2000). Reputation systems. *Communications of the ACM, 43*, 45–48. doi:10.1145/355112.355122

Rosenau, M. D. (1998). Successful project management: A step-by-step approach with practical examples. New York: John Wiley and Sons.

Ruthven, I., Lalmas, M., & van Rijsbergen, K. (2003). Incorporating user search behavior into relevance feedback. *Journal of the American Society for Information Science and Technology*, *54*, 529–539. doi:10.1002/asi.10240

Sacchi, S., & Burigo, M. (2008). Strategies in the information search process: Interaction among task structure, knowledge, and source. *The Journal of General Psychology*, *135*, 252–270. doi:10.3200/GENP.135.3.252-270

Shon, J., & Musen, M. A. (1999). The low availability of metadata elements for evaluating the quality of medical knowledge on the world wide web. In *Proceedings of American Medical Informatics Association Symposium* (pp. 945-949).

Shouhong, W. (2005). Business software specifications for consumers: Toward a standard format. *Journal of Organizational and End User Computing*, *17*(1), 23–37.

Song, J., Jones, D., & Gudigantala, N. (2007). The effects of incorporating compensatory choice strategies in Web-based consumer decision support systems. *Decision Support Systems*, *43*, 359–374. doi:10.1016/j.dss.2006.10.007

Standifird, S. S. (2001). Reputation and e-commerce: Ebay auctions and the asymmetrical impact of positive and negative ratings. *Journal of Management*, *27*, 279–295. doi:10.1016/S0149-2063(01)00092-7

Stein, E. W., & Zwass, V. (1995). Actualizing organizational memory with information systems. *Information Systems Research*, *6*, 85–117. doi:10.1287/isre.6.2.85

Stiff, J. B., & Mongeau, P. A. (2003). *Persuasive communications*. New York: The Guilford Press.

Svenson, O. (1979). Process descriptions of decision making. *Organizational Behavior and Human Performance*, *23*, 86–112. doi:10.1016/0030-5073(79)90048-5

Van der Linden, D., Frese, M., & Sonnentag, S. (2003). The impact of mental fatigue on exploration in a complex computer task: Rigidity and loss of systematic strategies. *Human Factors . The Journal of the Human Factors and Ergonomics Society*, *45*, 483–494. doi:10.1518/hfes.45.3.483.27256

Venkatesh, V., & Morris, M. (2000). Why don't men ever stop to ask for directions? Gender, social influence, and their role in technology acceptance and usage behavior. *MIS Quarterly*, *24*, 115–139. doi:10.2307/3250981

Wang, E., Klein, G., & Jiang, J. J. (2007). IT support in manufacturing firms for a knowledge management dynamic capability link to performance. *International Journal of Production Research*, *45*, 2419–2434. doi:10.1080/00207540601020437

Wang, R. Y., & Strong, D. M. (1996). Beyond accuracy: What data quality means to data consumers. *Journal of Management Information Systems*, *12*, 5–34.

Wathen, C. N., & Burkell, J. (2002). Believe it or not: factors influencing credibility on the web. *Journal of the American Society for Knowledge Science and Technology*, *53*, 134–144. doi:10.1002/asi.10016

White, R. W., Jose, J. M., & Ruthven, I. (2006). An implicit feedback approach for interactive information retrieval. *Information Processing & Management*, *42*, 166–190. doi:10.1016/j.ipm.2004.08.010

Whitten, J. L., Bentley, L. D., & Dittman, K. C. (2000). Systems analysis and design methods. Boston, MA: McGraw-Hill Higher Education.

Wu, J. H., & Wang, Y. M. (2006). Measuring KMS success: A respecification of the DeLone and McLean's model. *Information & Management*, *43*, 728–739. doi:10.1016/j.im.2006.05.002

Yang, K. W., & Huh, S. Y. (2007). Intelligent search for experts using fuzzy abstraction hierarchy in knowledge management systems. *Journal of Database Management*, *18*, 47–68.

Zhang, P., & Dillon, A. (2003). HCI and MIS: Shared concerns. *International Journal of Human-Computer Studies*, *59*, 397–402. doi:10.1016/S1071-5819(03)00109-5

Zimmer, J. C., Henry, R. M., & Butler, B. S. (2007/2008). Determinants of the use of relational and nonrelational information sources. *Journal of Management Information Systems*, *24*, 297–331. doi:10.2753/MIS0742-1222240310

Zuckerman, A., & Chaiken, S. (1998). A heuristic-systematic processing analysis of the effectiveness of product warning labels. *Psychology and Marketing*, *15*, 621–641. doi:10.1002/(SICI)1520-6793(199810)15:7<621::AID-MAR2>3.0.CO;2-H

ENDNOTE

1 Based on interviews with those using KMS in industry.

Chapter 2
Knowledge Appraisal and Knowledge Management Systems:
Judging What We Know

Hannah Standing Rasmussen
University of Western Ontario, Canada

Nicole Haggerty
University of Western Ontario, Canada

ABSTRACT

Knowledge management (KM) is a critical practice by which a firm's intellectual capital is created, stored and shared. This has lead to a rich research agenda within which knowledge management systems (KMS) have been a key focus. Our research reveals that an important element of KM practice—knowledge appraisal—is considered in only a fragmentary and incomplete way in research. Knowledge appraisal reflects the multi-level process by which a firm's knowledge is evaluated by the organization or individual for its value. The processes are highly intertwined with the use of the KMS. It therefore requires consideration of KA across multiple levels and types of knowledge across the entire KM cycle. To achieve this goal, we develop and present a taxonomy of knowledge appraisal practices and discuss their role in the KM lifecycle emphasizing implications for research and practice.

INTRODUCTION

If HP knew what HP knows, it would be three times more profitable.

Lew Platt, Former CEO of Hewlett Packard (Davenport & Prusak, 1998 xxi)

Lew Platt's classic quote illustrates the critical challenges and benefits to knowledge management—to excavate what is known from a firm's employees; to collect, store, and share it in some fashion and to then use it to gain greater business value. Knowledge management systems (KMSs) are often introduced into a firm in order to meet this challenge. Yet the introduction of KMSs into a firm often creates new challenges. Among these challenges, firms which introduce KMSs must deal with lack of use of a KMS by users and knowledge becoming outdated or lost with in the KMS (Birkinshaw & Sheehan, 2002). Additionally, from the user perspective, the same KMS which provides helpful access to stores of knowledge can also cause knowledge overload.

Overload represents the situation where a user has access to too much knowledge which they are unable to effectively search and sort through and this contributes to their eventual nonuse of the KMS (Kaser, 2004). Overload is not a new phenomenon. Prior work in KMS design has focused on how to deal with knowledge overload by designing better search techniques, sorting and ranking structures, and other technological solutions. For example, KnowledgeStorm, an Internet-based technology solution resource discusses a variety of KMS solutions that offer to "organize content and make it available to users," or to provide "a search solution" as well as "document management capabilities and the ability to streamline search functions, as well as store and manage scanned images and records from individual workstations into a central, secure repository" (KnowledgeStorm, 2007, p. 5). While valuable, these solutions do not tackle the main issue that organizations are often governed by a philosophy of "keep it all."

The practice of knowledge appraisal (KA) is a cognitive alternative to these technological solutions. KA is made up of the organizational and individual level processes by which a firm's knowledge (tacit and explicit) is evaluated within each step of the knowledge cycle. In the best examples within the literature, KA results in a better knowledge asset because it allows only the relevant, up-to-date, and correct knowledge to continue through the KM processes of using or discarding, adapting, and recreating knowledge. However, currently KA research and practice exists in various independent and fragmented activities. For example, knowledge appraisal practices can be embedded in KMSs via knowledge pricing schemes (Desouza, Yamakawa, & Awazu, 2003) or it can be informally practiced when an individual uses their own judgment and personal criteria for determining whether to create or use knowledge from the KMS or from connecting with a colleague (Gray & Meister, 2004).

Regardless of how or when KA is performed, the practice of KA within an organization is directly linked to how users interact, or do not interact, with an organization's KMS. The type of KA performed in an organization may radically alter the adoption and use of KMS by users, it may affect the amount of outdated knowledge used in an organization, and it may change the knowledge overload experienced by users of the KMS. Yet the fragmented way KA is approached in research and practice means that most organizations do not get full benefit from KA. By drawing together what we know and what we have yet to consider within the processes of knowledge appraisal as they occur throughout the knowledge management cycle and as practiced (or not practiced) by the organization and by individuals, this research seeks to shed a stronger light on "how we come to know what we know" and how managing that process can lead to better design practices and improved adoption and use of KMSs. Our aim is to integrate a variety of research including the library and information science field with practice-based examples to conceptualize the dynamics of KA processes and the degree to which they are intertwined with KMSs.

Thus, our efforts in this research is to (1) demonstrate the prevalence of a fragmented approach to appraisal, (2) to define appraisal and draw on archival theory to develop a theoretically based and more integrated, multifaceted view of appraisal that draws together the fragments of KA that we see in the literature, and (3) show how our approach to KA can be used in KMS design, development, and maintenance research and practice

In this conceptual article, we begin by examining and defining knowledge, knowledge management, and knowledge management systems. We then define knowledge appraisal within the context of four dimensions which we developed based on our review of the literature: organizational vs. individual level appraisal processes and tacit vs. explicit knowledge appraisal processes. This descriptive work summarizes what we observed in our review of the academic literature and enables us to develop a more thorough understanding of the multitude of ways in which KA currently manifests itself in practice. Following this, we develop a KA taxonomy which uses these dimensions to depict all of the ways in which KA practices appear throughout the knowledge management cycle and how KA influences and is influenced by KMSs. In this section we work in a jointly descriptive and prescriptive mode—discussing what practices constitute knowledge appraisal, but also reflecting on how organizations can use this insight to develop their knowledge assets more effectively. We conclude with a discussion of the implications of our work for design, development, and maintenance for KMSs and more broadly for KM and we propose areas of future research to extend this work.

BACKGROUND

Since there are many excellent reviews of the knowledge management research field (Alavi & Leidner, 2001; Spiegler, 2000),we focus here on those aspects of the field which are particularly influential to our work. We take as our core understanding, a definition of knowledge which reflects its dynamic, complex and multifaceted character. Knowledge is shaped by the context in which it is created and used. Thus, we define knowledge as "information combined with experience, context, interpretation, and reflection" (Davenport, Long, & Beers, 1998, p. 44). Our definition of knowledge is further enriched by Polanyi's (1966) distinction between tacit and explicit knowledge in which both tacit knowledge in people's heads and codified, and explicit knowledge, which exists in physical or digital form in reports, manuals, databases, work practices, and procedures is valuable.

Over the last 15 to 20 years, firms have come to see themselves as existing in a knowledge focused world. Almost all tangible resources can be purchased by any corporation. As a result, a firm's knowledge, an intangible resource, is one of the few ways that a firm can be seen as different from the other firms in the same market (Spender, 1996). Thus, in order to be competitive, corporations must create, find, capture, and share knowledge (Davenport & Prusak, 1998; Zack, 1999). This creation, locating, capturing, and sharing of knowledge and expertise reflects the core knowledge management (KM) practices as they are currently applied in firms. It is a very complex and expensive task. Despite the difficulty and expense associated with KM, it can be extremely rewarding and firms have invested substantially in knowledge management systems to capture benefits.

Knowledge Management Systems (KMSs) "are seen as the means to aid organizations in creating, sharing, and using knowledge" (Gallupe, 2001, p. 61). With a well-designed KMS, a corporation can make better use of their knowledge. A

KMS is typically defined as "systems designed and developed to give decision makers/users in organizations the knowledge they need to make their decisions and perform their tasks" (Gallupe, 2001, p. 63). These systems are made up of "people, tools, and technologies, and knowledge that interact to provide knowledge to people in the organization who need it" (Gallupe, 2001, p. 64). These systems, both the technology and people, are used throughout the four of the main process of KM: creating, storing/retrieving, transferring, and applying (Alavi & Leidner, 2001). These processes have been the focus of a large majority of the KM research. Researchers to date have focused on how and why knowledge is created (Nonaka & Takeuchi, 1995; Sabherwal & Becerra-Fernandez, 2003), shared (Gray, 2001), valued (Desouza et al., 2003), used (Gray & Meister, 2004), stored (Markus, 2001; Wijnhoven, 1999; Zack, 1999), and the value these actions give to the firm (Spender, 1996). Additionally, research has focused on how the adoption and design of KMSs (Gallupe, 2001; Stenmark & Lindren, 2004; Edwards, Shaw, & Collier, 2005).

While KMSs have offered great value to KM, they have not been without problems (Stenmark & Lindren, 2004). Research has also begun to acknowledge a critical problem of many KMSs—knowledge overload (Huber, 1991; Kaser, 2004). Knowledge overload occurs when the information or knowledge to be interpreted exceeds an individual or organization's attention and learning capacity to process the information or knowledge properly (Davenport & Prusak, 1998). The result of overload is a "bottleneck" in the flow of knowledge that must be managed in order to gain value from the knowledge (Davenport & Prusak, 1998). A large part of the bottleneck is due to the fact that KMSs are overflowing with knowledge that is incomplete, obsolete, or too context specific (Kaser, 2004). This is the result of the current mentality within organizations of not appraising knowledge and just keeping everything because "time is dear and digital space is cheap" (Kaser, 2004, p. 8). The bottleneck that results from this mentality creates substantial problems for users trying to interact with the KMS. The appraisal act is transferred entirely to the user. The users will always appraise retrieved knowledge to a certain extent; however, in situations like this the entire task of appraisal is transferred to the user. The user must take the time to appraise the knowledge they've retrieved from the KMS before continuing on with the task at hand. This can discourage KMS use, as users may avoid the KMS because of the time it takes to find and appraise the knowledge. The situation also creates conditions for costly mistakes where organizational decisions are based on incorrect knowledge due to the lack of proper appraisal techniques by the individual.

KNOWLEDGE MANAGEMENT SYSTEMS AND KNOWLEDGE APPRAISAL

One of the solutions to overload, as suggested by research in the field of library science (Dearstyne, 1993), is for both individuals and organizations to appraise the value of knowledge and then act in some way on that appraisal to organize, consolidate or eliminate "excess," outdated, or irrelevant knowledge. Because of the constraints of space, libraries have developed appraisal theory and practice to cope with managing the volume and quality of knowledge available by practicing appraisal and archiving books and other resources. An additional benefit of this practice is the time and effort saved on the part of users when trying to find relevant and up-to-date material (Dearstyne, 1993). We believe that both academic research and organizational practice can learn from recognizing that appraisal practices are already occurring in some fashion within all KM activities completed through a KMS and outside a KMS. Additionally, we believe that with a more systematic approach to applying such practices they could develop more strategic knowledge assets which represent what the firm values and is easy for users to find, use and develop. Thus, our efforts in this section are to (1) demonstrate the prevalence of a fragmented research approach to appraisal and (2) to define appraisal and draw on archival theory to develop a more theoretically based, integrated, and multi-faceted view of appraisal that draws together the fragments of KA that we see in the literature.

We define knowledge appraisal (KA) as the organizational and individual level tasks of examining both tacit and explicit knowledge, using criteria and judgments to evaluate it, and deciding if the knowledge should be created, used or reused, codified or kept tacit, kept active, archived or disposed/destroyed. Such appraisal practices can be performed regularly by the individual, as they create, use, search for, scan, and talk to people in order to find the knowledge they believe is the most suitable for their specific task. It can also occur more broadly at the organizational level, as the firm decides what knowledge has strategic value (or what does not and needs to be destroyed) and then acts to ensure this knowledge is available to knowledge users.

KNOWLEDGE APPRAISAL CONCEPTUAL FRAMEWORK

Based on our review of the literature and examination of organizational and individual knowledge management practices, we theorize that KA is a multifaceted process which is already occurring in fragmentary ways throughout firms—a finding which we review, with examples, in this section. It is performed by both individuals (Gray & Meister, 2004) and organizations (Zack, 1999) throughout the entire knowledge management cycle. It is governed by official rules and by informal methods. Additionally we acknowledge that KA acts can be explicit or tacit (Polanyi, 1966)—appraisal itself can be based on a codified set of rules/knowledge or appraisal can take place without the conscious processing of rules or practices. KA, regardless of whether it is done using the KMS or done without the KMS affects the use of the KMS by both the individuals and the organization. For example, KA, if done appropriately with the KMS, may increase the use of the KMS by individuals because the documents they get are up-to-date and relevant. KMS users learn that they do not have to spend very much time appraising the documents themselves because the documents are more likely to reflect the organization's strategy (or whatever the basis of the appraisal is) and thus are more likely to be appropriate. Alternatively, the KMS may not be used by an individual if they do not trust the knowledge in the KMS or it is difficult to find. The individual may appraise a coworker as a better source of knowledge than the KMS. Since KA is a dynamic, ongoing process, one situation can lead to another situation as well. For example, if the decision rules are not appropriate in the first example, the individual may choose to use their coworker as a source instead of the KMS the next time they need others' knowledge to accomplish their work. Additionally, in both situations the KMS could affect the type of KA used by the individual and the organization. For example if the KMS is a highly structured knowledge repository the organization may use decision rules to appraise knowledge. Alternatively, if the KMS is a based on a yellow pages approach, the organization may use an appraisal approach in which individuals are asked to rate and describe knowledge as they use and create it. Regardless, the type of KA and the type of KMS used are highly intertwined. If the KA and KMS are not complementary, then KMS use may not be as high as it could be. This is why it is so important for us to fully understand KA.

In order to more fully explore the many different KA practices that occur in an organization we outline the dimensions of KA below (see Figure 1), and then illustrate both the act of appraisal and the implications of these activities for the KMS, the individuals, and the organization. Figure 1 consists of two dimensions. The Organizational/

Figure 1. Knowledge appraisal conceptual framework

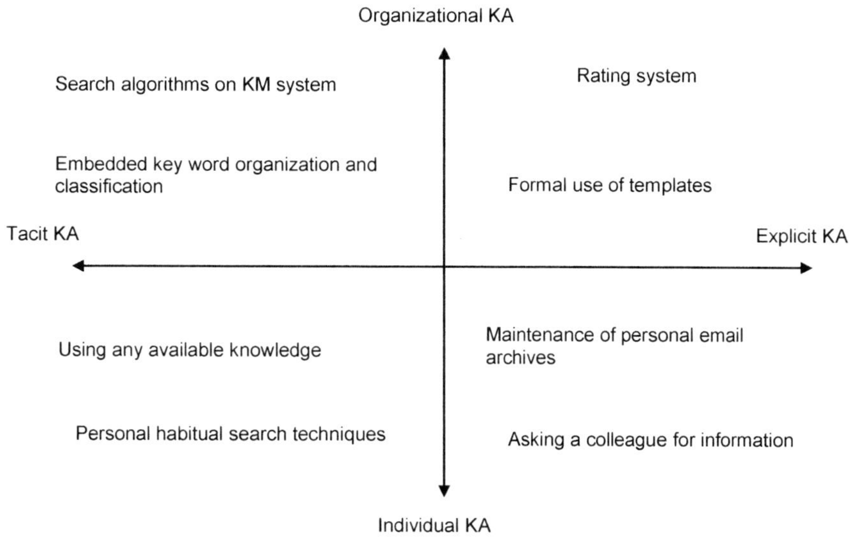

Individual dimension focuses on who is performing the KA activities. The Tacit/Explicit dimension focuses on how deliberate the act of KA is (as distinct from attributes of the knowledge itself). By combining these two dimensions we can fully understand the process of KA as performed by individuals and the KMS and how this affects the organization's knowledge asset. Below we discuss these two dimensions followed by explanations of each quadrant in Figure 1.

Dimension 1: Organizational/ Individual Knowledge Appraisal

Organizational KA occurs via pre-established forms, conventions, and requirements of knowledge within the organization (Davenport et al., 1998; Davenport & Prusak, 1998) and in light of its competitive and regulatory environment. Information technology can be used as a part of the KMSs to ensure that organizational KA is done properly. At the other end of the spectrum is individual knowledge appraisal. In our framework, individual KA is distinct from organizational practice and reflects what goes on inside people's heads as they act to find, analyze, integrate, forget, or eliminate knowledge to accomplish their tasks (Gray & Meister, 2004; Sternberg, 1999). Individual KA is not formally recognized or controlled as it resides within the individual. Individual acts of appraisal are completed in isolation, without reference to an organizationally established set of procedures. Different individuals may appraise the same knowledge very differently and, thus, create different knowledge, use different knowledge, and remove different knowledge. Additionally, Individual KA can be in conflict with an organization's KMS when individual acts of appraisal contradict the KMSs appraisal. Alternatively individual acts of appraisal can complement organizational appraisal. For example, an employee can receive documents from an organization's KMS that have already been appraised as valuable in most situations. This employee can then use individual appraisal acts to determine whether the document is valuable for his or her specific situation. Based on this, we can see how different the results can be for the usage of a KMS, and as a result the knowledge asset of the organization, depending on what types of appraisal acts are performed in an organization and how users interact with the KMS the organization uses. Thus, in order to ensure that the organization gets the most benefit from their KMS we need to understand this tension and design and encourage appraisal practices, both individual and organizational, which are in alignment between the organization, the individual, and the KMS.

Dimension 2: Explicit/Tacit Knowledge Appraisal

Explicit KA is defined as a deliberate act committed by individuals or the organization and demonstrates an intentionality and understanding of the meaning of behaviors and decisions to evaluate knowledge. Tacit KA refers to thoughts, decisions, and acts of appraisal that an individual or the organization is not directly or fully aware of and which is done without deliberate intent.

With these dimensions of knowledge appraisal processes broadly developed, we next review practice-based examples for each quadrant of Figure 1 which provide a fuller illustration of knowledge appraisal and which emphasize the use of KMSs in particular, since that is the critical mechanism by which organizations facilitate KM.

It is important to note that because knowledge is dynamic the dimensions do not exist in isolation. Often KA acts made in one dimension may evolve into acts made in another dimension. For example, at an organizational level, tacit appraisal acts often are the outcome of a former explicit act—the organization may explicitly embed valued knowledge in work practice, or may explicitly establish a ranking based search system based on valued criteria when designing a KMS database or corporate yellow pages. However, over time, the underlying embedded knowledge is forgotten and a form of organizationally endorsed, tacit appraisal is occurring—it slips into the background and yet it influences what knowledge is made available, what knowledge may fall into disuse, and thus gets forgotten, archived, or slated for disposal. Based on this we can see how different the results can be for the usage of a KMS, and, as a result, the knowledge asset of the organization, depending on if the appraisal act is tacit or explicit. Thus, in order to ensure that the organization gets the most benefit from their KMS we need to understand this tension between tacit and explicit practices. This will help with choices about KMS design and decisions about training which can teach and encourage appraisal practices, both individual and organizational, which are in alignment between the organization, the individual, and the KMS.

ORGANIZATIONAL-LEVEL EXPLICIT KNOWLEDGE APPRAISAL

Organizational, explicit knowledge appraisal occurs with established sets of procedures or with clear cut goals (i.e., strategic necessity) and the organization intentionally acts to appraise knowledge. The firm may use a variety of KMS mechanisms to accomplish this including information systems, KM teams, librarians, or networking events between selected people (Davenport & Prusak, 1998). Based on organizationally derived criteria, the appraiser decides whether the knowledge should be kept active, retired, or destroyed. Here we draw more heavily on archival literature as the activities in this quadrant are similar to the archival practices of deciding whether information should be kept active, retired, or destroyed (Grimard, 2004).

Knowledge is kept active when it is used, created, or kept in a place where it can be quickly accessed and easily understood. Knowledge retirement involves the pruning and careful preservation of knowledge that is considered valuable to the future but is not to be left in the active knowledge repository. This is due to the fact that it is not up to date, useful, or is repeated in several other places. This valuable knowledge is still stored in the KMS but not in an area where it can be easily or quickly accessed (Christianson, King, Ahrensfeld, 1991). It is moved so it is still accessible but not contributing to retrieval overload in the primary knowledge repository. Knowledge that is destroyed is the knowledge that is not valuable enough to be preserved or that may have lost is competitive efficacy and therefore must be destroyed to prevent its mistaken use (Grimard, 2004). The organization selects the documents, work practices, and knowledge to be destroyed primarily based on the goal to save essential, valuable knowledge (Dearstyne, 1993).

Organizations can appraise knowledge using their KMS to develop and enforce an established set of procedures and/or assess knowledge as their competitive environment evolves, based on strategic needs. In order to continually meet strategic needs, firms must develop their own appraisal processes within their KM practices to identify, create, share, archive, and destroy knowledge to reflect their competitive advantage. Sometimes this involves storing all reports, consulting engagements, project documents, and so forth, as forms of knowledge. Other times, organizations may act to consolidate prior knowledge to codify it into a new way of doing things via best practices and new business processes.

Organization level, explicit procedures can also aid an organization (and ultimately individuals) to intentionally forget. Organizational forgetting is the loss of a company's knowledge (deHolan, Phillips, & Lawrence, 2004). De Holan et al. (2004) distinguished between intentional and accidental forgetting. Intentional forgetting can result in increased competitiveness (deHolan et al., 2004), though this is very difficult. It occurs through two processes. The first process is unlearning, when knowledge has been appraised and is found to be hurting the organization. This knowledge is removed by the organization disorganizing the "part of its knowledge store" in which the knowledge resides (deHolan et al., 2004, p. 49). The other process of intentionally forgetting knowledge is through avoiding bad habits. This occurs when new knowledge is appraised and is found to be a potential source of harm to an organization. This harm could be due to the fact that the knowledge could be out-dated, incorrect, or it could result in knowledge overload. This knowledge is intentionally not placed into the organization's memory (deHolan et al., 2004).

Despite these benefits, this process of KA may not always be successful. For example, if the criteria are not chosen carefully and properly, with full participation from all stakeholders in the organization or if the organization's culture does not accept organizationally developed explicit KA, then the organization risks accidental forgetting, as well as the situation that by not establishing "what is important" then the emerging knowledge assets of the organization may not be of any strategic value.

Accidental forgetting is associated with the loss of valuable knowledge, which thus reduces a company's competitiveness as they relearn the loss knowledge (deHolan et al., 2004). They proposed two types of accidental forgetting: memory decay and failure to capture. Memory decay occurs when "a company forgets things that have long been embedded in it organizational memory" (deHolan et al., 2004, p. 47). Failure to capture occurs to new knowledge when a company "neglects to make valuable new information available to the rest of the organization" (deHolan et al., 2004, p. 48).

We believe that organizational, explicit KA is a critical foundation to successful KM practice with direct implications or the use of a KMS. All of these procedures are done through the various parts of the KMS. The human element of the KMS determines the criteria to evaluate the knowledge and the tools and technologies are used to perform the tasks. There are several examples in practice that show this process of KA as it occurs during the use of a KMS. For example, at Siemens, a team took part in an organizationally mandated, explicit knowledge appraisal activity when they established both a rating system and strong editorial control in order to provide quality control on their KMS called ShareNet (MacCormack & Volpel, 2002). The result was a more useful KMS for users to interact with and KM activities that reflect what the organization felt was strategically valuable. At Xerox customer-service engineers shared repair tips on the Eureka KMS system. These tips were created via evaluation processes used by subject-matter experts (as defined by the organization) before the tip could be placed into a database that all customer-service technicians had access to (Biren, 2000). These practices reflect an organizationally defined approach to knowledge appraisal with direct consequences for the quality and value of the resulting knowledge asset.

These examples demonstrate that often knowledge in a KMS is subjected to evaluation using an established set of procedures. The result of this process of appraisal, if done with appraisal criteria that were chosen carefully and properly with full participation from all stakeholders in the organization, will result in KA at each step of the KM cycle that will compliment the mandate of the organization (Grimard, 2004). As well, this constant adding, reshaping and pruning of the KMS will ensure that the knowledge asset that is being cultivated will be easy for users to interact with. This can help an organization to learn since this process of KA will allow knowledge to be encoded into the "routines that guide behaviour" (Levitt & March, 1988, p. 320). Ultimately these organizationally led, explicit choices shape knowledge assets within the KMS to reflect things that are important to the organization and this will ultimately help shape what the individual views as important and valuable knowledge.

ORGANIZATIONAL-LEVEL TACIT KNOWLEDGE APPRAISAL

Organizational, tacit knowledge appraisal acts are seen in our conceptualization to reflect situations in which a priori, organizational decisions become embedded in practices (like search and ranking systems in KMSs, or new procedures), but which over time, lose their "explicitness." Over time, such decisions take on a tacit quality for the organization because they move out of conscious awareness during KMS use or work practice and simply reflect "the way things are done." Individual using a KMS may not even be aware that the KMS is acting in particular ways based on a priori decisions embedded within the system. Alternatively, work groups acting within "best practices" may unconsciously enact the "way things are done" well past their usefulness and value. The result is that decisions can be made but individuals may not be fully aware of the implications of their actions. While performing this type of act the appraiser does not knowingly decide if the knowledge should be active (created, used, or kept easily accessible), retired, or destroyed on their own. Instead they decide if the knowledge should be active (created, used, or kept easily accessible), retired, or destroyed after it has already been appraised by the automated system.

The tools and technologies of the KMS perform this type of KA. This process of appraisal can be valuable to an organization because it would not be influenced by an individual or group concerns with being involved in potentially political behavior (Galunic & Weeks, 1999). For example, organizational, tacit KA can more easily enable an effort to develop the knowledge base by concealing identities and thus enable the appraisal of a junior consultant's work as valuable and a senior partner's work as appropriate for retirement or destruction. However, it could quite easily result in accidental organizational forgetting (deHolan et al., 2004), since the organization may forget embedded appraisal practices and be unaware of the long term implications of their actions. They may make decisions they would otherwise not make if they were aware of the long term implications of such practices.

Examples of this process of knowledge appraisal can be seen in the act of users at Buckman Laboratory using the search feature of a KMS to "find a list of abstracts concerning a particular person or subject area and then, based on those abstracts, decided which documents to download for viewing" (Fulmer, 2003, pp. 8). Knowledge value was appraised because if the knowledge in the database did not fit into the search terms the knowledge was not considered valuable enough to see (Grimard, 2004). This organization tacit appraisal had embedded the act of appraisal in the search algorithms. For example, the organizational procedure may be to limit the search to certain terms or certain authors. This limiting is an act of formal appraisal since it allows the individual to judge the worth of documents based on the search terms. However, it is tacit because the users are likely not fully aware that by following their own procedures (using particular search terms), the KMS is already appraising the value of the knowledge as only knowledge linked to the search terms is presented and thus assessed as potentially valuable.

INDIVIDUAL-LEVEL EXPLICIT KNOWLEDGE APPRAISAL

Individuals involved in individual-level explicit knowledge appraisal understand that they are participating in deciding whether the knowledge should be created, used, kept active, retired, or destroyed for their own, local, task-related purposes. However, their acts of appraisal are not officially recognized or formally developed by the organization (though they are likely, in part, influenced by what the organization formalizes). This process of knowledge appraisal can be more risky for the organization than organizational explicit knowledge appraisal since the individual involved may not be reflecting organizationally defined ways for appraising value. This may lead to appraisal that is more appropriate for each individual and not for the organization as a whole. The organization's knowledge may not be consistently appraised with the organization's goals in mind. This may lead to unintentional forgetting as well as direct how the knowledge assets of the firm emerge and the degree to which they are aligned with the firm's goals and routines. Alternatively, if the organizational culture is resistant to explicit organizational appraisal acts or the cognitive style of the employee does not fit into a formal, analytical process then individual explicit processes of KA may benefit the organization as they may result in serendipitous advantages such as intentional forgetting, organizational learning, as well as the alignment of the knowledge asset with the firm's goals and routines.

An example of this process of KA comes from practices at Booz-Allen & Hamilton in which an employee describes the process he went through to find a technology specialist to help him with a project.

So I e-mailed another colleague of mine who worked on the same assignment and who is a technology specialist and I said "what do you know about this subject?" He gave me a few things but he couldn't come to the meeting I'd set up. So he suggested another person. (Galunic & Weeks, 1999, pp. 13).

Through this process the individual took part in individual level explicit knowledge appraisal. He appraised the knowledge of the colleague based on his job title and prior work experience, and decided to use the knowledge given. This was an individual level explicit act because he consciously decided to use the colleague as a knowledge source based on his job title but he did not have a set of formal organizational procedures by which to decide that his colleague's knowledge is valuable. Often in this type of KA, the KMS is largely absent. Knowledge professionals are not involved nor are the tools and technologies of the KMS. The KMS may be used to find or identify knowledge but it is not used to appraise the knowledge. The implication of this is that the KMS may simply be seen by users as a storage facility rather than an enabling tool. In this situation the KMS is not fully adopted and the organization and users do not fully benefit from the investment the organization made. A small design change, allowing users to rate the knowledge they access for quality or usefulness, may change the way the KMS is used. This design change may also affect the organizational level KA. It could move organizational level tacit KA into organizational level explicit KA as the organization re-evaluates the historical lack of appraisal and makes changes to develop formal practices based on user insights.

INDIVIDUAL-LEVEL TACIT KNOWLEDGE APPRAISAL

A knowledge appraisal act that would fall into the individual-level tacit section of the conceptual framework would be an act that does not have a routine or policy and the individual involved was not performing the tasks with deliberate intent but instead is relying on prior experience, internally held beliefs, and other forms of tacit understanding. This process of KA is perhaps the most risky and difficult to observe; risky in that mindless use or discarding of knowledge may result in the knowledge assets of the firm being poorly aligned with the organization's strategy. This is because individuals may be unthinkingly incorporating available knowledge without cognitively processing appraisal acts which would reveal if it was (1) relevant, (2) current, (3) valuable, (4) mistaken, and so forth. However, individual tacit knowledge appraisal is commonly used by individuals on explicit and tacit knowledge. This is due to the ease of use of this KA act and the time consuming quality of other processes of KA. Additionally, this process of KA may suit many individuals' cognitive style and may complement many organizations' culture. While it is risky, it may also result in unique organization learning and forgetting.

An example of this process of knowledge appraisal occurred at Booz-Allen & Hamilton in which several junior employees used all knowledge on a specific subject found on their KM system in a report. The junior employees "had cobbled together a bunch of stuff that they didn't understand" (Galunic & Weeks, 1999, p. 12). This team of junior consultants had made an individual level tacit act of appraisal by using all of the knowledge without specific rules about what they would use and by assuming that all knowledge in the KMS was valuable without consciously appraising the knowledge as applicable to their project when they decided to use it. Again, with this type of KA, the KMS is often used to identify or find knowledge but not to consciously appraise it. Instead their use was based on the prevailing assumption of novice KMS users that everything in the KMS must be valuable.

As we have outlined, each process of KA predominately makes use of the firm's KMS—either by way of the knowledge assets stored in it or the communication it facilitates between users. Each type of KA has its risks and benefits to the organization and results in knowledge assets which evolve along lines which are either well aligned with organizational and individual goals or which are more divergent from them. With this foundation we now develop a taxonomy of appraisal practices that occurs throughout the knowledge management cycle and which can serve to inform research and practice in the development of KMSs in particular.

A KNOWLEDGE APPRAISAL TAXONOMY

Based on a review of these "lifecycle" frameworks, we select the well accepted model of Alavi and Leidner (2001) and outline four of the main processes of KM: creating, storing/retrieving, transferring, and applying. Within each, we integrate the phenomenon of KA to develop a taxonomy which is summarized in Table 1. Within our research, this taxonomy approach allows us to theorize about the relationship between different

Table 1. Knowledge appraisal taxonomy within the knowledge management cycle

Knowledge Process	Taxonomy of Knowledge Appraisal Acts			
	Org/Explicit	**Org/tacit**	**Ind./Explicit**	**Ind. Tacit**
Knowledge Creation/Use The development and use of new knowledge (Alavi & Leidner, 2001) Appraisal of the value of the knowledge—is it valuable enough to be created and used? Should it be retired, sent to secondary storage or discarded?	• Hiring librarians/archivists to formally appraise business value based on specific criteria of new knowledge before it is included in the KMS to be used • Formal use of templates and best practices based on knowledge already in KMS	• Organizationally endorsed informal "water cooler" meetings to brainstorm • Embedded decision rules regarding types of knowledge created (template, etc.) in KMS	• Consciously creating knowledge that "fits" individual specific criteria, that is, type of knowledge, amount, style, and so forth, for a task • Choosing which knowledge to use in a project based on a conscious set of individual criteria—author, age of document, type of document, format	• Using all knowledge available that fits embedded individual criteria, that is, automatically discarding as "irrelevant" knowledge from certain countries or certain projects
Storing/retrieving The collecting, storing, and retrieving of knowledge into a knowledge store or repository (Wijnhoven, 2003; Alavi & Leidner, 2001). Appraisal of the value of the knowledge—is it valuable enough to be made permanent? Should we assign a time limit and then discard it? Appraisal of the value of the knowledge—based on its value where should it be stored? Should it be immediately online in the KMS or archived in secondary storage?	• Core KM team develops standard to be used to decided which discussions in the forums should be permanent knowledge and which should be eliminated or digitally filed (Fulmer, 2003) • Constantly visible formal rating system and formal best practices embedded in KMS for retrieving knowledge.	• Embedded formal rating system throughout organization to decide what knowledge should be stored and provided • Embedded key word organization and classification that limits retrieval results • Validated tips placed into a searchable database (Biren, 2000).	• Personal validation of individual or source that is providing the knowledge before it is kept. • Maintenance of personal knowledge database, e-mail archives from sources deemed expert or of knowledge deemed valuable to specific projects and tasks.	• Collecting all or no knowledge regardless of value or source • Personal habitual search techniques
Knowledge Transfer The process of moving knowledge to places in the organization where it is needed and can be used (Alavi & Leidner, 2001). Appraisal of the value of the knowledge by the colleague—is his knowledge valuable enough to be sent to the employee? Should it be kept within particular geographical limits or business units?	• Formal best practices targeted to individual or group. • International sharing of knowledge via KMS, corporate yellow pages in conjunction with KM team who evaluates applicability in different settings (geography, industry, etc.)	• Automatic updates e-mailed throughout organization • Automatic global transfer of knowledge	• E-mailing trusted sources for knowledge • Using or developing social capital as a way of predefining appraisal criteria. • At Booz-Allen & Hamilton an employee described e-mailing colleague he trusted in order to find knowledge (Galunic & Weeks, 1999).	• Mass e-mailing for knowledge or sending knowledge indiscriminately • Forwarding all e-mails regardless of value to receiving party • Collecting all or no knowledge regardless of value or source
Knowledge Application (Reuse) The use of knowledge subsequent to its creation. It can be reused by the original creator or by someone entirely different. (Alavi & Leidner, 2001). Appraisal of the value of the knowledge created by one group by a different group– is it valuable enough to reuse? Should it be "destroyed" because it no longer has strategic value or lacks it in the new context?	• Best practices are developed and mandated for use • Re-evaluation of knowledge and appraisal practices • Formal use of best practices based on knowledge already in KMS • At Siemens a group used the experience of another group from Denmark to win a job contract in Malaysian (Maccormack & Volpel, 2002).	• Embedded decision rules regarding types of knowledge used • No re-evaluation of knowledge and appraisal practices	• Intentional use of knowledge from specific sources • Criteria use from one project applied to another	• All knowledge in given source used • Habitual sources and/or knowledge used

appraisal acts and the KM cycle. This is important because it allows us to create a classification framework to further our understanding of KA and to consolidate in one framework what is currently a fragmented understanding within research and practice. By doing this we can begin to understand appraisal as a dynamic process which is closely linked to KMS usage.

Knowledge creation signals the start of the KM cycle and reflects the stage at which the individual or organization actively creates new knowledge (Alavi & Leidner, 2001). During this process, knowledge appraisal is a key process in determining whether the knowledge being created is valuable enough to be remembered, if tacit or codified, and stored, if explicit. The KMS is used as the storage location to collect and place newly created knowledge into a knowledge repository (Wijnhoven, 2003).

The knowledge storing/retrieving stage is made up of the KMS activities that result in the knowledge in the organization being easily accessible and useable. Some of the KMS activities include codifying knowledge, deleting context, and filtering and pruning (Markus, 2001).

Organizations and individuals use KA in the packaging stage to decide whether the knowledge is valuable enough to be repackaged in order to be accessed by more people or whether it may lose its value by being repackaged. This stage is also used to choose the correct form of preservation (Markus, 2001). KA is used to decide how easily accessible the knowledge should be, based on its value—some knowledge may need to be instantly accessible. However, some knowledge may be viewed as required less frequently and for the sake of decreasing knowledge overload, be moved into an archive.

Retrieval, the process by which individuals find the knowledge they seek (Mills, 2004), is the next stage of the cycle. KA is used in the stage of knowledge retrieval to decide whether the knowledge is valuable enough to be retrieved.

Similarly, KA is used in the knowledge transfer stage, the process of moving knowledge to places in the organization where it is needed and can be used (Alavi & Leidner, 2001), to determine whether the knowledge is valuable enough to be transferred. Predetermined ranking systems, search algorithms, and knowledge markets can serve to appraise knowledge during these phases. Alternatively, at the individual level, users may reject formal, explicit appraisal and instead pursue a more trial and error implicit method of evaluating, using or discarding knowledge they collect.

Finally, organizations and individuals apply KA in the application/reuse stage to determine whether the knowledge is valuable enough to be applied or reused. At this stage knowledge is reused either by the original creator or by someone entirely different (Alavi & Leidner, 2001). Further, during this process, individuals and firms, over time, must consider the possibility of destroying knowledge to avoid knowledge overload.

Table 1 summarizes both the activities commonly studied in these KM processes as well as examples of different processes of KA, from a variety of sources, which can occur during these different activities. By developing these examples we seek to demonstrate the wide variety of KA processes from each of the four KA dimensions within each stage of the knowledge management lifecycle. Within this table we've also illustrated the way in which KA occurs through the use of a firm's KMS. Table 1 clearly demonstrates that KA occurs by both individuals and organizations, with both tacit and explicit knowledge, throughout KMS usage activities.

KNOWLEDGE APPRAISAL DYNAMICS: AN EXAMPLE EXPLANATION

In the previous section we have shown how KA occurs throughout the KM processes. In this section we intend to illustrate how to interpret Table

1 with examples focusing on how KMSs are used to aid the KA in the KM processes through which an organization creates or discovers, captures, shares, and applies knowledge (Alavi & Leidner, 2001; Sabherwal & Becerra-Fernandez, 2003). Additionally, we show how KA can improve the use of the KMS. We use only one column—the organizational explicit dimension of KA for this illustrative purpose.

KNOWLEDGE CREATION/USE

During the process of knowledge creation and use, the KMS is used as the storage location to collect and place newly created knowledge into a knowledge repository (Wijnhoven, 2003). Within the organizational explicit dimension, for example, the KMS is used not just as a storage location. The KMS can be used to develop a knowledge strategy (Zack, 1999) and map the knowledge they require to fulfill their strategy against the core, advanced, and innovative knowledge they possess (Zack, 1999). Identifying gaps and acting to fill in those gaps serves as the competitive impetus for knowledge appraisal practices. At Hill & Knowlton, the organization created a method of explicit, template-based knowledge creation included presentations, text documents, and case studies (Mark, 2004). The organization was aware and valued the explicit KA acts of template use and used a KMS that was designed for this type of knowledge and knowledge appraisal.

KNOWLEDGE STORING/ RETRIEVING

The knowledge storing/retrieving stage is made up of the KMS activities that result in the knowledge in the organization being easily accessible and useable. Some of the KMS activities include codifying knowledge, deleting context, and filtering and pruning (Markus, 2001).

Within the organizational explicit dimension, for example, the KMS can be used through the use of a constantly visible formal rating system to determine where to store knowledge. The KMS is also used in the organizational explicit dimension for retrieval, the process by which individuals find the knowledge they seek (Mills, 2004). KA is used in the stage of knowledge retrieval to decide if the knowledge is valuable enough to be retrieved.

Knowledge Transfer

The KMS is also used in the organizational explicit dimension in the knowledge transfer stage. Predetermined ranking systems, search algorithms, and knowledge markets can serve to appraise knowledge during this phase. Within the organizational explicit dimension, as an example, the KMS can be used to determine how easily accessible the knowledge should be, based on its value. For example, the organization may have determined that one of their criteria for retirement of knowledge is date created or last used. Thus, the KMS can be used to monitor dates of documents and then, for the sake of decreasing knowledge overload, move older or less used documents into an archive or out of the KMS.

Knowledge Application (Reuse)

Finally, organizations use the KMS to apply KA in the application/reuse stage to determine whether the knowledge is valuable enough to be applied or reused. We pointed out earlier that it is important to remember that the dimensions do not exist in isolation. It is also important to note that the KM stages do not exist in isolation either. Often KA acts made in one stage will affect the knowledge used in the next stage. For example, within the organizational explicit dimension, the KMS activity of codifying knowledge within the knowledge storing/retrieving stage can dramatically change the use of the knowledge later.

Specifically if the knowledge is codified in a way that removes problems of the knowledge being too context specific, then the knowledge may be used in a way that it would not have been used if it was not codified.

DISCUSSION

Knowledge management systems (KMSs) have become a critical organizational tool by which a firm's intellectual capital is created, stored, and shared. To date the research agenda in this field has focused on the various practices by which a firm creates, uses, stores, and retrieves knowledge and the risks and benefits that firms gain by pursuing the development and adoption of KMSs. However, our research reveals that KA, the processes by which individuals and organizations evaluate knowledge, has only received fragmentary attention in the research. Without an integrated understanding of KA, our research shows at least one of the major avenues by which KMSs become overloaded with redundant, partial, mistaken, or too context specific knowledge as well as valuable knowledge. It has been recognized that KMS with these characteristics are extremely difficult for users to make use of, thus leading to misuse, poor use which detract from realizing the business value of knowledge management. Our research has provided the first unified view of knowledge appraisal as a valuable knowledge management activity. Knowledge appraisal, as theorized by library science, gives us the language and framework for considering an important, dynamic KM practice which is only partially represented in research and practice but as we have demonstrated, has significant implications for the design and maintenance of KMS—the key tool employed by firms to achieve the benefits of managing their knowledge. Our taxonomy is a way of indicating a comprehensive set of both research opportunities and management practices to link KA into the knowledge management phenomenon more thoroughly and systematically.

KMS Design and Maintenance Implications

Throughout this article, we have drawn attention to many of the negative impacts on KMS design and maintenance that can occur when KA is not considered or is only considered in a fragmented manner. For example, KMSs can be designed in a manner that is inadvertently in conflict with the organization's KA strategy. This can result in a KMS that does not provide the knowledge that is considered valuable to the organization or does not provide it in a timely manner. Yet as we have illustrated, KMS and KA practices can complement each other and add value to an organization. Outlined below are some of the implications on KMS design and maintenance that may occur with the consideration of the KA framework.

It is important to note that design and maintenance implications are not just about how the technology is designed but how the KMS system (as reflected in people, processes, and technology) is designed. Thus, we outline implications regarding the design and maintenance of the KMS as defined earlier in our article as being made up of "people, tools, and technologies, and knowledge that interact to provide knowledge to people in the organization who need it," (Gallupe, 2001, p. 64). By doing this we can illustrate how the dynamic nature of appraisal can be used to improve the design and maintenance of a KMS.

A key figure in the design and maintenance of a KMS is the KM manager. This individual should adopt "appraisal" knowledge into his or her portfolio of responsibilities (just as librarians do from archival theory), revisit formalized organizational practices of appraisal often to ensure that they still are appropriate given the changing nature of organizational strategy, and be ready to change formalized organizational practices of appraisal when necessary. Additionally, KM managers need to be aware of KA practices throughout the framework that either complement the organizational strategy and could be brought into a more formal role or that are in conflict with the organizational strategy and need to be watched or actively discouraged. Additionally, the KM manager can consider how an organization's KA strategy may be in conflict with individual KA behaviors and design a KMS to either discourage the individual KA behavior or to somehow allow both to co-exist with less friction. This could be as simple as hiring librarians as part of the KMS to perform KA and to interpret the results for individuals.

Finally, the entire KM team, designers, managers, and knowledge workers need to consider how the dynamic nature of knowledge results in the four dimensions affecting each other and, as a result, the needs, requirements, and usage of the KMS. For example, the organizational explicit KA behavior of templates can create the conditions for the individual tacit KA behavior of discarding all knowledge that does not fit into the template regardless of value. If this occurs then the KMS will not be used to its full potential. Instead of the "people, tools, and technologies, and knowledge" (Gallupe, 2001, p. 64) being used to provide knowledge to people within the organization the technology is being used simply to discard knowledge. As a result the KM team would have to re-evaluate the use of templates and investigate practices, such as rating systems for knowledge that is not stored in the template, to ensure that the KA behavior is not damaging to the organization.

KMS Adoption and Use Implications

The adoption and use of a KMS still present some very challenging issues. Since many organizations today have made large investments in KMS, its nonadoption, or incomplete adoption, can result in lost productivity as systems are either not used at all or not used to their full capabilities (Jasperson, Carter, & Zmud, 2006). We have highlighted in this article the many ways that the fragmented nature of KA, as it exists now, can impair the adoption and use of a KMS. For example, a KMS that does not provide KA on the documents in its repository then the user may feel that other sources, coworkers or Internet search tools, are more useful or faster. However, the dynamic nature of KA can also improve the adoption and use of a KMS.

The adoption and use of a KMS is effected by the views and behaviors of everyone in the organization. However, the KM manager, and KM team, can play an important role in aiding the adoption and use of the KMS through the consideration of all aspects of the KA framework. For example, in this article we've considered how the dynamic nature of knowledge appraisal, defined by the four different but related dimensions, effects the needs, requirements, and usage of the KMS. The KM team needs to fully investigate the organizational culture, the individual preferences, and the KMS to ensure that the KA behaviors introduced, encouraged and discouraged by the organization, through the technology, tools, and people all are working together to improve the knowledge asset of the organization. Additionally, the KA performed in this way will ensure that the KMS usage will increase because the KMS will be maintained and made easier to use and useful.

CONCLUSION AND FUTURE WORK

By exploring KA throughout the KM cycle within the context of the KMS and understanding whether the process is either governed by organization or individual acts and whether it is either an explicit choice vs. a tacit, passive act, we can begin to determine when certain types of knowledge are created, retrieved, and used whereas other knowledge is not created, must be retired/archived, destroyed, or is intentionally or unintentionally forgotten. By developing an understanding of this, our research demonstrates the crucial linkages between the users' experience with KMS and important design considerations for developing highly usable KMS which contain knowledge which is clearly and dynamically linked to evolving firm strategy.

This line of theorizing also helps to illustrate the emergent nature of the knowledge assets developed in organizations and offers some explanation as to how and when actual knowledge assets within the KMS diverge from the strategic orientation of the firm.

By illustrating the processes of KA, we can begin to understand in more detail the motives and logic underlying the KM lifecycle and the way in which KMS use supports all aspects of the lifecycle and as a result we can begin to more fully understand the knowledge asset itself. The process of KA, in all parts of the KMS, is a crucial research phenomenon. In this article, we have developed a taxonomy which can be used to begin theorizing the various manifestations of these processes and the role they play in the knowledge management cycle. This article illustrates how more fully understanding the processes of KA will allow us to improve the design, development, and maintenance of the KMS and thus the knowledge asset of an organization.

This framework, however, also suggests many other questions. For example, there is a potential for conflict within organizations based on the four different processes of KA. If, for example, an individual uses tacit KA, using any and all knowledge that they can source and the organizational culture creates the expectation for explicit KA, which uses organizationally endorsed goals and processes then the individual's KA processes and results will be in conflict with the organization's expectations. Field work is needed in order to more fully explore this potential conflict and the consequences it has for both the individual and the firm. Additionally, there is the possibility that many of the issues in KM, the push for codification of knowledge, the difficulty in managing tacit knowledge, the challenges of knowledge overload, and KBS misuse or nonuse, may be further informed by KA. For example, in our view, formal, explicit, organizational-level KA practices which emphasize evaluating vast quantities of codified knowledge and discarding or destroying that which is no longer useful is a critical process to alleviate knowledge overload—a key condition for lack of knowledge sharing in firms. This practice is well developed in other fields, yet seems to contradict the general feeling in the KM field that "storage is cheap so save everything." Future research needs to investigate formal appraisal practices and their associated costs and link these practices to the individual level phenomenon of adoption of KMSs, knowledge use, and value creation.

Our research leads us to conclude that many companies take part in differing amounts of the four types of knowledge appraisal. However, additional research is needed to more fully understand the existence of KA and the reasons and implications for its existence or nonexistence in the organization, the individuals, and on the knowledge asset itself. By more fully exploring KA, we will begin to understand the pressures of knowledge at work in the modern organization and how, by judging what we know and subjecting it to appraisal, we strengthen the value of that knowledge.

REFERENCES

Alavi, M., & Leidner, D.E. (2001). Review: Knowledge management and knowledge management systems: Conceptual foundations and research issues. *Management and Information Systems Quarterly, 25*(1), 107-136.

Anderson, J. (1990). *Cognitive psychology and its implications.* New York: W.H. Freeman.

Biren, B. (2000). *Xerox: Building a corporate focus on knowledge.* Fontainebleau: INSEAD.

Birkinshaw, J., & Sheehan, T. (2002). Managing the knowledge life cycle. *MIT Sloan Management Review, 44*(1), 75-84.

Christianson, E.B., King, D.E., & Ahrensfeld, J.L. (1991). *Special libraries: A guide for management.* Washington: Special Libraries Association.

Davenport, T.H., Long, D.W.D., & Beers, M.C. (1998). Successful knowledge management projects. *Sloan Management Review, 39*(2), 43-57.

Davenport, T.H., & Prusak, L. (1998). *Working knowledge: How organizations manage what they know.* Boston: Harvard Business School Press.

Dearstyne, B.W. (1993). *The archival enterprise: Modern archival principles, practices and management technique.* Chicago: American Library Association.

deHolan, P.M., Phillips, N., & Lawrence, T.B. (2004). Managing organizational forgetting. *MIT Sloan Management Review, 45*(2), 45-54.

Desouza, K., Yamakawa, S., & Awazu, Y. (2003, September/October). Pricing organizational knowledge: An imperative. *Ivey Business Journal,* 1-5.

Edwards, J.S., Shaw, D., & Collier, P.M. (2005). Knowledge management systems: Finding a way with technology. *Journal of Knowledge Management, 9*(1), 113-125.

Fulmer, W.E. (2003). Fulmer, William E., Buckman Laboratories (A). Boston: Harvard Business School Publishing.

Gallupe, R.B. (2001). Knowledge management systems: Surveying the landscape. *International Journal of Management Practices, 3*(1), 61-77.

Galunic, C., & Weeks, J. (1999). *Managing knowledge at Booz-Allen & Hamilton: Knowledge online and off.* Fontainebleau: INSEAD.

Gray, P.H. (2001). The impact of knowledge repositories on power and control in the workplace. *Information Technology & People, 14*(4), 368-384.

Gray, P.H., & Meister, D.B. (2004). Knowledge sourcing effectiveness. *Management Science, 50*(6), 821-834.

Grimard, J. (2004). Program evaluation and archives: Appraising archival work and achievements. *Archivaria, 58*(2), 69-88.

Huber, G. (1991). Organizational learning: The contributing processes and the literatures. *Organization Science, 2*(1), 88-115.

Jasperson, J.S., Carter, P.E., & Zmud, R.W. (2005). A comprehensive conceptualization of post adoptive behaviors associated with information technology enabled work systems. *Management and Information Science Quarterly, 29*(3), 525-557.

Kaser, D.(2004). When all is nothing and something more. *Information Today, 21*(8), 16-17.

Knowledge Storm. (2007). Search results for knowledge management systems. Retrieved September 4, 2007, from http://www.knowledgestorm.com/SearchServlet?ksAction=Search&col=kslive&rf=0&srchtype=key&stype=&bi=1&ei=0&oq=null&vf=null&tId=&sId=&sSeq=1&regId=&lsTime=null&type=key&kw=knowledge+management+systems&isAdv=false&x=0&y=0)

Levitt, B., & March, J.G. (1998). Organizational learning. *Annual Review of Sociology, 14*, 319-340.

MacCormack, A., & Volpel, S. (2002). *Siemens ShareNet: Building a knowledge network.* Boston: Harvard Business School Publishing.

Mark, K.M., & Darren. (2004). *Hill & Knowlton: Knowledge management.* London: Ivey Management Services.

Markus, L.M. (2001). Toward a theory of knowledge reuse: Types of knowledge reuse situations and factors in reuse success. *Journal of Management Information Systems, 18*(1), 57-94.

Mills, J. (2004). Faceted classification and logical division in information retrieval. *Library Trends, 52*(3), 541-571.

Nonaka, I., & Takeuchi, H. (1995). *The knowledge-creating company.* New York: Oxford University Press.

Polanyi, M. (1966). *The tacit dimension.* New York: Anchor Day Books.

Sabherwal, R., & Becerra-Fernandez, I. (2003). An empirical study of the effect of knowledge management processes at individual, group, and organizational levels. *Decision Sciences, 24*(2), 225-260.

Spender, J.C. (1996). Making knowledge the basis of a dynamic theory of the firm. *Strategic Management Journal, 17,* 45-62.

Spiegler, I. (2000). Knowledge management: A new idea or a recycled concept? *Communications of the AIS, 3*(4), 2-26.

Stenmark, D., & Lindgren, R. (2004). Integrating knowledge management systems with everyday work: Design principles leveraging user practice. In *Proceedings of the 37th Annual Hawaii International Conference* (pp. 9-18).

Sternberg, R. (1999). *Cognitive psychology.* Orlando, FL: Harcourt Brace & Company.

Wijnhoven, F. (1999). Development scenarios for organizational memory information systems. *Journal of Management Information Systems, 16*(1), 121-146.

Wijnhoven, F. (2003). Operation knowledge management: Identification of knowledge objects, operation methods and goals and means for the support function. *The Journal of the Operational Research Society, 54*(2), 194-202.

Zack, M.H. (1999). Developing a knowledge strategy. *California Management Review, 41*(3), 125-145.

This work was previously published in the Journal of Organizational and End User Computing, Vol. 20, Issue 1, edited by M. Mahmood, pp. 17-34, copyright 2008 by IGI Publishing (an imprint of IGI Global).

Chapter 3
Rewarding End-Users for Participating in Organizational KM:
A Case Study

Mayasandra N. Ravishankar
National University of Singapore, Singapore

ABSTRACT

Organizations position their formal knowledge management (KM) initiatives as a continuous process of deriving strategic benefits from the knowledge resources dispersed in the various internal constituencies. While most organizations implement a rewards program attached to their KM initiative, the influence exerted by such programs on employees' responses to organizational KM is less well understood. In this context, this article focuses on the KM initiative of Rexon,[1] a leading Indian software services and products company recognised globally as a successful KM exponent. Adopting the case study methodology, we conducted intensive fieldwork for 6 months over a 2 year period at Rexon. Evidence from the case highlights how a KM-related rewards program was used to build awareness about organizational KMS and how employees responded to the rewards program. The theoretical and managerial contributions of the study are discussed.

INTRODUCTION

Formal knowledge management (KM) initiatives promise to trigger improvements in the utilization of an organization's knowledge resources. In the last decade or so, both the number of organizations embracing KM and the studies examining such efforts have risen steadily. Organizational interventions bracketed under the rubric of KM typically involve the implementation of an IT-based system designated as a knowledge management system (KMS) (Alavi & Leidner, 1999, 2001; Alavi & Tiwana, 2002; Gray, 2000; Schultze & Boland Jr., 2000). With rapid advancements in IT, initiating an organization-wide KM initiative has become relatively easier and studies have examined the organizational factors considered vital for realizing desired benefits from KM. While such studies argue that in the presence of certain important factors KM interventions produce intended results (Davenport, De Long, & Beers, 1998; Gold, Malhotra, & Segars, 2001; Holsapple & Joshi, 2000), other studies also highlight barriers to the adoption of KM initiatives[2] (Desouza, 2003a, 2003b; Fahey & Prusak, 1998; Ruggles, 1998; Walsham, 2001). Typically, such barriers are seen to include barriers to contributing documents to a KMS, to making use of available knowledge artifacts, to sharing documents, and so forth.

One important component built into a KM initiative to help overcome the barriers to adoption of a KMS is the rewards program. By rewards program we refer to the monetary and nonmonetary incentives that an organization offers to its employees for utilizing the organizational KMS. Though potentially the rewards program vitally influence the extent of interest in KM amongst the end-user communities and may also affect the successful implementation of the KM initiative in the long run, their influence on a organizational KM initiative is less well understood and very few empirical studies of the same are available. In this article, we address this gap by attempting to answer the questions: (1) How does an organizational rewards program influence employees' response to a KM initiative? and (2) How can organizations create an effective KM related rewards program?

We adopt the case study method and look into the implementation of an organization-wide KM initiative at *Rexon*, an India-based IT services company. The case study method remains one of the frequently adopted research methods, and the usefulness of the method is well documented (Benbasat, Goldstein, & Mead, 1987; Cavaye, 1996; Markus, 1983; Myers, 1994; Orlikowski, 1993). As Benbasat et al. (1987, p.370) point out, the relevance of the case study method is enhanced in light of the shift from purely technological issues to organizational issues in mainstream IT/IS research.

This article is organized as follows: In the next section, we review the existing literature on organizational KM. This is followed by a note on the research method and a description of Rexon's case. In the subsequent part of the article, we discuss the main findings and highlight the theoretical and managerial contributions of the study.

LITERATURE REVIEW

KM initiatives in organizations typically involve the implementation of one or more IT-based systems called Knowledge Management Systems (KMS), which are equipped to capture, store, and disseminate various forms of organizational knowledge (Alavi & Leidner, 1999, 2001; Alavi & Tiwana, 2002; Massey, Montoya-Weiss, & O'Driscoll, 2002; Newell, Huang, Galliers, & Pan, 2003). A typical KMS takes the shape of an intranet portal that acts as a window to an organization's specialized knowledge found in repositories and includes various initiatives such as discussion forums, newsgroups, and so forth, which promote greater meaningful interaction among employees (Ruppel & Harrington, 2001). The underlying focus of a KM initiative or a KMS is the creation of a dynamic platform that systematically collates expert knowledge, enabling organizational members to draw on the pooled expertise (Grover & Davenport, 2001; Massey et al., 2002; Von Krogh, Nonaka, & Aben, 2001).

The successful implementation of a KM initiative is usually determined by measures such as the ability of the KMS to provide specialized and customized knowledge to employees, to function as a platform that allows employees to connect to experts, and to reduce the time spent on routine tasks (Barrow, 2001; Hansen, Nohria, & Tierney, 1999; Sarvary, 1999). In addition to the traditional viewpoint of seeing organizational KM as being solely concerned with the implementation of a KMS, many researchers have also emphasized the importance of the social settings of the organization implementing a KM initiative (Gupta & Govindarajan, 2000; Von Krogh, 2002). Rather than adopting a purely structuralist perspective that sees a KMS implementation as either being a success or a failure, this approach sees KM as a continuous process of producing favorable changes in the social fabric of the organization (McInerney 2002; Tsoukas, 2001). This is indicative of a more complex position than that of simply implementing KM top-down and anticipating numerous strategic benefits.

Drivers and Limitations of KM

While KM initiatives indeed promise to be a source of creating and sustaining competitive advantage, a greater understanding of the drivers and limitations of the KM initiative implementation process will be gained by a closer examination of the unique embedded social contexts (Blackler, 1995; Brown & Duguid, 1991; Cohen & Levinthal, 1990; Pentland, 1995). This stream of literature recognizes and is sensitive to the complex demands of KM—like knowledge sharing and re-use—that necessitate paradigmatic shifts in the mindsets of organizational members (Constant, Kiesler, & Sproull, 1994; Dyer & Nobeoka, 2000; Hislop, 2002; Michailova & Husted, 2003). Thus, while IT is seen to play the role of an enabling agent in the process of managing organizational knowledge, researchers bestow more attention upon the intricacies of the subtle exchanges and transfer of knowledge taking place informally within and across different communities of practice (McDermott, 1999; Wenger & Snyder, 2000). The management of organizational knowledge through such communal interactions generally evolves with time and often gets embedded as routine and accepted approaches (Davenport, 2002).

Sociocultural Barriers

It has been pointed out that the unique social contexts put up significant if not insurmountable barriers to the integration of the KM process into the organizational environment (Brown & Duguid, 2001; Hansen, 2002; Kogut & Zander, 1996). Arguing at the more generic level of IT implementation, Robey and Boudreau (1999) have employed a *logic of opposition* and proposed four theories (*Organizational politics, Institutional theory, Organizational learning,* and *Organizational culture*) that both emphasize the centrality of organizational sociocultural barriers when dealing with IT implementation and also explain organizational consequences by investigating the barriers. Mapping the four theories to the specific case of organization-wide KM implementation would give researchers diverse but relevant perspectives for studying KM. The theory of *Organizational politics* directs us to the political undertones of the organization-wide KM and to how different interest groups might use KM as a platform for scoring political points over peers. *Institutional theory* provides a foundation for studying organizations where KM initiatives are in a constant state of flux owing to their inconsistencies with established organizational processes and practices. *Organizational learning* offers scope for studies that can look into how KM can transform organizational learning mechanisms both in the negative and positive senses. Lastly, Robey and Boudreau (1999, p.175) note three interesting perspectives of *Organizational culture,* namely *Integration, Differentiation,* and *Fragmentation,* that potentially affect IT-driven KM initiatives. While *Integration* identifies culture as a unified force that opposes IT driven change, *differentiation* focuses on conflicts within subcultures, and *fragmentation* highlights the inherent ambiguities in viewpoints across different subcultures, which clash with desired changes such as those sought by a organizational KM initiative.

While in the general context of IT strategies a number of studies have dwelt on *organizational culture* (Cabrera, Cabrera, & Barajas, 2001; Cooper, 1994; Kanungo, Sadavarti, & Srinivas, 2001; Klein & Sorra, 1996; Orlikowski, 1993; Romm, Pliskin, Weber, & Lee, 1991), in the specific case of KM implementation, studies have emphasized a relationship between organizational efforts to manage knowledge and the prevailing organizational culture (Davenport et al., 1998; Gold et al., 2001; Nonaka & Konno, 1998; Ruggles, 1998; Ruppel & Harrington, 2001); therefore, the challenge of a formal KM initiative is seen as the smooth integration of a KMS into the organizational activities such that it is not perceived as a head-on cultural intrusion into everyday work. This visualization of a successful KM initiative is what many researchers have referred to as the creation of a suitable *knowledge culture* (Davenport, 1997; Jarvenpaa & Staples, 2001). For instance, Ruppel and Harrington (2001) studied the different dimensions of organizational culture that supported the creation of an effective knowledge culture with respect to intranet implementation projects, while De Long and Fahey (2000) emphasized the cultural barriers to organizations-wide KM initiatives. Thus, it is deemed necessary to overcome the inhibitors and draw on the favorable conditions posed by *organizational culture* predispositions (Brown & Woodland, 1999) to create an effective *knowledge culture*. Here, the scope of *knowledge culture* is restricted insofar as it deals with behaviors and artifacts that are directly related to effective and better management of knowledge resources to meet organizational objectives.

A KM initiative could thus be accorded the rubric of what researchers refer to as a *culture change initiative* (Harris & Ogbonna, 2002; Wilkins & Dyer, 1988). Thus, where KM is a vehicle that has to continuously drive the organization towards an effective knowledge culture, organizational mechanisms that assist the creation of such a culture assume importance. One notable mechanism that organizations utilize to create an effective knowledge culture is the rewards program attached to the KM initiative.

KMS and Rewards

The rewards program could influence how end-users respond to the KM initiative and contribute to the organizational efforts at building an effective knowledge culture (Lee & Chen, 2005). In other words, employees' response to a KM initiative could be guided by the perceived attractiveness and relevance of the economic incentives associated with the rewards program (Desouza & Awazu, 2003; Desouza, Awazu, Yamakawa, & Umezawa, 2005). However, in KM research only a few empirical studies have attempted to understand how a rewards program influences the implementation of an organizational KM initiative (e.g., Burgess, 2005; Cabrera, Collins, & Salgado, 2006; Lucas & Ogilvie, 2006). Further, findings and recommendations made about KM-related rewards in such studies mostly stem from materials collated at a specific instant in time. For instance, a recent survey of 160 knowledge professionals in Singapore found that for interdependent tasks, rewards, and incentives have a significant positive relationship with employees' use of organizational knowledge repositories (Kankanhalli, Tan, & Wei, 2005). Another recent survey of 27 organizations in Korea (Bock, Zmud, Kim, & Lee, 2005) found that anticipated extrinsic rewards may actually have a negative effect on employees' attitudes towards sharing knowledge. By contrast, it emerged from a recent survey (Burgess, 2005) that a perception of greater organizational rewards encourages employees to spend more time sharing knowledge with employees outside their immediate work group.

In short, a review of the existing KMS literature suggests that rewards and incentives could be particularly crucial and, further, taking a longitudinal perspective of an organizational KM initiative could provide useful insights into the workings of a KM-related rewards program. Thus, in this article, we attempt to look at a typical rewards program attached to a KM initiative. In doing so, we adopt a longitudinal case study approach. In particular, we examine how a rewards program influences employees' response to an organizational KM initiative and how organizations can create an effective KM related rewards program.

RESEARCH METHODOLOGY

The study adopts the interpretivist paradigm, which argues that access to reality is contingent upon social attributes such as language, shared meanings, and artifacts (Butler, 1998; Klein & Myers, 1999; Lee, 1991; Orlikowski & Baroudi, 1991; Walsham, 1995a, 1995b). As Klein and Myers (1999, p. 69) note, interpretive research "attempts to understand phenomena through the meanings people assign to them." This study of the KM initiative at Rexon closely aligns with the interpretivist belief that "the same physical artifact, the same institution, or the same human action, can have different meanings for different human subjects, as well as for the observing social scientist" (Lee, 1991, p. 347). Following the traditions of the interpretivist research, we conducted fieldwork for a total of 6 months spread over a 2 year period at Rexon, a leading Indian IT firm. We felt that Rexon was a good choice for our study as it had recently implemented an organization-wide KMS and in a short span following the implementation had been well recognized globally as a leader in KM. In addition, there were numerous mentions in the global print-media about the "novel" KM rewards program at Rexon. Further, the head of the KM implementation team who we approached initially for the conduct of fieldwork was very supportive and assisted us in arranging a number of interviews.

In our study, we allowed for the emergence of a complete picture from the interviewees' responses to the KM initiative, and by interpreting the reasons they attributed to their responses. We utilized different sources of evidence. The main source of evidence was the 52 open-ended interviews conducted with developers and middle level managers from four different organizational business units, which we shall refer to as PU-1, PU-2, PU-3, and PU-4. The interviews also covered a nine-member central KM group (the KM implementation team). Given that the 6 months of intensive fieldwork was spread over a 2 year period, it was possible for us to better understand the rewards program, to follow employee responses to the rewards program over an extended length of time, and to keep track of the changes made to the rewards program.

Each interview lasted on an average about 80 minutes and was conducted at the headquarters of the company, which is home to more than 9,000 employees of Rexon. All the interviews were taped and transcribed with prior permission. The interview questions typically concerned the role of the interviewee, and the interviewee's understanding of and responses to the KM initiative. All the interviews were direct face-to-face interactions; follow-up discussions were conducted via telephone and e-mail. Most of the interviews were conducted in the late afternoon and evenings; this arrangement gave us the opportunity to utilize a good part of the mornings, interacting and meeting people informally without any appointments. Such interactions gave an ethnographic touch to the study and allowed us a more firm grasp over the issues at hand as we spent a considerable amount of time observing the employees from the four units participating in work and nonwork related activities. Further, we also accessed artifacts related to the evolution of KM at Rexon and documents of seminars conducted by the central KM group to market KM internally to the various business units. The multiple data collection methods that were followed enhance the validity of the findings and also serve the important methodological requirement of multiple interpretations (Klein & Myers, 1999). Qualitative data that assisted the case analysis included the transcripts of the taped interviews, follow-up discussions via e-mail and telephone, and notes related to informal interviews and the KM artifacts.

CASE DESCRIPTION

Rexon is a software services and products company based in India. Rexon provides consulting and IT services and products to close to 500 clients worldwide and has a presence in more than 20 countries. It generates revenues of more than $1.5 billion annually and employs more than 58,000 people. Software development, maintenance, and package implementation projects contribute about three-fourths of Rexon's revenue. Reengineering, testing, consulting, banking products, and engineering services constitute the other service and product offerings, and account for one-fourth of the company revenue. With an increasing number of firms looking to outsource the IT components of their business, Rexon provides software solutions, promising to reduce project completion time, respond to changing client requirements in real time, and save clients the cost of investing on large teams. Rexon offers solutions to customers via a distributed project management framework, which involves project teams at both on-site (customer site) and offshore locations (Rexon development centers). Usually, all projects that Rexon handles are broken down into on-site and offshore components.

While the initial planning, high-level design, acceptance testing and the implementation aspects of a project usually take place at the customer site, the prototyping, coding, detailed-design, system testing, documentation, application maintenance, and technical support components of a typical project are handled at the offshore development centers (DC). Clients are kept informed of the work at the DC through detailed schedules created at the beginning of each project, through status reports that are periodically mailed to the clients, and also via video-conferencing sessions with the client. The project plans and the status reports are sometimes also made available at client portals on the Internet. Within India, there are 17 DC that are connected to the India HQ through a mix of leased and ISDN circuits. Rexon DCs also have connectivity to client sites with high-speed satellite and fiber communication links incorporated into which are high levels of security and redundancy in order to avoid breakdowns. These links provide the necessary infrastructure for remote software development capability and maintenance. Major clients of Rexon include Airbus, Adidas, Dell, Franklin Templeton, and American Express. Rexon is organized into a number of business units called practice units (PU), which are defined based on the geographical origin of business, the industry focus, and the technology focus. The PU are complimented by a number of support departments such as Information Systems (IS), Human Resources (HR), Research and Communications (R & C), and so forth. Rexon administers an organization-wide KM initiative, which draws on the strong and proven IT capabilities of the organization and aims to cultivate, harness, and channel its knowledge resources towards better meeting organizational objectives. As a testimony to its status as a KM pioneer, Rexon has also won a number of internationally acclaimed KM related awards.

KMS at Rexon: Kstore

In a period of fast growth, Rexon has felt it imperative to have a formal structure to effectively manage its knowledge resources which—with the company employing over 40,000 software professionals today—are dispersed all over the world. In fact, as recently as 1997, less than 2,000 people worked for Rexon and presented a lesser challenge to the organization with regards to managing its knowledge resources. A software engineer with the KM group explained how KM activities were conducted informally in the early days:

In the early days, you had perhaps only a hundred people working at Rexon, and we operated from a single city. So the amount of knowledge exchange that could happen in such a small community was very high. Probably, we did not need a KMS in place for knowledge exchange. You could discuss just about anything over lunch and coffee. Even a one-hour informal seminar every month succeeded in getting across a fair amount of knowledge. So I think knowledge was managed mostly in informal ways, with the term KM not even coined at that point.

The organization-wide KM initiative gained increased visibility and a common platform with the implementation of an internally developed knowledge portal called Knowledge store (Kstore); it now represents the platform for Rexon's KM initiatives. Since the launch of the central KM portal, a nine-member team called the KM group has been formed to drive the organization-wide KM initiative. The KM group is a blend of senior project managers, software engineers, research analysts, and marketing personnel.

Kstore is built on a platform of Microsoft suite of servers (IIS, Site Server, and SQL Server). Organization-wide KM mainly involves voluntary submission of documents (also called knowledge assets) to Kstore and the subsequent use of these assets by other employees. The Kstore portal is also integrated with various existing systems for managing knowledge. With a secure ID, employees working at client locations can also access Kstore via the Web. The content in the Kstore repository is classified along four dimensions, namely the *knowledge domain*, the *type of knowledge*, the *target group*, and the *origin*. There are about 2,000 *knowledge domains*, which are arranged in a four level hierarchy; this taxonomy of knowledge areas is proprietary to Rexon. The *type of knowledge* classifies the content as case studies, project snapshots, publications/white papers, tutorials, experiential write-ups, and so forth. Employees are encouraged to contribute assets to the various knowledge areas via a content submission interface on Kstore, which is reviewed by a KM content editor for compliance with intellectual property (IP) regulations and by identified experts for relevance and quality. The *target group* classifier identifies by designation the possible audience that might be interested in the document/asset and also imposes hierarchical restrictions on access. The *origin* identifies the knowledge asset as either internally generated or externally generated. Kstore is also equipped with a powerful search engine with possibilities for both free text search and navigation-based content retrieval. One person in each project team of a business unit is identified as a "KM prime" who facilitates KM activities at the project level and encourages colleagues within the project team to participate in organization-wide KM. At the development center (DC) level, there are "DC KM champions" who interact regularly with the central KM group and co-ordinate activities at the DC level.

KM RELATED REWARDS PROGRAM

Rexon also administers a KM related rewards scheme, where employees accumulate KUs (Knowledge Units) by contributing, reviewing, and reusing Kstore assets. A KU represents a notional currency, and upon reaching some threshold value or points, they can be converted into rewards. Whenever an employee submits a document to Kstore, he accumulates KUs depending on how the document is rated by registered experts (these experts are employees who register with Kstore on a voluntary basis). The higher the rating given to the document, the greater is the number of KUs that accrue to the submission. The registered experts, too, get a few KUs for reviewing the document. Further, an employee also accumulates points whenever the employee uses a document or artifact available on Kstore in his everyday work. In such a case, the employee who originally sent in the document is also rewarded with KUs. A research analyst in the KM group explained further:

The rewards are in the form of cash coupons, which could be redeemed at a leading shopping stores chain in the city. Points can be accumulated by contributing documents, reviewing documents and reusing Kstore artifacts. So it is a highly attractive proposition for everyone.

The former head of the KM group, who was mainly responsible for the implementation of the KM initiative, explained the reasoning behind the KM initiative and why he considered the KU as central to building accountability in the initiative.

To build awareness among employees about KM, we need KUs. People who accumulate KUs become highly "visible" in the organizational environment. This makes people want to actively participate in KM. Also, in the process of giving "visibility," we are making them accountable in some sense, because if I am saying that a guy has done tremendous work and has been one of the leading knowledge contributors to the company, I am showcasing him in a big way. The inevitable effect is that other employees are going to hold him accountable. They naturally would want to know "What has this guy has actually contributed?" This forces the individual to make a substantial contribution and also ensure that the contribution is really worthwhile and not just a contribution aimed at boosting numbers. Thereby we are able to build in some kind of accountability.

Other members of the KM group also felt that mechanisms such as KUs were very essential to "push up" the awareness levels. They pointed out that the KM initiative can afford to focus on maintaining the credibility of the Kstore artifacts and move away from the focus on rewards only after a high level of awareness about the KM initiative is created in the organization. A marketing manager with the KM group noted:

As the KM awareness levels go up, maturity levels of the initiative are also bound to go up and we will need to do less and less of this explicit pushing. We won't have to keep on pushing KM down people's throat by saying "look if you do this you will get KUs, or if you do this the organization will benefit, and so forth." It would then become a natural way of doing things.

The encouragement offered by the KM group to employees in the different business units coupled with the promise of cash coupons as rewards made it possible for the KM initiative to gain ground organization-wide. However, the KM rewards program also created a number of challenges. A software engineer with business unit PU-1 observed:

I have recently submitted a document to Kstore and I now see another document on the same subject, submitted by another person, which matches my documents about 80%. This is surprising and it tells me that some people are not even honest. They submit documents just for the heck of it, and do not really care whether it is going to be used by anybody. They are just looking at piling up their KU and hoping to redeem it at the end of the day.

In the words of a senior software engineer with business unit PU-2:

Because of the KU factor, I submit a lot of documents such as white papers and case studies to Kstore. I also make it a point to include a hyperlink to my Kstore submissions in all e-mails I send out to friends at Rexon and in all my correspondence on the organizational bulletin board. This is an indirect way of promoting my Kstore submissions. I am basically saying "Go to Kstore and read my stuff." With thousands of people around, even if I post a "rotten tomato" at least a few hundred people will take a look at it. Most people are nice, they see no harm in giving KUs. Their attitude is "If some person is benefiting, what difference does it make to me, so let me give the person 5 points (the highest rating) straight away." In fact, with this tactic I have been very successful in accumulating KUs.

Members of the KM group also observed that there were a number of cases of employees submitting content to Kstore and asking their close friends and colleagues at Rexon to give a high rating to their submissions, so that they could easily obtain KUs and cash coupons. Whenever members of the KM group suspected such cases, they made it a point to warn employees and asked them to refrain from treating Kstore related activities as a frivolous exercise. However according to a software engineer with business unit PU-4, most people who ask their friends to give a high rating to their documents actually get away with doing so. He observed:

Had the KM group been seriously screening documents, every other guy who has at any point submitted a document to Kstore would have been caught. I don't blame anybody, because I believe its just human tendency. If I know a hundred people, why not use them. I just shoot a mail to 100 people saying read my submissions on Kstore. (Perhaps, it may be useful to you or it may not make sense to you, but please give me 5 points for it!).

Another software engineer with business unit PU-3 expressed his disappointment at not being able to accumulate KUs. He noted that since he was working on an uncommon technology platform, very few people organization-wide might actually be interested in any technical document he submits to Kstore. He noted:

One basic flaw with the rewards program is that only people who work on very common platforms and technologies are benefited. This is simply because their target audience is wider. If someone submits a document on Java, there might be 1,000 people reading and the person may get (say) 900 KUs and make 900 bucks. But I work on a new and uncommon technology and at most, two or three guys might read and find useful what I have written. But the system does not reward me in anyway.

In response to the initial challenges with the rewards program, the KM group introduced slight changes to the KU scheme to improve the quality of the submissions. While initially reviewers and end-users simply rated the documents based on a definite scale in a section called user comments, the user comments section was slightly modified in an attempt to improve quality. End-users were asked to rate a document at two levels. At the project level, the end-users had to indicate whether the concerned document was of any use to their project and were required to quantify and qualify the usefulness by converting it in terms of how much it has been useful and describing to what extent it was used. A year and a half into the implementation of the KM rewards program, a further change was incorporated into the rewards program. Employees continued to accumulate KUs, but were not given redeemable cash coupons any more. Employees who earned high KUs were given "certificates" in recognition of their active participation in the KM initiative. Unlike the cash coupons, these certificates had no monetary value and were merely a token appreciation of the employees' KM efforts. The head of the KM group reasoned that since there was a huge awareness about the KM initiative already in the organization-wide, continuing the cash coupons based rewards program could prove counter-productive. Interestingly, in many of our interviews conducted after the removal of the cash coupons, employees talked about being "hooked" to KM. While being aware that they might be recognized in some positive way for their participation in organizational KM, they nevertheless felt that they now participated in organizational KM simply because they wanted to. Many also observed that getting involved in KM had now become a part of their "culture." Indeed, statistics made available to us by the KM group showed that even after the removal of the cash coupon based reward structure, useful contributions to Kstore and the use of such resources on Kstore by employees continued to increase steadily.

DISCUSSION

Our study aimed to understand how an organizational rewards program influences employees' response to a KM initiative and how organizations can create an effective KM-related rewards program. We examined the responses of employees in four different business units of Rexon to organization-wide KM. The open ended interviews with the central KM group and software developers and middle level managers across different business units gave insights into the history of formal KM at Rexon and the dynamics of the rewards program that accompanied the KM initiative. We discuss the important findings of the study below.

"Rewards" as an Awareness Building Tool

While acknowledging the possibility that the quality of Kstore assets could suffer, the KM group felt that the cash coupon-based rewards program was an important tool to build an effective knowledge culture. In other words, the cash coupon-based rewards program was used as a deliberate tool by the KM group to build an organization-wide awareness about the KM initiative. Although different business units dealt with different clients and technologies and were therefore prone to different ways of working, it was felt that a greater exchange of ideas and knowledge sharing would at least be initiated because of the attractions offered by the rewards program. This suggests that the KM team and the top management were willing to see the KM initiative as a long-term investment that came with a number of initial challenges such as the KMS being deluged with information (Garud & Kumaraswamy, 2005) and the possibility of an increasing amount of redundant contributions from end-users.

Trivializing the Organizational KM Initiative

From the perspective of the end-users of the KMS, the rewards program presented an attractive proposition. They saw it as a great opportunity to accumulate KUs that could be redeemed at a shopping store later. Such a mindset resulted in the end-users focusing on contributing, reviewing, and reusing documents mostly with an idea to accumulate KUs. In other words, rather than see the KM initiative as an opportunity to build a strong knowledge base and responding accordingly, employees considered it trivial and only peripheral to their everyday work, whose only value lay in the rewards it offered. This perspective of the KM initiative taken by the end-users meant that they often resorted to dubious means to accumulate KUs. As a consequence, the KM group had to spend a significant amount of time trying to ensure that documents of a reasonable quality were contributed to the organizational KMS. Further, the inability of the rewards program to reward employees who worked on uncommon technologies meant that such end-users did not see any value of taking part in the KM initiative.

Phased Removal of the Rewards Program

Once the KM group was convinced that organization-wide awareness of the KM initiative had increased significantly, they considered it necessary to minimize the reward-centric focus of the initiative. This was done in two distinct phases. First, by enforcing stricter rules on the process by which employees accumulated rewards, the KM group attempted to focus more on creating useful content in the Kstore repository. Second, the cash coupon based rewards program was totally stopped and instead employees were only given certificates of merit for their participation in the KM initiative. Thus the KM team made sure that "rewards" were less of a factor in employees' involvement in the KM initiative. While "end-user interest" was generated initially mostly by the promise of rewards, subsequently the KM group started focusing more on the strategic underpinnings of the KM initiative by removing what was the most "lucrative" component of the initiative. This experience of managers at Rexon suggests that a reward centric focus while important initially might actually be detrimental to the success of the KM initiative in the long run. From Rexon's case, we observe that after sufficient awareness about the initiative is reached, undertaking a phased removal of a rewards centric approach to KM might help organizations create an effective knowledge culture. As noted earlier, after the restructuring of the rewards program at Rexon, which resulted in the removal of the cash coupon based reward structure, the number of contributions to Kstore actually increased. Further, the number of reviews of documents in Kstore also increased. This, in a way, further justified the phased removal of the rewards program in that the removal did not appear to in any way lessen the interest that the KM initiative had generated amongst employees. In short, Rexon's case shows how organizations may create an effective KM related rewards program by emphasizing on "attractive" rewards in the initial post-implementation stages. Subsequently, organizations could move towards restructuring the rewards program so that the rewards have a more symbolic rather than monetary value for employees.

CONCLUSION AND IMPLICATIONS

In this article, we have looked at the dynamics of a rewards program attached to an organization-wide KM initiative. We have traced the evolution of the formal KM initiative at Rexon that began with informal attempts to manage organizational knowledge and subsequently led to the initiation of an organization-wide KM initiative. We found that an organizational rewards program plays a very important role by generating a great deal of interest and awareness about the KM initiative amongst end-users. However, the rewards program, as seen in Rexon's case, may also lead to employees focusing purely on rewards and ignoring the main concerns of the KM initiative. Further, we found that a KM-related rewards program can be used as a strategy in the initial post-implementation phase to build awareness amongst end-user communities and once the awareness reaches a reasonable level, it can be removed in a phased manner. This would help organizations better focus on the long-term strategic concerns of the KM initiative.

Our study fills a gap in the existing KMS implementation literature that has tended to label KMS implementations either as successful or unsuccessful. The case has thrown light on the evolving nature of such outcomes and revealed the unfolding of consequences that cannot be inherently classified as successful or unsuccessful. Specifically, our study links the consequences of KM implementation, both intended and unintended, to the rewards program attached to the organizational KM initiative. While existing KM studies adopting objectivist stances have argued that rewards may either work or not work (Bock et al., 2005;

Kankanhalli et al., 2005), our case study presents a more complex picture of reality. It has pointed out that within the same organization, different kinds of rewards might be more effective during different phases of the KM initiative. In other words, our study underscores the importance of "time" in understanding employees' motivations (Steel & König, 2006) and subsequent responses to a KM initiative.

As limitations of our study, we note that our findings are the result of a single case study and therefore the generalizability of the findings to different organizational settings may be limited. Further, while our analysis broadly looked into employee responses to KM across different business units, it did not look into specific business unit level factors that might influence employee responses to a KM initiative. Such potentially unique factors (e.g., intellectual property restrictions) might further influence the structuring of KM-related rewards programs. Thus building on this study, future research could look into business unit level factors that impact employees' contributions and usage of an organizational KMS.

From a practitioner perspective, our study first suggests that while a rewards program may play an important role in generating awareness about KM, it is also vital that managers incorporate phased changes in the structuring of a KM-related rewards program. As seen in our case, such changes could take the form of a movement from a monetary rewards based structure to a nonmonetary rewards based structure. Second, after generating awareness about the KM initiative, managers may need to establish mechanisms to carefully monitor the quality of the contributions to the KMS and its usage. This could remove perceptions amongst employees that organizational KM is nothing more than a frivolous exercise. Third, given the increasing relevance of KM to organizations' business objectives, practitioners must seriously consider employing a dedicated team for the internal marketing and implementation of the KM initiative. Last, by incorporating initiatives that help foster a strong sense of identification towards the organization among employees, managers might ensure the continued success of organizational KM even after the removal of attractive KM related reward programs.

REFERENCES

Alavi, M., & Leidner, D.E. (1999). Knowledge management systems: Issues, challenges, and benefits. *Communications of the AIS, 1*(7), 2-35.

Alavi, M., & Leidner, D.E. (2001). Review: Knowledge management and knowledge management systems: Conceptual foundations and research issues. *MIS Quarterly, 25*(1), 107-136.

Alavi, M., & Tiwana, A. (2002). Knowledge integration in virtual teams: The potential role of KMS. *Journal of the American Society for Information Science and Technology, 53*(12), 1029-1037.

Barrow, D.C. (2001). Sharing know-how at BP Amoco. *Research Technology Management, 44*(3), 18-25.

Benbasat, I., Goldstein, D.K., & Mead, M. (1987). The case research strategy in studies of information systems. *MIS Quarterly, 11*(3), 369-386.

Blackler, F. (1995). Knowledge, knowledge work and organizations: An overview and interpretation. *Organization Studies, 16*(6), 1021-1043.

Bock, G.W., Zmud, R.W., Kim, Y.G., & Lee, J.N. (2005). Behavioral intention formation in knowledge sharing: Examining the roles of extrinsic motivators, social-psychological forces and organizational climate. *MIS Quarterly, 29*(1), 87-111.

Brown, J.S., & Duguid, P. (1991). Organizational learning and communities-of-practice: Towards a unified view of working, learning and innovation. *Organization Science, 2*(1), 40-57.

Brown, J.S., & Duguid, P. (2001). Knowledge and organization: A social-practice perspective. *Organization Science, 12*(2), 198-213.

Brown, R.B., & Woodland, M.J. (1999). Managing knowledge wisely: A case study in organizational behavior. *Journal of Applied Management Studies, 8*(2), 175-198.

Burgess, D. (2005). What motivates employees to transfer knowledge outside their work unit? *Journal of Business Communication, 42*(4), 324-348.

Butler, T. (1998). Towards a hermeneutic method for interpretive research in information systems. *Journal of Information Technology, 13*(4), 285-300.

Cabrera, A., Cabrera, E.F., & Barajas, S. (2001). The key role of organizational culture in a multi-system view of technology-driven change. *International Journal of Information Management, 21*(3), 245-261.

Cabrera, A., Collins, W.C., & Salgado, J.F. (2006). Determinants of individual engagement in knowledge sharing. *International Journal of Human Resource Management, 17*(2), 245-264.

Cavaye, A.L.M. (1996). Case study research: A multi-faceted research approach for IS. *Information Systems Journal, 6*(3), 227-242.

Cohen, W., & Levinthal, D. (1990). Absorptive capacity: A new perspective on learning and innovation. *Administrative Science Quarterly, 35*(1), 128-152.

Constant, D., Kiesler, S., & Sproull, L. (1994). What's mine is ours, or is it? A study of attitudes about information sharing. *Information Systems Research, 5*(4), 400-421.

Cooper, R. (1994). The inertial impact of culture on IT implementation. *Information Management, 27*(1), 17-31.

Davenport, T.H. (1997). *Information ecology.* Oxford: Oxford University Press.

Davenport, E. (2002). Mundane knowledge management and micro level organizational learning: An ethological approach. *Journal of the American Society for Information Science and Technology, 53*(12), 1038-1046.

Davenport, T.H., De Long, D.W., & Beers, M.C. (1998). Successful knowledge management projects. *Sloan Management Review, 39*(2), 43-57.

De Long, D., & Fahey, L. (2000). Diagnosing cultural barriers to knowledge management. *The Academy of Management Executive, 14*(4), 113-127.

Desouza, K.C. (2003a). Barriers to effective use of knowledge management systems in software engineering. *Communications of the ACM, 46*(1), 99-101.

Desouza, K.C. (2003b). Barriers to effective knowledge management: Why the technology imperative seldom works. *Business Horizons, 46*(1), 25-29.

Desouza, K.C., & Awazu, Y. (2003). Constructing internal knowledge markets: Considerations from mini-cases. *International Journal of Information Management, 23*(4), 345-353.

Desouza, K.C., Awazu, Y., Yamakawa, S., & Umezawa, M. (2005). Facilitating knowledge management through market mechanism. *Knowledge and Process Management, 12*(2), 99-107.

Dyer, J., & Nobeoka, K. (2000). Creating and managing a high performance knowledge-sharing network: The Toyota case. *Strategic Management Journal, 21*(3), 345-367.

Fahey, L., & Prusak, L. (1998). The eleven deadliest sins of knowledge management. *California Management Review, 40*(3), 265-276.

Garud, R., & Kumaraswamy, A. Vicious and virtuous cycles in the management of knowledge:

The case of Infosys Technologies. *MIS Quarterly, 29*(1), 2005, 9-33.

Gold, A.H., Malhotra, A., & Segars, A.H. (2001). Knowledge management: An organizational capabilities perspective. *Journal of Management Information Systems, 18*(1), 185-214.

Gray, P.H. (2000). The effects of knowledge management systems on emergent teams: Towards a research model. *Journal of Strategic Information Systems, 9*(2-3), 175-191.

Grover, V., & Davenport, T.H. (2001). General perspectives on knowledge management: Fostering a research agenda. *Journal of Management Information Systems, 18*(1), 5-21.

Gupta, A.K., & Govindarajan, V. (2000). Knowledge management's social dimension: Lessons from Nucor Steel. *Sloan Management Review, 42*(1), 71-80.

Hansen, M.T. (2002). Knowledge networks: Explaining effective knowledge sharing in multiunit companies. *Organization Science, 13*(3), 232-248.

Hansen, M.T., Nohria, N., & Tierney, T. (1999). What's your strategy for managing knowledge? *Harvard Business Review, 77*(2), 106-116.

Harris, L.C., & Ogbonna, E. (2002). The unintended consequences of culture interventions: A study of unexpected outcomes. *British Journal of Management, 13*(1), 31-50.

Hislop, D. (2002). Mission impossible? Communicating and sharing knowledge via information technology. *Journal of Information Technology, 17*(3), 165-177.

Holsapple, C.W., & Joshi, K.D. (2000). An investigation of the factors that influence the management of knowledge in organizations. *Journal of Strategic Information Systems, 9*(2-3), 235-261.

Jarvenpaa, S.L., & Staples, D.S. (2001). Exploring perceptions of organizational ownership of information and expertise. *Journal of Management Information Systems, 18*(1), 151-183.

Kankanhalli, A., Tan, B.C.Y., & Wei, K.K. (2005). Understanding seeking from electronic knowledge repositories: An empirical study. *Journal of the American Society for Information Science and Technology, 56*(11), 1156-1166.

Kanungo, S., Sadavarti, S., & Srinivas, Y. (2001). Relating IT strategy and organizational culture: An empirical study of public sector units in India. *Journal of Strategic Information Systems, 10*(1), 29-57.

Klein, H.K., & Myers, M.D. (1999). A set of principles for conducting and evaluating interpretive field studies in Information systems. *MIS Quarterly, 23*(1), 67-93.

Klein, K.J., & Sorra, J.S. (1996). The challenge of innovation implementation. *Academy of Management Review, 21*(4), 1055-1080.

Kogut, B., & Zander, U. (1996). What do firms do? Coordination, identity, and learning. *Organization Science, 7*(5), 502-518.

Lee, A.S. (1991). Integrating positivist and interpretivist approaches to organizational research. *Organization Science, 2*(4), 342-365.

Lee, C., & Chen, W.J. (2005). The effects of internal marketing and organizational culture on knowledge management in the information technology industry. *International Journal of Management, 22*(4), 661-672.

Lucas, L.M., & Ogilvie, D. (2006). Things are not always what they seem: How reputations, culture, and incentives influence knowledge transfer. *The Learning Organization, 13*(1), 7-24.

Markus, M.L. (1983). Power, politics, and MIS implementation. *Communications of the ACM, 26*(6), 430-444.

Massey, A.P., Montoya-Weiss, M.M., & O'Driscoll, T.M. (2002). Knowledge management in pursuit of performance: Insights from Nortel networks. *MIS Quarterly, 26*(3), 269-289.

McDermott, R. (1999). Why information technology inspired but cannot deliver knowledge management. *California Management Review, 41*(4), 103-117.

McInerney, C. (2002). Knowledge management and the dynamic nature of knowledge. *Journal of the American Society for Information Science and Technology, 53*(12), 1009-1018.

Michailova, S., & Husted, K. (2003). Knowledge-sharing hostility in Russian firms. *California Management Review, 45*(3), 59-77.

Myers, M.D. (1994). A disaster for everyone to see: An interpretive analysis of a failed IS project. *Accounting, Management, and Information Technologies, 4*(4), 185-201.

Newell, S., Huang, J.C., Galliers, R.D., & Pan, S-L. (2003). Implementing enterprise resource planning and knowledge management systems in tandem: Fostering efficiency and innovation complimentarity. *Information and Organization, 13*(1), 25-52.

Nonaka, I., & Konno, N. (1998) The concept of "Ba": Building a foundation for knowledge creation. *California Management Review, 40*(3), 40-54.

Orlikowski, W.J. (1993). CASE tools as organizational change: Investigating incremental and radical changes in systems development. *MIS Quarterly, 17*(3), 309-340.

Orlikowski, W.J., & Baroudi, J.J. (1991). Studying information technology in organizations: Research approaches and assumptions. *Information Systems Research, 2*(1), 1-28.

Pentland, B.T. (1995). Information systems and organizational learning: The social epistemology of organizational knowledge systems. *Accounting, Management, and Information Technologies, 5*(1), 1-21.

Robey, D., & Boudreau, M-C. (1999). Accounting for the contradictory organizational consequences of Information technology: Theoretical directions and methodological implications. *Information Systems Research, 10*(2), 167-185.

Romm, T., Pliskin, N., Weber, Y., & Lee, A. (1991). Identifying organizational culture clash in MIS implementation. *Information Management, 21*(2), 99-109.

Ruggles, R. (1998). The state of the notion: Knowledge management in practice. *California Management Review, 40*(3), 80-89.

Ruppel, C., & Harrington, S. (2001). Sharing knowledge through intranets. *IEEE Transactions on Professional Communication, 44*(1), 37-52.

Sarvary, M. (1999). Knowledge management and competition in the consulting industry. *California Management Review, 41*(2), 95-107.

Schultze, U., & Boland Jr., R.J. (2000). Knowledge management technology and the reproduction of knowledge work practices. *Journal of Strategic Information Systems, 9*(2-3), 193-212.

Steel, P., & König, C.J. (2006). Integrating theories of motivation. *Academy of Management Review, 31*(4), 889-913.

Tsoukas, H. (2001). What is organizational knowledge? *Journal of Management Studies, 38*(7), 973-993.

Von Krogh, G. (2002). The communal resource and information systems. *Journal of Strategic Information Systems, 11*(2), 85-107.

Von Krogh, G., Nonaka, I., & Aben, M. (2001). Making the most of your company's knowledge: A strategic framework. *Long Range Planning, 34*(4), 421-439.

Walsham, G. (1995a). Interpretive case studies in IS research: Nature and method. *European Journal of Information Systems, 4*(2), 74-81.

Walsham, G. (1995b).The emergence of interpretivism in IS research. *Information Systems Research, 6*(4), 376-394.

Walsham, G. (2001). Knowledge management: The benefits and limitations of computer Systems. *European Management Journal, 19*(6), 599-608.

Wenger, E.C., & Snyder, W.M. (2000). Communities of practice: The organizational frontier. *Harvard Business Review, 78*(1), 139-145.

Wilkins, A.L., & Dyer Jr., W.B. (1988). Toward culturally sensitive theories of culture change. *Academy of Management Review, 13*(4), 522-533.

ENDNOTES

[1] Rexon is a pseudonym.

[2] In this article, we use the terms "KMS" and "KM initiative" interchangeably. Though a KMS is only a subset of a KM initiative, we have taken this liberty since in this case study the KM initiative entirely revolved around the implementation of an organizational KMS.

This work was previously published in the Journal of Organizational and End User Computing, Vol. 20, Issue 1, edited by M. Mahmood, pp. 35-49, copyright 2008 by IGI Publishing (an imprint of IGI Global).

Chapter 4
Exploring System Use as a Measure of Knowledge Management Success

Murray E. Jennex
San Diego State University, USA

ABSTRACT

This article discusses system use as a measure of knowledge management success. It is proposed that for knowledge management systems (KMS) it is not the amount of use that is important, but rather the quality of that use and the intention to use the KMS when appropriate. Evidence is provided to support this proposition and a knowledge management system success model incorporating this proposition is discussed. Additionally, findings are provided that show that new users to an organization use the KMS differently than experienced users and implications of this difference are discussed.

INTRODUCTION

A premise of information systems (IS) is that for an IS to be successful, the intended system users must "use" the system. In this case, Rai, Lang, and Welker (2001) consider "use" to be the consumption of the outputs of the IS by the users as measured in terms such as frequency of use, amount of time of use, numbers of access to the IS, usage pattern, and so forth. General thinking is that the more an IS is used, the more successful the IS. This leads to the common use of quantity of "use," as previously defined, as a measure of IS success. For example, two of the more widely accepted IS models, the DeLone and McLean (1992, 2003) IS Success Model and the Davis (1989) Technology Acceptance Model (TAM), incorporate "use" as a measure of success (DeLone & McLean, 1992, 2003) or successful adoption (TAM). But is quantity of "use" a good measure of success for all systems, particularly a knowledge management system (KMS)?

Jennex (2005, p. iv) defines knowledge management (KM) as the practice of selectively applying knowledge from previous experiences of decision-making to current and future decision making activities with the express purpose of improving the organization's effectiveness. KMS are those systems designed to support KM. Alavi and Leidner (2001) describe the KMS as an IT-based system developed to support/enhance the KM processes of knowledge creation, storage/retrieval, transfer, and application. KM is an action discipline; knowledge needs to be used and applied for KM to have an impact. This implies that KM and KMS success, like IS success, can use quantity of "use" measures for determining KM success.

However, Jennex and Olfman (2005, 2006), while exploring KM/KMS success, make the assertion that as long as knowledge is used at some point, it is the quality of "use" and intent to use when appropriate that are better measures of KM/KMS success than quantity of "use" measures. While this may seem counter intuitive, that successful KM/KMS is not based on frequent use of knowledge, it is a defendable position although, neither Jennex and Olfman (2005) nor Jennex and Olfman (2006) provide support for this assertion. This article addresses this key issue and provides support for using quality of "use" and intent to use as appropriate measures for KM/KMS success.

This article will make a case for using "intent to use" as a measure of KM/KMS success rather than quantity of "use." To make this case, data gathered from a review of published research plus data gathered from a longitudinal study of KM/KMS in an engineering organization will be presented that illustrates that quantity of "use" measures fail to predict success and that "intent to use" measures may predict success. Additionally, the article will present an overview of quantity of "use" measures in predicting success by discussing the DeLone and McLean (1992, 2003) IS Success and the Technology Acceptance Models, and an overview of KM/KMS success models.

The value and contribution of this article is in helping researchers and practitioners understand the impact of "use" on KM/KMS success. This is an important contribution as research into identifying key KM/KMS success measures need to identify the right measures in their KM/KMS success models so that organizations implementing KM/KMS will understand what to monitor and measure.

BACKGROUND OF USE MEASURES

Information System Success and Use

DeLone and McLean (1992) is a seminal work proposing a taxonomy and interactive model for conceptualizing and operationalizing IS Success. The DeLone and McLean (1992) IS Success Model is based on a review and integration of 180 research studies that used some form of system success as a dependent variable. The model identifies six interrelated dimensions of success as shown in Figure 1. Each dimension can have measures for determining their impact on success and each other.

The key focus of the model is the relationships showing that system and information quality aspects of a system (information quality reflects having the correct data and system quality refers to the technical infrastructure and interface) lead to system use and user satisfaction. User satisfaction tends to increase use and use tends to lead to some level of user satisfaction, making these dimensions difficult to separate. System use then leads to system success. This relation has been accepted and demonstrated to be correct although Seddon (1997) has suggested that use is not an appropriate variable for a causal model as it is a behavior.

DeLone and McLean (2003) revisited the IS Success Model by incorporating subsequent IS

Figure 1. DeLone and McLean (1992) IS success model

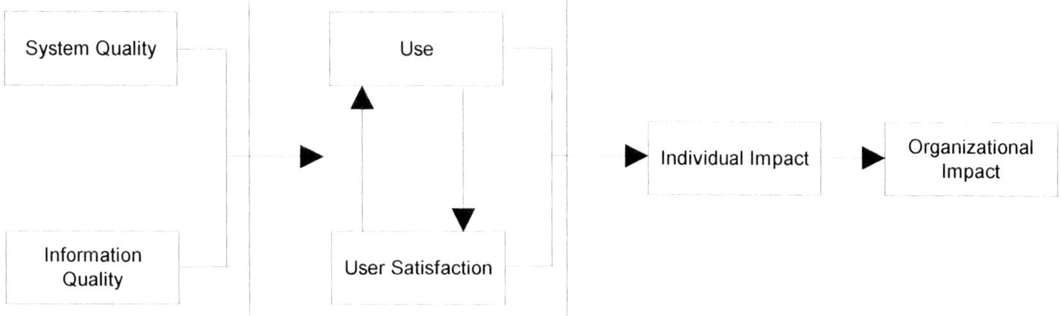

Success research and addressing criticisms of the original model. One hundred forty-four articles from refereed journals and 15 papers from the International Conference on Information Systems (ICIS) citing the IS Success Model were reviewed, with 14 of these articles reporting on studies that attempted to empirically investigate the model. The result of the article is the modified IS Success Model shown in Figure 2. Major changes include the additions of a Service Quality dimension for the service provided by the IS group, the modification of the Use dimension into a Use/Intent to Use dimension, and the combination of the Individual and Organizational Impact dimensions into an overall Net Benefits dimension. The modification of the use variable to include intent to use is important for this article. This modification takes into account the quality of use as well as the amount of use and recognizes that in some contexts it is better to monitor intent to use (a belief) rather than actual use (a behavior). This modification will be shown to be applicable to KM/KMS use.

Other researchers have also reported on the importance of use to system success. Goodhue and Thompson (1995) and Markus and Keil (1994) emphasized that the value of an information system is not in the system but in its effective and efficient usage. Additionally, they found that only when information systems are used can the desired purpose be achieved, and, conversely, the underutilization and nonuse of information systems frequently results in failure to meet an organization's objectives. Based on the same rationale, KM/KMS can make a difference only if used to enhance the application and reuse of knowledge; companies that have prospered are not the companies that implemented KM technology but those that applied it.

Technology Acceptance Model

Davis (1989) developed the technology acceptance model (TAM) as an explanation of the general case determinants of computer acceptance that are capable of explaining user behavior across a broad range of systems, technologies, and user populations. The model includes use as a determinant but indicates that use is determined by ease of use or perceived usefulness, attitude, and intention to use. TAM is a derivative of Fishbein and Ajzen's (1975) Theory of Reasoned Action (TRA) model. TRA focuses on situation specific personal beliefs and attitudes, and the effects of the beliefs of others who can influence the individual. The fundamental premise of TRA is that individuals will adopt a specific behavior if they perceive it will lead to positive outcomes (Compeau & Higgins, 2001). TAM is a TRA derivative tailored to the study of a broader range of user behavior in the context of IT acceptance (Davis, 1989).

The following are brief descriptions of the components of the model:

Figure 2. DeLone and McLean's (2003) revisited IS success model

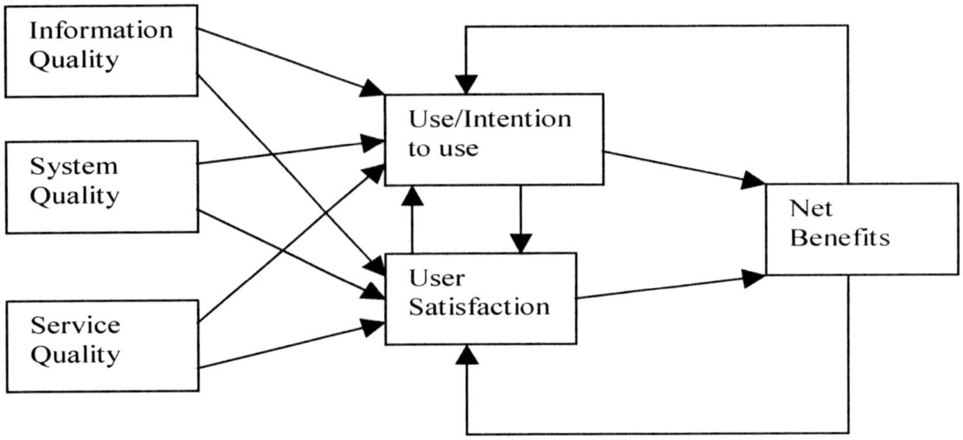

- Perceived Usefulness reflects that an individual's perception of usefulness influences their intention to use the technology primarily through the creation of a positive attitude. This is consistent with the TRA, which holds that attitude (an individual's positive or negative feelings about performing a behavior) influence behavioral intention.
- Perceived Ease of Use reflects the user's assessment of how easy a system is to learn and use. TAM includes ease of use as a separate belief construct based on the concept of self-efficacy (an individual's judgment of ability to organize and execute tasks necessary to perform a behavior).
- Attitude Towards Using reflects that an individual's perceptions of usefulness and ease of use influences intention to use a system through the creation of a positive attitude.
- Behavioral Intention to Use is a measure of the strength of one's intention to perform a specified behavior. The construct comes from TRA and is a predictor of an individual's behavior.
- System Usage is actual usage of the system and reflects that the users have accepted the system.

Knowledge Management Success

What is KM and KMS success? Jennex and Olfman (2006) consider KM and KMS success to be the same and Jennex, Smolnik, and Croasdell (2007, p. v) found a consensus definition of KM success to be:

KM success is a multidimensional concept. It is defined by capturing the right knowledge, getting the right knowledge to the right user, and using this knowledge to improve organizational and/or individual performance. KM success is measured using the dimensions of impact on business processes, strategy, leadership, efficiency and effectiveness of KM processes, efficiency and effectiveness of the KM system, organizational culture, and knowledge content.

Several KM success models have been proposed (Jennex & Olfman, 2005). Many of these are based on traditional information systems success models such as the DeLone and McLean IS Success Model (DeLone & McLean, 1992, 2003). These models suggest several factors contribute to system success including the amount of system "use." The above definition of KM Success also implies use as it is focused on the using of knowledge to

Figure 3. Technology acceptance model (Davis, 1989)

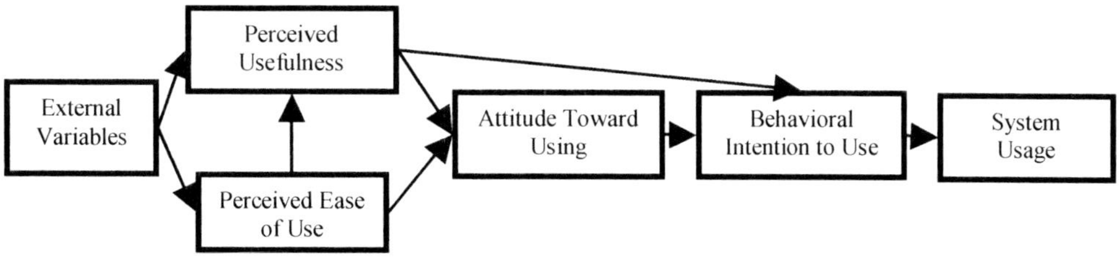

improve organizational performance. However, the above definition also focuses on the impact of knowledge use and it is this focus that will be argued to be the correct focus.

DeLone and McLean (2003) discuss the difficulties researchers have applying the DeLone and McLean IS Success Model to specific research contexts. Jennex, Olfman, Pituma, and Yong-Tae (1998) adopted the generic framework of the DeLone and McLean IS Success Model and customized and operationalized the dimensions to reflect the System Quality and Use constructs needed for an organizational memory information system. Jennex and Olfman (2002) expanded this KMS Success Model to include constructs for Information Quality and applied and operationalized the model to reflect the KM context. Jennex and Olfman (2006) modified the model to include suggestions from DeLone and McLean (2003) and concluded that intent to use rather than actual use is the appropriate measure.

Figure 4 shows the resulting KMS Success Model. This model evaluates success as an improvement in organizational effectiveness based on the impact from use of knowledge from the KMS. The dimensions are *System quality*, which defines how well the KMS performs the functions of knowledge creation, storage/retrieval, transfer, and application, how much of the knowledge is codified, and how the KMS is supported by the IS staff and infrastructure. *Knowledge/Information quality* ensures that the right knowledge with sufficient context is captured and available for the right users at the right time. *Service Quality* measures management support, KM governance, and organizational support of KM. *User Satisfaction* indicates the satisfaction of the users with their "use" of the KMS. This reflects that the KMS has been used but does not focus on the quantity of "use." *Perceived Benefit* measures perceptions of the benefits and impacts of the KMS by users and is based on the Perceived Benefit Model (Thompson, Higgins, & Howell, 1991). It is good for predicting that the KMS will be used when appropriate. *Net Impact* shows that an individual's use of a KMS will produce an impact on that person's performance in the workplace. Each individual impact will in turn have an effect on the performance of the whole organization. The association between individual and organizational impacts is often difficult to draw and is why all impacts are combined into a single dimension. This model recognizes that the use of knowledge may have good or bad benefits and allows for feedback from these benefits to drive the organization to either use more knowledge or to forget specific knowledge.

Lindsey (2002) proposed a KM effectiveness model based on combining Organizational Capability Perspective Theory (Gold, Malhotra, & Segars, 2001) and Contingency Perspective Theory (Becerra-Fernandez & Sabherval, 2001). The model defines KM effectiveness in terms of two main constructs: Knowledge Infrastructure Capability and Knowledge Process Capability, with the Knowledge Process Capability construct be-

Figure 4. Jennex & Olfman's (2006) KM success model

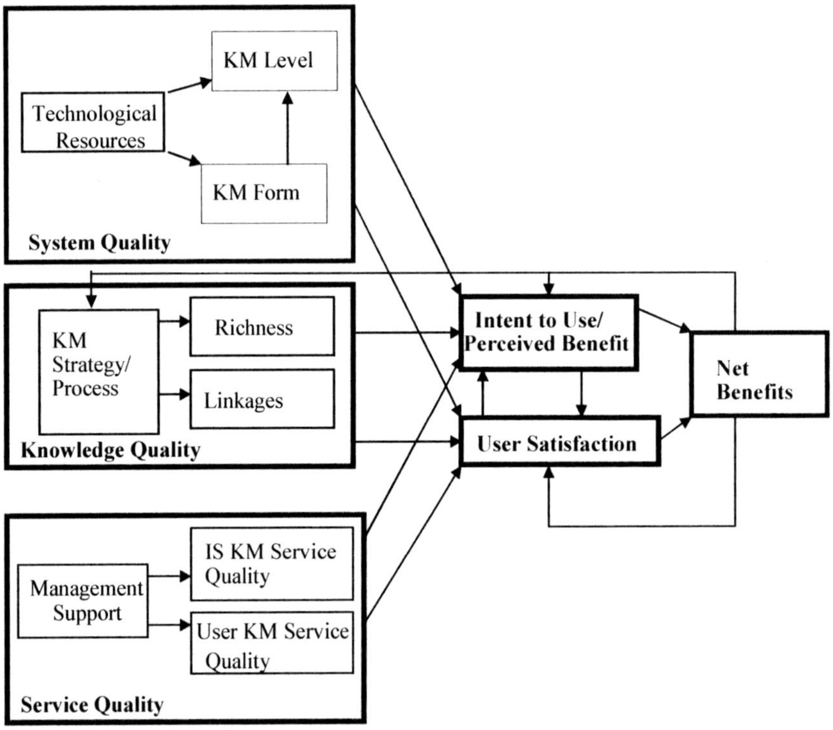

ing influenced by a Knowledge Task. Knowledge infrastructure capability represents social capital, the relationships between knowledge sources and users, and is operationalized by technology (the network itself), structure (the relationship), and culture (the context in which the knowledge is created and used). Knowledge process capability represents the integration of KM processes into the organization, and is operationalized by acquisition (the capturing of knowledge), conversion (making captured knowledge available), application (degree to which knowledge is useful), and protection (security of the knowledge). Tasks are activities performed by organizational units and indicate the type and domain of the knowledge being used. Tasks ensure the right knowledge is being captured and used. KM success is measured as satisfaction with the KMS. Use is implicitly incorporated into the model via the knowledge process capability and the tasks and is reflective of knowledge in action. Use in this model reflects actual use.

Massey, Montoya-Weiss, and O'Driscoll (2002) present a KM success model based on their Nortel case study. The model is based on the framework proposed by Holsapple and Joshi (2002) and reflects that KM success is based on understanding the organization, its knowledge users, and how they use knowledge. It recognizes that KM is an organizational change process and KM success cannot separate itself from the organizational change success with the result that KM success is essentially defined as improving organizational or process performance. Key components of the model are:

- *KM Strategy:* defines the processes using knowledge and what that knowledge is, the sources, users, and form of the knowledge, and the technology infrastructure for storing the knowledge.

- *Key Managerial Influences*: defines management support through leadership, allocation and management of project resources, and oversight of the KMS through coordination and control of resources and the application of metrics for assessing KMS success.
- *Key Resource Influences:* these are the financial resources and knowledge sources needed to build the KMS.
- *Key Environmental Influences:* describe the external forces that drive the organization to exploit its knowledge to maintain its competitive position.

Use is not explicitly discussed in this model but is implied through the definition of success that defines KM success as improving process performance; this implies that the knowledge stored in the KMS is used. Use in this model refers to a quality of use as well as actual use.

METHODOLOGY

KM/KMS has two sets of users, knowledge users who use the knowledge stored in the system and knowledge creator users who contribute knowledge to the system. Users may belong to both groups simultaneously. To support a discussion on KM/KMS use, data needs to be collected on each group of users' actual system use and the factors that led to this use. This article uses findings from three quantitative studies that looked at KMS use or KM success and data collected during a longitudinal case study of a KMS in an engineering organization. The methodologies for the quantitative studies are discussed with the findings from those studies. The methodology for the longitudinal case study is discussed below.

The longitudinal case study was conducted in three stages. The first stage was conducted in 1996. A survey instrument incorporating Thompson et al.'s (1991) perceived benefit model and actual system usage was administered to the total engineering population of 105 engineers. In addition, structured interviews were used to collect data on components of the KMS, KMS usage patterns, and KMS effectiveness. A response rate of 79% was achieved on the survey (83 respondents). Interviews were held with 5 managers, 5 supervisors, and 11 engineers. Interview subjects were selected for their knowledge of the organization and its processes. The same interviewer (the author) conducted and analyzed all the interviews. All data was collected within 2 months.

Stage 2, conducted in late 1998, utilized observation, a survey, and selected interviews. The survey focused on identifying drivers for capturing knowledge and was administered to all 98 members of the organization. A response rate of 22% was achieved (22 respondents) on this survey. Semistructured interviews were conducted with 10 members of the organization who were either new to the organization or to their position and were designed to determine if the KMS was usable by new personnel and if it transferred knowledge effectively. The same interviewer (the author) conducted and analyzed all the interviews. All data was collected within 2 months.

Stage 3, conducted in late 2001, used observation, interviews, and a document review. Twenty interviews were conducted. Six interviews were with the remaining new members from those interviewed during the second study. The remaining 14 interviews were conducted with selected managers, supervisors, and engineers (4 managers/supervisors and 10 engineers were selected). Selection was based on participation in the previous studies. Additionally, two interviews were conducted with Information Systems (IS) management and two interviews were conducted with the Reengineering Group management. The purpose of these interviews was to review processes, responsibilities, and procedures for managing knowledge in the engineering groups. The repeat interviews, again conducted by the author, followed the same script used in the second study.

The remaining interviews were unstructured. All data was collected within two months.

FINDINGS ON KMS USE

Quantitative Test of Relationship Between System Quality and Use of the KMS

Liu, Olfman, and Ryan (2005) tested the relationships between several of the dimensions from the Jennex and Olfman KMS Success Model. The goal was to quantitatively establish the relationship between these dimensions, KMS use, and KMS effectiveness using structured equation modeling. The key hypothesis with respect to use was that KMS use would have a positive effect on organizational learning (for this study the KMS was to facilitate organizational learning so improving individual and organizational learning is a measure of system success). Data was collected via a Web-based survey with respondents recruited from industry via an e-mail solicitation. Three hundred and sixty valid responses were collected. A low correlation was found between system utilization and knowledge application where knowledge application was the use of knowledge in decision-making. However, a high correlation was found between system utilization and changes in individual learning behavior indicating that use of the system was tied to how users formulate questions and use knowledge. Structured Equation Modeling found support for the impact of KMS use on individual learning but found insignificant or indirect impact of KMS Quality factors (system quality and information quality) on KMS use. Qualitative analysis of responses found several respondents concerned with the low utilization of their KMS with several listing system and information quality issues as the reasons for low system usage, somewhat contradicting the quantitative findings. Ultimately, this study found that the greatest impact on system use was the perceptions of users with respect to the usefulness of the KMS. This supports using an intent to "use" measure as these measures include usefulness to support predicting KMS use when appropriate.

Quantitative Test of TAM When Applied to KMS Adoption

Money and Turner (2005) applied TAM to the study of KMS with the goal of verifying the applicability of the TAM components to the study of the KMS research context. They used a Web-based survey derived from previous TAM research and administered to the employees of two firms wanting to obtain data on the adoption and use new KMS. Fifty-one responses were obtained of which 35 were usable. Thirteen of the rejected responses were rejected because the respondent indicated they did not use the system. Correlation and regression analyses verified all the TAM relationships with the exception of the relationship between system use and behavior intention to use. The lack of correlation between behavior intention to use and actual use with all other relationships being significant indicates that users saw benefit in, found it easy to use, and intended to use the system when appropriate, but did not predict the quantity of system use, that is, a user who saw significant benefit in the system was not likely to have more quantity of use than a user who did not see significant benefit. This suggests that intention to use the system is a more viable measure of KMS adoption than actual use.

Exploratory Study on Use and KM/KMS Success

Jennex et al. (2007) explored KM and KMS success. The goal was to identify a consensus definition of KM/KMS success and a set of measures that could be used to indicate KM/KMS success. An exploratory survey was generated using input from an expert panel, the editorial review board of the International Journal of Knowledge Management. The survey was distributed using a Web survey and e-mail solicitation. One hundred and three usable survey responses were received. Thirteen were from KM practitioners, 70 were from KM researchers, 6 were from KM students, and 14 were from academics interested in KM but not active KM researchers. Likert items were analyzed using means and standard deviations as no hypotheses have been proposed needing testing. While little consensus was observed in this survey, one item that was found to be agreed upon was that amount of use was not a good measure of KM/KMS success. Respondents were asked if a definition of KM success should include measures of pure KMS usage statistics. On a 5 point Likert scale where 5 was strongly agree and 1 was strongly disagree, the overall mean was 2.5 with a standard deviation of 1.2, indicating general disagreement with the statement.

Longitudinal Study of Knowledge User Use of the KMS

Knowledge user use was assessed using two different methods, a survey to measure current KMS usage and the perceived benefit of the KMS based on the Perceived Benefit Model (Thompson et al., 1991) and interviews. The survey found that the engineers used the KMS extensively, an average of 2.9 hours per day. However, this usage was not indicative of the value of the KMS as the interviews found that amount of KMS use were not a good indicator of the impact of KMS use. Several interviewees echoed the sentiment that it was not how often they used the KMS but rather it was the one time that they absolutely had to find knowledge or found unexpected knowledge that proved the worth of the KMS. An example of this was the use of the KMS to capture lessons learned and best practices associated with refueling activities (refueling is a high cost, high stress, short duration activity). These activities occur on an approximate 18-month cycle that was sufficient time to forget what had been learned during the last cycle or to have new members with no experience taking over these activities. So while this knowledge may be used infrequently, it was vital when it was used. The survey measuring perceived benefit assessed attitudes on factors important to predicting the knowledge users seeing value in the KMS. Table 1 summarizes the findings for each of the perceived benefit factors (5-point Likert scale, 5 is strongly agree) and leads to the conclusion that the KMS was perceived to be useful because the organizational culture encourages the engineers to use the KMS, the KMS was not complex to use, and the KMS supports them in performing their jobs. This survey was not repeated in the stage 2 and 3 studies since interviews revealed that the KMS was still being relied upon and used at about the same level as in stage 1.

Another interesting finding was in the longitudinal study of a group of new members to the organization. During interviews after they had joined the organization (members had been with the organization for approximately 6 months when interviewed) none of the new members indicated they used the KMS regularly to retrieve knowledge. Instead, they used the KMS to locate the name of someone who possessed the knowledge, then talked to that person. This seemed to counter the overall finding that the KMS was useful. However, during interviews conducted approximately 18 months later, all the new members used the KMS to retrieve knowledge and rarely, if ever, used the KMS to identify knowledge possessors for discussions. During the course of the interviews, it was determined that these new members to the organization needed to understand the context and culture of the knowledge that was stored in the KMS before they could use it. This context and culture were obtained by talking to knowledge possessors. Jennex (2006) discussed that for knowledge to be useful; the knowledge user had to know the culture and context in which the knowledge was generated. Context is the story around the knowledge generation that tells

Table 1. Perceptions affecting usage

Perceived Benefit Factor	Score	Result
Social factors	4.08	Organizational culture encourages use of the KMS
Complexity (inverse score)	2.38	Not complex, supports use of the KMS
Job fit, near terms	4.56	Fit current job well, supports use of the KMS
Job fit, long terms	3.36	Neutral
Fear of Job Loss	2.32	Not supported, no fear found

Note: score is based on a 5-point scale where 5 is "strongly agree."

what the knowledge applies to. Culture is that set of values the knowledge creator and user use to apply the knowledge; it reflects how the user will use that knowledge to make decisions. It is expected that this is normal behavior for new members in an organization and that they will need to obtain culture and context about their new organization before they will use the KMS to retrieve knowledge.

Knowledge Creator User Use of the KMS

The first stage found a successful and effective KMS. A major reason for this success was that the KMS held the right knowledge and made it available for use. Since no formal knowledge management initiative, organization, or organizational strategy had been observed to be in-place guiding engineers in what knowledge to capture, the second stage used a survey and interviews to discover what drivers existed to guide engineers in selecting what knowledge to capture in the KMS. Respondents were asked if they used the drivers, and if so, how important they were (3 point scale with 1-very important, 2-important, and 3-not very important), how frequently they were used (daily, weekly, monthly, yearly, and less than yearly), and the formality of the driver (formal, informal). As expected, the most important driver were formal Nuclear Regulatory Commission (NRC) requirements scoring 1.05 in importance (0.24 std. dev.) with 19 out of 22 respondents indicating they used it. Somewhat surprising was that the informal driver of the engineer thinking a knowledge item was important and then capturing it in some manner, was the second most important driver scoring 1.18 in importance (0.41 std. dev.) with all 22 respondents indicating they used it.

The key observation was that frequency of contribution use had little meaning because the driver's frequency of use was found to not be linearly related to importance. This observation indicates that there is not an obvious relationship between importance of a driver and use of the KMS for contributing knowledge because respondents were just as likely to rate a driver very important but resulting in monthly "use" as they were to rate the driver very important resulting in daily "use." Also, the perceived benefit findings fit here as knowledge creators were also knowledge users. Applying Table 1 findings indicates that knowledge creators will contribute knowledge when appropriate with the fear of job loss factor not being significant for these users being a critical indicator of future use. Table 2 lists the 15 most important drivers along with their frequency of use and correlation constant between importance and frequency.

DISCUSSION

Prior to discussing the above studies it is important to report that Jennex and Olfman (2002) also report that the subject KMS was found to be suc-

Table 2. Knowledge driver ratings

Driver or Reason Something is Captured in the KMS	n	Importance (Std Dev)	Frequency (Std Dev)	Correlation Constant
NRC requirement	19	1.05 (0.24)	3.26 (1.31)	0.339
You believe it is important to capture the knowledge	22	1.18 (0.41)	1.84 (1.30)	0.064
Procedure requirement	19	1.32 (0.47)	2.27 (1.03)	0.443
Near Miss Event	17	1.53 (0.64)	3.39 (0.96)	-0.354
Management/Supervisor directive	20	1.55 (0.70)	2.29 (1.36)	0.574
Site Event	18	1.56 (0.62)	3.21 (1.22)	-0.209
AR Assignment	20	1.60 (0.71)	2.19 (1.05)	0.277
Data/Trend Analysis	19	1.63 (0.49)	2.67 (0.90)	0.313
Lesson Learned	17	1.71 (0.59)	3.08 (0.76)	-0.320
Other Regulatory requirement	14	1.71 (0.65)	2.93 (1.54)	-0.559
Industry Event	20	1.75 (0.55)	3.44 (1.15)	0.226
Good Practice	19	1.79 (0.64)	2.67 (1.18)	-0.090
INPO Recommendation	15	1.80 (0.56)	3.47 (1.25)	-0.157
Group/Task Force recommendation	17	1.82 (0.35)	3.86 (1.03)	0.147
Co-Worker recommendation	18	1.83 (0.66)	2.56 (1.37)	-0.023

n=# of respondents using the driver; Importance: 1=Very Important, 2=Important, 3=Not Very Important; Frequency: 1=Daily, 2=Weekly, 3=Monthly, 4=more than monthly, less than yearly, 5=Yearly

cessful. Individual and organizational impacts on effectiveness were identified and in some cases, actual measurement of success was recorded. This is important when discussing the impact of "use" measures for indicating KMS success.

TAM and the IS Success Model both use quantity of "use" measures along with intent to use and quality of use measures. The KM Success Model does not use a quantity of "use" measure as long as the KM/KMS is used at some point and instead relies on intent to use. This article presents empirical data to support using intent to use measures instead of quantity of "use" measures in the KM context. All the studies presented support intention to use as the best measure of KMS use. The key findings from Liu et al. (2005) and Money and Turner (2005) are that intention to use does not correspond to quantity of "use" but does indicate the KMS will be used when appropriate. The reason is found in the longitudinal case study interviews with the discussion of the value of the knowledge. Knowledge users stated that it was knowledge used infrequently that was knowledge with the greatest value and impact. This implies that the KMS with the greatest impact is the KMS that may not be used all that frequently. This is contrary to the commonly accepted theories on IS Success and adoption and suggests that a KMS is very different from an IS. It also suggests that the key use dimension in the use of TAM and DeLone and McLean when applied to a KMS is intention to use. DeLone and McLean (2003) acknowledged that intention to use may be a more appropriate measure for some research contexts and these studies support that KM is an appropriate context for using intention to use in lieu of amount of use.

This is not a surprising finding. Reflecting on the longitudinal case study, Jennex and Olfman (2002) concluded that KM, organizational memory (OM), and organizational learning (OL) are related. The relationship is that the use of knowledge captured in the OM by the KMS results in changes in individual and/or organizational behavior with a subsequent impact on effectiveness. KM is an action discipline meaning that knowledge needs to be used to be considered useful. Use of knowledge results in learning and knowledge used frequently is soon "learned" and so its value in the KMS is perceived as less. Knowledge used infrequently is not easily "learned" and may be easily forgotten so its retrieval and use is considered of great value. This implies that frequency of "use" measures will not be effective measures of the value of the knowledge being used. Conversely, since a greater value is placed on knowledge that is used infrequently, measuring intent to use the KMS when appropriate is a more accurate reflection that the KMS will be used when it is needed. Finally, since KM success is focused on having an impact on the organization, it is reasonable to conclude that measures that reflect that knowledge with value will be used or contributed when appropriate are the appropriate measures for assessing KM/KMS success.

An additional concern with researchers has been getting knowledge creators to share their knowledge and to contribute to the KMS. The longitudinal case study suggests that frequency or amount of knowledge sharing is not as important as perceived. What is important is that there is a knowledge strategy that identifies critical knowledge and that knowledge creators supply this critical knowledge when appropriate. Again, using the amount of contributory use may not be appropriate. It is proposed that a new measure, intention to contribute, be used in conjunction with intention to use as the appropriate measure for KMS use when determining KMS success or adoption. This new measure can also be based on Thompson et al.'s (1991) Perceived benefit model.

Finally, the finding that there is a difference between how new members to an organization use a KMS and how experienced members use the KMS, while unexpected at first, is actually an expected finding once the impact of culture and context on knowledge use are taken into account. It is easier and perhaps only possible for new members to learn how an organization uses knowledge and make decisions by talking to experienced knowledge creators and users. New users during interviews made comments like:

Sure all the information is in the computer but the computer isn't as fast as simply asking the previous guy.

Not only does asking the previous engineer get me the answer faster but he can guide me to other sources and interpret my questions to give me the answers I need.

I treat all events as new events because it is easier and faster to get the information I need to fix the problem than it is to research the system about what happened before.

These same users made the following comments during interviews just 18 months later:

I always use the computer, all the information I need is there.

I go to the computer first, if the information isn't detailed enough for my purpose I can find out who did the work and then talk to them.

I rarely need to talk to anyone as all the history is in the databases and its fast and easy to use.

This indicates that how users use a KMS changes based on experience level. This has many impacts on KM researchers and practitioners. The first impact is on who is expected to benefit the most from KM. Many researchers and practitioners perceive KM as a way of helping new users to the organization find and utilize knowledge quicker. This probably will not happen as it appears new users may not use knowledge in the KM/KMS until after they have learned the decision-making culture and context of the organization. However, it also indicates that great benefits can be realized by experienced members. The second impact is on what knowledge needs to be captured by the KMS. The KMS needs to capture detailed knowledge and pointers to knowledge to satisfy both new an experienced users. Third, KMS training needs to be different for new and experienced members of the organization. New members need to know how to use the KMS to find sources of knowledge while experienced members need to be taught how to search and retrieve needed knowledge. Finally, use measures should be different. Intent to use is an acceptable measure for experienced members but this may not be a good measure for new members. This is an area for future research as none of the studies used in this article addressed the issue of measuring use by new members.

CONCLUSION

Jennex and Olfman (2005, 2006) explored KM/KMS success and asserted that quantity of "use" was not a good measure of success. This assertion was made without any evidence being offered in support. This article provides that evidence and comes to the key conclusion that a more appropriate use measure for evaluating KMS success or adoption is a combined intention to use and intention to contribute measure. The Perceived Benefit Model is an instrument that can be adapted to measuring either intention. Other models such as TAM2 may also be available and useful.

A secondary complementary conclusion is that measuring knowledge use is inappropriate and will lead to incorrect decisions on the effectiveness, adoption, or actual value of a KMS.

While perhaps not earth shaking in scope, these conclusions do change the way researchers and practitioners should view KMS success. KM and KMS do not need to be used extensively to be considered successful. Rather, it is the quality of use that is important. Knowledge that is used every day tends to be remembered and learned and ultimately loses value while knowledge that is used infrequently tends to be forgotten and so its retrieval and use has a greater impact on individuals and the organization. KM/KMS designers need to focus on identifying this higher value knowledge for capture and retention to ensure that KM/KMS users see the value in the KM/KMS.

Another key conclusion is that there is a difference in use behavior between new and experienced members of an organization. This is a very far reaching and potentially significant finding that can affect the design of KMS. This finding is reflected in the Jennex and Olfman KM Success Model (Jennex & Olfman, 2006) where it has been incorporated into the Knowledge Quality dimension through the constructs of richness and linkages where richness refers to rich, detailed knowledge and linkages refers to pointers to knowledge sources (see Figure 4). However, Jennex and Olfman (2006), while using this finding, did not provide support for it, and this article does that

Limitations

The studies used in this article have external validity concerns. Subject populations are small and tend to be focused within specific organizations or industries. This suggests that the conclusions may not be generalizeable to all KMS users. However, given that the three studies, when combined, look at several different organizations and industries, it is more appropriate to consider the small sample size as the greatest limitation. This limitation can only be overcome through more research but it is expected that further research will validate these findings rather than change them.

REFERENCES

Alavi, M., & Leidner, D.E. (2001). Review: Knowledge management and knowledge management systems: Conceptual foundations and research issues. *MIS Quarterly, 25*(1), 107-136.

Becerra-Fernandez, I., & Sabherwal, R. (2001). Organizational knowledge management: A contingency perspective. *Journal of Management Information Systems, 18*(1), 23-55.

Compeau, D., & Higgins, C. (1995). Computer self-efficacy: Development of a measure and initial test. *MIS Quarterly, 19*(2), 189-211.

Davis, F. (1989). Perceived usefulness, perceived ease of use, and user acceptance of information technology. *MIS Quarterly, 13,* 319-339.

DeLone, W.H., & McLean, E.R. (1992). Information systems success: The quest for the dependent variable. *Information Systems Research, 3,* 60-95.

DeLone, W.H., & McLean, E.R. (2003). The DeLone and McLean model of information systems success: A ten-year update. *Journal of Management Information Systems, 19*(4), 9-30.

Fishbein, M., & Ajzen, I. (1975). Belief, attitude, intention and behavior: An introduction to theory and research. Reading, MA: Addison-Wesley.

Gold, A.H., Malhotra, A., & Segars, A.H. (2001). Knowledge management: An organizational capabilities perspective. *Journal of Management Information Systems, 18*(1), 185-214.

Goodhue, D.L., & Thompson, R.L. (1995). Task-technology fit and individual performance. *MIS Quarterly 19*(2), 213-236.

Holsapple, C.W., & Joshi, K.D. (2002). Knowledge management: A three-fold framework.. *The Information Society.*

Jennex, M.E. (2005). What is knowledge management? *International Journal of Knowledge Management, 1*(4), i-iv.

Jennex, M.E. (2006). Culture, context, and knowledge management. *International Journal of Knowledge Management, 2*(2), i-iv.

Jennex, M.E., & Olfman, L. (2002). Organizational memory/knowledge effects on productivity, a longitudinal study. In *Proceedings of the 35th Hawaii International Conference on System Sciences, HICSS35, IEEE Computer Society.*

Jennex, M.E., & Olfman, L. (2005). Assessing knowledge management success. *International Journal of Knowledge Management, 1*(2), 33-49.

Jennex, M.E., & Olfman, L. (2006). A model of knowledge management success. *International Journal of Knowledge Management, 2*(3), 51-68.

Jennex, M.E., Olfman, L., Pituma, P., & Yong-Tae, P. (1998). An organizational memory information systems success model: An extension of DeLone and McLean's I/S success model. In *Proceedings of the 31st Hawaii International Conference on System Sciences, January, IEEE Computer Society Press.*

Jennex, M.E., Smolnik, S., & Croasdell, D. (2007). Knowledge management success. *International Journal of Knowledge Management, 3*(2), i-iv.

Lindsey, K. (2002). Measuring knowledge management effectiveness: A task-contingent organizational capabilities perspective. In *Eighth Americas Conference on Information Systems* (pp. 2085-2090).

Liu, S.C., Olfman, L., & Ryan, T. (2005). Knowledge management success: Empirical assessment of a theoretical model. *International Journal of Knowledge Management, 1*(2), 68-87.

Markus, M.L., & Keil, M. (1994, summer). If we build it, they will come: Designing information systems that people want to use. *Sloan Management Review*, 11-25.

Massey, A.P., Montoya-Weiss, M.M., & O'Driscoll, T.M. (2002). Knowledge management in pursuit of performance: Insights from Nortel Networks. *MIS Quarterly, 26*(3), 269-289.

Money, W., & Turner, A. (2005). Assessing knowledge management system user acceptance with the technology acceptance model. *International Journal of Knowledge Management, 1*(1), 8-26.

Rai, A., Lang, S., & Welker, R. (2002). Assessing the validity of IS success models: An empirical test and theoretical analysis. *Information Systems Research, 13*(1), 50-69.

Seddon, P.B. (1997). A respecification and extension of the DeLone and McLean model of IS success. *Information Systems Research, 8*(3), 240-253.

Thompson, R.L., Higgins, C.A., & Howell, J.M. (1991, March). Personal computing: Toward a conceptual model of utilization. *MIS Quarterly,* 125-143.

This work was previously published in the Journal of Organizational and End User Computing, Vol. 20, Issue 1, edited by M. Mahmood, pp. 50-63, copyright 2008 by IGI Publishing (an imprint of IGI Global).

Chapter 5
Collaborative Knowledge Management in the Call Center

Debbie Richards
Macquarie University, Australia

ABSTRACT

Collaboration is fundamental to the goals and success of knowledge management (KM) initiatives aimed at supporting decision making and problem solving. Yet many KM approaches and systems do not provide explicit mechanisms which allow knowledge to be collaboratively built up, validated and reconciled so that the more general goals of knowledge sharing and reuse can be achieved. In domains such as the call center, problems and solutions need to be created, retrieved, reworked and reused by multiple individuals and typically involves the use of multiple knowledge management tools, knowledge scattered across disparate sources and implicit "know-how". Acquiring, accessing, maintaining, sharing, reconciling and reusing knowledge in its various forms are particular challenges in the call center domain where the knowledge needed is complex and constantly changing made worse by short-term knowledge workers. The approach suggested allows knowledge, in the form of rules, to be incrementally acquired as the problem arises, in the form of cases, as part of the daily routine. Using the approach, knowledge workers are able to collaboratively and incrementally capture and maintain the heuristics they use daily for trouble-shooting. Further the system is designed to integrate to a wide variety of information and knowledge sources including legacy systems, recognizing the investment and value of such sources and minimizing the need to duplicate existing resources. This paper reports experiences and issues with knowledge management systems in the call center environment. A case study conducted during 2003-2006 is presented which describes how users found the incumbent systems and a prototype knowledge management system embodying the above approach.

DOI: 10.4018/978-1-60566-687-7.ch005

INTRODUCING THE CALL CENTER

In the period 2003-2006 we[1] have been working with the Sydney-based call center in a large multinational Information and Communication Technology (ICT) organization, which will be referred to as ORG X. Trouble-shooting failures or reduced system performance on the client's equipment was difficult and time consuming due to the complex environments involving multiple vendors, machines, software products and topologies, in an infinite number of combinations. It was no longer possible to expect a single expert to quickly find and resolve such issues. A better approach was needed, to allow both the accumulation of knowledge with guided trouble-shooting techniques, along with interfaces to all other relevant knowledge bases and data sources. The call center of ORG X received around 5,000 customer problem tickets per day globally, 1000 were emailed automatically from faulty equipment to the support center's case tracking software and another 4,000 per day came from customers, taking on average 2 hours to solve. According to their 2004 Annual Report, ORG X's cost of services as a whole were in the order of $US1 billion per annum. Better (re)use of trouble-shooting knowledge could save time and result in improvements to the bottom line.

Timely retrieval of the pertinent knowledge is an issue for all call centers involved in problem-solving. Additionally, while not necessarily true of ORG X, opportunities for career advancement in call centers are typically limited and motivation tends to be low with levels of 'churn' (the percentage of staff that need to be replaced) for call centers averaging around 31 percent, and as high as 51 percent among outsourced centers (Batt, Doellgast and Kwon, 2005). A knowledge management system which would allow call center workers to handle the routine problems more quickly and solve more of the interesting problems that were commonly passed to higher, usually more technical, levels of customer support, could provide greater employee satisfaction and stability as well improve the company's reputation and customer satisfaction.

A number of research instruments and techniques were used during this project. We began with an exploratory approach in the form of an indepth case study at our host organization together with review of vendor offerings and the related literature. The case study involved interviews, observation and surveys but moved into action research (as defined by Gummesson 2000) as we participated in the life of the organization and sought to improve the current knowledge management solution through the design, development and testing of a prototype.

Next let us consider the call center further by looking at the systems currently in use and the issues related to knowledge management.

CALL CENTER KNOWLEDGE MANAGEMENT AND SUPPORTING SYSTEMS

Traditional call center knowledge management software has supported case tracking of information such as customer details and the problem description including the product affected, operating system, version number, relevant error codes and who has been assigned to solve the case. These systems can be seen as an extension to Customer Relationship Management (CRM) systems. Integrating concepts related to CRM and KM recognizes the value of customers, the value of knowledge relating to products and services and the value of managing knowledge for, about and from customers (Gebert et al. 2003). Traditionally clients call front-line personnel but facilities for clients to directly enter, and sometimes solve their problems are becoming more common. In our domain the problem cases/tickets may be machine generated and electronically forwarded. The Internet has opened up the possibility of "customer coaching" or "one to one marketing" via technologies such as voice over IP (VOIP), conferencing and joint web browsing (Hampe, 1999).

Moving beyond the traditional model often requires redesign of workflows and user interfaces and upskilling of the call center staff. For example, Grundel and Schneider-Hufschmidt (1999) offered a custom built user interface for the call center environment in which calls and problems are passed from person to person and perhaps from a range of different device types, ranging from PCs to small handheld personal digital assistants (PDAs) using direct manipulation interfaces. XML to mark-up (web-based) documents is another key to supporting *Service Centers of the Future (ScotF)* (Schmidt and Wegner, 2000).

In a case study conducted in 3M's Call center (Mukund, 2002) it was found that large organizations offering a diverse range of products require sophisticated technologies to provide efficient and effective customer support. Similarly, in the customer care call center for Panafon, Greece's leading mobile phone operator in 2001, it was found that much of the knowledge that was needed was heuristic knowledge residing both in the minds of individuals and in the stories shared in their communities of practice which could be better managed for organizational re-use in a propositional knowledge based system (KBS) (Tsoukas and Vladimirou, 2001). Other techniques from the field of artificially intelligence (AI) have been suggested for the call center such as: machine learning (or data mining); neural networks; genetic algorithms and case based reasoning (CBR). However, most of these techniques rely on the availability of classified cases structured into attribute-value pairs. While CBR approaches, such as Chan, Chen and Geng (2000), do not require structured cases, there are a number of open issues limiting the technology including how to minimize the effort involved in manual indexing and how to adapt the retrieved case to the current case.

Some have noted that KMS require a multi-perspective approach. For example, Cheung et al. (2003) propose the multi-perspective knowledge based system (MPKBS). In keeping with our findings in ORG X, they note that in conventional approaches to customer service there is significant reliance on "know-how, experience and quality of the staff" (Cheung et al. 2003, p. 459) and that this knowledge needs to be captured and shared. However the perspectives they refer to are knowledge acquisition; knowledge diffusion; business automation; and business performance management which we see as multiple functionalities of the system rather than perspectives as there is no consideration of capturing or reconciling differences of opinion. They point out that in the CBR approach they have developed "the semantic context is difficult to be analysed by the computer. Therefore an encoding process is needed" (Cheung et al., 2003 p.460) and indexes need to be provided between the cases to the solution sets. The C-MCRDR approach, introduced later, addresses the CBR issues by using a combined CBR and KBS technique in which the indexing and encoding is performed by the system as users review cases and select features.

A key issue we identified from our own case study and the literature was the need for call center workers to make extensive use of external sources of knowledge to assist in the problem solving process. González, Giachetti and Ramirez (2005) call the drawing together of diverse knowledge sources in the organization, such as databases, files, experts, knowledge bases, and group chats, a "knowledge management-centric help desk" approach superior to the traditional technology focused approach to supporting the IT help desk function found in most organizations. Further, Parasuram and Grewal (2000) point out that CRM applications often fail because they do not integrate data from diverse sources or deliver the right information to the right people at the right time. Chang (2005) also believes that "disparate business processes and systems, compounded by the proliferation of customer contact points and channel, have created incompatible and disconnected views of customers" with failure to integrate to the business and legacy systems as key contributing factors to CRM failure rates around 55- 75% (Chang, 2005).

One of the ironies of the call center situation pointed out by Raestrup (2002) is that while many call centers are designed to handle problems that can occur globally, call center research, policies and work practices tend to differ and be decided at the national or regional level. This makes offering corporate solutions that fit all call centers even more problematic. Taylor et al. (2002) also note that despite technology integration, there is huge diversity across call centers making them difficult to characterize and improve. They cite empirical evidence that shows nine different workflows within two call centers in the financial sector.

Bendixen and Mitchell (2004) report on a case study in Vodacom Customer Care where the organization went to lengths to provide a pleasant environment, good training and an up-to-date knowledge base of their products. The success of these measures seem to have been counterbalanced by the addition of a quantitative performance measurement system to calculate staff bonuses which gave debatable and inconclusive results regarding improvements in productivity or satisfaction. The complex and diverse call center environment provides a difficult domain in which to provide a KM solution.

ORG X EXPERIENCES WITH EXISTING KMS

The experiences of ORG X were gathered through interviews (formal and informal), observation, survey and participation. This section selects, summarizes and synthesizes from the overall data collected. Vazey (2007) and Richards and Vazey (2005) provide more detail of the data collection instruments, specific questions, results and analyses.

ORG X was using a well-known[2] knowledge management solution together with a well-known case/ticket tracking system from another vendor. Typical of many KMS, when the knowledge management system was first introduced, it delivered significantly reduced time-to-resolution through application of Consortium for Service Innovation (CSI) knowledge management principles (CSI, 2006a). However, over time the solution offered was no longer adequate for the problems being faced. As is common in large organizations, they were reluctant to transition to the new products superceding the original systems due to the large investment and commitment in terms of training, measurement metrics and management reporting. Possibly more problematic, changing to a different system would involve major change at the cultural level.

The following statements, summarized from Vazey (2007), express the users' view of the incumbent KM systems recorded during a training session at ORG X:

1. Extremely poor response times leading to reluctant and reduced usage;
2. Many duplicate solutions and junk solutions;
3. Inability to search the ticket tracking tool to find past cases similar to the current case;
4. Limited searching in the knowledge base but there was no boolean or free text search facility;
5. The lack of a shared ontology or means to identify and resolve semantic conflicts resulted in inappropriate or missed hits.
6. Different KM tools used by different groups which were not integrated to allow knowledge sharing.

During the period 2004-2006, the first issue regarding system performance was to some extent addressed. To address the second issue a lengthy and costly exercise was undertaken to *scrub* the knowledge base resulting in significant improvement to the credibility and effectiveness of the knowledge management product as a knowledge storage solution.

A lot of knowledge had to be rediscovered daily by multiple people. Not only was the product knowledge being lost, the problem solving knowledge involving what questions to ask, how to identify the type of problem and how to find a solution was not being acquired. Das (2003) points out the importance of acquiring problem solving knowledge in call center KM initiatives to assist both knowledge users and providers to enhance productivity (Das, 2003). The following sentiment was frequently expressed: "*We can't find old solutions, even the ones we created ourselves!*" By tracking individual cases, it was found that some cases took just as long or sometimes even longer to solve when they reappeared as they had the first time they were seen (Richards and Vazey, 2005). It was these repeat incidents that made capture and retrieval of past solutions and proven processes most worthwhile.

Following Folcher (2003), who found that 1) the instrument used to conduct a dialogue between the expert and the caller and 2) the complexity of the problem will effect the knowledge-based artifact that has been progressively co-elaborated (resulting in the case being *worked up*), it was important to provide a technique which supported a dialogue and a range of problem complexities. Not only does the case need to evolve between the call center employee and the customer, cases will often require multiple employees to collaborate to specify the problem situation and/or the required solution. This need for cooperation and collaboration was identified in Adler and Simoudis (1992) where they examine the structure of help desk environments and the implications of this for distributed artificial intelligent (DAI) solutions.

In summary, ORG X needed a way of systematically gathering symptoms that provided a structured approach to both entering data into and retrieving data from a range of internal and external existing sources and formats including knowledge bases, case bases, manuals, documents, diagrams, and so on. The system needed to support evolution and incremental acquisition of the knowledge, including the problems and solutions, involving multiple individuals distributed by time and space who wanted to be able to rate the solutions, get feedback, and revise and revisit the knowledge as necessary. The knowledge acquisition approach needed to fit with the organizational culture, task workflow, require minimal training and be doable by the call-center worker.

THE COLLABORATIVE KNOWLEDGE MANAGEMENT APPROACH

In accordance with the findings of Adria and Chowdhury (2002), who studied the call centers at the group insurance company Sun Life and the Mayo Medical Clinic in Rochester, Minnesota, and our own KBS research with novice and domain experts (Richards 2000), user acceptance would be minimal unless knowledge workers were given control and ownership of their knowledge. This meant that knowledge acquisition and maintenance needed to be intuitive and also to fit into the daily routine. For this reason a knowledge acquisition technique known as Ripple Down Rules (RDR) (Compton and Jansen, 1989) was chosen, which does not require knowledge to be entered by a knowledge engineer but allows the user themselves to become the engineer. Additionally, the RDR approach uses cases to drive knowledge capture and support validation but uses rules to act as an index between cases. In ORG X we had problem tickets and solution cases in separate systems that needed to be linked and thereby close the feedback loop between problem and solution knowledge.

Starting with the strengths (Kang, Compton and Kang, 1995) and successes of RDR[3] we found that the call center application domain required a number of extensions (Vazey and Richards,

Figure 1. A partial C-MCRDR showing original MCRDR within the box

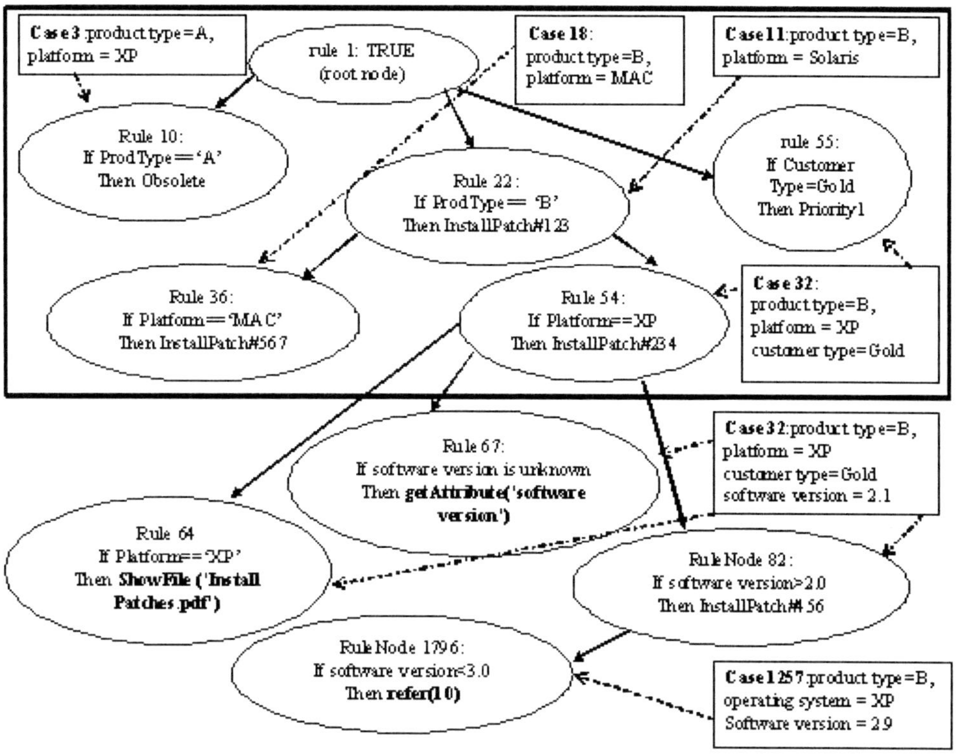

2004) to traditional Multiple Classification RDR (MCRDR) (Kang, Compton and Preston, 1995) including:

1) The need to support required when collaboratively acquiring knowledge from multiple and possibly conflicting sources of expertise;
2) The need to work up cases over an extended period of time.
3) The need to edit all aspects of the knowledge base including rules, cases and conclusions.
4) The need to distinguish between a classification and conclusion.

The modified knowledge representation is referred to in this paper as C-MCRDR, but known as 7Cs in Vazey (2007), representing the collaborative process by which problem cases are worked up and classified. Figure 1 shows a partial C-MCRDR knowledge base.

Within the solid line in Figure 1 we see an example of original MCRDR. An MCRDR knowledge base consists of rules and associated cases. When a case is presented to the system it is processed by the first rule, rule 1. As shown, this is the root node and is always true. This node can contain a default conclusion which covers the most common conclusion, such as "no conclusion" in the pathology report interpretation environment, and is a way of reducing the amount of knowledge needed to be captured to cover a domain. The inference engine then proceeds to test whether any of the child nodes are true. If a child node is true, all of its immediate children are evaluated, and so on, until the last true rule on each pathway is found. The conclusion at each

Table 1. Demonstrating the MCRDR Knowledge Acquisition Process using Figure 1

After meetings to discuss the knowledge domain and review of the data/case content and structure, a knowledge and/or software engineer designs and implements the interfaces to other information sources and systems. The empty knowledge base is set up with the default rule 1 which always evaluates to true. For this domain there is no default conclusion.
Customer A rings and describes a performance problem with product A running on one of their XP machines. Knowledge Worker A (KWA) creates a problem ticket containing the case details (case 3). Only the default rule fires so KWA needs to find a solution from outside the knowledge base. KWA looks up a product catalogue, informs the customer that this product is no longer supported by their company, suggests that they purchase Product D which provides similar functionality and offers to put the customer through to the sales department. To capture this knowledge for future reuse, the KWA creates a conclusion "Product Obsolete" and selects the "prodType=A" feature from the case (rule 10). Rule 11 (not shown) is also added which states "If ProdType=A then suggest Product D".
Customer B rings with a problem with product B running on a Solaris platform. KWA creates a new ticket with this information but the system has no knowledge about how to solve this situation. The KWA asks another colleague if they know if there is any problem with product B. They are told that patch 123 is needed. KWA rings back the customer and creates a new case (case 11) from the problem ticket and a new rule by entering the conclusion "InstallPatch123" and selecting the feature "ProdType =B" from case 11.
Customer C rings an hour later with the same problem with product B this time running on a Macintosh computer. The ticket is raised and the system informs KWA that Patch123 should be installed based on rule 22. However, Patch123 is for the Solaris platform. The rule had been too general. When KWA discovers from the technical staff that a different patch is needed for each operating system, rule 36 is added as an exception to rule 22. Some feature which differentiates the cornerstone case (case 11) from the current case (case 18) must be specified. The exception is needed because the platform is a MAC rather than a Solaris system.
At a later time Customer D rings with a problem with running Product B on a Window XP platform and rule 54 and case 32 are added. Rule 55 is also to indicate that the problem needs to be resolved quickly as the customer has paid for the top-level maintenance agreement (gold) and must be given priority.

final true node are the conclusions provided by the system.

In our example within the box, rules 54 and 55 would be last the true rules for case 32 and would return two conclusions "install Patch#234" and "Priority1". Each node has at least one case associated with it, known as its cornerstone case/s. Knowledge is validated in the context of the cornerstone case/s, which is the case that prompted the rule to be added, and all cases associated with all generations of connected child rule nodes. For example, the set of cornerstone cases for rule 22 are {11, 18, 32}. MCRDR uses an exception structure in which knowledge is never changed but overridden by one or more new rules. When a conclusion is given that the user does not agree with, they attach a new exception rule to the rule which gave the misclassification by selecting an existing conclusion or specifying a new conclusion and picking the features in the current case which differentiate it from the case associated with the rule which misfired. Table 1 provides a step-by-step description of how the MCRDR knowledge base may have formed.

Outside of the solid line some of the extensions supported by C-MCRDR (Vazey, 2007) are represented. As in MCRDR, multiple conclusions for each case may be given and each parent may have multiple children. However, C-MCRDR differentiates between classifications and conclusions, allowing a classification to be linked to multiple conclusions and reuse of conclusions across multiple classifications. In the approach (Vazey, 2007), classifications are classes or groups that share a set of features and they may be labeled using text or hyperlinks, or remain unlabelled. Figure 1 shows some labeled classifications (for example, "Obsolete", "Priority1"). A conclusion can be seen as one or more propositions, or final statements, including actions that one should take as a result of arriving at a given classification. Many conclusion types are available, such as the ones shown in Figure 1. For example, getAttribute ('attributeName') indicates that the user should be prompted to enter the value of a particular attribute; ShowFile('fileName') displays a file or provides a hyperlink to an uploaded file; advise('error-code') provides a hyperlink to a description of a particular error code; and refer(ruleNodeID) refers to a conclusions or classification provided at another RuleNode. Also unlike the MCRDR knowledge representation, it is possible for child nodes to have multiple parents and child Rule-Nodes may inherit the axiomatic behaviour of multiple parent RuleNodes using the refer() and/ or link() function.

The C-MCRDR approach supports case-driven KA in the same spirit as MCRDR, however, the system also encourages and supports top-down rule-driven KA. This allows users to enter the rules they already have in their head or may have even codified without relying on a case to motivate knowledge acquisition. C-MCRDR allows editing of any aspect of the knowledge base, including past cases and rules to cater for the call center environment where cases are being worked up and may continue to change over a period of months. This may involve multiple people who are globally distributed. To resolve conflicts which may arise when edits are made, the system keeps track of all seen cases, and the relationships between cases, rule nodes, conditions, classifications and conclusions. A key way in which conflict is identified and resolved is via the notion of live versus registered nodes, where live indicates that the system has determined that the node is the last TRUE rule on a pathway by the system and registered is where a human user has confirmed that the node should be active (that is, they agree). Through this mechanism users are advised when changes in areas of the global knowledge base relevant to them have occurred so that they may approve or disapprove a change. If the user disapproves, they add one or more refinement rules. If the rule is accepted the rule's status becomes live and registered. If nothing is done, then the rule is live but not registered. Another user at another time or place may choose to approve or reject the rule.

Referring back to Figure 1, outside the box we see a number of extensions to MCRDR. These differences include: rule-driven knowledge capture; working up a case; changing a case; identifying and reconciling inconsistencies (that is, live versus registered); being able to provide conclusions and classifications; and linking and referring to other rules and conclusions to enable greater reuse of knowledge. The process is described using a hypothetical example in Table 2.

LESSONS LEARNED WITH KMS FOR THE CALL CENTER

Reports of interaction with KMS for the call center are largely in the form of promotional testimonials at vendor websites. While scant and often anecdotal, in the research literature there is some mention of user interaction with KMS. Bose and Sugumaran (2003) note a number of limitations of their prototype KM-based CRM system including: the need for more knowledge to be captured; increased maintenance issues of the knowledge over time and lack of interface to third party software. Gebert et al. (2003) found that the KM tool in their customer call center case study had an unmanageable navigational structure that was poorly linked to the many needed sources and half of the time spent using the system was taken up with waiting for MS Word documents to open in the Web browser.

As an example of the benefits of reusing codified knowledge, Hansen, Nohria, and Tierney (1999) describe the Access Medical Center, which had captured 50% of the call-center market under consideration and was growing at a rate of 40% per year, a somewhat novel call center allowing patients to call in to receive a diagnosis. They note that depending on the organization, KM strategies can be differentiated on the basis of

Table 2. A hypothetical C-MCRDR Knowledge Acquisition history based on Figure 1

Customer D rings back and asks how to install the patch. Knowledge Worker B (KWB) describes the process. When the call is over KWB decides to create a document containing the installation process and creates rule 64 so that future customers will be notified about the file. This is an example of top-down rule driven knowledge acquisition.
Customer D rings again and informs knowledge worker C (KWC) that the solution they were given did not work. The C-MCRDR system assists the call center person to know what questions to ask in working up a case. Rule 67 added by another worker to capture knowledge they had previously gained requests that KWC ask which software version of product B is being used. The customer informs KWC that they are using version 2.1. Case 32 is updated with this new information and the system returns the conclusion "InstallPatch#456" (rule 82) which is the appropriate fix for software versions greater than 2.0. The system will record case 32 as live and notify users who are registered about any changes (and possible inconsistencies) that might have occurred to other parts of the knowledge base as a result of changing the case. Registered users will indicate whether they accept or reject the changes.
A year later a customer rings with a performance problem with product B running on Windows XP. The system requests the version number. The customer indicates that the version number is 2.9 (case 1257). The system responds with rule 64 and 82. However: Product B is no longer supported for versions less than 3.0 and rule 1796 concludes that the product is obsolete by linking to the conclusion for rule 10.

whether the organization takes a *codification* or *personalization* view of knowledge, where codification involves storing knowledge in repositories for use by others and personalization involves an individual directly sharing their knowledge with another individual.

Based on ORG X and the case studies mentioned from the literature, Table 3 summarizes the limitations/issues of existing KMS and what is needed.

Measurable goals of KMS in the call center environment include lower service cost, improved service and consistency in service (eGain 2004). Taking the view that KM and KMS are one and the same thing (Jennex, 2008), Jennex and Olfman (2006) have offered a KM success model which determines net benefit based on system quality, knowledge/information quality, service quality, user satisfaction and perceived benefit, In our context, success can be measured by the effectiveness and efficiency by which customer problems are handled, for example: reduced problem incidence, increased customer self-service, increased automation of problem diagnosis and solution matching, increased accuracy of solution matching as measured by reduced case revisits, increased solution re-use, reduced duplication of solutions, rapid fault and enquiry resolution times, increased customer satisfaction, increased in-line self-learning by support center staff, increased staff satisfaction, and reduced staff turnover. Return on investments (ROI) for KMS can be measured in terms of better efficiencies: reduced repeat calls, incorrect transfers, end-to-end call length, training time and staff premiums and increased call avoidance and first time fixes and reduced incoming phone calls for companies using web-based self-service trouble-shooting KM systems (eGain 2004). Further ROI gains can be made, but harder to measure, in reduced customer turnover, increased repeat business and sales (eGain 2004). As we can see, KMS can offer benefits to all stakeholders, which includes customers, knowledge-workers, management and the organization, and thus the solution must meet a wide range of goals including fitting in with the organizational culture and daily workflow.

The issues in Table 1 have been major design considerations for the approach we offer. The prototype KMS aims at addressing or minimizing these problems by supporting integration; rapid and incremental knowledge acquisition and maintenance and a simple navigational structure linking problems with solutions in whatever format they take and wherever they reside. A number of incentive schemes were suggested to be used in conjunction with the system to encourage knowledge usage and particularly entry and validation,

Table 3. Call center Issues and Requirements

Call center Issue/Limitation	KMS requirement
Knowledge distributed in multiple, including legacy and other vendor, systems.	KMS needs to handle and link knowledge in many different systems including some which are external to the organization
Similar cases/problems often recur. Finding past solutions can be difficult.	KMS needs to support queries, searching and navigation of problem and solution spaces. A link must exist between the two.
Much knowledge resides in people's heads and is difficult to transfer and reuse.	KMS must handle a wide range of types of knowledge, including tacit knowledge, involving different formats, locations, accessibility levels and availability.
Dynamic environments with changing technology, staff turnover and evolving knowledge resulting in inconsistencies, out-of-date and redundant knowledge.	Simple maintenance strategies which allow inconsistencies and multiple stakeholder/ knowledge worker viewpoints to be reconciled.
The sooner and closer the problem can be solved to the first point of contact the better for client, company and worker.	Knowledge acquisition, maintenance and usage needs to be shared by multiple levels of users not just technical users or knowledge engineers.
High staff churn, low morale, sometimes requires complex technical knowledge.	Training and incentives for adding, updating, sharing and reusing knowledge needs to be incorporated
Call centers have diverse needs.	KMS needs to be tailored to fit the local environment and allow personal, local and corporate knowledge to be captured.

but we recognize that these do not always lead to the desired outcomes. Ravishankar (2008) cites a number of studies which reported negative impacts of reward schemes on employee attitudes and knowledge sharing. One scheme which was successful was the one used by Rexon involving the concept of Knowledge Units (KU). Knowledge experts reviewed and awarded KU to individuals whenever they made a submission to the Kstore system. The experts accumulate KU for rating documents and anyone (re)using the knowledge in the system also accrued points. KUs translated to cash coupons redeemable at leading shopping chains. The rewards program not only encouraged KM it served to raise awareness about its importance.

To determine how users found the C-MCRDR prototype two studies were conducted. Following a training and introductory session, approximately 20 participants from two levels of customer support and covering two product groups were asked for their initial impressions of the system and whether they felt it would be useful. With the results in the affirmative (Vazey, 2007, Appendix A: Part B), the real proof was in the usage of the system over a period of time. Methods for usability testing of call center applications have been suggested. For example, Liddle (1998) recommends the use of scripts and role-playing customers. Poston and Speier (2008) provide a rating scheme which calculates decision accuracy based on a trade-off between search effort and evaluation effort. Bauman (1999) recommends a matrix-based approach with the criteria: self-descriptiveness, consistency, simplicity, compatibility, error tolerance, and feedback, to determine the experience of the customer based on call center data and customer activity tracking software. In a similar vein, our second evaluation study involved tracking the activity and data generated by the call center worker when using the prototype. The trial of the C-MCRDR prototype system involving 12 registered participants, reported in Vazey and Richards (2006), demonstrated that multiple users could collaboratively build up a trouble-shooting knowledge base using both bottom-up case-driven and top-down rule-driven knowledge acquisition according to the situation and their knowledge. After minimal training (one hour session attended by all participants) and seven hours (in total for all participants) of knowledge acquisition, knowledge workers were able to capture knowledge to cover a subdomain (specifically the problem cases which are automatically generated and emailed to the system by errant equipment) which was globally consuming somewhere between 4.5 hours, in the best case of 1 minute of resolution time, to 67.5 hours per day, using the more likely estimate of 15 minutes per case resolution time (though average resolution time of two hours was suggested by some participants). The estimated direct cost of resolving problems is this subdomain is $3.3 million per annum. Our system covered approximately 90% of errors in the chosen subdomain by handling 270 of the 300 cases per day. These time and cost savings after just 7 hours of collective knowledge acquisition effort are achieved by providing a mechanism to index solutions from a range of internal and external sources including existing legacy systems within the context of the existing task, workflow and processes.

CONCLUSION AND FUTURE DIRECTIONS

While the solution offered has been initially motivated by the problems facing high-volume call centres that support complex high-tech IT products it can be generalised to other call centers and problem domains which have problem cases to be classified or linked to solution cases.

We note that while widely accepted standards and metrics are still to emerge in this domain, there are movements in this direction as evidenced in the existence and growing membership of the Consortium for Service Innovation (CSI). Nevertheless, CSI acknowledge that "tools are tempting, but not a panacea" (CSI, 2006b, p.1). In one case study reported by CSI (CSI, 2006b), the challenge was found to be the need to manage the complexity of multi-tier, multi-platform implementations, bottlenecks imposed by knowledge quality assurance processes, solution redundancy and the need for additional data entry into customized KM tools resulting in poor quality entries. To address these challenges CSI advocate Knowledge Centered Support (KCS) based on the principles: Capture in the Workflow; Flag It or Fix It; Performance Assessment; and Leadership.

The C-MCRDR knowledge acquisition, maintenance and reuse cycle is a flag or fix it approach designed to fit with the ORG-X, and typical call center, workflow and also to sit on top of existing systems without the need for additional data entry. We note that our greatest impediment to the widespread uptake and expansion of our system across the organization is due to the lack of *leadership*, defined as "Visible, ongoing commitment by management reinforc[ing] the message that KCS was a long-term standard for delivering support" (CSI, 2006b, p. 2), in the context of our project and KMS. Through organizational restructure, we lost our champion and project sponsor. As found in the Kstore experience at Rexon, KM champions play a vital role in ensuring the success of any KM initiative together with sociocultural and political influences within the organization (Ravishankar, 2008). Despite the very promising preliminary results the project came to an abrupt halt. Confirming the sad truth, that success it is not based on what a KMS knows, but on who knows the KMS.

Anticipated future trends in KMS, applicable to knowledge management in ORG X, call centers in general and beyond the call center, include increased system intelligence via incorporation of ideas and technologies used in query matching/rewriting, data mining, information retrieval, agent technology, semantic web, natural language processing, XML, ontologies and Web services and other techniques from artificial intelligence increasingly being used behind today's search engines. These technologies offer benefits, but addressing human factors is a more pressing need. There are lessons to be learnt to support collaborative knowledge management from social software such as wikis, Communities of Practice, Blogs and even email. KMS and their interfaces need to support user modelling and allow greater end user participation and system ownership in line with increasingly sophisticated and demanding users. Rasmussen and Haggerty (2008) note that knowledge and cognitive overload due to access to too much knowledge, requires attention to be paid to what they term *knowledge appraisal* involving human consideration and evaluation of the knowledge presented from all dimensions (individual, organizational, tacit and explicit) and within each step of the knowledge cycle. The focus is on ensuring that only up-to-date, relevant and correct knowledge is stored and retrieved and that other knowledge is discarded, adapted or recreated. While performance assessment (validation) and knowledge evolution are central to our approach, as a future challenge a technique for identifying and perhaps removing stale or unused sections of the knowledge base may be helpful. Halverson, Erickson and Ackerman (2004) found that the attitudes of the service provider (that is, is your role a mentor or problem solver?) and local and organisational preferences and constraints combined to produce a *bricolage* of KM strategies and adoption models.

A collaborative approach involving integration with existing systems and work practices together with incentives and rewards for using the KM system were essential elements that we sought to deliver. Trials to date have validated the goals and prototype developed. However, like many other good ideas, if collaborative attitudes, approaches and actions are missing, disconnected knowledge silos or islands will prevail.

ACKNOWLEDGMENT

The author wishes to acknowledge the significant work and effort of Megan Vazey in the requirements, analysis, design, development and implementation of the extensions, prototype, surveys and trials over the past three years. Also many thanks to the corporate sponsor for funding and review of a draft of this paper, the Australian Research Council and Macquarie University for funding related to this project.

REFERENCES

Adler, M., & Simoudis, E. (1992). Cooperation and coordination in help desk organizations. In *Proc. of the 11th Int.l Workshop on Distributed Artificial Intelligence*, Glen Arbor, MI.

Adria, M., & Chowdhury, S. (2002). Making room for the call center. *Information Systems Management, 19*(1), 71–80. doi:10.1201/1078/43199.19.1.20020101/31479.10

Batt, R., Doellgast, V., & Kwon, H. (2005). *U.S. call center industry report 2004 national benchmarking report strategy, HR practices & performance* (CAHRS Working Paper #05-06). Ithaca, NY: Cornell University, School of Industrial and Labor Relations, Center for Adv. Human Resource Studies. htttp://digitalcommons.ilr.cornell.edu/cahrswp/6

Baumann, K. (1999). Matrix evaluation method for planned usability improvements based on customer feedback. In H.J. Bullinger and J. Ziegler (Eds.), *Human-computer interaction: Ergonomics and user interfaces* (pp. 701-705). Mahwah, NJ: Lawrence Erlbaum Associates.

Bendixen, M., & Mitchell, C. (2004). *Vodacom Customer Care*. Case Wits Business School, University of the Witwatersrand, South Africa.

Bose, R., & Sugumaran, V.Application of knowledge management technology in customer relationship management. *Knowledge and Process Management, 10*(1), 3–17. doi:10.1002/kpm.163

Chan, C. W., Chen, L. L., & Geng, L. Q. (2000). Knowledge engineering for an intelligent case-based system for help desk operations. *Expert Systems with Applications, 18*(2), 125–132. doi:10.1016/S0957-4174(99)00058-5

Chang, J. O. (2005). Toward a unified view of customer relationship management. *The Journal of American Academy of Business*, March 2005, 32-38.

Cheung, C. F., Lee, W. B., Wang, W. M., Chu, K. F., & To, S. (2003). A multi-perspective knowledge-based system for customer service management. *Expert Systems with Applications*, *24*, 457–470. doi:10.1016/S0957-4174(02)00193-8

Compton, P., Peters, L., Edwards, G., & Lavers, T. G. (2006). Experience with ripple-down rules. *Knowledge-Based System Journal*, *19*(5), 289–380. doi:10.1016/j.knosys.2006.05.001

Compton, P. J., & Jansen, R. (1989). A philosophical basis for knowledge acquisition. *3rd European Knowledge Acquisition for KBS W/shop* (pp. 75-89).

Consortium for Service Innovation. (CSI, 2006a). *The KCSsm Operational Model (Knowledge-Centered Support)* Version 3. Retrieved December 26, 2008 from http://www.serviceinnovation.org/included/docs/library/ programs/KCS_OpModel_V3.7.pdf

Consortium for Service Innovation. (CSI, 2006b). *Progress Software Application Support Services KCS at Work)*. Retrieved December 26, 2008 from http://www.serviceinnovation.org/included/docs/library/programs/ progress_casestudy.pdf

Das, A. (2003). Knowledge and productivity in technical support work. *Management Science*, *49*(4), 416–431. doi:10.1287/mnsc.49.4.416.14419

Edwards, G., Compton, P., Malor, R., Srinivasan, A., & Lazarus, L. (1993). PEIRS: A pathologist maintained expert system for the interpretation of chemical pathology reports. *Pathology*, *25*, 27–34. doi:10.3109/00313029309068898

eGain (2004). Knowledge management for customer service: Ingredients for success. eGain Communications Corporation. http://www.egain.com.

Folcher, V. (2003). Appropriating artifacts as instruments: When design-for-use meets design-in-use. *Interacting with Computers*, *15*(5), 647–663. doi:10.1016/S0953-5438(03)00057-2

Gebert, H., Geib, M., Kolbe, L., & Brenner, W. (2003). Knowledge-enabled customer relationship management: Integrating customer relationship management and knowledge management concepts. *Journal of Knowledge Management*, *7*(5), 107–123. doi:10.1108/13673270310505421

González, L. M., Giachetti, R. E., & Ramirez, G. (2005). Knowledge management-centric help desk: specification and performance evaluation. *Decision Support Systems*, *40*(2), 389–405. doi:10.1016/j.dss.2004.04.013

Grundel, C., & Schneider-Hufschmidt, M. (1999). A direct manipulation user interface for the control of communication processes—Making call handling manageable. In H.J. Bullinger & Ziegler, J. (Eds.), *Human-computer interaction: Communication, cooperation, and application design* (pp. 8-13). Mahwah, NJ: Lawrence Erlbaum Associates.

Gummesson, E. (2000). *Qualitative methods in management research.* London: Sage Publication.

Halverson, C. A., Erickson, T., & Ackerman, M. S. (2004). Behind the help desk: Evolution of a knowledge management system in a large organization. In *Proceedings of the 2004 ACM Conference on Computer Supported Cooperative Work* (pp. 304-313) (Chicago, Illinois, USA, November 06 - 10, 2004). CSCW '04. New York: ACM.

Hampe, J. F. (1999). Call center: technical and organizational challenges. Human-Computer Interaction: Ergonomics and User Interfaces. In *Proc. of 8th International Conference on Human-Computer Interaction (HCI International'99)* (pp. 1316-1320). Mahwah, NJ: Lawrence Erlbaum Associates.

Hansen, M. T., Nohria, N., & Tierney, T. (1999). What's your strategy for managing knowledge? *Harvard Business Review*, *77*(2), 106–116.

Jennex, M. (2008). Exploring system use as a measure of knowledge management success. *Journal of Organizational and End User Computing*, *20*(1), 50–63.

Jennex, M. E., & Olfman, L. (2006). A model of knowledge management success. *International*

... *Journal of Knowledge Management*, *2*(3), 51–68.

Kang, B., Compton, P., & Preston, P. (1995). Multiple classification ripple down rules: evaluation and possibilities. In *Proc. 9th Banff Knowledge Acquisition for Knowledge Based Systems Workshop.* Banff. Feb 26 - March 3 1995, Vol 1: 17.1-17.20.

Kang, B., Yoshida, K., Motoda, H., Compton, P., & Iwayama, M. (1996). A help desk system with intelligent interface. In P. Compton, R. Mizoguchi, H. Motoda & T. Menzies (Eds.), *Pacific Rim Knowledge Acquisition Workshop, (PKAW'96)* (pp. 313-332). Sydney, School of Computer Science and Engineering, UNSW.

Lazarus, L. (2000). Clinical decision support systems: Background and role in clinical support. Retrieved from http://www.pks.com.au/CDSS_White_Paper_doc.pdf

Liddle, R. J. (1998). Usability testing of a call center application: The importance and necessity of using scenario-driving scripts. In *Proc. of the Silicon Valley Ergonomics Conference and Exposition - ErgoCon '98* (pp. 31-32). Palo Alto, CA.

Mukund, A. (2002). CRM/KM Initiatives at 3M. Case. *ICFAI Center for Management Research (ICMR)*, India.

Parasuram, A., & Grewal, D. (2000). The impact of technology on the quality-value-loyalty chain: A research agenda. *Journal of the Academy of Marketing Science*, *28*(1), 168–175. doi:10.1177/0092070300281015

Poston, R., & Speier, C. (2008). Knowledge Management Systems Usage: Rating Scheme Validity and the Effort-Accuracy Trade-Off. *Journal of Organizational and End User Computing*, *20*(1), 1–16.

Raestrup, B. (2002). Call center agent network—A strategy against 'Cubicalization': A virtual community for call-center workers in the information industry. In H. Luczak, E. Cakir & G. Cakir (eds.), *Ergonomic Institut fur Arbeits- und Sozialforschung* (pp. 256-258). Forschungsgesellschaft mbH, Berlin.

Rasmussen, H. S., & Haggerty, N. (2008). Knowledge appraisal and knowledge management systems: Judging what we know. *Journal of Organizational and End User Computing*, *20*(1), 17–34.

Ravishankar, M. N. (2008). Rewarding end-users for participating in organisational KM: A case study. *Journal of Organizational and End User Computing*, *20*(1), 35–49.

Richards, D. (2000). The reuse of knowledge: A user-centered approach. *International Journal of Human-Computer Studies*, *52*(3), 553–579. doi:10.1006/ijhc.1999.0342

Richards, D., & Vazey, M. (2005). Closing the Gap Between Different Knowledge Sources and Types in the Call center. *Proc. Australian Conference in Information Systems (ACIS 2005)*, November 2005, Sydney, Australia.

Schmidt, H. W., & Wegner, L. M. (2000). Shared XML documents in service centers of the future. In *Proc. of the 1st Int.l Conf. on Web Information Systems Engineering (Workshops)* (105-112). IEEE Comput. Soc, Los Alamitos, CA.

Taylor, P., Hyman, J., Mulvey, G., & Bain, P. (2002). Work organization, control and the experience of work in call centers. *Work, Employment and Society*, *16*(1), 133–150. doi:10.1177/09500170222119281

Tsoukas, H., & Vladimirou, E. (2001). What is organizational knowledge? *Journal of Management Studies*, *38*(7), 973. doi:10.1111/1467-6486.00268

Vazey, M. (2007). *Case-driven collaborative classification*. Unpublished doctoral thesis, Macquarie University, Sydney, NSW.

Vazey, M., & Richards, D. (2004, August 9-13). Achieving rapid knowledge acquisition. In *Proc. Pacific Knowledge Acquisition W/shop (PKAW 2004)* (pp. 74-86). Auckland, New Zealand.

Vazey, M., & Richards, D. (2006, August 7-11). Evaluation of the FastFIX prototypes 5Cs CARD System. In *Proc. Pacific Knowledge Acquisition Workshop (PKAW 2004)* (LNAI 4303, pp. 106-117). Guilin, China.

ENDNOTES

1 The project reported in this paper was conducted with my PhD student Megan Vazey. Full details of the call center description (section 1), the complete set of survey questions, findings and results of observations and interviews (section 2) and detailed description of the C-MCRDR knowledge representation can be found in Vazey (2007).

2 our client prefers to maintain the anonymity of its existing vendors with whom they have had a successful working relationship

3 For a description of experiences with other successful RDR systems see Edwards et al. (1993) regarding the Pathology Expert Interpretation Reporting Systems (PEIRS); Lazarus (2000) and Compton et al. (2006) regarding LabWizard; and Kang et al. (2006) regarding the help desk domain.

Chapter 6 Diffusing Management Information for Legal Compliance:
The Role of the IS Organization within the Sarbanes-Oxley Act

Ashley Braganza
Cranfield University, UK

Ray Hackney
Brunel University, UK

ABSTRACT

Information systems are vital to successful compliance with Section 404 of the Sarbanes Oxley Act. However, there is little published academic literature which reports systematic studies that explain how IS organizations implement 404. Institutional theory was adopted as the lens through which to examine the experiences of 404 implementation in three global organizations. The methodology for the research involved in-depth case study analysis. We conclude that key implementation drivers for 404 are directives from senior authorities, financial and resource subsidies, standards being set and adhered to, and knowledge being deployed. The findings are believed to present significant insights into the complexities and role of IS in providing valid and appropriate approaches to 404 compliance.

INTRODUCTION

The Sarbanes Oxley Act (SOX) creates the deepest changes to the Securities Exchange Commission (SEC) rules since 1934 (107th Congress, 2002; Banham, 2003; Aberdeen Group, 2005). The act was passed in response to financial misstatements and high-profile corporate frauds such as Enron,

WorldCom, Tyco, and Global Crossing. The act aims to reduce the level and scale of financial fraud due to an organization's management being able to misrepresent its financial condition (Ferrell, 2004; Rone & Berman, 2004). Organization-wide strong governance—that is the formal and informal rules that guide organizational action and behavior—and robust controls are therefore seen as essential to avoiding future accountancy deficiencies.

Section 404 of the act requires organizations to provide external auditors with documentary evidence of the existence and effective functioning of processes, systems, and controls used to generate all financial and management information made available to the public. Since in most organizations, processes, systems, and controls are embedded in a wide range of information systems, the IS organization assumes a significant role in 404 compliance (Chan, 2004; Hackney, Burn, & Salazar, 2004;Coe, 2005).

This article analyzes the implementation of Section 404 within organizations through the lens of institutional theory. Unlike previous regulatory frameworks which are based on self-regulation, the act makes the management of effective internal controls mandatory. Furthermore, the act backs up the requirements for controls with severe penalties including fines and prison sentences for those in breach of its provisions. SOX is binding on all companies listed on any American Stock Exchange, and hence non-U.S. companies are subject to its provisions (Dalton & Dalton, 2005; Coffee, 2005). Therefore, companies incorporated in other legal jurisdictions, such as the UK, for example, can be prosecuted, for the first time, in U.S. courts for being in breach of SOX (Dewing & Russell, 2003). In the past, company officials, such as the chief executive officer (CEO) and chief financial officer (CFO), could only be prosecuted in the country of the company's incorporation.

TAXONOMY OF 404 INTERVENTION DRIVERS

There is a significant amount of practitioner literature available that provides managers with methods and procedures they need to consider when implementing Section 404 (Duffy, 2004; Ivancevich, Duening, Gilbert, & Konopaske, 2003; Mayer, 2003; Quall, 2004). However, as normal, the practitioner literature lacks a theoretical basis for the approaches being recommended and is akin to the plethora of prescriptions for successful implementation of information systems. As in the wider IS academic field, our aim is to examine the role of the IS organization when implementing Section 404 through a sound theoretical lens, based on valid methods, in order to provide conceptual insights for 404 implementation.

Section 404 adds to the body of corporate governance literature. The most common approach used to study corporate governance is agency theory (Dalton, Daily, Ellstrand, & Johnson, 1998; Dalton & Dalton, 2005), which stems from the seminal work of Berle and Means (1932). They argued that the separation of ownership (shareholders) and control (management) gave managers—agents—an opportunity to act in their own self-interest by making decisions or acting in ways to increase their financial prosperity rather than that of the shareholders (Fama, 1980; Jensen, 1993). A variety of methods are deployed to minimize the opportunities for promoting management's self-interest over that of shareholders. These are exemplified by managing the board's composition, strengthening the role of non-executive directors (Barnhart, Marr, & Rosenstein, 1994), and linking the board's compensation to shareholder returns (Cadbury, 1992; Dalton, Daily, Certo, & Roengpitya, 2003). These methods are essentially self-regulatory.

Prior to the SOX Act, the roles of executive and non-executive directors, as well as internal and external auditors, were considered to provide sufficient 'checks and balances' to avoid financial disasters on the scale of Enron. However, the SOX Act, and in particular Section 404, has swept away traditional forms of self-regulation by mandating organizations have transparent systems of internal controls. The act also places significant responsibilities and potential penalties upon audit firms, and through them, on organizations' management (Duffy, 2004; Ooms-Piepers & Degens, 2004). Agency theory appears to be of limited use because it neglects the effects that external institutions can have on organizations and their behavior. Agency theory takes a narrower perspective by focusing on internal actors (managers) and one external stakeholder (shareholders) (Daily, Dalton, & Canella, 2003). The theory is geared towards finding ways to minimize agency costs incurred by organizations to stockholders (Aguilera & Jackson, 2003) and barely addresses the power that external institutions can have on board behavior (Pfeffer, 1981; DiMaggio & Powell, 1983).

These limitations of agency theory are likely to yield superficial insights into the role of IS organizations in the implementation of 404. We argue that institutional theory enables deeper insights into 404 implementation as it takes into account multiple stakeholders within and outside organizations and the use of power and influence to bring about changes in practices (King et al., 1994). Institutional theory suggests that organizations conform with rules and regulations about appropriate conduct and behaviors to ensure legitimacy within their environment (Suchman, 1995). Institutional properties have been developed by numerous researchers (Covaleski & Dirsmith, 1988; Jepperson, 1991; Meyer & Rowan, 1977; Scott, 1987; Zucker, 1987; Avgerou, 2000; Crowston & Myers, 2004; DiMaggio & Powell, 1991; Goodstein, 1994; Greenwood & Hinings, 1996; Oliver, 1991; Teo, Wei, & Benbasat, 2003).

King et al. (1994) use institutional theory to develop a taxonomy to categorize IT interventions at institutional and organizational levels (Robey & Boudreau, 1999). We argue that Section 404 requires organizations to intervene to change controls and processes embedded in information systems and have accordingly adapted King et al.'s taxonomy for the study of 404 implementation for the following reasons. First, they recognize an institution to be a social entity that can bring to bear both influence and power over other social entities. In the context of Section 404, the SEC has sanctions that it can use to modify actions of institutions such as within audit companies. These companies can sway client organizations' behaviors to ensure the system of internal controls is approved (Kurien et al., 2004).

King et al. (1994) suggest the need for power-based and influence-based implementation tactics. Power-based tactics change behaviors through the use of penalties. Influence-based tactics affect behavior through social processes such as negotiation and politics (Jasperson et al., 2002). Second, King et al.'s taxonomy acknowledges the social aspects of interventions, which involve recipients and implementers of the intervention. The interactions between the groups are dynamic and complex. In 404 interventions, there are several levels of implementers and recipients. At the highest level are institutions such as the U.S. Congress and the Public Company Accounting Oversight Board in the role of implementers and audit firms, and organizations as recipients. Within organizations, SOX program teams act as implementers and IS departments can act as implementers and/or recipients. Line managers are recipients because they need to change their working practices in response to the intervention. Third, King et al.'s framework distinguishes between 'supply-push' and 'demand-pull' interventions. Supply-push is characterized as a force arising from the production of a change. Demand-pull interventions emanate from users' willingness to use the product of the intervention. The taxonomy for 404 interventions is illustrated in Figure 1 based on King et al.'s original classification.

King et al.'s (1994) taxonomy describes IT intervention drivers that we have reinterpreted,

Figure 1. A taxonomy of intervention drivers

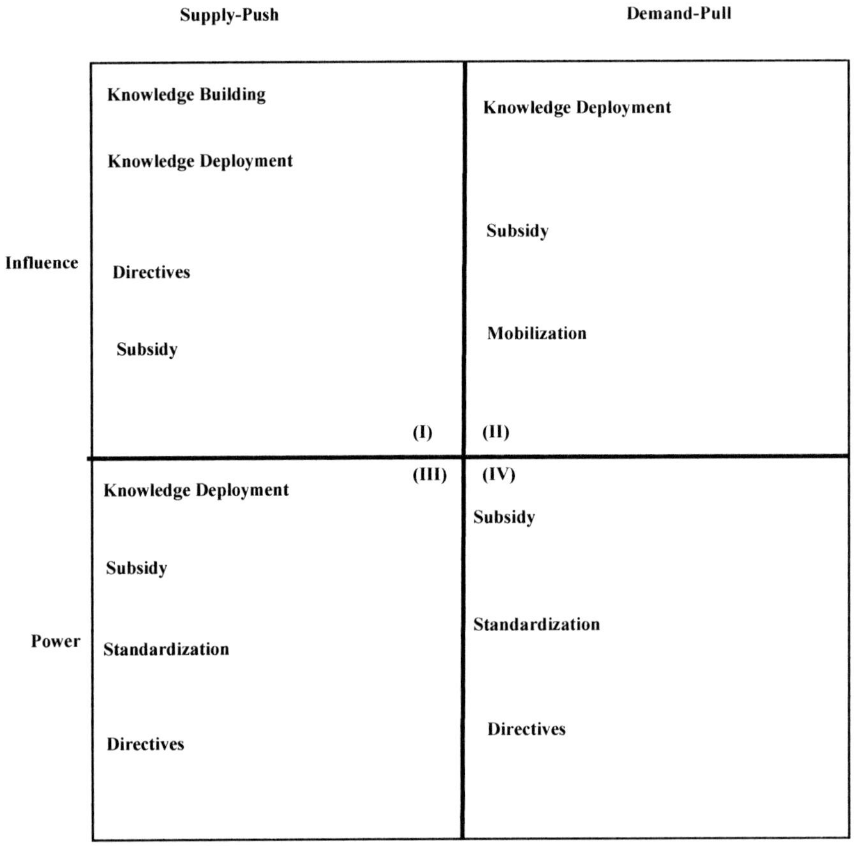

in this study as Section 404 intervention 'drivers'. The six drivers are described briefly in Table 1.

RESEARCH METHODOLOGY AND CASE STUDY DATA

This study is based on an multi-case study approach (Yin, 1989) where the design allows researchers to take a more holistic view of phenomena (Eisenhardt, 1989b) and especially where the aim is to explore an area that has received little previous research attention (Benbasat, Goldstein, & Mead, 1987).

Organizations affected by 404 can be split into two broad categories: (1) listed companies—that is, those whose shares are traded on a U.S. stock exchange, that have to achieve clean 404 certification; and (2) audit firms that have to attest to internal controls. This study is based on two listed companies and one global audit firm. The three specific case study settings for this research were chosen based on theoretical, rather than statistically representative, criteria (Eisenhardt, 1989b). All three had to be large organizations with a global presence and therefore subject to meeting 404 requirements. The organizations had to have implemented 404 in a UK division in order to analyze the initial effects of their implementation tactics.

The primary sources of data were the Sarbanes Oxley program team and the IT division. The aim was to gather mostly qualitative and non-quantitative data (Blaikie, 2000). A variety of data-gathering

Table 1. A description of 404 intervention drivers (adapted from King et al., 1994)

Intervention Driver	Section 404 Context
Knowledge Building	Finding out about Section 404 and its requirements, e.g., research into internal controls
Knowledge Deployment	Making information about 404 available to people, e.g., through training courses
Subsidy	Covering the costs of 404 implementation through the provision of budgets and human resources
Mobilization	Promoting and publicizing 404 and its implications, e.g., through internal communications that endorse the benefits and making people aware of 404
Directives	Putting in place rules and procedures that people have to follow
Standardization	Setting standards that lead people to follow prescribed courses of action

techniques were used, including semi-structured interviews with key roles in 404 implementation (including the program director, IT director, IT manager, and finance manager) and internal documents such as written reports. Additional data was collected through informal discussions that were held both face-to-face and over the phone. The data gathering strategy was flexible as this study sought to find a representative and unbiased set of data (Orlikowski & Baroudi, 1991). Open-ended questions to conduct the interviews were developed into an interview schedule using theoretical constructs based on the taxonomy described earlier in this article. The research process involved interviews lasting about two to three hours each.

The Case of Alpha

Alpha Group is one of Europe's largest UK-based global financial services organizations. It offers a full range of banking services under a number of well-known brands. The group comprises eight customer-facing divisions, in addition to six group and central divisions. Each divisional head reports into the group chief executive. This case study focuses on the Group Technology Division (GTD). GTD defines the group's overall technical architecture, and develops and operates the majority (over 80%) of its systems and technical platforms. GTD's scope for 404 covered its processes, significant business processes, and controls for documentation. Alpha's overall SOX program started in November 2004.

The Case of Beta

Beta is the UK consulting division of Omega Group, a large U.S.-based global professional services group with operations in over 25 countries. Omega started a formal SOX program in the U.S. first because American organizations had to be 404 compliant by the end of 2004, whereas overseas subsidiaries had to be compliant by 2005. Omega adopted a program management approach to SOX implementation.

The Case of Gamma

Gamma is a wholly owned subsidiary of Zeta. Zeta is a UK-based professional services firm registered with the PCAOB. Zeta is a global firm, and about 40 countries in which it operates, including the U.S. and UK, are influenced by SOX. Gamma offers a range of audit and non-audit services. Gamma is structured in various client facing and internal divisions. Section 404 has direct and indirect implications on all of Gamma's divisions. This case focuses on the implementation of 404 within IS services in Gamma.

Table 2. The case of alpha

Intervention Driver	Alpha
Knowledge Building	• Established a Central SOX program team with a program director and people from group accounts and internal audit • Conducted a pilot in the lending process with external auditors • Pilot study produced 404 documentation • Applied documents to test existing controls in the lending process • Central team and auditors used pilot findings to develop practical approaches to implement 404 • Did little knowledge building with external consultants • Relied on external auditors and PCAOB (Public Company Accounting Oversight Board) Web site • Program director and central team IT representative studied competitors' approaches to 404 implementation for information systems to remain consistent with competitors
Knowledge Deployment	• Created a central committee that included the group chief accountant, group internal audit, project managers, and the SOX program director • Created a standard Group Technology Division governance structure • Created a Project Control Committee (PCC) with representatives from relevant Group Technology Division departments and the committee rep • Central program team created a Web site on the intranet to store documents and templates • Appointed a representative to interface to each business division, with one rep dedicated to Group Technology Division • GROUP Technology Division appointed a program manager to take 404 implementation forward within the division
Subsidy	• Alpha covered the costs of supporting 12 significant committees including a central committee, which reported to the group finance director • Spending estimated to be several million dollars • Budgets created as implementation progressed • No budgets were refused or expenditure turned down
Mobilization	• Created a one-day seminar for heads of finance at divisional level and their staff • Seminar co-facilitated by SOX program director and an external audit partner • Seminars outcomes: create awareness of SOX and 404, alert senior managers to resources required for 404 implementation, and facilitate creation of implementation plan • Seminar attendees were individuals directly involved with SOX implementation • Organized forums by the larger global accountancy and audit firms to reconfirm their approach
Directives	• Central committee mandated each division to use agreed documentation • Central committee allowed divisions some flexibility to manage their teams according to that division's environment, but with certain minimum requirements to be achieved
Standardization	• Selected the COSO[1] framework as the overall entity level controls framework • Adopted a centralized approach towards both entity and activity level controls, including application and general IT controls • Group Technology Division and the central committee rep developed 404 compliance approach using GTD's existing Process Framework, documentation, and controls testing standards • Used COBIT[2] framework to model the approach • Undertook research to ensure COBIT met COSO framework requirements
Outcomes	• Discussed proposed methodology with external auditors • Auditors ratified Alpha's 404 compliance methodology as acceptable • PCC applied Group Technology Division's process framework on significant business cycles and controls to achieve 404 compliance within the division • Established templates to document processes and controls and attest documentation • Assessments showed that existing controls were adequate and already in place • Existing IT controls assessed as 404 compliant, including controls for the following GTD processes: change management; performance and capacity management; data back-up and recovery; security and continuity services; services operation and monitoring; incident management; user requirements; design, development, and testing of solutions • Developed an overarching process to manage GTD processes • One of the central team's overarching concerns was to ensure that Alpha was compliant in all respects, but was not going beyond 404's basic requirements

Table 3. The case of beta

Intervention Driver	Beta
Knowledge Building	• Omega appointed the U.S.-based Global Finance function as overall sponsor for SOX implementation • Omega monitored SOX legislation development through the various Congress and Senate approval stages and therefore accumulated knowledge of SOX and 404 • The Global Finance function developed documentation, e.g., templates to capture, on paper and in spreadsheets, 404 control procedures • Gathered information through the use of questionnaires covering, among other things, control objectives, control activities, and overall status • The questionnaires covered five business cycles, i.e., revenue, expenditure, company-level controls called 'Tone from the Top', treasury and payroll, and financial reporting • Beta and its IT department relied on the Global Finance function for information about SOX • Beta's IT and finance departments were responsible for completing the questionnaires
Knowledge Deployment	• U.S. global chief financial officer given responsibility for liaising between Global Finance and overseas subsidiaries • Beta's SOX program board comprises the UK CFO and CEO and included members of Omega's program board • Beta sent people from the U.S. to the UK; people from the UK were sent to Australia • Beta's IT department's supported Global Finance in ensuring the accuracy and validity of information contained in the documentation • Beta's IT department corrected controls so that they did not appear to be that inadequate or broken in the 404 documentation • Beta's IT department liaised with global IT for implementing 404 documentation within Beta • Beta IT had almost no direct contact with people in the UK business
Subsidy	• No precise value can be placed on costs, but they are estimated in terms of millions of dollars • Beta used internal resources, with 41 people from the IS department alone dedicated to 404 documentation • Twelve individuals were at the center of completing the SOX documentation • Costs were calculated as the implementation progressed, and IS and finance budgets increased accordingly
Mobilization	• Managers from Omega's finance department delivered presentations to explain SOX and 404 to Beta's management team and individuals working on SOX documentation • Managers from Beta's internal finance department made presentations to operational managers to explain the documentation they needed to complete • Operational managers had to complete prescribed templates, which were often the wrong version • Beta's finance department implemented procedures to ensure latest versions of templates were communicated
Directives	• Beta already had controls in place to cover levels of internal oversight, operations of the board, and delegation of power from board to subsidiary committees • Beta documented control narratives, internal control systems, and control objectives in prescribed templates • SOX implementers tested conclusions, monitored project completion, and assessed Beta's compliance based on the documentation produced • Beta's IT department played a key role in proving system compliance based on the control narratives in the documentation • IT expanded control narratives and led the definition of how Beta operated its internal controls
Standardization	• Omega's global IT function, based in the U.S., developed an assessment method for IT controls based on the COBIT framework • Global IT sent assessment method to Beta's IT department in the UK • Beta's IT department created templates (based on the assessment method) for documenting processes and controls, and shared these with other firms within Omega Group
Outcomes	• Beta conducted internal assessments of its documented controls • Beta's board concluded the organization had documented a robust system of internal controls and no new controls needed to be introduced in the SOX documentation • Individuals working on specific business cycles identified areas where Beta could enhance its documented controls • Aimed to achieve best practice and consistency across Beta's documented business cycles

Table 4. The case of gamma

Intervention Driver	Gamma
Knowledge Building	• Zeta's U.S.-based audit and legal partners accessed information directly from the PCAOB • A specific division within Zeta U.S.—The Professional Risk and Technical Quality Group—developed training material for subsidiary firms to use • Gamma appointed a UK steering and project team • Gamma's steering and project teams used much of Zeta's 404 compliance work
Knowledge Deployment	• Gamma established a steering group for SOX • Steering group chaired by senior partner and included people at regional compliance level, regional audit partners, internal legal council, and IT people • Steering group assumed overall responsibility for independent compliance and regulation, and defined the brief for 404 compliance • Zeta's Professional Risk and Technical Quality Group answered internal queries from member firms • Same group addressed public and client events, and wrote articles and instruction documents on SOX • Zeta coordinated internationally with member firms to develop one set of information • Developed repositories of SOX knowledge on the intranet which are accessible globally by those involved with 404 • Steering and project team meetings were held in London
Subsidy	• Moving people with 404 knowledge around the globe meant that there were significant amounts of travel and related costs • About 100 individuals with 404 knowledge and experience traveled from the U.S. to the UK for between 6 and 12 months as well as to other countries that lacked 404 knowledge • No overall 404 implementation budget, therefore no clarity of overall spending to achieve 404 compliance • Costs estimated to be in the region of $10 million; one system alone cost about $1 million • No expenditure was refused
Mobilization	• Use of written formal communication, regionalization, training, knowledge bases, links, changing methodologies, etc. aided 404 implementation • Regional representatives on steering groups communicated with each other to maintain regional level coordination
Directives	• U.S. created audit systems which were rolled out in the UK and other countries affected by SOX • Audit systems allowed for deviation from mandated practices in different countries due to variations in local audit practices and client relationships
Standardization	• Zeta developed standards for IT general controls which all subsidiaries had to follow strictly • Zeta produced standards for end user computing applications such as the use of spreadsheets which has to be followed • The firm used COBIT as the basis for setting IT control objectives
Outcomes	• Zeta, globally, and Gamma, in the UK, developed the capability to conduct SOX/404 audits • The organization developed consistent audit methods that could be applied globally

ANALYSIS, SYNTHESIS, AND RESULTS

For each intervention driver, the findings are condensed into a theoretical proposition for 404 implementation.

Knowledge Building

All three cases created a central team to take responsibility for developing knowledge about SOX and its implementation in their organization. These teams focused on producing templates that could be used to assess and prove that controls were in place. Beta and Gamma's parent companies have their head offices based in the U.S., and these parent companies were involved with developing and monitoring this legislation while it was going through its various stages of approval. These cases had the opportunity to build up significant amounts of knowledge as a result. Alpha, on the other hand, being UK-based, had no involvement with SOX in its formative stages. Alpha had to rely on briefings from audit firms and the PCAOB Web site for information. It had to build its knowledge base about the documentation to be used for 404 certification from first principles. As the Alpha program director stated:

At the start of the program I got called into the group finance director's office and asked to lead the Sarbanes Oxley program. I had never heard of this before and thought 'what is this thing?'

In addition to the central team, each organization created SOX implementation teams at subsidiary or local levels. These teams had to develop their own knowledge base, and this was done through a variety of tactics such as seminars and briefings. Knowledge building focused on the documentation to be produced for the central team. Alpha developed its documentation in the context of its lending process. The pilot was run by the central team and involved a small number of people from the group technology and the external auditors. It chose this process because it was complex:

We wanted to tackle the lending because we felt if we could do it for lending all the others would be easier. (Program Manager, Alpha)

Beta, on the other hand, had to complete lengthy questionnaires that were then sent back to the U.S. to be compiled. These questionnaires were filled in by the IT and finance functions on behalf of the business. In Gamma, a central department based in the U.S. developed documents and templates for the subsidiaries to use internally and with external clients. Local subsidiaries were not expected to develop their own knowledge base about 404 documentation.

What becomes apparent in all three cases is that this intervention driver was about finding out about the requirements of the PCAOB, and creating documents and templates that could be used to prove adequate controls were in place. Once the documentation—whether in the form of templates or questionnaires—was in place, these were completed by people in the finance function with support from IT managers. People managing the day-to-day business in these organizations had little or no involvement in building knowledge about 404, and the introduction of controls needed to ensure compliance. End users were not involved with documenting the controls that were being proposed by the central teams.

The above discussion leads to the first theoretical proposition.

Theoretical Proposition #1

Proposition 1a: *Knowledge building in the context of Section 404 is focused on documenting controls on paper rather than affecting practice.*

Proposition 1b: *Lack of end user involvement can limit the extent to which controls are actually used in practice*

Knowledge Deployment

The three case study organizations established committees and teams to oversee 404 implementation. This is exemplified by Alpha's Project Control Committee, Beta's Program Board, and Gamma's Steering Group (I) (the roman numerals refer to the four quadrants of Figure 1). Information about SOX was disseminated from the center to the subsidiaries through the committees and teams. The central teams pushed knowledge about 404 from the center to subsidiaries using technology. They developed repositories on their intranets to store documents and templates created centrally (I). The repositories contained information about 404 and its requirements, presentation material, guidelines, templates, and roll-out plans. Only those directly involved with developing and completing 404 templates accessed the 404 intranet sites. The repositories were not promoted to people beyond the teams and committees involved with 404 implementation.

The SOX Web site was a powerful way of getting information to the finance people…We didn't tell the head of operations and his direct reports (about the central SOX repository) because they weren't completing the questionnaires. (Finance Manager, Beta)

The organization used face-to-face briefings and more personal communications media such as transferring people from one country to another for extended periods of time. However, these communications were to people directly involved with the implementation of 404 documentation. The aim of these communications was to create demand for 404 compliance within the finance and IT communities that were directly involved with completing 404 documentation (II). The extent to which the case study organizations stimulated demand for 404 controls from the end users was very limited (II).

The documentation and templates created by the central teams were mandatory. In other words, each division or subsidiary had to complete the documentation within strict timescales. The importance of the documentation was stressed in communications, yet subsidiaries did not necessarily provide the resources required to complete the documentation. The SOX program teams in each organization were working to the deadlines set in legislation and hence had to ensure timescales were adhered to.

We put together a list of divisions that were late. At first there was a great deal of resistance to publishing the list but then we sent the list to the CFO…none of the teams wanted to be seen as late…I'd get calls from directors asking if they were in the red zone ahead of the list going out. (Program Director, Alpha)

People didn't see the importance of sticking to deadlines. It (404 implementation) was not core business for people in finance and IT so 'why bother?' was an attitude we had to overcome. (IT Manager, Beta)

The organizations used the tactic of 'name and shame' to ensure knowledge was deployed and timescales adhered to (III).

The above discussion leads to the second theoretical proposition.

Theoretical Proposition #2

Proposition 2a: *Knowledge deployment tactics are used to create demand in implementer communities rather than end user communities.*

Proposition 2b: *Power-based tactics are used by implementers to 'push' Section 404 document completion to other implementers and stopped short of involving end user communities.*

Subsidy

Each case study organization subsidized the implementation of 404 documentation. The costs in all three cases ran into several million dollars. Subsidies were used to create demand by meeting the costs of maintaining committee and team members' time (II). The costs of people moving for extended periods of time between countries and associated living and other costs were all absorbed by the organization (II). From a supply-push perspective (III), subsidies were used to allow program and project team members to ensure 404 documentation was completed properly.

The message was 'pay what it takes to do the documentation'…I cannot recall a discussion about withholding funding related to 404 activities. (Global IT Director, Gamma)

No pressure was brought to bear to cap expenditure…we had to meet the quality standards to meet the requirements of (404). (Program Director, Alpha)

Subsidies were used to provide sufficient resources to push through the implementation of 404 documentation. Access to funding gave project teams the ability to influence decision makers who said they did not have sufficient resources to implement 404.

We got the message out—that if you hear 'we need it for next Tuesday' it has to be done by next Tuesday. So people get around to doing it when they can because they are stretched for resources. I was able to say— 'you need resources then here's the budget to get some'. It changed their perception. (IT Manager, Beta)

The consistent message across all three organizations is that funding was not a problem. However, two of the organizations, Beta and Gamma, could not quantify the overall spending on 404 implementation. In these organizations, budgets were diffused across different finance and IT departments in different subsidiaries. As the finance manager at Beta put it: "We made up the costs as we went along...what we spent was funded." Alpha held budgets centrally which was controlled by the program director; however, many of the costs at divisional level were masked from the central view.

The above discussion leads to the third theoretical proposition.

Theoretical Proposition #3

Proposition 3a: *Creating high-quality Section 404 documentation is more important than the overall spending to achieve Section 404 implementation.*

Proposition 3b: *Budgets for Section 404 documentation are fragmented across finance and IT departments, but not end user operational departments.*

Directive

Each organization created a set of documentation that had to be completed. This documentation was created by the central teams, and subsidiary companies and divisions had no choice but to ensure the documentation was completed.

The 404 processes are mandatory...its top-down coming from the U.S. down to the subsidiaries. (Compliance Partner,[3] Gamma)

Our business in now becoming rules based...the extent to which judgment can be exercised is being removed. (Global IT Director, Gamma)

IT controls were also mandatory. IT operations such as password controls, managing access to systems for starters and leavers, and access violations are mandated by the central teams; further, documentation supporting these controls had to be completed.

Organizations used controls and processes that were already in place (I). For example, Beta had controls for issues such as the delegation of power from the board to subsidiary committees and the operations of the board. These were adopted in their current form. Alpha followed a similar approach:

We repackaged existing processes and controls as 404 processes and controls. (Program Manager, Alpha)

The top-down mandatory approaches adopted by these organizations suggest that implementers drove the completion of 404 documentation (I, III).

The extent to which demand pull was used was limited to the flexibility that project teams were allowed to meet local conditions (IV). For example, Gamma's audit systems allowed for some variations due to local country audit practices, and Alpha allowed divisions to manage teams to fit with that division's culture. In both cases, however, there were still a set of directives that had to be followed.

The above discussion leads to the fourth theoretical proposition.

Theoretical Proposition #4

Proposition 4a: *The completion of Section 404 documentation is made mandatory to be accomplished.*
Proposition 4b: *Organizations allow for local customization of Section 404 documentation to match local conditions*

Mobilization

Communications to raise awareness of SOX were carried out to a very narrow group of people: those directly involved in the Sarbanes Oxley program. According to one program director:

We didn't take the view that we needed to create awareness. Communications were sent only to people actually doing (404) work, e.g., process improvement teams. Awareness was not really necessary as many staff are in operational roles and they don't need to understand (404) requirements. Communication was facilitated through the central program team on a need-to-know basis. (Program Director, Alpha).

In another case, the direction of communications was top-down with little time for questions from users. The pressure was on getting 404 compliance done and out of the way.

The focus was on 'are you on time and are you going to do it (complete the documentation)... don't ask questions 'just do it' was the impression from the global team. 'Get it done and clear it out of the way so we can get back to business'. (IT Manager, Beta)

These views suggest that Section 404 does not require the organization to 'do' anything differently in the business. The underlying view is that 404 requires financial processes and controls, especially as many of these are embedded in information systems, to be documented. The assumption underpinning this view is that, provided this documentation is in place for the external auditors to test, the board can claim a sound set of internal controls in the financial statements are in place and that the organization has met the requirement of 404.

There are bigger, more important things happening (than 404). General business managements' view is that the requirements of the act are not asking us to do anything different from what we have been already doing. We were already doing it (processes and internal controls) but we needed to put in place the documentation so that the auditors are able to identify with it. (Program Director, Alpha)

Most people don't know what Sarbanes Oxley is and need not be aware of it either. (Compliance Partner, Gamma)

When I raised the question, 'How should we do this process?', the reaction I got was 'Don't ask. That will only delay the implementation and delay getting a tick in the box...Get the documentation out of the way and then get back to business'. (IT Manager, Beta)

This finding is surprising as SOX requires processes and controls to be in place and documented wherever it is possible that these can have a material affect on figures reported in financial statements. Mobilization requires the use of influence over people who have to adopt procedures and change processes that are 404 compliant. Current theory suggests that this requires the development of mutually shared assumptions and alignment with the prevailing rational arguments being made for 404 compliance in the organization (Robey & Markus, 1984). Yet there appears to be little effort being made to involve wider participation across the business. A common occurrence is the use of spreadsheets to handle figures to prepare reports. This can happen at many different organizational levels: a local office, country head office, and the global headquarters. The use of spreadsheets, databases, and project plans occurs in all business cycles and processes contained in COSO and COBIT frameworks. Examples include inventory controls, pricing, account analysis and reconciliations, and program changes. This suggests a much wider audience than those in the finance and IT departments ought to be aware of 404, its implementation and implications.

The above discussion leads to the fifth theoretical proposition.

Theoretical Proposition #5

Proposition 5a: *Communications are limited to those directly involved in Section 404 implementation with little communications with end user communities.*

Proposition 5b: *End users have little or no knowledge of Section 404 and its impact on the day-to-day operations in the business.*

Proposition 5c: *Section 404 documentation is perceived as a box-ticking exercise which can limit its ability to prevent future financial scandals.*

Standard Setting

All the case study organizations used COSO and COBIT as the standards for setting their controls. SOX requires organizations to select and adopt a control framework. Many organizations have adopted the COSO framework for entity-level controls. However, COSO does not cover specific IT-related controls, and consequently, the IT Governance Institute published COBIT (1994), which is a set of standards that address operational and compliance control objectives that organizations can adopt. Within these broad frameworks, all three organizations developed their own assessment methods, templates, and control objectives (III). As stated earlier, the documentation that supported these standards was compulsory and had to be completed (III).

People (in subsidiaries) were told to document their processes using specific templates. They had to capture the controls. (IT Manager, Beta)

The effect of standardization was to centralize controls and processes. In Gamma, Zeta produced the standards centrally and then rolled them out across subsidiary firms. These firms attempted to push back the extent to which the center was "interfering with local operations," according to the compliance partner. However, local subsidiaries had very limited room to negotiate.

Our ultimate sanction against a subsidiary firm is to withdraw the use of the brand…If you don't comply (with the standards) we will remove the brand.(Global IT Director)

The above discussion leads to the sixth theoretical proposition:

Theoretical Proposition #6

Proposition 6: *Implementers use standards to drive the completion of Section 404 documentation.*

DISCUSSION

The common theme that emerges from these cases is that the introduction of Sarbanes Oxley, in general, and the requirements of Section 404, in particular, were limited to finance and IT departments. The rest of the business, namely end user departments, has a very small role to play, if involved at all in some instances. Each case organization used implementation tactics that involved supply-push from implementers using influence (I). Knowledge-building tactics included developing the legislation during its passage from inception through to approval into statute; dealings with the PCAOB, auditors, and legal council; workshops and seminars; and pilots. Virtually all the knowledge building focused on the documentation that needed to be completed so that the organization's external auditors could certify compliance. Each organization's central SOX team created forms and templates that showed, on paper, that controls were in place. Knowledge deployment involved the rollout of these forms and templates. The organizations established Web sites on their intranets to store and share documents and templates. The implementers agreed which of the extant controls could continue to be used, retagging these as being 404-compliant controls. This had the effect of cutting down on the amount of effort and gaining the support of people in subsidiaries and departments that already had controls in place that they perceived to be adequate. Subsidiaries were used extensively to build within and share knowledge between those directly involved with 404 implementation, exemplified by steering group, committee, project, and program teams.

The case organizations used demand-pull and influence tactics (II), and these too focused on those directly involved with 404 implementation. Central teams were usually the first to learn about 404, and they shared their knowledge with subsidiaries and divisions affected by 404 through workshops and electronic means. The direction of communication was top-down with little effort being made to create real demand. Individuals directly involved with 404 implementation were not encouraged to change or improve extant processes and controls. This approach tended to reduce the implementation of 404 to 'box ticking': to demonstrate that controls have been documented with little regard to what was going on in the actual business. The overarching concern was to complete the documentation within the timescales set by the legislation itself. Communications about 404 implementation to people in end user operational communities were negligible. Nonetheless, organizations had to subsidize the tactics used such as flying people with knowledge of 404 requirements to different countries.

The use of supply-push and power tactics (III) is highly prevalent when achieving 404 implementation. Although the case study organizations used influence-based tactics, they resorted to power-based tactics to push through 404 implementation. The publication of names of executives and program directors who were behind schedule or below quality levels exerted significant force on those people to adhere to the timescales and quality targets set by central teams. Organizations took a top-down approach, making completion of documents and templates mandatory. Individual finance and IT departments in subsidiaries or divisions were given little leeway, with sanctions being made available for use by senior executives. Lack of resources could not be used as an excuse for failing 404 implementation. Implementers had access to funding as and when they needed it. This lever could be used to bring in resources from other parts of the group or from external sources such as contractors to ensure subsidiaries achieved the outcomes necessary.

The demand-pull and power tactics (IV) softened some of the supply-push/mandatory forces at work. Subsidiaries outside the U.S. needed to comply with local laws and customs. For example, the ways in which relationships with customers are managed in, say the UK, could not be made to change overnight, and hence, documenting controls that reflected new ways of dealing with customers simply set up the organization to fail. Therefore, variations from the global standards and directives were allowed to ensure subsidiary organizations agreed to complete 404 documentation. The ways in which teams, in individual subsidiaries or divisions, were managed during the completion of the documentation varied to take into account cultural characteristics between different parts of the same organization in the same country and between different countries.

The overarching detraction from the implementation of Section 404 is that the legislation calls for controls to be documented. The audit firms and the organizations that have to be 404 compliant have interpreted this to mean the mapping of processes and controls. This has generated huge amounts of paper as organizations produce details of controls. On paper, therefore, organizations appear to be meeting the requirements of 404. However, the extent to which the organizations actually work in accordance with the documented controls is questionable. The concern is that we may see the emergence of another Enron in spite of Section 404.

OUTCOMES OF 404 IMPLEMENTATION

We discern two major outcomes from the implementation of Section 404 of the Sarbanes Oxley Act. The first is that each organization fulfilled 404 certification requirements in the timescales stipulated by the act. The documentation and templates completed were sufficient for external auditors to ratify that, on paper at least, all material risks had adequate controls associated with them. Many organizations used their existing control regimes to form the large part of 404 controls. The organizations rarely identified the need to introduce a new control, which given the breadth and scope of a 404 implementation is surprising. We would expect organizations to identify a small number of new controls that could be introduced. However, this was, by and large, not the case.

The second outcome is that there is a very low expectation that behaviors of people will change with respect to risk and controls, at any level of the organization. The overwhelming feeling seems to be one of 'tick the boxes and get back to business as usual'. One interviewee, with experience of several large global organizations, said:

Executives are using 404 as a way of minimizing change rather than driving change through the organization. They don't want to tackle the really hard issue of changing behaviors towards how people manage risk. (Compliance Partner, Gamma)

This was reinforced by one program director:

We concluded that there was no need to change existing processes and controls...There was no need to change behaviors and attitudes. (Program Director, Alpha)

Arguably, without changes in behaviors and attitudes, it is quite difficult to see how 404 documentation can truly prevent another Enron. Organizations appear to be taking a rule-driven legalistic approach rather than dealing with deeper social relationships, inadequate operational processes, and poor 'real' IT governance (Weill & Ross, 2005). This is reflected in the recent academic literature which reinforces rule-driven approaches (Haworth & Pietron, 2006; Krishnan et al., 2005). Until organizations and academics seriously address these issues, the vast amount of time and resources spent on documenting 404 risks and controls may not result in effective compliance.

CONCLUSION

The research in this article presents a systematic analysis of three multinational organizations in relation to their compliance with Section 404 of the Sarbanes-Oxley Act. The importance of appropriate IS was determined in this respect where standards, procedures, and applications are critical for successful accountancy processes. A number of significant implementation drivers are reported that will reduce the potential for financial deficiencies. As a result, it is believed the integration of institutional theory with observed practice provides valuable insights into meeting the challenges of SOX and subsequent IT governance.

REFERENCES

107th Congress of the United States of America. (2002). *The Sarbanes-Oxley Act of 2002.* HR3763, Washington, DC.

Aberdeen Group. (2005). *SOX compliance and automation.* Boston: Author.

Aguilera, R.V. & Jackson, G. (2003). The cross-national diversity of corporate governance: Dimensions and determinants. *Academy of Management Review, 28*(3), 447–465.

Anand, V., Ashforth, B.E., & Joshi, M. (2004). Business as usual: The acceptance and perpetuation of corruption in organizations. *Academy of Management Executive, 18*(2), 39–53.

Argyris, C. (1971). Management information systems: The challenge to rationality and emotionality. *Management Science, 17*(6), 275–292.

Avgerou, C. (2000). IT and organizational change: An institutionalist perspective. *Information Technology and People, 13*(4), 234–262.

Banham, R. (2003). Period of adjustment. *Journal of Accountancy, 195*(2), 43(6).

Barnhart, S., Marr, W., & Rosenstein, S. (1994). Firm performance and board composition: Some new evidence. *Managerial and Decision Economics, 15,* 329–340.

Beath, C.M. (1991). Supporting the information technology champion. *MIS Quarterly, 15*(3), 355–372.

Benbasat, I., Goldstein, D., & Mead, M. (1987). The case research strategy in studies of information systems. *MIS Quarterly, 11,* 369–386.

Berghel, H. (2005). The two sides of ROI: Return on investment vs. risk of incarceration. *Communications of the ACM, 48*(4), 15–20.

Berle, A., & Means, G. (1932). *The modern corporation and private property.* New York: Macmillan.

Cadbury, A. (1992). *The financial aspects of corporate governance.* Report of the Committee on the Financial Aspects of Corporate Governance, Gee and Co., London.

Coffee, J.C. Jr. (2005). Internal controls: The scarlet letter. *Corporate Governance Advisor, 13*(1), 1–6.

Chan, S. (2004). Sarbanes-Oxley: The IT dimension. *The Internal Auditor,* (February), 31–33.

Coe, M.J. (2005). Trust services: A better way to evaluate IT controls. *Journal of Accountancy,* (March), 69–75.

Blaikie, N. (2000). *Designing social research.* Oxford: Blackwell.

COBIT. (1994). *Control objectives for information and related technology.* Rolling Meadows, IL: IT Governance Institute.

COSO. (1994). *Internal control—integrated framework.* Committee of Sponsoring Organizations of the Treadway Commission.

Covaleski, M.A., & Dirsmith, M.W. (1988). An institutional perspective on the rise. Social transformation, and fall of a university budget category. *Administrative Science Quarterly, 33*(4), 562–587.

Crowston, K., & Myers, M.D. (2004). Information technology and the transformation of industries: Three research perspectives. *Journal of Strategic Information Systems, 13,* 5–28.

Damianides, M. (2005). Sarbanes-Oxley and IT governance: New guidance on IT control and compliance. *Information Systems Management,* (Winter), 77–85.

Daily, C.M., Dalton, D.R., & Canella, A.A. Jr. (2003). Corporate governance: Decades of dialogue and data. *Academy of Management Review, 28*(3), 371–382.

Dalton, D.R., & Dalton, C.M. (2005). Sarbanes-Oxley legislation and the private company: If not for marriage then certainly engagement. *Journal of Business Strategy, 26*(2), 7–8.

Dalton, D.R., Daily, C.M., Certo, C., & Roengpitya, T. (2003). Meta-analyses of financial performance and equity: Fusion or confusion? *Academy of Management Journal, 46,* 13–26.

Dalton, D.R., Daily, C.M., Ellstrand, A.E., & Johnson, J.L. (1998). Meta-analystic reviews of board composition, leadership structure, and financial performance. *Strategic Management Journal, 19,* 269–290.

Dewing, I.P., & Russell. (2003). Post-Enron developments in UK audit and corporate governance regulation. *Journal of Financial Regulation and Compliance, 11*(4), 309–322.

DiMaggio, P.J., & Powell, W.W. (1983). The iron cage revisited: Institutional isomorphism and collective rationality in organizational fields. *American Sociological Review, 48*(2), 147–160.

DiMaggio, P.J., & Powell, W.W. (1991). Introduction. In W.W. Powell & P.J. DiMaggio (Eds.), *The new institutionalism in organization analysis* (pp. 1–38). Chicago: University of Chicago Press.

Duffy, M.N. (2004). Section 404 opens a door. *Journal of Accountancy, 197,* 8.

Eisenhardt, K.M. (1989a). Agency theory: An assessment and review. *Academy of Management Review, 14,* 57–74.

Eisenhardt, K.M. (1989b). Building theories from case study research. *Academy of Management Review, 14*(4), 532–550.

Fama, E.F. (1980). Agency problems and the theory of the firm. *Journal of Political Economy, 88*(21), 288–307.

Fama, E.F., & Jensen, M.C. (1983). Separation of ownership and control. *Journal of Law and Economics, 26,* 301–325.

Ferrell, O.C. (2004). Business ethics and customer stakeholders. *Academy of Management Executive, 18*(2), 126–129.

Goodstein, J.D. (1994). Institutional pressures and strategic responsiveness: Employer involvement in work-family issues. *Academy of Management Journal, 37*(2), 350–382.

Greenwood, R., & Hinings, C.R. (1996). Understanding radical organizational change: Bringing together the old and new institutionalism. *Academy of Management Review, 21*(4), 1022–1054.

Hackney, R.A., Burn, J., & Salazar, A. (2004). Strategies for value creation in e-markets: Towards a framework for managing evolutionary change. *Journal of Strategic Information Systems, 13*(3), 91–103.

Haworth, D., & Pietron, L.R. (2006). Sarbanes-Oxley: Achieving compliance by starting with ISO 17799. *Information Systems Management, 23*(1), 73–87.

Ivancevich, J.M., Duening, T.N., Gilbert, J.A., & Konopaske, R. (2003). Deterring white-collar crime. *Academy of Management Executive, 17*(2), 114–127.

Jasperson, J.S., Carte, T.A., Saunders, C.S., Butler, B.S., Croes, H.J.P., & Zheng, W. (2002). Review: Power and information technology research: A meta-triangulation review. *MIS Quarterly, 26*(4), 397–459.

Jensen, M.C. (1993). The modern industrial revolution, exit, and the failure of internal control systems. *Journal of Finance, 48,* 831–880.

Jepperson, R.L. (1991). Institutional effects, and institutionalism. In W.W. Powell & P.J. DiMaggio (Eds.), *The new institutionalism in organizational analysis* (pp. 143–163). Chicago: University of Chicago Press.

King, J.L., Gurbaxani, V., Kraemer, K.L., McFarlan, F.W., Raman, K.S., & Yap, C.S. (1994). Institutional factors in information technology innovation. *Information Systems Research, 5*(2), 139–169.

Kling, R., & Iacono, S. (1984). The control of information systems development after implementation. *Communications of the ACM, 27*(12), 1218–1226.

Knights, M., & Reed, K. (2004). UK PLC dealt Sarbox deadline. *Accountancy Age,* (3), 7–9.

Haworth, D., & Pietron, L.R. (2006). Sarbanes-Oxley: Achieving compliance by starting with ISO 17799. *Information Systems Management, 23*(1), 73–87.

Kurien, P., Rahman, W., & Purushottam. (2004). The case of re-examining IT effectiveness. *Journal of Business Strategy, 25*(2), 29–36.

Legare, T.L. (1995). Minimizing resistance to technological change. *Information Systems Management, 12*(4), 59.

Levine, H.G., & Rossmoore, D. (1994). Politics and the function of power in a case study of IT implementation. *Journal of Management Information Systems, 11*(3), 115–133.

Maitland, A. (2004). BT chairman criticises US governance. *Financial Times, 22*(1).

Markus, M.L., & Benjamin, R.I. (1996). Change agentry—the next IS frontier. *MIS Quarterly, 20*(4), 385–407.

Mayer, A.F. (2003). Preparing for Basel II by optimizing Sarbanes-Oxley. *Journal of Bank Cost & Management Accounting, 16*(3), 27(7).

McFarlan, F.W., & McKenney, J.L. (1983). The information archipelago—governing the new world. *Harvard Business Review, 61*(4), 91–99.

McWhinney, W. (1992). *Paths of change: Strategic choices for organizations and society.* Newbury Park, CA: Sage.

Meyer, J.W., & Rowan, B. (1977). Institutional organizations: Formal structures as myth and ceremony. *American Journal of Sociology, 83,* 340–363.

Ooms-Piepers, M., & Degens, R.M.I. (2004). SOX 404 business en tool alignment. *Compact KPMG, 31*(4), 26–33.

Oliver, C. (1991). Strategic responses to institutional processes. *Academy of Management Review, 16*(1), 145–179.

Orlikowski, W.J., & Baroudi, J.J. (1991). Studying information technology in organizations: Research approaches and assumptions. *Information Systems Research, 2*(1), 1–28.

Pfeffer, J. (1981). *Power in organizations.* Marshfield, MA: Pitman.

Quall, J.C. (2004). Implementing Section 404: A practical approach to the Sarbanes-Oxley Act. *CPA Journal, 74*(8), 52.

Robey, D., & Markus, M.L. (1984). Rituals in information system design. *MIS Quarterly, 8*(1), 5–15.

Robey, D., & Boudreau, M.C. (1999). Accounting for the contradictory organizational consequences of information technology: Theoretical directions and methodological implications. *Information Systems Research, 10*(2), 167–185.

Rone, J., & Berman, A. (2004). Musing on post-Enron reforms. *Journal of Accounting, Auditing and Finance, 19*(3), 331–342.

Sabherwal, R., & King, W.R. (1992). Decision processes for developing strategic applications of information systems: A contingency approach. *Decision Sciences, 23*(4), 917–943.

Saunders, C.S. (1981). Management information systems, communications, and departmental power: An integrative model. *Academy of Management Review, 6*(3), 431–442.

Scott, W.R. (1987). The adolescence of institutional theory. *Administrative Science Quarterly, 32*(4), 493–511.

Suchman, M.C. (1995). Managing legitimacy: Strategic and institutional approaches. *Academy of Management Review, 20,* 571–610.

Swartz, N. (2003). The cost of Sarbanes-Oxley. *Information Management Journal, 37*(5), 8.

Teo, H.H., Wei, K.K., & Benbasat, I. (2003). Predicting intention to adopt interorganizational linkages: An institutional perspective. *MIS Quarterly, 27*(1), 19–49.

Tractinsky, N., & Jarvenpaa, S.L. (1995). Information systems design decisions in a global versus domestic context. *MIS Quarterly, 19*(4), 507–534.

Weill, P., & Ross, J. (2005). A matrixed approach to designing IT governance. *MIT Sloan Management Review, 46*(2), 26–34.

Yin, R.K. (1989). *Case study research: Design and methods* (revised ed.). Newbury Park, CA: Sage.

Zucker, L. (1987). Institutional theories of organization. *Annual Review of Sociology, 13,* 443–464.

ENDNOTES

1. COSO is the set of guidelines published by the Committee of Sponsoring Organizations of the Treadway Commission.
2. COBIT stands for Control Objectives for Information and related Technology. See *www.isaca.org* for further information.
3. A *compliance partner* is the partner responsible for the compliance line of business in Gamma.

This work was previously published in the Journal of Organizational and End User Computing, Vol. 20, Issue 2, edited by M. Mahmood, pp. 1-24, copyright 2008 by IGI Publishing (an imprint of IGI Global).

Chapter 7
The Role of Expertise in the Evaluation of Computing Architectures:
Exploring the Decision Models of Expert and Novice IS Managers

Akhilesh Bajaj
University of Tulsa, USA

ABSTRACT

Recently, there has been considerable interest in evaluating newer computer architectures such as the Web services architecture and the network computer architecture. In this work we investigate the decision models of expert and novice IS managers when evaluating computing architectures for use in an organization. This task is important because several consumer choice models in the literature indicate that the evaluation of alternative products is a critical phase that consumers undergo prior to forming an attitude toward the product. Previous work on evaluating the performance of experts vs. novices has focused either on the process differences between them, or on the performance outcome differences, with work in MIS focusing primarily on process differences. In this work, we utilize a methodology that examines both aspects, by constructing individual decision models for each expert and novice in the study. There is a growing consensus in the management literature that while experts may follow different processes, very often their performance does not differ significantly from novices in the business domain.

INTRODUCTION

One of the most important decisions that information system (IS) managers make is the selection of a computing architecture for their organization. This decision is even more difficult today, with several architectural choices available, including distributed Web services, a centralized server with disk-less clients, and more traditional client/servers (Haag, Cummings, & McCubbrey, 2003).

The importance of computing architectures has been recognized in several past studies. Nezlek, Jain, and Nazareth (1999) state:

Appropriate architectures allow organizations to meet current as well as projected information needs, and to successfully adopt new information processing paradigms in a cost-effective manner.

In a classic summary of the early debate between centralized and decentralized architectures, King (1983) recognizes that the debate between the pros of centralized IS management vs. distributed user control of software and data has flourished since the 1960s. Melling (1994) illustrates how new technologies lead to new choices for IS managers when selecting architectures. Nieh, Yang, and Novik (2000) recognize that thin-client architectures may reduce the total cost of ownership to an organization, and compare different thin-client architectures across broadband networks. The choice of one or more architectures determines several subsequent decisions important to the IS department, such as:

- **What application software will be purchased:** For example, a thin-client architecture will necessitate the purchasing of server-type applications that are served across a "fat" network.
- **Who will drive the purchasing:** Consider a traditional client-server architecture that puts significant computing power on every end user's desk. This will lead to user-driven purchasing of several applications (Spinellis 1998).
- **What kind of personnel will be available to maintain the systems:** If a novel architecture such as a Web service-based architecture is selected, personnel costs may be higher.
- **What level of security is attainable:** As an example, a decision to adopt a thin-client architecture, with a centralized server for the variety of application software and the data, will probably lead to higher levels of security and control, but to less flexibility from the user perspective.

For this study, we define an architecture to be a computing infrastructure that significantly affects the purchasing and maintenance of hardware and software in an organization. Examples include: (a) the client-server architecture, where data and processing are shared between a client and a server; (b) the network appliance architecture with disk-less network computers that provide the graphical user interface, with data and processing centralized on the server; and (c) the fully distributed Web-services architecture enabled by emerging standards such as J2EE (Java 2 Enterprise Edition) and .Net (Baker & O'Sullivan, 2001). Rapid innovation in the area of IS implies that *often the evaluation of new technologies such as computing architectures is performed by less experienced IS managers in conjunction with senior IS managers.* The primary purpose of this work is to examine the decision models used by expert and novice IS managers when given the task of evaluating computing architectures for use by an organization, and to investigate: (a) whether there is a significant difference between their performance, and (b) whether they follow different internal processes when conducting their evaluations.

The difference between experts and novices has interested researchers in both psychology as well as diverse business sub-disciplines. Regardless of discipline, almost all studies have focused on particular tasks that were given to experts and novices, whose processes and/or output performances were then compared for that task. The studies show mixed results about the existence and magnitude of difference in performance between experts and novices. Next, we discuss illustrative studies in psychology as well as the business literature.

Earlier Work in Psychology

In the psychology literature, work on measuring expertise can be broadly divided into the *binary* perspective and the *developmental* perspective. The developmental perspective focuses on the emergence of knowledge rather than the end-states of novice or expert. For example, a five-stage sequence of developmental stages was proposed in Dreyfus and Dreyfus (1986) which ranged from novice to expert: *novice, advanced beginner, competent, proficient,* and *expert.* These stages differ not just along experience, but also along the commitment to the problem (increasing with expertise), the degree to which knowledge has been automated, and the degree of awareness of theory behind knowledge (Campbell & Bello, 1996). The goal in the developmental approach is to come up with explanations of the evolution of the novice to the different stages of expertise.

In contrast, the *binary* perspective (Anderson, 1995) has dominated the study of expertise in computer systems. Classic studies in the binary perspective include Chase and Simon (1973) and Chi, Feltovich, and Glaser (1981). Work using this perspective presumes that: (a) novice-expert is a binary distinction, (b) novice knowledge and expert knowledge can be compared statically, and (c) experts are people with more experience (designated the Power Law of Practice by Anderson, 1995). A review of the binary perspective on expertise in Glaser (1989) states that experts structure their knowledge into meaningful chunks, that their knowledge is more procedural than declarative, and that the knowledge of experts has a theory or schema that can undergo change.

In Charness (1976) and Chase and Simon (1973), master chess players showed expertise in remembering meaningful chess positions from chess games, but failed to show any expertise in remembering random placements of chess pieces on the chess board, when compared to novices. In another study, Boster and Johnson (1989) found that expert fishermen cluster fish species (the task) on both functional and morphological criteria, while novices cluster on morphological criteria alone. Similar results were observed earlier by Chi (1984). In Randel and Pugh (1996), 28 electronic warfare technicians were classified into one of three categories: expert, intermediate, or novice. The task was to examine warfare scenarios, and the performance was the ability to recall spatial relationships between warships in the scenarios, as well as the ability to recall meaningful non-spatial patterns that developed in each scenario. Experts were shown to be different from novices in that they focused more on the classification of the situation, and demonstrated better recall of hostile ships and better recall of non-spatial relevant information.

In contrast to the work described above, several studies have not detected performance differences. The ability of expert, trainee, and novice medical physicians and students to diagnose complex medical cases was studied by Hassebrock, Johnson, Bullemer, Fox, and Moller (1993). A verbal protocol analysis revealed little difference between their abilities to recall relevant information, prior to making the diagnosis. Kirlik, Walker, Fisk, and Nagel (1996) argue that in complex, dynamic environments, human decision making does not use cognitively intensive processes, but rather perceptually guided, automatic processes that are heuristic in nature. Empirical work in Brehmer (1990) also indicates that often, individuals do not develop explicit internal models of complex environments, a prerequisite for expertise. In Frederico (1995), expert and novice naval officers were asked to classify naval tactical situations. The findings indicated no difference between the two groups in terms of the number of superficial features used vs. deeper principles.

The above studies from psychology indicate that for tasks that require both a superficial perceptual component and a deeper cognitive component, such as chess, there is usually a difference in performances between experts and novices. However, *there are many tasks where deeper cognitive knowledge, and domain specific principles, even if they exist in research literature, are not used to perform the task.* To the best of our knowledge, there is no prima facie method of determining whether experts' and novices' performances will differ on a particular task, without empirical testing.

Previous Work in Business

In the business literature, expert-novice differences have been studied in several sub-disciplines. Bouwman (1984) conducted a protocol analysis on five accounting students and three professors to investigate their processes of interpreting accounting statements. He found that the experts tended to be more proactive in their analysis, while novices tended to interpret the data more passively. A study testing the accuracy of predictions about consumer behavior situations was conducted by Armstrong (1991), where no difference was found between the accuracy of the predictions, suggesting that knowledge of business research in the area was not used by experts when analyzing the situations and making predictions. In Mackay and Elam (1992), a protocol analysis of 12 subjects revealed no difference between expert and novice performance in the healthcare domain, when they were both inexperienced in spreadsheet technology. In Day and Lord (1992), 38 CEOs were found to have a greater variance in categorizing organizational problems than 30 MBAs. Also, the CEOs tended to rely on previously developed heuristics vs. the novice MBAs who relied on more formal models of evaluation. A similar finding was obtained by a study in marketing (Maheswaran, Sternthal, & Gurhan 1996) that found that novices were influenced by the more superficial presentations and formats of advertisements, while experts were more focused on fewer, content-based dimensions, the choice of dimension being based on their past experience. In another study, Spence and Brucks (1997) found that for problems with moderate levels of difficulty, experts tended to use fewer, more focused inputs, and in contradiction to other studies, their solutions tended to be more tightly clustered than novices. In the management information systems (MIS) literature, Schenk, Vitalri, and Davis (1998) conducted a protocol analysis of seven novice and 18 expert systems analysts. They found that the experts adopted a very different process from the novices; however, performance differences were not considered in the study. In Austin and Mawhinney (1999), a protocol analysis of two experts and two novices revealed small differences in the accuracy of some tasks, but no clear discernable differences in performance. Marshall (2002) examined 90 accounting experts and 60 novices, and concluded there was no discernible difference between the process followed by, or the performance of, the two groups.

The above studies in the area of business suggest that while experts may sometimes follow different processes than novices, *there is usually little difference in their performance outputs when asked to perform tasks in the business domain.* In the MIS sub-discipline, as discussed above, most of the past work on expert/novice differences has involved a protocol analysis of subjects and has aimed at identifying the processes that experts follow. However, there is a paucity of work in MIS that measures the *performance* differences between experts and novices. In this work, we investigate both the process followed by experts and novices, as well as the performance outcome for an important task faced by MIS managers: evaluating new computing architectures for their organizations. We utilize a novel methodology that creates individual decision models of each subject. Thus, apart from the theoretical contributions, this work also contributes methodologically to the area.

The rest of this article is organized as follows. In the next section, we describe the research study.

We then discuss the findings, and conclude with the contributions and limitations of this study, as well as future research.

THE RESEARCH STUDY

The Task

In this work, the task is the *evaluation* of computing architectures for use in an organization. The importance of the task of product evaluation has long been recognized in the consumer behavior literature, which is replete with 'hierarchy of effects' models. These models suggest a pre-purchase sequence of psychological states of increasing comprehension and desire, and culminating in the 'strong conviction' which determines the action (such as purchase) and its outcome (Engell, Blackwell, & Kollat, 1978; Foxall, 1983; Rogers, 1983). Thus, the following model is proposed in Rogers (1983): *awareness → interest → evaluation → trial → adoption.* Another hierarchy of effects model is proposed in Engell et al. (1978): *perceived information → problem recognition → search → evaluation of alternatives → beliefs → attitudes → intentions → choice.* A summary of several of these models is presented in Foxall (1983). Past studies in consumer behavior clearly establish that the *evaluation* of alternative products is a prerequisite to the formation of *attitudes* about these products, which precedes any purchase decision. The process in our study parallels the steps followed by the subject upon arriving at an evaluation model, and the performance is the final evaluation model.

Modeling the Evaluation Phase

In order to model the evaluation phase of the expert and novice groups in our study, we use conjoint analysis (CA), which is a well-known method in mathematical psychology (Luce & Tukey 1964) and marketing (Green & Rao, 1971), but which has been used infrequently in MIS research. CA determines the contributions of various predictor variables in determining an individual's evaluation model and establishes a valid model of the individual's judgment that is useful in predicting overall acceptance in the population of any combination of values, one for each predictor variable (Hair, 1992).

For a CA study, a *product class* is considered, along with a set of subjects who can evaluate products in that class. A set of *attributes* (predictor variables) is selected to describe the product class. The possible *levels* of each attribute are selected. A *product* in the product class is then simply a *combination of attribute levels* (one level value per attribute).

In a typical CA study, the researcher first constructs a set of products (in our case, architectures) by combining the possible attributes (or factors) at various levels for each attribute. The hypothetical products are presented to subjects, who provide an *overall evaluation* of each product, relative to the others (usually by giving each one a score). CA is advantageous in that first, subjects have to consider all attributes *jointly* vs. considering them in isolation, as in most other decision modeling techniques. This consideration of the product as a whole better reflects real-world evaluation strategies and necessitates a *tradeoff* between attributes for each subject, again similar to real-world decision making. Second, an individual evaluation model is created for *each subject* (vs. merely collecting one data point for each subject), thereby allowing the detection of inconsistent decision making in a subject.

The steps we followed in the CA study are outlined in Figure 1. Next, we describe each of these steps in detail.

Identification of Factors and Hypothesis Formulation

In order to create the evaluation model, we needed to identify factors (attributes) that would best de-

Figure 1. List of steps constituting the CA study

1. Identify factors important in the decision space of IS managers when evaluating computing architectures.
2. Select appropriate levels for each factor (attribute).
3. Operationalize each factor in a manner suitable for a face-to-face study.
4. Create study packet and pilot test for clarity of measures, time taken for one study, any other implementation problems or possible biases.
5. Select subjects.
6. Administer the study to each subject individually, in the presence of the researcher.
7. Analyze data and present results.

scribe computer architectures (the product) *from the point of view of the subjects of our study.* A list of factors that are considered important by senior IS managers was presented in Bajaj (2000). This list is reproduced in Table 1.

The second step in Figure 1 is to specify levels for each factor. In all cases, the levels chosen were high, medium, and low, except for the *centralization/decentralization* factor, which was either centralized or distributed. We constructed the following additive decision model for each subject:

$$EvaluationScore = \propto_1 SQ + \propto_2 CENT + \propto_3 COST + \propto_4 ACC + \propto_5 BCOMP + \varepsilon \qquad (1)$$

Equation 1 is evaluated for each subject in our study. For clarity in hypothesis formulation, we represent the parameter values of n subjects in the expert group as $\propto_{1i}$, $\propto_{2i}$,...$\propto_{5i}$,and the parameter values of m subjects in the novice group as $\propto_{1j}$, $\propto_{2j}$, $\propto_{5j}$.

Past work (Day & Lord, 1992; Maheswaran et al., 1996) indicates that experts tend to use fewer inputs when performing a task. These inputs are based on their earlier experience. Given that all our experts manage MIS in the business domain, we hypothesize that they will, as a group, "zero in" on one or two factors when evaluating architectures. Novices, on the other hand, tend to be scattered with regard to the inputs they use. Based on these findings, we posit hypotheses H1 and H2:

Hypothesis H1: *The expert group will differ from the novice group in their decision models on each of the factors that are considered when evaluating computing architectures for an organization.*

Since there are five factors, H1 has five subparts. The **null** hypotheses are:

$H1_0$(a): $\overline{\alpha_{1i}} = \overline{\alpha_{1j}}$
$H1_0$(b): $\overline{\alpha_{2i}} = \overline{\alpha_{2j}}$
$H1_0$(c): $\overline{\alpha_{3i}} = \overline{\alpha_{3j}}$
$H1_0$(d): $\overline{\alpha_{4i}} = \overline{\alpha_{4j}}$
$H1_0$(e): $\overline{\alpha_{5i}} = \overline{\alpha_{5j}}$

Hypothesis H2: *The part-worths of the five factors in the expert groups will be unequal, with some factors having a higher part-worth than the expected value of 20% (since there are five factors, adding up to 100%).*

The **null** hypothesis is:

$H2_0$: $\overline{\alpha_{1i}} = \overline{\alpha_{2i}} = \overline{\alpha_{3i}} = \overline{\alpha_{4i}} = \overline{\alpha_{5i}}$

Table 1. Empirically derived list of factors that describe a computing architecture (from Bajaj, 2000)

Factor	Broad Definition
Software Quality (SQ)	The quality of software[1] associated with the architecture. This can include response time to end users, quality of user interface, and features provided by the software.
Centralization vs. Distributed (CENT)	A centralized architecture means that software resides in a centralized location, and most of the hardware investment is also centralized.
Costs (COST)	The costs of an architecture include the costs of acquisition of hardware and software, the costs of maintenance of hardware and of controlling different versions of the software, and the costs of personnel trained in maintaining the hardware and software.
Acceptance of the Architecture (ACC)	This factor represents the degree to which a particular architecture has been accepted by IS magazines, the media, model organizations, and software and hardware vendors.
Backward Compatibility of the Architecture (BCOMP)	This factor models the degree to which an architecture will cause changes in the organization. Changes include: converting old data to be read by the new architecture, and retraining users to use and IS personnel to maintain the software and hardware.

Some of the earlier work indicates that experts tend to show more variance in their performance than novices. Boster and Johnson (1989) proposed that this is because experts have different types of knowledge that they use to perform the task. Day and Lord (1992) also found that experts showed greater variance in the categorization of business problems than novices. This was attributed to the richer experience of the experts, which led to differing interpretations of the problems. However, a contradictory viewpoint emerges from other works. For example, Spence and Brucks (1997) found that experts' solutions tended to be more tightly clustered, when asked to specify the values of real estate for sale. Shanteau (1988) stated that experts tend to agree more about which input information is important than do novices. Given the focused nature of the task in this study, we test the hypothesis that experts will show a smaller variance in performance than novices.

Hypothesis H3: *The expert group will show smaller variance than the novice group in each of the factors that are considered when evaluating computing architectures for an organization.*

The **null** hypotheses are:

$H3_0$(a): $\text{var}(\alpha_{1i}) >= \text{var}(\alpha_{1j})$
$H3_0$(b): $\text{var}(\alpha_{2i}) >= \text{var}(\alpha_{2j})$
$H3_0$(c): $\text{var}(\alpha_{3i}) >= \text{var}(\alpha_{3j})$
$H3_0$(d): $\text{var}(\alpha_{4i}) >= \text{var}(\alpha_{4j})$
$H3_0$(e): $\text{var}(\alpha_{5i}) >= \text{var}(\alpha_{5j})$

There is consensus in earlier work that *novices tend to use more elaborate or formal bottom-up methods* to perform a task because they utilize explicit knowledge, whereas experts tend to rely more on heuristics acquired through experience (tacit knowledge), and follow more "automatic" processes to perform the task (Cowan, 1986; Day & Lord, 1992; Dutton & Jackson, 1987; Mackay & Elam, 1992; Randel & Pugh, 1996). Our fourth hypothesis tests if expert and novice managers display this expected difference in the utilization of more formal or elaborate models when performing the task.

Hypothesis H4: *The proportion of subjects in the novice sample using elaborate models when evaluating computing architectures for an orga-*

nization will be greater than the proportion of subjects in the expert sample.

Next we describe the construction and testing of the instrument used in the study.

Construction and Testing of the CA Instrument

The SPSS statistical package was used to generate an orthogonal design, which consisted of 16 possible computing architectures. In a standard additive model, like the one in Equation 1, an orthogonal design is required which does not include all possible combinations of factor levels (Hair, 1992). The computing architectures were each characterized by one value for each of the five factors in Table 1. In addition, we also generated four *holdout* architectures, to test the internal validity of the responses of each subject (i.e., the consistency of their evaluation model). The actual scores that the subject gave to the architectures in the holdout sample were compared against scores predicted by the evaluation model that was generated by the 16 architectures that comprised the orthogonal design. Thus, each subject was given the same 20 architectures, of which 16 were used to estimate their individual decision model and four were used to test their actual vs. estimated scores. The 20 architectures are shown in Appendix 1.

The third step in Figure 1 is to *operationalize* the factors. A richer operationalization of factors is permissible here than with a mail-out survey, since each subject was administered the study by the same researcher in person. This allowed reliability and validity controls to not just be dependent on the instrument (which implies a leaner operationalization), but to be implemented on site also. For each factor we gave the definition (as in Table 1) and a *reason* why the factor was important. The reasons were kept moderate, so as not to bias the subjects in favor of any factor. In the case of *software quality, backward compatibility,* and *acceptance,* the reason was formulated to make the factor's effect moderately positive (i.e., higher was better than medium, which was better than lower, based on the reason). In the case of *costs,* the example served to make the effect negative. The *centralization/decentralization* factor was treated differently. The pros and cons of centralization vs. distribution are well documented in the IS literature (e.g., Allen & Boynton, 1991; King, 1983). Hence, we gave one reason why centralization may be beneficial and another reason why distribution may be beneficial. The idea behind all the reasons was to simply highlight to the subject the pros of each factor, and to achieve relatively uniform awareness among the subjects about what each factor meant. Note that this does not create any upward bias for any one factor, since CA involves *trading off* between factors, and so any importance given by a subject to one factor has to come at the expense of another factor.

The fourth step was the *construction and pilot testing of a study packet* that would be used in the actual study. The 20 architectures were printed on separate cards of identical length, breadth, and thickness. We pilot tested the study with three graduate students with high, moderate, and low IS experiences respectively. No compensation was provided to the graduate students for this. Based on their feedback, we made the following changes in the packet: Since the order of appearance of a factor on a card was important, we created five different study packets. Across the study packets, each factor showed up first in all the cards of one packet, second in all the cards of another packet, and so forth. Of course, the *same* 20 architectures were presented in each packet; only the order of factors describing each architecture on a card was changed across the five packets. The cards would be shuffled before being handed out to each subject, and the cards were titled from A–T, with the explicit mention to the subjects that the letters were chosen at random. We also ensured that the operationalization of each factor was easily understood by all three pilot study subjects. All three subjects reacted very similarly to the study, which increased our confidence in the reliability of the final study. One final study packet (out of five) is shown in Appendix 2.

Next we describe the selection of subjects used for the study.

Subjects for the Study

In the MIS literature, the selection of a computing architecture is considered a significant decision (Chau & Tam, 1997). It is also not a decision that usually entails any organizational changes, rather it only impacts the IS department (Bajaj, 2000; Chau & Tam, 1997). Hence an evaluation of a computing architecture is more likely to be performed by IS managers than if it were an innovation that impacted the entire organization (see Swanson, 1994, for a categorization of organizational innovations).

We used two groups of subjects. The *expert* group was carefully screened to consist of senior IS managers of randomly selected large corporations. We interviewed each potential subject to ensure that these managers were decision makers in terms of making significant new investments in IS within the organization. The *novice* group consisted of final-year graduate IS students from a U.S. university, the majority of whom already had job offers as fresh IS managers in large corporations or as consultants who would interact with such managers. The demographics of the two groups are shown in Tables 2 (expert group) and 3 (novice group). The expert group not only had longer average job tenure than the novice group, but they had also spent a significant portion of their time dealing with issues of purchasing IS for the organization. The novice group had no experience in this area at the organizational level, even though they had some years of job experience in the IS area prior to joining the IS program. Thus, in our study, the chief distinguishing feature between experts and novices was their years of experience in actually performing the task of architecture selection. This is widely accepted in the binary perspective literature as being *the* distinguishing factor between experts and novices. For example, in their summary of the binary perspective literature, Campbell and Bello (1996) indicate that "experts are people with a certain amount of experience, rather than people who satisfy specific criteria of knowledge or skill."

To select the first group, we used a database of 232 large firms located in a city in the United States. A large firm is defined in the database as having more than 250 employees. From this population of 232 firms, we generated a *random* sample of 30 firms. The senior IS manager of each firm was contacted, and a personal meeting was set up for the study. Special care was taken to ensure that each subject was indeed the chief decision maker for IS purchases within that firm (or division of a larger firm). All the subjects were contacted over a period spanning two months. In our judgment, no external events of sufficient magnitude[2] occurred so as to bias subjects in the latter or earlier periods of the study. Of the 30 managers contacted, one declined to participate, one firm did not exist any longer, two IS managers were not responsible for making decisions, and three did not return our calls. This left us with a sample size of 23 and a response rate of 76.6%. The demographics of the 23 IS managers who agreed to participate are shown in Table 2.

The population for the second group of subjects consisted of 49 final-year graduate IS students, most of whom had already accepted jobs as fresh IS managers. An incentive of US$20 was offered to each novice subject to participate in the study. We should note that this incentive was not necessary for the expert group, since they were senior IS managers who expressed interest in participating in the study and had committed an hour of their time. Novice subjects were instructed that they would need to put in a reasonable level of cognitive effort in evaluating the different architectures, in order to be consistent in their decision making,

Table 2. Demographics of subjects in the expert group

Subject No.	Gender	Years of Experience	Approximate Number of Machines Manager is Responsible For	Environment They are Most Comfortable Managing*	SIC Code of Organization or Services Provided by Organization
1.	M	18	400+	Client/Server	SIC 99
2.	M	7	100+	Mainframes	Design and build coil processing systems
3.	M	20	155	Client/Server	SIC 3612
4.	F	20	1,000+	Client/Server	SIC 89, 28
5.	M	32	135+	Mainframes	SIC 3316, 3362, 3533
6.	M	6	78	Fully Distributed	Supply hi-tech personnel
7.	F	13	350+	Mainframes	Distribute heavy construction equipment
8.	M	8	500+	Client/Server	Hospital systems
9.	M	11	1,200+	Fully Distributed	SIC 3465, 3711, 3713
10.	M	15	20,000+	Mainframes, Client/Server, Fully Distributed	SIC 3334, 3353, 3354
11.	M	15	42	Client/Server	SIC 99
12.	M	12	1,000+	Client/Server	SIC 6711, 6722
13	M	20	30,000+	Fully Distributed	SIC 3355, 3857
14.	F	20	40,000+	Client/Server	SIC 2819, 1051, 3399
15.	M	17	200+	Mainframes	SIC 3544
16.	M	8	950	Mainframes	SIC 4011
17.	M	27	250	Mainframes	SIC 3317, 3531
18.	M	3	50	Client/Server	SIC 3316
19.	M	6	475	Client/Server	SIC 99
20.	M	20	28,000+	Mainframes, Client/Server, Fully Distributed	Banking
21.	M	9	80+	Client/Server	SIC 70.72
22.	M	25	20,000+	Mainframes, Client/Server	SIC 1011, 1211,1311, 3312, 4923
23.	M	13	150	Mainframes, Client/Server	SIC 2829

* *This information is shown to demonstrate that our sample set was indeed varied and not biased towards any particular architecture.*

and that they would be entered in a drawing for US$50 as long as they took the study seriously. Of the 49 novices contacted, 25 participated in the study, giving a response rate of 51%. The demographic data for the 25 subjects in the second group is shown in Table 3.

Table 3. Demographics of the subjects in the novice group

Subject No.	Gender	Years of Full-Time Experience in IS	Future Organizational Position
1.	M	1	IS Consultant
2.	M	2	Unknown
3.	F	0	IS Consulting
4.	F	3	IS Consulting
5.	M	0	IS Consulting
6.	F	3	IS Consulting/IS Manager
7.	M	0	IS Consultant
8.	M	1	IS Consulting
9.	M	0	IS Consultant
10.	M	2	Senior IS Consultant
11.	M	0	Systems Analyst
12.	M	0	IS Project Manager
13.	M	0	IS Consulting
14.	M	2	Senior Analyst
15.	M	6	Systems Administration
16.	M	3.5	In-House IS Support
17.	F	0	IS Consultant
18.	M	0	In-House IS Manager
19.	M	0	IS Consultant
20.	M	0	IS Consulting
21.	M	1.5	IS Consulting
22.	M	2	IS Analyst
23.	F	0	IS Consultant
24.	M	1	Unknown
25.	M	4.5	IS Research

Validity and Reliability Checks when Administering the Study

We now describe how we ensured reliability and construct validity with each subject in the actual CA study. Each study was conducted with one subject, in the presence of the same researcher. The instructions in the packet asked the subject to read the written descriptions of the factors. The next step in the study was for the researcher to answer any questions the subject may have had regarding the descriptions of the factors, and to ensure that the subject had an understanding of how each factor was different from the other. Particular care was taken to distinguish between *cost* and the other factors. It was specified that only explicit, tangible costs needed to be considered, and not intangible costs like "loss of user productivity." This dialogue with the subjects was necessary to ensure that all subjects had a *similar understanding* of the five factors. At this stage, they were also asked if, in their opinions, *any important factors had been omitted.* This was an additional check on whether our factors were complete.[3] Once the researcher was satisfied that the subject had a good understanding of the different factors, the subject was asked to rank the cards in descending order of preference. No time limit was to be set for the ranking, though it typically was expected to take between 20 and 30 minutes to perform. It is important to note that agreement of a set of factors among subjects would not imply lower variance in their performance, since the evaluation model of each subject consisted of the *tradeoffs* he or she would make between these factors. Once the cards were rank ordered, the subject was to give a score of 100 to the highest card and a score of 1 to the lowest card. The remaining cards were each to be given any score, as long as a strict order was maintained. These scores were the (metric) dependent variable in the study and represented the likelihood of adoption of the architecture on that particular card.

When conducting the study, we asked the experts to rank the *cards in the context of what would be adopted in his or her organization,* as opposed to a general ideal norm that the subject may have of architectures. We asked the novices *to make their evaluations based on their best understanding of the needs of a large organization, drawing on their previous experiences with organizations.* Our aim was to make the evaluation task as realistic as possible, given the limitations of the experimental design.

In order to study the use of formal, elaborate evaluation methods (Hypothesis 4), the researcher conducting the study gave a score of 1 to each subject who performed written calculations when sorting the cards or assigning scores, and a score of 0 to ones that did not perform any formal, written calculations.

Data Analysis

In our case the dependent and independent constructs were metric. Hence, we used dummy variable regression analysis (using the Microsoft Excel package) to estimate a part-worth decision model for each subject in each group. *Internal validity* in a CA study translates to determining whether each subject's decision model represents a consistent logic or not. Internal validity of each individual subject's model was tested based on the *hold out sample* of four architectures for each subject. The Wilcoxon rank test[4] (Wonnacott & Wonnacott, 1984, p. 472) was used for this. The test ranks observations from different populations (in this case, the two populations are predicted and actual scores for the four holdout architectures) and then answers the question: Are the two populations significantly different from each other? For the first group in all 23 cases, the IS managers had valid internal decision models. For the second group, all 25 subjects also had valid decision models. Thus all subjects in both groups were retained for analysis.

Based on the dummy variable coding scheme for the 16 architectures (as represented by the factors) we used, the part-worth estimates are on a common scale. Hence, the overall relative importance of each independent factor for a subject can be computed in a straightforward manner by looking at the range of dummy variable coefficients across the levels of that factor. For each subject, the part-worth values for the five factors represent their individual decision model. The individual models for all the subjects in both groups are shown in Appendix 3.

For each subject, the expected part-worth of each factor is 20% (since there are five factors). We summarize the results across the expert and the novice groups in Table 4. The first metric shown in Table 4 is the *mean* relative part-worth of each of the five factors and the confidence intervals of these means. Since the mean part-worth can be biased by extreme values in the sample, we use a second metric, which gives the percentage of subjects in the group that indicated a higher than the expected 20% relative part-worth for each of the five factors. Note that while we obtained an

Table 4. Summary statistics for the evaluation models of the expert and novice samples

Factor	Mean Part-Worths (standard deviation)		95% Confidence Intervals*		Importance **	
	Experts	Novices	Experts	Novices	Experts	Novices
Acceptance	15.9 (14.8)	14.65 (9.89)	9.41 – 22.38	10.51-18.78	17%	16%
Backward Compatibility	12.9 (5.1)	22.04 (14.77)	10.66 – 15.13	15.86-28.21	13%	44%
Software Quality	40.2 (16.9)	39.4 (17.2)	32.8 – 47.6	32.21-46.58	86%	88%
Centralization/Distribution	16.4 (13.3)	12.2 (13.8)	10.58 – 22.22	6.43-17.97	39%	20%
Costs	14.4 (10.2)	11.7 (7.74)	9.93 – 18.86	8.46-14.94	26%	16%

* *Degrees of freedom = 18*
** *This is the percentage of subjects for whom the relative part-worth was > 20% for this factor*

individual-level decision model for each subject (shown in Appendix 3), Table 4 shows the *aggregate* statistics of the decision models across each group.

F-tests were conducted to test Hypotheses 1 and 2. The null hypotheses (that the two are equal) were not rejected in all cases of H1, except for the case of backward compatibility, where novices had a significantly higher mean (also see the confidence intervals of all the factors in Table 4). Hypothesis 2, which posits that experts will zero in on a small set of factors, was supported. Table 5 lists the P-values. For Hypothesis 3, we conducted an F-test to test the difference in variance between the two samples and, again, the only null hypothesis to be rejected was for backward compatibility, where the novices showed a *greater* variance than the experts. These F-tests for variance are also listed in Table 5. Finally, to test Hypothesis 4, it was observed that nine novices out of 20 used some formal utility model (utilizing pen and paper) when evaluating the computing architectures. No experts used any formal models utilizing pen and paper. A confidence interval of difference in proportions (Wonnacott & Wonnacott, 1984), also shown in Table 5, indicates that novices are significantly more likely to use formal models than experts for this task. Hence, our study found support for Hypothesis 4.

DISCUSSION AND IMPLICATIONS

Performance Differences

The stimulus environment for managers consists of large amounts of data from various sources. Firms often depend on managers' expertise to deal with these complex decision environments (Day & Nedungadi, 1994; Spence & Brucks, 1997). While the cognitive literature in psychology clearly indicates a difference between the cognitive *processes* of experts and novices (Chi, Glaser, & Farr, 1988), this may or may not translate to better *performance* in judgment and decision making (Spence & Brucks, 1997). Indeed, reviews of studies on expertise in behavioral decision theory generally offer a pessimistic view of expertise (Armstrong, 1985; Camerer & Johnson, 1991; Johnson, 1988). As Johnson (1988, p. 212) states:

Table 5. Summary of hypothesis testing results

Hypothesis No.	Hypothesis Statement	P-value or Confidence Interval	Hypothesis Supported?
H1(a)	Mean part-worth of Acceptance is different in both groups.	0.719	No
H1(b)	Mean part-worth of Backward Compatibility is different in both groups.	0.007	Yes
H1(c)	Mean part-worth of Software Quality is different in both groups.	0.869	No
H1(d)	Mean part-worth of Centralization is different in both groups.	0.289	No
H1(e)	Mean part-worth of Costs is different in both groups.	0.292	No
H2	The part-worths of the five factors will be unequal for experts.	$9.6*10^{-14}$	Yes
H3(a)	Variance of part-worth of Acceptance is different in both groups.	0.056	No
H3(b)	Variance of part-worth of Backward Compatibility is different in both groups.	0.00	Yes
H3(c)	Variance of part-worth of Software Quality is different in both groups.	0.941	No
H3(d)	Variance of part-worth of Centralization is different in both groups.	0.883	No
H3(e)	Variance of part-worth of Costs is different in both groups.	0.176	No
H4	More novices will use formal evaluation models than experts.	0.172-0.548 (confidence interval for difference between proportions)	Yes

$\alpha = 0.05$ in all cases

The superiority of experts to novices is often surprisingly small, or, in some cases, non-existent... the surprisingly poor performance of experts has been replicated across a broad range of seemingly unrelated task domains.

Camerer and Johnson (1991) call the contrast between poor expert performance in the behavioral decision-making literature with the findings of clear process differences in the cognitive processing literature the *process-performance paradox* in expert judgment.

While experts do perform better in environments where mental models can be tested and improved, they appear to perform poorly with tasks that are more subjective, such as decision making in the business environment (Shanteau, 1992). This explains why the business literature is replete with examples of experts performing little better than novices in terms of the quality of their decision outputs (Armstrong, 1991; Austin & Mawhinney, 1999; Mackay & Elam, 1992; Marshall, 2002). Past work in the MIS sub-discipline, however, has ignored the process-performance paradox, and focused largely on the process differences between experts and novices. Our findings here break new ground in the area, by considering the performance of expert and novice IS managers, along with the process differences.

The lack of support for H1(a), (c), (d), and (e) indicates that expert IS managers do not differ significantly from novices in their final evaluation models of computing architectures—that is, their evaluation performance is similar. From Table 4, it is clear that the most important factor for both groups is software quality. There is striking similarity in the percentage of subjects in each group who thought it significant in both groups (86% and 88%). The confidence intervals for the mean part-worths for software quality are very similar for both groups also, as shown in Table 5. Thirty-nine percent of the senior IS managers considered centralization/distribution significant, while 20% of fresh IS hires considered it significant, with an overlap between the confidence intervals. Both groups' consideration of acceptance was also similar: 17% of senior IS managers and 16% of fresh IS hires considered acceptance significant, and the confidence intervals for the mean part-worth for acceptance in both groups also overlap; 26% of senior IS managers and 16% of fresh IS hires considered costs significant, again with an overlap in the confidence intervals of the two groups for cost. The only significant difference was for backward compatibility, where 13% of the experts thought it significant, vs. 44% of the novices. The mean part-worth confidence interval bounds for backward compatibility are also significantly higher in the case of novices (no overlap).

The strong support for H2 implies that experts do tend to "zero in" on one or two factors as a group. This finding is in agreement with research in non-MIS business domains, where senior managers selectively filter inputs when making judgments (Day & Lord, 1992; Maheswaran et al., 1996). The surprising finding in our study was that novice MIS managers utilized the same filter and ended up using the same inputs for their decision models. This further supports our finding that performance differences between expert and novice IS managers cannot be detected for the important task in this study.

The dichotomy in the literature on whether experts show more or less variance than novices in their performance is not completely resolved in our study. The lack of support for hypothesis H3(a), (c), (d), and (e) indicates that no difference in variance can be detected on factors where both groups agree. However, the backward compatibility factor, which was considered more important by significantly more novices, also shows greater variance among the novices than the experts. Thus, while our study offers some support for the view that novices perform with greater variance, the lack of support for four out of five hypotheses indicates that, in general, the variance differences are not significant.

The novices in our study were full-time graduate students who were not currently working in organizations, though several had some prior work experience. It is possible that the experts would consider the power and politics in their organization when making their evaluations, whereas novices could not, since they were not working in any organizations as yet. This difference between experts and novices would be true even if we had used freshly hired managers in an organization as novices and asked them to evaluate the architectures in the context of their new organizations. Our findings indicate that even if experts do incorporate an awareness of power and politics in their evaluation of computing architectures, it does not lead to significantly different *evaluations* than novices. This is further supported in Swanson (1994) and Chau and Tam (1997), where the selection of an IS architecture is recognized as a decision that will significantly affect the IS department, but not the overall organization.

Process Differences

The cognitive processing literature indicates a clear difference between the processing methods of experts and novices. For example, Chi et al. (1981) and Larkin, McDermott, Simon, and Simon (1980) found that experts categorize problems on a deeper basis, using solution procedures or other underlying concepts, while novices classify problems on the basis of shallow surface features.

Experts tend to adopt more efficient, top-down strategies for decision making, as opposed to the bottom-up strategies adopted by novices. The strong support for H4 indicates that novices in our study adopted formal pencil-and-paper procedures when evaluating the different computing architectures. These formal procedures consisted of actually assigning weights (or utilities) to each factor, before evaluating the architectures, and then computing a score for each architecture on paper, before ranking and scoring it. None of the experts in our study adopted such an analytical approach. Instead, the experts ranked and scored the architectures in an intuitive, "wholistic" manner, with no pencil-and-paper calculations. Subsequent interviews with some of the experts confirmed that they viewed each architecture in its entirety and used a synthesis of their earlier experiences when ranking and scoring it. Our findings lend further support to the widely held observation that experts do follow different cognitive processes from novices when performing judgment tasks, in our case utilizing heuristics rather than bottom-up utility calculations. One possible explanation for the observed process difference could be that experts quickly discarded impractical architectures within their organizational context, while novices, who did not have a specific organizational context in mind, would consider each factor more carefully and expend greater effort in arriving at their evaluation model. However, it is important to note that, as observed for many managerial tasks in past studies, the heuristics followed by experts in our study do not appear to reflect rich experience, or any knowledge of deep, domain-specific principles that would lead to *performance* differences.

Practical Implications

Our findings are also likely to be interesting to IS practitioners. We demonstrate, for the first time, that expertise does not influence the final evaluation of IS architectures. This implies that customer segmentation in the IS market should not be based on expertise; rather, other dimensions such as industry or geography can be applied. Second, the major factor in the majority of our subjects' decision models was software quality. Promoters of new architectures such as Web services and thin clients should be aware that the major issue to focus on is software quality, with its many sub-dimensions. Factors such as whether an architecture is centralized or not and the actual costs of the architecture are much less important in the decision space of IS managers than the quality of software available on the architecture.

LIMITATIONS, CONTRIBUTIONS, AND FUTURE RESEARCH

Limitations of the Study

Unlike mail-out surveys, where quantitative measures of construct validity and reliability exist, conducting face-to-face data collection places greater burden on the researcher for ensuring validity and reliability. In this work, we have documented in detail the steps we took, and any replication of this work will require similar work on the part of the researcher.

Another limitation of this study is that only the expert group was asked to define the factors they would consider in an evaluation of computing architectures. We did ask both groups if any factors had been omitted, and received negative responses from them. However, it is conceivable that the novice group may have come up with a different set of factors if they had been interviewed in a manner similar to the experts.

Third, because of time and resource constraints, the decision models that comprise our data sets belong to individuals. As with most important organizational tasks, the decision to actually adopt computing architectures may be made at a committee level. Even so, as already discussed, the decision models of IS managers are likely to be an important input into this process. While almost every other study in the area has focused on one task, it is possible that significant performance differences may exist between expert and novice IS managers for other tasks. The validity of our findings will be enhanced as more studies are undertaken for other tasks.

Fourth, unlike mail-out surveys where larger sample sizes may be obtained, the method of face-to-face data collection constrains the sample size of both groups. The limitations of a smaller sample size include lower power, though extremely high sample sizes reduce standard error so that even miniscule differences become statistically significant (Wonnacott & Wonnacott, 1984). While the face-to-face data collection approach allowed us to implement a study with richer constructs and methodology than a mail-out survey, a survey would generally allow a larger sample size. Nevertheless, the similarity between the evaluation models of experts and novices (the performance) is striking in this study, and we believe provides good exploratory-level evidence that differences in the evaluation models are small. As an example, Table 6 indicates the effect size values for the hypotheses that tested differences between mean par- worths of the two samples, where the null hypothesis was not rejected. We note that an effect size of 0.2 or less is considered *low* in most studies. To illustrate, an effect size of 0.2 implies only a 14.7% *non-overlap* in the distributions of the expert and novice samples, while an effect size of 0.1 implies only a 7.7% non-overlap. In general, the smaller the effect size, the stronger the support for lack of difference between the two samples.

Finally, the measure of performance in our study is the actual evaluation models arrived at by the subjects, after considering different architectures. An alternate performance measure would be the actual performance of the selected architecture within the organization. Measuring this would require an extended longitudinal study and was not possible given the resource constraints of this study. However, this remains a possibility for future research.

Contributions

Our work makes contributions to both theory and practice. On the theoretical front, first, we extend earlier work in the MIS literature that focused on process differences between expert and novice IS managers, without regard to performance differences. Here, for the first time, we examine the performance differences between the groups for an important task. Our findings of significant process difference, but little performance difference, are

Table 6. Effect size when testing for differences between mean part-worths

Hypothesis	Hypothesis Statement	P-Value	Hypothesis Supported	Effect Size
H1(a)	Mean part-worth of Acceptance is different in both groups.	0.719	No	0.04
H1(b)	Mean part-worth of Backward Compatibility is different in both groups.	0.007	Yes	N/A
H1(c)	Mean part-worth of Software Quality is different in both groups.	0.869	No	0.023
H1(d)	Mean part-worth of Centralization is different in both groups.	0.289	No	0.153
H1(e)	Mean part-worth of Costs is different in both groups.	0.292	No	0.147

supported by the literature in other (non-MIS) business areas. Rather than assume expert-novice differences in performance and seek to establish a cause by studying the process, future work in MIS should first establish performance differences before delving further. This is especially true if the task under study is unstructured and subjective. Second, our findings contribute to the business literature in general and add weight to the growing body of evidence that while process differences do exist, performance differences between expert and novice managers for several tasks are not detected. This suggests that several tasks in the business domain are not structured and may not have a core set of domain-specific principles that are better understood by experts than novices. Third, we confirm findings from the psychology, business, and MIS literatures that experts adopt a top-down, heuristic methodology when performing a task and draw on earlier experience, while novices resort to bottom-up, elaborate methods that do not draw on elaborate methods. Fourth, on the methodological front, we extend work in MIS, which has traditionally used self-reported perceptual measures to test a variety of models. We utilize and extensively document a methodology that allows for the objective testing of task performance differences, and provide what we hope is one model for future work on expert-novice differences in the MIS area.

Our findings also contribute to industry. Since evaluation is a prerequisite to purchase, MIS vendors are likely to be interested in the similarity of the evaluation models of expert and novice MIS managers. For the task examined here, market segmentation of IS managers based on experience may not be necessary from a vendor's perspective. While, as discussed earlier, the decision to actually adopt computing architectures may be made at a committee level, the decision models of IS managers are likely to be an important input into this process. The importance of software quality vs. centralization, cost, backward compatibility, and market-base of a product also sends a clear message to vendors to focus on developing higher quality software and emphasize that in their communication to MIS managers.

FUTURE WORK

It is clear from our work that, as in other business areas, the process-performance paradox is alive and well in the MIS domain. In future work, it will be very interesting to understand which managerial tasks actually lend themselves to expertise—that is, what the tasks are where the performance of expert and novice managers differs. While it is clear that performance differences will exist for highly structured tasks such as programming and systems development, as the IS manager moves higher up the ladder and the tasks get progressively more unstructured, which tasks lend themselves to expertise? Of equal importance will be understanding the importance of these tasks in determining the success of the organization as well as the manager.

Second, our work considered several aspects of computing architectures and found that the software quality aspect was the most important. It will be interesting to extend our work by unraveling this factor and understanding which aspects of software quality are considered important by IS managers.

Third, backward compatibility was considered important by 44% of the novices, but only 13% of the experts. This is an interesting finding, since intuitively one would expect senior managers to be aware of the importance of integrating new systems with legacy applications. It would be interesting to get a more finely granular perspective on what constitutes backward compatibility and why it is not considered by senior IS managers to the degree one would expect.

Finally, the method of measuring process differences in our study used differences in variance and level of formal explicit bottom-up modeling as indicators of process difference. These are 'black-box' measures that provide exploratory evidence. This study indicates that novice IS managers utilize explicit knowledge when evaluating computing architectures, while experienced managers rely more on tacit knowledge. Further examination of this difference is warranted in future studies. A follow-up study that utilizes a 'white-box' approach, such as protocol analysis, for example, can shed further light on the cognitive processes followed by expert vs. novice IS managers, when performing the evaluation task.

ACKNOWLEDGMENT

We thank the editor-in-chief, associate editor, and three anonymous reviewers whose comments have greatly enhanced the quality of this article.

REFERENCES

Allen, B.R., & Boynton, A.C. (1991). Information architecture: In search of efficient flexibility. *MIS Quarterly,* 435–445.

Anderson, J.R. (1995). *Cognitive psychology and its implications.* New York: W.H. Freeman.

Armstrong, J.S. (1985). *Long range forecasting: From crystal ball to computer.* New York: John Wiley & Sons.

Armstrong, J.S. (1991). Prediction of consumer behavior by experts and novices. *Journal of Consumer Research, 18*(2), 251(6).

Austin, J., & Mawhinney, T.C. (1999). Using concurrent verbal reports to examine data analyst verbal behavior. *Journal of Organizational Behavior Management, 18*(4), 61–81.

Bajaj, A. (2000). A study of senior information systems managers' decision models in adopting new computing architectures. *Journal of the Association of Information Systems, 1*(4).

Baker, S., & O'Sullivan, D. (2001). Positioning CORBA, J2EE, Web services and other middlewares. *Proceedings of the 3rd International Symposium on Distributed Objects and Applications* (pp. 359–360).

Boster, J.S., & Johnson, J.C. (1989). Form or function: A comparison of expert and novice judgments of similarity among fish. *American Anthropologist, 91*(4), 866–889.

Bouwman, M.J. (1984). Expert vs. novice decision making in accounting: A summary. *Accounting, Organizations and Society, 9*(3–4), 325–327.

Brehmer, B. (1990). Strategies in real-time decision making. In R. Hogarth (Ed.), *Insights in decision making* (pp. 262–279). Chicago: University of Chicago Press.

Camerer, C.F., & Johnson, E.J. (1991). The process performance paradox in expert judgment: How can experts know so much and predict so badly? In K.A. Ericsson & J. Smith (Eds.), *Toward a general theory of expertise: Prospects and limits* (pp. 195–217). New York: Cambridge University Press.

Campbell, R.L., & Bello, L.D. (1996). Studying human expertise: Beyond the binary paradigm. *Journal of Experimental and Theoretical Artificial Intelligence, 8*(3–4), 277–291.

Charness, N. (1976). Memory for chess positions: Resistance to interference. *Journal of Experimental Psychology: Human Learning and Memory, 2,* 641–653.

Chase, W.G., & Simon, H.A. (1973). The mind's eye in chess. In W.G. Chase (Ed.), *Visual information processing.* New York: Academic Press.

Chau, P.Y.K., & Tam, K.Y. (1997). Factors affecting the adoption of open systems: An exploratory study. *MIS Quarterly,* (March), 1–23.

Chi, M.T.H. (1984). Knowledge derived categorization in young children. In D.R. Rogers & J.A.

Sloboda (Eds.), *Acquisition of symbolic skills* (pp. 327–334). New York: Plenum.

Chi, M.T.H., Feltovich, P.J., & Glaser, R. (1981). Categorization and representation of physics problems by experts and novices. *Cognitive Science, 5,* 121–152.

Chi, M.T.N., Glaser, R., & Farr, M.J. (1988). *The nature of expertise.* Hillsdale, NJ.

Cowan, D.A. (1986). Developing a process model of problem recognition. *Academy of Management Review, 11,* 763–776.

Day, D.V., & Lord, R.G. (1992). Expertise and problem categorization: The role of expert processing in organizational sense making. *Journal of Management Studies, 29*(1), 35–47.

Day, G.S., & Nedungadi, P. (1994). Managerial representations of competitive advantage. *Journal of Marketing, 58*(April), 31–44.

Dreyfus, H.L., & Dreyfus, S.E. (1986). *Mind over machine: The power of human intuition and expertise in the era of the computer.* New York: The Free Press.

Dutton, J.E., & Jackson, S.E. (1987). The categorization of strategic issues by decision makers and its links to organizational action. *Academy of Management Review, 12,* 76–90.

Engell, J.F., Blackwell, R.D., & Kollat, D.T. (1978). *Consumer behavior.* Hillsdale, IL: Dryden.

Foxall, G.R. (1983). *Consumer choice.* New York: St. Martin's Press.

Frederico, P.-A. (1995). Expert and novice recognition of similar situations. *Human Factors, 37*(1), 105(18).

Glaser, R. (1989). Expertise and learning: How do we think about instructional processes, now that we have discovered knowledge structures? In D. Klahr & K. Kotovsky (Eds.), *Complex information processing: The impact of Herbert A. Simon* (pp. 269–282). Hillsdale, NJ: Lawrence Erlbaum.

Green, P.E., & Rao, V.R. (1971). Conjoint measurement for quantifying judgmental data. *Journal of Marketing Research, 8*(August), 355–363.

Haag, S., Cummings, M., & McCubbrey, D.J. (2003). *Management information systems for the information age.* New York: McGraw-Hill/Irwin.

Hair, J.F. (1992). *Multivariate data analysis with readings.* New York: Macmillan.

Hassebrock, F., Johnson, P.E., Bullemer, P., Fox, P.W., & Moller, J.H. (1993). When less is more: Representative and selective memory in expert problem solving. *American Journal of Psychology, 106*(2), 155(35).

Johnson, E.J. (1988). Expertise and decision under uncertainty: performance and process. In M.T.H. Chi, R. Glaser, & M.J. Farr (Eds.), *The nature of expertise.* London: Lawrence Erlbaum.

King, J.L. (1983). Centralized versus decentralized computing: Organizational considerations and management options. *Computing Surveys, 15*(4), 319–349.

Kirlik, A., Walker, N., Fisk, A.D., & Nagel, K. (1996). Supporting perception in the service of dynamic decision making. *Human Factors, 38*(2), 288(12).

Larkin, J.H., McDermott, J., Simon, D.P., & Simon, H.A. (1980). Expert and novice performance in solving physics problems. *Science, 208,* 1335–1342.

Luce, D.R., & Tukey, J.W. (1964). Simultaneous conjoint measurement: A new type of fundamental measurement. *Journal of Mathematical Psychology, 1*(February), 1–27.

Mackay, J.M., & Elam, J.J. (1992). A comparative study of how experts and novices use a decision aid to solve problems in complex knowledge domains. *Information Systems Research, 3*(2), 150–172.

Maheswaran, D., Sternthal, B., & Gurhan, Z. (1996). Acquisition and impact of consumer expertise. *Journal of Consumer Psychology, 5*(2), 115–133.

Marshall, D.P. (2002). Solving accounting problems: Differences between accounting experts and novices. *Journal of Education for Business, 77*(6), 325–329.

Melling, W.P. (1994). Enterprise information architectures: They are finally changing. *Proceedings of ACM SIGMOD,* Minneapolis, MN.

Nezlek, G.S., Jain, H.K., & Nazareth, D.L. (1999). An integrated approach to enterprise computing environments. *Communications of the ACM, 42*(11), 82–90.

Nieh, J., Yang, S.J., & Novik, N. (2000). *A comparison of thin client computing architectures.* CUCS-022-00, Columbia University, USA.

Randel, J.M., & Pugh, H.L. (1996). Differences in expert and novice situation awareness in naturalistic decision making. *International Journal of Human Computer Studies, 45,* 579–597.

Rogers, E.M. (1983). *Diffusion of innovations.* New York: The Free Press.

Schenk, K.D., Vitalri, N.P., & Davis, K.S. (1998). Differences between novice and expert systems analysts: What do we know and what do we do? *Journal of MIS, 15*(1), 9–50.

Shanteau, J. (1988). Psychological characteristics and strategies of expert decision makers. *Acta Psychologica, 68,* 203–215.

Shanteau, J. (1992). Competence in experts: The role of task characteristics. *Organizational Behavior and Human Decision Processes, 53,* 252–266.

Spence, M.T., & Brucks, M. (1997). The moderating effects of problem characteristics on experts' and novices' judgments. *Journal of Marketing Research, 34,* 233–247.

Spinellis, D. (1998). The computer's new clothes. *IEEE Software, 15*(6), 14–17.

Swanson, E.B. (1994). Information systems innovation among organizations. *Management Science, 40*(9), 1069–1092.

Wonnacott, T.H., & Wonnacott, R.J. (1984). *Introductory statistics for business & economics.* New York: John Wiley & Sons.

ENDNOTES

1 The software associated with any architecture can be split into several levels, starting from the operating system at the bottom, moving up to application systems like database management systems, moving up to end user applications such as database form applications. Each level's quality depends on the levels below it. In this study, we define software as all the software that all members of the organization would interact with. Thus, IS staff may interact with the operating system and the next higher level, while end users may react only with the highest levels. Ultimately, the goal of an organizational IS is, of course, to deliver end user software, and in our definition of software quality, we stress this focus.

2 A hypothetical example of such an event is: a particular architecture that is highly centralized is accepted as a worldwide standard, biasing all subjects in favor of centralized architecture.

[3] All of the subjects in the study described next indicated that the five factors covered their decision space.

[4] An analysis of variance could not be used, since the populations are small (four observations each). A larger population would have meant a larger holdout sample, which could have cognitively overloaded the subjects, thus leading to serious biases in their responses.

APPENDIX 1

The 20 hypothetical architectures (16 for the orthogonal set + four holdout) generated by SPSS.

Architecture name	Backward Compatibility Level	Software Quality Level	Centralized/Distributed Level	Costs Level	Acceptance of the Architecture Level
Architecture A	Medium	Medium	Centralized	Medium	Low
Architecture B	Low	Low	Centralized	Low	Low
Architecture C	High	Medium	Distributed	Low	Medium
Architecture D	High	High	Distributed	High	Low
Architecture E	Medium	Low	Distributed	Low	Low
Architecture F	Low	Low	Distributed	Low	Low
Architecture G	Low	Medium	Centralized	High	Low
Architecture H	Medium	Low	Distributed	High	High
Architecture I	Low	Medium	Distributed	Low	High
Architecture J	Low	High	Distributed	Medium	Low
Architecture K	Low	High	Centralized	Low	High
Architecture L	Low	Low	Centralized	High	Medium
Architecture M	Low	Low	Distributed	Medium	Medium
Architecture N	Medium	High	Centralized	Low	Medium
Architecture O	High	Low	Centralized	Low	Low
Architecture P	High	Low	Centralized	Medium	High
Architecture Q	High	Low	Centralized	Medium	Low
Architecture R	Low	High	Distributed	Low	High
Architecture S	Medium	Medium	Distributed	Low	Low
Architecture T	High	High	Centralized	Medium	Low

APPENDIX 2

Description of the Study Packet

Demographic Information

(1) Name:

(2) Organizational address:

(3) Organizational position and duties:

(4) Years of experience in the IS area:

(5) Highest educational degree:

(6) Gender:

(7) What best describes the computing environment you feel most comfortable managing (check one, please):

- ☐ Mainframe-based systems
- ☐ Client-server systems
- ☐ Intranet-based systems
- ☐ Fully distributed systems

Please read the following *carefully,* in order to understand the study.

This study looks at what issues IS managers like yourself consider, when selecting *computing architectures* for your organization. There are several computing architectures that are available. Examples of computing architectures include:

- mainframe systems with terminals;
- client-server systems (client and server machines dividing up the processing);
- the proposed architecture of diskless network computers running off an intranet server; and
- a fully networked architecture, where each machine is a server by itself and communicates with every other machine.

A computing architecture gives rise to a large number of hardware products, as well as software. In many cases, it has profound effects on how organizations conduct their business, since the software and hardware the organization uses changes with the architecture. For example, an architecture shift from mainframe to client-server systems significantly changed the software and hardware that end users' use.

In this study, we assume that a computing architecture is *completely described* by the following *factors*:

1. **Software quality:** The quality of software associated with the architecture. This can include response time to end users, quality of the user interface, and features provided by the software, and so forth. Since users interface with the system via software, overall this factor could play an important role in determining how satisfied end users are with the software and the system.

In this study, a computing architecture's software quality has one of three levels: **low, medium,** or **high.**

2. **Centralization vs. distributed nature:** Some computing architectures are inherently more centralized than others. A centralized architecture means that software resides in a centralized location, and most of the hardware investment is also centralized. Thus, a mainframe architecture and an intranet architecture with network computers are centralized. The client-server architecture and the fully distributed architecture are distributed—that is, the software and hardware investments

are scattered on user machines. A centralized architecture is usually easier to maintain, while a distributed architecture usually provides greater freedom to end users in terms of being able to install their own local software and so forth.

In this study, an architecture is either considered **centralized** or **distributed.**

3. **Costs:** Each computing architecture comes associated with its own costs. The costs include the costs of acquisition of hardware/software, the cost of maintenance of hardware, the costs of controlling different versions of software, the availability of people trained in the maintenance of hardware/software of the computing architecture, and so on.

In this study, an architecture can have **low, medium,** or **high** costs associated with it.

4. **Acceptance of the architecture:** This factor represents the degree to which a particular computing architecture has been accepted by IS magazines, the media, model organizations you look up to, software vendors who write software that you use, and so forth. This factor can influence how senior managers like the CEO, CFO, and so forth in your organization feel about the architecture (they are more likely to buy into an accepted architecture). An architecture with low acceptance is not necessarily bad: it could just be new.

In this study, an architecture can have **low, medium,** or **high** acceptance.

5. **Backward compatibility of architecture:** This factor models the degree to which a computing architecture will cause changes in your organization. The changes can be of many types, for example: the ability to have your organization's existing information read by software in the new architecture, the need to retrain users in the new software of the architecture (maybe the word processor and spreadsheets look different), the learning curve of your IS staff in maintaining the hardware/software in the architecture, and so forth. This factor can also be important in determining the initial satisfaction of your end users and IS staff.

In this study, an architecture can have a **high, medium,** or **low** backward compatibility.

You will now be presented with 20 different computing architectures. These architectures do not have names, but are arbitrarily labeled from A–T. *Each architecture will be described in terms of the five factors we just discussed.* As an IS manager, we would like you to do the following:

- Please sort these 20 architectures (on the 20 different cards) in descending order of preference (from most preferred on the top of the pile to least preferred at the bottom).
- After you have sorted the cards, please write a number on each card that gives a numerical value to your preference, from 1–100. The least preferred architecture (at the bottom of the pile) will be given a score of 1, while the most preferred architecture will be given a score of 100. The cards in between should be given a preference score (between 1 and 100). Naturally, each card should have a preference score lower than the card above it and higher than the card below it. *However,*

the scores need not be spaced equally. It is entirely up to you to choose the score you wish to give each architecture. Note that the *entire architecture should be given one preference score,* based on how appealing it is to you.

Also, in case you change your preferences, you may reorder the cards in the heap at any time during the study. If you do alter the order, please make sure you alter the preference scores as well—that is, the preference score of every card is still between the scores of the cards above and below it.

Since we shall be reusing the cards, please use the pencil provided to write on the cards. All the factors discussed earlier have been summarized on a single sheet, for your convenience. Please feel free to refer to this.

Below is an example of one architecture on a card. In all, the packet had 20 cards, one for each architecture. Note that in this packet, the *centralized/distributed* factor is listed first for all the cards. There were four other packets created, each having a different order of factors.

ARCHITECTURE A

Centralized/Distributed: Centralized
Costs: Medium
Acceptance of the Architecture: Low
Backward Compatibility of the Architecture: Medium
Software Quality: Medium

APPENDIX 3

Table A1 presents the individual decision models for each expert IS manager. Here, *Acceptl* implies the factor acceptance with level "low," and so on.

The relative part-worths for each factor (for each expert) are shown in Table A2.

Table A3 presents the individual decision models for each novice. Here, *Acceptl* implies the factor acceptance with level "low," and so on.

The relative part-worths for each factor (for each novice) are shown in Table A4.

Table A1. The dummy variable coefficients for each level of each factor for each expert

Subject	Acceptl	Acceptm	Accepth	BCl	BCm	BCh	SQl	SQm	SQh	Cent	Dist	Costsl	Costsm	Costsh
1.	-23.2	1	22.25	-4.75	-1.87	6.625	-24.5	2.666	21.91	1.437	-1.43	2.25	2.875	-5.15
2.	-8.25	7.75	0.5	-5.91	1.083	4.833	-48.4	23.95	24.45	0.312	-0.31	6.416	-2.08	-4.33
3.	-9.16	-2.41	11.53	-1.83	0.166	1.66	-20.8	6.916	13.91	-12	12	-0.16	17.08	-16.9
4.	-3.25	2.375	0.875	-0.41	2.83	-2.41	-12.9	-4.04	16.95	14.43	-14.4	14.08	10.45	-24.5
5.	-1.08	-1.95	3.041	-7.91	-5.16	13.0	-28.4	7.958	20.45	11.31	-11.3	3.25	-0.62	-2.62
6.	6	-5	-1	-0.66	-4.16	4.833	-17.5	2.12	15.37	-24.5	24.5	1.166	2.041	-3.20
7.	-6	-4.12	10.12	-6.33	-5.20	11.54	-41.1	17.08	24.08	9.375	-9.37	7.33	10.20	-17.5
8.	-6.08	-4.70	10.79	-10.0	1.041	9.041	-6.75	-0.62	7.37	-15.1	15.18	-29.0	21.54	7.541
9.	-22.5	12.12	10.37	-10	7	3	-27	9.75	17.25	8.5	-8.5	17.5	0.375	-17.8
10.	2.416	1.916	-4.33	-15.9	3.833	12.08	-36.0	11.29	24.79	6.437	-6.43	10.75	4.75	-15.5
11.	-8.25	-9.25	17.5	0.583	10.45	-11.0	-38.5	4.91	33.66	-5.18	5.18	0.583	7.458	-8.04
12.	0.416	0.416	-0.83	-7.41	-0.79	8.208	-29.5	-3.33	32.91	3.562	-3.56	7.25	0.375	-7.62
13.	3.08	-1.66	-1.41	0.416	-12.8	12.41	-28.7	0.125	28.62	-15.8	15.81	-4.58	3.416	1.166
14.	-2.83	10.79	-7.95	-14.8	7.291	7.541	-36	8	28	1	-1	3.833	-3.29	-0.54
15.	-40.5	15.75	24.75	-12.5	0	12.5	-5.5	3.75	1.75	-2.37	2.375	-3.5	3.5	0
16.	-6.08	3.666	2.416	-6.58	2.791	3.791	-40.2	5.125	35.12	-0.81	0.812	2.25	-0.5	-1.75
17.	1.5	1.5	-3	-4.33	1.291	3.041	-20.8	6.666	14.16	24.62	-24.6	-3.5	3.5	0
18.	-37.2	6.75	30.5	-8.75	2.125	6.625	-18.0	7.79	10.2	-4.93	4.937	8.75	-2.25	-6.5
19.	-0.16	4.70	-4.54	-8	2	6	-32.5	-3.3	35.87	-9.5	9.5	2.66	0.416	-3.08
20.	-1.5	2.875	-1.37	-5	-2	7	-23.5	-2.12	25.62	19.12	-19.1	0	-5.25	5.25
21.	-15.9	4.458	11.45	-13.0	9.916	3.166	-29.2	21.87	7.375	12.81	-12.8	10.41	-6.45	-3.95
22.	-11.0	-6.20	17.29	-10.0	8.541	1.541	-18.9	10.08	8.833	18.68	-18.6	5.08	13.33	-18.4
23.	-0.66	6.083	-5.41	-9	6.25	2.75	-27.6	1.583	26.08	-4.87	4.875	11.33	7.583	-18.9

Table A2. Relative part-worths of the five factors for each expert

Subjects	Acceptance	Backward Compatibility	Software Quality	Centralization/Distribution	Costs
1.	39.82	9.96	40.70	2.52	7.00
2.	14.41	9.68	65.65	0.56	9.68
3.	17.74	2.99	29.70	20.51	29.06
4.	5.20	4.85	27.60	26.67	35.68
5.	4.84	20.31	47.28	21.89	5.68
6.	10.27	8.40	30.69	45.74	4.90
7.	11.06	12.26	44.77	12.86	19.04
8.	12.87	14.59	10.77	23.16	38.61
9.	24.00	9.01	30.68	11.79	24.52
10.	5.01	20.78	45.18	9.55	19.48
11.	18.27	14.69	49.36	7.09	10.59
12.	1.23	15.41	61.65	7.03	14.67
13.	3.74	19.88	45.18	24.90	6.30
14.	16.41	19.58	56.02	1.75	6.24
15.	58.65	22.47	8.31	4.27	6.29
16.	9.64	10.26	74.54	1.61	3.96
17.	4.36	7.15	33.94	47.76	6.79
18.	49.59	11.25	20.77	7.23	11.16
19.	7.95	12.03	58.75	16.33	4.94
20.	3.83	10.50	43.00	33.48	9.19
21.	19.01	15.97	35.50	17.80	11.72
22.	19.55	12.83	19.98	25.75	21.88
23.	9.54	12.66	44.61	8.09	25.10

Table A3. The dummy variable coefficients for each level of each factor for each novice

Subject	Acceptl	Acceptm	Accepth	BCl	BCm	BCh	SQl	SQm	SQh	Cent	Dist	Costsl	Costsm	Costsh
1.	-2.83	-1.08	3.916	-13.3	-1.45	14.79	-33.1	10.58	22.58	-7.5	7.5	-1.5	1.5	0
2.	-5.58	3.66	1.916	-0.75	-1.37	2.125	-48.0	12.54	35.54	2.062	-2.06	-5.25	5.5	-0.25
3.	-3.75	-9.62	13.37	-23.0	13.04	10.04	-29.9	-1.16	31.08	0.312	-0.31	7.083	9.583	-16.6
4.	-15.2	-1.5	16.75	-7.58	2.416	5.166	-35.3	17	18.25	7.937	-7.93	1.916	6.291	-8.20
5.	-32.8	11.79	21.04	-11	1.25	9.75	-14.8	0.291	14.54	5.5	-5.5	-4.33	5.166	-0.83
6.	-12.5	-0.25	12.75	-15.6	6.708	8.958	-26.3	7.041	19.29	-4.25	4.25	17.33	-1.79	-15.5
7.	1.166	-3.08	1.916	-10.3	-0.45	10.79	-27.6	-1.29	28.95	-1.5	1.5	15	5.875	-20.8
8.	-11.0	3.416	7.666	-14.2	-1.12	15.37	-36.2	5.875	30.37	-5.56	5.562	4.583	4.083	-8.66
9.	-3.33	-3.20	6.541	-8.5	3.25	5.25	-25.1	4.083	21.08	-15.7	15.75	2.333	3.458	-5.79
10.	-4.58	-0.08	4.666	-6.08	0.291	5.791	-33.2	-3	36.25	0.437	-0.43	0.25	-0.12	-0.12
11.	-5.58	0.291	5.291	-5.41	-3.66	9.083	-34.0	12.41	21.66	-12.4	12.43	-4.41	3.333	1.083
12.	-2.58	0.541	2.041	-3.91	-0.04	3.958	-11.5	-1.70	13.29	-26.6	26.68	0.75	3.625	-4.37
13.	-5.75	1.875	3.875	-41.2	8	33.25	-9.08	1.291	7.791	-1.68	1.687	5.25	0.375	-5.62
14.	-11.8	1.916	9.916	-14.6	1.208	13.45	-20.1	-1.91	22.08	-9.37	9.37	10.16	9.916	-20.0
15.	-6	-8	14	-15.5	6.875	8.625	-9.5	1.125	8.375	-13.7	13.75	1.5	-0.62	-0.87
16.	-11.1	8.458	2.708	-7.33	1.916	5.416	-41.5	20.12	21.37	-1.12	1.125	8.333	-2.66	-5.66
17.	-2.66	5.708	-3.04	-37.6	11.45	26.20	-17	3.125	13.87	0.625	-0.62	0.166	0.666	-0.83
18.	-10.4	6.083	4.333	-17.7	4	13.75	-20.2	2.875	17.37	-7.06	7.062	0.916	4.916	-5.83
19.	-10.5	4.791	5.791	-18.2	-2.37	20.62	-25.4	-0.16	25.58	-5.06	5.062	-0.75	3	-2.25
20.	-30.2	1.875	28.37	-16.4	5.083	11.33	-3.41	3.583	-0.16	6.187	-6.18	17.91	1.916	-19.8
21.	-11	1.875	9.125	-32.5	18.5	14	-28.5	10.5	18	-2.75	2.75	-7	4.125	2.875
22.	-9.58	2.416	7.166	-9.25	-6	15.25	-15.9	13.83	2.083	-6.06	6.062	8.583	0.958	-9.54
23.	2.916	-5.83	2.916	1.083	0.208	-1.29	-14.7	3	11.75	-20.5	20.56	5.083	2.458	-7.54
24.	-9.75	4.75	5	-13.4	-2.41	15.83	-33.9	9.958	23.95	2.937	-2.93	1.916	10.41	-12.3
25.	2	-2.62	0.625	-9.66	-3.04	12.70	-41.8	9.166	32.66	-0.5	0.5	2	5.125	-7.12

Table A4. Relative part-worths of the five factors for each novice

Subjects	Acceptance	Backward Compatibility	Software Quality	Centralization/Distribution	Costs
1.	6.21	25.89	51.32	13.81	2.76
2.	8.31	3.15	75.17	3.71	9.66
3.	15.65	24.57	41.50	0.43	17.86
4.	24.88	9.91	41.59	12.34	11.27
5.	43.27	16.67	23.59	8.84	7.63
6.	18.45	17.99	33.33	6.21	24.02
7.	4.11	17.37	46.56	2.47	29.50
8.	13.45	21.26	47.80	7.98	9.51
9.	8.93	12.43	41.81	28.47	8.36
10.	10.07	12.93	75.65	0.95	0.41
11.	9.56	12.75	49.01	21.87	6.81
12.	4.68	7.97	25.19	54.05	8.10
13.	8.35	64.64	14.64	2.93	9.44
14.	15.41	19.93	29.94	13.29	21.43
15.	23.44	25.70	19.04	29.29	2.53
16.	17.60	11.43	56.39	2.02	12.56
17.	8.24	60.12	29.06	1.18	1.41
18.	14.93	28.51	34.05	12.78	9.73
19.	13.46	31.96	41.93	8.32	4.32
20.	40.85	19.34	4.88	8.62	26.31
21.	14.99	37.99	34.64	4.10	8.29
22.	16.54	24.20	29.38	11.98	17.90
23.	9.58	2.60	29.00	45.01	13.82
24.	11.30	22.41	44.35	4.50	17.43
25.	4.03	19.50	64.92	0.87	10.68

This work was previously published in the Journal of Organizational and End User Computing, Vol. 20, Issue 2, edited by M. Mahmood, pp. 25-60, copyright 2008 by IGI Publishing (an imprint of IGI Global).

Chapter 8
End User Types:
An Instrument to Classify Users Based on the User Cube

Chittibabu Govindarajulu
Delaware State University, USA

Bay Arinze
Drexel University, USA

ABSTRACT

Contemporary end users are more knowledgeable about computing technologies than the end users of the early '80s. However, many researchers still use the end user classification scheme proposed by Rockart and Flannery (1983) more than two decades ago. This scheme is inadequate to classify contemporary end users since it is based mainly on their knowledge and ignores other crucial dimensions such as control. Cotterman and Kumar (1989) proposed a user cube to classify end users based on the development, operation, and control dimensions of end user computing (EUC). Using this cube, users can be classified into eight distinct groups. In this research, a 10-item instrument is proposed to operationalize the user cube. Such an instrument would help managers to identify the status of EUC in their firms and to take appropriate action. Based on the data collected from 292 end users, the instrument was tested for construct, convergent, and discriminant validities. Researchers can use this instrument to study the interaction between constructs such as development and control with end user computing satisfaction (EUCS).

INTRODUCTION

End user computing (EUC) has been around since the late 1970s. Contemporary end users are more knowledgeable about computing technologies than ever before. They develop not only simple applications such as spreadsheets, but also sophisticated *graphical user interface* (GUI)-based applications and dynamic Web applications with back-end database connectivity. There is no dearth of EUC research in the information systems literature. Research in this area ranges from benefits of user computing (Rivard & Huff, 1984; Brancheau, Vogel, & Wetherbe, 1985; Lee, 1986; Leitheiser & Wetherbe, 1986; Davis & Bostrom, 1993) to risks (Alavi & Weiss, 1986) and problems (Guimaraes, 1999) associated with user-developed applications. However, in the fundamental area of end user classification, more research is required. Most existing studies classify end users based on Rockart and Flannery's (1983) classification scheme. This scheme primarily uses end user computing knowledge as a base for classification and ignores other dimensions associated with the contemporary EUC environment such as control.

EUC became widespread due to users relying less on centralized information technology (IT) departments for their computing needs. In other words, personal computers allowed users to exert control over their own information needs. In current EUC environments, users play different roles, such as developers of applications and controllers of the EUC environment. In spite of active involvement of end users in organizational computing, they are not yet well understood. This often leads to inefficient management of EUC, poorly designed training programs, and decreased productivity, among other effects. Since the concept of EUC begins with end users, researchers need to understand the various constructs associated with them, such as development, operation, and control. These constructs may help to better understand end user computing satisfaction and productivity. Rockart and Flannery's (1983) scheme does not reflect the different characteristics of contemporary end users. Cotterman and Kumar (1989) presented a user cube and classified users into eight distinct types based on three dimensions represented by users—developer, operator, and controller. This quantitative approach to end user classification has been largely ignored by researchers. Hence, an attempt has been made in this article *to operationalize the user cube.* The instrument presented in this article classifies end users into eight different types and represents a means of quantifying the EUC 'culture' in an organization. The benefit to organizations in understanding the extent and type of their EUC use is in informing and guiding the types of support infrastructure and tools provided to its users.

PRIOR END-USER CLASSIFICATION SCHEMES

Prior EUC research has provided different end user typologies. McLean (1979) divided users into two main categories, namely: the *data processing professional* (DPP) and the *data processing user* (DPU). DPPs develop application programs for use by others and are thus typical IT personnel. DPUs are end users who are further divided by McLean into *DP amateurs* (DPAs) and *non-DP-trained users* (NTUs). The DPAs develop applications for their own use while the NTUs use applications written by others. Rockart and Flannery (1983) presented a fine-grained classification of end users that is widely accepted and used by IS researchers. The different end user groups they identify are:

- **Non-programming end users:** do not program or use report generators. Access to computerized data is through a limited, menu-driven environment or a strictly followed set of procedures. Examples include data entry personnel.
- **Command-level users:** perform simple inquiries, often with a few simple calculations such as summation, and generate unique reports for their own purposes. An example would be shop-floor supervisors who generate staffing reports for each shift.
- **End user programmers:** utilize both command and procedural languages directly for their own personal information needs. They develop their own applications, some of which are used by other end users. An

example would be a financial analyst using spreadsheet applications.

- **Functional support personnel:** are sophisticated programmers supporting other end users within their particular functional areas. These are individuals who, by virtue of their prowess in EUC languages, have become informal centers of systems design and programming expertise within their functional areas.
- **End user computing support personnel:** are most often located in a central support organization such as an "information center."
- **DP programmers:** are similar to traditional COBOL shop programmers except that they program in end user computing languages.

Since the last two categories specifically refer to IT professionals such as programmers and help desk personnel, they are usually ignored. A closer look at these types reveals that user knowledge of computing is the main criterion for classification. These classifications, while useful when EUC was in its infancy, are not appropriate today in identifying different groups of end users. Contemporary end user groups also *control* EUC activities around them. In fact, the relevance of control dimension is evident from the various definitions of EUC. Davis (1982) defined EUC as:

...the organization of computing resources and design of information systems applications such that: (1) the application systems provide direct, immediate support for user activities, (2) information requirements are specified by the user and may be changed by the user as the system is used, and (3) the development and use of the system is controlled by the user.

According to Kasper and Cerveny (1985), EUC is:

...the capability of users to have direct control of their computing needs.

Cotterman and Kumar (1989) state:

End users are those who are consumers or producer/consumers of information. Producer/consumers of information are those who operate, develop, or control the computer based information system (CBIS), while at the same time using its output.

Thus, while control has been identified as an important characteristic of EUC, it has been mostly ignored by all end user classification schemes except one. Cotterman and Kumar (1989) identified control as one of the three dimensions of EUC along with operation and development. Based on these dimensions, they classified end users into eight distinct types (user cube): user-consumer, user-operator, user-developer, user-controller, user-operator/developer, user-developer/controller, user-operator/controller, and user-operator/developer/controller.

Availability of affordable personal computers and software, coupled with end users' desire to manage their own information needs without relying on centralized IT departments, has largely fueled EUC growth. However, this growth is not without IT management issues. In addition to the risks identified in the literature (Alavi & Weiss, 1986), a study by Rainer and Carr (1992) reported differences in end user support expectations and information center support services. They found that users placed high importance on data-related support while helpdesks did not. This highlights the hesitancy of IT departments to provide more end user data access. In other words, the 'tug of war' for control over data is a good indicator that control is an integral characteristic of EUC. The Cotterman and Kumar classification, therefore, is *more precise* and reflective of EUC than other classifications. Figure 1 presents the user cube.

Figure 1. The user cube

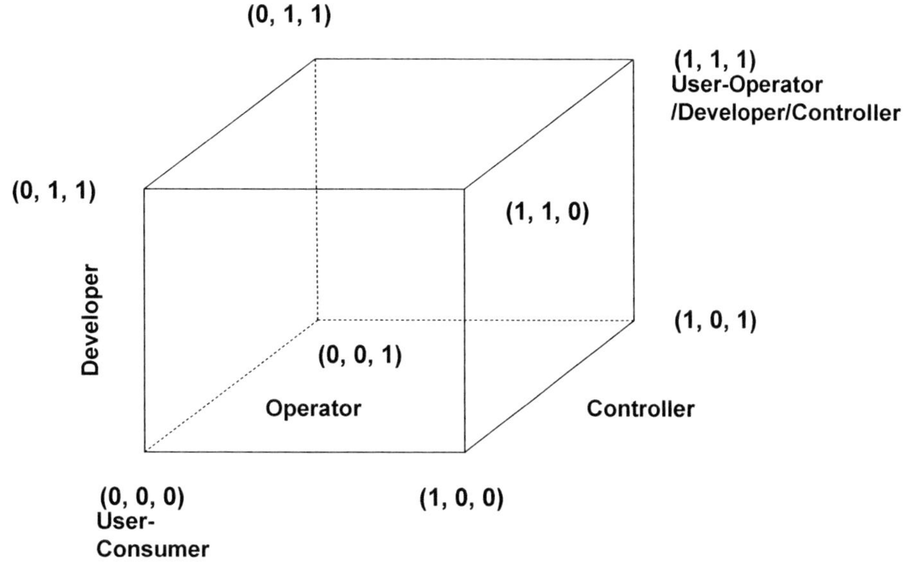

According to Cotterman and Kumar (1989), finer classifications are possible if points on the edges and inside the cube are considered. However, for simplicity, this research focuses on the eight user types represented by the eight edges of the cube. They are:

1. **User-consumer (0,0,0):** These users do not develop, operate, or control EUC applications. Examples are accounting or warehousing clerks who mainly use enterprise applications and have no contact with EUC applications, other than perhaps static reports.
2. **User-operator (1,0,0):** These end users only use applications developed by others. However, they do not develop applications or control EUC activities. Marketing staffers for example, may use internally developed EUC applications they did not develop and do not control.
3. **User-developer (0,1,0):** These users primarily develop end user applications for others. An example would be marketing or financial specialists who develop spreadsheet-based applications for use by their colleagues within the department, but do not themselves use the applications.
4. **User-controller (0,0,1):** These users neither develop nor use applications, but control EUC activities by virtue of their positions within their organizations. A good example would be the head of a finance unit who oversees the use of an internally developed EUC spreadsheet-based application.
5. **User-operator/developer (1,1,0):** User-operators/developers develop applications and use these applications for their decision making. An accounting specialist who develops a custom spreadsheet primarily for his or her own use would be classified as a user operator/developer.
6. **User-developer/controller (0,1,1):** These users develop applications and control EUC activities. A marketing department project lead who supervises EUC application development for staffers and manages the application's use is an example of a user-developer/controller.

7. **User-operator/controller (1,0,1):** User-operators/controllers use end user applications and control EUC activities as well. Examples are unit managers who use an internal EUC application, and by virtue of their position, control EUC activities within their unit.
8. **User-operator/developer/controller (1,1,1):** These users develop applications, use them, and control EUC activities. An accounting specialist who develops a custom spreadsheet for his or her own use and retains autonomous control of the system is an example of this type of user.

It should be noted that Cotterman and Kumar make a clear distinction that user-consumers (0, 0, 0) only use reports/printouts from end user applications and hence they are purely 'consumers'.

NEED FOR AN INSTRUMENT

As discussed above, earlier classification schemes (e.g., McLean, 1979; Rockart & Flannery, 1983) fail to capture all the characteristics of the end user. Understanding the dimensions of use, development, and control is crucial and a necessary precursor to designing effective training programs and efficient support mechanisms among others. Research has identified several support mechanisms for EUC, such as helpdesks, information centers, local MIS staff, Web support, and informal support. While early research showed end user satisfaction with information centers (Bergeron & Berube, 1988), later studies reveal end user dissatisfaction with information centers (Rainer & Carr, 1992; Mirani & King, 1994; Nord & Nord, 1994). One recent study reported that helpdesks are minimally used by end users (Govindarajulu, 2002). Also, prior research shows that end users prefer decentralized local MIS staff support over centralized helpdesk support (Govindarajulu, Reithel, & Sethi, 2000). Several reasons can be attributed to this. First, local MIS staff typically support only a few departments and hence understand their business and software needs better than helpdesk staff who support many departments and multiple software packages. Second, local MIS staff may be more accessible to users than helpdesk staff. Finally, contemporary end users are more knowledgeable about computing technologies and hence may not be satisfied with the basic support provided by helpdesk staff. While several support sources are available for end users, it is not clear which support sources are used by end users for their support needs, such as software support and data support. Such knowledge can help in the design of effective support mechanisms that increase user productivity, reduce risks arising from EUC, and aid in effectively managing EUC in general. Hence, clearly identifying various end user groups is vital. Without a clear understanding of user groups, any attempts to manage EUC will not achieve the desired results.

An instrument to classify users can also help to identify the different roles users play. For example, if a significant number of end users develop applications, then management can take appropriate actions such as encouraging development through redesigned support structures, increasing budgets for EUC, or even training in end user application development. Alternately, management may devise new policies to control unwanted and redundant end user application development.

Similarly, if the control dimension is dominant among end users, management may need to strictly enforce or relax policies to keep EUC in check. A dominant control dimension may also mean that the 'tug of war' between end users and centralized IT departments for control over data is highly pronounced and such a situation may require immediate management attention. On the other hand, in engineering departments of manufacturing firms, end user control over computer-aided design (CAD) systems may have to be permitted in order to spur innovation. For academic researchers, the instrument provides a way to describe the type of participants in the study and to study specific groups of end users in various EUC settings.

INSTRUMENT DEVELOPMENT

Based on Cotterman and Kumar's (1989) definition of the dimensions, an 11-item instrument was designed, as presented in Table 1. Specifically, the four control items and the four development items were based *primarily* on the definitions for control and development. According to Cotterman and Kumar (1989):

Development is the performance of any or all tasks of the system development process, whether traditional systems development lifecycle or prototyping. It consists of the specification of system requirements, system design, programming, and/or system implementation and conversion.

This definition includes all of the key aspects of development, and hence the four development items map directly to this definition. The control dimension is defined as:

...the decision-making authority to acquire, deploy, and use the resources needed to develop and operate the computer-based information systems. It includes the authority to acquire and deploy computer hardware and software; to assign development priorities; to initiate, manage, and implement development projects; to collect,

Table 1. Instrument to classify end users

EUC Dimensions and Items on the Questionnaire	Scale						
Development Please rate:	No Active Involvement						Involvement
(1) Your involvement in the design of end user applications	1	2	3	4	5	6	7
(2) Your involvement in the specification of end user application requirements	1	2	3	4	5	6	7
(3) Your involvement with respect to actual coding of end user applications	1	2	3	4	5	6	7
(4) Your involvement in the implementation of the applications developed by them and/or by others	1	2	3	4	5	6	7
Operation Please rate the extent of your use of end user applications:	Low Extent						High Extent
(1) Developed by you	1	2	3	4	5	6	7
(2) Developed by others in the department	1	2	3	4	5	6	7
(3) Developed by others in the firm	1	2	3	4	5	6	7
Control Please rate:	No Complete Authority						Authority
(1) Your decision-making authority to acquire hardware (hard disks, RAM, etc.) for the department	1	2	3	4	5	6	7
(2) Your decision-making authority to acquire software (MS Office, Corel Suite, etc.) for the department	1	2	3	4	5	6	7
(3) Your authority to initiate, manage, and implement new end user applications	1	2	3	4	5	6	7
(4) Your authority to collect, store, and use data for the end user applications	1	2	3	4	5	6	7

store, and use data; to acquire and assign personnel responsible for developing the CBIS; and to operate the system.

Again, the control items map directly to this definition.

Cotterman and Kumar (1989) define operation as:

...the initiation and termination of system operation, monitoring, or operation of hardware and software, and the execution of manual tasks necessary for the operation of a CBIS.

By this definition, they attempt to distinguish between operation and use. However, in this research, operation is defined as the *use of applications* through the operation of end user applications and consumption of results from those applications. This is necessary because the primary intent of operating an application is to *use* it for decision making. Accordingly, the operation dimension items reflect our definition. A 'pure consumer' will be an end user who uses only the outputs such as printouts of sales reports and/or balance sheets produced by end user applications. They represent the edge (0, 0, 0) on the user cube.

METHODOLOGY

A structured questionnaire was designed for data collection. In addition to the instrument, the survey contained a section to collect additional demographic information such as respondent industry, job title, and years of experience with information technology. The questionnaire was then converted to a Web page for data collection using the Internet. For a pretest, the Web page address was e-mailed to faculty and staff of a midwestern university. The resulting 125 responses were used to refine the survey. This mainly involved rewording and reordering of several items on the survey. A seven-point scale was used to measure respondents' self-perception of how well they represented the operation, development, and control dimensions.

To facilitate final data collection, the site address was widely advertised in various Usenet groups, list servers, and so forth. Once a respondent completed the survey, the response was written to a database file using active server page (ASP) technology. To prevent duplicate responses, an algorithm was used to ensure that only one response was received from each respondent. An end user is one who uses computers as part of his or her everyday work for decision making, and he or she is not involved in information systems design, development, and/or implementation. The above definition was conspicuously placed at the beginning of the survey to exclude IS/IT professionals from taking this survey. A total of 292 useful responses were received during the two-week time period the survey was posted online.

Demographics

The respondents represent a wide variety of industries. A detailed breakup of the spread is presented in Figure 2. Approximately 60% of the respondents had 10 or more years of experience working with computers, while 85.6% of respondents had five or more years of experience. About 36% of the respondents were in the 21- to 35-years age range, while another 37% were in the 36- to 49-years age range. Table 2 presents the type of end user applications developed by respondents, and the results are consistent with earlier research findings (Govindarajulu & Reithel, 1998). Spreadsheet applications seemed to be popular among respondents followed by presentations. It is interesting to note that end users seemed to be keeping up with technology. About 25% of the respondents had developed dynamic Web pages with backend database connectivity. Data analysis showed that 66% of the respondents used

Figure 2. Respondent industry type

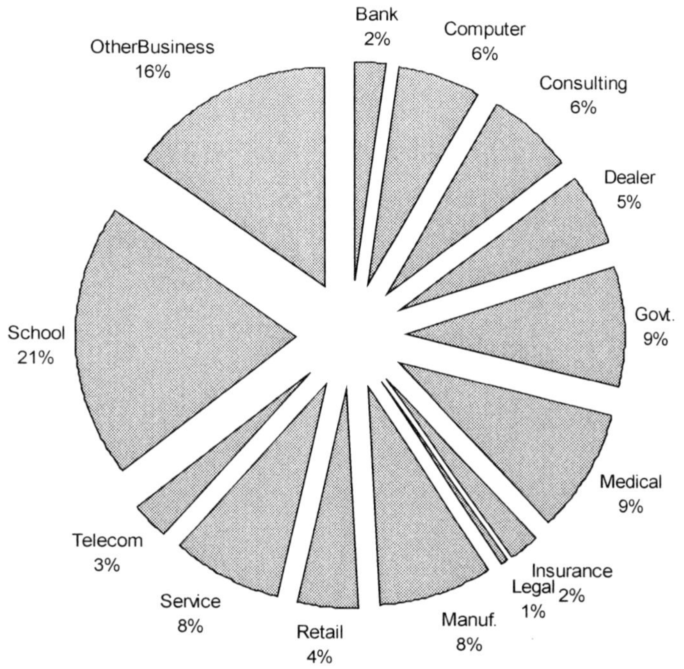

Table 2. End user-developed applications

Types of Applications	Percentage of Respondents
Spreadsheets	74.0
Presentations	60.6
Database Related	54.5
Static Web Pages	40.1
Graphical	37.3
Dynamic Web Pages	25.0
GUI Based	19.5

applications they developed, while 40% and 20% reported that others in the department and other departments respectively used their applications. To better understand the type and complexity of applications developed by end users, respondents were asked to specify the number of different levels of applications they had developed. They are given below:

- **Level 1 application:** Development of simple applications such as presentations (e.g., PowerPoint presentations) and/or creation of static Web pages using MS Word or other editors.
- **Level 2 application:** Medium-sized applications which include development of one or more of the following: spreadsheet applications using financial or statistical formulas; a statistical package such as SAS/SPSS; database applications that use SQL type queries; dynamic Web pages that use some scripting, database connectivity, and so forth.
- **Level 3 application:** Development of complex programs that involve extensive use of advanced features of COBOL or GUI-based languages such as Visual Basic/Visual FoxPro/Visual C++ and so forth. Applications involving CAD/CAM can be included here.

Table 3. Initial factor loadings with 11 items

Items	Factor 1	Factor 2	Factor 3
Developer1	.215	**.881**	-.003
Developer2	.359	**.789**	.093
Developer3	.116	**.847**	-.073
Developer4	.331	**.751**	.141
Operator1	.298	**.457**	.441
Operator2	.009	.078	**.893**
Operator3	.012	-.054	**.877**
Controller1	**.912**	.185	-.047
Controller2	**.913**	.181	-.034
Controller3	**.852**	.367	.074
Controller4	**.791**	.323	.155

Extraction Method: Principal Component Analysis; Rotation Method: Varimax; Rotation converged in five iterations.

While 41% of the respondents reported that they had developed six or more Level 1 applications, 25% and 11% reported developing six or more Level 2 and Level 3 applications respectively. The data clearly shows the range and depth of end user applications, implying that EUC applications are becoming more advanced.

RESULTS

To check for the end user classification instrument's validity, factor analysis was performed. End user classification using the instrument is presented later in this section.

Factor Analysis

Construct validity measures how well the instrument measures the construct. Exploratory factor analysis yielded three factors with eigenvalues greater than 1.0. A total dataset of 292 responses is greater than the required minimum to conduct factor analysis on an instrument with 11 items and hence expected to yield fruitful results.

While the items for control and development dimensions loaded clearly, one operation item—'use of end user applications developed by the respondent'—had a weak loading with development factor. A closer analysis reveals that this item does not capture the operation dimension as expected since it represents the operation of self-developed applications; also 57% of the respondents do not represent the developer dimension (see Table 8). Thus, this item was dropped from the instrument. Subsequent factor analysis with 10 items resulted in three factors. These three factors (presented in Table 4) account for more than 80% of the variance.

Cronbach's alpha values for the instrument indicate scale reliability (see Table 5). All the values exceed 0.75 indicating acceptable internal consistency (Nunnally, 1978).

Confirmatory Factor Analysis

In order to assess the validity of the scales, a confirmatory factor analysis (CFA) using LISREL 8.0 (Jöreskog & Sörbom, 1996) was conducted. In the CFA model, each item is restricted to load on its pre-specified factor. The overall goodness

Table 4. Result of final exploratory factor analysis with 10 items

Items	Factor 1	Factor 2	Factor 3
Developer1	.221	**.883**	-.002
Developer2	.366	**.796**	.093
Developer3	.120	**.849**	-.075
Developer4	.338	**.753**	.133
Operator2	.009	.090	**.898**
Operator3	.016	-.031	**.905**
Controller1	**.912**	.185	-.055
Controller2	**.913**	.181	-.043
Controller3	**.855**	.362	.052
Controller4	**.796**	.314	.123

Extraction Method: Principal Component Analysis; Rotation Method: Varimax; Rotation converged in five iterations.
Developer1–Developer4: Development dimension items
Operator1–Operator2: Operation dimension items
Controller1–Controller4: Control dimension items

Table 5. Reliability of constructs

Factors (No. of items)	Alpha	N
Development (4)	0.8869	292
Operation (2)	0.7766	288
Control (4)	0.9318	292

of fit of the measurement model was examined by using seven common fit statistics (χ^2/df ratio, NNFI, IFI, CFI, GFI, RMSEA, and SRMR) shown in Table 6. As seen from the fit indices generated by the measurement model, the data fit the model moderately to well (χ^2_{32} (N = 292) = 193.32, NNFI = .89, IFI = .92, CFI = .92, GFI = 0.87, RMSEA = 0.14, SRMR = .06) by exceeding or almost meeting the recommended thresholds commonly suggested within the literature.

The chi-square test assessed the goodness-of-fit between the reproduced and observed correlation matrices. Wheaton, Mutchen, Alwin, and Summers (1997) suggest that the chi-square to degree of freedom ratio (χ^2/df) is reasonable for values of five or less. The ratio for the saturated model was 6.04 and is slightly above the acceptable fit level recommended by Wheaton et al. (1997). As noted by Bentler and Bonnett (1990), the chi-square test is sensitive to sample size, and therefore additional fit indices are necessary to adequately assess the model fit to the data. The NNFI (Benter & Bonnett, 1980), IFI (Bollen, 1989), and CFI (Bentler, 1990) represent other goodness-of-fit criteria not sensitive to sample size (Bentler & Long, 1993). These three indices improve the fit of the hypothesized model over the null model, in which all observed variables are specified as uncorrelated. These indices have expected values of 1.00 when the hypothesized model is true in the population. Acceptable thresholds for NNFI, IFI, and CFI are > .90 (Kelloway, 1998). In the CFA analysis conducted for the current study, the NNFI of 0.888 is slightly below the recommended threshold of 0.90, while the IFI of 0.921 and CFI of 0.920 exceeded the 0.90 thresholds established as a good fit to the data. GFI provides an indication of the amount of variance and covariance accounted for by the model (Diamantopoulos & Siguaw, 2000). The GFI in this study is 0.869, which is slightly below the GFI value of 0.90 threshold for a good fit to the data (Diamantopoulos & Siguaw, 2000; Kelloway, 1998). Although the GFI level could be improved by dropping additional items, the procedure to drop additional items was stopped in order to preserve the content of the operator measure.

The RMSEA is an estimate of the discrepancy between the original and reproduced covariance matrices (Wheaton et al., 1997). Browne and Cudeck (1993) suggest that an RMSEA of .10 or less indicates an acceptable fit. The RMSEA of 0.142, for the current measurement model, exceeded the recommended level, indicating that the residuals do not fit the data well. The SRMR is a measure of the discrepancies between the implied and

Table 6. Fit indices

Fit Index	Recommended Value	Measurement Model	Source
χ^2/df	≤ 5.00	6.04	Wheaton et al., 1997
NNFI	≥ 0.90	0.888	Kelloway, 1998
IFI	≥ 0.90	0.921	Kelloway, 1998
CFI	≥ 0.90	0.920	Kelloway, 1998
GFI	≥ 0.90	0.869	Diamantopoulos & Siguaw, 2000
RMSEA	≤ 0.10	0.142	Steiger, 1990
SRMR	≤ 0.05	0.058	Kelloway, 1998

Table 7. Discriminant validity test using AVE comparison

Constructs	Items*	Composite Reliability	AVE
Developer	D1, D2, D3, D4	0.888	0.666
Operator	O1, O2	0.518	0.379
Controller	C1, C2, C3, C4	0.933	0.776

**D1, D2, D3, D4—Developer items; O1, O2—Operator items; C1, C2, C3, C4—Controller items*

observed covariance matrices (Kelloway, 1998). SRMRs less than .05 indicate a good fit to the data (Diamantopoulos & Siguaw, 2000), although this fit index is sensitive to the scale of measurement of the model variables (Kelloway, 1998). The SRMR of 0.058 for the current analysis slightly exceeds the recommended threshold.

Recognizing the adequate model fit for the measurement model, further analysis was conducted to assess the psychometric properties of the scales. This assessment of the construct validity considered the dimensions of convergent validity and discriminant validity. Convergent validity was assessed by three measures, as shown in Tables 4 and 7: factor loading, composite construct reliability, and average variance extracted (Fornell & Larcker, 1981).

The composite construct reliabilities for the developer and the controller constructs are well within the commonly accepted range of 0.70 or greater (Gefen, Straub, & Boudreau, 2000). The composite reliability for the operator construct did not make this threshold. Finally, the average variance extracted (AVE) measures the amount of variance captured by the construct in relation to the amount of variance due to measurement error (Fornell & Larcker, 1981). The AVEs for the developer and controller constructs were all above the recommended level of 0.50 (Hair, Anderson, Tatham, & Black, 1998), which meant that more than 50% of the variances observed in the items were explained by their underlying constructs. The AVE for the operator construct failed to meet this threshold, and only 38% of the variance obtained in the items was explained by the underlying construct. Therefore, the developer and controller constructs in the measurement model had adequate convergent validity, while the operator construct requires additional modification and restructuring in order to adequately capture the underlying construct.

Classification Analysis

A seven-point scale was used to solicit responses for categorizing respondents as developers, operators, controllers, or any combination of these (see Table 8). If the average score of the items in each factor was equal to or above 4 (midpoint of Likert scale), then the respondent was assigned to that category. For example, respondent 21 had an average score of 6.25 for the development (D) factor, 3 for the operation (O) factor, and 6.5 for the control (C) factor. Hence, the respondent was classified as a user-developer/controller. It is important to point out that this respondent presented a measure of the operation dimension, but it was ignored. As Cotterman and Kumar (1989) note, it is possible to classify end users to more than eight types.

Table 8 shows that the 18.5% of respondents represent all the dimensions vis-à-vis development, operation, and control. The dimension analysis shows that approximately 43%, 44%, and 60% of the respondents represent the development, operation, and control dimensions respectively. It is surprising to note that 60% of the respondents represent the control dimension. End user computing became widespread primarily due to users becoming self-reliant for their information needs by developing their own applications with or without support from others. User independence from a centralized IT department is apparent from the analysis. In other words, the data shows that a majority of the respondents control their end user computing environment. To determine whether the instrument classified users accurately, job titles of respondents were compared between controllers and non-controllers (classified using the instrument) to check whether controllers hold higher administrative positions than non-controllers or not. Respondents were asked to select one among the six job titles that closely matched their current title. The choices provided are: (1) operator/technician, (2) clerical staff, (3) supervisor, (4) middle-level manager, (5) upper-level manager, and (6) CEO/CIO level administrator. Table 9b shows that there is a significant difference between these groups.

Table 9a shows that more respondents in the controller category hold higher administrative positions than respondents in the non-controller category. This is logical since by virtue of their administrative positions, controllers should be able to control the end user computing environment better than non-controllers. Similarly, more respondents in the non-controller category hold lower administrative positions than respondents in the controller category (except for the title *operator/technician*).

Comparisons were also made between developers and non-developers based on the number

Table 8. Respondent end user classification

End User Types	Frequency	Percent
User-Consumer	56	19.2
User-Developer	15	5.1
User-Operator	41	14.0
User-Controller	45	15.4
User-Developer/Operator	6	2.1
User-Operator/Controller	26	8.9
User-Developer/Controller	49	16.8
User-Developer/Operator/ Controller	54	18.5

of Level 1, Level 2, and Level 3 applications developed. Tables 10a through 10c show that significant differences exist between these groups of respondents in the number of applications developed. These analyses show that the instrument validity remains strong.

To compare how well this classification scheme compares with Rockart and Flannery's (1983) scheme, respondents were presented with Rockart and Flannery's description of the four user types (presented above) and asked to select one that best describes them. The respondent selections were compared against their development dimension scores. To facilitate this comparison, respondents were divided into four equal groups based on their average development scores (see Table 11). In this comparison, respondents who have low development dimension scores (D_1) should represent non-programming end users and those with high scores should represent functional support personnel (D_4). The cross-tabulation presented in Table 9 shows interesting results. As expected, the development dimension groups match Rockart and Flannery user types to some extent. For each Rockart and Flannery type, the corresponding developer dimension number is the highest in each row. Thus, there is limited support for the conclusion that the instrument subsumes Rockart and Flannery's classification scheme.

DISCUSSION OF RESULTS AND LIMITATIONS

The results of the main study, when compared with the pilot study, were really not that different. Both results indicate that the validity of the instrument is strong and presents a quantitative, alternative, and accurate way of classifying end users based on the user cube. The researchers in the operationalization of end user classification have long ignored control, a major factor in the

Table 9a. Non-controller/controller title cross tabulation*

Count	Title						Total
	1	2	3	4	5	6	
Non-Controller	13	29	19	18	4	0	83
Controller	24	9	14	43	27	25	142
Total	37	38	33	61	31	25	225

N = 163 for controllers, 107 for non-controllers. Since some respondents did not fill out job title question, N differs for controllers/non-controllers from the value in Table 8.

Table 9b. Chi-square tests

	Value	df	Asymp. Sig. (2-sided)
Pearson Chi-Square	55.188[a]	6	.000
Likelihood Ratio	63.848	6	.000
N of Valid Cases	225		

[a]0 cells (.0%) have expected count less than 5. The minimum expected count is 9.22.

Table 10. t-tests for number of applications means for developers vs. non-developers

t-test for Equality of Means						
t	df	Sig. (2-tailed)	Mean Difference	Std. Error Difference	95% Confidence Interval of the Difference	
					Lower	Upper
6.088	274	.000	0.83	.136	.561	1.097

(a) t-test for number of Level 1 applications means for developers vs. non-developers
N = 116 for developers (mean = 2.88), 160 for non-developers (mean = 2.05)

t-test for Equality of Means						
t	df	Sig. (2-tailed)	Mean Difference	Std. Error Difference	95% Confidence Interval of the Difference	
					Lower	Upper
7.263	270	.000	.92	.126	.667	1.164

(b) t-test for number of Level 2 applications means for developers vs. non-developers
N = 113 for developers (mean = 2.47), 159 for non-developers (mean = 1.55)

t-test for Equality of Means						
t	df	Sig. (2-tailed)	Mean Difference	Std. Error Difference	95% Confidence Interval of the Difference	
					Lower	Upper
5.501	263	.000	.52	.094	.331	.701

(c) t-test for number of Level 3 applications means for developers vs. non-developers
N = 109 for developers (mean = 1.67), 156 for non-developers (mean = 1.15)

spread of EUC. Now, researchers can study end user dynamics more closely to explore the interactions between dimensions such as control, and other constructs such as end user satisfaction. For practitioners, using the instrument provides an immediate benefit of identifying which dimensions are predominant within their firms. For example, if the control dimension is predominant, this may be viewed as a threat by centralized IT departments since end user groups may attempt to gain access to centralized IT resources such as corporate data. Conversely, in a more decentralized culture, this same attribute may represent a positive, namely the opportunity for the IT department to reduce the amount of support (and thus, costs) provided to the group.

Similarly, if the development dimension is predominant, management might take measures to minimize the risks of EUC by providing appropriate support or devising control policies. The final 10-item instrument has the following three factors: (1) development, (2) operation, and (3) control. Demographic data shows that contemporary end users develop advanced applications such as dynamic Web pages. Spreadsheets still

Table 11. Rockart-Flannery and developer dimension comparison

	Developer Dimension Scores*				Total
Rockart-Flannery Types	D_1	D_2	D_3	D_4	
Non-programming end user	21	10	6	2	39
Command-level users	28	54	18	7	107
End user programmers	6	21	32	18	77
Functional support personnel	2	10	18	33	63
Total	57	95	74	60	286

Average developer dimension score for D1 is 0–1.75, D2—greater than 1.75 and <= 3.5, D3—greater than 3.5, and <= 5.25, D4—greater than 5.25 and <= 7.0

seem to be the most popular end user applications developed by 74% of the respondents.

It is imperative to note some of the limitations of this study. First, the response rate could not be determined since the data was collected using the Internet by posting a Web-based survey and advertising using news and Usenet groups. The memberships in these groups are dynamic, and hence it is difficult to assess the response rate. However, respondents represent a wide variety of industries and are from various levels of management. This is expected to nullify any possible biases in data. Second, since data was collected through a Web page, non-Internet users are not represented by the sample. Given the wide acceptance and use of Internet, this may not be a serious limitation. Given the desirability of improved factor analysis, future research might impose tighter controls on access to the online survey in order to improve the model fit. Third, sub-factors within each construct may be possible. For example, end users may have control over application initiation and data collection, but may not have the authority to decide hardware and software purchases. In such instances, the control dimension needs two factors. Fourth, classifying job titles into higher- and lower-level administrative positions involves a great deal of subjectivity. Finally, the items used in the operation construct may be too generic, and hence the instrument may be improved by refining the items in this construct. It can also be argued that the operation dimension itself is limited in its usefulness of classification since the main purpose of operation is to use the applications for decision making. Hence, other dimensions such as *decision-making effectiveness* (through use of EUC applications), *application usage*, or *application usefulness/effectiveness in making better decisions* may be more appropriate than the operation dimension. The operation dimension may therefore be a major weakness of the user cube and the reason why this classification scheme is not paid much attention in IS research. Additional research is crucial to test/modify this dimension. The instrument, however, serves as a good starting point to researchers and practitioners alike to study end user groups in more depth.

REFERENCES

Alavi, M., & Weiss, I.R. (1985–1986). Managing the risks associated with end-user computing.

Journal of Management Information Systems, 2(3), 5–20.

Bentler, P.M. (1990). Comparative fit indexes in structural models. *Psychological Bulletin, 107*(2), 238–246.

Bentler, P.M., & Bonnett, D.G. (1980). Significance tests and goodness of fit in covariance structures. *Psychological Bulletin, 88,* 588–606.

Bentler, P.M., & Long, J.S. (1993). *Testing structural equation models.* Newbury Park, CA: Sage.

Bergeron, F., & Berube, C. (1988). The management of the end-user computing environment: An empirical investigation. *Information and Management, 14*(3), 107–113.

Bollen, K.A. (1989). *Structural equations with latent variables.* New York: John Wiley & Sons.

Brancheau, J.C., Vogel, D.R., & Wetherbe, J.C. (1985). An investigation of the information center from the user's perspective. *Data Base, 17*(1), 4–17.

Browne, M.W., & Cudeck, R. (1993). Robustness of normal theory methods in the analysis of linear latent variant models. In K.A. Bollen & J.S. Long (Eds.), *Testing structural equation models* (pp. 136–162). Newbury Park, CA: Sage.

Cotterman, W.W., & Kumar, K. (1989). User cube: A taxonomy of end users. *Communications of the ACM, 32*(11), 1313–1320.

Davis, G.B. (1982). *Caution: User developed systems can be dangerous to your organization.* MISRC-WP-82-04, MIS Research Center, University of Minnesota, USA.

Davis, S.A., & Bostrom, R.P. (1993). Training end users: An experimental investigation of the roles of the computer interface and training methods. *MIS Quarterly, 17*(1), 61–85.

Diamantopoulos, A., & Siguaw, J. (2000). *Introducing LISREL.* Thousand Oaks, CA: Sage.

Fornell, C., & Larcker, D.F. (1981). Evaluating structural equation models with unobservable variables and measurement error. *Management Science, 40*(4), 440–465.

Gefen, D., Straub, D.W., & Boudreau, M.-C. (2000). Structural equation modeling and regression: Guidelines for research practice. *Communications of the AIS, 4*(7), 1–70.

Govindarajulu, C. (2002). The status of help desk support: A survey. *Communications of the ACM, 45*(1), 97–100.

Govindarajulu, C., & Reithel, B.J. (1998). Beyond the information center: An instrument to measure end-user computing support from multiple sources. *Information & Management, 33*(5), 241–250.

Govindarajulu, C., Reithel, B.J., & Sethi, V. (2000). A model of end user attitudes and intentions toward alternative sources of support. *Information & Management, 37*(2), 77–86.

Guimaraes, T. (1999). Empirically testing the relationship between end-user computing problems and information center success factors. *Decision Sciences, 30*(2), 393–413.

Hair, J.T., Anderson, R.E., Tatham, R.L., & Black, W.C. (1998). Multivariate data analysis (5th ed.). Upper Saddle River, NJ: Prentice Hall.

Joreskog, K.G., & Sorbom, D. (1996). *Lisrel 8: User's reference guide.* Chicago: Scientific Software International.

Kasper, G.M., & Cerveny, P.C. (1985). A laboratory study of user characteristics and decision-making performance in end-user computing. *Information and Management, 9*(2), 87–96.

Kelloway, E.K. (1998). *Using Lisrel for structural equation modeling: A researcher's guide.* Thousand Oaks, CA: Sage.

Lee, D.M.S. (1986). Usage patterns and sources of assistance for personal computer users. *MIS Quarterly, 10*(4), 313–325.

Leitheiser, R.L., & Wetherbe, J.C. (1986). Approaches to end-user computing: Service may spell success. *Journal of Information Systems Management, 3*(1), 9–14.

McLean, E.R. (1979). End users as application developers. *MIS Quarterly, 3*(4), 37–46.

Mirani, R., & King, W.R. (1994). The development of a measure for end-user computing support. *Decision Sciences, 25*(4), 481–498.

Nord, G.D., & Nord, J.H. (1994). Perceptions and attitudes of end users on technology issues. *Journal of System Management, 45*(11), 12–15.

Nunnally, J.C. (1978). *Psychometric theory.* New York: McGraw-Hill.

Rainer, K., & Carr, H. (1992). Are information centers responsive to user needs? *Information and Management, 22*(2), 113–121.

Rivard, S., & Huff, S.L. (1984). User developed applications: Evaluation of success from the DP department perspective. *MIS Quarterly, 8*(1), 39–49.

Rockart, J.F., & Flannery, L.S. (1983). The management of end-user computing. *Communications of the ACM, 26*(10), 776–784.

Steiger, J.H. (1990. Structural model evaluation and modification: An internal estimation approach. *Multivariate Behavioral Research, 25,* 173–190.

Wheaton, B., Mutchen, B., Alwin, D.F., & Summers, G.F. (1977). Assessing reliability and stability in panel models. In D.R. Heise (Ed.), *Assessing reliability and stability in panel models* (pp. 84–136). San Francisco: Jossey-Bass.

This work was previously published in the Journal of Organizational and End User Computing, Vol. 20, Issue 2, edited by M. Mahmood, pp. 61-81, copyright 2008 by IGI Publishing (an imprint of IGI Global).

Chapter 9
Social and Usage-Process Motivations for Consumer Internet Access

Thomas F. Stafford
University of Memphis, USA

ABSTRACT

Differences between light and heavy users of America Online are investigated using theoretical expectations derived from recent research on uses and gratifications theory. Measures of Internet-usage-process gratifications and Internet socialization gratifications were utilized to test for differences between light and heavy Internet users in the consumer market, and it was expected that heavy users would be more socially motivated in their Internet use while light users would be more motivated by gratifications related to usage processes. However, results indicate that both heavy and light users are more motivated by usage factors, although the difference between usage and social motivation was more pronounced for heavy users. Heavy users are more socially motivated than light users, but both heavy and light users show a significant preference for process uses and gratifications as compared to social uses and gratifications for Internet use.

INTRODUCTION

Looking back on its consumer-market introduction and early growth phases, the Internet has dramatically changed society in terms of its communication and consumption behaviors. It was predicted soon after its introduction to the general public that the Internet would have important social implications (Artle & Averous, 1973), and recent years have been spent recognizing and observing this social impact as it has manifested itself in the consumer marketplace. The proliferation of Internet service providers (ISPs), instant messaging, e-mail, chat rooms, Web logging, and the like are all emblematic of the new and important social role that Internet use plays in daily life.

In the process of adopting the Internet as a communication channel, society has been evolving away from traditional mass-exposure media in favor of the emerging interactive medium (Drèze & Zufryden, 1997; Stafford & Stafford, 1998), in which users actively involve themselves (i.e., interact) with the medium to personally direct its content retrieval and display. Along the way, individual communication patterns have also evolved toward a more network-enabled interactive social model as individuals proceed to utilize the new communications capabilities of the Internet medium to interact with each other (Rogers & Albritton, 1995). While much of the recent focus on the Internet has been on the transactional properties of the medium for e-commerce purposes, scholars have always recognized that the evolution of the Internet would serve both transactional and communicative goals (Drèze & Zufryden; Eighmey & McCord, 1998; Lohse & Spiller, 1998).

This study reports on consumer motivations related to the use of the Internet via the America Online (AOL) Internet-access service; although there are a number of ways to gain access to the Internet, including always-on business and government broadband network connections, the predominant consumer-market mode of access for the majority of users is still through ISP services ("U.S. Home Broadband Penetration," 2004), of which AOL holds an appreciable share of the market (IDC, 2004). Hence, what is learned about Internet use in a broad study of AOL users can be representative of the broader consumer market for Internet use (Stafford, Stafford, & Schkade, 2004).

Uses and gratifications theory (U&G) is utilized to investigate Internet-related motivations and enjoyments, and associated uses. A large sample of America Online users is surveyed, and subsequent analysis is performed with U&G measures to identify differences between heavy and light users with regard for their preference for, and motivations related to, uses and gratifications for Internet use.

LITERATURE AND HYPOTHESES

Researchers freely recognize the media-like capabilities and characteristics of the Internet (Armstrong & Hagel, 1996; Eighmey & McCord, 1998; Kannan, Chang, & Whinston, 1998; Turban, Lee, King, & Chung, 2000). In considering the Internet from a media-use perspective, robust theoretical models from previous investigations of various media can be applied; one of these is uses and gratifications, which is a special model of communications theory useful for understanding the adoption of new computer-mediated communication technologies.

Uses and Gratifications for Internet Use

U&G is a theory-driven approach to understanding media-use motivations and might be characterized by an inductive method for developing classifications of different motivations and functions of media use (Ruggiero, 2000; Weiser, 2001). The theoretical perspective of U&G concentrates on motives for and consequences of media use (Rubin, 1985), with the underlying presumption that individuals are motivated, as opposed to random or mindless, in their media use (Katz, 1959). U&G describes why consumers use a particular medium and what functions the medium they choose serves for them (Katerattanakul, 2002) by building profile groupings of related uses and theoretically associated gratifications. The major assumptions of U&G are that media audiences are goal directed and seek out media and messages to satisfy specific needs (Johnson & Kaye, 2003; Papacharissi & Rubin, 2000; Ruggiero). The U&G approach to understanding media use involves identifying basic needs, and identifying the related actions to engage in media use related to those needs, in order to determine the need-satisfying gratifications that arise from motivated media use (Foucault & Scheufele, 2002).

In the U&G tradition, media use is said to be associated with psychological motivations that prompt audience members to purposefully select media and media content in order to satisfy needs arising from these motivations (Lin, 1999). Hence, the terms *uses* and *gratifications* refer loosely to media-use activities that arise from unmet needs in audience members (uses), and the gratifying need-satisfaction process that results from engaging in motivated media use triggered by some need (gratifications). Uses and resulting gratifications are generally interrelated so far as media consumption is concerned since the need-satisfaction effect occurs contemporaneously with the media-consumption act (Matthews & Schrum, 2003; Ruggiero, 2000).

The U&G approach to media research is largely descriptive (Matthews & Schrum, 2003), using multivariate analysis to build U&G profiles of various usage and gratification areas (cf., Ebersole, 2000; Korgaonkar & Wolin, 1999; McDonald-Russell, 2002; Mitchell, 1999; Ruggiero, 2000; Stafford & Stafford, 2001; Weiser, 2001). The typical approach is designed to identify needs related to the use of media as part of understanding how needs related to media use are met in their use. Shown in Figure 1, Fawkes and Gregory's (2000) visual depiction of the process is instructive and aids greatly in the understanding of the processes and audience variables involved in the uses and gratifications for media. This depiction of the general theoretical concept demonstrates that needs arise from audience-member motivations, leading to expectations that drive media exposure, which results in needs being met: the ubiquitous gratifications arising from media use in the U&G paradigm.

U&G theory was comprehensively applied in studies of the television medium as a technological innovation decades ago (cf., Katz, 1959; Klapper, 1963; McGuire, 1974). Findings from U&G television studies have already been applied in Internet research (Eighmey & McCord, 1998; Kaye & Johnson, 2002; Rafaeli, 1988), but only by applying measures previously developed for specific television use. However, Internet-specific U&G measures have recently been demonstrated in the MIS (management information system) literature (Stafford, 2001; Stafford et al., 2004).

Internet uses and needs are well understood within the U&G framework (Eighmey & McCord, 1998; Newhagen & Rafaeli, 1996), and many U&G theorists believe that uses and gratifications is a research tradition eminently suited for Internet study (Johnson & Kaye, 2003; Lin, 1999; Ruggiero, 2000; Weiser, 2001), primarily because of the active-audience tenet of the U&G paradigm in the context of the necessity of active audience interaction with the medium for Internet use (Lin; Papacharissi & Rubin, 2000).

Applications of U&G theory from studies that predate the Internet consistently found motivations that were dichotomized between general areas of media content or media-usage processes (Cutler & Danowski, 1980). Modern Internet analogs to TV-based process and content gratification profiles have been identified (Stafford & Stafford, 1998; Stafford et al., 2004); they generally characterize content gratifications as related to information-content access and related Internet learning activities, while process gratifications are generally

Figure 1. Uses and gratifications illustrated

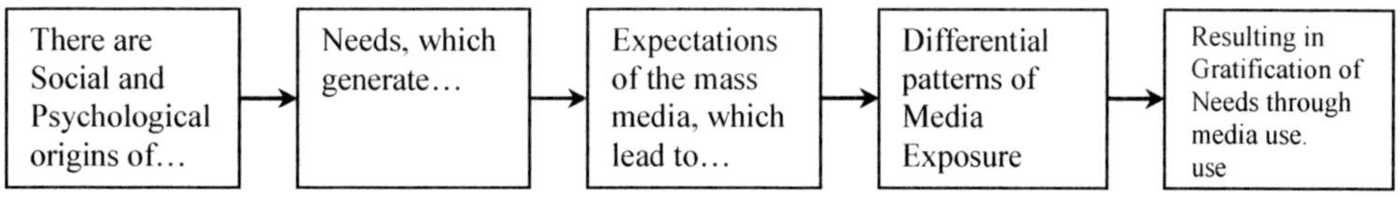

characterized as involving either searching or surfing Internet-usage behavior.

Even though television U&G studies and early Internet studies based on television measures found the same consistent process and content dichotomy of motivations, more recent Internet-specific U&G research has identified a new dimension of social gratifications for Internet use, in recognition of the interactive social dynamics that are supported by the network (Ebersole, 2000; Mitchell, 1999; Stafford & Stafford, 2001). The two basic motivations for media use in television research have always been media usage processes and media content motivations. However, more recent Internet-adoption research utilizing U&G (Stafford, 2003) examines three motivational dimensions (process, content, and social motivations, unlike TV research, which only focused on usage process and media content). This recent Internet-usage research has shown that the key motivations for Internet use tend to center on just two of the three motivational dimensions—usage processes and social motivations—and that content-based motivations play a less distinctive role in differentiating between different groupings of users. Hence, there is reason to expect that the primary differentiation between heavy and light Internet users will be the degree to which process gratifications vs. social gratifications predominate as a primary reason for going online rather than the differential influence of online content (Stafford, 2003). For this reason, the theoretical focus here is on differences between heavy and light Internet users as distinguished by audience responses to usage processes and social Internet uses and gratifications.

Internet-Usage Rates and Social Implications

A long-standing critical characterization of the U&G paradigm is that it is a functionalist approach that may lack the power to predict individual differences between users (Matthews & Schrum, 2003). This potential shortcoming is reconciled in the robust means-end orientation of Internet U&G studies that give specific consideration to the interplay between audience activity levels and gratifications (Ruggiero, 2000). Motivations related to the process of Internet use and the social benefits of Internet use have the most promising capabilities to differentiate between groups of users who access a given technology such as the Internet more or less frequently (Adams, Nelson, & Todd, 1992; Emmannouildes & Hammond, 2000; Kraut, Mukhopadhyay, Szczypula, Kiesler, & Scherlis, 1999; Savloainen, 1999). Audience activity levels are a credible link between sought gratifications and motivations underlying the gratifying use of the Internet (Johnson & Kaye, 2003) because of the inherent interrelation between degree of use and degree of gratification, in addition to the unique aspect of the Internet medium for fostering active audience use as compared to other more passive media.

There are several ways to look at motivations for Internet use as related to user activity levels. One approach is demographic; it has been observed that heavy users frequently use the Internet for social purposes (Emmannouildes & Hammond, 2000; Karahanna & Straub, 1999), and Internet utilities related to social interaction can be considered a motivating factor influencing Internet use. For example, e-mail represents a key reason for initiating online sessions (Emmannouildes & Hammond; Savloainen, 1999). In the home, where much consumer use of the Internet transpires, e-mail appears to be the primary motivation for use of the Internet (Kraut et al., 1999).

Research Hypotheses

Lighter users of the Internet are generally highly motivated by the need to learn how to use the technology through direct experience (Stafford, 2003) and, hence, might be expected to have largely process-related Internet uses and gratifications. In contrast, heavy users have experience and should not be particularly gratified by the learning processes found in usage experience, but are more motivated by the utility of the online medium—in particular, social communication uses of the Internet such as e-mail (Emmannouildes & Hammond, 2000). In the present study, heavy and light users in the consumer market are operationally defined based on user responses to a semantic differential scale that asks, "How frequently do you use the Web?" User responses were benchmarked against the sample mean for the usage frequency question, and specific expectations for differences between subsequent categorizations of heavy and light users of the AOL Internet service are as follows.

H1: *Heavy Internet users should be significantly more motivated than light users by social uses and gratifications.*

H2: *Light Internet users should be significantly more motivated than heavy users by process uses and gratifications.*

METHOD

With the cooperation of Digital Marketing Services, the internal online research division for Internet service provider AOL, data for analysis were collected at AOL's online research site, Opinion Place, from a large sample of AOL users. Nine hundred fifteen individuals, compensated for their participation with American Airlines frequent-flyer points, completed usable surveys. During the time this survey was active, 12,890 individuals were screened by AOL at the Opinion Place site and were randomly assigned to 18 currently active AOL studies, of which this study was one. Queuing software ensured that each respondent, once selected for any of the 18 studies, could not participate again for a fixed period of time (2 months).

Sample characteristics for the 18 rotating studies were reported in the aggregate by AOL, and the pool of respondents available for assignment to the study pool was considered to be reasonably balanced across age, income, gender, and geographical location. A strict condition of outside access to company data at AOL's internal research division is the maintenance of individual anonymity of respondents, and the author was not permitted to ask specific respondents for demographic information. However, AOL's proprietary demographic studies conducted on the available participant pool for the period, summarized in Table 1, demonstrate that there were only minor demographic differences between participants recruited through Opinion Place, general users of the AOL service, and Internet users at large. In light of the demographic analysis conducted by AOL, and in consideration of other available research (Stafford et al., 2004), the data were considered representative of AOL users, and in light of demographic similarities demonstrated in Table 1, they were also reasonably representative of broader consumer Internet-user characteristics.

Respondents were presented with a questionnaire adapted from a recent uses and gratifications study of Internet use (Stafford, 2001; Stafford et al., 2004) providing a validated list of measures characteristic of Internet-specific uses and gratifications in accordance with the Gerbing and Anderson's (1988) structural equation modeling method of scale validation. The instrument included measures for both usage-process gratifications and social gratifications, and the scales used are represented in Table 2.

In the current survey, each measurement scale exhibited good levels of internal consistency. The social gratification scale produced a coefficient alpha of 0.80, and the usage process gratification scale produced an alpha of 0.8354. Convergent and discriminant properties of the candidate scales are also very good, as evidenced by the factor loading structure demonstrated in Stafford's (2001) analysis, shown in the appendix.

Respondents were instructed to indicate how important each specific aspect of using the Internet

Table 1. Sample characteristics and comparisons (source: AOL's Digital Marketing Services research)

	Internet	AOL	Opinion Place	U.S. Population
Gender				
- Male	46%	45%	30%	48%
- Female	54%	55%	70%	52%
Age				
- 18 – 24	12%	14%	10%	13%
- 25 – 34	19%	18%	24%	19%
- 35 – 44	24%	23%	28%	22%
- 45 – 54	24%	25%	22%	18%
- 55 +	21%	20%	17%	28%
Married	66%	63%	56%	53%
Income				
- $25K and less	9%	9%	19%	29%
- $26K – $49K	28%	27%	37%	28%
- $50K – $99K	41%	41%	34%	29%
- $100K or more	22%	23%	10%	13%
Children at Home	43%	43%	48%	33%
Location				
- Northeast	19%	20%	24%	19%
- Midwest	24%	23%	21%	23%
- South	32%	32%	37%	36%
- West	26%	25%	18%	22%

was to them, personally, by using the scales to indicate their opinion. Each potentially gratifying aspect of Internet use was presented with a seven-point semantic differential scale anchored by *very important* and *very unimportant*. As discussed above, the general expectation of this study was that heavy Internet users would be more socially oriented in their use of the network and its applications, while light users would be more usage-process oriented. This translates into the expectation that media-usage processes (i.e., process gratifications) would be more characteristic of light users, while Internet-mediated socialization would characterize heavy users.

In order to assess hypotheses related to differential Internet-usage levels, the respondent group was divided into categorizations of light and heavy usage groups based on a comparison of individual responses to the sample mean for responses to the semantic differential scale that asked, "How frequently do you use the Web?" Direct observational measures of user online activity were unavailable for this survey due to restrictions imposed by AOL's privacy policy, so a self-report measure of usage was required. Although self-reports are often considered less desirable than objective observations of behavior (Nisbett & Wilson, 1977), the typical problem with self-report validity is in regard to the potential lack of respondent accessibility to underlying cognitive processes that generate the reports as opposed to the actual reports themselves (Ericson & Simon, 1980).

Self-reports that are structured upon a defensible theory of how participants produce such responses can be quite valid as an alternative to objective measures (Ericson & Simon, 1980). In this case, real measures of actual usage time as a self-reported construct can be problematic, as shown in previous research (Gershuny & Rob-

Table 2. U&G measures (adopted from Stafford, 2001)

Social Gratifications (α = 0.80)

Chatting (live interactions)
Very Important ___:___:___:___:___:___:___ Very Unimportant

Friends (people who are important to you)
Very Important ___:___:___:___:___:___:___ Very Unimportant

Interaction (communicating with people)
Very Important ___:___:___:___:___:___:___ Very Unimportant

People (social interactions, in general)
Very Important ___:___:___:___:___:___:___ Very Unimportant

Process Gratifications (α = 0.8354)

Resources (online services and utilities that you use)
Very Important ___:___:___:___:___:___:___ Very Unimportant

Search Engines
Very Important ___:___:___:___:___:___:___ Very Unimportant

Searching (looking for specific information)
Very Important ___:___:___:___:___:___:___ Very Unimportant

Surfing (browsing the Web, not necessarily with a specific goal)
Very Important ___:___:___:___:___:___:___ Very Unimportant

Technology (information technology; computer systems that you access, learn about, or use when online)
Very Important ___:___:___:___:___:___:___ Very Unimportant

Web Sites
Very Important ___:___:___:___:___:___:___ Very Unimportant

inson, 1988; Jacobs, 1998), but the more relative assessment of usage frequency is actually a robust and theoretically defensible construct with a long history of experimentation to support it (Hasher & Zacks, 1979, 1984). In fact, as compared to more deliberative recall tasks such as remembering the duration of prior events, a robust body of psychological research supports the contention that people are surprisingly accurate at answering questions about the frequency of occurrence of some event, without even being aware of how they acquired the relevant information in the first place (Hasher & Zacks, 1984). This ability to automatically assess the frequency of events seems to be a basic operating characteristic of the human information-processing system that inevitably encodes into memory fundamental aspects of experiences, most specifically the frequency of their occurrence (Hasher & Zacks, 1979).

For this reason, it was determined that the usage-level question would be structured to assess the frequency of usage rather than structured to ascertain the time duration of usage. The usage-level question asked, "How frequently do you use the Web?" and the scale was anchored by *frequently* and *infrequently*. The usage-level scale was purposefully constructed with eight response points (without a specific midpoint) to prevent neutral responses in order to assure that a choice would be made by respondents that indicated some specific degree of either frequent or infrequent use. Users were categorized for analysis into light and heavy user groups based on a comparison to the sample mean for the question, which was 5.78. Three hundred forty-seven users were below the mean, while 568 were above the mean. This split operationally defined light and heavy users for purposes of analysis.

As an initial test, analysis of variance was performed in SPSS 10.0 based on the mean split of the sample and the process and social gratifications measures shown in Table 2. Results demonstrated distinctive differences between light and heavy users, but not in the directions expected.

RESULTS

ANOVA Tests

As shown in Table 3, there were differences (significant at levels better than $\alpha = 0.05$) for every variable in both process and social gratification dimensions between light and heavy Internet users. However, differences between heavy and light user groups were not all as expected. Heavy users did rate Internet social gratifications higher than did light users, but heavy users also rated usage-process gratifications higher than did the light users. H1 is confirmed, given that heavy users did display higher ratings than light users for social U&G variables. However, since light users did not display higher usage-process ratings, H2 is rejected.

The expectation that light users would be most motivated by usage processes and that heavy users would be most motivated by social uses and gratifications were not confirmed given the pattern of means for heavy users between process and social U&G variables. What emerges is a pattern of results that demonstrate that both heavy and light users are more motivated by Internet-usage processes even though expected differences between heavy and light users related to social uses and gratifications were discerned.

There are several general trends to consider. First, means across both usage levels were typically in the *important* range, consisting of scores that ranged above the midpoint of 4 for the seven-point scales that were used. There was a single exception to this: Mean scores for the *chatting* component of the social-gratification dimension were just at or a little below the scale midpoint for both light and heavy users.

The sharpest distinctions between light and heavy Internet users were in the form of the means for *interaction* on the social-gratification dimension and for *surfing* on the Internet-usage-process gratification. The light users were much less motivated than heavy users by both *interaction* and *surfing*. The highest mean on the social dimension across both heavy and light user groups was for *friends*, and the highest mean for the process dimension across both groups was *Web sites*. The lowest means were for the *chatting* aspect of the social dimension and the process variable *surfing*. Clearly, light users were not entirely process oriented, but it also can be said

Table 3. ANOVA results

Variable	Gratifications	$F_{1,806}$	p > F	Usage Group Means (sd)		
				Heavy	Light	Δ_{mean}
Chatting	Social	23.527	0.000	4.023	3.340	0.683
Friends	Social	12.359	0.000	5.773	5.352	0.421
Interaction	Social	50.099	0.000	5.278	4.406	**0.872**
People	Social	24.827	0.000	5.132	4.522	0.610
Resources	Process	48.707	0.000	6.190	5.553	0.637
Search Engines	Process	45.430	0.000	6.160	5.455	0.705
Searching	Process	55.237	0.000	6.305	5.654	0.651
Surfing	Process	146.51	0.000	5.835	4.386	**1.449**
Technology	Process	21.346	0.000	5.870	5.380	0.490
Web Sites	Process	86.811	0.000	6.312	5.487	0.825

that they were not as socially motivated as heavy users, either. Even so, the strongest means for the light user group were the usage gratifications of *resources* and *searching.*

Within-Subjects Analysis

Theoretical considerations generated the expectation that heavy users would be more socially oriented while light users would be more oriented toward usage processes in their motivations for Internet use. Instead, analysis indicates that heavy users and light users alike are more process oriented in their motivations. Moreover, means (as shown in Table 3) appear to be stronger for process U&G variables than for social variables. Given the lack of coherence with expectations generated from theoretical review, additional analysis is warranted to more fully understand the differences between heavy and light users in terms of their characteristic Internet-usage motivations.

First, a component-scale score was developed for the two areas of motivation. The variables *chatting, friends, interaction,* and *people*, representing social motivations, were summed and divided by the number of scale elements to provide an average social dimension rating per participant. The same process was followed for the media-usage-process variables *resources, search engines, searching, surfing, technology,* and *Web sites.* The resulting summed-scale scores served as overall measures of the respective gratification dimensions, and they were useful for assessing potential differences within usage groupings on motivation type and for detecting potential interactions between motivation type and usage-group level.

A within-subjects test was performed to assess for potential interactions between usage groups (heavy vs. light) and usage dimensions (media process motivation vs. social motivation). The resulting test for differences produced a significant effect for the usage dimension ($F_{1,913}$ = 411.42, p = 0.000), but the interaction effect for usage group by usage dimension did not reach significance even at the α = 0.10 level ($F_{1, 913}$ = 2.42, p = 0.135). Demonstrated graphically in Figure 2, the analysis of group means confirmed what was already apparent in earlier analysis: Heavy users had significantly higher scores than light users for both usage process (6.112 vs. 5.32, respectively) and social motivations (5.052 vs. 4.41, respectively). While it cannot be said, based on these results, that there are gratifications that are more or less specific to heavy users vs. light users, it does appear to be the case that there is a powerful effect for usage processes in motivating online services use among all users surveyed.

The list of means and individual variable tests are provided in Table 4.

Figure 2. Mean differences by usage group for gratifications

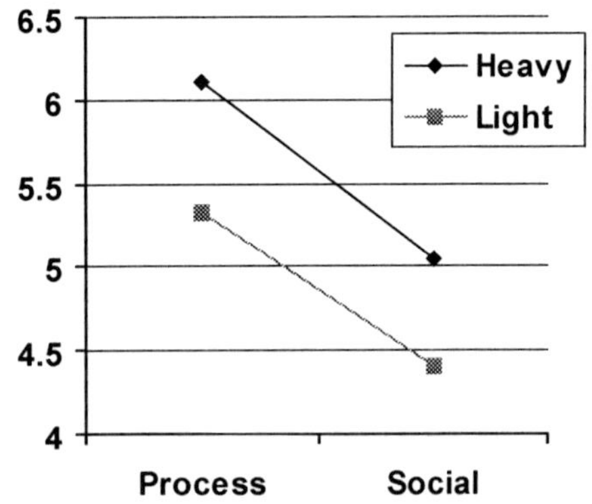

DISCUSSION

Among 915 AOL users, heavy and light users alike, Internet-usage-process U&G variables were consistently rated most important in considerations of ongoing Internet usage. Emerging views suggest that the ready availability of easy-to-use service providers like AOL can be highly predictive of Internet use in the consumer market (Rai, Ravichandran, & Samaddar, 1998). Certainly, ease of technology use is well established as a predictive variable related to actual usage levels (Venkatesh & Davis, 2000), and the prevalence of process-based uses and gratifications over social motivations among both heavy and light users in this study may be reflective of the robust association between ease of use and intention to use, as demonstrated in the technology-acceptance literature.

Heavy users, as predicted by prior research on demographics of Internet usage, are more socially motivated in their Internet use than light users.

Table 4. Motivation and usage group analysis

Variable	$F_{1,911}$	Usage Group Mean (sd) High	Usage Group Mean (sd) Low
Process Sum Score	411.42, p = 0.000	6.112 (.816)	5.32 (1.081)
Resources	53.431, p = 0.000	6.190 (1.04)	5.553 (1.42)
Search Engines	51.308, p = 0.000	6.160 (1.24)	5.455 (1.54)
Searching	59.546, p = 0.000	6.305 (1.04)	5.654 (1.32)
Surfing	153.61, p = 0.000	5.835 (1.44)	4.386 (1.84)
Technology	21.133, p = 0.000	5.870 (1.35)	5.380 (1.45)
Web Sites	95.350, p = 0.000	6.312 (1.00)	5.487 (1.38)
Social Sum Score	411.42, p = 0.000	5.052 (1.34)	4.405 (1.39)
Chat	13.431, p = 0.000	4.023 (2.09)	3.340 (1.95)
Friends	4.8360, p = 0.000	5.773 (1.55)	5.352 (1.71)
Interaction	27.071, p = 0.000	5.278 (1.61)	4.406 (1.69)
People	12.707, p = 0.000	5.132 (1.58)	4.522 (1.66)

Social communicative functionality is probably something one learns to use the Internet for after continued experience with the medium and its applications. In consideration of previous communication innovations, the telephone diffusion process is instructive. Phone adoption trends seem to have evolved in response to both economic and social desires in society (Flynn & Preston, 1999). When considering simple telecommunications functionality, the phone diffusion process was more influenced by social variables related to lifestyle (Dordick, 1993), yet when telephone technology was adapted to provide more media-like services, such as audio information services over the phone system, distinct media motivations surfaced to explain adoption patterns (Atkins, 1995). Interestingly, one of the most important societal characterizations of telephones has been that of a public good that acts through information exchange effects to reduce transaction costs in normal life (Artle & Averous, 1973). The Internet has widely been considered to have similar economic effects (Bakos, 1998), yet in comparison to telephones, it is something considerably more than just a communication resource. Hence, the social motivations related to communication across the Internet would appear to be just one part of a very rich and useful medium; this may be another reason why usage-process motivations seem to predominate among this sample. Users may consider communication functionality as but one small part of a large and useful media-usage process in the online world.

The Internet is also quite different from media innovations that have been studied before using the U&G paradigm, and the motivations for using it are not like those we have seen with previous media or communications innovations (Rai et al., 1998). Aside from the well-understood utility of networked computing, the Internet also provides a robust interpersonal communications venue that operates in parallel, perhaps even in synergy, with the machine communications venue provided by the network. As such, it would appear to represent an entirely new mode of human discourse and interaction (Rogers & Albritton, 1995). Certainly, there is more than enough anecdotal evidence of the power of e-mail as a motivation for heavier Internet use (Emmannouildes & Hammond, 2000; Kraut et al., 1999), and we have known for some time that heavy Internet users find social uses for the Internet, even if other uses are more cogent in explaining motivation for use.

Writers frequently characterize the Internet as an interactive medium while implying, most likely, not only the self-directed aspect of user direction of the display of the medium, but also its facilities and capabilities to support human interpersonal interaction through its many telecommunications applications. Experienced heavy users, operating with the benefit of greater experience and understanding, naturally would be the ones mostly like to perceive this potent combination of functionalities, and this may be the reason for the results we see here. If anything, the more you learn about the Internet, the more you use it, and the more you find to use it for.

Implications

The balance of customers available for recruitment to purchase Internet services is likely to be the less-than-heavy users who are not already committed to a service on a regular basis, so results that guide the improvement of Internet services for light users are particularly interesting to industry (D. Gonier, personal communication, July 2001). The results of this study do not so much provide affirmative guidance as to how to motivate light users to make better use of Internet services as much as they demonstrate that heavy users, in general, are more motivated to use Internet services than light users; this makes sense in the context of the beneficial effects of experience with the medium. However, in considering where the largest differences are between heavy and light usage groups, there are some suggestions for how to improve the usage experience for light users.

In general, light users are seen here to be more process motivated than socially motivated in their Internet use. This finding is theoretically consistent with the expectation that light users will be motivated to use the service more in the process of learning how to use it: a "practice makes perfect" effect (Stafford, 2003). Yet, of all the process variables reported in Table 3, *surfing* not only has the lowest score for light users on the process dimension, but it also represents the greatest difference between light and heavy users for the process dimension. Though it cannot be said with certainty, it may be useful to speculate that light users could benefit from navigational aids in their online experience—that a more gratifying Internet experience would arise from easier navigation in online browsing. This is a point that may bear additional scrutiny in future research.

A similar point could be made with respect to the low score by light users for *chatting*. AOL has been aware for some time of the need to find ways to guide and tutor users in the use of some of their online utilities (D. Gonier, personal communication, July 2001), and online coaches that interactively guide less experienced users in chat and navigation activities may well prove to be a useful feature.

To the extent that Internet service providers are anxious to retain heavier users, results indicate that heavy users prize the usage processes of the Internet. The strongest ratings among the heavy user group in this study were for process variables such as *Web sites*, *surfing*, *search engines*, and *resources*. Service providers would do well to ensure trouble-free and seamless service connectivity to maintain satisfaction among a usage group that is clearly motivated by usage-process gratifications. However, given that heavy users are also socially motivated, service providers would also do well to look to increasing the quality and range of applications that provide social connectivity.

Certainly, the market-share opportunities in the Internet service industry are in the recruitment of new users, so light users have a certain attraction (D. Gonier, personal communication, July 2001); however, it can also be said that with heavier users of Internet services, ISPs have a dramatically better revenue opportunity due to potential e-commerce utilization by more active customers, so heavy users also have their attraction in the Internet business. Results found here can provide actionable guidance to management in the industry, for purposes of customer retention among a less populous but more lucrative market segment, with regard to both competitive service improvements that may attract more new recruits and services that heavy users find compelling.

Limitations

The data for this study were drawn from users of the AOL Internet-access service. While a majority of consumer-market users obtain their online access through ISPs such as AOL, surveying AOL members is not the same thing as assessing generic Internet use. Demographic comparisons, shown in Table 1, demonstrate convincing similarities between the AOL sample base, the U.S. population, and Internet users in general. Even so, the sample frame for this study is limited by its character: Data were obtained from the sample frame used by the commercial research division of AOL, and conclusions generalize best to this specific context.

The categorization of light and heavy users was operationalized in accordance with a mean split based on a user self-report of Internet-usage frequency. Although this was the only option available when collecting data through AOL's research division, it is still an operationalization that is limited in comparison to direct behavioral measures of actual time spent online. Theoretical arguments made about the veracity of usage-frequency self-reports notwithstanding, the findings reported here should be considered in the context of this limitation.

CONCLUSION

Nine hundred fifteen AOL users were surveyed in an effort to determine whether theoretical expectations about the social utility of Internet use drawn from uses and gratifications theory would pertain to the new media-usage models that are emerging in recent Internet studies. While it was found that light users are not as usage-process motivated as expected, and that heavy users are less process oriented than light users, it was also found that there is a strong social component to Internet use, particularly among the heavy users. If customer retention is important, it is suggested that ISP operators focus on ensuring reliable, trouble-free use for their high-volume customers since they are likely to be more motivated by the usage processes related to the Internet. Yet, operators ought to be thinking about how to prevent undue restrictions and inconveniences related to the social use of the Internet for these heavy-use customers as well since heavy users appear to be equally process and socially motivated in their network use.

REFERENCES

Adams, D. A., Nelson, R. R., & Todd, P. A. (1992). Perceived usefulness, ease of use, and usage of information technology: A replication. *MIS Quarterly, 16*, 227-247.

Armstrong, A. G., & Hagel, J. (1996). The real value of online communities. *Harvard Business Review, 74*, 134-141.

Artle, R., & Averous, C. (1973). The telephone system as a public good: Static and dynamic aspects. *Bell Journal of Economics & Management Science, 4*, 89-100.

Atkins, D. (1995). Audio information services and the electronic media environment. *Information Society*, pp. 75-83.

Bakos, Y. (1998). The emerging role of electronic marketplaces on the Internet. *Communications of the ACM, 41*, 35-42.

Cutler, N. E., & Danowski, J. A. (1980). Process gratification in aging cohorts. *Journalism Quarterly, 57*, 269-277.

Dordick, H. S. (1993). America calling: A social history of the telephone to 1940. *Telecommunications Policy, 17*, 397-398.

Drèze, X., & Zufryden, F. (1997). Testing Web site design and promotional content. *Journal of Advertising Research, 37*, 77-91.

Ebersole, S. E. (2000). *Adolescents' use of the World Wide Web in ten public schools: A uses and gratifications approach.* Unpublished doctoral dissertation, Regent University, Virginia Beach, VA.

Eighmey, J., & McCord, L. (1998). Adding value in the information age: Uses and gratifications of sites on the World Wide Web. *Journal of Business Research, 41*, 187-194.

Emmannouildes, C., & Hammond, K. (2000). Internet usage: Predictors of active users and frequency of use. *Journal of Interactive Marketing, 14*, 17-32.

Ericson, K. A., & Simon, H. A. (1980). Verbal reports as data. *Psychological Review, 87*, 215-251.

Fawkes, J., & Gregory, A. (2000). Applying communication theories to the Internet. *Journal of Communication Management, 5*, 109-124.

Flynn, R., & Preston, P. (1999). The long-run diffusion and techno-economic performance of national telephone networks: A case study of Ireland, 1922-1998. *Telecommunications Policy, 23*, 437-457.

Foucault, B. E., & Scheufele, D. A. (2002). Web vs. campus store? Why students buy textbooks online. *Journal of Consumer Marketing, 19*, 409-423.

Gerbing, D. W., & Anderson, J. C. (1988). An updated paradigm for scale development incorporating unidimensionality and its assessment. *Journal of Marketing Research, 25*, 186-192.

Gershuny, J., & Robinson, J. P. (1988). Historical changes in household division of labor. *Demography, 25*, 537-552.

Hasher, L., & Zacks, R. T. (1979). Automatic and effortful processes in memory. *Journal of Experimental Psychology: General, 108*, 356-388.

Hasher, L., & Zacks, R. T. (1984). Automatic processing of fundamental information: The case of frequency of occurrence. *American Psychologist, 39*, 1372-1388.

Hoffman, D. L., & Novak, T. P. (1996). Marketing in hypermedia computer-mediated environments: Conceptual foundations. *Journal of Marketing, 60*, 50-68.

IDC. (2004). *U.S. consumer ISP market share.* Retrieved August 8, 2004, from http://www.idc.com/getdoc.jsp?containerId=30731

Jacobs, J. A. (1998). Measuring time at work: Are self-reports accurate? *Monthly Labor Review, 121*, 42-53.

Johnson, T. J., & Kaye, B. K. (2003). Around the World Wide Web in 80 ways. *Social Science Computer Review, 21*, 304-325.

Kannan, P. K., Chang, A., & Whinston, A. B. (1998). Marketing information on the I-way. *Communications of the ACM, 41*, 35-40.

Karahanna, E., & Straub, D. W. (1999). The psychological origins of perceived usefulness and perceived ease-of-use. *Information & Management, 35*, 237-250.

Katerattanakul, P. (2002). Framework of effective Web site design for business-to-consumer Internet commerce. *INFOR, 40*, 57-70.

Katz, E. (1959). Mass communication research and the study of popular culture: An editorial note on a possible future for this journal. *Studies in Public Communication, 2*, 1-6.

Kaye, B. K., & Johnson, T. J. (2002). Online and in the know: Uses and gratifications of the Web for political information. *Journal of Broadcasting & Electronic Media, 46*, 54-71.

Klapper, J. T. (1963). Mass communication research: An old road resurveyed. *Public Opinion Quarterly, 27*, 515-527.

Korgaonkar, P. K., & Wolin, L. D. (1999). A multivariate analysis of Web usage. *Journal of Advertising Research, 38*, 53-68.

Kraut, R., Mukhopadhyay, T., Szczypula, J., Kiesler, S., & Scherlis, B. (1999). Information and communication: Alternative uses of the Internet in households. *Information Systems Research, 10*, 287-303.

Lin, C. A. (1999). Online service adoption likelihood. *Journal of Advertising Research, 39*, 79-89.

Lohse, G. L., & Spiller, P. (1998). Electronic shopping. *Communications of the ACM, 41*, 81-87.

Matthews, D., & Schrum, L. (2003). High-speed Internet use and academic gratifications in the college residence. *The Internet and Higher Education, 6*, 125-144.

McDonald-Russell, D. E. (2002). *Profiling music consumers for viral marketing purposes: A test of the efficacy of combining uses and gratifications theory with the diffusion of innovation model.* Unpublished doctoral dissertation, University of Missouri, Columbia.

McGuire, W. J. (1974). Psychological motives and communication gratification. In J. Blumler & E.

Katz (Eds.), *The uses of mass communications: Current perspectives on gratifications research.* Beverly Hills, CA: Sage Publications.

Mitchell, W. S. (1999). *Social and psychological factors associated with Internet use in the home: A uses and gratifications study.* Unpublished doctoral dissertation, Bowling Green State University, Bowling Green, OH.

Moody, S. A. (2002). *Public radio on the Web: A uses and gratifications analysis.* Unpublished doctoral dissertation, University of Nevada, Reno.

Newhagen, J., & Rafaeli, S. (1996). Why communication researchers should study the Internet: A dialogue. *Journal of Communication, 46*, 4-13.

Nisbett, R. E., & Wilson, T. D. (1977). Telling more than we can know: Verbal reports on mental processes. *Psychological Review, 84*, 231-259.

Papacharissi, A., & Rubin, A. M. (2000). Predictors of Internet use. *Journal of Broadcasting & Electronic Media, 44*, 175-196.

Rafaeli, S. (1988). Interactivity: From new media to communication. In R. Hawkins, J. Wieman, & S. Pingree (Eds.), *Advancing communication science: Merging mass and interpersonal processes.* Newberry Park, CA: Sage Publications.

Rai, A., Ravichandran, T., & Samaddar, S. (1998). How to anticipate the Internet's global diffusion. *Communications of the ACM, 41*, 97-106.

Rogers, E. M., & Albritton, M. M. (1995). Interactive communication technologies in business organizations. *Journal of Business Communication, 32*, 177-195.

Rubin, A. M. (1985). Uses and gratifications: Quasi-functional analysis. In J. Dominick & J. Fletcher (Eds.), *Broadcasting research methods.* Boston: Allyn & Bacon.

Ruggiero, T. E. (2000). Uses and gratifications theory in the 21st century. *Mass Communication & Society, 3*, 3-37.

Savloainen, R. (1999). The role of the Internet in information seeking: Putting the networked services in context. *Information Processing & Management, 35*, 765-782.

Stafford, T. F. (2001). Measuring consumer motivations to use marketspace. In *ICIS Diffusion Interest Group in Information Technology (DIGIT) Proceedings.* Retrieved from http://mis.uah.edu/sigadit/workshops/files/DIGIT_2001_Stafford.pdf

Stafford, T. F. (2003). Differentiating between innovators and laggards in the uses and gratifications for Internet services. *IEEE Transactions on Engineering Management, 50*, 427-435.

Stafford, T. F., & Stafford, M. R. (1998). Uses and gratifications of the World Wide Web: A preliminary study. In *Proceedings of the 1998 American Academy of Advertising Conference*, Pullman, WA.

Stafford, T. F., & Stafford, M. R. (2001). Identifying motivations for the use of commercial Web sites. *Information Resources Management Journal, 14*, 22-30.

Stafford, T. F., Stafford, M. R., & Schkade, L. L. (2004). Determining uses and gratifications for the Internet. *Decision Sciences, 35*, 259-288.

Turban, E., Lee, J., King, D., & Chung, H. M. (2000). *Electronic commerce: A managerial perspective.* Upper Saddle River, NJ: Prentice Hall.

U.S. home broadband penetration. (2004). *Broadband Business Report, 14*, 1.

Venkatesh, V., & Davis, F. D. (2000). A theoretical extension of the technology acceptance model: Four longitudinal field studies. *Management Science, 46*, 86-204.

Weiser, E. B. (2001). The functions of Internet use and their social and psychological consequence. *CyberPsychology & Behavior, 4*, 723-743.

APPENDIX

Factor Loading Matrix (adapted from Stafford, 2001)

Variable Eigenvalue	**Factor 1 (Processes)** *10.96*	**Factor 2 (Content)** *3.0*	**Factor 3 (Social)** *2.0*
Access	0.125	0.360	-0.004
Answers	0.187	0.320	0.018
Browsing	0.449	0.111	0.04
Chatting	0.03	0.02	**0.681**
Communication	0.106	0.187	0.246
Current	0.07	0.07	0.08
E-Mail	0.172	0.05	0.09
Easy	0.08	0.05	0.07
Education	0.118	**0.581**	0.109
Entertainment	0.08	0.002	0.282
Freedom	0.05	0.288	0.176
Friends	0.01	0.01	**0.612**
Fun	0.101	0.06	0.243
Games	-0.03	0.004	0.120
Government	0.107	0.256	-0.006
Homework	0.148	0.318	0.210
Ideas	0.282	0.424	0.174
Information	0.291	**0.617**	0.02
Interaction	0.257	0.08	**0.661**
Interesting	0.217	0.246	0.135
Knowledge	0.227	**0.660**	-0.02
Learning	0.224	**0.679**	0.07
Money	0.05	0.180	0.09
New	0.260	0.261	0.241
News	0.06	0.275	0.03
Newsgroups	0.160	0.141	0.445
People	0.174	0.138	**0.709**
Progressive	0.314	0.402	0.203
Relaxing	0.116	0.114	0.205
Research	0.234	**0.542**	-0.02
Resources	**0.522**	0.370	0.03
Search Engines	**0.644**	0.125	0.07
Searching	**0.657**	0.274	0.04
Shopping	0.307	0.03	0.05

continued on the following page

APPENDIX CONTINUED

Software	0.479	0.183	0.120
Speed	0.347	0.203	0.135
Sports	-0.02	-0.04	0.223
Stocks	0.07	-0.06	-0.04
Surfing	**0.553**	0.02	0.136
Technology	**0.566**	0.220	0.04
Updates	0.445	0.157	0.130
Variety	0.463	0.04	0.135
Weather	0.157	0.107	0.122
Web Sites	**0.564**	0.203	0.07
Work	0.307	0.221	0.06

This work was previously published in the Journal of Organizational and End User Computing, Vol. 20, Issue 3, edited by M. Mahmood, pp. 1-21, copyright 2008 by IGI Publishing (an imprint of IGI Global).

Chapter 10
General and Specific Computer Self-Efficacy:
An Empirical Comparison of their Strength in Predicting General and Specific Outcomes

James P. Downey
University of Central Arkansas, USA

R. Kelly Rainer Jr.
Auburn University, USA

Summer E. Bartczak
University of Central Arkansas, USA

ABSTRACT

Computer self-efficacy is known to operate at multiple levels, from application-specific sub-domains like spreadsheets to a judgment of ability for the entire computing domain (general computer self-efficacy-GCSE). Conventional wisdom and many recent studies contend that the level of self-efficacy (specific to general) should match the level of its related constructs to maximize predictive power (Bandura, 1997; Chen, et al., 2001; Pajares, 1996). This thinking claims, for example, that GCSE should be used with a general attitude like computer anxiety (and vice versa). This study examines whether such a limitation is theoretically and empirically sound, given that SE judgments generalize across domains. Results indicate any self-efficacy judgment (specific or general) significantly relates to both general **and** *domain-specific constructs. These results suggest that an individual's cognitive processing of ability level is multi-faceted; that is, every SE judgment consists of general and specific components. The implication is that CSE is simultaneously generalizable and formative in nature. The results also suggest that the relationship between general and specific CSE is mediated by one's ability level in the specific domain.*

DOI: 10.4018/978-1-60566-687-7.ch010

INTRODUCTION

The exploration of the relationship between the individual and computers by researchers and practitioners has evolved into a significant stream of knowledge and research concerning the individual and his/her perceptions, beliefs and capabilities concerning technology. The reference discipline for much of this work rests in social and cognitive psychology, where the basic premise is that an individual behaves in a predictable way that is a function of environmental and/or cognitive factors. One influential model was Bandura's (1986) Social Cognitive Theory, which explained human behavior in terms of a continuous reciprocal interaction between cognitive, behavioral, and environmental determinants. This "triadic reciprocality" suggests that behavior is depends on and is determined by both environmental and cognitive factors (p. 23). The most prominent of the cognitive factors is self-efficacy (SE), which is an individual's perception of his/her ability to successfully carry out a task or activity. Self-efficacy is not just an ability perception; it provides a generative mechanism that orchestrates the motivation and effort required to complete the task. It helps determine which activities are attempted, the effort in pursuing that activity, and persistence when encountering obstacles (Bandura, 1986; 1997; Gist & Mitchell, 1992). Self-efficacy also applies to computing behavior. Computer self-efficacy, defined as an individual's judgment of computing capability, is a significant influence on attitudes toward technology (Harrison & Rainer, 1992) and performance (Agarwal, Sambamurthy, & Stair, 2000).

Self-efficacy has been shown to operate at multiple levels; for example, an individual can make judgments of ability for specific applications (such as database or spreadsheet self-efficacy and labeled AS-CSE for application specific CSE) or a judgment of ability for the entire computing domain, labeled general computer self-efficacy, or GCSE (Marakas, Yi, & Johnson, 1998). These levels, frequently labeled as specific or general CSE, have been operationalized and used in numerous studies, with varying degrees of success.

Although extant studies confirm a linkage between self-efficacy and various computing behaviors, there is relatively little research which empirically examines the distinctions between general and specific self-efficacy and in particular, their predictive validity. Which level of self-efficacy, for example, should be used in a given study? Research maintains that the level of self-efficacy (specific to general) should match the level of the study outcomes (Ajzen, 1991; Pajares, 1996). Chen, Gully, and Eden (2001) refer to this as "specificity matching" and maintain that matching levels is crucial for predictive power (p. 64).

Although this approach makes intuitive sense, there have been several studies in information technology (IT) where cross-leveling (using different levels for self-efficacy and outcomes) relationships have been significant. For example, GCSE (using the instrument of Compeau & Higgins, 1995a), had a significant relationship with spreadsheet ease of use (Agarwal et al., 2000), affect and anxiety (Compeau, Higgins, & Huff, 1999), and word processing/spreadsheet declarative knowledge (Compeau & Higgins, 1995b).

We contend that the reason for these findings is due to the nature of self-efficacy judgments and the way specific and general judgments interact. The relationship between specific and general self-efficacy has been largely unexplored. Although it is generally accepted that one of the three dimensions of self-efficacy, the generality dimension, is the degree to which a SE judgment applies to other domains (Bandura, 1997; Gist & Mitchell, 1992), we believe that the way this operates in individuals is primarily through the relationship between general and specific self-efficacy. But how these influences occur and their impact on the way an individual perceives his ability in any domain has not been empirically examined.

This chapter empirically examines the nature of self-efficacy judgments. While antecedent factors which influence the formation of any self-efficacy judgment are well known (e.g., mastery and vicarious experiences, among others, Bandura, 1986), the components of an actual SE judgment require clarification. We propose that AS-CSE judgments (such as spreadsheet SE) consist in part of the individual's perception of ability for the entire computing domain (or GCSE); this we label the generality dimension. This occurs through a process we call the "generality effect", and is why some studies have significant cross-leveling results. A clarification of the interaction between self-efficacy judgments is crucial to our understanding of the cognitive processing which occurs in individuals and will further awareness in an area important to organizations. SE is known to be an important factor in the success of organizational training, making it a crucial construct to both researchers and practitioners.

GCSE AND THE GENERALITY DIMENSION

GCSE is an individual judgment of ability across all computing domains (Marakas et al., 1998). Compeau and Higgins (1995a) describe it as a perception of ability for different hardware and software configurations. It is not application specific, but rather is an individual's overall computing ability belief without regard to applications, environments, or tasks. Conceptually, it can be considered the sum of all computer sub-domain CSEs (Marakas et al., 1998). This point is worth noting: one way to conceptualize GCSE is that it is formed from the SE judgments of all constituent domains in computing (e.g., AS-CSEs and other component computing SEs). This was demonstrated empirically in a study where AS-CSEs were summed into a GCSE which demonstrated significant relationships with outcome variables (Downey, 2006). We call this the "contribution effect", in that all component CSEs can be combined to form GCSE.

Self-efficacy has three distinct but related dimensions, including strength, magnitude, and generality (Bandura, 1986; Compeau & Higgins, 1995a). Strength is an assessment of confidence in successfully completing a task. Magnitude (called "level" by Bandura), refers to task difficulty levels; the higher the SE, the more difficult the task the individual believes they can accomplish. The third dimension, generality, is the degree to which the self-efficacy judgment applies to other tasks in other domains. Eden and Kinnar (1991) consider generality as that which transfers among domains; it is described as a "product of a lifetime of experience ... not amenable to change under short-lived conditions" (p. 772). We contend that what transfers between specific domains is GCSE. As an individual makes specific CSE judgments (e.g., spreadsheet AS-CSE), those judgments are influenced by their perception of overall computing ability, or GCSE. This is the generality effect which we define (in a computing context) as the process by which general CSE influences SE judgments of component sub-domains. GCSE is therefore trait-like, in that it is slow to change and influences multiple activities (Agarwal et al., 2000; Bandura, 1997).

How this process occurs is complex and not the intent of this study. Bandura lists five processes through which generality occurs, including the existence of similar sub-skills in domains and developing generic self-judgment skills that apply to all self-efficacy judgments, like assessing task demands or evaluating possible courses of action to accomplish the task (see Bandura, 1997).

We intend to demonstrate the generality effect in this chapter obliquely by empirically establishing that cross-level relationships are significant. We consider empirically establishing cross-level relationships a worthwhile endeavor of itself, particularly considering the literature which recommends specificity matching. Conceptually we believe GCSE judgments transfer to specific judgments. If cross-level relationships are significant, that is if AS-CSEs are significant predictors of general level outcomes, *and* GCSE significantly predicts domain specific performance, this suggests that there is an interaction between the judgments of self-efficacy. We contend that the reciprocal interaction between GCSE and component domain CSEs undermines the theoretical soundness of specificity matching and suggests generality and contribution effects.

THEORETICAL MODEL AND HYPOTHESES

This chapter compares the predictive power of general and specific (AS-CSEs) self-efficacy by examining the strength of their relationships with common outcomes. To allow a comparison of cross-level relationships, some outcomes are general and some domain-specific. The theoretical model is presented in Figure 1. The model suggests that general level outcomes (attitudes and overall computing competence), and specific-level outcomes (application-specific competence and performance), are a function of *both* GCSE and AS-CSEs.

According to specificity matching, AS-CSEs (which are domain- or application-specific) should be significant predictors of domain specific competence and GCSE should be a significant predictor of general domain outcomes. The generality effect suggests that an individual's judgment of efficacy for applications is in part a function of the individual's GCSE (displayed as the down pointed arrow in the figure). When an individual judges their ability in a specific domain, part of the cognitive processing that occurs includes their perceived ability in the full domain (Marakas et al., 1998). Given the linkage between GCSE and AS-CSEs, we contend that GCSE should have a significant relationship with domain-specific outcomes, including competencies. Similarly, because AS-CSEs contribute to (or form) GCSE, AS-CSEs should have significant relationships with general computer outcomes.

Outcomes of CSE (Attitudes and Competence)

An attitude has been defined as "a learned predisposition to respond in a consistently favorable or unfavorable manner" towards a domain (Fishbein & Ajzen, 1975, p. 6). It is an internal state that influences personal choice (Gagne, 1984). Computer attitudes influence how an individual reacts to the computing environment. Both theory and research suggests that there is a significant relationship between CSE and computer attitudes. How an individual "feels" about a domain, their emotional arousal towards the domain, is influenced by what he/she thinks their capability is in that domain (Marakas et al., 1998).

Computer Anxiety

Computing anxiety is a fear of computers or of computer use (Loyd & Gressard, 1984). Computer anxiety is influenced by a variety of emotional and environmental factors (Marakas et al., 1998). Self-efficacy influences how individuals interpret their experiences, which influences anxiety and other emotions (Bandura, 1997). Studies show that persons with high CSE have less anxiety, while those with low CSE exhibit higher anxiety (Johnson & Marakas, 2000). This leads to the first hypothesis:

Hypothesis 1: Both GCSE and AS-CSEs will have a negative relationship with computer anxiety, a general level construct.

Computer Affect

Another important computing attitude is that of affect, or the feeling of like or dislike towards computing. Affect is a different construct than anxiety (Kernan & Howard, 1990). An individual could simultaneously dislike computing and have little anxiety towards it. A person's attitude towards computing is a critical factor in user acceptance as well as computer usage (Al-Jabri & Al-Khaldi, 1997). Individuals tend to pursue activities they like while avoiding disliked activities. Affect, and in particular positive affect or computer liking, has a significant relationship with CSE (Rainer & Harrison, 1993). Therefore:

Hypothesis 2: Both GCSE and AS-CSEs will have a positive relationship with computer affect (liking), a general level construct.

Computing Competence

The relationship between self-efficacy and performance is one of the strongest in the literature. Individuals with higher self-efficacy in a domain tend to perform better at tasks in that domain and have higher competence (Bandura, 1997; Compeau & Higgins, 1995b; Munro, Huff, Marcolin, & Compeau, 1997). The acquisition of skills or competencies is accomplished through a process which includes gaining declarative knowledge, integrating this knowledge, and putting it to use through procedural knowledge (Kanfer & Ackerman, 1989). Declarative knowledge is un-

Figure 1. Theoretical model

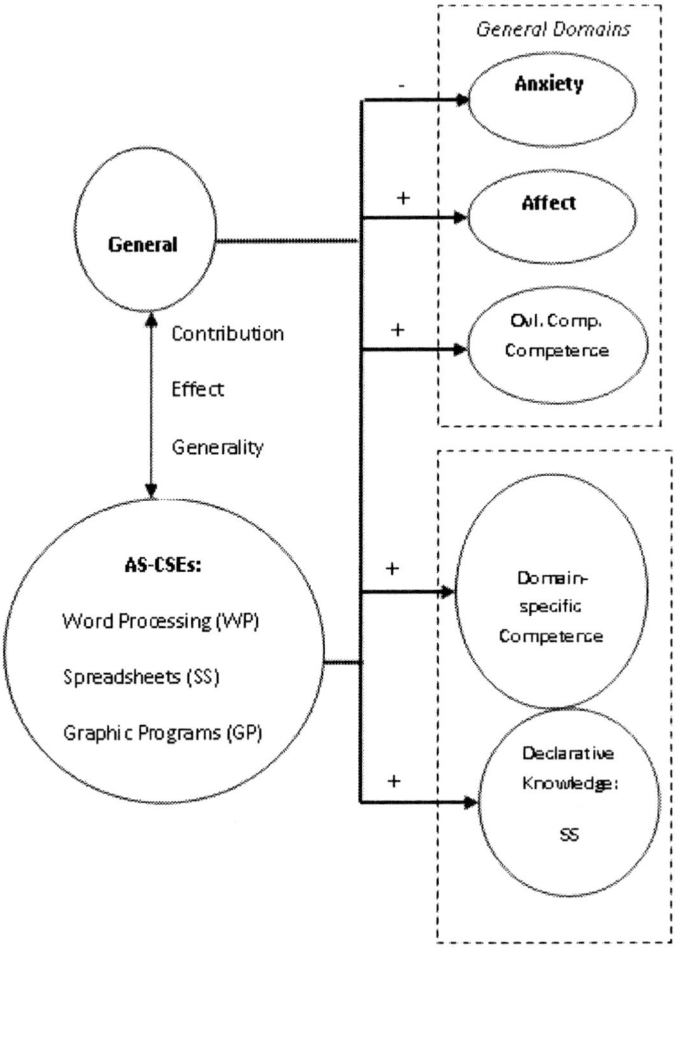

derstanding "facts and things" (Anderson, 1985, p. 199), or "verbal knowledge" (Kraiger, Ford, & Salas, 1993). Self-efficacy influences each phase of skill acquisition (Marcolin, Compeau, Munro, & Huff, 2000). Competence may be measured at either the general level (full or overall computing domain) or at individual application levels (e.g., spreadsheet competence). Both GCSE and AS-CSEs should significantly influence competence at either level. Therefore:

Hypothesis 3: Both GCSE and AS-CSEs will have a positive relationship with overall computer competence (a general level construct) and application-specific competence and performance (domain-specific constructs).

RESEARCH METHODOLOGY

The population for this study is Midshipmen in the U.S. Navy's commissioning program. This research was part of an ongoing study to determine the effectiveness of technology training for newly commissioned officers. There are 57 universities that currently have a Naval Reserve Officers Training Corps program as well as the US Naval Academy, with Midshipmen in the process of earning college degrees and receiving commissions in the Navy or Marine Corps. The Naval Academy (because of its size) plus thirteen universities with NROTC programs were chosen at random to participate from across the U.S. Universities included the US Naval Academy, South Florida, Florida, Missouri, Kansas, Minnesota, South Carolina, Penn State, Idaho, Ohio State, Washington, Purdue, Oregon State, and Vanderbilt. Each university was sent 24 surveys, while the Naval Academy received 61. Of the 373 surveys sent, 310 completed responses were received for an overall response rate of 83%. The average age of respondent was 21.1 (sd = 2.91); 267 were male (86%) and 45 were female. On average, responders had 2.4 years of college (sd = .99).

Study Measures

Attitudes

Anxiety and affect were measured using the anxiety and computer liking subscales of the Computer Attitude Scale developed by Loyd and Gressard (1984). This instrument was validated by Al-Jabri and Al-Khaldi (1997). Woodrow (1991) stated that the subscales were reliable enough to be administered separately. Both scales used a seven-point scale, where 1 is "completely disagree" and 7 is "completely agree".

Computing Competence

Computer competence was measured at both an overall level (entire computing domain) as well as six individual application domains, using an instrument adapted by Munro et al. (1997). The application domains included word processing (abbreviated in this paper as WP), spreadsheets (SS), graphics programs (GP), databases (DB), email programs and web page development. The instrument asked respondents the number of domain packages they used, number of academic or training courses taken in the domain, and thoroughness of current knowledge of the domain (on a scale of 0 = "No Knowledge", to 7 = "Complete Knowledge"). For overall computing competence, the six application domains were added to the respondent's reported expertise in two other domains, "other" software and hardware (with several items each).

Declarative Knowledge

Declarative knowledge was measured for the domains of word processing and spreadsheets using an actual fourteen item multiple choice test. The items were specific to the applications of

Microsoft Word and Microsoft Excel. The items on each test were derived from the "intermediate" level of expertise provided from Microsoft (Microsoft Corporation, 2003). Care was taken to eliminate confounding by an application effect, where a respondent could score below their actual knowledge level because they had expertise in a non-Microsoft application. Each respondent indicated the application they knew best and only those who indicated Word and Excel were included. Each survey recipient received only one of the performance tests, randomly divided. The performance test was optional, but 202 respondents completed one of the tests (out of 310, a 65% return). Of these, 97 usable tests on Excel and 105 usable tests on Word were received.

Application CSEs

Application-specific CSE was calculated for each of the six application domains. All of the items in each of the six scales were task-based and started with the same stem, "I believe I have the ability to…", followed by the actual task within the domain. Following the recommendation of Bandura (1986), each AS-CSE included both magnitude ("Yes" or "No") and strength (1-10). Following the recommendation of Lee and Bobko (1994), each application CSE score was derived from averaging the strength of only those tasks that the respondent believed they could accomplish.

The AS-CSE (spreadsheet) instrument was developed by Johnson and Marakas (2000). The other five AS-CSEs were self-developed, but similar in scope and design to the spreadsheet scale. All were pilot tested successfully; reliability and validity (convergent and discriminant) are provided in the results section.

GCSE

GCSE was measured using the ten item GCSE instrument of Compeau and Higgins (1995a). This instrument uses the "unfamiliar" software stem with an unspecified task. Like each AS-CSE instrument, this scale also included magnitude and strength and the score was derived in the same manner.

ANALYSES OF FINDINGS

Measurement Model

To assess the measurement model, we first examined the reliability and factor structures of each construct, followed by convergent and discriminant validity.

CSE Scales

Each of the six CSE measures was factor analyzed independently. Results indicated that all six AS-CSE constructs were unidimensional and every item in each scale loaded most highly on its applicable latent construct, suggesting convergent validity. Four items were eliminated due to low factor loadings (two from WP-CSE, one each from SS-CSE and GP-CSE). When GCSE was factor analyzed, however, the scale was two-dimensional. To retain a one dimensional construct, two of the ten items were eliminated (items 9 and 10). Reliabilities were high. Table 1 presents construct means, standard deviations, and correlations of all CSE scales.

Next, validity was assessed. All seven SE scales were factor analyzed simultaneously. Each item loaded highest on its own construct, rather than other variables, suggesting construct validity (Netemeyer, Bearden, & Sharma, 2003). Factor loadings are provided in the Appendix. Average variance extracted (AVE) was then computed. AVE should be greater than .50 to justify using a construct and discriminant validity is indicated if its square root is greater than other construct correlations (Fornell & Larcker, 1981). The shaded diagonal elements in Table 1 provide results of this test, indicating satisfactory validity.

Table 1. Descriptive data for CSE scales

Construct	Mean	SD	Reliability	Correlations and Average Variance Extracted						
				(1)	(2)	(3)	(4)	(5)	(6)	(7)
(1) WP	9.12	1.42	.95	**.88**						
(2) SS	7.47	2.60	.97	.45	**.90**					
(3) GP	7.68	1.87	.95	.63	.55	**.88**				
(4) DB	3.59	3.23	.99	.12*	.40	.21	**.95**			
(5) Email	8.86	2.05	.92	.58	.34	.51	.18	**.89**		
(6) Web	5.30	3.60	.98	.30	.40	.25	.49	.31	**.93**	
(7) GCSE	6.87	1.83	.93	.43	.48	.41	.39	.32	.39	**.85**

Off diagonal elements are correlations. Shaded elements along the diagonal represent the square root of AVE (average variance shared between the construct and their measures). All correlations significant at $p < .01$ except one indicated by * (significant at $p < .05$).

Attitude Scales

The two attitude scales were examined in a like manner as the CSE scales. Anxiety (mean = 1.83; sd = 1.0) and liking (mean = 4.73; sd = 1.2) had a correlation of -.58. Reliabilities were .92 and .91 respectfully. Each item loaded on its own factor. An analysis using square root of AVE indicated sufficient discriminant validity .88, greater than correlation of -.58.

Competence and Knowledge Scales

Computer competence was measured for six application domains and for overall computing, plus there were two performance tests in the domains of word processing and spreadsheets. Means, standard deviations, and correlations are provided in Table 2 for the six application domains and overall computing competence.

Respondents' competence levels ranged from higher competence (WP and Email) to lower competence (DB and Web). All correlations were significant between domain competencies, suggesting in part the similarities present in these software applications (such as the Windows environment).

Because each respondent received only one of the objective performance tests, and to ensure there was no distribution effect, t-tests were conducted to determine if there were any differences between the group that received (and returned) the WP test, the group returning the SS test, and the group that returned neither. Tests indicated there were no significant differences between the groups in college major, age, gender, college class, or university attending. The WP objective test (n = 105; mean = 7.80; sd = 2.5) had a correlation with the WP competence measure of .367 ($p < .01$). The SS test (n = 97; mean = 9.50; sd = 3.6) had a correlation with the spreadsheet competence measure of .596 ($p < .01$). The high correlations, particularly in the spreadsheet domain, provide some degree of convergent validity.

Hypotheses Testing

Given a satisfactory measurement model, the hypotheses were then tested. Regression analysis was chosen (instead of structural equation modeling) in order to facilitate testing the *differences* in predictive power of various self-efficacy measures on general and specific outcomes using the Cohen and Cohen (1983) multiple regression procedure.

Hypothesis testing was conducted in two steps and the results presented in Table 3 (general outcomes) and Table 4 (specific outcomes). First,

Table 2. Descriptive data for competencies

Construct	Mean	SD	Correlations						
			(1)	(2)	(3)	(4)	(5)	(6)	(7)
(1) Email Competence	7.81	2.3	1.0						
(2) WP Competence	7.39	1.9	.64	1.0					
(3) GP Competence	5.49	2.2	.55	.55	1.0				
(4) SS Competence	5.11	2.0	.46	.54	.58	1.0			
(5) Web Competence	2.84	3.3	.40	.40	.35	.38	1.0		
(6) DB Competence	2.06	2.4	.29	.33	.34	.42	.45	1.0	
(7) Ovl Competence	53.9	22.1	.68	.69	.66	.68	.66	.61	1.0
n = 310. All correlations significant at p < .01									

simple regressions were run between the indicator (independent variable or IV, the CSEs) variables and each dependent variable (DV, the outcomes) to ascertain whether each CSE significantly predicted the dependent outcome. This step provides an initial assessment of whether all CSEs (general and specific) significantly predict both general and domain-specific outcomes. The second step consisted of determining whether there was a significant difference in predictive strength between GCSE and AS-CSEs for both general and specific outcomes. If specificity matching is sound, GCSE should be a *significantly better* predictor of general outcomes and AS-CSEs should be *significantly better* in predicting specific outcomes. This step was accomplished by running a multiple regression which included both CSEs to determine significant predictors and then conducting a formal t-test procedure to test the difference. For the general outcomes, the multiple regressions included as IVs both GCSE and all six AS-CSEs. For the specific outcomes, multiple regressions included GCSE and one AS-CSE (the one that matched the domain; for example, with DB competence as the DV, DB-CSE and GCSE were used as IVs). Only those IVs which significantly predicted the DV are included in the multiple regression columns of Table 3.

Using the multiple regression results, a formal t-test was then conducted which compared the predictive power of significant IVs in accordance with the multiple regression procedure of Cohen and Cohen (1983). The t-test is given by Equation (1):

$$t = \frac{\beta_i - \beta_j}{SE\beta_i - \beta_j}$$

$$SE\beta_i - \beta_j = \sqrt{\frac{1 - R^2}{n - k - 1}(r^{ii} + r^{jj} - 2r^{ij})} \qquad (1)$$

where SE is standard error, β are standardized regression coefficients, R^2 is squared multiple correlation, r is the inverse correlation (from the inverse correlation matrix), k is number of independent variables, and n is number of observations.

For general outcomes, results indicate that all self-efficacies, application-specific and general, had a significant relationship with every general outcome. Thus, all specific measures of CSE significantly predict general outcomes. This provides support for hypotheses 1-3. In the test to determine whether GCSE or AS-CSEs were stronger predictors, results varied by DV. For anxiety, the multiple regression (where there were seven CSE independent variables) resulted in three significant variables (GCSE, GP-CSE, and Email-CSE, noted in the multiple regression columns). The t-tests to determine whether GCSE

Table 3. General outcome results

	Anxiety					Computer Affect					Overall Competence				
	Simple Regression		Multiple Regression		t-test diff.	Simple Regression		Multiple Regression		t-test diff.	Simple Regression		Multiple Regression		t-test diff.
	R^2	β	β	t	GCSE vs. AS-CSE	R^2	β	β	t	GCSE vs. AS-CSE	R^2	β	B	t	GCSE vs. AS-CSE
GCSE	.23	-.48	-.33	-6.4		.31	.56	.40	7.0		.29	.54	.23	4.7	
WP	.19	-.44				.13	.36				.18	.42			
SS	.15	-.39				.18	.42	.14	2.2	t = 3.3 p< .01	.30	.55	.19	3.5	t = .54 NS
GP	.19	-.44	-.18	-3.3	t = 1.6 NS	.11	.34				.20	.45	.15	3.0	t = 1.1 NS
DB	.03	-.19				.08	.29				.21	.46	.12	2.5	t = 1.4 NS
Email	.19	-.44	-.24	-4.5	t = 1.0 NS	.06	.25				.14	.37			
Web	.08	-.28				.13	.36	.12	2.1	t = 4.1 p< .01	.31	.56	.29	6.1	t = .82 NS
n = 310. All regressions shown significant at p < .01. For multiple regressions, only significant IVs are included.															

was stronger than either of the two AS-CSEs were not significant, indicating that all three predicted equally well. For overall competence, there were five significant IVs. But like anxiety, there was no significant difference between the predictive strength of GCSE and any significant AS-CSE. This suggests that both forms of CSE have relationships with anxiety and overall competence that are similar in strength. For computer liking, there was a difference. The general instrument was significantly stronger than either of the two significant AS-CSEs (web and spreadsheets).

Table 4. Specific outcomes results

	Simple Regression				Multiple Regression				t-test difference
	GCSE		AS-CSE		GCSE		AS-CSE		GCSE vs. AS-CSE
Competence	R2	β	R2	β	β	t	β	t	
WP	.18	.42	.23	.48	.27	5.0	.36	6.7	t = 1.0 NS
SS	.17	.42	.45	.68	.12	2.6	.62	13.0	t = 5.7 p < .01
GP	.11	.33	.22	.47	.17	3.0	.41	3.0	t = 2.6 p < .01
DB	.11	.33	.37	.61	.12	2.4	.57	11.7	t = 5.3 p < .01
Email	.13	.37	.14	.38	.27	5.0	.30	5.5	t = .30 NS
Web	.13	.36	.42	.65	.13	2.8	.60	12.8	t = 5.7 p < .01
WP Test	.07	.28	.16	.41	.15	1.5	.33	3.3	t = 1.1 NS
SS Test	.24	.49	.37	.61	.20	2.0	.50	5.0	t = 1.6 NS
n = 310 for all competencies; n = 105 for WP test; n = 97 for SS test.									

For the domain-specific outcomes (note that in Table 4 the DVs are in rows), both GCSE and the appropriate AS-CSE significantly predicted all DVs, again providing support for hypotheses 1-3. But results varied in determining whether GCSE or the AS-CSE was a stronger predictor for these domain-specific outcomes. If specificity matching holds, the AS-CSEs should be stronger. Using the t-tests from the multiple regression results, for half of the DVs the AS-CSE was a significantly stronger predictor, including the competencies of spreadsheets, graphic programs, database, and web design (thus supporting specificity matching). For the other half, including both actual performance tests, there was no significant difference in the predictive power of GCSE versus the AS-CSE.

DISCUSSION, LIMITATIONS, AND CONCLUSION

This chapter was designed to examine self-efficacy judgments and the relationship between them. When an individual makes domain-specific computer self-efficacy judgments (e.g., spreadsheet SE), these judgments are made within a cognitive context that takes into account (among other factors) past experience in the domain, task demands, and their perception of ability for the entire computing domain (GCSE). We posited that the process by which this occurs, which we call the generality effect, implies that one's GCSE generalizes or transfers to the specific CSE judgment. It was also suggested that the relationship between general and specific CSE is reciprocal, that specific CSEs influence or form GCSE (Downey, 2006; Marakas et al., 1998). To demonstrate this, we hypothesized that GCSE should significantly influence domain-specific performance and AS-CSEs should significantly influence general outcomes, which is contrary to the concept of specificity matching, which suggests that one should match general SE and general outcomes (and specific SE and specific outcomes).

In general, results of the study confirm these hypotheses. GCSE was a significant predictor (as expected) of all three general outcomes (anxiety, affect, and overall computer competence) but also of *all* specific domain competencies (and performance tests). Specific CSEs were significant predictors of domain-specific competencies, but also of *all* three general-level outcomes. Because cross-level relationships were significant, and because the strength of the predictive power in some cases was not significantly different, this suggests that there is a reciprocal relationship among specific and general CSE. Therefore, we suggest a person's judgments of CSE are multi-faceted: specific-CSEs influence GCSE and GCSE generalizes to specific CSE judgments.

This study extends previous research in two important ways. First the notion that self-efficacy measures and outcomes should be the same level (i.e., specificity matching) is called into question. Cross level relationships were always significant and in some cases there was no difference in predictive power between same level and cross level relationships (true for anxiety, overall computing competence, WP test and competence, email competence, and spreadsheet test). It was not true for affect and four specific competencies (SS, GP, DB, and web).

Secondly, this study clarifies the relationship between specific and general CSE. Previous studies have noted positive correlations between the two, but this study suggests that this relationship is also mediated by an individual's ability level in the domain. The influence of GCSE was similar in strength to that of AS-CSE in the domains of email and word processing, the two domains with the highest ability levels. For the other four domain competencies, AS-CSE was significantly stronger. This suggests that as an individual masters a domain (such as WP or email), the influence of specific-CSE weakens and the influence of GCSE gains strength. For domains not mastered, specific

CSE is stronger. Further study on the effect of domain ability in this relationship is warranted.

There are several limitations that should be mentioned. As with any cross-sectional instrument, common method bias and other related limitations arise. Attempts were made to reduce the influence of these biases and limitations, by including multiple items for each measure to increase reliability and validity (Netemeyer et al., 2003). The use of two objective performance tests was another method used to mitigate the extent of common method variance. Generalizability to a general population must be approached with caution. This population is one in a Navy commissioning program and may be different from the American population at large. In particular there was a gender discrepancy in this sample. While gender bias could exist, there was no difference between the two gender populations in this study for any demographic variable (age, class, major, or college attended), indicating that bias may not have been a significant factor.

Given the design of this study, the proposed interaction between self-efficacy judgments cannot be proved. This limitation is common to most cross-sectional studies where the dependent variable was not directly manipulated. Alternative explanations cannot be ruled out. Although the results suggest this to be the case, further study is paramount to make such a conclusion.

The conventional wisdom of matching specificities (SE and outcomes) in studies is called into question by the results of this study. We believe CSE judgments are multi-faceted, that there is a reciprocal interaction between general and specific SEs which reduces the enhanced predictive power when levels are matched. In some cases, this interaction is sufficient to offset completely any advantage gained in predictive power by specificity matching, which was seen in the outcomes of anxiety, overall computing competence, WP test and competence, email competence, and the spreadsheet test.

We posit these relationships in Figure 2. General CSE transfers to all sub-domain CSEs. What actually transfers and whether it is different for each sub-domain CSE is not clear from this study; however its influence on how an individual uses

Figure 2. Proposed relationship among CSEs

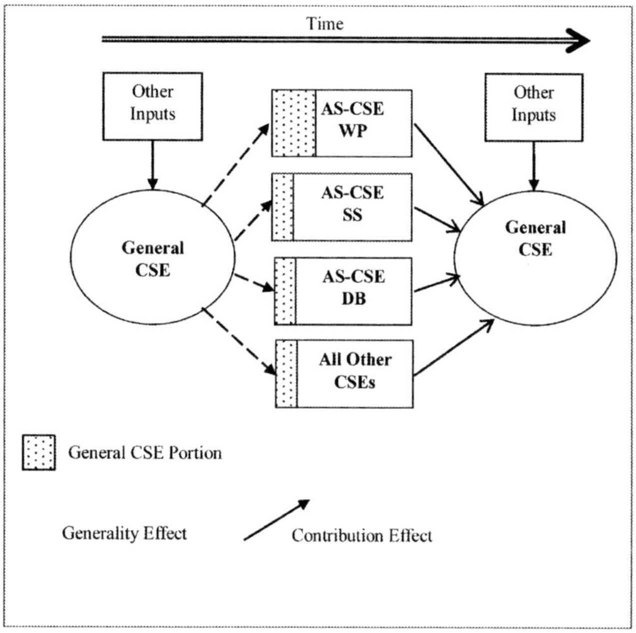

it to make sub-domain SE judgments appears to be different (indicated by a different sized GCSE portion in Figure 2). This study suggests that individual's rely on GCSE more in making SE judgments for domains where they had more ability (such as email and word processing). This refines previous research that suggested when mastery of a domain is reached, the cognitive analysis that goes into SE judgments is bypassed and prior performance becomes most important (Bandura, 1997). Marakas et al. (1998) proposed that at the point of mastery, GCSE should become a more important predictor of performance than specific CSE. This study found that GCSE was not more important, but that it was *equally effective* as a predictor of mastered domain performance.

Our goal in this chapter was to further refine the nature of computer self-efficacy and in particular the relationship between its general and specific forms. We believe that understanding the interaction between these levels of efficacy will lead to a greater awareness of the cognitive processes that occur in individuals. This should assist both practitioners and researchers in training environments were SE remains one of the most useful constructs. This chapter also provides empirical evidence which suggests that single dimension scales (GCSE or application specific) may be used in studies involving any level (general or specific) outcomes.

REFERENCES

Agarwal, R., Sambamurthy, V., & Stair, R. M. (2000). Research report: The evolving relationship between general and specific computer self-efficacy – An empirical assessment. *Information Systems Research, 11*(4), 418–430. doi:10.1287/isre.11.4.418.11876

Ajzen, I. (1991). The theory of planned behavior. *Organizational Behavior and Human Decision Processes, 50*, 179–211. doi:10.1016/0749-5978(91)90020-T

Al-Jabri, I. M., & Al-Khaldi. (1997). Effects of user characteristics on computer attitudes among undergraduate business students. *Journal of End User Computing, 9*(2), 16–22.

Anderson, J. R. (1985). *Cognitive psychology and its implications*. New York: Freeman.

Bandura, A. (1986). *Social foundations of thought and actions*. Englewood Cliffs, NJ: Prentice-Hall.

Bandura, A. (1997). Self-efficacy: The exercise of control. New York: W.H. Freeman and Company.

Chen, G., Gully, S., & Eden, D. (2001). Validation of a new general self-efficacy scale. *Organizational Research Methods, 4*(1), 62–83. doi:10.1177/109442810141004

Cohen, J., & Cohen, P. (1983). *Applied multiple regression/correlation analysis for the behavioral sciences*. Hillsdale, NJ, Lawrence Erlbaum Associates.

Compeau, D., Higgins, C. A., & Huff, S. (1999). Social cognitive theory and individual reactions to computing technology: A longitudinal study. *MIS Quarterly, 23*(2), 145–158. doi:10.2307/249749

Compeau, D. R., & Higgins, C. A. (1995a). Computer self-efficacy: Development of a measure and initial test. *MIS Quarterly, 19*(2), 189–202. doi:10.2307/249688

Compeau, D. R., & Higgins, C. A. (1995b). Application of social cognitive theory to training for computer skills. *Information Systems Research, 6*(2), 118–143. doi:10.1287/isre.6.2.118

Downey, J. (2006). Measuring general computer self-efficacy: A surprising comparison of three instruments in predicting performance, attitudes and usage. In *Proceedings of the Thirty-Ninth Annual Hawaii International Conference on System Sciences*.

Eden, D., & Kinnar, J. (1991). Modeling Galatea: Boosting self-efficacy to increase volunteering. *The Journal of Applied Psychology*, *76*(6), 770–780. doi:10.1037/0021-9010.76.6.770

Fishbein, M., & Ajzen, I. (1975). *Belief, attitude, intention and behavior: An introduction to theory and research*. Reading, MA: Addison-Wesley.

Fornell, C., & Larcker, D. F. (1981). Evaluating structural equation models with unobservable variables and measurement error. *JMR, Journal of Marketing Research*, *18*(1), 29–50. doi:10.2307/3151312

Gagne, R. M. (1984). Learning outcomes and their effects: Useful categories of human performance. *The American Psychologist*, *39*, 377–385. doi:10.1037/0003-066X.39.4.377

Gist, M. E., & Mitchell, T. R. (1992). Self-efficacy: a theoretical analysis of its determinants and malleability. *Academy of Management Review*, *17*(2), 183–211. doi:10.2307/258770

Harrison, A. W., & Rainer, R. K. (1992). The influence of individual differences on skill in end-user computing. *Journal of Management Information Systems*, *9*(1), 93–111. doi:10.1080/10580539208906858

Johnson, R. D., & Marakas, G. M. (2000). Research report: The role of behavioral modeling and computer skills acquisition-toward refinement of the model. *Information Systems Research*, *11*(4), 402–417. doi:10.1287/isre.11.4.402.11869

Kanfer, R., & Ackerman, P. L. (1989). Motivation and cognitive abilities: An integrative/aptitude-treatment interaction approach to skill acquisition. *The Journal of Applied Psychology*, *74*(4), 657–690. doi:10.1037/0021-9010.74.4.657

Kernan, M., & Howard, G. S. (1990). Computer anxiety and computer attitudes: an investigation of construct and predictive validity issues. *Educational and Psychological Measurement*, *50*, 681–690. doi:10.1177/0013164490503026

Kraiger, K., Ford, J. K., & Salas, E. (1993). Application of cognitive, skill-based, and affective theories of learning outcomes to new methods of training evaluation. *The Journal of Applied Psychology*, *78*(2), 311–328. doi:10.1037/0021-9010.78.2.311

Lee, C., & Bobko, P. (1994). Self-efficacy beliefs: Comparison of five measures. *The Journal of Applied Psychology*, *79*(3), 364–369. doi:10.1037/0021-9010.79.3.364

Loyd, B. H., & Gressard, C. (1984). Reliability and factorial validity of computer attitude scales. *Educational and Psychological Measurement*, *44*, 501–505. doi:10.1177/0013164484442033

Marakas, G. M., Yi, M. Y., & Johnson, R. D. (1998). The multilevel and multifaceted character of computer self-efficacy: Toward clarification of the construct and an integrative framework for research. *Information Systems Research*, *9*(2), 126–163. doi:10.1287/isre.9.2.126

Marcolin, B. L., Compeau, D. R., Munro, M. C., & Huff, S. L. (2000). Assessing user competence; conceptualization and measurement. *Information Systems Research*, *11*(1), 37–60. doi:10.1287/isre.11.1.37.11782

Microsoft Corporation. (2003). [On-line].http://office.microsoft.com/ marketplace/default.aspx?

Munro, M. C., Huff, S. L., Marcolin, B. L., & Compeau, D. R. (1997). Understanding and measuring user competence. *Information & Management, 33*, 45–57. doi:10.1016/S0378-7206(97)00035-9

Netemeyer, R. G., Bearden, W. O., & Sharma, S. (2003). *Scaling procedures: Issues and applications*. Thousand Oaks, CA: Sage Publications.

Pajares, F. (1996). *Assessing self-efficacy beliefs and academic outcomes: The case for specificity and correspondence*. Paper presented at the annual meeting of the American Educational Research Association, New York.

Rainer, R. K., & Harrison, A. W. (1993). Toward development of the end user computing construct in a university setting. *Decision Sciences*, *24*(6), 1187–1202. doi:10.1111/j.1540-5915.1993.tb00510.x

Woodrow, J. E. (1991). A comparison of four computer attitude scales. *Journal of Educational Computing Research*, *7*(2), 165–187.

APPENDIX

Appendix Table 1. Factor analyses of all CSE constructs

	1	2	3	4	5	6	7
GCSE1						**.77**	
GCSE2						**.76**	
GCSE3						**.82**	
GCSE4						**.82**	
GCSE5						**.74**	
GCSE6						**.76**	
GCSE7						**.72**	
GCSE8						**.67**	
WP1				**.74**	.32		
WP2				**.77**			.33
WP3				**.77**	.32		.33
WP4				**.71**			
WP5				**.72**			
WP6				**.78**			
WP7				**.72**			
WP8				**.78**			
WP9				**.72**			
SS1			**.74**				
SS2			**.79**				
SS3			**.80**				
SS4			**.84**				
SS5			**.82**				
SS6			**.85**				
SS7			**.84**				
SS8			**.81**				
SS9			**.74**				
GP1				.30	**.81**		
GP2					**.81**		
GP3					**.76**		
GP4				.32	**.81**		
GP5					**.80**		
GP6					**.79**		
GP7					**.68**		
DB1	**.88**						
DB2	**.89**						
DB3	**.91**						
DB4	**.89**						
DB5	**.88**						

DB6	**.87**						
DB7	**.91**						
DB8	**.92**						
DB9	**.91**						
DB10	**.90**						
EM1							.75
EM2							**.88**
EM3							**.85**
EM4							.76
EM5							**.86**
Web1		**.85**					
Web2		**.85**					
Web3		**.88**					
Web4		**.86**					
Web5		**.89**					
Web6		**.88**					
Web7		**.86**					
Web8		**.85**					

Chapter 11
Design of the PromoPad: An Automated Augmented-Reality Shopping Assistant

Wei Zhu
Michigan State University, USA

Charles B. Owen
Michigan State University, USA

Hairong Li
Michigan State University, USA

Joo-Hyun Lee
Cheil Communications, Korea

ABSTRACT

Augmented-reality technologies as a new way of human-computer interaction make possible real-time modification of our perception of reality without active user interference. This article introduces the prototype of an augmented-reality shopping-assistant device, the PromoPad, based on a handheld tablet PC allowing see-through vision with augmentations. While this new interaction utilizing augmented reality that places products into contextual settings can enhance shopping experience and suggest complementary products, it also has challenges and issues when used in a public environment such as a store setting. This article discusses the design and implementation of the PromoPad, and addresses the issues and possible solutions. The concept of dynamic contextualization is further investigated in this setting with a list of possible context modifications and their relation to advertising and the psychology of consumer purchasing.

INTRODUCTION

This article presents the design of the PromoPad, an augmented-reality shopping assistant that provides a new way of human-computer interaction in a new setting. Augmented-reality technologies have been enhancing people's perception interaction with the real world using computer-generated virtual objects. Furthermore, augmented-reality technologies change the way that people interact with the computer and the real world. By the new way of human-computer interactions, users interact and manipulate with the real world and real objects with the aid of computers without the users' active operation of a keyboard or mouse. Considerable amount of research work has been conducted in the area of augmented reality and human-computer interaction in various application domains (Mackay, 1996; Rauterberg, Mauch, & Stebler, 1996; Rekimoto & Nagao, 1995). The shopping environment, however, poses more challenges not yet well explored. First, a friendly user interface and negligible user interference are essential characteristics for such a system. Second, the amount of information that can be delivered to the user is vast so that how to effectively provide the most relevant information to the user without cluttering his or her view becomes a major concern. Cluttering the display can significantly degrade the quality and performance of the tasks that the user and the PromoPad are performing (Rosenholtz, Li, Mansfield, & Jin, 2005). Third, the users of the system come from different backgrounds and possess difference skill levels. They might not use the system like our laboratory staff; they might use and move the system differently as they move around. Hence, robustness and stability are other key points that lead to the success of this design. These challenges are deliberated throughout the design and implementation of the system and will be addressed in detail in this article.

The application of augmented reality in store settings is promising. Given the fact that 70% of purchase decisions are made in the store (Armata, 1996) and retail grocery shopping in the United States alone is a $450 billion business (U. S. Census Bureau, 2001), computer-aided shopping assistants can be an important tool that can affect both planned and potential purchase decisions. Recent research in advertising shows that a virtual experience simulating 3-D product visualization results in more product knowledge, better brand attitude, and elevated purchase intention relative to traditional advertising (Li, Daugherty, & Biocca, 2002). This work draws on technical capabilities in the augmented-reality community in combination with theoretical concepts from consumer responses to advertising in order to demonstrate and evaluate the concept of dynamic contextualization.

The PromoPad system, built on the concept of dynamic contextualization (Zhu, Owen, Li, & Lee, 2004), uses a tablet PC (personal computer) as a see-through display (Milgram & Kishino, 1994) to provide personalized assistant information to an individual customer. Using dynamic contextualization, the PromoPad not only actively discovers and takes advantage of the context of the user and the environment at a single point (Chen & Kotz, 2000), but also modifies the context to allow retailers to direct users' interests in real time using augmented-reality technologies. These discoveries and modifications of the context are means to improve human-computer interaction and enrich user experience. Augmented reality, as distinct from virtual reality, is the modification of the perception of reality. In this system, the tablet PC is equipped with a small camera on its back, and the display presents the camera image as if the tablet were transparent. Because the image is processed, augmentation graphics can be used to add to the visible context, and erasures or occlusions can be used to remove context by diminishments; all of these operations occur in real time (Azuma, 1997). Several empirical studies on the effectiveness of augmented-reality technologies in terms of human-computer interaction provide sufficient evidence that augmented-reality systems improve the operational performance in an instructing assembly task, training, and guiding tourists (Boud, Haniff, Baber, & Steiner, 1999; Tang, Owen, Biocca, & Mou, 2002; Vlahakis et al., 2002). This work explores the benefits of augmented reality in a more natural and user-centric setting, that is, a shopping environment. Moreover, the design principles of this system can be easily adapted to other application domains that require negligible user interference, automated context-related information presentation, and friendly usage in public environments.

The PSA (Asthana, Cravatts, & Krzyzanoowski, 1994), MyGrocer (Kourouthanassis & Roussos, 2003), and Project Voyager (Chan, 2001) are all prototype shopping assistants that display product reviews, promotions, and pricing information. Our PromoPad system addresses different issues from different points of view and, hence, proposes different solutions. In addition to providing assistant information, the PromoPad focuses on providing the most relevant information to improve the shopping experience.

This article discusses the design issues of the PromoPad system. An analysis of user studies will be included in a separate work.

The rest of the article is organized as follows. The second section gives a brief introduction of the PromoPad's user interface. Next we discuss context-aware automated shopping assistance and dynamic contextualization in detail. The article then talks about the methods to evaluate the PromoPad system, and finally it concludes and discusses the direction of future work.

INTERFACE DESIGN

As we mentioned in the introduction, the first challenge of such a system is that it has to be user friendly and requires no active user interference. The PromoPad possesses these characteristics inherently as it is designed to be a natural and intuitive computing device. Unlike conventional users of computing devices, users of the PromoPad are not required to actively operate the system by legacy input devices. Without interrupting the shopping process, the system provides consumers with useful information at a glance, as natural as seeing a physical sign in the store. On the other hand, if the shopper intends to inspect a particular product, she or he can instantly access additional information through the system.

The target design of the PromoPad is a lightweight device that can slip into a cradle in the shopping cart and be portable by the user for easy shopping assistance. The primary focus of the PromoPad project is operation when removed from the cradle as an augmented-reality shopping assistant. The system consists of a front-end client component and a back-end server component.

The front-end client component is the component that the users interact with. It includes a tablet PC and a camera that is attached to the back of the tablet PC. The front end is designed to track the 3-D position, orientation, and context of the consumer; to track shelf and cart stock; and to generate and display graphical information utilizing data retrieved from the back-end server. The tablet PC is used as a mediating device to deliver graphical information because it is lightweight and its large display can provide both user convenience and rich information. With a camera attached to the back, the tablet PC works as a video see-through display and is aware of the position and orientation of the customer in the store (Tuceryan et al., 1995). What the consumer will see on the display is determined by the user's current location in the store, the user's shopping preference and history, and the product context retrieved from the store database. Figure 1 shows a typical usage of the front-end component.

The back-end component can be one or more servers that contain store inventory databases, customer profiles, and business logic, from which information in the databases is filtered and returned to the front-end component.

Figure 1. Using the PromoPad in a store setting

AUTOMATED CONTEXT-AWARE ASSISTANCE

Using augmented reality in a shopping environment, the information that can be delivered to the user's attention can be vast. It can include the introduction of a new product, a sales sign, or information about a related product. We would have no trouble to clutter the user's view in the tablet PC with a large amount of information. This would make the user unable to interact with the real world, which breaks the principle of augmented-reality technologies. Thus, how to selectively display the most interesting and important information for each individual user becomes a major concern. The system must filter the information stream and provide relevant information that can be accommodated in the tablet display. For example, if the system chooses to flood the user with a large amount of promotion information, price comparisons, and in-store advertising, then the system accomplishes little more than what could be accomplished by handing the customer a thick flier. The new capability of the PromoPad is that it can selectively display information that is related to the product under inspection and information that is tailored to individual needs. In other words, the information that is presented to the user is highly related to the context of the user and the product under inspection. We develop three criteria to determine the relevance of a piece of information to a specific user at a single point in the store:

- User's location and orientation
- User's previous shopping history and pattern
- Product complementary in the store database

We discuss the details of these three criteria in this section.

USER'S LOCATION AND ORIENTATION

The user's location and orientation determine what products the user is inspecting. When the consumer is using the PromoPad during his or her shopping trip, it is reasonable to assume that the

Figure 2. Experimental shelf with fiducial images

position and the orientation of the tablet PC are a reasonable approximation of the position and orientation of the consumer as well. A variety of auto ID systems are in development that will allow high-quality tracking of products relative to the PromoPad and knowledge of purchase (cart insertion) decisions.

With an in-store tracking system, the PromoPad is aware of its 3-D position relative to store shelves and products. Considerable ongoing research has been exploring the use of ultrasonic, RFID (radio-frequency identification), infrared, and vision-based technologies to achieve location awareness (Bishop, Allen, & Welch, 2001; Hightower & Borriello, 2001). The tracking method for such a system, however, is challenging. The quality of the tracking system directly determines the robustness and scalability of the whole system. A vision-based fiducial system and its improvement proposed by Owen, Xiao, and Middlin (2002) is robust (high correlation) and fast (consistently under 2 ms). The fiducial images serve as visual clues that accurately tell the system where the camera is looking. However, 256 possible fiducial images are not scalable enough to identify all the necessary products in a typical store setting. Therefore, we use a hybrid tracking system that uses RFID to track down the approximated position of the user and vision-based fiducial system to determine the accurate position and orientation of the user. Figure 2 shows our experimental shelf with several fiducial images on the bottom.

The location information required for the PromoPad is considerably more rigorous than that of traditional context-aware computing systems. Owen, Zhou, Tang, and Xiao (2003) discuss many issues relative to the augmentation of imagery for augmented-reality applications such as the PromoPad. Augmented reality requires modification of the camera image. Achieving pixel-resolution registration of computer graphics with store shelf contents requires high-accuracy knowledge of the location and orientation of the PromoPad. Visual fiducial systems provide sufficient accuracy for high-quality image modifications.

With the tracking system, the PromoPad is aware of the 3-D position and orientation of the consumer relative to the product and store shelves. It then sends a query to the back-end server and displays feedback on the tablet PC. For example, when the consumer is in the dairy aisle, the server returns the promotional information for various milk brands.

User Profile

The user profile includes such data as brand preference, buying history, and shopping pattern. The user profile also includes individual and aggregate behaviors based on shopping habits and demographics. Each time the consumer checks out, purchases are recorded in the store membership database. These systems are already common in many stores that include loyalty cards, and there is evidence that many consumers utilize these systems (Mauri, 2003). From loyalty-card systems or future automated variations, stores can create personal profiles based on the previous purchases that the consumer has made. For nonmember consumers, a generic profile with demographic manipulations can be used.

The consumer will scan her or his member card or log in as a member before using the PromoPad. Based on history information, the system applies business logic at the database inquiry. The system is able to answer questions like "How likely is it that the customer will buy a carton of milk on this visit?" or "How interested is this customer in some toys for 2- to 3-year-old girls?" or "Will the customer like this brand of frozen pizza?" Carefully applying data mining techniques and planning business logic, the system can even predict more sophisticated conditions (Hastie, Tibshirani, & Friedman, 2001). Answers to these questions help the system to predict whether or not the consumer will be interested in certain classes of information. If the answer is affirmative, then the system will consider that the consumer is definitely interested in this information and delivers it to the consumer using store directions and emphasis of the product on the shelf. If the answer is moderately positive, then it can consider this information may trigger an impulse purchase. If the answer is strongly negative, then it interprets that the consumer will not like this information or related products, and hence the system will not bother the consumer at all.

Product Context

Product context is the set of complementary products that are associated with the focal product or the product under inspection. A complementary product is a product that enjoys an associative relationship with the focal product. By contextualizing the focal product with a matching product, image, or symbol, the consumer's attitude toward the focal product can be influenced. Product contextualization can include functional, aesthetic, or sociocultural complements of the focal product (Englis & Solomon, 1996).

Functional complementary products are products that can be consumed jointly in order to facilitate some operational relationship. For example, golf clubs can be functionally complemented by golf balls, bags, shoes, and so forth. A user purchasing hot dog buns is likely to purchase the hot dogs to place in them. Hence, functionally complementary products can have very close relationships that influence simultaneous purchase.

Aesthetic complementary products are products that are consumed because they form an inherently pleasant relationship with each other. Consumers' motivation in using these products is the aesthetic pleasure derived from their juxtaposition. For example, a baroque painting in a baroque-designed house gives aesthetic complementarity to the house. Aesthetic complementarity is often highly subjective; hence, it is not currently included in our experiment design, though use of experts may allow for aesthetic suggestions.

Sociocultural complementary products are groups of products that involve consumption activities and/or products that hold little or no inherent relationship to each other, but are instead related through a sociocultural process of association and ascription of meaning. Groupings are valued for the ability to communicate social messages within a particular culture at a particular historic moment. For example, we may easily socioculturally associate BMWs with MBAs, Rolex watches, and so forth. Tie-dyed tshirts are always socioculturally associated with patched blue jeans, army fatigue jackets, and so on. Table 1 lists some examples of product complementarity as used in the base PromoPad evaluation products database.

Dynamic Contextualization with Augmented Reality

Dynamic contextualization is a process of contextual information rendering in multimedia form in response to cognitive needs of users when they are interacting with real objects in a changing physical environment. It is an extension of the concepts of product contextualization and virtual product contextualization. Researchers define product contextualization as the placement of the product in a particular setting that will resonate with the consumers and make clear the product's consumption practices (Englis & Solomon, 1996). Product contextualization is often seen in store displays and advertisement. In electronic commerce, product contextualization can be easily simulated with 3-D visualization, which can offer a variety of ways for the consumer to arrange a focal product with other complimentary products on the computer screen. Researchers use virtual contextualization to refer to the placement of complimentary products along with a focal product in 3-D visualization in order to affect the user's perception of the focal product (Li, Daugherty, & Biocca, 2001). For example, the user can arrange a set of furniture in different settings in 3-D on a Web site to select the preferable combination. Research demonstrated that virtual contextualization can lead to better consumer experience and brand attitude, and hence influences purchase intention (Host, 2001).

Dynamic contextualization is superior to virtual contextualization in that it is a combination of both direct experience and virtual experience, resulting in an enhanced product experience. Augmented reality lies between the real world and complete virtual reality (Milgram & Kishino, 1994). Users can add virtual objects to their perception of the real world to create an augmented reality. Although consumers can view various combinations of a focal product with different complimentary products in virtual contextualization, their product experience is simulated and virtual in the sense that they have no direct contact with a real focal product. In dynamic contextualization using augmented-reality technologies, consumers can inspect a real focal product in a virtual context that is simulated to meet their cognitive needs. Consumers can not only see the real product, but also instantly access additional product information on the tablet PC, such as complementary products and background information of the focal product. Such an enhanced consumer experience in dynamic contextualization is even richer than merely a direct product experience.

Dynamic contextualization modifies the user's perception of reality by either augmenting context

Table 1. Product complementarity examples

Focal Products	Functional Complementarity	Sociocultural Complementarity
Digital camera	Photo paper, memory card, printer for digital camera, picture-editing software	Vacation package, plane ticket, ballpark tickets
Pen	Notebook, highlighter, pencil jar	Hair tie
Wine	Wine stand, corkscrew, glasses	Crystal container, romantic dinner, travel package to winery
Shampoo	Conditioner, hair dryer, hair gel, body wash	Fruits, herbs

or diminishing context. The latter is referred to as diminished reality in the literature (Mann & Fung, 2001; Zokai, Esteve, Genc, & Navab, 2003).

Augmenting Context

Augmenting context is the most common implementation of augmented-reality systems, as suggested by the name of augmented reality. By adding context to the focal product, the PromoPad is able to give consumers more information about the focal product that is not possible in traditional media. Theoretically, the added context can be coupons, advertisements, or complementing products as discussed in the previous section. Based on the advertiser's needs, these pieces of information could be 2-D pictures or 3-D objects that appear beside, in the foreground, or in the background of the focal product, or immersed into the shelf display. It is actually possible to have content in the display with depths deeper than the physical shelf, allowing a virtual extension of the store space. Figure 3 illustrates the augmentation of a box of spaghetti with an image of cooked spaghetti with sauce.

Likewise, the PromoPad can place information such as complementary settings of the product into the background of the focal product. Although it may not draw the consumer's active attention, the new information affects the consumer's attitude toward this product. The immersive setting will function in a similar fashion. Putting the augmentations in the background or immersing them into the layout is more technically challenging. The contour of the front objects needs to be determined and modeled using an occlusion model so that the front objects accurately occlude the virtual object in the background. In an immersive setting, the depth of the virtual object needs to be compared with all the real objects or other virtual objects that may occlude it. Figure 4 gives an example of augmenting the background. A comparison of a store brand and a name brand appears in the background.

Diminishing Context

Whereas augmenting context highlights the focal product by delivering augmented virtual objects to the consumer, diminishing context emphasizes the focal product by hiding the surrounding product

Figure 3. Augmenting the box of spaghetti with cooked spaghetti and sauce

items, most likely noncomplementary products or competing brands. Figure 5 illustrates this idea by virtually removing the competition from the surrounding settings. Removing the competition gives more room to display information for the product that the retailer plans to introduce to the consumer or to increase the sales volume at that period of time.

Both augmentations and diminishments allow retailers to apply business strategy and direct users' interests. Table 2 lists several possible examples of augmentations and diminishments to the focal products, which are listed in Table 1, other than coupons and sales offers.

EVALUATING THE PROMOPAD SYSTEM

The design and development of the PromoPad prototype have focused on the development of the appropriate technologies for implementation and acquisition of the theory in support of dynamic contextualization as discussed in this article. The feasibility of applying augmented reality on a tablet PC as a shopping assistant will next be assessed in lab and field experiments so as to determine the real benefit of dynamic contextualization. As a multidisciplinary project involving researchers from both computer science and advertising, research questions of this user

Figure 4. Augmenting the background

Figure 5. Diminishing context

Table 2. Examples of augmentations and diminishments

Focal Products	Augmentations	Diminishments
Digital camera	Picture slideshow, feature demonstration, accessories	Outmoded models, security locks and latches, film camera
Pen	Notebook, grade report, back-to-school picture	Crayon, scissors
Wine	Glasses, roses, picture of a grand banquet	All bottles other than the bottle under inspection
Shampoo	Hair dryer, fruits, picture of model with beautiful hair	Hair dye

* *This is determined by the user profile, hence it is user dependent*

study include (a) whether direct experience can be significantly enhanced with virtual experience that is simulated by real-time rendering of 3-D objects during a typical shopping process, (b) how direct experience with different types of products (geometric, material, or mechanical) can be affected by different complementary associations (functional, aesthetic, or sociocultural), (c) what the roles are that consumer product knowledge and needs for cognition play in the formation of enhanced product experience, (d) what obstacles exist for the tablet PC to be used as an effective shopping assistant in a store setting, (e) how participants assess the human-computer interaction provided by the PromoPad, (f) how efficient and accurate the tracking and information retrieval are in the system, (g) whether the system is ergonomically friendly, and (h) how realistic the rendered imagery is perceived to be.

A shopping setting will be created in the lab where participants will be invited to test the PromoPad system. Example physical products that were selected from pretests (as reported in previously) will be used in pilot studies. Based on pilot-study results, the research questions, design of the system, and measures will be revised and further tested with a sample of consumers in a real store environment to increase the external validity of the study.

Three kinds of data will be collected in experimental sessions. First, the shopper's interaction with all objects on the screen will be tracked and the patterns of interaction will be analyzed to reveal what information is of interest to the shopper, how long it takes for the shopper to process the information, and what sequences the shopper follows to access different product information. The tracking data also can help examine the usability of the system design. Second, the shopper's overall experience with the products and the shopping process will be measured, along with several dependent variables such as presence, brand knowledge, brand attitude, purchase intention, and decision confidence. Third, the quality of the system design will be assessed by examining variables such as reaction time, accuracy of data, and user friendliness.

The internal and external validity and the reliability of all measures will be assessed before scale scores are used for analysis. To answer the research questions, a series of statistical analyses will be conducted.

CONCLUSION

This article presents the concept of a shopping assistant that utilizes augmented-reality technologies to provide personalized advertising and in-store shopping assistance based on dynamic contextualization. This PromoPad system is a step toward ubiquitous computing in the highly lucrative grocery-shopping segment. The development goal is to offer a pleasant and inviting shopping experience that is mediated by an augmented-reality-based tablet PC. Beyond traditional context awareness, this article developed the concept of dynamic contextualization, which suggests the modification of context to direct the interest flow of users. Dynamic contextualization, the real-time modification of context, can be enabled by augmented-reality technologies with augmentations and diminishments. Dynamic contextualization is based on, but extends beyond, the spatial and temporal context of the user. Location context, user context, and product context are integrated in this design to address the requirements of an intelligent context-aware shopping assistant.

The design methodology of the PromoPad system can be extended to other circumstances such as tourism guides, training assistants, and so forth. Nevertheless, designers of other systems need to deliberately consider the context factors based on the requirements of the application domain.

Although this article has addressed several important issues in designing the PromoPad, it has not discussed the privacy issue in the project. The privacy issue arises when the retailers collect consumption activities and try to predict the consumer's interest based on previous shopping behavior. It is necessary to balance the trade-off between automation and privacy to meet the needs of both retailers and consumers. Consumers may be willing to sacrifice a certain degree of their privacy in return for certain value, and retailers definitely should respect the privacy of their customers. The goal of this study is to maximize the automation, and the privacy issue is beyond the scope of this article.

ACKNOWLEDGMENT

This work is supported by a Microsoft research grant.

REFERENCES

Armata, K. (1996). Signs that sell. *Progressive Grocer, 17*(21).

Asthana, A., Cravatts, M., & Krzyzanoowski, P. (1994). An indoor wireless system for personalized shopping assistance. In *IEEE Workshop on Mobile Computing Systems and Applications*, Santa Cruz, CA. IEEE Computer Society Press.

Azuma, R. T. (1997). A survey of augmented reality. *Presence: Teleoperators and Virtual Environments, 6*(4), 355-385.

Bishop, G., Allen, B. D., & Welch, G. (2001). *Tracking: Beyond 15 minutes of thought.*

Boud, A. C., Haniff, D. J., Baber, C., & Steiner, S. J. (1999). Virtual reality and augmented reality as a training tool for assembly tasks. In *1999 International Conference on Information Visualisation.*

Chan, W. (2001). *Project Voyager: Building an Internet presence for people, places, and things.* Cambridge, MA: Massachusetts Institute of Technology.

Chen, G., & Kotz, D. (2000). *A survey of context-aware mobile computing research.* Dartmouth College, Department of Computer Science.

Englis, B. G., & Solomon, M. R. (1996). Using consumption constellations to develop integrated marketing communications. *Journal of Business Research, 37*(3), 183-191.

Hastie, T., Tibshirani, R., & Friedman, J. (2001). *The elements of statistical learning.* Springer-Verlag.

Hightower, J., & Borriello, G. (2001). *A survey and taxonomy of location systems for ubiquitous computing.* University of Washington, Department of Computer Science and Engineering.

Host, B. (2001). The impact on consumer behavior by virtual reality: Survey in the German furniture market. In *Proceedings of the 2001 Experiential E-Commerce Conference*, East Lansing, MI.

Kourouthanassis, P., & Roussos, G. (2003). Developing consumer-friendly pervasive retail systems. *IEEE Pervasive Computing.*

Li, H., Daugherty, T., & Biocca, F. (2001). Characteristics of virtual experience in electronic commerce: A protocol analysis. *Journal of Interactive Marketing, 15*(3), 13-30.

Li, H., Daugherty, T., & Biocca, F. (2002). Impact of 3-D advertising on product knowledge, brand attitude, and purchase intention: The mediating role of presence. *Journal of Advertising, 31*(3), 43-57.

Mackay, W. E. (1996). *Augmenting reality: A new paradigm for interacting with computers.* Orsay Cedex, France.

Mann, S., & Fung, J. (2001). VideoOrbits on eye tap devices for deliberately diminished reality or altering the visual perception of rigid planar patches of a real world scene. In *International Symposium on Mixed Reality (ISMR2001).*

Mauri, C. (2003). Card loyalty: A new emerging issue in grocery retailing. *Journal of Retailing and Consumer Services, 10*(1), 13-25.

Milgram, P., & Kishino, F. (1994). A taxonomy of mixed reality visual displays. *IEICE Transactions on Information Systems, E77-D*(12).

Owen, C. B., Xiao, F., & Middlin, P. (2002). What is the best fiducial? In *The First IEEE International Augmented Reality Toolkit Workshop*, Darmstadt, Germany.

Owen, C. B., Zhou, J., Tang, K. H., & Xiao, F. (2003). Augmented imagery for digital video applications. In *CRC handbook of video databases.* CRC Press LLC.

Rauterberg, M., Mauch, T., & Stebler, R. (1996). The digital playing desk: A case study for augmented reality. In *Fifth IEEE International Workshop on Robot and Human Communication*, Tsukuba, Japan.

Rekimoto, J., & Nagao, K. (1995). The world through the computer: Computer augmented interaction with real world environments. In *Symposium on User Interface Software and Technology (UIST'95).* ACM Press.

Rosenholtz, R., Li, Y., Mansfield, J., & Jin, Z. (2005). Feature congestion: A measure of display clutter. In *Proceedings of the SIGCHI Conference on Human Factors in Computing Systems*, Portland, OR.

Tang, A., Owen, C., Biocca, F., & Mou, W. (2002). Comparative effectiveness of augmented reality in object assembly. In *Proceedings of ACM CHI 2002*, Darmstadt, Germany.

Tuceryan, M., Greer, D. S., Whitaker, R. T., Breen, D., Crampton, C., Rose, E., et al. (1995). Calibration requirements and procedures for a monitor-based augmented reality system. *IEEE Transactions on Visualization and Computer Graphics, 1*(3), 255-273.

U.S. Census Bureau. (2001). *Unadjusted and adjusted estimates of monthly retail and food service sales by kinds of business.*

Vlahakis, V., Ioannidis, N., Karigiannis, J., Tsotros, M., Gounaris, M., Stricker, D., et al. (2002). Archeoguide: An augmented reality guide for archaeological sites. *IEEE Computer Graphics and Applications, 22*(5), 38-50.

Zhu, W., Owen, C. B., Li, H., & Lee, J.-H. (2004). Personalized in-store e-commerce with the PromoPad: An augmented reality shopping assistant. *The Electronic Journal for E-Commerce Tools & Applications, 1*(3).

Zokai, S., Esteve, J., Genc, Y., & Navab, N. (2003). Multiview paraperspective projection model for diminished reality. In *The Second IEEE and ACM International Symposium on Mixed and Augmented Reality (ISMAR '03)*, Tokyo.

This work was previously published in the Journal of Organizational and End User Computing, Vol. 20, Issue 3, edited by M. Mahmood, pp. 41-56, copyright 2008 by IGI Publishing (an imprint of IGI Global).

Chapter 12
Thinking Outside of the Ballot Box:
Examining Public Trust in E-Voting Technology

Susan K. Lippert
Drexel University, USA

Ekundayo B. Ojumu
IBM Global Services, USA

ABSTRACT

Electronic voting, or e-voting, is a relatively closed process that contains inherent risks associated with the potential for voting irregularities, translation errors, and inappropriate manipulation (Oravec, 2005). To develop a greater understanding of trust issues surrounding the use of e-voting, an investigation into the public trust and the relationship between trust and electronic voting technology were assessed. Men and women of various ethnicities, ages, educational backgrounds, technological experiences, political affiliations, and prior experience with e-voting participated in this study. Rogers' (1995) taxonomy of adopters—innovators, early adopters, early majority, late majority, and laggards—was used to classify individuals based on their willingness to participate in e-voting. A principle-components factor analysis (PCFA) with separate tests for discriminant validity and multiple-regression analyses were used to confirm the hypotheses. The findings suggest that innovators and early adopters are more likely to trust technology and express an intention to use an e-voting system.

INTRODUCTION

Electronic voting, or e-voting, has been found to contain inherent risks for irregularities, errors, and inappropriate manipulation (Oravec, 2005). E-voting is the use of software and hardware to facilitate voting by individuals from either remote or poll-specific locations through a computer information system for casting votes. E-voting systems should ensure the privacy and authenticity of the voter, enable the individual to record only one vote, and remain secure from any unauthorized individuals tampering with the technology in an attempt to cast fraudulent votes.

The 2004 election in the United States encountered several problems with the e-voting process including technological issues when the New Orleans e-voting machines failed, resulting in frustrated voters and unwanted litigation (*E-Voting Problems Reported as Election Gets Under Way*, 2004). Additionally, an e-voting machine in Ohio added almost 4,000 votes for George W. Bush (Liptak, 2004) while in North Carolina, more than 4,500 votes were lost due to a storage problem (*Computer Loses 4,500 Votes*, 2004). These issues provide examples of technological and procedural anomalies associated with e-voting and underscore the need for protocols that ensure the verifiability of actual votes cast.

The United States is not alone in the use and development of e-voting. In fact, Ireland, Australia, the United Kingdom, and India have established independent commissions to investigate the use of e-voting technologies (Commission on Electronic Voting, 2005). The Government of Ireland established a commission on e-voting in March 2004 to evaluate a computer-aided voting and counting system proposed for use during the June 2004 elections. The commission indicated that it did not have a "requisite degree of confidence" in the chosen system based on issues of system testing, source-code reliability, accuracy of the software, and the security of the system. A key overriding factor cited in the report was the limited amount of time available to review the system prior to the proposed usage date.

Australian voters were first introduced to the Australian Capital Territory (ACT) e-voting system in the October 2001 election. This system was again used for parliamentary elections in October 2004 (*ACT Legislative Assembly*, 2001). This e-voting system uses personal computers as voting terminals and authenticates the votes with the use of a bar code. These voting terminals are connected to a secure server in each polling location. In the Australian model, individuals are not able to vote over public networks such as the Internet (*ACT Legislative Assembly*).

The Office of the Deputy Prime Minister in the United Kingdom is considering the use of e-voting for its next general election in 2008 (*Implementing Electronic Voting in the UK*, n.d.). While the UK government has yet to decide on a specific e-voting policy, it has a wide variety of possibilities under consideration including (a) enabling individuals to vote by telephone from home, (b) casting a ballot from a mobile phone, (c) using the Internet, or (d) recording choices through digital television configurations. Regardless of the specific application selected, there remain a number of issues of concern with the introduction of e-voting practices. These concerns include protecting privacy, maintaining security, enabling secrecy, and generating public confidence in e-voting systems (*Implementing Electronic Voting in the UK*, n.d.).

The Election Commission of India (2005) has considered the use of electronic voting machines (EVMs) as an alternative to traditional paper ballots used for electing candidates. The EVM contains a control unit and a balloting unit listing each candidate with a light adjacent to the button that the voter presses to indicate a selected candidate choice. Both components of the EVM operate through a battery power pack. The Election Commission suggests that the use of EVMs speeds the counting process, offers secrecy of voting data, and contains security features to ensure the integrity of recorded votes.

Internet usage varies greatly. As of 2005, it is estimated that 13.9% or 889 million individuals of the estimated 6.4 billion in the world are Internet users (*Internet Usage Statistics*, n.d.). The seven world regions differ in the percentage of the population that has Internet access: In Africa it is 1.5%; Asia, 8.4%; Europe, 35.5%; the Middle East, 7.5%; North America, 67.4%; Latin America and the Caribbean, 10.3%; and Oceania and Australia, 48.6% (*Internet Usage Statistics*). Table 1 provides a comparison of the percentage of Internet users with the total citizenship in selected industrialized countries as of February 2005.

Given the diversity in the percentage of Internet users in each of these countries, the challenges of implementing e-voting in each locale differ. The differences between the proposed systems by country vary in terms of the user interface, the procedures used to facilitate the voting process, the degree of computerization, and the location from which the individual is able to vote. The similarity between these systems is that they automate the electoral process.

THE UNITED STATES AND ELECTRONIC VOTING

In October 2002, the 107th U.S. Congress passed the public law known as the Help America Vote Act of 2002 (HAVA; Public Law 107-252) that authorized $3.8 billion in federal spending, of which a substantial portion was allocated to U.S. states to replace their punch-card and current voting machines (*Help America Vote Act of 2002*, 2002). Direct-recording electronic (DRE) voting machines and touch-screen systems electronically record a vote during polling (Dill, Mercuri, Neumann, & Wallach, 2004; Dill, Schneier, & Simons, 2003). DREs, introduced in the 1970s, are the first computerized voting systems. Touch-screen DREs are considered the most versatile and user friendly of any current voting system (Fischer, 2003). The presence and use of these systems is expected to increase substantially under provisions of the Help America Vote Act of 2002 due to the requirement that, beginning in 2006, each polling place used in a federal election have at least one voting machine that is fully accessible for persons with disabilities (Fischer). The use of DREs is a security issue due to the absence of ballots, thorough audit trails, and concrete assurances that votes cast are properly recorded and processed (Neumann, 1990).

The e-voting technology currently available in the United States is in the initial stages of testing, and the U.S. Federal Election Commission (2004) recognizes that unclear standards exist on how to successfully perform the tasks necessary for electronic polling. Contrary to popular belief,

Table 1. Internet usage by population

Country	Percentage of Internet Users	Total Country Population	Average Annual Earnings in 2003[1]
United States	67.8% [2]	296 million	$37,610
Australia	66.2%[3]	20.5 million	$21,650
United Kingdom	58.7%[4]	60.4 million	$27,350
Ireland	51.2%[5]	4.0 million	$26,960
India	3.6%[6]	1.1 billion	$530

[1] *Global/World Income Per Capita/Head 2004* (2004)
[2] *Internet Usage for the Americas* (n.d.)
[3] *Internet Usage and Population in Oceania* (n.d.)
[4] *Internet World Stats* (n.d.)
[5] *Internet World Stats* (n.d.)
[6] *Internet Usage in Asia* (n.d.)

Internet voting does not reduce the administrative costs of an election due to the purchase and maintenance costs of polling equipment at the various regulatory levels (B. Jones, 2000). Therefore, what motivating factors could make this evolution of the electoral process appropriate for electronic voting? Empowerment, expediency, and improved efficiency might influence this fundamental change in the way that society exercises its voting privileges.

The March 2000 Democratic presidential primary in Arizona was the first binding public election in the United States to use Internet voting technology. The 1996 American presidential election turnout of 49% was the lowest since Calvin Coolidge was elected in 1924 and the second lowest presidential election turnout since the election of John Quincy Adams in 1824 (Phillips & Von Spakovsky, 2001). These statistics raise concern regarding the populace's involvement in the electoral process. Lack of involvement may be partially attributable to voters' disenfranchised sentiment toward the electoral process. As the motivation for this study, we suggest that voters' lack of trust in the technology used to facilitate the voting process affects the degree of individual participation using e-voting systems.

The 2000 Caltech-MIT Voting Technology Project found that in elections from 1988 to 2000, the accuracy of touch-screen machines or DREs resulted in less reliable results than paper ballots (Boutin, 2004). The process is subject to errors, manipulation, and fraud (Neumann, 2004), which may be exacerbated with the use of e-voting. Although paper ballots can be lost, which has occurred in a number of elections, the recovery of these ballots remains a potential. The loss of an e-vote is permanent and unrecoverable. In August 2000, the Reform party solicited validity systems to facilitate their presidential nomination process by offering Internet voting as an alternative to traditional methods such as mail-in and telephone balloting (Weiss, 2001). The validity systems' Internet-based voting system was claimed to have successfully recorded 5,000 votes despite 35 reported attempts by individuals of hacking into the voting system (Weiss). The Internet-based system was not compromised and thereby demonstrated the potential to successfully use an Internet-based technology for e-voting.

Public concern perpetuates the notion that computerizing the voting process could put those unfamiliar with computers at a disadvantage. Additionally, access issues remain an equality issue when initially evaluating e-voting technology, also known as the digital divide. In two independent studies (Ornstein & Schenkenberg, 1996; Phillips & Von Spakovsky, 2001) that compared online access and use, the findings suggest differences in public representation in the electoral process as a function of access and familiarity with technology.

The purpose of this study is to test predictive validity and relational hypotheses based on Rogers' (1995) characteristics of adopters as compared to perceptions of trust in e-voting systems, the intention to adopt e-voting technology, and the willingness to vote using this technology.

THEORETICAL GROUNDING

Innovation Diffusion Theory

Rogers' (1995) innovation diffusion theory (IDT) is a widely accepted theory to explain the process by which new innovations are accepted by members of a social system. IDT suggests that the diffusion process occurs as individuals accept and use new practices, ideas, or objects such as a new technology. Social systems, according to Rogers, consist of individuals or groups who share a common goal or objective, connecting them as a social structure. Each member of the social system makes his or her own adoption decision based partially on his or her own subjective evaluations, but also on the evaluation of others who previously adopted the technology. Experiences of earlier adopters are communicated to members of the individual's network of peers through informal or formal communication channels. Based on Rogers' definition, we suggest that members of the general voting populous represent a social system.

Diffusion is the process by which an innovation is communicated through channels over time among members of a social system. As part of this process, there are four components to the diffusion: (a) the innovation, (b) the communication process, (c) time, and (d) the social system. As individuals within the general voting populous interact with Internet-based technologies, it is common that they communicate their experiences to others who are important to them. This process is represented in Rogers' (1995) discussion of diffusion. Yet, not all individuals adopt the technology at the same rate nor will they have the same level of interest in the continued use of the innovation. Rather, individuals adopt a technology over time based on their innovativeness, which represents the degree to which a member of a social system adopts an innovation earlier than other individuals within the same system. According to Rogers, innovativeness manifests as a behavioral change rather than just an attitudinal or cognitive shift.

In order to capture these differences between potential adopters, Rogers (1995) developed a taxonomy of five classifications of adopters based on the speed with which each adopts a new innovation. A key differentiation between each category of adopter is innovativeness. Rogers suggests that innovativeness is relative in that one individual expresses greater or less interest than others in the system. The five adopter categories within the taxonomy include (a) innovators, (b) early adopters, (c) early majority, (d) late majority, and (e) laggards. In studying these types of users, Rogers noticed a normal frequency distribution associated with each different category of adopter. Rogers suggests that adopters from the same category share similar socioeconomic status, personality characteristics, values, and communication behavior.

MODEL DEVELOPMENT AND HYPOTHESES

This study examines three dependent variables: (a) perceptions of technology trust, (b) intention to adopt, and (c) willingness to vote through e-voting technology. Figure 1 summarizes the research model incorporating the hypothesized relationships.

Dependent Variables

Three dependent variables are considered in this study: (a) perceptions of technology trust, (b) intention to adopt, and (c) willingness to vote.

Perceptions of Technology Trust

Technology trust is an individual's willingness to be vulnerable to a technology based on the individual's expectations that the technology is predictable, reliable, and useful (Lippert, 2001). This form of trust is unique because the object of trust is an inanimate artifact rather than another individual. The trust assessment formed by an individual toward the technology results from the individual's attitude based on past experiences and expectations of how the system will function in the future. The individual makes the assumption that data entered into the system will be accurately maintained and available for later retrieval. An evaluation is made by the individual each time he or she interacts with the technology. Understanding how individuals learn to trust in technology is becoming more important as individual and organizational dependence on information systems mature (S. Jones, Wilikens, Morris, & Masera, 2000).

Using a technology for a new task, such as e-voting, requires a significant degree of trust and

Figure 1. Research model

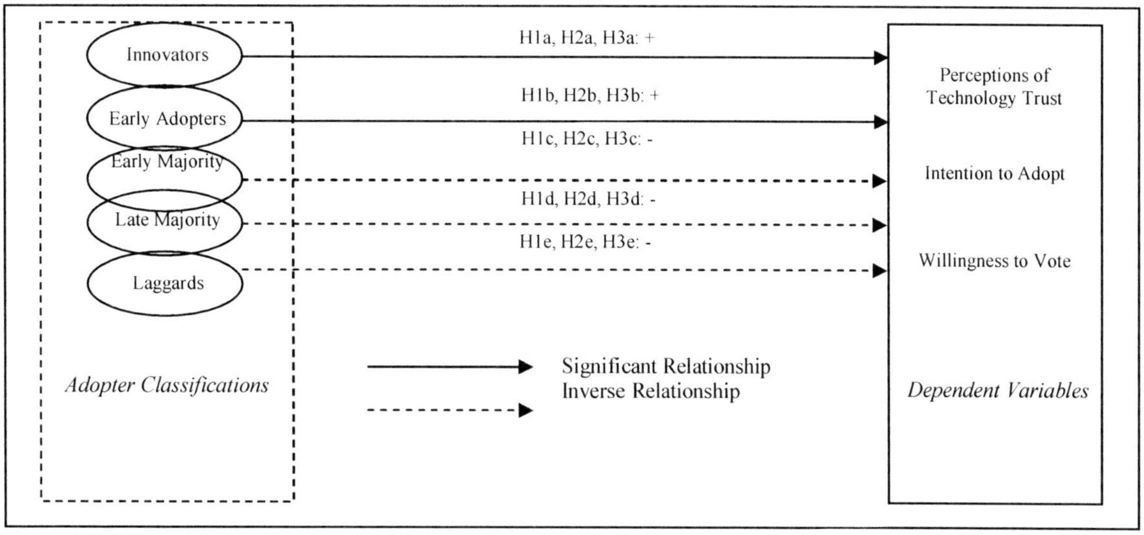

manifests in a willingness to assume the risks associated with the technology's use. The willingness to take a risk is a common characteristic of all trust situations (Costigan, Ilter, & Berman, 1998). In order for trust to exist, past experiences are needed to establish familiarity with the situation and lessen the level of perceived risk (Johnson-George & Swap, 1982). Additionally, as individuals engage in a series of interactions that result in successful outcomes, their perceptions of trust will increase (Dahl & Pedersen, 2005). In other words, an individual's familiarity with a given technology coupled with a sense of trust that the technology will function as expected combines to shape the individual's attitude and subsequent behavior. Technology trust is particularly applicable to situations involving the use of an innovation because the individual's interaction with the system is a classic man-machine interface. An individual's standards and perceptions of technology trust will influence the nature of the interaction with the technology.

According to Rogers (1995), innovators are intellectual risk takers who are able to cope with a high degree of ambiguity. Since e-voting technologies are relatively unknown to the majority of the U.S. population, innovators are likely to enjoy the novelty of the innovation and be willing to trust the technology to function effectively and consistently without any malfunctions. Innovators understand the value and convenience that e-voting enables and will continue to perceive the technology to be worthy of trust. Early adopters, as well, will gain insights from the innovators who trust the e-voting technology and are likely to express trust early in the acceptance process. The remainder of the adopters, however, will not trust the e-voting system at an early state since the technology is so new. Individuals who are classified as early majority, late majority, and laggards will not express a trust in the e-voting technology because they are not familiar enough with the technology to assign trust to the system. Therefore, we have the following hypothesis:

H1: *Individuals classified as innovators and early adopters will indicate that they trust the e-voting technology. Individuals classified as early majority, late majority, and laggards will not express trust in e-voting technology.*

Intention to Adopt

The theory of reasoned action (TRA; Fishbein & Ajzen, 1975) provides a basis for predicting human behavior through two key assumptions that underlie the theory. These two assumptions include (a) that an individual's action is preceded by the conscious decision to behave in a particular manner, and (b) once the individual has made the decision to act, he or she will not be inhibited by external limitations or unconscious beliefs (Bagozzi & Warshaw, 1990). Fishbein and Ajzen contend that an individual's intention to behave is determined by two predominant factors: (a) an individual's attitude toward an activity and (b) the subjective norms about the behavior.

An individual's attitude is influenced by her or his assessment that engaging in a specific behavior will lead to a desired outcome. Subjective norms are based on beliefs about whether or not a behavior exhibited by an individual will gain approval from her or his referent group(s). The TRA assumes that individuals behave rationally and voluntarily. Therefore, if behaviors are volitional, then understanding intentions to behave should increase behavior predictability. Thus, TRA can be useful in understanding the degree to which citizens are willing to adopt e-voting systems. The use of TRA as a theoretical basis for understanding intention to adopt a new technology is substantiated by a number of studies (e.g., Agarwal & Prasad, 2000; Davis, 1989). Venkatesh and Morris (2000) extended the technology acceptance model (TAM) to include the influence of subjective norms on the adoption decision by both men and women.

Rogers (1995) suggests that innovators are likely to adopt an innovation based on its novelty and the opportunity of working with the new system. As such, individuals classified as innovators are likely to express an interest in trying the new e-voting technology before others in their social group. Likewise, early adopters are likely to express an interest in the new innovation. Since early adopters serve as role models for their friends and colleagues, they can influence later adopters—early majority, late majority, and laggards—through the subjective norms process described in TRA. Early adopters are more likely to express an intention to adopt e-voting technology in the initial stages when the system is relatively unknown. However, since e-voting technology has not become a mainstream voting protocol, it is unlikely that the early majority, late majority, and laggards will express an intention to adopt e-voting systems. Based on Rogers's classification of adopters, the following hypothesis is offered.

H2: *Individuals classified as innovators and early adopters will express an intention to adopt e-voting technology. Individuals classified as early majority, late majority, and laggards will not express an intention to adopt e-voting technology.*

Willingness to Vote

Willingness to vote represents the degree to which an individual is prepared to vote using e-voting technology. When an innovation is introduced, individuals adopt the innovation at different times and for different reasons. When an innovation is introduced into a social system, some individuals are more open to adaptation than others (Lefebvre & Lefebvre, 1996). The degree to which an individual is open to change will affect his or her rate of acceptance. Rogers' (1995) work suggests that change becomes self-sustaining when about 15% to 20% of a target population accepts an innovation. Early adopters are the most influential agents for change because they have links to both the innovators and the more conservative members of the social system. Individuals may differ based on the innovation being introduced. For example, an individual may be an early adopter for ATM (automated teller machine) banking technology but classified within the late majority for Internet-based banking. The difference may be attributable to his or her level of trust in the two technologies; past experiences, both positive and negative; and input received from members of his or her social system deemed important. The characteristics, as described by Rogers, that an individual voter identifies with will influence the level of technology trust in the innovation and the individual's proclivity to use the new system. Understanding the depth of an individual's tendency to trust technology will be significant in the development and successful deployment of e-voting. In order for e-voting to become mainstream, it is important that a majority of citizens express a willingness to vote. As such, we present the following hypothesis.

H3: *Individuals classified as innovators and early adopters will express a willingness to vote if e-voting is used at their precinct. Individuals classified as early majority, late majority, and laggards will indicate that they are not willing to vote with e-voting technology at this time.*

METHODOLOGY

Questionnaire Measures

Three classes of measures were used in this study: (a) adopter measures and items, (b) dependent variables, and (c) demographics.

Adopter Measures and Items

Seven-point Likert-scales were used to measure respondents' perceptions toward the specific scale items. Response options ranged from *strongly disagree* (1) to *strongly agree* (7), with interval-created data from an ordinal response pattern. Questions were used to classify individuals into one of five categories—innovators, early adopters, early majority, late majority, or laggards—based on Rogers' (1995) taxonomy of adopters. These questions were developed for this study and represent new measures. Three items were used to assess an individual's classification as an innovator. These were "I care about technology," "I like to try new technologies just to see if they work," and "I am interested in learning new technologies." Two questions were used to measure an individual's classification as an early adopter. These two items include "I have high expectations for the new technology" and "I look at the technology for what it can do from a business perspective." Three questions were used to classify the early majority. The three items are "Product quality is important in the decision to use or recommend the new technology," "The availability of repair service is important in the decision to use the new technology," and "I look to other people, whose opinions I respect, for recommendations when buying new technologies." Two items were used to assess an individual's classification as late majority and include "I have a fear of high-technology products" and "I tend to stop using new technology shortly after trying it." Two questions were used to classify laggards and include "I believe a new technology will often fail" and "The costs of high-tech products are not worth the money invested." Means of the items were calculated to produce composite scores. A score was generated for each respondent across the five adopter categories. Each participant was classified within a specific category based on his or her highest generated mean score.

Dependent Variables

Technology trust was assessed using a modified three-item version of Lippert's (2001) technology trust measure: "I can rely on technology to be working when I need it," "I have faith that technology will function as I expect it," and "I have a high degree of confidence that technology will be working when I need it." Intention to adopt was assessed using a two-item scale by Agarwal and Karahanna (2000): "I plan to use electronic voting in the future" and "I expect my use of electronic voting to continue in the future." Willingness to vote was measured using a two-item scale developed for this study: "If e-voting was used in my area, I would be less likely to vote" and "If e-voting was not used in my area, I would be more likely to vote."

Demographics

The demographic variables measured are age, gender, educational level, years of work experience, years using technology, cultural orientation, party registration, participation in the most recent gubernatorial election, and participation in the most recent presidential election.

Data Collection

To evaluate public perception regarding e-voting technology, 165 men and women from New Jersey, Pennsylvania, and Georgia participated in a study to evaluate trust in technology, intention to adopt, and willingness to use e-voting systems. Study participants volunteered to complete a self-report questionnaire. The data captured perceptions from men and women of various ethnicities ranging from 18 to 60+ years of age with differing work and technological experiences. An individual's political party affiliation and educational background were also polled. The degree of their past participation in the electoral process was queried.

RESULTS

Sample Description and Statistics

Of the 165 survey participants, 76 were men and 89 were women; 6.6% of the male respondents reported that they had a high school diploma or some college, 25% reported a college degree, and 68.4% indicated having completed graduate work. Female respondents reported comparable education levels: 10.1% reported completion of a high school diploma or some college, 29.2% reported a college degree, and 60.7% indicated completion of graduate work. The average age of all participants was 32.8 years. The average work experience of men and women was similar; men had an average of 8.2 years and women reported 8.3 years of work experience. The average number of years reported of technology experience varied slightly. Men reported 9.2 years of technology experience while women reported 10.3 years. Ethnic distribution of the study participants were 63.0% Caucasian, 13.3% African American, 7.3% Hispanic, 9.1% Asian American, and 7.3% other. Registered party affiliation was 53.3% Republican, 36.4% Democrat, 7.3% independent, and 3.0% other. The study respondents were asked if they participated in the recent local or statewide elections: 75.8% responded *yes* and 24.2% responded *no*. When asked if they participated in the last presidential election, their answers differed significantly: 90.9% responded *yes* while 9.1% indicated *no*.

Tests of Discriminant Validity

The items used to measure innovators, early adopters, early majority, late majority, and laggards were subjected to a principal-components analysis with a varimax rotation. The results provided strong evidence for the independence of the self-reported scales used to measure the independent variables. Five factors with eigenvalues greater than 1 emerged from the data, with the rotated factors accounting for 79.02% of the variance. Items used to measure each of the five groups loaded strongly onto their respective constructs with minimal cross-loading based on the 0.40 loading threshold. Specifically, the items used to measure early majority loaded onto Factor 1 (0.75 or better), innovators onto Factor 2 (0.64 or better), laggards onto Factor 3 (0.85 or better), early adopters onto Factor 4 (0.82 or better), and late majority onto Factor 5 (0.88 or better).

Similarly, the items used to measure technology trust, intention to adopt, and willingness to vote were subjected to a principal-components analysis with varimax rotation. The results provided strong evidence for the independence of the self-reported scales used to measure the dependent variables. Three factors with eigenvalues greater than 1 emerged from the data, with the rotated factors accounting for 77.69% of the variance. Items used to measure technology trust loaded strongly onto Factor 1 (0.82 or better), items used to measure intention to use technology loaded only onto Factor 2 (0.85 or better), and the items used to measure willingness to vote only loaded onto Factor 3 (0.88 or better). There was minimal cross-loading onto the other factors.

Descriptive Statistics and Reliabilities

In Table 2, reliabilities, means, standard deviations, numbers of items for each scale, and numbers of respondents for each category are shown. Respondents received weighted scores across the entire classification schema as noted in Tables 2 and 3. The variables used in this study were not dichotomous variables. The alpha statistics indicated that internal reliability for each scale was high ($\alpha = 0.73$ or higher).

In Table 3, reliabilities, means, standard deviations, and the numbers of items for each construct used in this study are provided. The descriptive statistics indicate that respondents expressed a reserved trust in the technology and in the intention to use the technology, and were generally not willing to vote using e-voting technologies.

Predictors of Technology Trust, Intention to Adopt, and Willingness to Vote

A general linear model regression approach was undertaken to analyze the predicted hypotheses. Fifteen separate regression analyses were run to test the hypotheses. Based on convention, the probability threshold was set at the 0.05 level. Hypotheses that proposed a positive relationship were supported when $p < 0.05$. For negatively proposed relationships, the hypotheses were supported when $p > 0.05$. Hypotheses 1, 2, and 3 were

Table 2. Reliabilities, means, standard deviations, and numbers of items by classification

Classification	Means	Standard Deviations	α	Number of Items in Scale	n
Innovators	5.24	0.88	0.753	3	25
Early Adopters	5.49	0.92	0.751	2	36
Early Majority	5.30	1.05	0.754	3	69
Late Majority	3.42	1.44	0.810	2	23
Laggards	4.12	1.41	0.791	2	12

Table 3. Reliabilities, means, standard deviations, and numbers of items by construct

Construct	Means	Standard Deviations	A	Number of Items in Scale
Technology Trust	4.90	0.92	0.804	3
Intention to Use	5.17	1.37	0.789	2
Willingness to Vote	3.59	1.46	0.731	2

evaluated resulting in somewhat mixed findings in that 13 of the 15 proposed relationships were supported. Table 4 includes a summary of the proposed relationships tested and the subsequent results.

Hypotheses 1a through 1e were all supported. This suggests that innovators and early adopters are likely to trust the e-voting technology while individuals classified as early majority, late majority, and laggards expressed that they currently

Table 4. Hypotheses

Hypothesis	Investigation	Proposed Relationship	Beta	t Value	F-Score	Statistical Significance	Probability Threshold	Hypothesis Supported
H1a	Innovators → Technology Trust	+	0.376	5.465	5.749	0.000	P < 0.05	Yes
H1b	Early Adopters → Technology Trust	+	0.461	6.269	8.612	0.000	P < 0.05	Yes
H1c	Early Majority → Technology Trust	-	-0.078	-1.126	0.819	0.262	P > 0.05	Yes
H1d	Late Majority → Technology Trust	-	-0.088	-1.242	0.862	0.216	P > 0.05	Yes
H1e	Laggards → Technology Trust	-	0.140	1.898	8.305	0.060	P > 0.05	Yes
H2a	Innovators → Intention to Adopt	+	0.190	2.197	9.479	0.029	P < 0.05	Yes
H2b	Early Adopters → Intention to Adopt	+	0.205	2.388	9.628	0.018	P < 0.05	Yes
H2c	Early Majority → Intention to Adopt	-	-0.080	-0.996	0.348	0.321	P > 0.05	Yes
H2d	Late Majority → Intention to Adopt	-	0.008	0.092	0.223	0.927	P > 0.05	Yes
H2e	Laggards → Intention to Adopt	-	0.193	2.410	3.726	0.017	P > 0.05	No
H3a	Innovators → Willingness to Vote	+	0.537	9.091	7.615	0.000	P < 0.05	Yes
H3b	Early Adopters → Willingness to Vote	+	0.340	5.905	3.380	0.000	P < 0.05	Yes
H3c	Early Majority → Willingness to Vote	-	0.047	0.815	0.287	0.416	P > 0.05	Yes
H3d	Late Majority → Willingness to Vote	-	-0.264	-4.269	0.160	0.000	P > 0.05	No
H3e	Laggards → Willingness to Vote	-	0.127	2.061	6.134	0.061	P > 0.05	Yes

do not trust these systems. Hypotheses 2a to 2d were supported; 2e was found to be inconsistent with the original hypothesis. Innovators and early adopters indicated that they intend to adopt e-voting systems. Individuals classified as early majority and late majority indicated that they do not intend to adopt e-voting technologies at this time. Uncharacteristically, individuals classified as laggards indicated that they intend to adopt e-voting systems. Hypotheses 3a to 3c and 3e were supported; Hypothesis 3d was not consistent with the original hypothesis. Innovators and early adopters expressed a willingness to adopt e-voting systems. Early majority and laggards indicated that they are not willing to adopt these technologies at this point in time. Surprisingly, individuals classified as late majority indicated that they would be willing to adopt these systems.

There were two hypotheses that resulted in unexpected outcomes. The first was Hypothesis 2e, which postulated a negative relationship between laggards and their intention to adopt e-voting technology. However, this study found that individuals classified as laggards indicated a positive intention to adopt e-voting technology. This finding could be attributable to errors in construct validity within the laggard scale. An alternative explanation for the unexpected outcome resides in possible report bias, where laggards misclassified themselves because of misunderstanding or intention to influence the results of the study.

The second unexpected outcome was associated with Hypothesis 3d, which postulated a negative relationship between individuals classified as late majority and a willingness to vote using e-voting technology. This study found that these individuals reported a willingness to use e-voting technology. This may be explained through an intervening variable associated with the novelty of new technology. Individuals classified within the late majority may well operate from a belief system that e-voting technology is considered to be the standard of the future. Additionally, the assertion that e-voting technology will be used within the majority of voting precincts in the immediate future may explain the apparent reporting of the individuals.

For the purpose of the regression analysis, the following control variables were used: gender, education, age, work experience, technology experience, ethnicity, party affiliation, and participation in the most recent gubernatorial election and the most recent presidential election.

DISCUSSION

The study results supported the proposition that the degree of technology trust can affect an individual's intention to use e-voting as a means to participate in the electoral process. The adoption of innovation classifications according to Rogers' (1995) theory is an important consideration in understanding individual intention and willingness to use an e-voting system and to trust technology. Individuals who classified in the first two categories reported that their intention to use an e-voting system was high. Age had a minor effect, such that younger individuals who were classified as innovators expressed a greater intention to use an e-voting option. Gender made a slight difference in that those men in the early majority category demonstrated a more likely intention to use e-voting systems. Consistent with Rogers' theory, individuals in our investigation within the innovators and early-majority groups found technology trust to be of great importance. Expectedly, individuals classified as early majority are not risk averse but are cautious and careful in adopting new technology.

Gefen and Straub (1997) found that men and women differ in their perceptions of e-mail technology and suggest that gender differences should be considered when evaluating the use of innovations. Venkatesh and Morris (2000) assert that the moderating effect of gender is important to understanding user acceptance of new technologies since men and women make different decisions about adopting and using innovations. Venkatesh, Morris, and Ackerman (2000) investigated the roles of gender and age independently and found that gender moderated both men's and women's intention to adopt immediately following a training experience. They also found no gender differences for the short-term, continued, and long-term use of the technology. This suggests that gender differences are most apparent in the initial decision-making phases.

Notably, there was no difference in participants' intent to use e-voting systems based on party allegiance, and no differences for the relationship between the degree of trust in the technology and intent to use an electronic polling system. Interestingly, no significant difference was found as a function of cultural identification, age, education level, technology experience, or gender with regard to technology trust. However, both men and women who were classified as representatives of the innovators and early majority expressed a stronger intention to use e-voting technology. This investigation revealed a number of significant implications of the public's technology trust in e-voting systems, namely:

1. the general trust in technology weighs heavily on individual choices about using e-voting systems,
2. technology trust is a near-linear function that decreases as constituents are classified from innovators to laggards, and
3. technology trust is generalized from specific technology interactions and associated with adoption behavior.

The goals of any e-voting structure are to record the intent of the individual voter and to tally the sum of the voting choices. Voting systems that do not meet both of these goals are undesirable. Security, as a characteristic of accuracy, is defined as safeguards that prohibit changes to one vote, ballot stuffing, or the loss of votes.

Security

A key finding is that the level of trust that constituents have in the security of the technology is a primary consideration. In order to protect constituents from invasion of privacy, misuse of their voting records, or misrepresentation of their intentions, developers of electronic systems need to pay particular attention to security issues as these systems are deployed. While the degree of security is a perception that changes with time and experience, the perceptions of an individual that he or she is using a system that is more convenient, more efficient, and more accurate are all based in the general beliefs about the characteristics of the system to protect them from a known or unknown harm. Secure systems that have little or no history of error or unauthorized disclosure will always be favored by voters over less secure systems. An important point is that the perception of security is simply that: a perception that oftentimes is based in inferences instead of data. The context of the general privacy of one's voting choices is affected by the current system as well as the developing use of e-voting alternatives.

Voting Locations

Internet voting systems are grouped into three general categories: (a) poll site, (b) kiosk, and (c) remote (*National Science Foundation Internet Voting Workshop Report*, 2001). Poll-site Internet voting occurs when voters cast their ballots from any polling place that contains the Internet voting platform. Kiosk voting occurs when voters cast ballots from traditional polling sites located in convenient locations such as shopping malls, libraries, or schools. For both poll-site and kiosk voting systems, election officials control the voting platform including the hardware and software used to vote and the physical environment of the voting location. Remote Internet voting occurs when individuals are able to cast ballots from any Internet-accessible location such as from home, school, or the office. This type of Internet voting provides the greatest convenience to voters and facilitates voting to all individuals with Internet access. A significant downside to remote Internet voting is the potential security risks and the inability of election officials to control the voting platform and physical environment in which the ballot was cast.

IMPLICATIONS

Implications for Election Officials, Election Systems, and Technologists

The results of this study offer implications for three different groups: (a) election officials, (b) election systems, and (c) information technologists. First, based on the hypotheses, research model, and findings, election officials should be aware of and responsive to the wide variance in the degree to which voters trust information technology and their willingness to use electronic voting. Practically, this can mean that electronic voting could change the voting profile since every voter will treat the system in a different way. This might be significant for a particular voting precinct since voters characterized by selected demographic profiles might be less represented as a function of the voting medium. Some voters are likely to be receptive to the technology as a function of its novelty—the innovators, as suggested by Rogers (1995)—while others are less likely to see the value of using e-voting technology under any circumstances—the laggards, as suggested by Rogers. While common sense tells us that not all voters are the same, the introduction of an information technology adds another variable to the process of voting. As such, election officials would benefit from developing an awareness of general factors likely to influence technology acceptance across populations and different technologies. The use of TAM by Davis (1989) or the supply chain internalization model (SCIM) by Forman and Lippert (2005) might serve as starting points for the identification of additional factors likely to influence the adoption and acceptance process of e-voting technologies. These models could be applied to the application of e-voting technology as a means for further investigation.

Second, this study suggests that the design of election systems will also have some effect on the e-election process. Election systems' ballot design, voting location, security issues, accuracy concerns, and privacy considerations all become more important when using an electronic voting system because of the inherent trust in technology issues associated with the e-voting technology. Election systems become more complex as a function of the introduction and use of a technology to assist in recording and processing voter choices. Voters with limited technology experience may be concerned with issues of attribution: the possibility that their votes might be attributable to them through the use of the system. These privacy and security concerns are likely obstacles to individuals' willingness to adopt e-voting systems. These challenges may be magnified when extended to other cultures where variances in country-specific requirements for the development and implementation of e-voting systems may further exacerbate usage differences between voters. Additionally, regulations and procedures in different countries may also explain variances in overall acceptance of e-voting within certain geographic locations.

Finally, there are minimal implications from the results of this study on information technologists. The mission for information technologists is to apply ever-increasing standards of information processing to the design, development, and use of specialized technologies. Systems design, application, implementation, and adoption criteria become factors for technologists to consider as electronic voting systems are planned, designed, tested, evaluated, and implemented. Information technologists will also need to consider how to address end-user concerns regarding ease-of-use issues and the privacy and security anxiety associated with voting via these systems.

LIMITATIONS

There are several limitations to this study despite our best efforts to guard against these constraints. In order to generate the categories into which the participants were placed, the determination was based on an individual's highest score. This process will have an effect on the degrees of freedom and also limits the individual as classified into a single category. We recognize that the categorization based on highest mean score, in some cases, was insignificantly different from the second highest score. We accepted that limitation in order to establish distinct classifications for each subject.

Second, as is the case with much of work on technology acceptance, the survey used in this study contains self-report measures. Consistent with the work of scholars (Schmitt, 1994; Spector & Brannick, 1995), the reported correlations may suffer common method bias. This is acknowledged as a limitation of this study, although common in most studies that investigate technology acceptance (*ISWorld.net*, 2007).

A final limitation of this study is statistical significance error, in which the potential for making Type 1 errors is confounded by probability thresholds that are selected based on convention.

FUTURE EFFORTS

Providing the opportunity for each eligible voter to exercise his or her choice with optimized efficiency and accuracy is a goal of e-voting. The outcome of the development and application of e-voting systems is shaped by informed participants. Knowing that Internet technology is not a secure tool is important in future developments to allow for the incorporation of its use in the electoral process. The encryption of information to minimize data fraud (Neumann, 2004) and voter signature services for vote validation are just a few of the essential features that need to be introduced for the successful advancement of Internet voting (Watson & Cordonnier, 2001). Minimization of the digital divide is also critical to future efforts. Ensuring that all individuals have equal opportunities and ability to participate in the voting process will reinforce a democratic system. Overall, education on the software and tools that will support the electoral process will strengthen public trust in the technology, and in turn make individuals more apt to utilize and participate in the system.

There should be further examination and planning to ensure that the development of an Internet-based voting system can progress in an effective manner. It is recommended that a series of well-planned, controlled experiments testing the feasibility of Internet voting be undertaken. In particular, investigations should target (a) special populations of voters, such as individuals living in the subordinate end of the digital divide, typically minorities and low-income families, (b) traditionally partisan states, and (c) special types of elections, such as local elections with low turnout. Internet security issues must be addressed so that voters can have confidence in the integrity of online voting. The threat of electioneering the voting process must continue to be a concern for voters and election officials. The extent to which e-voting is being developed by the government and other organizations must be monitored and standardized. This form of voting can be dangerous if used to adjust the final and real vote (Watson & Cordonnier, 2001).

Ultimately, the digital divide must be narrowed so that all voters will have a completely equal opportunity to vote over the Internet. Legal and regulatory modifications must be evaluated to see what is needed to make Internet voting practical, efficient, and reliable. Taking into account that election law varies at the federal, state, county, and local levels, it is likely that laws in many states will have to be changed to make this possible. Hoffman (2004) suggests that elections enable the selection of intermediaries to be empowered, but that the Internet disintermediates specific control of the electoral process. Issues such as competitive pricing of technology systems and economic market forces could facilitate lowering barriers for states and individuals wishing to participate in an online electronically inspired voting system. Investment in the infrastructure of local and national polling systems is warranted for the expansion of this form of voting. A public that initially resists then gradually accepts technology for fundamental personal and public processes is likely to accept e-voting.

Anonymity of voting records protects the voter's identity from any intrusion that would otherwise link a voter to her or his selection. Anonymity is defined as universal secrecy since the only person who will have knowledge will be that individual. The anonymity of the voter's ballot must be preserved. The voting system must be tamper resistant and comprehensive so that it is usable by the entire voting population, regardless of age, technological ability, competence, or disability. Challenges associated with e-voting include insider attacks, network vulnerabilities, and the challenges of auditing. The most fundamental problem with e-voting is that the entire election hinges on the correctness, robustness, and security of the software within the voting terminal. Errors in the code resulting in security-relevant flaws are a potential problem. The absence of a verifiable audit trail makes the use of such systems an issue.

Scalability is a consideration in the implementation of e-voting. Voting systems need to be able to efficiently process large populations of voters concurrently. In the 2000 U.S. presidential election, 111 million people voted (*U.S. Census Bureau Newsroom*, 2005), and in the 2004 elections in India, almost 380 million cast their ballot (*India Election 2004 Statistics, Facts and Figures*, 2004). Voting systems need to be able to handle multiple choices since a voter casts his or her choice for electing national and local representatives and frequently for national and local propositions. A final consideration in scalability is the need for voting systems to produce and transmit results in a timely manner.

This study explored electronic voting as an innovative process for understanding public trust in e-voting systems. The findings indicate the feasibility for the continued development of electronic voting systems with recognition of selected cautions and characteristics of the voting populous. E-voting can be feasible and efficient, and improve voter turnout through ease and convenience in the electoral process.

REFERENCES

ACT Legislative Assembly election electronic voting and counting system review executive summary. (2001). Retrieved from http://www.elections.act.gov.au/CompExecSumm.htm

Agarwal, R., & Karahanna, E. (2000). Time flies when you're having fun: Cognitive absorption and beliefs about information technology usage. *MIS Quarterly, 24*(4), 665-694.

Agarwal, R., & Prasad, J. (2000). A field study of the adoption of software process innovations by information systems professionals. *IEEE Transactions on Engineering Management, 47*(3), 295-308.

Bagozzi, R. P., & Warshaw, P. R. (1990). Trying to consume. *Journal of Consumer Research, 17*(2), 127-140.

Boutin, P. (2004). Is e-voting safe? *PC World, 22*(6), 121-125.

Commission on Electronic Voting. (2005, June 20). Retrieved from http://www.cev.ie/htm/about/index.htm

Computer loses 4,500 votes. (2004, November 4). Retrieved from http://www.wired.com/news/evote/0,2645,65601,00.html

Costigan, R. D., Ilter, S. S., & Berman, J. J. (1998). A multi-dimensional study of trust in organization. *Journal of Managerial Issues, 10*(3), 303-317.

Dahl, M. S., & Pedersen, O. R. (2005). Social networks in the R&D process: The case of the wireless communication industry around Aalborg, Denmark. *Journal of Engineering and Technology Management, 22*(1-2), 75-92.

Davis, F. D. (1989). Perceived usefulness, perceived ease of use, and user acceptance of information technology. *MIS Quarterly, 13*(3), 319-340.

Dill, D. L., Mercuri, R., Neumann, P. G., & Wallach, D. S. (2004, September 10). *Frequently asked questions about DRE voting systems.* Retrieved from http://www.verifiedvoting.org/drefaq.asp#s1q1

Dill, D. L., Schneier, B., & Simons, B. (2003). Voting and technology: Who gets to count your vote? *Communications of the ACM, 46*(8), 29-31.

Election Commission of India. (2005, June 28). *Electronic voting machine.* Retrieved from http://www.eci.gov.in/ EVM/ index.htm

E-voting problems reported as election gets under way. (2004, November 2). Retrieved from http://www.itworld.com/Tech/2987/041102evoteprobs/

Fischer, E. A. (2003, November 4). *Election reform and electronic voting systems (DREs): Analysis of security issues.* Retrieved from http://www.notablesoftware.com/papers/ RL32139.pdf

Fishbein, M., & Ajzen, I. (1975). *Belief, attitude, intention and behavior: An introduction to theory and research.* Reading, PA: Addison-Wesley Publishing Company.

Forman, H., & Lippert, S. K. (2005) Toward the development of an integrated model of technology internalization within the supply chain context. *International Journal of Logistics Management, 16*(1), 4-26.

Gefen, D., & Straub, D. W. (1997). Gender differences in the perception and use of e-mail: An extension to the technology acceptance model. *MIS Quarterly, 21*(4), 389-400.

Global/world income per capita/head 2004. (2004). Retrieved from http://www.finfacts.com/biz10/globalworldincomepercapita.htm

Help America Vote Act of 2002, Public Law 107-252. (2002, October 29). Retrieved from http://www.electionline.org/site/docs/pdf/hr3295.pl107252.final.pdf

Hoffman, L. J. (2004, September 15). *Internet voting: Will it spur or corrupt democracy?* Retrieved from http://www.cfp2000.org/papers/hoffman2.pdf

Implementing electronic voting in the UK. (n.d.). Retrieved from http:// www.odpm.gov.uk/ stellent/groups/odpm_localgov/documents/page/odpm_locgov_605188-01.hcsp#P50_1197)

India election 2004 statistics, facts and figures. (n.d.). Retrieved from http://www.neoncarrot.co.uk/h_aboutindia/india_election_stats.html

Internet usage for the Americas, Internet user statistics and population stats for 51 countries and regions: North America, Central America, South America and the Caribbean. (n.d.). Retrieved from http://www.internetworldstats.com/stats2.htm

Internet usage in Asia (Internet users & population statistics for 35 countries and regions in Asia). (n.d.). Retrieved from http://www.internetworldstats.com/stats3.htm

Internet usage and population in Oceania (South Pacific Islands, New Zealand, and Australia Internet users and population statistics). (n.d.). Retrieved from http://www.internetworld stats.com/stats6.htm

Internet usage statistics: The big picture, world Internet users and population stats. (n.d.). Retrieved from http://www.internetworldstats.com/stats.htm

Internet world stats, usage and population statistics: European Union. (n.d.). Retrieved from http://www.internetworldstats.com/europa.htm#ie

ISWorld.net, qualitative research page, Section 7: Glossary. Quantitative, positivist research methods in information systems: Common method bias. (n.d.). Retrieved from http://dstraub.cis.gsu.edu/88/quant/7glossary.asp

Johnson-George, C., & Swap, W. C. (1982). Measurement of specific interpersonal trust-construction and validation of a scale to access trust in a specific other. *Journal of Personality and Social Psychology, 43*(12), 1306-1317.

Jones, B. (2000, January). *California Internet task force: A report on the feasibility of Internet voting.* Retrieved from http://www.ss.ca.gov/executive/ivote/final_ report.htm

Jones, S., Wilikens, M., Morris, P., & Masera, M. (2000). Trust requirements in e-business. *Communications of the ACM, 43*(12), 80-87.

Lefebvre, E., & Lefebvre, L. (1996). *Information and communication technologies: The impact of their adoption on small and medium-sized enterprises.* Retrieved from http://www.idrc.ca/

Lippert, S. K. (2001). *An exploratory study into the relevance of trust in the context of information systems technology.* Unpublished doctoral dissertation, George Washington University.

Liptak, A. (2004, November 7). *Voting problems in Ohio set off an alarm.* Retrieved from http://www.nytimes.com/2004/11/07/politics/campaign/07elect.html?ex=1117252800&en=21af6b0293e451c3&ei=5070)

National Science Foundation Internet voting workshop report. (2001, March). Retrieved from http://lorrie.cranor.org/voting/ipi-voting-report.pdf

Neumann, P. G. (1990). Risks in computerized elections. *Communications of the ACM, 33*(11), 170.

Neumann, P. G. (2004). The problems and potentials of voting systems. *Communications of the ACM, 47*(10), 28-30.

Oravec, J. A. (2005). Preventing e-voting hazards: The role of information professionals. *Journal of Organizational and End User Computing, 17*(4), i-iv.

Ornstein, N., & Schenkenberg, A. (1996). The promise and perils of cyber democracy. *The American Enterprise, 7*(2), 53.

Phillips, D. M., & Von Spakovsky, H. A. (2001). Gauging the risks of Internet elections. *Communications of the ACM, 44*(1), 73-85.

Rogers, E. M. (1995). *Diffusion of innovations.* New York: Free Press.

Schmitt, N. (1994). Method bias: The importance of theory and measurement. *Journal of Organizational Behavior, 15*(5), 393-398.

Spector, P. E., & Brannick, M. T. (1995). The nature and effects of method variance in organizational research. In C. L. Cooper & I. T. Robertson (Eds.), *International review of industrial and organizational psychology* (pp. 249-274). Chichester, United Kingdom: Wiley.

U.S. Census Bureau newsroom. (2005, July 6). Retrieved from http://www.census.gov/Press-Release/www/releases/archives/facts_for_features/001643.html

U.S. Federal Election Commission. (2004, September 13). Retrieved from http://www.fec.gov/pages/vssfinal/vss_implementation.html

Venkatesh, V., & Morris, M. G. (2000). Why don't men ever stop to ask for directions? Gender, social influence, and their role in technology acceptance and usage behavior. *MIS Quarterly, 24*(1), 115-139.

Venkatesh, V., Morris, M. G., & Ackerman, P. L. (2000). A longitudinal field investigation of gender differences individual technology adoption decision-making processes. *Organizational Behavior and Human Decision Processes, 83*(1), 33-60.

Watson, A., & Cordonnier, V. (2001). *Information technology improves most of the democratic voting processes.* Retrieved from http://ieeexplore.ieee.org/iel5/7561/20604/00953092.pdf?tp=&arnumber=953092&isnumber=20604

Weiss, A. (2001). Click to vote. *Association for Computing Machinery: NetWorker, 5*(1), 18-24.

This work was previously published in the Journal of Organizational and End User Computing, Vol. 20, Issue 3, edited by M. Mahmood, pp. 57-80, copyright 2008 by IGI Publishing (an imprint of IGI Global).

Chapter 13
End Users' Acceptance of Information Technology: A Rasch Analysis

Geoffrey N. Soutar
University of Western Australia, Austraila

Steven Ward
Murdoch University, Australia

ABSTRACT

While there has been research on the diffusion of a particular type of innovation, few if any studies have examined the acceptance of a set of innovations (behavioral innovativeness) over time. This study using the Rasch methodology found evidence that computer hardware innovations are adopted in a particular order. The same could not be said for computer software, whose acceptance may be application based. This study applied a theoretical framework based on the diffusion of innovation literature (See Rodgers 1995). Data was collected via a telephone survey of 302 computer users. Scores obtained from Rasch analysis were used as the dependent variable (that of behavioral innovativeness) in a regression analysis, against factors such as **overall innovativeness**, **use innovativeness**, *opinion leadership/acceptance, product class knowledge and use of sources of information. Determinates of the level of behavioral innovativeness were found to be personality traits of innovateness, (a willingness to trial new technology) and use innovateness (how innovatively existing information technology was used). The level of recent purchases in the last month of information technology items, a measure of leading edge use was also positively associated with acceptance of new technology. The research findings suggest that computer hardware manufacturers can assume that there is an order of acceptance of new technology and so can predict from the knowledge of existing hardware the acceptance of innovations in the future. Computer manufacturers can also effectively target early adopters of their technology given the results of this study.* **Rasch modeling** *can also be beneficial for organizations wishing to market diverse computer packages to users, as it allows a numerical scoring of a users acquisition profile or use of information technologies.*

DOI: 10.4018/978-1-60566-687-7.ch013

INTRODUCTION

Steenkamp, Hofstede and Wedel (1999) estimated that two thirds of new products fail, at an average cost of around $US 15 million for each such product. However, they also noted that many major companies, such as Gillette and Hewlett-Packard, rely on new products for profits and growth. Thus, consumer's acceptance of new products is vital, which means a greater understanding of the consumer diffusion process is crucially important to many organizations.

Rogers (1958) initial research suggested the kinds of consumers who would be most willing to accept innovations and this group have generally been termed "innovators". It is believed that such consumers influence opinion leaders who, through word of mouth, spread an innovation through a population. Innovation researchers have tended to examine this process by looking at the acceptance of one product at a time, although Midgley and Dowling (1993) were a notable exception. However, Gatignon and Robertson (1985) have argued that, for some products, such as personal computers and entertainment systems, multiple purchases are possible, as is a migration to better performing units. In such categories, the purchase of ancillary units (or perhaps software in the case of computers) is also possible. They suggested that, in such situations, research should focus on how an innovation fitted into existing consumption patterns, rather than looking at a single product's acceptance.

The present paper is an attempt to broaden our understanding of the diffusion process by considering diffusion as a product class phenomenon. It is suggested that the acceptance of innovations within a product class depends on people's ownership of related items within that class, although use innovativeness and past purchase behavior may influence the adoption of new items within the class (e.g., more online purchasing can lead to a demand for computer security software). These issues are addressed in the review provided in the next section.

It can be argued that consumers do not purchase individual computer items but, rather, packages of hardware and software. A good way to examine the acceptance of product class assortments or items belonging to a set of related products is to use **Rasch modeling**, as it models the acquisition of different technologies from established products to innovations and, consequently, this approach was used in the present study. The study also examined some of the factors that might influence the acceptance of information technologies and these factors are also discussed in the subsequent review.

A REVIEW OF RELEVANT LITERAURE

The Dependent Variable: Behavioral Innovativeness

As discussed earlier, the present study investigated the adoption of a set of innovations within a product class (see Midgley and Dowling 1978). A product class is a hierarchy of items, or units that can be purchased over time. In the case of personal computers, these units or items can be hardware, software or peripherals, such as printers and modems. Innovative behavior, or behavioral innovateness, can be considered to be to the extent to which a user adopts most of these items, with "newer" items being the most recently purchased. However, a major problem, noted by Midgley and Dowling (1978 p. 238), is the availability of time series data through which forecasts of innovative behavior may be made. Another problem for researchers is that there is no way to predict whether innovative behavior is unidimensional, occurring in a set order across a population of interest.

Past research using cross sectional data has suggested a unidimensional order of acquisition for many consumer durables and financial assets (e.g. Kasulis et al., 1979, Clarke and Soutar,

1982, Dickinson and Kirzner and 1986, Soutar and Cornish-Ward 1997). Innovative products seem to be the last to be purchased, after more established products have been accepted. This supports the possibility that innovative behavior may be unidimensional in some cases.

There is, however, a question as to the how to test the dimensionality of purchase order. Is there a simple ladder consumers "climb" to obtain certain combinations of software, hardware and peripherals or are there sets of ladders (orders) for different sets of information technology? Another concern is whether the order varies among different segments and some research has examined differences between renters and house owners, but with very limited success. It is, however, important to derive an acquisition order using a measurement model that can evaluate the goodness of fit of a set of items (e.g. a set of durables goods or financial assets, computer hardware and software items) and of the people who purchase these products as this would resolve both issues.

In the present study, a post hoc measurement model was used. That is, a predetermined order of purchase acquisition was not developed before examining the data. This approach was used, as there is no established taxonomy. As already noted, past research into consumer durables and financial assets has favored this approach and two major measurement approaches have been suggested, namely:

1. The conditional probability approach, suggested by Pyatt (1964) and further developed by Hebden and Pickering (1974), and
2. The Guttman Scalogram Analysis used by Parousch (1965), Kasulis et al. (1979), Clarke and Soutar (1982) and Dickson, Lusch and Wilkie (1983).

Both suggestions have problems, as they are dependent on the number of items used. Guttman scaling has other disadvantages as the derived probability estimates are based on a zero-one probability model. As Dickinson et al. (1983, p. 435) noted, this method has been found to be "somewhat lacking." The Guttman model's restrictions have resulted in the suggestion of the Rasch model as an alternative approach in a number of areas as it is not dependent on the number of items considered and allows for probabilities other than zero or one (Andrich, 1988). The Rasch model is one of a family of logit models that has been primarily used in educational research to examine the difficulty of test items, especially in the binary correct-incorrect case. Such a situation is analogous to that of consumers who own or do not own particular hardware, software and/or peripherals items. "Difficulty," here, represents the order of hardware, software and/or peripherals purchased. Based on Wright (1977, p. 99) and following Soutar, Bell and Wallis (1990), the appropriate logit model can be shown as:

$$P_{vi} = \exp(B_v - D_{i)}/[1+\exp(B_v - D_i)] \qquad (1)$$

where:

P_{vi} = Probability of a person v owning hardware, software and/ or peripherals item (in other words, a measure of a probability of expected innovative behaviour).
B_v = Location of person v on the Rasch scale.
D_i = Location of the hardware, software and/ or peripherals item on the Rasch scale.

The B_v parameter provides a measure of a person's ownership of hardware, software and /or peripherals item, while D_i relates to "difficulty" of owning a particular hardware, software and/ or peripherals item and, so, is a measure of the market penetration (or adoption) of the various items. The model simulates a longitudinal order of adoptions of items, using cross-sectional data. Thus, the Rasch model's B_v parameter can be used as a measure of behavioral innovativeness.

The Rasch model enables both item and person fit to be computed (Wright, 1977, p. 102). Con-

Figure 1. The independent variable innovativeness

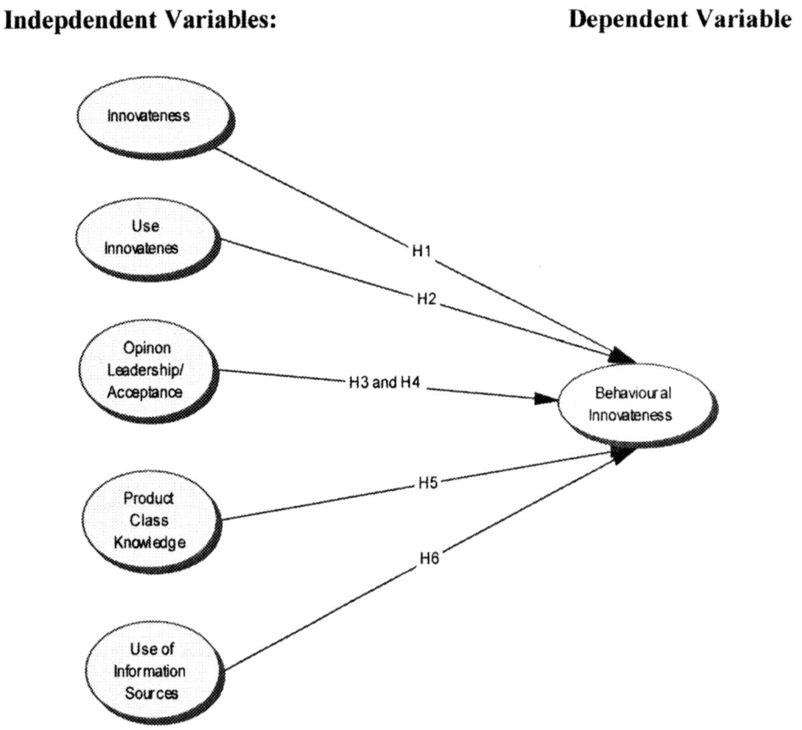

sequently, the dimensionality of the acquisition order can be answered through the closeness of the observed item fit to the model's implied order. The model also allows an examination of each respondent's pattern of adoption, compared to that expected by the model, enabling an investigation of the presence of subgroups whose patterns do not fit a general model. The model also allows an examination of a person's position in the hierarchy of adoption of a set of innovations and, so, allows comparisons of different adopter groups, such as innovators, early adopters and so on.

Finally, as is pointed out in the following section, several other constructs seem to be related to behavioral innovativeness. Since the values obtained from **Rasch modeling** can be considered intervally scaled, regression analysis can be used to examine such hypothesized relationships.

The Independent Variables

The potential explanatory variables that were examined are shown in Figure 1. The personality factors of innovativeness, use innovativeness opinion leadership and acceptance, as well as product class knowledge, the use of information sources and personal background are suggested to impact on innovativeness. The variables, which are similar to those suggested in prior research (e.g. Rogers 1995; Mudd 1990; Gatignon et al. 1985), were used to develop the hypotheses tested in the present study.

Innovativeness is a general personality trait that has been defined as "the degree to which an individual makes innovation decisions independently of the communicated experience of others" (Midgley and Dowling, 1978, p 235). Hirschman (1980) suggested that general **innovativeness** is a part of *vicarious innovation*, which is necessary, but not sufficient, for the early adoption of an innovation (or *actualized innovativeness*). These researchers, as well as Foxall (1995), Goldsmith (1990) and Venkatraman and Price (1990), all used self-report measures to estimate such a tendency, rather than the post hoc behavioral measure suggested by Rogers (1995).

Hirschman (1980) has argued that consumer novelty seeking and creativity are important antecedents to **innovativeness**, while others (e.g. Foxall 1995; Goldsmith 1990; Venkatraman and Price 1990; Leavitt and Walton 1975, 1988) have suggested that **innovativeness** is impacted by risk taking, openness to change and a willingness to experiment. Foxall (1995) supported this view as he suggested that **innovativeness** is a problem solving process in which accepted methods (or products) are adapted creatively to solve problems.

Venkatraman and Price (1990) suggested that **innovativeness** has a cognitive and a sensory dimension. The cognitive dimension deals in part with the need to solve problems, while the sensory component deals with novelty seeking and experimentation. Empirical evidence, however, has not supported such a two dimensional model. These and other generalized **innovativeness** measures, while initially promising, have been poor predictors of the acceptance of innovations.

As might be expected, simple product class based **innovativeness** measures have been better predictors. Goldsmith and Hofacker (1991) found that a shorter, domain specific measure of **innovativeness** was a reasonable predictor of people's awareness and purchase of an innovations (in their case new rock music). The measure was unidimensional, had high alpha and test-rest reliabilities (greater than 0.80) and there was considerable support for its construct validity. Goldsmith, Friedman and Eastman (1995) showed that domain specific **innovativeness** measures were also better predictors of electronic and fashion innovations than were general measures. Recent research in information science (Vishwanath 2005) found overall **innovativeness** is associated with the likelihood of adoption, which suggests:

H1: IT behavioral innovativeness is positively related to consumers' **innovativeness**.

The prediction of the acceptance of innovations may depend on other factors, however. An important but related issue is how existing products (e.g. software) within a class (personal computers) are used. This construct is called ***use innovativeness*** and is discussed next.

Use Innovativeness

While innovativeness is a predisposition to accept an innovation, **use innovativeness** is a related construct that focuses on the ways products or services are used in novel and creative ways. **Use innovativeness** can apply as much to old products and services as to new ones (Price and Ridgway 1983). A consumer can be use innovative if, for example, they use an old product in a new or novel way (e.g using baking soda to remove carpet stains). Alternatively, they might use existing or new products in different ways (e.g. a consumer could use a computer for a wide variety of purposes, such as keeping financial records, developing websites, shopping online and conducting detailed statistical analysis). Like innovativeness, **use innovativeness** can be seen as a personality trait. Price and Ridgway (1983) suggested **use innovativeness** has five aspects, which they termed Creativity-Curiosity, Risk Preferences, Voluntary Simplicity, Creative Re-Use and Multiple Use Potential. They found these factors were good predictors of students' innovative use of handheld calculators.

Price and Ridgway (1983) argued that **use innovativeness** can extend product lifecycles, further the growth of existing products and improve new product acceptance (by suggesting new uses and targeting consumers who are use innovative). It also seems that a tendency to use products and services in innovative ways implies a greater acceptance of new products and services. Ram and Hyung-Shik (1994) found **use innovativeness** was positively associated with the time of adoption of new technology (personal computers and video recorders), as earlier adopters were more use innovative, suggesting:

H2: IT behavioral innovativeness is positively related to consumers' use innovativeness.

Opinion Leadership and Opinion Seeking

A crucial element in the diffusion of an innovation is the extent to which it is accepted by opinion leaders (Rodgers 1995). Opinion leaders spread an innovation more effectively than the mass media by visible demonstration or by word of mouth communication. Opinion leaders also have greater exposure to the mass media, a greater degree of social interaction, higher socio-economic status and are more innovative than are followers (Baumgarten 1975 and Midgley and Dowling 1993). They are crucial change-agents who champion innovation and are well positioned to become aware of and adopt innovations (Chau and Hui 1998), suggesting:

H3: IT behavioral innovativeness is positively related to consumers' opinion leadership status.

While opinion leadership seems to lead to the adoption of innovations, so too can the acceptance of opinion leadership because those seeking opinions are also socially orientated and are likely to searching for new information or news about particular developments in a field (Tsang and Zhou 2005) and thus may become aware of innovations more earlier and thus may have a greater propensity to adopt, suggesting:

H4: IT behavioral innovativeness is positively related to consumers' opinion seeking status.

Product Class Knowledge

Product knowledge is seen as another important determinant of the acceptance of an innovation (Hirschman 1980). Knowledgeable consumers are more aware of and have a good understanding of innovations. They are also likely to be heavy users with greater product experience and expertise, or lead users of new technology who, because of their knowledge, see new innovations as less complex and are therefore more likely to adopt it earlier than other consumers (Schreier, et al. 2007), suggesting:

H5: IT behavioral innovativeness is positively related to consumers' product class knowledge.

Product class knowledge seems to be multidimensional as it consists not only of what consumers know, but also their belief about what they know. What consumers know is termed "actual", or "objective", knowledge (Cole, Gaeth, Chakraborty and Levin 1992 and Park, Fieck and Mothersbaugh 1992) and is usually assessed through a factual test (Brucks 1985; Cole, Gaeth, Chakraborty and Levin 1992 and Sujan 1985). Knowledge includes experience (often self-reported), which is based on frequency of purchase and ownership (Anderson, Engledow and Becker 1979; Bettman and Park 1980; Cole, Gaeth, Chakraborty and Levin 1992 and Kiel and Layton 1981). What consumers believe they know is often termed "subjective" knowledge (Park, Fieck and Mothersbaugh 1992). Experience and perceived knowledge may overlap as both are usually assessed through self-report data.

Research suggests subjective knowledge and experience motivate consumer search and impact on product involvement or interest (Cole, Gaeth, Chakraborty and Levin 1992; Park, Fieck and Mothersbaugh 1992). Importantly, self-reported knowledge has been linked to experience and found to be more related to product judgment and evaluation than is objective knowledge (Broniarzyk, Hutchinson and Alba 1992; Park, Fieck and Mothersbaugh 1992). Further, objective knowledge seems to be of more relevance to a consumer's task ability, such as the proper of use of information and decision making effectiveness (Cole, Gaeth, Chakraborty and Levin 1992). It appears that experience and subjective knowledge have greater relevance than does objective knowledge in consumer decision-making processes. A major reason for this may be consumers' reliance on experience to guide current decisions (Park, Fieck and Mothersbaugh 1992).

Use of Information and Background

Gatignon and Robertson (1985) cited a number of studies that have suggested people who have greater exposure to the mass media and, hence, have used a greater number of sources of information, were more likely to adopt an innovation. Midgley and Dowling (1993) found consumers who had higher magazine readership tended to adopt fashion styles earlier than did other people, while Rodgers (1995) and Shuptrine (1977) found people who adopted earlier tended to be younger, better educated and wealthier, suggesting:

H6: IT behavioral innovativeness is positively related to consumers' information use.
H7: IT behavioral innovativeness is negatively related to age.
H8: IT behavioral innovativeness is positively related to consumers' educational status.
H9: IT behavioral innovativeness is positively related to consumers' income.

The study undertaken to examine these relationships and the results of the various analyses are outlined in the following sections.

THE PRESENT STUDY

The present study was similar to previous studies as it used a cross-sectional approach to obtain the needed data. A questionnaire was designed that included the various scales needed to examine the various hypotheses and also asked respondents to indicate whether or not they owned the various hardware and software items that are shown in Table 2. Respondents were asked if their computer had one or more of the 14 hardware items, which included both internal components and external peripherals, such as printers, scanners and zip drives. Respondents were also asked whether their computer had one or more of 25 software programs. This list included the year and type of operating system (*Apple* versus *Microsoft*), as well as, in some cases, the brand names of software, such as *Adobe, Microsoft and Apple.* The list of software and hardware items was generated through a series of depth interviews with five computer experts prior to the main study who were asked about the items they considered would be a part of a state of the art computer.

The Sample

The data were collected by a commercial market research organization on weekends during March 2002 using random telephone dialing throughout a Metropolitan Area of a large Australian City. Three hundred and two responses were obtained, although the response rate being low (17%). The final sample was evenly split on gender and included mainly people who were employed in administrative or white-collar occupations (48%). One third of respondents had a university qualification and a similar proportion (32%) had incomes of between $US 33600 and $US 50400.

The Scales Used

To examine the various hypotheses of interest, it was necessary to obtain information about respon-

Table 1. Scales used to represent the constructs

Construct	Source of the Scale	Number of Items	Mean (Std Dev)	Alpha Reliability
Innovativeness	Goldsmith and Hofacker (1991)	5	11.57 (4.88)	0.87
Use Innovativeness	Girardi et al. (2003), based on Price and Ridgway (1983)	9	28.47 (6.64)	0.79
Opinion Leadership	Flynn et al. (1996)	3	6.57 (12.5)	0.89
Influenced by Opinion Leaders	Flynn et al. (1996)	3	12.00 (2.84)	0.87
Objective Knowledge	Rao and Monroe (1988)	6	1.00 (1.21)	n.a.
Subjective Knowledge	Rao and Monroe (1988)	1	2.88 (1.32)	n.a.
Shopping Knowledge	Rao and Monroe (1988)	5	2.65 (1.74)	n.a.
Experience: Days since last purchase No. items of IT in the last month	Rao and Monroe (1988)	2	293 (489) 5 (9)	n.a.
Information Use Readership of: *Aust PC user.* *Aust. Personal Computer Internet.* *au* *Net Guide* *Official Playstation* *PC Powerplay* Hours on the Internet per week gaining knowledge about computers.	Midgley and Dowling (1993)	7	1.57 (1.19)* 1.41 (1.00) 1.11 (.56) 1.20 (.68) 1.10 (.51) 1.10 (.51) 1.65 (4.66)	n.a.

Note: *Scaled as 1 (never), 2 (once a year), 3 (once every six months), 4 (every two months) and five (once every month)

dents' innovativeness, use innovativeness, opinion leadership, knowledge and use of information. To do this, a number of constructs were included in a questionnaire that was distributed to a sample of consumers, as discussed subsequently. The list of constructs can be seen in Table 1 and the items used to measure the various constructs are shown in the Appendix. In most cases, Likert-type scales that ranged from strongly disagree (1) to strongly agree (7) were used to collect the desired data.

Analysis of the Acceptance of Information Technology

The Rasch Unidimensional Measurement Model (RUMM) program (Andrich et al. 2000) was used to analyze the ownership data by estimating the model described in Equation 1. The fit between the data and the model were determined through two major indices. The item-trait test (a chi-square) examines the consistency of the item parameters across respondents, combining all of the items to provide an overall test-of-fit. The item-respondent test examines respondents' response patterns across items and for items across respondents. The fit statistics approximate a distribution with a mean near zero and a standard deviation near one. Negative values imply a response pattern that fits the model too closely, probably because there are response dependencies (Andrich 1985), while large positive values imply a poor fit, probably because of noise in the data or an inappropriate set of items.

As equation 1 implies, the model provides an estimate of each respondent's place along the ownership scale and this score can be considered to be interval scaled. Consequently, regression analysis was used to examine the relationships between

Table 2. Hardware And Software Items Included In The Study

Hardware Item	Proportion Owning		Software Item	Proportion Owning
Modem	92		Internet Browser	87
Video Card	51		Email	85
CD Burner	38		Spreadsheet	82
Zip Drive	33		Photography	50
PCI Digital Dolby Audio	31		Database	47
3D Card	30		Educational	45
512 Mb of RAM	29		Wed Design	32
19 inch LCD Monitor	16		Multimedia	21
DVD Writer	16		Video Editing	19
Ultra Scuzzy HD	8		Statistical	16
			Voice Activated	15
Average Number Owned	3.4			5.0

the background data collected within the study and people's ownership of computer hardware and software. The results obtained in the various analyses are outlined in the next section.

THE RESULTS OBTAINED

As noted earlier, people were asked whether they owned each of the hardware and software items shown in Table 1. As can be seen in Table 2, the proportion owning the items varied greatly. While 92% of respondents owned a modem, only 8% owned an ultra scuzzy hard drive. Similarly, while 87% of respondents had an internet browser, only 15% had voice-activated software. Interestingly, the total number of software items owned was greater than the number of hardware items owned, indicating the diversity of use of computers.

As was noted in the previous section, the ownership data for both the hardware and software items were analyzed using the Rasch model and these data sets are examined in turn. One of the ten hardware items (the modem) did not fit the model well, perhaps because it was almost universally owned and, using a similar approach to a backward stepwise regression, the item was removed from the analysis. The remaining nine items fitted the model well, as can be seen in Table 3.

The spread of items and respondents can also be displayed graphically, as in Figure 2. Respondents were reasonably well spread across the scale, although they were more concentrated at the lower than at the higher end, suggesting the Rasch model provides a useful amount of information about people's hardware ownership pattern. The spread of the items was not as good, however. While the standard deviation of the respondents was 1.43, the standard deviation of the items was 0.89, suggesting there were too few items in the tails of the distribution. It would seem further research is needed to identify additional items that might provide better differentiation.

A similar analysis was undertaken for the eleven software items shown in Table 2. In this case, four items had to be removed before a reasonable fit was found and, even then, the powers of the tests-of-fit were only reasonable and the reliability coefficient was only 0.50, suggesting software ownership may not be unidimensional and that other analysis approaches (such as correspondence analysis) may be more appropriate. Consequently,

Table 3. The Hardware scale (Item-Person Interaction)

Hardware Item		
Scale Location in logits	Chi Square Probability	Video Card
-1.30	0.66	CD Burner
-0.74	0.43	Zip Drive
-0.45	0.07	PCI Digital Dolby Audio
-0.27	0.39	512 Mb of RAM
-0.18	0.95	3D Card
-0.12	0.15	19 inch LCD Monitor
0.63	0.13	DVD Writer
0.65	0.26	Ultra Scuzzy HD
1.69	0.94	

subsequent analysis was only undertaken with the hardware data. Individual respondent fits were examined by comparing ownership profiles with the model's predictions (Andrich 1988). Only one respondent had a residual outside the accepted limit, suggesting there was a consistent pattern across the sample and suggesting there was no point in looking for segments, as there was uniformity in ownership patterns.

The results confirm previous research that suggested consumers purchase important and complementary items in a particular order (McFall 1969; Kasulis, Lusch & Stafford 1979; Clarke & Soutar 1982; Soutar, Bell & Wallis 1990; Soutar & Ward 1997). What is also apparent is that consumers purchase computer hardware components (possibly as part of a package when they upgrade) in a hierarchical order, with more innovative, or

Figure 2. Person and item fit

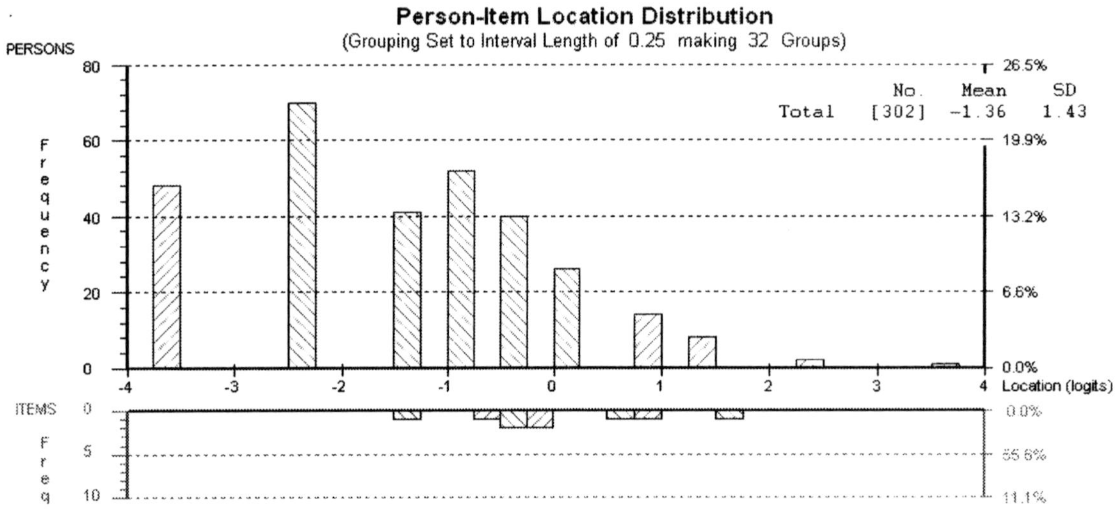

Table 4. Regression results for behavioural innovateness

Variable	B	SE.B	Beta
A. Demographic and Background Variables			
Constant	-1.16	.42	
Readership of *Australian PC User Magazine*	.24	.08	.26**
B. Demographic and Background Variables + Consumer Knowledge Variables			
Constant	-1.17	.42	
Number of Items purchased in the last month	.05	.01	.29**
C. Demographic and Background Variables + Consumer Knowledge Variables+ Innovateness +Use Innovateness + Opinion Leadership			
Constant	-2.72	.32	
Innovateness	.05	.02	.22**
Use Innovateness	.03	.01	.18**
Number of Items purchased in the last month	.04	.01	.23**

**=p<.01, *=p<.05,
A. Multiple R-squared = .12, Adjusted R-squared = .06
B. Multiple R-squared = .21, Adjusted R-squared = .14
C. Multiple R-squared = .30, Adjusted R-squared = .22
Note: Only significant results are shown.

new, items purchased most recently. Decisions to purchase software, however, may be more complex and may depend on a user's requirements, knowledge and background.

Respondents' scores on the Rasch model were used to measure their behavioral innovativeness. This measure reflects the acceptance of a series of innovations (computer hardware components purchased as part of a PC) over a period of time, which is similar in conception to the suggestion that innovative behavior is a product class phenomenon consisting of a series of product adoptions (see Midgley and Dowling 1978, p. 230), rather than a simple measure of acceptance.

The Regression Results

Initial data screening, based on the standardised scores of the variables, found two outliers with absolute Z scores greater than 1.96 (Tabachnick and Fidell 1996). The first had a positive response bias as the respondent had agreed with most of the questions, while the second had purchased 100 items of computer hardware and software in the last month, which may have reflected business rather than consumer purchases. Both cases were excluded from the subsequent analysis.

Hierarchical regression analysis (Cohen and Cohen 1983) was used to evaluate the nine hypotheses outlined earlier in the paper. The independent variables were entered in three separate blocks, starting with the variables of least theoretical significance which were, as in most studies, the demographic and background variables (H6 to H9) and the information sources (referred to as panel A in Table 4). The second block included product class knowledge (H5) (referred to panel B in table 4). The third block included the independent variables of greatest theoretical interest, namely innovativeness (H1) **use innovativeness** (H2), opinion leadership (H3) and opinion followership (H4) (referred to panel C in Table 4).

Hierarchical regression was used as it is "the only basis on which variance partitioning can proceed with correlated independent variables (and) is a useful tool for estimating the effects of each cause" (Cohen and Cohen 1983, p. 120-121). The regression analysis results are shown in Table 4.

There were a number of significant relationships that explained a reasonable proportion of the variation in the behavioral innovativeness scores ($R^2 = 0.31$, $F_{(24,232)} = 3.74$, $p<0.01$). The regression model that included product class knowledge, innovativeness and **use innovativeness** had a significantly higher R^2 than did the model that included only the demographic and background variables (R^2 change from A to C = 0.18, $Fchange_{(8,208)} = 6.98$, $p<0.01$). The final model (C) suggested the significant predictors of behavioral innovativeness were innovativeness, **use innovativeness** and past shopping experience, as shown by the number of relevant items purchased during the previous month.

The results suggest innovativeness (H1), **use innovativeness** (H2) and product class knowledge and experience (H3 AND H5) are significant predictors of behavioral innovativeness. Opinion leadership (H3), opinion seeking (H4) information use, age and income (H6 to H9) did not predict behavioral innovativeness, although the readership of *Australian PC Magazine* initially did so (Table 4, panel A). This variable may have been a suppressor variable (Tabachnick and Fidell 1996) in that it originally increased R^2 because it was correlated with other important predictor variables, such as opinion leadership (correlation = 0.40, $p<0.01$), the number of items purchased last month (correlation = 0.30, $p<0.01$) and innovativeness (correlation = 0.37, $p<0.01$).

DISCUSSION

The results obtained suggested there was a unidimensional order for the purchase of computer hardware, but that the computer software decision appears to be more complex and a multidimensional innovation pattern may exist for such products. For example, it may be that consumers purchase different products for different sets of software applications (e.g. statistical software, web animation software, different operating systems). Interestingly, the results suggest it cannot be assumed consumers will accept software innovations from software companies in any particular order.

There is a unidimensional order for computer hardware, however. For computer manufacturers such as Dell and chip manufacturers such as Intel, this is a useful finding as it appears consumers will trade up (hence the unidimensional order of computer hardware). These companies can also make a reasonable prediction that the acceptance of one level of technology is likely to lead the future adoption of new technology. The study also suggested that the acceptance of a new technology is influenced by how innovative consumers are, which supports previous findings (Goldsmith and Hofacker 1991; Goldsmith et al 1985; Venkataraman and Price 1990 and Foxall 1995) and how innovatively they use existing information technology (Price and Ridgway 1983). Such innovative consumers are likely to be leading edge users, (Schreier 2007) as can be seen by the high level of their recent purchases of information technology. These results only relate to consumers in 2002. Future research needs to be undertaken to see if subsequent innovations have changed the present results.

Additional research should also look at long-term adoption as determined by different end user groups (Jurison 2000) and the role of culture and overload (ability to understand and use technology, see Thatcher et al. 2003). Further insights into decision making involved in the acceptance of new technology could also be made from qualitative research (Chatman 1986).

The present research needs to be considered within the broader context of the technology acceptance model (or TAM, see King and He 2006; Hernandez et al. 2008; Hashim 2008; Lu et al. 2009). TAM research focuses on the acceptance of one technology at a time. Further, a meta-analysis of TAM research (King and He 2006) suggests a low prediction of the uptake of new technology (an average beta coefficient of 0.18). There is much to be gained by the using the Rasch methodology to study a series of technology adoptions and the components in the TAM model, such as perceived ease of use and usefulness. Other meta-analysis research found experience moderated the relationship between perceived ease of use and usefulness (Li, Qi, and Shu 2008), suggesting there is scope to combine both approaches in future research.

There were some limitations to the study. The research used a cross sectional, rather than a longitudinal, design, which may be useful when examining the **diffusion of innovations**. Future researchers also need to see how consumers consider bundles of hardware and software items when they purchase IT products. Given the possibilities of different technologies bundles, researchers may want to consider the acceptance of individual hardware and software items.

The Rasch approach used suggested market penetration and behavioral innovativeness measures. Future researchers may wish to examine the acceptance of computer software for specific applications and of competing computer operating systems. With the digital revolution pushing consumers to consider convergent technologies (e.g. Mobile or Cell telephones, the Internet and Digital Television), the Rasch approach may be a valuable tool for researcher and managers trying to come to terms with changing demand patterns in the information age.

REFERENCES

Anderson, R., Engledow, J., & Becker, H. (1979). Evaluating the relationships among attitude towards business product satisfaction, experience, and search effort. *JMR, Journal of Marketing Research, 16*(3), 394–400. doi:10.2307/3150714

Andrich, D. (1985). A latent trait model for items with response dependencies: Implications for test construction and analysis. In S.E. Embretson (Ed.), *Test design: Developments in psychology and psychometrics* (pp. 245-275). Orlando: Academic Press.

Andrich, D. (1988). *Rasch models for measurement*. Thousand Oaks, CA: Sage Publications.

Andrich, D., Sheridan, B., Lyne, A., & Luo, G. (2000). *RUMM: A windows-based Item analysis program employing Rasch unidimensional measurement models*. Murdoch University, Perth, WA.

Baumgarten, S. (1975). The innovative communicator in the diffusion process. *JMR, Journal of Marketing Research, 22*(1), 12–18. doi:10.2307/3150653

Bettman, J., & Park, W. (1980). Effects of prior knowledge and experience and phase of the choice process on consumer: A protocol analysis. *The Journal of Consumer Research, 7*(3), 234–248. doi:10.1086/208812

Bienstock, C., Royne, M., Sherrell, D., & Stafford, T. (2008). An expanded model of logistics service quality: Incorporating logistics information technology. *International Journal of Production Economics, 113*(1), 203–222. doi:10.1016/j.ijpe.2007.03.023

Boyd, T., & Charlotte, M., H. (1999). The link between attractiveness of extrabrand attributes and the adoption of innovation. *Journal of the Academy of Marketing Science, 27*(3), 306–319. doi:10.1177/0092070399273002

Broniarzyk, S., Hutchinson, J., & Alba, J. (1992). What consumers 'really know' and what they know: investigations into the determinants of confidence and performance. *Advances in Consumer Research. Association for Consumer Research (U. S.), 19*, 191.

Chatman, E. (1986). Diffusion theory: A review and test of a conceptual model in information diffusion. *Journal of the American Society for Information Science American Society for Information Science, 37*(6), 377–386.

Chua, P., & Hui, K. (1998). Identifying early adopters of new IT products: A case of Windows 95. *Information & Management, 33*(5), 225–230. doi:10.1016/S0378-7206(98)00031-7

Clarke, Y., & Soutar, G. (1982). Consumer acquisition patterns for durable goods: The Australian evidence. *The Journal of Consumer Research, 8*(4), 456–460. doi:10.1086/208887

Cohen, J., & Cohen, P. (1983). *Applied multiple regression: Correlation analysis for the behavioral sciences.* Hillsdale, NJ: Lawrence Erlbaum.

Cole, C., & Gaeth, G. Chakraborty, & Levin, I. (1992). Exploring the relationship among self-reported knowledge, objective knowledge and consumer decision making. *Advances in Consumer Research. Association for Consumer Research (U. S.), 19*, 191.

Dickinson, J., & Kirzner, E. (1986). Priority patterns of acquisition of financial assets. *Journal of the Academy of Marketing Science, 14*(1), 43–49. doi:10.1007/BF02722156

Flynn, L., Goldsmith, R., & Eastman, J. (1996). Opinion leaders and opinion seekers: Two new measurement scales. *Journal of the Academy of Marketing Science, 24*(2), 137–147. doi:10.1177/0092070396242004

Foxall, G. (1995). Cognitive styles of consumer initiators. *Technovation, 15*(5), 269–288. doi:10.1016/0166-4972(95)96600-X

Foxall, G., & Seema, B. (1993). Cognitive style and use-innovativeness for applications software in home computing: Implications for new product strategy. *Technovation, 13*(5), 311–323. doi:10.1016/0166-4972(93)90004-F

Gatignon, H., & Robertson, T. S. (1985). A propositional inventory for new diffusion research. *The Journal of Consumer Research, 11*(4), 849–867. doi:10.1086/209021

Girardi, A., Soutar, G., & Ward, S. (2003). Assessing price and ridgeway's use innovateness scale. In *Proceedings of the Australian and New Zealand Academy of Management Conference, Fremantle, Australia* (pp. 1-12).

Goldsmith, R. (1990). The validity of a scale to measure global innovativeness. *The Journal of Applied Business Research, 7*(2), 89–97.

Goldsmith, R., & Hofacker, C. (1991). Measuring consumer innovativeness. *Journal of the Academy of Marketing Science, 19*(3), 209–221. doi:10.1007/BF02726497

Goldsmith, R., Hofacker, C., & Eastman, J. (1995). The generality/specificity issue in consumer innovativeness research. *Technovation, 15*(10), 601–612. doi:10.1016/0166-4972(95)99328-D

Goslar, M. (1987). Marketing and the adoption of microcomputers: An application of diffusion theory. *Journal of the Academy of Marketing Science, 15*(2), 42–48. doi:10.1007/BF02723401

Greenacre, M. (1993). *Correspondence analysis in practice, Boca Raton, Fla.* London: Chapman & Hall/CRC.

Hashim, J. (2008). Factors influencing the acceptance of web-based training in Malaysia: Applying the technology acceptance model. *International Journal of Training and Development, 12*(4), 253–264. doi:10.1111/j.1468-2419.2008.00307.x

Hernandez, B., Jimenez, J., & Martin, J. (2008). Extending the technology acceptance model to include the IT decision maker: A study of business management software. *Technovation, 28*(3), 112–121. doi:10.1016/j.technovation.2007.11.002

Hirschman, E. (1980). Innovativeness, novelty seeking and consumer creativity. *The Journal of Consumer Research*, *7*(3), 283–295. doi:10.1086/208816

Jurison, J. (2000). Perceived value and technology across four end users groups. *Journal of End User Computing*, *12*(4), 21–28.

Kasulis, J., Lusch, R., & Stafford, E. (1979). Consumer acquisition patterns for durable goods. *The Journal of Consumer Research*, *6*(1), 47–55. doi:10.1086/208747

Kiel, G., & Layton, R. (1981). Dimensions of consumer information seeking. *JMR, Journal of Marketing Research*, *18*(2), 233–239. doi:10.2307/3150957

King, W., & He, J. (2006). A meta-analysis of the technology acceptance model. *Information & Management*, *43*(6), 740–755. doi:10.1016/j.im.2006.05.003

Leavitt, J., & Walton, J. (1975). Development of a scale for innovativeness. *Advances in Consumer Research. Association for Consumer Research (U. S.)*, *2*, 545–554.

Leavitt, J., & Walton, J. (1988). *Openness of information processing as a moderator of message effects on behavior.* Working Paper, College of Business Administration, Ohio State University.

Li, Y., Qi, J., & Shu, H. (2008). Review of relationships among variables in TAM. *Tsinghua Science and Technology*, *13*(3), 273–278. doi:10.1016/S1007-0214(08)70044-0

Lu, Y., Zhou, T., & Wang, B. (2009). Exploring Chinese users' acceptance of instant messaging using the theory of planned behaviour, the technology acceptance model, and the flow theory. *Computers in Human Behavior*, *25*(1), 29–39. doi:10.1016/j.chb.2008.06.002

Midgley, D. (1976). A simple mathematical theory of innovative behavior. *The Journal of Consumer Research*, *3*(1), 31–41. doi:10.1086/208648

Midgley, D., & Dowling, G. (1978). Innovativeness: the concept and its measurement. *The Journal of Consumer Research*, *4*(4), 229–242. doi:10.1086/208701

Midgley, D., & Dowling, G. (1993). A longitudinal study of product form innovation: The interaction between predispositions and social messages. *The Journal of Consumer Research*, *19*(4), 611–625. doi:10.1086/209326

Mudd, S. (1990). The place of innovativeness in models of the adoption process: An integrative review. *Technovation*, *10*(2), 119–136. doi:10.1016/0166-4972(90)90032-F

Park, W., Feick, L., & Mothersbaugh, D. (1992). Consumer knowledge assessment: How product experience and knowledge of brands, attributes, and features affect what we think. *Advances in Consumer Research. Association for Consumer Research (U. S.)*, *19*, 193–198.

Parousch, J. (1965). The order of acquisition of consumer durables. *Econometrika*, *33*(1), 225–234. doi:10.2307/1911897

Price, L., & Ridgway, N. (1983). Development of scale to measure use innovativeness. *Advances in Consumer Research. Association for Consumer Research (U. S.)*, *10*, 681–682.

Ram, S., & Jung, H. (1994). Innovativeness in product usage: A comparison of early adopters and early majority. *Psychology and Marketing*, *11*(1), 57–67. doi:10.1002/mar.4220110107

Rao, A., & Monroe, K. (1988). The moderating effect of prior knowledge on cue utilization in product evaluations. *The Journal of Consumer Research*, *15*(2), 253–264. doi:10.1086/209162

Rodgers, E. (1958). Catgorizing the adopters of agricultural practices. *Rural Sociology, 23*(4), 346–354.

Rodgers, E. (1995). *Diffusion of innovations* (4th Ed.). New York: The Free Press.

Schreier, M., Oberhauser, S., & Prügl, R. (2007). Lead users and the adoption and diffusion of new products: Insights from two extreme sports communities. *Marketing Letters, 18*(1-2), 15–30. doi:10.1007/s11002-006-9009-3

Shuptrine, K. (1977). Identifying innovative behavior patterns using canonical analysis. *Journal of Business Research, 5*(3), 249–259. doi:10.1016/0148-2963(77)90014-5

Soutar, G., Bell, R., & Wallis, Y. (1990). Consumer acquisition patterns for durable goods: A Rasch analysis. *Asia Pacific International Journal of Marketing, 2*(1), 31–39. doi:10.1108/eb010212

Soutar, G., & Cornish-Ward, S. (1997). Consumer acquisition patterns for durable goods and financial assets: A Rasch analysis. *Applied Economics, 29*(7), 903–911. doi:10.1080/000368497326561

Steenkamp, J., Hostede, F., & Wedel, M. (1999). A cross-national investigation into the individual and national cultural antecedents of consumer innovativeness. *Journal of Marketing, 63*(2), 55–69. doi:10.2307/1251945

Sujan, M. (1985). Consumer knowledge: Effects on evaluation strategies mediating consumer judgments. *The Journal of Consumer Research, 12*(1), 31–46. doi:10.1086/209033

Tabachnick, B., & Fidell, L. (1996). *Using multivariate statistics* (3rd Edition). New York: Harper and Collins Publishers.

Thatcher, J., Strite, M., Stepina, L., & Liu, Y. (2003). Culture, overload and personal innovativeness with information technology: Expanding the nomological net. *Journal of Information Systems, 44*(1), 74–81.

Tsang, A., & Zhou, N. (2005). Newsgroup participants as *opinion* leaders and seekers in online and offline communication environments. *Journal of Business Research, 58*(9), 1186–1193. doi:10.1016/j.jbusres.2004.05.002

Venkatraman, M., & Price, L. (1990). Differentiating between cognitive and sensory innovativeness. *Journal of Business Research, 20*(4), 293–315. doi:10.1016/0148-2963(90)90008-2

Vishwanath, A. (2005). Impact of personality on technology adoption: An empirical model. *Journal of the American Society for Information Science and Technology, 58*(8), 803–811. doi:10.1002/asi.20169

Wright, B. (1977). Solving measurement problems with the Rasch Model. *Journal of Educational Measurement, 14*(1), 97–116. doi:10.1111/j.1745-3984.1977.tb00031.x

Zeithaml, V., & Gilly, M. (1987). Characteristics affecting the acceptance of retailing technologies: A comparison of elderly and Non-elderly consumers. *Journal of Retailing, 63*(1), 49–68.

Zhang, S., Zhao, J., & Tan, W. (2008). Extending TAM for online learning systems: An intrinsic motivation perspective. *Tsinghua Science and Technology, 13*(3), 312–317. doi:10.1016/S1007-0214(08)70050-6

APPENDIX

Appendix Table 1. Items use to measure the constructs

Scale
Innovativeness
In general I am the first of my circle of friends to buy anything in information technology
If I heard something new was available in information technology then I would probably buy it
Compared to my friends I own a lot of items of information technology
In general, I am the first of my circle of friends to know the names of new items of information technology
I will buy anything new in information technology even if I haven't heard of it
Use Innovativeness
Even if I don't have the right tool for the job, I can usually improvise I never throw something away that I might use later In general, I would rather alter an old product to work in a new situation than purchase a new product specifically for that purpose After the useful life of a product, I can often think of ways to use the parts of It for other purposes I do not enjoy a product unless I can use it to its fullest capacity I use products in more ways than most people It's always impossible to improve upon a project by adding new features After purchase of a product, I try to keep track of new accessories that come out in the market I enjoy expanding and adding onto projects that I'm involved in on a continuing basis *Opinion Leadership*
My opinion on information technology seems to count with a lot of people People that I know pick something in information technology based on my advice I often influence people s opinions about information technology
Opinion Seeking
When I consider buying anything in information technology, I always ask for advice I usually ask other people what type of information technology I should buy I feel more comfortable buying something in information technology when I have gotten advice".
Objective Knowledge Respondents were asked what was the meaning of the following computer terms; RAM, ROM, 486-processor, Config.sys, bandwidth, and bit. The responses were scored 1 for a correct answer and zero for an incorrect answer and then the results were summed to give a score of objective knowledge.
Subjective Knowledge I know more about personal computers compared to the average person
Shopping Knowledge List five factors that would be helpful for a friend or relative selecting a computer. These were scored in a similar fashion to the objective knowledge responses, a one for a correct answer and zero for an incorrect answer. *Experience:* Days since last purchase No. items of IT in the last month
Information Use Readership of: *Aust PC user.* *Aust. Personal Computer Internet.au* *Net Guide* *Official Playstation* *PC Powerplay* Hours on the Internet per week gaining knowledge about computers.

Chapter 14
Information Technology Supported Communication – Group Cohesion, Agreeability, and Performance: The Role of Media Richness

Michael B. Knight
University of Wisconsin –Green Bay, USA

D. Scott Hunsinger
John A Walker College of Business, Appalachian State University, USA

J. Michael Pearson
Southern Illinois University at Carbondale, USA

ABSTRACT

Research over the past few decades has identified that organizations have been faced with social/economic pressure to utilize information technology and to facilitate communication via technological modes. These technology drive communications, under media richness theory, have been found to impact group cohesion and performance. The communications that are dependent on media richness are affected by individual user characteristics. Further group impacted by technology driven communication often experience varying levels of individual member agreeability, which further affect cohesion and performance. The individual users who participate in group projects must communicate, and ultimately can have different performance and cohesion outcomes based on the mode of communication used. This study identifies significant differences between groups, using specific media to communicate cohesion, the change in cohesion, agreeability and performance. Over the past few decades, organizations have faced increased pressure to utilize information technology (IT) to expand markets, to support increased communication between constituents, to streamline organizational decision making, and to improve employee productivity. Unfortunately, the results are contradictory as to the success IT has had in helping organizations achieve these goals. On one hand, several studies have reported beneficial returns on investment with the aforementioned implementation of information technology (Bourquard, 2004;

DOI: 10.4018/978-1-60566-687-7.ch014

Chienting, Jen-Hwa Hu, & Hsinchun, 2004; Dehning & Richardson, 2002; Hinton & Kaye, 1996; McGrath & Schneider, 2000; Violino, 1998; Willcocks & Lester, 1991). On the other hand, research also seems to suggest that technology can sink an organization when IT is not in alignment with the strategic goals of the organization (Arlotto & Oakes, 2003; Hinton & Kaye, 1996; PITAC, 1999; Violino, 1998; Willcocks & Lester, 1991). Adding to this dilemma, the marketplace has been turning to global expansion, becoming more demographically diverse, and relying more on the use of workgroups and teams (Stough, Eom, & Buckenmyer, 2000). These work teams historically have performed in homogenous settings and have met primarily face-to-face (FTF). These teams typically used little technology to interact. Lawler, Mohrman, & Ledford (1992) found that organizations that use teams more often have a positive outcome in decision making, employee trust and employee tenure. Considering the advances in communication media over the past twenty years, information technology has become a part of the everyday operations of most businesses. The requirement of the employee to use this technology has become essential to organizational success. With the organizational dependence on the employee to use information technology, plus the increased use of teams in the workplace, organizations may fail to provide workers with the support and training needed to develop cohesive groups resulting in improved performance and member satisfaction (Sarbaugh-Thompson & Feldman, 1998; Yoo, 2001). Several studies have concluded that teams that communicate successfully have had positive team performance (Rice, 1979; Tuckman, 1997; Zaccaro & Lowe, 1988). However, the independent variables considered in the aforementioned research vary greatly and seem to show inconsistency in identifying indicators that could be used to help with the implementation of technology that supports team performance. This study looks at face to face (FTF) and virtual teams, the personality trait of agreeability and the impact of specific communication technology on cohesion and performance. We use the media richness theory to facilitate our literature review and to guide the development of our hypotheses.

COHESION

Through a meta-analysis of the group dynamics literature, Forsyth (1990, 1999) suggested that the key to group processes was cohesion. In these two studies, Forsyth noted that cohesion was the "glue" that holds a group together and that cohesion was the "strength" that bonds and links groups together. Forsyth (1999) further suggested that cohesive groups possess the common characteristics of cooperation, satisfaction, and enjoyment.

Another meta-analysis by Bettenhausen (1991) suggested that group cohesion was one of the most studied constructs in group literature between 1986 and 1990 and that a consensus on the definition of cohesion was not found. Authors seemed to identify cohesion in terms that best fit their relevant study. For example, Frank (1997) and Langfred (1998) defined cohesion as an individual's feeling of belongingness to a group or the amount that members of a group like each other. Festinger (1950) stated that cohesion was the degree to which group members support each other and are motivated to remain together as a group.

According to Murdack (1989) and his review of literature, cohesiveness is simply attraction-to-group, while Evans and Dion (1991) interpreted cohesion as an individual's desire to remain in the group. Or as Tuckman (1997) suggested, cohesion is an outcome of the group development process. Cartwright and Zander (1968) stated that close and frequent interactions with group members would result in an individual's greater attraction to the group, while Bollen and Hoyle (1990) had reservations about using the term "attraction to a group" because attraction may be the cause of cohesion, rather than the effect of membership. Knight and Pearson (2004) further refined the definition of cohesion through a conglomeration of definitions to say cohesion is "members' beliefs that they are accepted, liked, secure, and belong to the collective decision making body of the group."

For the purposes of this study, we will use the conglomeration definition provided by Knight and Pearson (2004). Hoegl (2001) identified cohesion as one of six dimensions that make up teamwork quality and developed a second order construct to measure the interaction within a group. The six dimensions, which included cohesion, communication, coordination, balance of member contribution, mutual support, and effort, were shown to be related to teamwork quality. Additionally, the research revealed that the two areas that are most directly related to performance, and thus relevant to this study, were cohesion and communication, which directly relate to group effectiveness and efficiency.

Evan and Dion (1991) conducted a meta-analysis which examined group cohesion and performance. They reported that the relationship between cohesion and performance is a positive one and that frequency and duration of communication contributes to successful performance. Zaccaro and Lowe (1988) reported that cohesion is multidimensional, and it is a necessity to identify both the level and nature of cohesion in order to predict performance.

Treadwell, Lavertue, Kumar, & Veeraraghavan (2001) repeated the educational environment study of Wood, Kumar, Treadwell, & Leach, (1998); however, they modified the instrument (the Group Cohesion Scale) and validated a new 25 item multidimensional scale to identify levels and nature of cohesion in an educational setting. Steiner (1972) suggested that a group can actually experience a loss of productivity when the group is not coordinated effectively, or when group members are individually incompatible in personality with each other (Yalom & Rand, 1966).

Further studies that identify the positive aspects of cohesion on group dynamics and performance include Wech, Mossholder, Steel, and Bennett's (1998) study that identified higher collective cohesion correlated with significant improvements in communication among group members, and Rempel and Fisher's (1997) study that reported higher problem solving capabilities with groups that attained higher levels of cohesion. Furthermore, groups with increased quality and quantity of output were reported by Langfred (1998) to have higher cohesion.

Treadwell et al. (2001) posited the idea that cohesion has a healthy effect on group behavior and suggested that cohesion may reduce or eliminate social loafing (Karau & Hart, 1998), absenteeism (Carron, Widmeyer, & Brawley, 1988) and drop out rates (Robinson & Carron, 1982). Furthermore, Treadwell et al. (2001) identified changes in cohesion over time and suggested that interaction method may moderate cohesion development. Hence the following hypotheses are postulated:

H1: Groups with higher final group cohesion will have higher decision quality (performance).

H2: Groups using rich media (face-to-face) will have increased final group cohesion.

H3: Groups using semi-rich media (WebCT) will not have increased final group cohesion.

H4: Groups using lean media (e-mail) will have decreased final group cohesion.

Considering the aforementioned studies, in which cohesion has been identified as an influence on group performance (Steiner,1972), and may be affected by group interaction frequency and interaction quality (Wood et al, 1998), to date, there are very few studies considering cohesion and the aspects of personality in virtual teams. Therefore, a study identifying relationships between cohesion and personality factors in virtual teams seems supported.

PERSONALITY FACTOR

An individual's personality has been found to influence the interaction process within groups (Hackman and Morris 1975, McGrath 1964, Goodman Ravlin, and Argote 1986). More recent theory and research provide convincing evidence that systematic relations exist among personality dimensions and mood (Emmons & Diener, 1985; Meyer & Shack, 1989; Suh, Diener, & Fujita, 1996; Watson & Tellegen, 1985). Additionally, as a group increases in membership, increased difficultly in communication and decrease in performance occur (Nieva et al 1978, Champion et al 1993, Guzzo and Dickson 1996). McGrath's (1964) model suggests that members within a group have abilities, attitudes, backgrounds, and personality characteristics. In fact, the literature is quite comprehensive when looking at personality characteristics for individuals. Within the psychology literature alone, there are hundreds of studies that have been undertaken for the purpose of identifying the personality and behavioral aspects of individuals and their interpersonal qualities (Mershon & Gorsuch 1988, Costa & McCrae 1992, Ashton, Jackson, Paunonen, Helmes, & Rothstein 1995, Goldberg, L. R. 1999).

Barrick and Mount (1991) and Digman (1990) identified five factors that were meaningful across disciplines and could be used for both domestic and international research. These five factors included neuroticism, extraversion, agreeability, openness to experience and conscientiousness (the Big Five). Bruck and Allen (2003) defined each of these factors. Of interest to this study is the definition of Agreeability. Agreeability is termed as "An individual's interpersonal tendencies to be helpful, sympathetic to others, cooperative, and/or good-natured" (Bruck and Allen, 2003).

Each of the big five factors are related to other important subsets of variables related to group performance (Goldberg, 1999). A list of 280 personality constructs was identified on the International Personality Inventory Pool (IPIP) website (IPIP 2001). This website provides numerous constructs that have *yet to be explored* or published on in the information technology or strategy literature. Of interest to this study will be Agreeability, a group's cohesion, and resulting performance and satisfaction.

AGREEABILITY

Researchers have become increasingly interested in the attributes of personality and the effectiveness of group work as well as the conflict levels between group members (Bono 2002). Behling (1998), for example, claimed Conscientiousness as one of the most valid predictors of performance for most jobs, second only to general intelligence. More recently Hurtz and Donovan (2000), through a meta-analysis, state that the Big Five attributes of personality as measured in past literature have had construct validity threats ranging from collection methods to interrater agreement in classification and prediction capability. They found that for interpersonal facilitation, agreeableness rivaled both conscientiousness and emotional stability in its estimated true validity. This finding supports Van Scotter and Motowidlo's (1996) finding that although agreeableness does not influence task performance in given job types, it does appear to influence interpersonal facilitation.

McCrea and Costa (1992) found that individuals who can be described as agreeable also are perceived as being trusting, cooperative, and compliant. As defined, agreeableness, therefore, refers to how individuals relate with others and how considerate they are of others' feelings and opinions. Agreeable people see others as mostly honest and trustworthy; they are straightforward and frank, willing to help out, yielding rather than aggressive in conflict, modest and unpretentious, and caring, nurturing, and supportive. Agreeableness would seem, based on the research of Suls (1998), to be valuable in assessing and addressing issues of conflict, as well as being a possible moderating variable to cohesion. Agreeability has been previously examined and related to extraversion and neuroticism in the Big Five personality factors (Costa & McCrae, 1987). However, both traits, extraversion and neuroticism, have been most strongly associated with positive and negative affect (both state and trait) respectively (Larsen & Ketelaar, 1991; Watson & Clark, 1992). Further investigation has revealed limited research addressing agreeability and the relationship to cohesion and performance when modified by the use of technology to communicate. Therefore we postulate the following:

H5: Agreeability will positively impact final cohesion.
H6: Agreeability will positively impact the change in cohesion.

SAMPLE

Three hundred sixty-two (362) upper level undergraduate students enrolled in management courses at a large midwestern state university participated in class assigned requirements and completed the research portion for 1% extra credit. The classes included two courses in management, one course in human resources management, one course in policy and strategy, and one course in group and organizational dynamics. Of the possible 405 individual participants, 392 completed all three surveys. After removing the 13 incomplete responses from the data, groups were identified that did not have full member participation. These groups (5 WebCT groups) were eliminated from the study. A second screening was conducted to insure that participants communicated using the assigned medium. A review of the WebCT data strings revealed that two WebCT groups met face-to-face. A review of the email accounts for groups assigned to email revealed that only three groups mentioned meeting face to face. And a review of the face-to-face contact journals revealed that eight groups participated using email. These groups that violated media restrictions were eliminated from the study. As a result, 362 responses, from a possible 405, were used in this study. Table 1 shows the demographics for this study.

Table 1. Demographics

		Frequency	Percent
Gender	Male	217	59.9
	Female	145	40.1
Age	Average age = 22.8	362	100
Group Experience	Average number of group experiences = 7.39	362	100
Ethnic background	Caucasian	274	75.7
	African American	55	15.2
	Hispanic/Chicano	5	1.4
	American Indian	1	.3
	Asian / Pacific Islander	17	4.7
	Not-mentioned	10	2.8
	Total	362	100.0
Missing	System		0
Total		362	100.0

PROCEDURE

The students were randomly assigned via computer into three-person groups. No consideration was given in the formation stage of the groups to produce groups that were more homogeneous than others on the variables of age, gender, or ethnic background. Groups were informed of the contact options available to them as Verbal = face to face meeting, WEBCT = live on-line meeting, and Email = delayed exchange of information.

Groups participated in ice breaker exercises over the course of a week within the confines of the assigned medium. (Ice breakers are a way to begin a group interaction). These activities help relax participants, making them more receptive to listening and contributing. An ice breaker can also serve to build a group atmosphere.

Harris (2004) suggests that an ice breaker consists of multiple leading type questions that can be answered and shared among participants. Harris suggests that these questions can encourage participants to let down barriers, share their sense of humor with others, and release information about themselves. The open ended questions, regardless of communication mode, included in the current study were "What is your name? Why did you pick this school for your education? Why did you pick your major? Is it wrong to cheat on a test? Why or why not? If you could be an M&M, what color would you be and why?"

In order to facilitate group communication, each group assigned a group leader. This leader coordinated communication and assignment delivery per the assigned mode of communication. Each group was provided with the same task adopted from the ISWorld website (2004) of published intellective and preference tasks. The study utilized a preference task that required greater amounts of inter-group communication and collaboration (Huang, Wei, Watson, and Tan, 2003).

In the newly adopted task, the individual group members, for each group, were randomly assigned one of three "peer" organizations for which they became knowledgeable, regarding that organization's policy on dishonesty. Each individual participant was required to answer the following:

1. What is your assigned organizations dishonesty policy?
2. Determine what you MUST do regarding ethical/unethical behavior based on the dishonesty policy?
3. What would you have to do if this is a repeat offense (meaning the violator is dishonest a 2nd or 3rd time)

The individual participants then communicated their assigned organizations policy on dishonesty to their assigned group through the assigned communication medium. The groups were required to arrive at a consensus and develop a dishonesty policy that incorporated the "best" features of the other peer organization's policies. A written report (a policy document) was turned in as the official group's position.

The group members all were to receive the same grade as assigned for the group. The goal was to achieve the highest grade possible: 100%. The policies submitted by the groups were graded by two different teaching assistants. Of the submitted cases for grading, no groups experienced a variance in the assigned score by the two graders of greater than 5%. In these cases where grade assignment was greater than 5% the head instructor independently graded the case and assigned the final grade.

Table 2. Cronbach alpha for scales

SCALE	Cronbach's Alpha	N of Items
COHESION T1	.893	25
COHESION T2	.884	25
Agreeability	.863	10

MEASURES, METHODS, AND RESULTS

Groups were measured for cohesiveness and agreeability at the beginning of the project after the ice breaker exercise, and a second cohesiveness scale was collected at the end of the project before grades were given as feedback. As shown in Table 2, the scales of agreeability (IPIP, 2003) and the Group Cohesion Scale (Treadwell et al, 2001) were tested for reliability using Cronbach's coefficient alpha. The Cronbach's coefficient alpha for the scales exceeds the minimum requirement and is considered reliable for survey use (Hair, 1998).

Before conducting an ANOVA, the cohesion scale was computed for each observation. As shown in Figure 1, the FTF groups reported the highest cohesion both at the start and the end of the project (76.23, 78.23), the WebCT groups reported the next highest cohesion (74.32, 75.93), and the Email groups reported the lowest (73.45, 71.48). Additionally, as shown in Figure 2, the ANOVA test did reveal significant differences between the groups in cohesion and the change in cohesion.

Figure 1. ANOVA descriptive –cohesion

Item	group	N	Mean	Std. Deviation	Std. Error
total starting cohesion (Ct_1)	WebCT	115	74.3217	6.95921	.64895
	Email	126	73.4524	6.78187	.60418
	FTF	121	76.2314	8.20849	.74623
total ending cohesion (Ct_2)	WebCT	115	75.9391	9.55068	.89061
	Email	126	71.4841	11.07338	.98650
	FTF	121	78.2810	9.76492	.88772
change in cohesion ($Ct_2 - Ct_1$)	WebCT	115	1.6174	10.80901	1.00795
	Email	126	-1.9683	11.92707	1.06255
	FTF	121	2.0496	10.23788	.93072

Figure 2. Overall ANOVA results - cohesion

		Sum of Squares	df	Mean Square	F	Sig.
total starting cohesion (Ct_1)	Between Groups	495.694	2	247.847	4.597	.011
	Within Groups	19355.831	359	53.916		
	Total	19851.525	361			
total ending cohesion (Ct_2)	Between Groups	2950.893	2	1475.446	14.251	.000
	Within Groups	37168.488	359	103.533		
	Total	40119.381	361			
change in cohesion ($Ct_2 - Ct_1$).	Between Groups	1201.690	2	600.845	4.938	.008
	Within Groups	43678.741	359	121.668		
	Total	44880.431	361			

The ANOVA results in Figures 1 and 2 reveal significant differences between groups on the cohesion construct at the start of the task p= .011, F=4.597, the end of the task p<.001, F=14.251, and the overall change in cohesion p=.008, F=4.938.

Performance Measurement (Decision Quality)

As shown in Figure 3, the FTF groups achieved the highest decision quality with a mean grade score of 87.93, WebCT groups achieved the second highest decision quality with a mean grade score of 86.74, and Email groups achieved the poorest decision quality with a mean grade score of 85.60.

In addition, an ANOVA was run between the groups to identify if the grades assigned were significantly different between the media groups. The results indicate that the differences between media groups are not significant at the .05 level (see Figure 4). However, the results of a least significant difference (LSD) Post hoc test, shown in Figure 5 suggest that the mean difference between the grades assigned to the Email group

Figure 3. Average assigned grade

Group type	N	Minimum	Maximum	Mean	Std. Deviation
WebCT GROUP	115	65	99	**86.74**	8.492
EMAIL GROUP	126	65	98	**85.60**	8.603
Face-to-Face group	121	65	100	**87.93**	8.743

Figure 4. ANOVA - performance

	Sum of Squares	df	Mean Square	F	Sig.
Between Groups	332.928	2	166.464	2.243	.108
Within Groups	26644.663	359	74.219		
Total	26977.591	361			

Figure 5. Post hoc test - LSD

(I) Group type	(J) Group type	Mean Difference (I-J)	Std. Error	Sig.	95% Confidence Interval Lower Bound	95% Confidence Interval Upper Bound
1	2	1.136	1.111	.307	-1.05	3.32
	3	-1.186	1.122	.291	-3.39	1.02
2	1	-1.136	1.111	.307	-3.32	1.05
	3	-2.322(*)	1.097	.035	-4.48	-.17
3	1	1.186	1.122	.291	-1.02	3.39
	2	2.322(*)	1.097	.035	.17	4.48

Legend: 1 = WebCT, 2 = Email, 3 = Face-to-face
* The mean difference is significant at the .05 level.

and grades assigned to the FTF group are actually significantly different (p=.035).

Before conducting an ANOVA for agreeability, the reported data was summated for each group. As shown in Table 3, the WebCT groups reported the highest agreeability (42.26), the FTF groups reported the next highest agreeability (41.86), and the Email groups reported the lowest (41.07). However, as shown in Table 4, the ANOVA test did not reveal significant differences between the groups in agreeability.

As shown in Table 5, the groups with higher cohesion had higher performance (decision quality). A correlation analysis (Table 5) was then conducted between ending cohesion, change in cohesion, performance and the personality trait of agreeability. This analysis resulted significant correlations. As shown in table 6, ending cohesion and performance where significantly correlated with a p value of <.05, explaining 11.6% of the relationship. Additionally, the results suggest a significant positive relationship between agreeability and the variables of performance, cohesion and the change in cohesion to be significant at both the P<.01 P<.000. The correlated relationship between group performance and agreeability is significant (P=.008) explaining 13.9% of the relationship. Additionally, the correlated relationship between ending cohesion and the change in cohesion as relating to agreeability is also significant, explaining 41.4% and 31.8% of the relationship respectively.

DISCUSSION

The results of the statistical analyses in this study explored data from groups using different media to communicate, the personality trait of agreeability, and the associated outcomes of performance. The

Table 3. ANOVA descriptive – constructs

		N	Mean	Std. Deviation	Std. Error	95% Confidence Interval for Mean		Minimum	Maximum
						Lower Bound	Upper Bound		
totlagree	1	115	42.2696	5.82542	.54322	41.1934	43.3457	26.00	55.00
	2	126	41.0714	6.15296	.54815	39.9866	42.1563	18.00	53.00
	3	121	41.8678	6.89558	.62687	40.6266	43.1089	15.00	55.00
GRADE	1	115	86.74	8.492	.792	85.17	88.31	65	99
	2	126	85.60	8.603	.766	84.09	87.12	65	98
	3	121	87.93	8.743	.795	86.35	89.50	65	100
avgch2	1	115	75.9391	9.55068	.89061	74.1748	77.7034	42.00	97.00
	2	126	71.4841	11.07338	.98650	69.5317	73.4365	42.00	97.00
	3	121	78.2810	9.76492	.88772	76.5234	80.0386	33.00	97.00
chngech	1	115	1.6174	10.80901	1.00795	-.3793	3.6141	-25.00	38.00
	2	126	-1.9683	11.92707	1.06255	-4.0712	.1347	-36.00	45.00
	3	121	2.0496	10.23788	.93072	.2068	3.8923	-23.00	29.00

Table 4. ANOVA - all constructs

		Sum of Squares	df	Mean Square	F	Sig.
totlagree	Between Groups	90.375	2	45.187	1.134	.323
	Within Groups	14306.885	359	39.852		
	Total	14397.260	361			
GRADE	Between Groups	332.928	2	166.464	2.243	.108
	Within Groups	26644.663	359	74.219		
	Total	26977.591	361			
avgch2	Between Groups	2950.893	2	1475.446	14.251	.000
	Within Groups	37168.488	359	103.533		
	Total	40119.381	361			
chngech	Between Groups	1201.690	2	600.845	4.938	.008
	Within Groups	43678.741	359	121.668		
	Total	44880.431	361			

Table 5. Means analysis

	Change In Cohesion	Ending Cohesion	Decision Quality- Performace	Agreeability
Web CT Groups	1.6174	75.93	86.74	42.26
Email Groups	-1.9683	71.48	85.60	41.07
FTF Groups	2.0496	78.28	87.93	41.86

multiple ANOVA tests reveal significant differences between the groups for the dimensions of cohesion, ending cohesion, change in cohesion, agreeability and performance, while the least significant difference post hoc test provided secondary confirmation of the significant differences between groups.

The purpose of the study was to better understand the impact of media richness on group cohesion, while identifying the differences between groups in the outcomes of performance in consideration of personality attributes. The findings imply that a communication medium does have an impact on a group's cohesion and further an impact on a relationship between the personality trait of agreeability, performance and the development of cohesion in groups. Specifically, cohesion development seems to be greatest in groups that communicate via FTF medium, while cohesion development seems to decline in groups that communicate exclusively by Email. Groups using WebCT showed an improvement in cohesion, but not as great an improvement as that found in FTF groups.

IMPLICATIONS

These findings have important implications. First, when organizations are seeking to develop groups or teams, the use of technology for communication needs should be considered carefully. Although previous studies have focused on the ease of use of technology, or the cost savings through the use of technology, we contend that organizations should not restrict newly formed groups to the use of a

Table 6. Correlation analysis

		Total agree	Performance	Ending cohesion	Change in Cohesion
Total agree	Pearson Correlation	1	.139(**)	.414(**)	.318(**)
	p-value (2-tailed)		.008	.000	.000
	N	362	362	362	362
Performance	Pearson Correlation	.139(**)	1	.116(*)	.080
	p-value (2-tailed)	.008		.027	.127
	N	362	362	362	362
Ending cohesion	Pearson Correlation	.414(**)	.116(*)	1	.768(**)
	p-value (2-tailed)	.000	.027		.000
	N	362	362	362	362
Change in cohesion	Pearson Correlation	.318(**)	.080	.768(**)	1
	p-value (2-tailed)	.000	.127	.000	
	N	362	362	362	362

** Correlation is significant at the 0.01 level (2-tailed).
* Correlation is significant at the 0.05 level (2-tailed).

specific communication technology but provide media options for rich communication needs. Additionally, we suggest that organizations provide groups with opportunities for richer communication on a regular basis. This rich communication could be in conjunction with a training or initial group assignment. Furthermore, we suggest that solely relying on a specific technology for communication will have a negative affect on the newly formed group and ultimately affect the organization through the loss of cohesion.

Second, the use of a rich communication medium for groups has a positive relationship with a group's cohesion over time. Our findings suggest that in a given period of time, WebCT groups experienced greatest positive change in cohesion in all group types. Additionally, Email groups in this study experienced a loss in cohesion. We contend that the awareness and understanding of how communication media affect groups are critical for the decision making bodies of an organization. Additionally, we suggest that individuals in the position of assigning members to a group should understand the implications of communication media and how they will affect group cohesion over time. Additionally, the personality trait of agreeability is correlated to performance and cohesion.

Through this understanding, individuals in charge of group assignment can provide the appropriate level of media and maximize the cohesion groups can achieve.

Of significant interest to most organizations is the relationship between a group's cohesion, agreeability and the ending performance. Specifically, the greater the final group cohesion, the better a group will perform on a given project (i.e., FTF groups reported the greatest ending cohesion and achieved the highest performance, while Email groups reported the lowest ending cohesion and achieved the lowest performance). Although the differences between FTF and email groups were significant, the differences between WebCT and FTF were not significant. It would seem from the results of this research that the virtual groups may be in danger of not performing to the best of their ability, given a media option for communication. This finding could be taken as an implication that managers may need to provide additional options to the traditional email or WebCT meeting.

We found that cohesion is directly correlated to performance and suggest that while organizations are continuing a quest to increase individual and organizational performance, organizations should provide organizational workgroup opportunities to become more cohesive. As stated earlier, one way to help groups to become more cohesive would be to provide the opportunity to communicate more frequently via a rich media, rather than a lean media such as email. Additionally, groups can become more cohesive through opportunities to utilize greater blocks of time, thus needing less frequent communication. These practices increase cohesion, and ultimately, increase performance. We suggest that technologies that have greater media richness, such as WebCT and MS Net Meeting, be considered a valuable option to organizations that are implementing virtual groups. This study supports the idea that performance is related to cohesion and that semi-rich mediums can provide a trade-off between cohesion development and group performance. The performance in this study accounted for less than 2% difference between FTF groups and WebCT groups. Although WebCT group performance was less than the FTF group, WebCT groups communicated less often and with less duration. These efficiencies of using less time to communicate, that were found in the WebCT group, may justify the difference (loss) in performance for some organizations.

The trait of agreeability is directly correlated to performance. While organizations are continuing a quest to increase individual and organizational performance, it would seem clear that organizations should look for ways to develop agreeability within teams. The relationship between agreeability and cohesion is also quite interesting and there may be further implications for the formation of groups and the trait of agreeability to be researched. While the other personality factors of the Big Five are not included in this study further research should be conducted to include them as potential factors in cohesion and performance.

As stated earlier, one way to help groups to become more cohesive would be to provide the opportunity to communicate more frequently via a richer medium. Or, to have groups utilize greater blocks of time rather than more frequency (Knight, 2005), thus needing less frequency of communication. Therefore, based on the findings of this study, development of cohesion may be related to the development of agreeability. These practices increase cohesion, potentially increase agreeability, and ultimately, increase performance.

REFERENCES

Arlotto, P., & Oakes, J. (2003). *Return on investment: Maximizing the value of healthcare information technology.* Chicago: Healthcare Information & Management Systems Society.

Ashton, M. C., Jackson, D. N., Paunonen, S. V., Helmes, E., & Rothstein, M. G. (1995). The criterion validity of broad factor scales versus specific facet scales. *Journal of Research in Personality, 29*, 432–442. doi:10.1006/jrpe.1995.1025

Barrick, M. R., & Mount, M. K. (1991). The big five personality dimensions and job performance: A meta-analysis. *Personnel Psychology, 44*, 1–26. doi:10.1111/j.1744-6570.1991.tb00688.x

Behling, O. (1998). Employee selection: Will intelligence and conscientiousness do the job? *The Academy of Management Executive, 12*, 77–86.

Bettenhausen, K. L. (1991). Five years of groups research: What we have learned and what needs to be addressed. *Journal of Management, 17*, 345–381. doi:10.1177/014920639101700205

Bollen, K. A., & Hoyle, R. H. (1990). Perceived cohesion: A conceptual and empirical examination. *Social Forces, 69*, 479–504. doi:10.2307/2579670

Bono, J. (2002). The role of personality in task and relationship conflict. *Journal of Personality, 70*(3), 311. doi:10.1111/1467-6494.05007

Bourquard, J. (2004). IT–Big investment, bigger returns. *State Legislatures, 30*(4), 18–22.

Carron, A. V., Widmeyer, W. N., & Brawley, L. R. (1988). Group cohesion and individual adherence to physical activity. *Journal of Sport & Exercise Psychology, 10*(2), 127–138.

Cartwright, D., & Zander, A. (1968). *Group dynamics.* New York: Harper Row.

Champion, M. A., Medsker, G. J., & Higgs, A. C. (1993). Relations between work group characteristics and effectiveness: Implications for designing effective work groups. *Personnel Psychology, 46*, 823–850. doi:10.1111/j.1744-6570.1993.tb01571.x

Chienting, S., Jen-Hwa Hu, P., & Hsinchun, C. (2004). Technology implementation management in law enforcement. *Social Science Computer Review, 22*(1), 24–37. doi:10.1177/0894439303259881

Costa, P., & McCrae, R. (1987). Validation of the five-factor model of personality across instruments and observers. *Journal of Personality and Social Psychology, 52*(1), 81. doi:10.1037/0022-3514.52.1.81

Costa, P. T., & McCrae, R. R. (1992). *NEO PI-R. The revised NEO personality inventory.* Odessa, FL: Psychological Assessment Resources.

Dehning, B., & Richardson, V. (2002). Returns on investments in information technology: A research synthesis. *Journal of Information Systems, 16*(1), 7–31. doi:10.2308/jis.2002.16.1.7

Digman, J. M. (1990). Personality structure: Emergence of the five-factor model. *Annual Review of Psychology, 41*, 417–440.

Emmons, R. A., & Diener, E. (1986). Influence of impulsivity and sociability on subjective well-being. *Journal of Personality and Social Psychology, 50*(6). doi:10.1037/0022-3514.50.6.1211

Evans, S., & Dion, K. (1991). Group cohesion and performance – A metaanalysis. *Small Group Research, 22*, 175–186. doi:10.1177/1046496491222002

Festinger, L., Schachter, S., & Back, K. (1950). *Social pressures in informal groups.* Stanford, CA: Stanford University Press.

Forsyth, D. (1990). *Group dynamics* (2nd ed.). Pacific Grove, CA: Brook/Cole Publishing.

Forsyth, D. (1999). *Group dynamics* (3rd ed.). Pacific Grove, CA: Brook/Cole Publishing.

Frank, J. D. (1997). Some determinants, manifestations, and effects on cohesiveness in therapy groups. *The Journal of Psychotherapy Practice and Research, 6*(1), 59–70.

Goldberg, L. R. (1999). A broad-bandwidth, public domain, personality inventory measuring the lower-level facets of several five-factor models. In I. Mervielde, I. Deary, F. De Fruyt, & F. Ostendorf (eds.), *Personality psychology in Europe, 7* (pp. 7-28). Tilburg, The Netherlands: Tilburg University Press.

Goodman, P. S., Ravlin, E., & Argote, L. (1986). Current thinking about groups: Setting the stage for new ideas. In P.G.a. Associates (ed.), *Designing effective work groups* (pp. 1-33). San Francisco: Jossey-Bass, Inc.

Guzzo, R. A., & Dickson, M. W. (1996). Teams in organizations: Recent research on performance and effectiveness. In J.T. Spence, J.M. Darley & D.F. Foss (eds.), *Annual Review of Psychology,* (pp. 307-338). Palo Alto, CA: Annual Reviews, Inc.

Hackman, J. R., & Morris, C. G. (1975). Group tasks, group interaction process, and group performance effectiveness: A review and proposed integration. In L. Berkowitz (ed.), *Advances in experimental social psychology* (pp. 45-99). New York: Academic Press.

Hair, J., Anderson, R., Tatham, R., & Black, W. (1998). *Multivariate data analysis* (5th ed.) Englewood Cliffs, NJ: Prentice Hall.

Harris, D. (2004). Your favorite icebreakers. *Training (New York, N.Y.)*, 23.

Harris, D. (2004, May). Your favorite icebreakers. *Training (New York, N.Y.)*, 23.

Hinton, M., & Kaye, R. (1996). Investing in information technology: A lottery? *Management Accounting (London)*, *74*, 52.

Hoegl, M. G. (2001). Teamwork quality and the success of innovative projects: A theoretical concept and empirical evidence. *Organization Science*, *12*(4), 435. doi:10.1287/orsc.12.4.435.10635

Huang, W., Wei, K., Watson, R. T., & Tan, B. (2003). Supporting virtual team-building with a GSS: An empirical investigation. *Decision Support Systems*, *34*(4), 359. doi:10.1016/S0167-9236(02)00009-X

Hurtz, G., & Donovan, J. (2000). Personality and job performance: The Big Five revisited. *The Journal of Applied Psychology*, *85*(6), 869. doi:10.1037/0021-9010.85.6.869

International Personality Item Pool. (2001). A scientific collaboratory for the development of advanced measures of personality traits and other individual differences. Retrieved December 12, 2004 from http://ipip.ori.org/

Karau, S., & Hart, J. (1998). Group cohesiveness and social loafing: Effects of a social interaction manipulation on individual motivation within groups. *Group Dynamics*, *2*, 185–191. doi:10.1037/1089-2699.2.3.185

Knight, M. B. (2005). *An empirical evaluation of groups and the use of technology to communicate*. Unpublished Dissertation.

Knight, M. B., & Pearson, J. M. (2004). Cohesion via technology: Information technology, individual personality and group cohesion. *Decision Science Institute conference* (pp. 5122-5126). Boston.

Langfred, C. W. (1998). Is group cohesiveness a double-edged sword? An investigation of the effects of cohesion on performance. *Small Group Research*, *29*(1), 124. doi:10.1177/1046496498291005

Larsen, R., & Ketelaar, T. (1991). Personality and susceptibility to positive and negative emotional states. *Journal of Personality and Social Psychology*, *61*(1), 132. doi:10.1037/0022-3514.61.1.132

Lawler, E., Mohrman, S., & Ledford, G. (1992). *Employee involvement and total quality management: Practices and results in Fortune 1000 companies.* San Francisco: Jossey-Bass.

McGrath, G., & Schneider, A. (2000). Measuring intranet return on investment. Retrieved November 15, 2004 from http://intrack.com/intranet/ireturn.shtml

McGrath, J. (1964). *Social psychology: A brief introduction.* New York: Holt.

Mershon, B., & Gorsuch, R. L. (1988). Number of factors in the personality sphere: Does increase in factors increase predictability of real-life criteria? *Journal of Personality and Social Psychology*, *55*, 675–680. doi:10.1037/0022-3514.55.4.675

Meyer, G. J., & Shack, J. R. (1989). Structural convergence of mood and personality: Evidence for old and new directions. *Journal of Personality and Social Psychology*, *57*(4), 691. doi:10.1037/0022-3514.57.4.691

Murdack, G. (1989). Defining group cohesiveness: A legacy of confusion? *Small Group Behavior, 20*, 37–49. doi:10.1177/104649648902000103

Nieva, V., Fleishman, E., & Rieck, A. (1978). *Team dimensions: Their identity, their measurement, and their relationships* (Report No. DAHC19-78-C-0001). Washington, D.C: Advanced Research Resources Organizations.

PITAC. (1999). *Information technology research: Investing in our future.* Retrieved November 15, 2004 from http://www.itrd.gov/pitac/report/

Rempel, M., & Fisher, R. (1997). Perceived threat, cohesion, and group problem solving in intergroup conflict. *The International Journal of Conflict Management, 8*(3), 216. doi:10.1108/eb022796

Rice, R., & Monkarsh, W. (1979). Time-phased interrelationships of group atmosphere, group performance, and leader style. *The Journal of Applied Psychology, 64*(4), 401. doi:10.1037/0021-9010.64.4.401

Robinson, T. T., & Carron, A. V. (1982). Personal and situational factors associated with dropping out versus maintaining participation in competitive sports. *Journal of Sport Psychology, 4*, 364–378.

Sarbaugh-Thompson, M., & Feldman, M. (1998). Electronic mail and organizational communication: Does saying "hi" really matter? *Organization Science, 9*(6), 685–69. doi:10.1287/orsc.9.6.685

Steiner, I. D. (1972). *Group processes and productivity.* New York: Academic Press.

Stough, S., Eom, S., & Buckenmyer, J. (2000). Virtual teaming: A strategy for moving your organization into the new millennium. *Industrial Management & Data Systems, 100*(8), 370–378. doi:10.1108/02635570010353857

Suh, E., Diener, E., & Fujita, F. (1996). Events and subjective well-being: Only recent events matter. *Journal of Personality and Social Psychology, 70*(5), 1091–1092. doi:10.1037/0022-3514.70.5.1091

Treadwell, T., Ashcraft, D., & Kumar, V. K. (2001). *A pedagogy for collaborative on-line research and learning: The CORAL Model.* Retrieved August 13, 2004 from http://coral.wcupa.edu/about/pedagogy.doc

Treadwell, T., Lavertue, N., Kumar, V.K., & Veeraraghavan, V. (2001). The group cohesion scale-revisited: Reliability and validity. *Action Methods 3.*

Tuckman, B. W., & Jensen, M. A. C. (1997). Stages of small group development revisited. *Group & Organizational Studies, 2*, 419–427. doi:10.1177/105960117700200404

Van Scotter, J. R., & Motowidlo, S. J. (1996). Interpersonal facilitation and job dedication as separate facets of contextual performance. *The Journal of Applied Psychology, 81*, 525–531. doi:10.1037/0021-9010.81.5.525

Violino, B. (1998). ROI in the real world. *Information Week, 679*, 60–72.

Watson, D., & Clark, L. (1992). Affect, personality, and social activity. *Journal of Personality and Social Psychology, 63*(6), 1011. doi:10.1037/0022-3514.63.6.1011

Watson, D., & Tellegen, A. (1999). The two general activation systems of affect: Structural findings, evolutionary considerations, and psychobiological evidence. *Journal of Personality and Social Psychology, 76*(5), 820–839. doi:10.1037/0022-3514.76.5.820

Wech, B., Mossholder, K., Steel, R., & Bennett, N. (1998). Does work group cohesiveness affect individuals? *Small Group Research*, *29*(4), 472. doi:10.1177/1046496498294004

Willcocks, L., & Lester, S. (1991). Information systems investments: Evaluation of the feasibility stage of projects. *Technovation*, *11*, 283–302. doi:10.1016/0166-4972(91)90027-2

Wood, D., Kumar, V., Treadwell, T., & Leach, E. (1998). Perceived cohesiveness and sociometric choice in ongoing groups. *The International Journal of Action Methods*, *51*(3), 122.

Yalom, I., & Rand, K. H. (1966). Compatibility and cohesiveness in therapy groups. *Archives of Gen. Psych*, *15*, 267–275.

Zaccaro, S. J., & Lowe, C. A. (1988). Cohesiveness and performance on an additive task: Evidence for multidimensionality. *The Journal of Social Psychology*, *128*, 547–558.

APPENDIX

Appendix Table 1. GCS-R

1 = Strongly Disagree 2 = Disagree 3 = Agree 4 = Strongly Agree
1. Group members are accepting of variations in each other's culture, customs, habits, and traditions.
2. There are positive relationships among the group members.
3. There is a feeling of unity and togetherness among group members.
4. Group members usually feel free to share information.
5. Problem solving processes would be disrupted if one or two members are absent.
6. The group members feel comfortable in expressing disagreements in the group.
7. Problem solving in this group is truly a group effort.
8. Group members influence one another.
9. I dislike going this group's meetings.
10. The group members seem to be aware of the group's unspoken rules.
11. Discussions appear to be unrelated to the concerns of the group members.
12. Most group members contribute to decision making in this group.
13. Group members are receptive to feedback and criticism.
14. Despite group tensions, members tend to stick together.
15. It appears that the individual and group goals are inconsistent.
16. An unhealthy competitive attitude appears to be present among group members.
17. Group members usually feel free to share their opinions.
18. Minimal attempts are made to include quieter members of this group.
19. Group members respect the agreement of confidentiality.
20. People would be concerned when a group member is absent from the groups members.
21. Group members would <u>not</u> like to postpone group meetings.
22. Many members engage in "back-biting" in this group.
23. Group members usually feel free to share their feelings.
24. If a group with the same goals is formed, I would prefer to shift to that group.
25. I feel vulnerable in this group.

Appendix Table 2. Agreeableness construct

	10-item scale (Alpha = .82)
+ keyed	I Am interested in people.
	I Sympathize with others' feelings.
	I Have a soft heart.
	I Take time out for others.
	I Feel others' emotions.
	I Make people feel at ease.
– keyed	I Am not really interested in others.
	I Insult people.
	I Am not interested in other people's problems.
	I Feel little concern for others.

Chapter 15
Ratings Schemes in e-Commerce

Robin S. Poston
University of Memphis, USA

Marla B. Royne
University of Memphis, USA

ABSTRACT

Evidence has been growing that suggests Internet-based opinion systems influence users' purchase decisions. One of the most popular systems are the rating schemes found on Web sites such as eBay.com, expertcentral.com, bizrate.com, epinions.com, slashdot.net, moviefone.com, citysearch.com, etc. Rating schemes affect user productivity by changing their ability to search and find products and services on the Internet. Regrettably, ratings schemes can provide misleading information because those inputting ratings have personal subjective opinions, or they want to manipulate other users' behaviors. For example, an author of a book may ask family and friends to rate his or her book highly and his or her competitors' books poorly. This chapter provides a robust summary of the rating scheme literature and delineates the sources of rating scheme bias and the potential effects of this bias on how users utilize ratings. In a research study, data were gathered from 73 upper-division undergraduates completing a preliminary survey with open- and closed-ended questions and 164 additional students completing an exploratory survey to support the preliminary survey results. Based on the research findings, the chapter discusses preliminary insights and develops a set of propositions to encourage a more rigorous and in-depth examination of rating scheme bias by both practitioners and academicians.

INTRODUCTION

Finding products on the Internet is now a relatively easy task since search engines such as Google.com have become commonplace. A simple keyword search can potentially produce thousands of results, but poring through these results can be daunting, and finding high-quality items within the long list is even less straightforward (Drennan, Mort & Previte, 2006; Hodkinson & Kiel, 2003; Lueg, Moore & Warkentin, 2003). For example, a search on Google.com for an Italian restaurant in Chicago

DOI: 10.4018/978-1-60566-687-7.ch015

produces hundreds of listings with little means for the end-user to determine which choices are best. To address this problem, Internet sites are increasingly adopting rating schemes to help users make online choices for goods and services. Popular rating schemes can be found at eBay.com (Keser, 2003; Melnik & Alm, 2002); expertcentral.com and bizrate.com (Resnick, Zeckhauser, Friedman & Kuwabara, 2000); epinions.com, slashdot.org, moviefone.com, and citysearch.com (Dellarocas, 2003); and so forth. Rating schemes offer users the opportunity to submit feedback on goods and services so future online users can utilize this information in their own purchase decisions.

Rating schemes are designed to let parties enter ratings as feedback, usually after the completion of an online e-commerce transaction; ratings are then aggregated to create a trustworthiness or reputation score. This score is subsequently used by other online consumers to decide whether or not to engage in future transactions. Rating schemes are a type of reputation system that is collaborative in nature because it is based on the inputs of multiple online consumers. This makes ratings schemes related to systems that utilize online collaborative filtering, word-of-mouth input, reputation information, recommendation ideas, and feedback text (Josang et al. 2007).

For rating schemes to be successful, they must have the following properties: (1) they must be long lived, where every transaction prompts an expectation of future transactions, (2) their ratings about current transactions are captured and distributed, and (3) their ratings about past transactions must guide decisions about future transactions (Resnick et al., 2000). Through a variety of available rating schemes, today's online consumers share opinions and experiences about companies, products, and services with other individuals outside of their personal network of family, friends, and acquaintances by contributing to blogs, user feedback forums, search engines, or shopping review sites (e.g. pricescan.com) (Davis and Khazanchi, 2008). This means the personal ties between raters and consumers are weak because the raters and the consumers relying on the ratings do not have a personal relationship (Chatterjee, 2001). This weak tie establishes an opportunity for misleading ratings to be published and shared.

Thus, rating schemes vary in the amount of bias and manipulation incorporated into them (Dellarocas, 2003; Melnik & Alm, 2002; Resnick et al., 2000). Ratings are inherently subjective and voluntarily provided, resulting in a possible mismatch between the quality of the rated object and the rating given (Melnik & Alm, 2002). Alternatively, individuals who submit ratings may manipulate them to influence others' thinking or to enhance their own reputation. In addition to a rater's true feeling about the object, ratings naturally have a random component, meaning it may be impossible to derive a perfect rating. Thus, this chapter examines (1) if users understand the inherent bias in rating and subsequently discount ratings based on the level of perceived bias involved; or (2) whether users treat ratings similar to other forms of feedback, specifically word-of-mouth advice and advertising.

The purpose of this chapter is to delineate the sources of rating scheme bias and the potential effects of this prejudice on how end-users utilize ratings by reporting results from two exploratory surveys. Our intent is to gather preliminary insights and then develop a research program to encourage practitioners and academicians to examine how online consumers use rating scheme information. First, we discuss the sources of rating scheme bias and ways of mitigating this bias, and the current research literature on rating schemes. Then we explore the feelings and opinions of users to determine the potential impact of these subjective ratings. Next, we present results from a preliminary survey that provide direction for a second exploratory study. Results from the second survey are then discussed. Finally, based on findings from the two studies, we offer a series of propositions for future research to encourage a more rigorous examination of rating scheme bias.

SOURCES OF RATING SCHEME BIAS

Ratings may be biased for several reasons. First, raters may use products in inappropriate contexts, which results in poor perceptions and low ratings (Resnick et al., 2000). For example, an end-user may buy spreadsheet software instead of word processing software to write a report and may rate the software as "low" because it is cumbersome to use in the task. Second, individuals who submit ratings may manipulate these ratings in an attempt to influence others' behaviors or to enhance their own reputations (Resnick et al., 2000). For instance, the author of a book may enter positive ratings of his or her own book and negative ones of competing books. Regardless of the reasons, bias may simply be inherent because ratings are based on personal opinions or tastes. Moreover, ratings may always contain some randomness along with the rater's true feeling about the object, suggesting that deriving a rating perfectly may be impossible. Ratings can also be subject to flaming (i.e., intentionally angry, hostile, or abusive), exhibiting greater bias and error. Finally, the approaches used to entice online consumers to submit ratings may influence feedback. For example, some online retailers (e.g., ebags.com) send e-mails to past and current customers asking them to submit feedback for purchased products in exchange for discount coupons toward future purchases. It is possible that these customers may be influenced by the coupon to provide more positive ratings than their true feelings about the products.

DESIGNS TO MITIGATE AND DISCLOSE BIAS

Although some end-users know that ratings may be biased, they cannot overcome this prejudice (Resnick et al., 2000). Given user vulnerability, several Web sites attempt to mitigate these concerns. For example, Google.com aggregates across large numbers of raters, while eBay.com only permits ratings from those directly involved in transactions. Epinions.com uses a double rating system that includes a mechanism for rating raters. Amazon.com includes a "real name" label for raters to imply that those who identify themselves may be more honest. Bizrate.com recently barred two retailers from its site after detecting efforts to manipulate ratings (Resnick et al., 2000). In addition, many online rating schemes require raters to be registered, provide the total number of ratings reported by each person, and encourage text explanations and other indicators of rating credibility.

RESEARCH ON RATINGS SCHEMES

Considerable research uses eBay's Feedback Forum to examine the performance of existing rating schemes (Standifird, 2001). Here, buyers and sellers rate each other's performances on the current transaction to inform potential future participants about both parties' current behavior. Negative ratings may discourage participants from engaging in a transaction with that particular buyer or seller. The Feedback Forum attempts to help buyers identify trustworthy sellers, encourage sellers to be trustworthy, and discourage participation from those who are not trustworthy (Keser, 2003; Standifird, 2001). To understand feedback behavior, eBay, and Epinions conducted customer focus groups. Their findings show that people care about their own rating scores and prefer metrics that are easily understood (e.g., if ratings are aggregated, they want to know how the individual ratings were weighted) (Dellarocas, 2003). Another study suggests that eBay would have experienced less growth and more fraud had they not implemented their rating system (Keser, 2003). These findings suggest that rating schemes offer a means of reputation management to foster trust among transaction partners (Keser, 2003).

Other research explores ways of eliciting truthful ratings (Chevalier & Mayzlin, 2006; Smith, Menon & Sivakumar, 2005). Because most rating schemes are voluntary, the absence of incentives for raters may keep them from providing feedback or encourage them to provide intentionally or unintentionally deceptive ratings (Ekstrom, Garcia & Bjornsson, 2005). Some researchers propose concrete incentives to individuals to both provide ratings and truthfully report their opinions. In addition, some schemes can punish those manipulating ratings for personal gain by locking them out of the system (Dellarocas, 2003).

Additional research examines ways to implicitly extract ratings to eliminate the ability for untruthful submissions (Constant, Sproull & Kiesler, 1996). This includes data mining techniques that can automatically extract ratings from public networked data structures such as the Web, Usenet groups, and so forth (Sabater, 2004). Data mining and statistical analysis of past ratings are techniques to monitor or eliminate abnormal ratings. These techniques use a large amount of information about raters' social standings, past behaviors, and online habits to infer a reputation to identify dishonest raters (Sabater, 2004).

Most rating systems are based on centralized designs where ratings are solicited and stored in a single repository, and controlled by a single organization (e.g., eBay, Epinions, Amazon). Motivated by issues of privacy and scalability, some researchers examine distributed rating schemes (Sabater, 2004). Here, software agents receive rating information from a variety of sources, including direct experience, feedback from third parties, and implicitly extracted data. Researchers are working on ways to make these schemes resilient to the influence of strategic software agents created to influence ratings for their owners' benefits or malicious agents created to merely render the system ineffective (Dellarocas, 2003).

In addition to rating scheme design, Hennig-Thurau, Gwinner, Walsh & Gremler (2004) conducted a study of motivations among consumers who share their opinions online (i.e., electronic word-of-mouth behavior). The authors concluded that the motivations for submitting ratings are consumers' need for social interaction, desire for economic incentives, concern for others, and potential to enhance their self worth. In summary, the performance and effectiveness of existing rating schemes (e.g., eBay's Feedback Forum) and the ways these ratings schemes influence users' decisions and actions have received considerable attention in the literature. The mechanisms for extracting ratings as well as providing truthful ratings to users have been widely studied. A summary of the current research literature addressing rating scheme issues is provided in Table 1. Note that the references to online word-of-mouth, reputation systems, recommendation agents, and feedback systems are all forms of rating schemes designed to help consumers make important purchasing decisions. This list of current research has been grouped by how each paper informs Measuring Rating Scheme Outcomes, Measuring Rating Scheme Trust, and Improving Rating Scheme Outcomes.

However, despite the growing body of literature on this topic, little research has specifically examined end-user perceptions of ratings schemes and their utilization in purchasing decision contexts. To address this gap in the literature, this chapter examines whether users understand the biases present in online rating schemes. The next section describes a preliminary survey designed to capture users' perceptions of rating schemes.

STUDY 1: PRELIMINARY SURVEY

Survey Administration

To understand individual beliefs about these schemes, we developed and administered a survey that assessed the uses and perceptions of ratings as well as the perceived biases of those ratings. A portion of the survey asked respondents if they

Table 1. Summary of rating scheme current literature

Study	Area	Research Method	Findings for Rating Schemes	Theory
Measuring Rating Scheme Outcomes				
Davis and Khazanchi 2008	Attributes of online word-of mouth (WOM) predict e-commerce sales	Rating data collected from a leading multi-product retail e-commerce company	Online WOM attributes of volume, valence, visual cues, and reviewer type do not explain sales, and moderator variables (product category and promotion) do not explain sales, but product views by themselves can explain sales. Products that are visited by customers and have images are more likely to result in sales, and specific products that have higher online WOM via volume of comments impact sales.	Cognitive consequence of expectation and perception
Nikolaeva and Sriram 2006	Consumers update beliefs about a product after recom-mendations and factors affecting increase in product's expected utility after recommendations	A Monte Carlo simulation of how these factors influence the effectiveness of recommendations	Value of recommendation depends on the preference structure of the consumer, the attributes of the product, and the characteristics of the population of consumers. Retailers should include more information in recommendations when the products are less common or when there is large variability of user tastes.	Consumer search behavior
Mithas et al. 2006/2007	Effect of Web site design elements on customer loyalty	Survey data from 43 Web sites across business domains	Web site features affect customer loyalty to site and vary depending on site's domain. Relationship between site content and customer loyalty stronger for information-oriented than for transaction-oriented sites. Relationship between functionality and customer loyalty is stronger for transaction than for information-oriented sites. Government sites enjoy greater WOM effect than commercial sites. Transaction sites score higher on customer loyalty than information-oriented sites.	Customer loyalty
Pavlou and Dimoka 2006	Role of feedback text comments in reputation systems which differentiate among sellers and create price premiums for trustworthy sellers	Content analysis of publicly available text comments of sellers in eBay's online auction matched with data from buyers that transacted with the sellers	Text comments convey useful reputation information about a seller's prior transactions that cannot be captured by numerical ratings. Feedback text builds buyer's trust in seller's benevolence and credibility, which differentiate among sellers by influencing the price premiums that a seller receives from buyers. References to seller behavior in the sellers' comments create price premiums for reputable sellers by engendering buyer's trust in the sellers' benevolence and credibility. The addition of comments and benevolence explains variance in price premiums.	Economics and Trust
Zhao et al. 2006	On-line mediation services alleviate consequences of asym-metric informa-tion in C2C markets	Analytical model building	Rating schemes facilitate on-line transactions by (1) inducing traders to negotiate efficiently in the presence of ex post discrepancy, and (2) enabling sellers with higher chances of selling a high-quality product to signal their superiority and earn a price premium.	Game theory

continued on the following page

Table 1. continued

Zhou et al. 2008	Effects of feed-back systems on seller incentives to provide high quality products with asym-metric informa-tion	Analytical model building	Auction system without a feedback-based reputation system may not be sustainable. Using a feedback system can lead to sustainable market outcomes, but three practices – the changing of identifications by dishonest sellers, shilling, and failure to leave feedback – can negate the system.	Game theory
Dellarocas 2006	Consumers are influenced by online opinion forums and firms whose products are being discussed manipulate con-sumer perceptions by posting costly anonymous mes-sages that praise their products	Analytical model building	If every firm's manipulation strategy increase with firm's true quality, manipulation increases the information value of a forum to consumers. And manipulations benefit consumers. If accuracy of honest opinions that firms manipulate is high, firms are better off if manipulation was not possible. Firms spend resources on this profit-reducing activity because if they don't, perceptions will be biased against them. Social cost of manipulation can be reduced with technology. As amount of user-contributed online content increases, firms, not consumers gain.	Game theory
Sigala 2006	Relations between online features and customer satisfac-tion	Survey of interna-tional and multicultural student audience about a travel web site	Information provision: High power distance (PD) use site's expertise, authority, status, recommendations, certifications, logos for establishing trust and security. High PD customers expect push rather than pull of information. High PD customers expect one-way hierarchical communication, directions and suggestions from company's experts for selecting a product, configuring its production, and purchasing it; while low PD expect two-way personalized communications with staff.	Hofstede's (1994) cultural dimensions
Xiao and Benbasat 2007	Recommendation agents use, provid-er credibility, and factors related to product, user, and user–agent interac-tion, influence de-cisions, outcomes, and evaluation of agents	Develop conceptual model with proposi-tions	Identifies the specific features, such as input, process, and output design characteristics that affect users' evaluations.	Human information process-ing, Interpersonal similarity, Trust formation, technology acceptance model, and satisfaction
Liang et al. 2006/2007	Personalized content recommen-dation and user satisfac-tion	2 experiments were conducted	Personalized services reduce information overload and increase user satisfaction, but the effects are moderated by motivation for information access. The effect is stronger for users whose motivation is in searching for a specific target. Content recommendation is more useful for KMS where users are looking for specific knowledge, rather than for general purpose Web sites whose customers come for scanning. User involvement in the process affects a user's perception, but has effect on overall satisfaction.	Information overload, uses and gratifications, and user involvement

continued on the following page

Table 1. continued

Kumar and Benbasat 2006	Recom-mendations and consumer reviews influence on perceived usefulness and social presence	Experiment conditions via filtering the content of Amazon in real time	Recommendations and consumer reviews increase both the usefulness and social presence of the website.	Social exchange
Fuller et al. 2007	Changing influence of reputation informa-tion on decisions regarding an e-vendor	Experiment about Books-a-Million.com	Reputation information was initially strongly related to trusting beliefs regarding the e-vendor, direct experience to the web site reduced reputation's effects.	Social judgment theory
Standifird and Weinstein 2007	Market-based transaction costs	Measure market-based transaction costs indirectly by examining variations in market prices when selling Morgan Silver Dollars on eBay	Reputation of both the seller and the coin-rating agency employed influences the price premium obtained. Use of a coin-rating agency with a poor reputation more damaging than the use of no coin-rating agency. Reputation of sellers and third-party verification agencies influence transaction costs.	Transaction cost economics
Measuring Rating Scheme Trust				
Kim et al. 2008	Trust and perceived risk influence decisions and what kinds of trust and risk antecedents play a role in consumer trust-building	Survey data to test research model	Antecedents of trust and risk: Cognition-based: privacy protection, security protection, system reliability, information quality; Affect-based: reputation, presence of third-party seals, referral, recommendation, buyers' feedback, WOM; Experience-based: familiarity, Internet experience, e-commerce experience; and personality-oriented: disposition to trust, shopping style.	Consumer decision-making
Josang et al. 2007	Systems used to derive measures of trust and reputation for online transaction	Overview of existing systems, and analysis of current trends and development	Problems and solutions: Low incentive for providing ratings; Bias toward positive rating; Unfair ratings; Change of identities; Quality variations over time; Discrimination; and Ballot box stuffing.	None
Wenhong and Cook 2007/2008	Antecedent factors that lead to the trust of third-party trust assurance programs	Survey	Integrity and Competence impact consumer trust. Perceived reputation only had effect for people with low trust propensity. Third-party trust programs, www.bizrate.com, assist consumers in their evaluation of online retailers via a rating system (e.g., a four-star or smiley-face scale). Ratings of online retailers are based on aggregated consumer feedback and other observable data.	Trust
Wang and Benbasat 2008	Reasons users trust online recom-mendation agents in the early stages of its use	Experiment using quantitative data about trust and written protocols that explain the reasons for the trust	In the early stages of trust formation, 4 positive reasons (i.e., knowledge-based, interactive, calculative, and dispositional) are associated with higher trust in agents and two negative reasons (i.e., calculative and interactive) are associated with lower trust in agents.	Trust formation in interpersonal and organizational contexts

continued on the following page

Table 1. continued

Improving Rating Scheme Outcomes				
Lauw et al. 2008	Scores assigned to the same object may deviate due to the potential bias of raters	Experiments on real-life and synthetic data sets	Propose a rating approach based on the following observations: 1) evaluation is "subjective," as raters and objects have varying bias and controversy, respectively, and 2) bias and controversy are mutually dependent.	Computer science
Dellarocas and Wood 2008	Method allows partners of an exchange to report satisfaction and to "see through" reporting bias to derive unbiased estimates of private outcomes	Apply method of extracting information from transactions where trading partners choose to remain silent from a large data set of eBay feedback	eBay traders are more likely to post feedback when satisfied than when dissatisfied and exhibit positive and negative reciprocation. Analysis derives unbiased estimates of the risks that are associated with trading on eBay that are more realistic than those suggested by a naïve interpretation of the high levels of positive feedback found on that system.	Computer science
Krukow et al. 2008	Algorithm for a better reputation system	Analytical model building (eBay's Feedback Forum)	Reputation system with information using exact semantics, represented in a very concrete form. The systems can provide exact security guarantees that relate a present authorization to a precise property of past behavior.	Event-structure model and formal declarative language
Dellarocas 2006	How often reputation mechanism should update a trader's reputation profile	Analytical model building (eBay's Feedback Forum)	For trading with moral hazard and noisy ratings. If the per-period profit margin of sellers is high, do not publish every single rating received but rather only update a trader's public reputation profile every so many transactions with a summary statistic of the trader's most recent ratings. This induces higher average levels of cooperation and market efficiency than publishing all ratings as they are posted.	Game theory
Liu and Issarny 2007	How to stimulate reputation information sharing and enforce honest recom-mendation elicitation	Simulation based evaluation	Present a system to facilitate trustworthy evaluations. The system shows robustness against lies, and stimulates honest and active recommendations. The latter is realized by ensuring that active and honest raters obtain the most number of honest (helpful) recommendations and thus suffer the least number of wrong decisions. The system empowers an entity to distinguish (1) between trustworthy / untrustworthy service providers and (2) between honest / dishonest raters.	Probability theory
Dewally and Ederington 2006	Signaling strategies that sellers of high-quality goods and services employ to differen-tiate products from lower quality	Compare 4 strategies using data from eBay's comic book auction market	Signaling strategies include (1) development of a reputation for quality, (2) third-party certification, (3) warranties, and (4) information disclosure. eBay invites all buyers and sellers to rate their satisfaction with the other party and then posts the results. While imperfect, these feedback ratings provide a much better measure of reputation than before.	Signaling strategies

continued on the following page

Table 1. continued

Kennes and Schiff 2007	Reputation system that monitors and publishes informa-tion about sellers be-havior in a search market with asym-metric informa-tion	Analytical model building	Reputations influence search patterns of buyers and provide for market-based punishment of bad behavior. A reputation system that rewards honesty can enhance welfare by allowing good sellers to truth-fully signal their type. However, the same system can be prone to strategic ma-nipulation by sellers who have low-quality products. Alternative system which assigns reputations based on product quality rather than honesty is superior.	Signaling theory
Gregg and Scott 2006	Whether on-line reputation systems are a useful mecha-nism for buyers to avoid fraudulent auctions	Content analysis of complaints posted to understand fraud and the role of reputation systems in document-ing, predicting, and reducing fraud	(1) number of fraud allegations found in on-line reputation system exceeds the number of fraud allegations made through official channels, (2) recent negative feedback posted in an online reputation system is useful in predicting future on-line auction fraud, and (3) experienced on-line auc-tion buyers are in a better position to use reputation system data to avoid fraudulent auctions.	Signaling theory

treat ratings similar to other forms of feedback, specifically word-of-mouth advice and advertising, to examine how end-users perceive differences among these methods of communicating product information. Both closed- and open-ended questions were included, along with demographic information. Our goal was to (1) understand general feelings and opinions about ratings and their biases; and (2) develop a foundation for future research on the topic.

We used a sample of upper-division undergraduate business students because the majority of online consumers tend to be computer-savvy, and students meet this criterion (Leung, 2004; Mackay & Elam, 1992). Novice computer users devote substantial effort and attention to interacting with the computer rather than focusing on the facets of the task, including the information provided such as ratings and indicators of rating credibility (Mackay & Elam, 1992). By using student subjects from a college of business, we get feedback from those who have online purchasing experience and familiarity with online rating schemes. However, we recognize that additional research is needed to examine whether our findings can be replicated with other populations of Internet users, including nonstudent groups.

The survey was administered to students in several business classes at a major southern university. Data were gathered over a two-week period on a paper-based instrument. The 73 individuals who responded to the questionnaire were 57% male, 88% junior and senior standings, and 69% between 20 and 29 years old. To code and analyze the qualitative data from the open-ended survey questions, we employed the methods suggested by Miles and Huberman (1984). First, for each individual question, one of the authors coded the responses into themes. To establish an independent assessment of the reliability of the coding, two "blind" coders (graduate students who were not involved in the study) read and coded respondent answers according to the themes. To establish an initial inter-rater reliability, the coders completed a small sample from the first few respondents; the Cohen's Kappa was .71. The coders then discussed the discrepancies and developed coding rules to reconcile these discrepancies. After completing the rest of the coding, the final Cohen's Kappa was .96. Given this level of agreement, the coding approach was deemed reliable (greater than the threshold of .70) (Landis & Koch, 1977).

Findings

Findings indicate that most respondents use but do not contribute ratings: 68% of respondents use ratings to make purchase decisions, while 65% say they have never posted a rating. These findings support the notion of "free-riding" in rating schemes (Ba & Pavlou, 2002). Furthermore, the high percentage of those using ratings indicates many respondents believe ratings are helpful in making purchase decisions. Despite the high level of rating use, a majority (59%) of respondents think that ratings reflect others' opinions about products and that these opinions are biased. That is, individuals recognize that ratings are personal opinions and therefore are influenced by the raters' personal beliefs.

To further explore these issues, we asked and coded open-ended questions about what ratings represent and why people take the time to submit ratings. Answers to these questions are summarized in Table 2 and Table 3. The two most frequent responses to a question assessing what ratings represent are (1) personal opinions of others (57%) and (2) input from peers to help in decision-making (23%). The three most frequent answers to why people submit ratings are (1) to help others make the right decisions (21%), (2) to share strong feelings (18%), and (3) to input their thoughts and feelings (17%).

Most respondents (73%) believe ratings are different from advice from friends. Not surprisingly, more than half (53%) said that they would rely more on input from friends who know their individual preferences as compared to unknown raters. In contrast, some respondents (20%) state they would rely more on ratings since the raters had actually purchased and used the product. Answers to open-ended questions regarding these issues are presented in Table 4. The two most frequent responses to how ratings compare to advice from friends are that (1) friends can be trusted more than ratings (28%) and (2) friends are known, while the source of ratings is not known (26%).

Interestingly, 64% of the respondents believe ratings are similar to sales promotions or advertising. Yet despite knowing that ratings are biased, respondents still feel that ratings are less biased than advertising and therefore more useful in making purchase decisions. Additional insight on these issues can be found in Table 5. The two most frequent answers to how ratings compare to advertising are (1) because any publicity or

Table 2. Coded survey responses of what ratings represent

Coded Response Themes	Number of Respondents	Percentage of Total
The personal opinions of others	54	57%
Input from peers to help me make a decision	22	23%
Feedback from someone with first-hand experience with the rated object	5	5%
Opinions that may or may not equal your own opinion	5	5%
The real validity of rated object	3	3%
Advertising	3	3%
Expert's judgments	2	2%
Nonexpert's judgments	1	1%
Totals	95	100%

providing of information is like advertising (28%) and (2) because ratings influence people's decisions (25%).

More than half of the respondents (55%) believe attempts to mitigate and disclose biases are not particularly helpful, although 45% believe that these designs do have some advantages. Respondents were asked about indicators of rating credibility (e.g., badges associated with ratings), which suggests the raters' expertise and trustworthiness. Results from open-ended questions about these issues are shown in Table 6. The two most common perceptions of rating credibility indicators are that these indicators (1) specify the credibility of the raters (20%) and (2) provide confidence in the ratings (17%). Alternatively, other respondents feel that the indicators do not instill trust in either the indicator or the rating (17%).

Table 3. Coded survey responses of why people submit ratings

Coded Response Themes	Number of Respondents	Percentage of Total
Help others make the right decisions	19	21%
Share feelings when they really like or hate something	16	18%
Simple to input their thoughts or feelings about something	15	17%
Help others avoid bad stuff or find the good stuff	12	13%
Tell or share their experiences	10	11%
Influence others' thoughts and actions	6	7%
For money or some other benefit	3	3%
To provide feedback to the company	3	3%
Because they feel they have knowledge about something	2	2%
To promote a product or service	2	2%
Fill time when they have nothing else to do	1	1%
Totals	89	100%

Table 4. Coded survey responses of how ratings compare to advice from friends

Coded Response Themes	Number of Respondents	Percentage of Total
I can trust my friends more than ratings	17	28%
I know my friends so I know the source of the advice	16	26%
My friends know me so they know my likes and dislikes	8	13%
My friends have my best interest in mind	4	7%
Friends might not have first-hand experience with the object	4	7%
Ratings are better than friends because we all have different opinions	3	5%
Ratings are better than friends because everyone's opinion counts	3	5%
Friends try to convince you to agree with their opinions	2	3%
I can ask questions to my friends	1	2%
My friends are my peers and are better than ratings	1	2%
Ratings are better than friends because friends can be wrong	1	2%
Ratings are better than friends because friends will tell you anything	1	2%
Totals	61	100%

Table 5. Coded survey responses of how ratings compare to advertising

Coded Response Themes	Number of Respondents	Percentage of Total
Any publicity or giving out information (like ratings) is like advertising	18	28%
Like advertising, people are influenced by ratings	16	25%
Ratings can be either positive or negative while advertising is mostly positive	13	20%
Ratings are like word-of-mouth sharing of honest opinions by a third party	7	11%
Ratings are about the quality of or information about the object	3	5%
The people providing the ratings have no interest in selling the product	2	3%
Raters have already bought the rated object and know about it	2	3%
Advertising is blatantly biased, while ratings are based on true rater experiences	2	3%
Advertising is bound by law to be credible, while ratings are not	1	2%
Getting opinions from lots of others is not advertising	1	2%
Totals	65	100%

Table 6. Coded survey responses of perceptions of indicators of rating credibility

Coded Response Themes	Number of Respondents	Percentage of Total
They indicate the credibility of the raters	8	20%
They give me confidence in the ratings	7	17%
They do not instill trust in the indicator or the rating	7	17%
They help you find out more about those who are providing the ratings	6	15%
They do not help determine if those providing the ratings share the same interests and preferences with me	4	10%
A higher level indicator means the rating has greater believability	3	7%
Even with the indicator, I may still disagree with the rating	3	7%
They do not tell me anything about the raters' characters	3	7%
Totals	41	100%

Most respondents (68%) think it is unacceptable for raters to have a stake in the rated object, but a little more than half (53%) think it is acceptable for raters to be affiliated with someone who has a stake in the particular item. For example, although an author should not rate his or her own book, it is acceptable for the author's friend to do so. Respondents are split in their feelings about who is responsible for reducing rating bias. About half (51%) think the raters themselves should be held responsible, while a few (14%) think Web site managers should be held accountable. Yet almost one-third (29%) of the respondents believe it is irrelevant whether ratings are biased or not. Overall, our results suggest that perceived rating bias does exist and that potential buyers are aware of this bias. Based on these findings, a second survey was developed to assess the levels of agreement on several topics identified from the preliminary survey.

STUDY 2: EXPLORATORY SURVEY

Survey Administration

The second survey was administered to capture additional input about the coded response themes identified in the preliminary survey. More specifically, the questionnaire included a series of statements developed from the existing literature on ratings and the results of the initial survey. The purpose of this survey was to support and enhance the findings from the first study. A Likert scale was used to obtain respondents' levels of agreement or disagreement with each of the items representing the response themes from the preliminary survey. Participants were asked to respond to a five-point scale (1 = strongly agree and 5 = strongly disagree) for each statement using conditional branching to tailor the survey to the respondent's specific rating usage patterns. Specific instructions provided to the participants are included in the Appendix with all of the questionnaire items. The researchers used feedback from graduate students and modified the statements to achieve a higher level of content validity.

The survey targeted students who did not participate in the preliminary survey but were part of a similar population. We collected data for one week using an online instrument. A total of 164 students completed the survey, receiving course credit for their participation. As indicated in the Appendix, 57.9% of respondents were 20 to 29 years old, 54.3% were male, and 45.7% were junior or senior undergraduates. The second survey results will be integrated into discussions to support the research propositions.

Survey Results

Overall, this second survey supported the findings of the first preliminary survey. For example, most respondents use but do not contribute ratings: 70% (68% in first survey) of respondents use ratings to make purchase decisions, while 66% (65% in first survey) said they had never posted a rating. In addition, the analysis of the individual items provides some interesting insights. For example, although there is, on average, a feeling that ratings are biased, some credence is given to raters because of their experience with the product and because ratings are not like advertising, which is believed to be deliberately biased. The combined results from the two surveys offer insight into rating perceptions and biases, and provide direction for future research. These directions for future research has been captured through a series of propositions presented graphically in Figure 1 and are discussed below.

Propositions

This section develops a series of propositions to encourage practitioners and academicians to investigate how end-users utilize rating schemes and manage the inherent biases that accompany these schemes. These propositions are illustrated in Figure 1 and are organized under two overarching dimensions: (1) sources of rating scheme bias and (2) designs to mitigate and disclose bias. These two dimensions are developed from a combination of the existing literature and our survey findings. First, sources of rating scheme bias can be intentional or unintentional, based on the rater or rating context, and motivated by rewards. All of these sources of bias may influence whether end-users utilize the information provided by rating schemes. Second, designs to mitigate and disclose bias can inform end-users about the reliability of ratings, which may influence whether end-users utilize the rating schemes. The following sections discuss each proposition in detail.

Figure 1. Propositions for using ratings in e-commerce

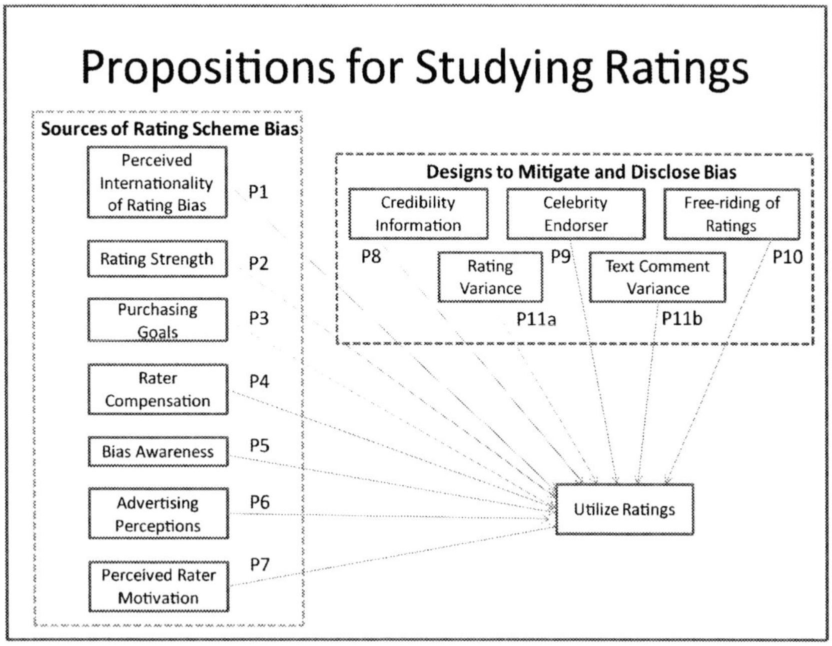

Sources of Rating Scheme Bias

Rating usage may be influenced by the perception that rating bias is intentional (Melnik & Alm, 2002; Resnick et al., 2000). Our preliminary results indicate people are aware of and accept inherent rating bias because ratings reflect the opinions of other people. One first-survey respondent stated, "Ratings represent people's varying opinions, not to be taken as a be-all or end-all, but something to look at very subjectively." Our findings also suggest people discount ratings from those individuals with a stake in product sales. For example, 68% of the first-survey respondents and 87% of the second-survey respondents indicate that it is *unacceptable* for an author to rate his or her own book, commenting that they would "not pay attention to" or they would "completely disregard" ratings from such an author. One first-survey respondent said he "would not use a rating if the rater had an interest or a monetary gain" in the rated product. However, respondents are not strongly opposed to friends of those with a stake in sales rating the product, as they believe that friends have less incentive to influence purchase decisions. In fact, 53% of the first-survey respondents and 40% of the second-survey respondents claim that it is *acceptable* for an author's friend to rate the book, stating that they would "take it into consideration" or they would "accept" such ratings as inputs. However, the second-survey respondents generally agree that they would treat ratings from the author (mean = 1.8) and an author's friend (mean = 2.1) skeptically, and they disagree with statements that they would accept the ratings from an author (mean = 3.9) or the author's friend (mean = 3.6) just like any other feedback.

Additionally, 34% of the first-survey respondents and 40% of the second-survey respondents believe ratings are unlike traditional advertising because they come from "people being helpful and giving their opinions," while traditional advertising is "strictly a way to make something look good." This means online consumers may discount information that they think contains blatant intentional bias but may not discount information that they believe comes from less intentionally biased opinions (Dellarocas, 2003; Xue & Phelps, 2004). That is, end-users may accept the bias that accompanies ratings or the opinions of others (i.e., similar to word-of-mouth communications), and therefore, they find the bias in opinions (i.e., ratings) more useful than the bias intentionally incorporated into traditional advertising messages. Therefore, we offer the following proposition:

- **Proposition 1:** Users who perceive that rating bias is unintentional will utilize ratings more than those who perceive that rating bias is intentional.

Extreme ratings may suggest renegade raters and outliers, but these ratings stand out, making them difficult for consumers to discount (i.e., not incorporate) when making purchase decisions (Ekstrom et al., 2005; Smith et al., 2005). Our results indicate that people are cognizant that more passionate people tend to contribute ratings, and this is acknowledged when utilizing this information in their purchase decisions. First-survey respondents state, "Raters submit ratings when they either really like or hate something and they want others to feel the same" or "are critics and use it as a forum to bitch about something … or they may have been moved in a direction (pro or con) and wish to reflect that impact they received to others." Second-survey respondents agree that ratings provide an outlet for people to voice their opinions (mean = 1.9) and that people enter ratings to share their feelings when they really like or dislike something (mean = 1.7).

Communications research suggests peoples' attitudes can differ in both their direction (positive or negative) and their strength (Chevalier & Mayzlin, 2006; Standifird, 2001). Given that a rating is generally selected from a scale of 1 = poor to 5 = outstanding, direction is the rating's path toward the different endpoints of the scale, while strength is indicated by the distance from the rating value to the midpoint of the scale. The more extreme/strong the rating value is (i.e., greater the distance from the midpoint), the greater it stands out (Dellarocas, 2003). Direction and strength of word-of-mouth communications, especially when negative, have an effect on brand attitudes, particularly for unfamiliar brands (Hennig-Thurau & Walsh, 2003; Hennig-Thurau et al., 2004). Users may utilize extreme rating values, especially when they are negative, because these are more salient and difficult to ignore. Thus:

- **Proposition 2:** Users will utilize ratings more when they perceive them to be extreme (positive or negative).

Consumers may use ratings to save time and/or learn more about the marketplace; these motives exist even when people also use word-of-mouth channels (Dellarocas, 2003; Hennig-Thurau & Walsh, 2003). People seek out information to (1) reduce the risk of buying inappropriate items, (2) lower the time spent searching, (3) learn how to use products, (4) learn how goods and services will enhance their social position, (5) be involved with a virtual consumer community, and (6) learn about competing products available in the marketplace (Hennig-Thurau & Walsh, 2003). First-survey respondents stated, "Ratings are a good first step to see how you will like something," "a way to see people's overview about a subject," and "helpful when you are unsure about what you want or think is best." Second-survey respondents agree that ratings offer both the positives and negatives about something (mean = 2.0).

Ratings are typically provided along with accompanying explanatory text comments that consumers can use to gain insights into the features and quality of goods and services prior to making a purchase decision (Ekstrom et al., 2005; Smith et al., 2005). Our first survey indicates respondents "like to read what others have to say before making a purchase" and "use others' judgments as a way to affirm or progress decisions." Ratings and accompanying text—similar to word-of-mouth input—provide information for end-users to make more efficient and effective purchase decisions. When the goal is to make a purchase decision rather than simply browse the Internet, ratings may be more useful by providing direction and insight into the decision process (Melnik & Alm, 2002). First-survey respondents mention, "Ratings are good for purchasing books but not clothing which you must try on," "I look at ratings to decide on purchasing a product," and "ratings are good especially with big purchases like buying cars." Thus, we propose the following:

- **Proposition 3:** When users seek information for a purchase decision, they utilize ratings more than when they do not have a specific purchase decision to make.

End-users may equate ratings to sales promotions and traditional advertising whether or not ratings are solicited and/or raters are compensated (Ekstrom et al., 2005; Forman et al., 2008; Smith et al., 2005). By definition, traditional advertising is paid communications; otherwise, it is not considered advertising (Belch & Belch, 2004). Second-survey respondents who believe ratings are similar to traditional advertising agree that, like advertising, people are influenced by ratings (mean = 1.8). In contrast, those who do not believe ratings are similar to advertising agree that raters have bought the particular item and therefore have first-hand knowledge about it (mean = 1.9).

Yet some ratings are solicited and effectively "paid for" with discount coupons from the seller, and users may perceive these ratings to be more like traditional advertising (Smith et al., 2005). However, users do not usually know if such a transaction occurred. Our study found that 64% of the first-survey respondents and 60% of the second-survey respondents feel that ratings are like traditional advertising. Comments from the first-survey include, "Ratings are like advertising because ratings influence people's opinions on products," "duh, these ratings are designed to influence you to make a purchase or not," and "any publicity is good publicity even if it's a bad rating."

Although discount coupons from the seller may affect a rater's feelings or attitudes, this does not necessarily translate into a positive rating (Cosley, Lam, Albert, Konstan & Riedl, 2003). In fact, research demonstrates that rewards undermine product evaluations under certain conditions (Constant et al., 1996). Regardless of their actual influence on product ratings, rewards or coupons still may be perceived as payment for the ratings and therefore equivalent to traditional advertising. That is, if end-users perceive ratings to be "purchased," they may treat this input more like traditional paid advertising. Thus, we propose:

- **Proposition 4:** Users who are unaware that raters received compensation forsubmitting ratings will utilize ratings more than those who are aware of the compensation.

End-users may continue to use ratings even when the bias is known (Cosley et al., 2003; Komiak, Wang & Benbasat, 2005; Mayer, Huh & Cude, 2005). More specifically, our results suggest that despite beliefs about biased ratings, people still use the information in their purchase decisions. One first-survey respondent stated, "Ratings are/can be informative and sometimes very amusing," while another noted, "Ratings are good when you are trying to research your options and get a feel of what people really think of different products, etc." It is possible that users are satisfied or have no alternative means to gather better information for decision-making. Moreover, purchasing risks may be taken into consideration. For example, users may knowingly use biased ratings when purchasing low-cost items or items with low-cost return policies.

Meanwhile, second-survey respondents generally disagree with the statement that ratings were unbiased (mean = 3.6). Decision-making theory suggests users should discount (i.e., give less weight to) ratings when they are biased and therefore should not incorporate these ratings in their decisions (Payne, Bettman & Johnson, 1993). Studies show people weigh advice based on characteristics of the source and of themselves (Yaniv, 2004). Similarly, people weigh ratings like they would weigh advice in making purchase decisions. Yaniv (2004) found that (1) people tend to place more weight on their own opinion than an adviser's opinion; (2) experts discount advice more than non-experts; (3) people weigh advice less as the distance of the advice from their own opinion increases; and (4) people assess the weight to place on advice to improve their decisions but not to an optimal level. Therefore, users may utilize ratings but discount them more when bias is explicitly apparent than when the bias seems not to exist. One first-survey respondent stated, "Ratings are useful, but must be met with some skepticism. You cannot know that they are genuine." Thus, the following is proposed:

- **Proposition 5:** Users unaware of extant rating bias will utilize ratings more than those who are aware of rating bias.

Similarly, end-users may recognize the existence of rating bias but still prefer to use rating information over traditional advertising information (Komiak et al., 2005; Mayer et al., 2005). One first-survey respondent stated, "Advertising is usually used to get people to buy or use a product. ...I find advertising is strictly a way to make something look good. Ratings do not always do this." Another respondent says, "Advertising is very blatantly biased in most cases, while ratings are usually someone's true experiences without any added 'fluff.'" Second-survey respondents generally agree that ratings are like word-of-mouth sharing of opinions (mean = 1.9).

Traditional advertising is persuasive and seeks to communicate with large audiences in a cost-effective manner, create brand images and symbolic appeals for a company or brand, and/or strike a responsive chord with consumers by attracting attention and generating sales (Belch & Belch, 2004). The purpose of advertising may be to generate immediate response or action from customers or to develop awareness or a positive image for its product over a longer period of time. In contrast to advertising, the motivation and subjectivity of those supplying ratings are generally accepted as less coercive and more helpful—similar to word-of-mouth input. People are more comfortable accepting advice from less coercive sources. Thus, the following is offered:

- **Proposition 6:** Users will utilize ratings more than they will utilize traditional advertising.

Individual motivations for submitting ratings may influence whether or not end-users utilize that information in purchase decisions (Cosley et al., 2003; Dellarocas, 2003; Resnick et al., 2000). Survey results suggest that people are aware of the different reasons for submitting ratings and that some motivations may be more benevolent and altruistic than others. For example, one first-survey respondent noted, "They enter them (ratings) to inform people who come after them and make purchases," while another suggested that ratings are provided to "either warn others of problems or tell them how good their encounter with the company was." One person says that raters "are either very pleased with the service received and want people to know or very unhappy with the service and want to warn future customers of problems they may face." Others note that some ratings are clearly self-serving (i.e., when an author enters ratings about his or her own book). For instance, first-survey respondents say they would be skeptical of an author's ratings because "it is a slighted opinion, hard for one to see his/her own faults," "the ratings would be biased and I would ignore it," and "of course he/she would give it a good rating."

Existing research on positive and negative word-of-mouth communication reveals several underlying motives for providing help to others (Hennig-Thurau & Walsh, 2003; Hennig-Thurau et al., 2004). People provide recommendations when they have a strong sense of involvement with the product or with sharing information about the product (Hennig-Thurau & Walsh, 2003). Self-involvement suggests consumers may feel the need for self-confirmation to reassure himself or herself in front of others. In this case, the end-users providing feedback seek attention, show expertise, feel like a leader, boast about insider information, advocate their status, confirm their own judgment, or assert their superiority (Hennig-Thurau & Walsh, 2003). Other-involvement suggests consumers feel the need to "give" something to another person or "share" their pleasure and express that they care, feel love, or show friendship. One study finds self-involvement existed in 24% of the word-of-mouth situations, while other-involvement existed in 20% of the situations analyzed (Hennig-Thurau et al., 2004).

When raters' motivations are perceived as benevolent and altruistic consistent with other-involvement (i.e., end-users just want to help others by giving honest feedback), ratings are more likely to be used in purchase decisions (Wakefield & Whitten, 2006). On the other hand, when motivations are perceived as malevolent and selfish, consistent with self-involvement (i.e., end-users are giving feedback to persuade others), ratings are more likely to be discounted in purchasing decisions. Thus, we propose:

- **Proposition 7:** Users who perceive rater motivations to be benevolent and altruistic will utilize ratings more than those who perceive rater motivations to be malevolent and selfish.

Designs to Mitigate and Disclose Bias

One possible approach to mitigating and disclosing bias is to develop a system that provides information on rating credibility (Ekstrom et al., 2005; Xue & Phelps, 2004). However, our results indicate that end-users generally do not use rating credibility information; 55% of the first-survey respondents (65% of the second-survey respondents) indicate they do not use "badges," which designate a rater's level of experience (i.e., to indicate credibility). One first-survey respondent stated, "Just because someone reviews a lot of items, it does not make them a #1 reviewer." Another respondent said, "I do not take the person seriously if they have an outrageous badge," and a final respondent answered, "I still do not know anything about the person giving the rating." Second-survey respondents who believe badges are helpful in determining if ratings are worthwhile agree that badges help in finding out who those individuals are that provide the ratings (mean = 1.9). Those who do not believe ratings are helpful agree that raters still could have different tastes and opinions than themselves (mean = 1.8).

These findings are consistent with existing research, suggesting that knowledge workers ignore credibility indicators for ratings in a complex task (Poston & Speier, 2005). Here, it was discovered that ratings were used in decisions about which knowledge objects to use in a decision task; however, credibility indicators of those ratings were not used (Poston & Speier, 2005). Also, our results suggest people care little about rating credibility information. Rather, many first-survey respondents believe that credibility information is irrelevant and redundant because rating bias is assumed and inherent. These same respondents state that ratings are more useful than credibility information because ratings provide direct information about the purchasing task. These same respondents indicate they are less likely to use rating credibility information because it is only indirectly related to their purchasing task (i.e., it is information about ratings and not the product of interest). Thus, we propose the following:

- **Proposition 8**: Users will utilize ratings more than they will use rating credibility information.

Although credibility information may not matter for the average rater, it may be important for celebrity raters (i.e., celebrities endorsing products by submitting ratings) (Sengupta, Goodstein & Boninger, 1997; Silvera & Austad, 2004). Existing advertising research suggests that endorsers or spokespersons are more effective when there is a fit or match between them and the product they are endorsing. This body of research argues that the endorser and the product will produce associations with other concepts in consumers' minds, based on their experiences with and attitudes about both (Sengupta et al., 1997; Silvera & Austad, 2004). In turn, the coupling of endorser and product becomes part of an individual's association set, so when one is seen, the other comes to mind immediately (Till & Busler, 2000). This effect is even stronger when the endorser has expertise in the area of the product (Fink, Cunningham & Kinsicki, 2004). Some Web sites, such as Amazon.com, associate "famous names" with badges to indicate that the rater is a celebrity. These "famous name" badges may provide end-users with input on whether to use rating information, particularly when the person is rating a product related to his or her area of expertise. Thus:

- **Proposition 9:** Users will utilize ratings associated with celebrity endorsers more than they will utilize ratings associated with non-celebrity endorsers.

"Free-riding" abounds on the Internet (Ba & Pavlou, 2002) and may influence rating usage. Free-riders use ratings to make a purchase decision but do not contribute back to the rating pool (Ba & Pavlou, 2002). From a retailer's perspective, free-riding dissuades retailers from paying the cost of providing information prior to a sale (i.e., rating schemes) because end-users may purchase a product based on the information from one retailer but buy the product from another retailer who has a lower price (Belch & Belch, 2004). In this way, retailers who did not provide the rating schemes free-ride on those who provide and pay for the service (Belch & Belch, 2004). In rating schemes, some individuals do not contribute ratings but do use them in making purchase decisions. Our survey found 68% of the first-survey respondents (70% of the second survey) use online ratings, but only 35% (34% in the second survey) have ever submitted a rating. Those that use but do not submit ratings are free-riding on those who do provide feedback.

Using data from the second survey, we compare the opinions of free-riders to nonfree-riders. The results suggest that both groups use ratings, but free-riders believe that ratings and associated text comments are more helpful in making good purchase choices than those who do not free-ride ($t = 4.89$, $p = .03$). Free-riders are likely following a goal-driven approach to making a purchase decision (Gerstiner & Holthausen, 1986). Nonfree-riders tend to use ratings to be part of a community, participate in the experiences of others, and keep up with what is new more than those who free-ride. This suggests that free-riders may use ratings to fulfill purchase goals, while nonfree-riders use ratings for more entertainment and social goals. Thus, we propose the following in a purchase decision context:

- **Proposition 10:** Those who free-ride rating schemes utilize ratings more than those who do not free-ride ratings schemes.

Users may place greater weight on ratings when both positive and negative feedback about goods and services is included. Inoculation theory argues that counter argumentation (i.e., minor negatives that "inoculate" the end-user from future negatives) leads to greater perceived message credibility (Polyorat & Alden, 2005). That is, when both positive and negative details about the goods and services are given, users tend to believe all of the information more than when only one-sided details are provided. Two-sided information leads to higher attitudes toward a new brand introduction than the more traditional, one-sided approach (which lacks "innoculative" material) (Polyorat & Alden, 2005).

Consistent with inoculation theory, when rating schemes contain both positive and negative information about goods and services, end-users will assign more credibility to the overall ratings themselves (Ekstrom et al., 2005; Xue & Phelps, 2004). Our first survey supports this notion, as one respondent commented, "Most advertising is positive. I have seen some ratings that were not so positive, actually negative," and another respondent stated, "Ratings let people know the good and the bad things about a product before they purchase it." One individual simply stated, "Some people will submit positive comments/ratings about products they like and negative comments/ratings about products they do not like." Ratings that reflect both positive and negative views of the goods and services may be seen, therefore, as more credible and thus more useful than ratings that are all positive or all negative. That is, users will utilize ratings more when both positive and negative ratings (i.e., greater rating variance) are present for a goods and services than when only one direction is present (i.e., less rating variance). Thus, we propose the following for a group of ratings about one product: free-riding on those who do provide feedback.

Using data from the second survey, we compare the opinions of free-riders to nonfree-riders. The results suggest that both groups use ratings, but free-riders believe that ratings and associated text comments are more helpful in making good purchase choices than those who do not free-ride ($t = 4.89$, $p = .03$). Free-riders are likely following a goal-driven approach to making a purchase decision (Gerstiner & Holthausen, 1986). Nonfree-riders tend to use ratings to be part of a community, participate in the experiences of others, and keep up with what is new more than those who free-ride. This suggests that free-riders may use ratings to fulfill purchase goals, while nonfree-riders use ratings for more entertainment and social goals. Thus, we propose the following in a purchase decision context:

- **Proposition 11:** Those who free-ride rating schemes utilize ratings more than those who do not free-ride ratings schemes.

Users may place greater weight on ratings when both positive and negative feedback about goods and services is included. Inoculation theory argues that counter-argumentation (i.e., minor negatives that "inoculate" the end-user from future negatives) leads to greater perceived message credibility (Polyorat & Alden, 2005). That is, when both positive and negative details about the goods and services are given, users tend to believe all of the information more than when only one-sided details are provided. Two-sided information leads to higher attitudes toward a new brand introduction than the more traditional, one-sided approach (which lacks "innoculative" material) (Polyorat & Alden, 2005).

Consistent with inoculation theory, when rating schemes contain both positive and negative information about goods and services, end-users will assign more credibility to the overall ratings themselves (Ekstrom et al., 2005; Xue & Phelps, 2004). Our first survey supports this notion, as one respondent commented, "Most advertising is positive. I have seen some ratings that were not so positive, actually negative," and another respondent stated, "Ratings let people know the good and the bad things about a product before they purchase it." One individual simply stated, "Some people will submit positive comments/ratings about products they like and negative comments/

ratings about products they do not like." Ratings that reflect both positive and negative views of the goods and services may be seen, therefore, as more credible and thus more useful than ratings that are all positive or all negative. That is, users will utilize ratings more when both positive and negative ratings (i.e., greater rating variance) are present for a goods and services than when only one direction is present (i.e., less rating variance). Thus, we propose the following for a group of ratings about one product:

- **Proposition 12a:** Users will utilize ratings more when ratings have greater variance than when ratings have less variance.

As noted, ratings can be accompanied by explanatory text comments that end-users can use for gaining insights into the features and quality of products prior to a purchase decision (Hodkinson & Kiel, 2003; Lueg et al., 2003). Similar to multiple ratings provided for one product, multiple comments tend to be included in the explanatory text for one rating. These comments can be multifaceted, including both positive and negative viewpoints. Combined with inoculation theory, this suggests that users may assign more credibility to ratings accompanied by both positive and negative comments in the explanatory text. Users will utilize ratings more when both positive and negative comments (i.e., greater text comment variance) are present for a product than when only one direction is present (i.e., less text comment variance). Thus, we propose for the text comments supporting one rating submitted for one product:

- **Proposition 12b:** Users will utilize ratings more when text comments have greater variance than when text comments have less variance.

Research Approach for Testing Propositions

To help practitioners and academicians perform a rigorous and in-depth examination of rating scheme bias, in this section we propose a laboratory experiment design for testing the propositions offered in this chapter. The purpose of a laboratory experiment is to study relationships under controlled and randomized conditions in order to develop new theories, to test predictions derived from theory, and to refine existing theories and hypotheses. At the expense of high external validity (i.e., generalizability), properly conducted laboratory experiments can achieve high levels of internal validity (Kerlinger, 1992) by isolating the effects of particular factors through careful manipulations and controlled conditions. This controlled environment is ideal for studying the propositions offered in this chapter. Although other research methods (i.e., surveys, projective techniques) could explore additional user perceptions about rating schemes, these methods cannot manipulate the variables discussed in the propositions offered earlier in this chapter.

We propose that researchers create a simulated retail Internet site along with a rating system to assist end-users in making decisions about hypothetical goods and services. By creating a simulated online retail environment, the design, the interface layout, and the information displayed would all be controlled. This interface would provide a predefined list of options for purchase along with associated rating values and/or text comments. Study participants would be asked to use the information available to make purchase decisions. The information would be manipulated as needed for each proposition.

More specifically, all participants across all treatment conditions would see a list of the same search results (i.e., list of options for purchase). To control for potential order effects that might influence purchase decisions, the order of the results should vary. Hypothetical ratings for each purchase option would also be displayed, and each option would be an active link, so the system can capture each respondent's option choices, the order of those choices, and the final purchase option. The list of options would be stable across treatment conditions, but the attributes of the ratings would vary to determine how these attributes influence participants' behaviors across treatment conditions.

Appropriate manipulations would be developed for each proposition. For example, to test Proposition 1, perceptions of the intentionality of rating bias must be manipulated into high and low levels. The high-intention manipulation could involve text statements disclosing the rating source as an owner, salesperson, or other individual who would benefit from the product's sale and thus have an incentive to positively influence consumers. The low-intention manipulation could disclose the rating source as an average consumer who simply wants to share his or her experience and help others in their purchase decisions; this person has no monetary or other incentive to influence users about the product. Other examples include manipulating rating strength (Proposition 2), purchasing goal specificity (Proposition 3), and perceptions of rater compensation (Proposition 4). All the remaining propositions could be tested in a similar manner, and manipulation checks would allow for the assessment of each manipulation. Analysis of variance (ANOVA) allows for testing of the propositions. In addition, researchers should analyze the click stream data to determine how ratings influence participant behaviors and option selections. We encourage future research to use this and other means to examine these propositions in an empirically rigorous manner.

CONCLUSION

The purpose of this chapter was to delineate the sources of rating scheme bias and the potential effects of this prejudice on end-user opinions by reporting results from both a preliminary survey and an exploratory survey. A key contribution of this chapter lies in the development of a framework of rating use in e-commerce (see Figure 1), which delineates various facets of ratings scheme bias as well as designs to mitigate and disclose the bias. Grounded in the results of two surveys, the framework suggests several important sources of rating scheme bias where perceived intentionality of rating bias, rating strength, purchasing goals, rater compensation, bias awareness, advertising perceptions, and perceived rater motivations all may influence how online users utilize rating schemes. The figure also identifies important sources of designs to mitigate and disclose bias where credibility information, celebrity endorsement, free-riding of ratings, rating variance, and text comment variance all may influence how online users utilize rating schemes. This chapter delineates and develops a set of propositions for using rating schemes in e-commerce, which warrant further inquiry. We also offer a research plan for testing these propositions in a rigorous empirical manner. Future research should build on these ideas and expand the analysis to compare end-user behaviors across different online tasks, a variety of goods and services, and diverse types of end-user groups. Moreover, future investigations should seek nonstudent samples to both replicate our preliminary findings and test our propositions. Finally, future research should rigorously develop and validate uni-dimensional scales for the various facets of perceived rating bias initiated by this study.

From a practical standpoint, rating scheme designers should focus on providing end-users with information about rating scheme bias and incorporating more ways to mitigate and disclose the bias. Based on our preliminary findings, many users accept rating bias but are willing to use ratings for help in making decisions. Thus, designers should embed additional types of rating information into rating schemes, knowing users will likely use it. Also, online retail firms would be well-advised to encourage users to participate in rating schemes by submitting and using ratings, as well as to craft marketing messages that highlight rating attributes to encourage users to use the rating systems. These firms should also recognize the important influence that rating schemes have on online consumers' perceptions and behaviors.

Our findings suggest that users believe raters have a tendency to be biased toward a certain product, and the presence of this bias in online ratings is acceptable. Ratings—similar to word-of-mouth communications—do matter in consumer decisions (Ba & Pavlou, 2002; Melnik & Alm, 2002). As a result, rating schemes proliferate on the Internet, yet our understanding of how and when they influence end-user decisions is lacking. Moreover, monitoring and managing rating bias is a problem because there is no central authority to govern feedback systems, and little uniformity exists in rating submission policies and procedures. But as online product search and purchase continue to increase (Hodkinson & Kiel, 2003; Lueg et al., 2003), so will the growth and use of online rating schemes. Consequently, additional research on this topic is critical, and this chapter provides a framework to develop a rigorous and in-depth look at rating scheme bias and its potential effects on end-user purchase decisions.

REFERENCES

Ba, S., & Pavlou, P. A. (2002). Evidence of the effect of trust building technology in electronic markets: Price premiums and buyer behavior. *MIS Quarterly*, *26*(3), 243–268. doi:10.2307/4132332

Belch, G. E., & Belch, M. A. (2004). *Advertising and promotion: An integrated marketing communications perspective* (6th ed.). New York: McGraw-Hill.

Chatterjee, P. (2001). Online reviews: Do consumers use them? *Advances in Consumer Research. Association for Consumer Research (U. S.)*, *28*(1), 129–133.

Chevalier, J., & Mayzlin, D. (2006). The effect of word of mouth on sales: Online book reviews. *JMR, Journal of Marketing Research*, *43*(3), 345–354. doi:10.1509/jmkr.43.3.345

Constant, D., Sproull, L., & Kiesler, S. (1996). The kindness of strangers: The usefulness of electronic weak ties for technical advice. *Organization Science*, *7*(2), 119–135. doi:10.1287/orsc.7.2.119

Cosley, D., Lam, S. K., Albert, I., Konstan, J. A., & Riedl, J. (2003). Is seeing believing? How recommender interfaces affect users' opinions. *Proceedings for CHI*, *5*(1), 585–592.

Davis, A., & Khazanchi, D. (2008). An empirical study of online word of mouth as a predictor for multi-product category e-commerce sales. *Electronic Markets*, *18*(2), 130–141. doi:10.1080/10196780802044776

Dellarocas, C. (2003). The digitization of word of mouth: Promise and challenges of online feedback mechanisms. *Management Science*, *49*(10), 1407–1425. doi:10.1287/mnsc.49.10.1407.17308

Dellarocas, C. (2006). How often should reputation mechanisms update a trader's reputation profile? *Information Systems Research*, *17*(3), 271–285. doi:10.1287/isre.1060.0092

Dellarocas, C. (2006). Strategic manipulation of internet opinion forums: Implications for consumers and firms. *Management Science*, *52*(10), 1577–1593. doi:10.1287/mnsc.1060.0567

Dellarocas, C., & Wood, C. A. (2008). The sound of silence in online feedback: Estimating trading risks in the presence of reporting bias. *Management Science*, *54*(3), 460–476. doi:10.1287/mnsc.1070.0747

Dewally, M., & Ederington, L. (2006). Reputation, certification, warranties, and information as remedies for seller-buyer information asymmetries: Lessons from the online comic book market. *The Journal of Business*, *79*(2), 693–729. doi:10.1086/499169

Drennan, J., Mort, G. S., & Previte, J. (2006). Privacy, risk perception, and expert online behavior: An exploratory study of household end-users. *Journal of Organizational and End User Computing*, *18*(1), 1–22.

Ekstrom, M., Garcia, A. C. B., & Bjornsson, H. (2005). Rewarding honest ratings through personalized recommendations in electronic commerce. *International Journal of Electronic Business*, *3*(3/4), 392–410. doi:10.1504/IJEB.2005.007280

Fink, J. S., Cunningham, G. B., & Kinsicki, L. J. (2004). Using athletes as endorsers to sell women's sport: Attractiveness vs. expertise. *Journal of Sport Management*, *18*(1), 350–367.

Forman, C., Ghose, A., & Wiesenfeld, B. (2008). Examining the relationship between reviews and sales: The role of reviewer identity disclosure in electronic markets. *Information Systems Research*, *19*(3), 291–313. doi:10.1287/isre.1080.0193

Fuller, M. A., Serva, M. A., & Benamati, J. (2007). Seeing is believing: The transitory influence of reputation information on e-commerce trust and decision making. *Decision Sciences*, *38*(4), 675–699.

Gerstiner, E., & Holthausen, D. (1986). Profitable pricing when market segments overlap. *Marketing Science*, *5*(1), 55–69. doi:10.1287/mksc.5.1.55

Gregg, D. G., & Scott, J. E. (2006). The role of reputation systems in reducing on-line auction fraud. *International Journal of Electronic Commerce*, *10*(3), 95–120. doi:10.2753/JEC1086-4415100304

Harr, R., & Wiberg, M. (2008). Lost in translation: Investigating the ambiguity of availability cues in an online media space. *Behaviour & Information Technology*, *27*(3), 243–262. doi:10.1080/01449290600874865

Hennig-Thurau, T., Gwinner, K. P., Walsh, G., & Gremler, D. D. (2004). Electronic word-of mouth via consumer-opinion platforms: What motivates consumers to articulate themselves on the Internet? *Journal of Interactive Marketing*, *18*(1), 38–52. doi:10.1002/dir.10073

Hennig-Thurau, T., & Walsh, G. (2003). Electronic word-of-mouth: Motives for consequences of reading customer articulations on the Internet. *International Journal of Electronic Commerce*, *8*(2), 51–74.

Hodkinson, C., & Kiel, G. (2003). Understanding Web information search behavior: An exploratory model. *Journal of Organizational and End User Computing*, *15*(4), 27–48.

Hofstede, G. (1994). Management scientists are human. *Management Science*, *40*(1), 4–13. doi:10.1287/mnsc.40.1.4

Josang, A., Ismail, R., & Boyd, C. (2007). A survey of trust and reputation systems for online service provision. *Decision Support Systems*, *43*(2), 618–644. doi:10.1016/j.dss.2005.05.019

Kennes, J., & Schiff, A. (2007). Simple reputation systems. *The Scandinavian Journal of Economics*, *109*(1), 71–91. doi:10.1111/j.1467-9442.2007.00481.x

Kerlinger, F. N. (1992). *Foundations of behavioral research*. Orlando, FL: Harcourt Brace & Company.

Keser, C. (2003). Experimental games for the design of reputation management systems. *IBM Systems Journal*, *42*(3), 498–506.

Komiak, S.Y.X., Wang, W., & Benbasat, I. (2005). Trust building in virtual salespersons versus in human salespersons: Similarities and differences. *e-Services Journal*, 49-63.

Krukow, K., Nielsen, M., & Sassone, V. (2008). A logical framework for history-based access control and reputation systems. *Journal of Computer Security*, *16*(1), 63–101.

Kumar, N., & Benbasat, I. (2006). The influence of recommendations and consumer reviews on evaluations of Websites. *Information Systems Research*, *17*(4), 425–439. doi:10.1287/isre.1060.0107

Lauw, H. W., Ee-Peng, L., & Ke, W. (2008). Bias and Controversy in Evaluation Systems. *IEEE Transactions on Knowledge and Data Engineering*, *20*(11), 1490–1504. doi:10.1109/TKDE.2008.77

Leung, L. (2004). Net-generation attributes and seductive properties of the Internet as predictors of online activities and Internet addiction. *Cyberpsychology & Behavior*, *7*(3), 333–348. doi:10.1089/1094931041291303

Liang, T., Lai, H., & Ku, Y. (2006/2007). Personalized content recommendation and user satisfaction: Theoretical synthesis and empirical findings. *Journal of Management Information Systems*, *23*(3), 45–70. doi:10.2753/MIS0742-1222230303

Liu, J., & Issarny, V. (2007). An incentive compatible reputation mechanism for ubiquitous computing environments. *International Journal of Information Security*, *6*(5), 297–311. doi:10.1007/s10207-007-0029-7

Lueg, J. E., Moore, R. S., & Warkentin, M. (2003). Patient health information search: An exploratory model of Web-based search behavior. *Journal of Organizational and End User Computing*, *15*(4), 49–61.

Mackay, J. M., & Elam, J. J. (1992). A comparative study of how experts and novices use a decision aid to solve problems in complex knowledge domains. *Information Systems Research*, *3*(2), 150–172. doi:10.1287/isre.3.2.150

Mayer, R. N., Huh, J., & Cude, B. J. (2005). Cues of credibility and price performance of life insurance comparison Web sites. *The Journal of Consumer Affairs*, *39*(1), 71–94.

Melnik, M. I., & Alm, J. (2002). Does a seller's e-commerce reputation matter? Evidence from eBay auctions. *The Journal of Industrial Economics*, *50*(3), 337–349.

Miles, M. B., & Huberman, A. M. (1984). *Qualitative data analysis: A sourcebook of new methods*. Newbury Park, CA: Sage Publications.

Mithas, S., Ramasubbu, N., Krishnan, M. S., & Fornell, C. (2007). Designing web sites for customer loyalty across business domains: A multilevel analysis. *Journal of Management Information Systems*, *23*(3), 97–127. doi:10.2753/MIS0742-1222230305

Nikolaeva, R., & Sriram, S. (2006). The moderating role of consumer and product characteristics on the value of customized on-line recommendations. *International Journal of Electronic Commerce*, *11*(2), 101–123. doi:10.2753/JEC1086-4415110205

Pavlou, P. A., & Dimoka, A. (2006). The nature and role of feedback text comments in online marketplaces: Implications for trust building, price premiums, and seller differentiation. *Information Systems Research*, *17*(4), 392–414. doi:10.1287/isre.1060.0106

Payne, J. W., Bettman, J. R., & Johnson, E. J. (1993). *The adaptive decision maker*. Cambridge, UK: Cambridge University Press.

Polyorat, K., & Alden, D. L. (2005). Self-construal and need-for-cognition effects on brand attitudes and purchase intentions in response to comparative advertising in Thailand and the United States. *Journal of Advertising*, *34*(1), 37–48.

Poston, R. S., & Speier, C. (2005). Effective use of knowledge management systems: A process model of content ratings and credibility indicators. *MIS Quarterly*, *29*(2), 221–244.

Resnick, P., Zeckhauser, R., Friedman, E., & Kuwabara, K. (2000). Reputation systems. *Communications of the ACM*, *43*(12), 45–48. doi:10.1145/355112.355122

Sabater, J. (2004). Evaluating the ReGreT system. *Applied Artificial Intelligence*, *18*, 797–813. doi:10.1080/08839510490509027

Sengupta, J., Goodstein, R. C., & Boninger, D. S. (1997). All cues are not created equal: Obtaining attitude persistence under low-involvement conditions. *The Journal of Consumer Research*, *23*(1), 351–361. doi:10.1086/209488

Sigala, M. (2006). Culture: The software of e-customer relationship management. *Journal of Marketing Communications*, *12*(3), 203–223. doi:10.1080/13527260600811787

Silvera, D. H., & Austad, B. (2004). Factors predicting the effectiveness of celebrity endorsement advertisements. *European Journal of Marketing*, *38*(11/12), 1509–1526. doi:10.1108/03090560410560218

Smith, D., Menon, S., & Sivakumar, K. (2005). Online peer and editorial recommendations, trust, and choice in virtual markets. *Journal of Interactive Marketing*, *19*(3), 15–37. doi:10.1002/dir.20041

Standifird, S. S. (2001). Reputation and e-commerce: eBay auctions and the asymmetrical impact of positive and negative ratings. *Journal of Management*, *27*(1), 279–295. doi:10.1016/S0149-2063(01)00092-7

Standifird, S. S., & Weinstein, M. (2007). The transaction cost economics of market-based exchange: The impact of reputation and external verification agencies. *International Journal of the Economics of Business*, *14*(3), 409–431. doi:10.1080/13571510701597510

Till, B. D., & Busler, M. (2000). The match-up hypothesis: Physical attractiveness, expertise and the role of fit on brand attitude, purchase intent and brand beliefs. *Journal of Advertising*, *29*(3), 1–14.

Wakefield, R. L., & Whitten, D. (2006). Examining end-user perceptions of third-party organization credibility and trust in an e-retailer. *Journal of Organizational and End User Computing*, *18*(2), 1–19.

Wang, W., & Benbasat, I. (2008). Attributions of trust in decision support technologies: A study of recommendation agents for e-commerce. *Journal of Management Information Systems*, *24*(4), 249–273. doi:10.2753/MIS0742-1222240410

Wenhong, L., & Cook, D. P. (2007/2008). An empirical study of trust of third party rating services. *Journal of Computer Information Systems*, *48*(2), 66–73.

Xiao, B., & Benbasat, I. (2007). E-commerce product recommendation agents: Use, characteristics and impact. *MIS Quarterly*, *31*(1), 137–209.

Xue, F., & Phelps, J. E. (2004). Internet-facilitated consumer-to-consumer communication: The moderating role of receiver characteristics. *International Journal of Internet Marketing and Advertising*, *1*(2), 121–136. doi:10.1504/IJIMA.2004.004016

Yaniv, I. (2004). Receiving other people's advice: Influence and benefit. *Organizational Behavior and Human Decision Processes*, *93*(1), 1–14. doi:10.1016/j.obhdp.2003.08.002

Zhao, X., Fang, F., & Whinston, A. B. (2006). Designing on-line mediation services for c2c markets. *International Journal of Electronic Commerce*, *10*(3), 71–93. doi:10.2753/JEC1086-4415100303

Zhou, M., Dresner, M., & Windle, R. J. (2008). Online reputation systems: Design and strategic practices. *Decision Support Systems*, *44*(4), 785–797. doi:10.1016/j.dss.2007.10.001

APPENDIX

Appendix Table 1. Exploratory survey

Survey Questions (Likert scale Strongly agree=1; Strongly disagree=5)	N	Mean	Std. Dev.
Instructions: Below is a screen print of customer reviews at Amazon.com for *Harry Potter and the Sorcerer's Stone* by J.K. Rowling. Notice that it includes ratings with stars and a text comment by several reviewers. [Screen print was inserted here.] Now think of a Web site that you use (such as epinions.com or cnet.com) where products and/or services are reviewed by others; then please answer the following:			
Have you ever used an online rating/review to assist you in making a purchasing decision?			
Yes = 115 (70%); No = 49 (30%)			
Have you ever posted a rating/review on a Web site?			
Yes = 56 (34%); No = 108 (66%)			
Instructions: Please select from the scale to show how much you agree or disagree with each statement.			
What is your opinion of ratings and comments in general?			
Ratings are helpful but not crucial input for decisions.	164	2.41	1.01
I enjoy using ratings.	164	2.36	0.85
Ratings give you the positives and negatives about something.	164	1.96	0.86
I do not use ratings.	164	3.81	0.98
Ratings are very helpful.	164	2.16	0.75
I like to check out others' views on things.	164	2.02	0.83
I use ratings but I am skeptical about them.	164	2.71	0.98
Ratings are unbiased.	164	3.58	1.07
Ratings are useless unless you know the source of the ratings.	164	2.84	0.99
Ratings provide an outlet for people to voice their opinions.	164	1.93	0.73
Ratings are useless for some but not all things.	164	2.67	0.92
Ratings on the Internet represent:			
Experts' judgments.	164	3.60	1.07
Input from peers to help me make a decision.	164	2.05	0.70
The personal opinions of others.	164	1.84	0.64
Help for me to make good choices.	164	2.46	0.85
The real validity of the rated object.	164	3.00	0.91
Feedback from someone with first-hand experience with the rated object.	164	2.17	0.76
Opinions that may or may not equal my own opinions.	164	1.96	0.66
Advertising about the product or service.	164	2.48	0.94
People enter ratings and comments because they want to:			
Input their thoughts about something.	164	1.76	0.49
Help others make the right decisions.	164	2.21	0.88
Tell or share their experiences.	164	1.78	0.63
Share feelings when they really like or dislike something.	164	1.71	0.61
Express their criticism about things because they are inherently critical.	164	2.51	0.99
Influence others' thoughts and actions.	164	2.34	0.82
Fill time when they have nothing else to do.	164	3.09	1.08
Add their voice because every opinion counts.	164	2.34	0.92
Receive money or some other financial benefit.	164	3.15	1.12

Promote a product or service.	164	2.52	0.94
Provide feedback to the company.	164	2.13	0.84

Appendix Table 2.

Survey Questions (Likert scale Strongly agree=1; Strongly disagree=5)	**N**	**Mean**	**Std. Dev.**
Which input would you rather use to make a decision? Friends or Ratings			
Friends = 144 (88%); Ratings = 20 (12%)			
Instructions: Please select from the scale to show how much you agree or disagree with each statement.			
Those answering Friends saw the next set of questions.			
I would rather get advice FROM MY FRIENDS than use ratings when making a purchase decision because:			
I know my own friends; that is, I know the source of the advice.	144	1.46	0.55
Friends are first-hand, known people.	144	1.56	0.66
I can trust my friends.	144	1.64	0.72
I can ask questions to my friends.	144	1.44	0.51
My friends know me; that is, they know my likes and dislikes.	144	1.63	0.72
I take advice from my friends to heart.	144	1.94	0.76
My friends are my peers.	144	1.78	0.76
Those answering Ratings saw the next set of questions.			
I would rather USE RATINGS than get advice from my friends when making a purchase decision because:			
Friends can be wrong.	20	2.40	1.05
Friends try to convince you to agree with their opinion.	20	2.00	0.86
Friends do not have first-hand experience with the object being purchased.	20	2.70	1.08
Friends will tell you anything.	20	3.15	1.14
All participants answered the next set of questions.			
I sometimes USE the advice from online ratings when making a purchase decision because:			
People providing the ratings (raters) are more genuine.	164	2.90	1.01
Raters have actual experience with the rated object.	164	2.15	0.82
I sometimes DO NOT use the advice from online ratings when making a purchase decision because:			
I do not know who is giving the ratings.	164	2.26	1.01

I cannot be sure of the motives of people providing the ratings (the raters).	164	2.06	0.92
I cannot be sure if my likes and dislikes are similar to the raters' likes and dislikes.	164	1.94	0.83
The people providing the ratings (the raters) have no interest in selling the product.	65	2.60	0.84
Ratings are information about the quality of the object.	65	2.02	0.62
Raters have already bought the rated object and know about it.	65	1.94	0.58
Advertising is bound by law to be credible while ratings are not.	65	2.34	1.06
Getting opinions from lots of other people is not advertising.	65	2.28	0.94
Advertising is blatantly biased, while ratings are based on true rater experiences.	65	2.18	0.93
Ratings are by real people, not advertising agencies.	65	2.18	0.81
Ratings are not pushed on you, while advertising is pushed on you.	65	2.15	0.97
I would treat ratings from the author's friend skeptically.	164	2.07	0.87
I would treat ratings from an author just like any other rating.	164	3.94	0.99
I would treat ratings from an author's friend just like any other rating.	164	3.62	1.11
I would ignore a rating from an author.	164	2.37	1.11
I would ignore a rating from an author's friend.	164	2.62	1.16

Appendix Table 3.

Survey Questions (Likert scale Strongly agree=1; Strongly disagree=5)	**N**	**Mean**	**Std. Dev.**
Instructions: Please select from the scale to show how much you agree or disagree with each statement.			
All participants answered the next set of questions.			
I use ratings:			
Because contributions by others help me to make the right decision.	164	2.28	0.94

To benefit from others' experiences before I buy.	164	2.21	0.88
Because I get information on the quality of products faster.	164	2.25	0.95
Because I save time shopping when informing myself with ratings.	164	2.49	1.09
Because I find answers when I have difficulties with a product.	164	2.46	1.04
To find advice and solutions for my problems.	164	2.49	1.03
Because I can confirm that I made the right buying decision.	164	2.66	1.08
Because I feel better knowing that I am not the only one with a problem.	164	2.44	1.09
Because I can see if others think of a product in the same way.	164	2.16	0.87
Because I like to compare my own evaluation with that of others.	164	2.30	0.99
Because I really like being part of such a community.	164	3.27	1.10
Because I enjoy participating in the experiences of others.	164	3.13	1.06
Because I am interested in what is new or "in."	164	2.93	1.20
Because I get a reward or money for using ratings.	164	3.48	1.31

Appendix Table 4.

Survey Questions About Demographics (radio buttons provided to allow participants to select the correct category)	
Instructions: Please select what describes you best.	
All participants answered the next set of questions.	
Age	Under 20 = 56 (34%); 20–29 = 95 (58%); 30–39 = 8 (5%); 40+ = 5 (3%)
Gender	Male = 89 (54%); Female = 75 (46%)
Year	Freshman / Sophomore = 89 (54%); Junior / Senior = 75 (46%)
Income	Under 25k = 117 (71%); 25-50k = 23 (14%); 50k+ = 24 (15%)
Frequency of Online Purchase	Never=18 (11%); 1–2 times/yr=84 (51%); 1–2 times/month=56 (34%); 1–2 times/week=6 (4%)

Chapter 16
Validating the End-User Computing Satisfaction Instrument for Online Shopping Systems

Chung-Tzer Liu
Soochow University, Taiwan

Yi Maggie Guo
University of Michigan – Dearborn, USA

ABSTRACT

End-user satisfaction has always been an important component of Information Systems (IS) success. This is also true for online applications, including online shopping systems, where in addition to being a customer, the shoppers play the role of end-users. Shoppers may not come back to or make a purchase on a Web site if they have an unsatisfactory experience. In this research, we focus on this aspect of online shopping by examining shoppers' experiences as end-users.

INTRODUCTION

Electronic commerce has proliferated during the last decade. In order for people to more effectively use technology in the global online business environment, a better understanding of the factors influencing a successful implementation is needed (Khalil & Elkordy, 1999; Shayo, Guthrie & Igbaria, 1999). It has been demonstrated that shopper satisfaction with a Web store is a crucial determinant of important outcomes, such as revisiting and purchase intentions (O'Cass & Fenech, 2003). Several instruments for measuring user satisfaction with a Web store have been proposed and developed (McKinney, Yoon & Zahedi, 2002; Szymanski & Hise, 2000).

A key difference between shopping through the Web and shopping in other environments is that Web shopping resides in an Internet-mediated environment (Fenech & O'Cass, 2001). Compared to the shoppers in a brick-and-mortar store, online shoppers play a dual role: that of "the shopper" in the traditional sense and that of "the end-user" interacting with a computer information system (Koufaris, 2002). Part of the system is the Web site, which is the store with which online shoppers interact. Thus, we can study online shopper satisfaction using two perspectives: (1) the marketing perspective and (2) the computing perspective. From the marketing perspective, abundant research has focused on factors contributing to customer satisfaction, such as perceived value, service quality, and image (Ball, Coelho & Machas, 2004; Chen & Dubinsky, 2003; Dodds, Monroe & Grewal, 1991; Jamal & Goode, 2001; Wang, Lo & Yang, 2004; Woo & Ennew, 2005; Yang & Fang, 2004). From the computing perspective, end-user satisfaction is considered to be one of the most critical aspects of success, and its measurement has been one of the major concerns in the IS field (DeLone & McLean, 1992). We posit that in addition to the marketing perspective, testing an existing IS instrument dealing with end-user satisfaction with online shopping systems can be a valuable approach. In this study, we conduct a research to validate an instrument called the End-User Computing Satisfaction (EUCS) from the computing perspective for use in the online shopping context. EUCS is a 12-item questionnaire regarding user satisfaction with an information system (Doll & Torkzadeh, 1988). It consists of five constructs: content, accuracy, format, ease of use, and timeliness. EUCS has already been applied and validated for various computer applications such as Decision Support Systems (DSS) (McHaney, Hightower & White, 1999), Enterprise Resource Planning (ERP) applications (Somers, Nelson & Karimi, 2003), and for a Web site (Abdinnour-Helm, Chaparro & Farmer, 2005). These studies have demonstrated the stability of psychometric properties of EUCS across applications and user groups. However, because the task of online shopping has its own characteristics, there is no guarantee that EUCS will be as effective for online shopping systems as for other kinds of computer systems. The main focus of this research is to try to bridge the gap by validating EUCS for online shopping systems. Once the hypothesized psychometric properties of this instrument are demonstrated to be consistent with those in prior studies, we can confidently use the instrument as a measure of end-user satisfaction in the online shopping context. In addition, we compare our results with those of three particular prior studies that focused on various kinds of information systems so we can study the differences among dimensions of EUCS in various situations. Our research will provide online practitioners with not only a tool to evaluate the end-user satisfaction with their systems, but also insights on how to interpret the result when using EUCS.

RELATED WORK

User Satisfaction and System Success

The implementation of IS has been an uncertain process; some systems are successful and others are not. Hence, IS success is an important outcome of IS implementation and one of the major dependent variables in IS research. There is a persistent quest for measures of IS success, and studying what factors contribute to IS success has been a major concern of both researchers and practitioners (DeLone & McLean, 1992). User satisfaction is considered a critical component of IS success with the assumption that dissatisfied users will not accept and use the system (Cyert & March, 1963). Users will be dissatisfied if the system does not meet their information needs. User information satisfaction (UIS) refers to the extent to which users perceive that the available information system meets their requirements and is often used as an indicator of user perception of the effectiveness of an information system (Bailey & Pearson, 1983; Doll & Torkzadeh, 1988). Therefore, the search for appropriate measurement variables for user satisfaction has both academic and practice relevance.

This search has resulted in a bewildering array of instrument choices (McHaney, Hightower & Pearson, 2002), and many researchers in MIS have assessed the success of applications and IS implementations using these measures of user satisfaction (Cyert & March, 1963; DeLone & McLean, 1992; Doll & Torkzadeh, 1988; Ives, Olson & Baroudi, 1983). Among these measures is End-User Computing Satisfaction (EUCS) (Doll & Torkzadeh, 1988), which has been widely used as either the sole or one of the outcome variables (Abdinnour-Helm et al., 2005; Gelderman, 1998; Hendrickson, Glorfeld & Cronan, 1994; McHaney & Cronan, 2001; Zviran, Glezer & Avni, 2006). EUCS was first developed as a 12-item, multifaceted instrument requiring subjective self-reports of five subscales that measure end-user satisfaction of the content, accuracy, format, ease-of-use, and timeliness of a computer application. The overall user satisfaction is a global, second-order construct (Doll & Torkzadeh, 1988).

The reasons for the wide adoption of user satisfaction as the measure of systems' success are bittersweet, as pointed out by some researchers (DeLone & McLean, 1992). On the one hand, user satisfaction has a high degree of face validity, and reliable tools have been developed for its measurement, including EUCS. On the other hand, other measures with strong conceptualization are not readily available. Nevertheless, EUCS is a reliable measure for end-user satisfaction. Continued use, testing, and refinement of this measure, at least as part of the measure of IS success, will address the criticisms that MIS research lacks standardization, well-defined outcome measures, and methodological rigor (Jarvenpaa, Dickson & DeSanctis, 1985; Straub, 1989).

EUCS has been tested in various studies over the past decade: computer simulation applications (McHaney & Cronan, 1998), DSS (McHaney et al., 1999), ERP systems (Somers et al., 2003), in a different cultural environment (McHaney et al., 2002), and for other varieties of software (Abdinnour-Helm et al., 2005; Doll & Xia, 1997; Doll, Xia & Torkzadeh, 1994). In all the studies, EUCS has shown good psychometric stability. EUCS should be reinvestigated in relation to emerging technologies and utilizing new data to demonstrate the robustness of the measurement model (Klenke, 1992; Somers et al., 2003). A study examining the EUCS instrument across a wide variety of contexts and population subgroups has shown that the structural weights are not equivalent across subgroups; thus, it is a context-sensitive measure of system success (Doll, Deng, Raghunathan, Torkzadeh & Xia, 2004). The current research is a continuation of this effort to expand the application of EUCS into a newer context: online shopping systems.

Satisfaction with Online Shopping Systems

Online shopping is an important business model in e-commerce. One essential factor for an online business to succeed is the success of the computer systems supporting the e-commerce. Thus, the effectiveness of online shopping systems is an important area to study. There have been several approaches used already. One approach focuses on Web sites. The Web site of a business is an important part of an online shopping system. From the customers' point of view, interacting with the Web site is "shopping." For most customers, the Web site is the major point of contact with the business. The Web site of an online business is where the effectiveness of their whole online shopping system is shown. This means that user satisfaction with a Web site can be used as an indicator of the success of an online shopping system. Some prior research into Web site effectiveness has focused on site content in general. Many studies have simply dealt with a technical assessment of the basic contents and hypertext structures of Web sites (Perry & Bodkin, 2000; Ranganathan & Ganapathy, 2002). Others have concentrated on principles developed from human factors research in computer interface design. Human-computer interface design factors (Lu & Yeung, 1998) and usability principles (Agarwal & Venkatesh, 2002; Palmer, 2002; Zviran et al., 2006) have been applied to the development and assessment of commercial Web applications.

Some researchers have taken the approach of identifying the key factors influencing consumer choice among various forms of shopping (Yang, Ahmed, Ghingold, Boon, Mei & Hwa, 2003). In this approach, the features of an online business are analyzed in terms of their values to Web users. Researchers have found that online shopping is preferred for convenience and for functional purchases, while store-based shopping is preferred for the ability to examine goods physically and for the shopping atmosphere (Nicholson, Clarke & Blakemore, 2002). Although "functional" compatibility of a newer technology with a previously adopted technology is preferred (Perse & Courtright, 1993), extra design features of Web sites (such as the use of multimedia) provide not only utilitarian values but also hedonic values to online shoppers (van der Heijden, 2004; Zhang & von Dran, 2000), thereby contributing to user satisfaction (Shim, Shin & Nottingham, 2002; Zhang & von Dran, 2000).

Yet another approach to studying electronic commerce effectiveness is to focus directly on one of the important dependent variables: online customer satisfaction. As in other retailing environments, positive attitude is a significant contributor to the adoption of a shopping channel (Shim & Eastlick, 1998). Customer satisfaction leads to purchase intention (Macintosh & Lockshin, 1997), loyalty (Oliver, 1999), and other desirable outcomes (Gummerus, Liljander, Pura & Van Riel, 2004; Jarvenpaa & Todd, 1996-1997). Therefore, customer satisfaction is one of the determinants of the success of an online business. This approach tries to define online customer satisfaction and examines various aspects of it. The dual role of being a shopper and a computer end-user at the same time makes it a challenge to measure online shoppers' satisfaction (Koufaris, 2002). A number of studies has focused on customer satisfaction (Devaraj, Fan & Kohli, 2002; McKinney et al., 2002; Schaupp & Belanger, 2005; Szymanski & Hise, 2000; Wang & Tang, 2004). However, these studies focus mainly on the role of the shopper. Only one study tries to measure the overall online customer satisfaction from both the marketing and computing perspectives. In that work, a total of 10 aspects of customer and information services is included (Cho & Park, 2001).

In the current study, we build on the effort to study online shopping system success from the point of view of end-users by seeking a measure for end-user satisfaction. Specifically, we test an existing IS instrument, End-User Computing Satisfaction (EUCS), in the online shopping context. We realize the other important aspect of online shopping satisfaction is customer satisfaction from a marketing perspective. However, the focus of the current study is end-user satisfaction with online shopping systems from a computing perspective.

EUCS for Online Shopping Systems

We believe the five dimensions of EUCS are all applicable in electronic commerce and important factors for online businesses to succeed. The fact that online shopping systems' end-users are also shoppers means that these dimensions may have additional meanings (Abdinnour-Helm et al., 2005). First, as any other kinds of information systems, a retailing Web site has to provide complete, correct, and relevant *content* to its end-users (i.e., customers) in order to build customer confidence in the Web site (Barnes & Vigden, 2002; Cai & Fun, 2003; Palmer, 2002; Wolfinbarger & Gilly, 2003). It has been found that complete and correct product and service information strengthens customer satisfaction and leads to a favorable consumer attitude (Elliott & Speck, 2005; Park & Kim, 2003).

Second, *accuracy* is the result of correct technical functioning of the systems of an online business. The accuracy of a system is necessary for success. The Web site must be free of broken links and missing pages, be robust enough to withstand peak traffic, and be available at all times. Whether a retail Web site is functionally robust affects loyalty (Parasuraman, Zeithaml & Malhotra, 2005). In addition, it is imperative that there be a reliable and accurate online transaction system in place to accurately process customer orders and payments (Cai & Fun, 2003; Yang & Fang, 2004).

Third, whether the information is displayed in a clear and logical *format* is as important as in other systems. For productivity systems, such as ERP and DSS, the way in which information is presented makes a difference in end-user performance and thus user satisfaction (Smelcer & Carmel, 1997; Vessey, 1994). In the case of online shopping systems, better designed format and well organized content aids the shoppers in carrying out purchasing activities more efficiently and fosters a positive attitude (Elliott & Speck, 2005; Parasuraman et al., 2005).

Fourth, for any technology, *ease of use* is a very influential factor. It affects not only user attitude toward the technology but also how useful the technology is perceived to be by the users (Davis, 1989; Gefen, Karahanna & Straub, 2003). Ease of use is an element of online shopping quality (Wolfinbarger & Gilly, 2003) and found to affect customer attitude (Elliott & Speck, 2005; Ribbink, van Riel, Liljander & Streukens, 2004; Santos, 2003; Yang & Fang, 2004).

Finally, *timeliness* means online shopping systems must offer two things: a fast response time and current information. Online shoppers can get frustrated easily if the downloading time is too slow; they also expect the Web site information to be updated frequently (Loiacono, Watson & Goodhue, 2002; Palmer, 2002; Santos, 2003; Wolfinbarger & Gilly, 2003). Fast transaction speed leads to high perceived usefulness and willingness to use for online banks (Liao & Cheung, 2002). One way to generate a positive customer attitude is to provide up-to-date information about products, services, news, and promotions (Elliott & Speck, 2005).

RESEARCH METHOD

In the past, four plausible alternative models for the EUCS instrument have been examined using confirmatory factor analysis techniques (Doll et al., 1994). In the first model, it is hypothesized that there is one first-order factor with 12 items as indicators. In the second model, the 12 items are grouped into five uncorrelated first-order factors. In contrast, the third model allows the five first-order factors to be correlated, while in the fourth model, it is further hypothesized that one second-order factor, user satisfaction, causes the five first-order factors. Both the third and the fourth models have shown a good fit in terms of the fit indices, with the fourth best representing the underlying theoretical factor structure (Doll et al., 1994; Somers et al., 2003). Therefore, the current study focuses on the third and fourth models to study the psychometric properties of the instrument in the online shopping context.

Survey questionnaires were distributed to a convenient sample of Web users who had prior online shopping experience. Both undergraduate and graduate students from a university in Taiwan were asked to participate in the research. The respondents came from a variety of departments and with various majors. Respondents were also encouraged to ask their friends and family members to complete the survey. We tried to make the sample as representative of the online population and as heterogeneous as possible. We do realize, however, that using a sample that consists mainly of college students raises the concern of generalizability. College students tend to be heavy computer users and highly skilled at using the Internet. On the other hand, research shows that such a sample is acceptable in online shopping research because college students are not dissimilar to the general online population, and they are often the target market for online purchasing (Abdinnour-Helm et al., 2005; Han & Ocker, 2002; Lee & Lin, 2005). From the viewpoint of customer relationship management, companies pay more attention to the long-term life time value of their customers, which means that college students are considered a key target market for the long-term success of companies (Lim & Dubinsky, 2004). Thus, the sample involved in the current study should have high potential value for companies in the future, and the results of this study should provide insights into how companies can acquire and retain this target market.

The questionnaire consisted of three major parts. In the first part, items measuring computing satisfaction were adopted from the EUCS (Doll & Torkzadeh, 1988). A total of 12 questions were included to measure the respondents' satisfaction with online shopping systems with which they had previous experience. The responses were described in a five-point Likert-type scale in which 5 was "almost always" and 1 was "almost never." The second part included three items measuring attitude, which was adapted from Lai and Li (2005). Responses for attitude were described in a five-point Likert-type scale as self-reported agreement toward a statement, in which 5 was "strongly agree" and 1 was "strongly disagree." In the third part of the questionnaire, the basic demographic information and shopping history were collected from the respondents.

Among the 445 collected questionnaires, 23 were incomplete, leaving 422 for the final analysis. The demographics of the respondents are shown in Table 1. Fifty-seven percent of the respondents were females, and 43% were male. The majority (51%) of the respondents were younger than 25 years old, while 39% were 26 to 35 years old. Very few (2%) of the respondents were older than 46. Also, most of the respondents had a college degree (50%) or higher (16%); the rest (less that 34%) had a high school diploma or less. In terms of computer competency, a significant number of respondents (81%) considered themselves to be experienced users, whereas only 13% did not consider themselves to be experienced. The majority (57%) had been shopping online for six months to two years; the next largest group (22%) was those with two to four years of experience; while 18% had begun online shopping within the last six months. Many of the respondents were frequent online shoppers who shop every month (12%) or shop every on to three months (55%). In other words, we can make the following profile: the majority of the respondents were under 35 years old and had a college degree and a high level of computer competency. They had more than half a year's experience with online shopping as well as with an online shopping frequency of more than once every three months.

DATA ANALYSIS AND RESULTS

The First-Order Model and Second-Order Model

In order to determine whether the EUCS instrument is a valid and reliable measure for online shopping systems, LISREL 8.54 was used to test the research model. First, confirmatory factor analysis was run on the measurement model. The measurement model was one with five identified dimensions as first-order factors. The five factors were correlated with each other. The observed variables (i.e., the items) were indicators of the five factors and had nonzero loading to corresponding factors and zero loadings on other

Table 1. Basic profile of respondents

Sample size	422	
Sex		
Male	183	(43%)
Female	239	(57%)
Age		
25 and below	216	(51%)
26 to 35	166	(39%)
36 to 45	33	(8%)
46 and above	7	(2%)
Education		
High school and below	144 (34%)	
College (associate and bachelor)	210 (50%)	
Graduate degree and above	68 (16%)	
Computer Competency		
Very bad	1	(0%)
Not good	55	(13%)
Good	340	(81%)
Very good	26	(6%)
Online shopping experience		
Less than 6 months	75	(18%)
6 months to 2 years	240	(57%)
2 years to 4 years	94	(22%)
4 years and above	13	(3%)
Average online shopping		
Every month or less	50	(12%)
Every 1 month to 3 months	230	(55%)
Every 3 months to 6 months	97	(23%)
Every 6 months or above	45	(11%)

factors. All error terms for the measured items were uncorrelated.

The first-order measurement model showed a reasonable model fit. The measurement properties are listed in Table 2. When assessing a model, there are several measures of fit that can be adopted. Since χ^2 is sensitive to the sample size and is normally significant when the sample size is large, it is not suitable for testing the construct validity (Bentler & Bonett, 1980; Homburg & Rudolph, 2001; Tan, 2001). In light of the limitation of χ^2, the ratio of χ^2 to degrees of freedom (df) can be adopted. The value of 3.80 (χ^2= 167.22, df= 44) in this study indicates a marginal fit because a ratio between 2 and 5 indicates a reasonable fit (Marsh & Hocevar, 1985). The overall fit of a model can also be assessed by the normed fit index (NFI), goodness-of-fit index (GFI), adjusted goodness-of-fit index (AGFI), and root mean square residual (RMSR) (Doll & Torkzadeh, 1988). A well-fitted model should have an NFI greater than .90 (.97 in this study); the GFI and AGFI should be greater

Table 2. Measurement properties

	Mean	SD	Loading [a]	t-value
Content (Cronbach's Alpha = .85, AVE = .59)				
C1. Do online shopping systems provide the precise information you need?	3.41	.76	.78	18.34
C2. Does the information content meet your needs?	3.38	.81	.78	18.40
C3. Do online shopping systems provide reports that seem to be just about exactly what you need?	3.31	.73	.77	17.89
C4. Do the systems provide sufficient information?	3.32	.78	.74	16.97
Accuracy (Cronbach's Alpha = .78, AVE = .64)				
A1. Are online shopping systems accurate?	3.40	.77	.76	17.20
A2. Are you satisfied with the accuracy of online shopping systems?	3.35	78	.83	19.32
Format (Cronbach's Alpha = .75, AVE = .61)				
F1. Do you think the output of online shopping systems is presented in a useful format?	3.41	.70	.74	16.10
F2. Is the information on online shopping systems clear?	3.31	.72	.81	17.75
Ease of use (Cronbach's Alpha = .79, AVE = .68)				
E1. Are online shopping systems user friendly?	3.43	.69	.71	14.21
E2. Are online shopping systems easy to use?	3.55	.71	.92	18.28
Timeliness (Cronbach's Alpha = .72, AVE = .57)				
T1. Do you get the information you need in time?	3.42	.77	.81	17.56
T2. Do online shopping systems provide up-to-date information?	3.14	.85	.70	14.87

Note: [a]. standardized loadings estimated by LISREL 8.54
AVE: average variance extracted

than .80 (.94 and .89 in this study, respectively); the RMSR should be smaller than .05 (.024 in this study). In addition, the comparison fit index (CFI) was .98 and the root mean square of error approximation (RMSEA) had a value of .08 in this study. Based on these criteria, the goodness of fit measures of this model were satisfactory (Lai & Li, 2005).

The purpose of this study was to validate EUCS for online shopping systems and to compare our results with those of previous research of EUCS

Figure 1. The second-order model of the study

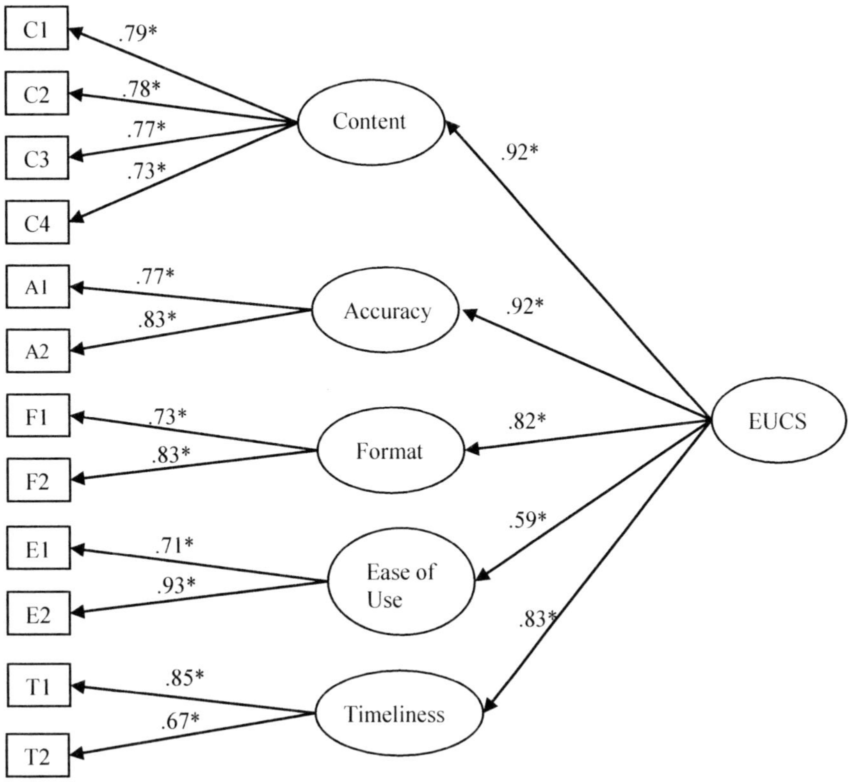

*. P<.001

for other kinds of systems. In previous research, in addition to the first-order model, a second-order factor of overall user satisfaction was thought to explain the five first-order factors (Doll & Torkzadeh, 1988; McHaney et al., 1999; Somers et al., 2003). Such a model has shown good model fit in these studies. In this study, we also tested a second-order model of user satisfaction with online shopping systems. The five first-order reflective factors of user satisfaction are content, accuracy, format, ease of use, and timeliness. The model was consistent with those in previous studies (see Figure 1). The model showed a reasonable fit. The ratio of χ^2 to degrees of freedom was 4.11, GFI was .93, AGFI was .88, NFI was .96, CFI was .97, RMSEA was .086, and RMSR was .029. All five factors loaded on the second-order factor significantly and strongly (path coefficients >.59). This result indicates the existence of a second-order factor of user satisfaction with online shopping systems.

Reliability and Validity

The Cronbach's alphas for each factor are listed in Table 2. They were .85, .78, .75, .79, and .72 for content, accuracy, format, ease of use, and timeliness, respectively. The reliability of all 12 items was .91. All values were above the acceptable level of reliability of .70 (Nunnally & Bernstein, 1994).

Next, we examined construct validity of the instrument from three aspects: convergent, discriminant, and nomological validity. First, to assure convergent validity, all item loadings for corresponding factors should be significant (t value should be greater than 1.96) and above .60 (Bagozzi & Yi, 1988), while the average variance extracted (AVE) estimates should be greater than .50 (Fornell & Larcker, 1981). The AVE is the percentage of variance in the items as explained by the constructs and indicates the extent of convergence among the items measuring the same construct. As shown in Table 2, the t values of the items ranged from 14.21 to 19.32, and the standardized loadings ranged from .70 to .92. In this study, the AVE of content was .59, that of accuracy was .64, that of format was .61, that of ease-of-use was 0.68, and that of timeliness was .57. All values were greater than .50. Hence, the convergent validity was supported.

Second, we assessed discriminant validity of the instrument, which means that one construct can be empirically differentiated from other similar constructs. A series of confirmatory factor analyses was performed on the constrained models. The unconstrained model is the first-order measurement order without setting values for correlations among factors. A constrained model is one with a correlation between a pair of factors fixed at one. Such a model has one more degree of freedom than the unconstrained model, assuming there is no discriminant validity between the two factors with a correlation of one. The difference in χ^2 was calculated between each constrained model and the unconstrained model. The minimum difference in χ^2 between a constrained model and the unconstrained model was 25, which was greater than $\chi^2_{(0.999,1)} = 10.83$. This demonstrated that discriminant validity had been achieved.

Finally, nomological validity of the instrument was examined. A nomological network consists of the construct of interest and other theoretically related constructs. By examining whether the instrument behaves as expected within the network, we can determine its nomological validity. Prior research has supported the positive impact of satisfaction on customer attitude (Cho & Park, 2001; Elliott & Speck, 2005). Therefore, we tested a structural model that related the overall computing satisfaction to shoppers' overall attitude to online shopping (Figure 2). Attitude was measured by the following three items: (1) "In my opinion, it is desirable to shop online"; (2) "I think it is good for me to shop online"; and (3) "Overall, my attitude toward online shopping is favorable." The structural model showed a good fit. The ratio of χ^2/df was 3.08 (χ^2=258.75, df=84), NFI was .96, GFI was .92, CFI was .97, AGFI was .89, RMSEA was .07, and RMSR was .029. In addition, as expected, overall satisfaction had a significantly positive effect on attitude, as shown by the path coefficient of .38. Therefore, the nomological validity of this instrument was supported.

DISCUSSION

The interpretation of the validity results in the last section is straightforward. As with other systems, user satisfaction with online shopping systems consists of five factors: content, accuracy, format, ease of use, and timeliness. The results of both first-order and second-order models gave strong evidence of the reliability and validity of this five-factor structure. Our results showed that the five factors significantly affected overall user satisfaction with online shopping systems, which in turn affected their attitude toward online shopping. This provides strong evidence of the validity of the EUCS instrument as an effective measure for online shopping systems.

We based the discussion of results in conjecture with the results from previous research. In addition to the results of the current study, Tables 3 and 4 contain results reported in three previous studies (Doll et al., 1994; McHaney et al., 1999; Somers et al., 2003). A comparison of all these yields further insights. First, the second-order model in the current study showed a good fit in terms

Figure 2. A nomological model of EUCS and attitude

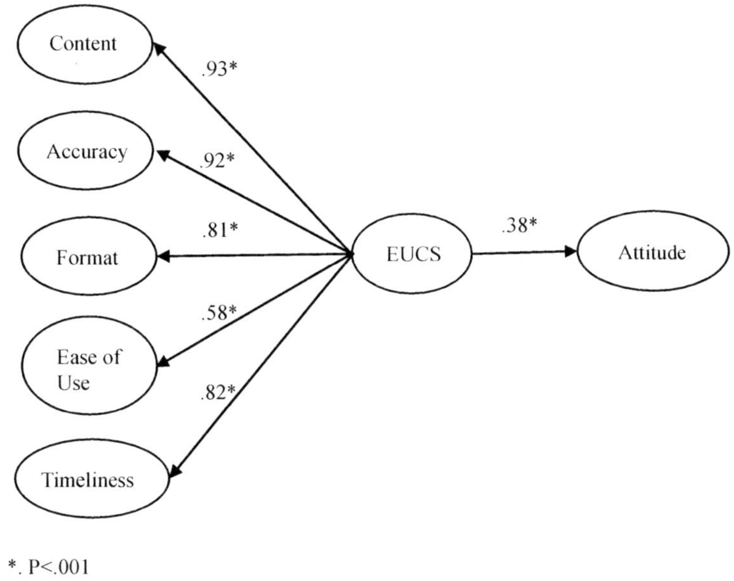

Table 3. A comparison of goodness of fit measures of EUCS second-order models

Goodness of Fit Measures	Current Study	Doll, Xia, and Torkzadeh (1994)	McHaney, Hightower, and White (1999)	Somers, Nelson, and Karimi (2003)
Sample Size	422	409	123	407
Chi-Square (df)	201.58(49)	185.51(50)	145.15(44)	385.33(49)
Chi-Square/df	4.11	3.71	3.30	7.86
NFI	.964	.940	.899	.900
GFI	.926	.929	.866	.918
AGFI	.882	.889	.762	.810
RMSR	.029	.035	.051	.034

of goodness-of-fit indices (NFI =.96, GFI =.93, AGFI=.88, and RMSR=.029). An examination of Table 3 shows that the model in the current study has a better fit as evidenced by better values in the goodness-of-fit indices. This demonstrates that the applicability of the EUCS to online shopping systems is at least as good as for other applications, such as decision support systems and enterprise resource planning applications.

Next, we looked at the highest coefficients among the factors to discover and compare the most important aspects of user satisfaction when end-users deal with various systems. Table 4 lists standardized parameter estimates for these factors. Table 4 and Figure 2 show that the two highest coefficients in the current study are content and accuracy, while in all three previous studies content and format were listed as the highest (Table 4). This means that both content and format are the most important factors for user satisfaction in general computing systems (Doll et al., 1994), DSS (McHaney et al., 1999), and ERP applica-

Table 4. A comparison of standardized structural coefficients (β) and t-values

	Current Study		**Doll, Xia, and Torkzadeh (1994)**		**McHaney, Hightower, and White (1999)**		**Somers, Nelson, and Karimi (2003)**	
Factor	β(t value)	R^2	β(t value)	R^2	β(t value)	R^2	β(t value)	R^2
Content	**.92**(16.47)	0.84	**.91**(17.67)	0.83	**.96**(15.22)	0.91	**.97**(18.33)	0.95
Accuracy	**.92**(15.41)	0.84	.82(16.04)	0.68	.77(10.86)	0.59	.78(14.32)	0.62
Format	.82(12.70)	0.67	**.99**(18.19)	0.98	**.86**(12.70)	0.73	**.94**(13.81)	0.88
Ease of Use	.59(8.35)	0.35	.72(13.09)	0.52	.63(8.30)	0.40	.87(13.24)	0.76
Timeliness	.83(15.73)	0.69	.88(13.78)	0.78	.71(9.74)	0.51	.84(13.40)	0.71

Note: Values in bold represent the two highest loadings for each study.

tions (Somers et al., 2003). This difference of coefficients does not imply that EUCS is not a good measure for Web-based shopping systems; rather, it suggests that the Internet and the Web are somewhat different than those other "traditional" computing systems.

Since it has been one of the factors with the highest coefficients in all the studies listed, the importance of content is obvious. This observation confirms our common understanding of the major concerns and expectations of end-users. The core of an information system is its content, which should be precise and complete. This is the top requirement necessary to ensure system success; sometimes it is even the reason for new system development.

When carrying out online activities, especially shopping, users are more concerned about information accuracy than about format. This can be explained by the less-controlled nature of the Web. Since it is a general perception that information from the Web is less trustworthy, it is not surprising that online shoppers prefer accuracy over format. In contrast, for productivity systems, such as ERP and DSS, the way information is presented makes a difference to end-user performance (Smelcer & Carmel, 1997; Vessey, 1994), which of course makes format more critical to user satisfaction. This comparison not only provides evidence of the applicability of EUCS for various applications and systems because it is a comprehensive measure of general but distinctive aspects of user satisfaction, but also suggests that using EUCS can provide insights into user satisfaction in particular situations. For instance, the practical implication for managers and designers of online shopping systems is that they should provide relevant, complete, and accurate information.

Moreover, we found that ease-of-use factor in the current study has significant t value but relatively low loading (.59) compared with four other factors. In Table 2, items of ease of use have high mean values. This indicates that end-users feel online shopping systems are easy to use. This means that ease-of-use is a necessary but not the most important contributor to the end-user computing satisfaction for online shopping systems. Therefore, online retailers and Web site designers should pay more attentions to other aspects of user experience, such as accuracy and content, to improve end-user computing satisfaction.

CONTRIBUTIONS

Our study replicated a widely used instrument of end-user computing satisfaction: EUCS (Doll & Torkzadeh, 1988). The purpose of the study was to validate the instrument as a measure for end-user satisfaction with online shopping systems. Following the approach in previous studies (Doll et al., 1994; McHaney et al., 1999; Somers et al.,

2003), we further examined EUCS in the context of online shopping. Our study provided strong evidence that EUCS is a multifaceted construct consisting of five subscales: content, accuracy, format, ease of use, and timeliness. Although we focused on online shopping systems, we are confident that EUCS can also be applied to other kinds of online businesses, such as online auction systems and information portals. For researchers, the major contribution of this study lies in the area of measurement. EUCS was rigorously validated, thus enabling researchers to use the instrument with increased confidence, especially for online shopping and Internet applications. In this regard, this research can serve as an example for instrument validation.

Moreover, not only does the instrument provide an overall assessment of end-user computing satisfaction, but also the magnitude of the path coefficients provides useful insights into the relative importance of each subscale. The instrument can be used to detect major areas of end-user satisfaction or dissatisfaction for a particular system, thereby enabling managers to focus on those factors that contribute most significantly to overall satisfaction and to improve systems in an efficient and effective manner. We are also able to compare path coefficients across types of information systems, including online shopping systems, to gain insights about user satisfaction in various contexts and to provide general guidelines for system development.

Satisfaction with the online shopping experience is very important in that it has an impact on the bottom-line profitability of sellers. The shopper's satisfaction with the Web site is an integral part of overall satisfaction. Our research thus contributes to the understanding of shoppers as end-users in e-commerce and provides online retailers with a tool to evaluate their systems in terms of end-user computing satisfaction. Our research also suggests that accuracy and content are the two most important information needs of online shoppers. Thus, in order to better serve shoppers, Web sites should pay close attention to accuracy and content.

The results of this study offer particular insights into the situations where buyers' information needs and requirement for system reliability are more important than other aspects of the transaction, such as B2B e-commerce. In B2B e-commerce, buyers tend to use information and systems such as procurement systems or supply chain systems in a way more like the end-users in other studies from which EUCS originated, making EUCS more applicable in a context like this. A study focusing on B2B buyers would be valuable.

Although our sample was limited, it provides us a chance to study a specific potential market. First, college students represent a large and lucrative segment of both present and future markets. Second, the Asian e-commerce is becoming increasingly important and has great potential for growth (Grau, 2005). In Asia, Taiwan has a relatively mature e-commerce environment with broadband connections and an e-commerce population (Shiu & Dawson, 2002). In China, although there is a long way to go for e-commerce to become a viable means of shopping, the number of Internet users has already surpassed that of the huge US market (The Associated Press, 2007). Thus, not only is Taiwan an example for other Asian markets to follow, it also represents what those currently underdeveloped markets could become in the future.

FUTURE RESEARCH

Online shoppers are both shoppers and system users. Although in this study their needs as shoppers are considered, overall the EUCS instrument is a measure of their satisfaction toward online shopping systems as end-users. Customer service is just as important as the quality of the online shopping system in determining the quality of the customer relationship and customer loyalty (Ribbink et al., 2004). In the current study, we only focused on one important aspect of online shopping: the online customer's end-user computing satisfaction. E-commerce customer satisfaction, however, is much more complex than this. We plan to take both roles of the online shopper into account in the future. That is, our research model will be extended to include both aspects of satisfaction of online shopping: customer satisfaction and end-user computing satisfaction. Factors thought to be crucial to customer satisfaction, such as trust and service quality, will be incorporated into a comprehensive model.

The research method and the sample presented limitations of this study. Using a single source survey may cause common method bias in our data. Various data collection methods can be used in the future to reduce this threat. Using a sample that mainly consisted of college students raised concerns of generalizability. A more diverse sample would provide greater insights into factors affecting online shoppers' evaluations of an online shopping system. We plan to replicate the research using a different sample in terms of user computer skills and cultural background in the future. That would provide us with a valuable opportunity to compare and contrast the results.

In summary, we studied one important variable having an influence on Internet commercial systems: user satisfaction. We conducted a validity study for online shopping systems utilizing the widely used EUCS. As a result of our study, EUCS is better understood, and its applicability as a standardized measure of advanced information technologies has been extended to online shopping. Thus, EUCS can provide a summary evaluation for researchers and a means of formally evaluating commercial Web sites for practitioners in terms of end-user computing satisfaction.

REFERENCES

Abdinnour-Helm, S.F., Chaparro, B.S., & Farmer, S.M. (2005). Using the end-user computing satisfaction (EUCS) instrument to measure satisfaction with a Web site. *Decision Sciences, 36*(2), 341–364.

Agarwal, R., & Venkatesh, V. (2002). Assessing a firm's Web presence: A heuristic evaluation procedure for the measurement of usability. *Information Systems Research, 13*(2), 168–186.

The Associated Press. (2007). China to surpass U.S. Internet users. *MSNBC.com*. Retrieved January 24, 2007, from http://www.msnbc.msn.com/id/16785918/

Bagozzi, R., & Yi, Y. (1988). On the evaluation of structural equation models. *Journal of the Academy of Marketing Science, 16*(1), 74–94.

Bailey, J.E., & Pearson, S.W. (1983). Development of a tool for measuring and analyzing computer user satisfaction. *Management Science, 29*(5), 530–545.

Ball, D., Coelho, P.S., & Machas, A. (2004). The role of communication and trust in explaining customer loyalty: An extension to the ECSI model. *European Journal of Marketing, 38*(9/10), 1272–1293.

Barnes, S.J., & Vigden, R.T. (2002). An integrative approach to the assessment of e-commerce quality. *Journal of Electronic Commerce Research, 3*(3), 114–127.

Bentler, P.M., & Bonett, D.G. (1980). Significance tests and goodness of fit in the analysis of covariance structures. *Psychological Bulletin, 88*, 588–606.

Cai, S., & Fun, M. (2003). Internet users' perceptions of online service quality: A comparison of online buyers and information searchers. *Managing Service Quality, 13*(6), 504–519.

Chen, Z., & Dubinsky, A.J. (2003). A conceptual model of perceived customer value in e-commerce: A preliminary investigation. *Psychology & Marketing, 20*(4), 323–347.

Cho, N., & Park, S. (2001). Development of electronic commerce user-consumer satisfaction index (ECUSI) for Internet shopping. *Industrial Management and Data Systems, 101*(8), 400–405.

Cyert, J., & March, J.G. (1963). *A behavior theory of the firm*. Englewood Cliffs, NJ: Prentice-Hall.

Davis, F.D. (1989). Perceived usefulness, perceived ease of use, and user acceptance of information technology. *MIS Quarterly, 13*(3), 319–340.

DeLone, W.H., & McLean, E.R. (1992). Information systems success: The quest for the dependent variable. *Information Systems Research, 3*(1), 60–95.

Devaraj, S., Fan, M., & Kohli, R. (2002). Antecedents of B2C channel satisfaction and preference: Validation e-commerce metrics. *Information Systems Research, 13*(3), 316–333.

Dodds, W.B., Monroe, K.B., & Grewal, D. (1991). Effect of price, brand, and store information on buyers' product evaluations. *Journal of Marketing Research, 28*(3), 307–319.

Doll, W.J., Deng, X., Raghunathan, T.S., Torkzadeh, G., & Xia, W. (2004). The meaning and measurement of user satisfaction: A multigroup invariance analysis of the end-user computing satisfaction instrument. *Journal of Management Information Systems, 21*(1), 227–262.

Doll, W.J., & Torkzadeh, G. (1988). The measurement of end-user computing satisfaction. *MIS Quarterly, 12*(2), 259–274.

Doll, W.J., & Xia, W. (1997). A confirmatory factor analysis of the end-user computing satisfaction instrument: A replication. *Journal of End User Computing, 9*(2), 24–31.

Doll, W.J., Xia, W., & Torkzadeh, G. (1994). A confirmatory factor analysis of the end-user computing satisfaction instrument. *MIS Quarterly, 18*(4), 453–461.

Elliott, M.T., & Speck, P.S. (2005). Factors that affect attitude toward a retail Web site. *Journal of Marketing Theory and Practice, 13*(1), 40–51.

Fenech, T., & O'Cass, A. (2001). Internet users' adoption of Web retailing: User and product dimensions. *Journal of Product & Brand Management, 10*(6), 361–381.

Fornell, C., & Larcker, D.F. (1981). Evaluating structural equation models with unobservable variables and measurement error. *Journal of Marketing Research, 18*(1), 39–50.

Gefen, D., Karahanna, E., & Straub, D.W. (2003). Trust and TAM in online shopping: An integrated model. *MIS Quarterly, 27*(1), 51–90.

Gelderman, M. (1998). The relation between user satisfaction, usage of information systems and performance. *Information & Management, 34*(1), 11–18.

Grau, J. (2005). Asia-Pacific e-commerce: Spotlight on China, Japan and South Korea. *eMarketer.com*. http://www.emarketer.com/Report.aspx?ecom_asia_jul05

Gummerus, J., Liljander, V., Pura, M., & Van Riel, A. (2004). Customer loyalty to content-based Web sites: The case of an online health care service. *Journal of Services Marketing, 18*(3), 175–186.

Han, H., & Ocker, R.M. (2002). Is it worthwhile to target university students? *Decision Line*, (September/October), 18–20.

Hendrickson, A.R., Glorfeld, K., & Cronan, T.P. (1994). On the repeated test-retest reliability of the end-user computing satisfaction instrument: A comment. *Decision Sciences, 25*(4), 655–667.

Homburg, C., & Rudolph, B. (2001). Customer satisfaction in industrial markets: Dimensional and multiple role issues. *Journal of Business Research, 52*(1), 15–33.

Ives, B., Olson, M.H., & Baroudi, J.J. (1983). The measurement of user information satisfaction. *Communications of the ACM, 26*(10), 785–793.

Jamal, A., & Goode, M.M.H. (2001). Consumers and brands: A study of the image of self-image congruence on brand preference and satisfaction. *Marketing Intelligence & Planning, 19*(7), 482–492.

Jarvenpaa, S.L., Dickson, G..W., & DeSanctis, G. (1985). Methodological issues in experimental IS research. *MIS Quarterly, 9*(2), 141–156.

Jarvenpaa, S.L., & Todd, P.A. (1996-1997). Consumer reactions to electronic shopping on the World Wide Web. *International Journal of Electronic Commerce, 1*(2), 59–88.

Khalil, O., & Elkordy, M. (1999). The relationship between user satisfaction and systems usage: Empirical evidence from Egypt. *Journal of End-User Computing, 11*(2), 21–28.

Klenke, K. (1992). Construct measurement in management information systems: A review and critique of user satisfaction and user involvement instruments. *INFOR, 30*(4), 325–348.

Koufaris, M. (2002). Applying the technology acceptance model and flow theory to online consumer behavior. *Information Systems Research, 13*(2), 205–233.

Lai, V.S., & Li, H. (2005). Technology acceptance model for internet banking: An invariance analysis. *Information & Management, 42*(2), 373–386.

Lee, G..-G., & Lin, H.-F. (2005). Customer perceptions of e-service quality in online shopping. *International Journal of Retail & Distribution Management, 33*(2), 161–176.

Liao, Z., & Cheung, M.T. (2002). Internet-based e-banking and consumer attitude: An empirical study. *Information & Management, 39*(4), 283–295.

Lim, H., & Dubinsky, A.J. (2004). Consumers' perception of e-shopping characteristics: An expectancy-value approach. *Journal of Services Marketing, 18*(7), 550–513.

Loiacono, E.T., Watson, R.T., & Goodhue, D.L. (2002). WebQual: A measure of Website quality. *Proceedings of the American Marketing Association: Winter Marketing Educators' Conference.* Austin, Texas, 432–438.

Lu, M.T., & Yeung, W.L. (1998). A framework for effective commercial Web application development. *Internet Research: Electronic Networking Applications and Policy, 8*(2), 166–173.

Macintosh, G., & Lockshin, L.S. (1997). Retail relationships and store loyalty: A multi-level perspective. *International Journal of Research in Marketing, 14*(5), 487–497.

Marsh, H.W., & Hocevar, D. (1985). Application of confirmatory factory analysis to the study of self-concept: First-and higher-order factor models and their invariance across groups. *Psychological Bulletin, 97*(3), 562–582.

McHaney, R., & Cronan, T.P. (1998). Computer simulation success: On the use of the end-user computing satisfaction instrument: a comment. *Decision Sciences, 29*(2), 525–534.

McHaney, R., & Cronan, T.P. (2001). A comparison of surrogate success measures in on-going representational decision support systems: An extension to simulation technology. *Journal of End User Computing, 13*(2), 15–25.

McHaney, R., Hightower, R., & Pearson, J. (2002). A validation of the end-user computing satisfaction instrument in Taiwan. *Information & Management, 39*(6), 503–511.

McHaney, R., Hightower, R., & White, D. (1999). EUCS test-retest reliability in representational model decision support systems. *Information & Management, 36*(2), 109–119.

McKinney, V., Yoon, K., & Zahedi, F. (2002). The measurement of Web-customer satisfaction: An expectation and disconfirmation approach. *Information Systems Research, 13*(3), 296–315.

Nicholson, M., Clarke, I., & Blakemore, M. (2002). One brand, three ways to shop: Situational variables and multichannel consumer behavior. *International Review of Retail, Distribution and Consumer Research, 12*(2), 131–148.

Nunnally, J.C., & Bernstein, I.H. (1994). *Psychometric theory.* New York: McGraw-Hill.

O'Cass, A., & Fenech, T. (2003). Web retailing adoption: Exploring the nature of Internet users Web retailing behaviour. *Journal of Retailing and Consumer Services, 10*(2), 81–94.

Oliver, R.L. (1999). Whence customer loyalty? *Journal of Marketing, 63*(4), 33–44.

Palmer, J.W. (2002). Web site usability, design, and performance metrics. *Information Systems Research, 13*(2), 151–167.

Parasuraman, A., Zeithaml, V., & Malhotra, A. (2005). E-S-QUAL: A multiple-item scale for assessing electronic service quality. *Journal of Services Research, 7*(3), 213–233.

Park, C.-H., & Kim, Y.-G. (2003). Identifying key factors affecting consumer purchase behavior in an online shopping context. *International Journal of Retail & Distribution Management, 31*(1), 16–29.

Perry, M., & Bodkin, C. (2000). Content analysis of Fortune 100 company Web sites. *Corporate Communications, 5*(2), 87–96.

Perse, E.M., & Courtright, J.A. (1993). Normative images of communication media: Mass and interpersonal channels in the new media environment. *Human Communication Research, 19*(4), 485–503.

Ranganathan, C., & Ganapathy, S. (2002). Key dimensions of business-to-consumer Web sites. *Information & Management, 39*(6), 457–465.

Ribbink, D., van Riel, A.C.R., Liljander, V., & Streukens, S. (2004). Comfort your online customer: Quality, trust, and loyalty on the Internet. *Managing Service Quality, 14*(6), 446–456.

Santos, J. (2003). E-service quality: A model of virtual service quality dimensions. *Managing Service Quality, 13*(3), 233–246.

Schaupp, L.C., & Belanger, F. (2005). A conjoint analysis of online consumer satisfaction. *Journal of Electronic Commerce Research, 6*(2), 95–111.

Shayo, C., Guthrie, R., & Igbaria, M. (1999). Exploring the measurement of end-user computing success. *Journal of End-User Computing, 11*(1), 5–14.

Shim, J.P., Shin, Y.B., & Nottingham, L. (2002). Retailer Web site influence on customer shopping: An exploratory study on key factors of customer satisfaction. *Journal of the Association for Information Systems, 3,* 53–76.

Shim, S., & Eastlick, M.A. (1998). The hierarchical influence of personal values on mall shopping attitude and behavior. *Journal of Retailing, 74*(1), 139–160.

Shiu, E.C.-C., & Dawson, J.A. (2002). Cross-national consumer segmentation of Internet shopping for Britain and Taiwan. *The Service Industries Journal, 22*(1), 147–166.

Smelcer, J., & Carmel, E. (1997). The effectiveness of different representations for managerial problem solving: Comparing maps and tables. *Decision Sciences, 28*(2), 391–420.

Somers, T.M., Nelson, K., & Karimi, J. (2003). Confirmatory factor analysis of the end-user computing satisfaction instrument: Replication within an ERP domain. *Decision Sciences, 34*(3), 595–621.

Straub, D.W. (1989). Validating instruments in MIS research. *MIS Quarterly, 13*(2). 147–169.

Szymanski, D.M., & Hise, R.T. (2000). e-Satisfaction: An initial examination. *Journal of Retailing, 76*(3), 309–322.

Tan, K.C. (2001). A structural equation model of new product design and development. *Decision Sciences, 32*(2), 195–226.

van der Heijden, H. (2004). User acceptance of hedonic information systems. *MIS Quarterly, 28*(4), 695–704.

Vessey, I. (1994). The effect of information presentation on decision making: A cost-benefit analysis. *Information & Management, 27*(2), 103–119.

Wang, Y., Lo, H.-P., & Yang, Y. (2004). An integrated framework for service quality, customer value, satisfaction: Evidence from China's telecommunication industry. *Information Systems Frontiers, 6*(4), 325–340.

Wang, Y.-S., & Tang, T.-I. (2004). A validation of the customer information satisfaction instrument for digital market context. *International Journal of Electronic Business, 2*(6), 567–582.

Wolfinbarger, M., & Gilly, M. (2003). eTailQ: Dimensionalizing, measuring and predicting retail quality. *Journal of Retailing, 79*(3), 183–198.

Woo, K.-s., & Ennew, C.T. (2005). Measuring business-to-business professional service quality and its consequences. *Journal of Business Research, 58,* 1178–1185.

Yang, X., Ahmed, Z.U., Ghingold, M., Boon, G.S., Mei, T.S., & Hwa, L.L. (2003). Consumer preferences for commercial Web site design: An Asia-Pacific perspective. *Journal of Consumer Marketing, 20*(1), 10–27.

Yang, Z., & Fang, X. (2004). Online service quality dimensions and their relationships with satisfaction: A content analysis of customer reviews of securities brokerage services. *International Journal of Service Industry Management, 15*(3/4), 302–326.

Zhang, P., & von Dran, G.M. (2000). Satisfiers and dissatisfiers: A two-factor model for Website design and evaluation. *Journal of the American Society for Information Science, 51*(4), 1253–1268.

Zviran, M., Glezer, C., & Avni, I. (2006). User satisfaction from commercial Web sites: The effect of design and use. *Information & Management, 43*(2), 157–178.

This work was previously published in the Journal of Organizational and End User Computing, Vol. 20, Issue 4, edited by M. Mahmood, pp. 74-96, copyright 2008 by IGI Publishing (an imprint of IGI Global).

Compilation of References

107th Congress of the United States of America. (2002). *The Sarbanes-Oxley Act of 2002.* HR3763, Washington, DC.

Abdinnour-Helm, S.F., Chaparro, B.S., & Farmer, S.M. (2005). Using the end-user computing satisfaction (EUCS) instrument to measure satisfaction with a Web site. *Decision Sciences, 36*(2), 341–364.

Aberdeen Group. (2005). *SOX compliance and automation.* Boston: Author.

ACT Legislative Assembly election electronic voting and counting system review executive summary. (2001). Retrieved from http://www.elections.act.gov.au/CompExecSumm.htm

Adams, D. A., Nelson, R. R., & Todd, P. A. (1992). Perceived usefulness, ease of use, and usage of information technology: A replication. *MIS Quarterly, 16*, 227-247.

Adler, M., & Simoudis, E. (1992). Cooperation and coordination in help desk organizations. In *Proc. of the 11th Int.l Workshop on Distributed Artificial Intelligence*, Glen Arbor, MI.

Adria, M., & Chowdhury, S. (2002). Making room for the call center. *Information Systems Management, 19*(1), 71–80. doi:10.1201/1078/43199.19.1.20020101/31479.10

Agarwal, R., & Karahanna, E. (2000). Time flies when you're having fun: Cognitive absorption and beliefs about information technology usage. *MIS Quarterly, 24*(4), 665-694.

Agarwal, R., & Prasad, J. (1999). Are individual differences germane to the acceptance of new information technologies? *Decision Sciences, 30*, 361–391. doi:10.1111/j.1540-5915.1999.tb01614.x

Agarwal, R., & Prasad, J. (2000). A field study of the adoption of software process innovations by information systems professionals. *IEEE Transactions on Engineering Management, 47*(3), 295-308.

Agarwal, R., & Venkatesh, V. (2002). Assessing a firm's Web presence: A heuristic evaluation procedure for the measurement of usability. *Information Systems Research, 13*(2), 168–186.

Agarwal, R., Sambamurthy, V., & Stair, R. M. (2000). Research report: The evolving relationship between general and specific computer self-efficacy – An empirical assessment. *Information Systems Research, 11*(4), 418–430. doi:10.1287/isre.11.4.418.11876

Aguilera, R.V. & Jackson, G. (2003). The cross-national diversity of corporate governance: Dimensions and determinants. *Academy of Management Review, 28*(3), 447–465.

Ajzen, I. (1991). The theory of planned behavior. *Organizational Behavior and Human Decision Processes, 50*, 179–211. doi:10.1016/0749-5978(91)90020-T

Alavi, M., & Leidner, D.E. (1999). Knowledge management systems: Issues, challenges, and benefits. *Communications of the AIS, 1*(7), 2-35.

Alavi, M., & Leidner, D.E. (2001). Review: Knowledge management and knowledge management systems: Conceptual foundations and research issues. *MIS Quarterly, 25*(1), 107-136.

Alavi, M., & Tiwana, A. (2002). Knowledge integration in virtual teams: The potential role of KMS. *Journal of the American Society for Information Science and Technology, 53*, 1029–1037. doi:10.1002/asi.10107

Alavi, M., & Weiss, I.R. (1985–1986). Managing the risks associated with end-user computing. *Journal of Management Information Systems, 2*(3), 5–20.

Alden, D. L., Stayman, D. M., & Hoyer, W. D. (1994). Evaluation strategies of American and Thai consumers. *Psychology and Marketing, 11*, 145–161. doi:10.1002/mar.4220110205

Al-Jabri, I. M., & Al-Khaldi. (1997). Effects of user characteristics on computer attitudes among undergraduate business students. *Journal of End User Computing, 9*(2), 16–22.

Allen, B.R., & Boynton, A.C. (1991). Information architecture: In search of efficient flexibility. *MIS Quarterly*, 435–445.

Anand, V., Ashforth, B.E., & Joshi, M. (2004). Business as usual: The acceptance and perpetuation of corruption in organizations. *Academy of Management Executive, 18*(2), 39–53.

Anderson, J.R. (1995). *Cognitive psychology and its implications.* New York: W.H. Freeman.

Anderson, R., Engledow, J., & Becker, H. (1979). Evaluating the relationships among attitude towards business product satisfaction, experience, and search effort. *JMR, Journal of Marketing Research, 16*(3), 394–400. doi:10.2307/3150714

Andrich, D. (1985). A latent trait model for items with response dependencies: Implications for test construction and analysis. In S.E. Embretson (Ed.), *Test design: Developments in psychology and psychometrics* (pp. 245-275). Orlando: Academic Press.

Andrich, D. (1988). *Rasch models for measurement.* Thousand Oaks, CA: Sage Publications.

Andrich, D., Sheridan, B., Lyne, A., & Luo, G. (2000). *RUMM: A windows-based Item analysis program employing Rasch unidimensional measurement models.* Murdoch University, Perth, WA.

Argyris, C. (1971). Management information systems: The challenge to rationality and emotionality. *Management Science, 17*(6), 275–292.

Arlotto, P., & Oakes, J. (2003). *Return on investment: Maximizing the value of healthcare information technology.* Chicago: Healthcare Information & Management Systems Society.

Armata, K. (1996). Signs that sell. *Progressive Grocer, 17*(21).

Armstrong, A. G., & Hagel, J. (1996). The real value of online communities. *Harvard Business Review, 74*, 134-141.

Armstrong, J.S. (1985). *Long range forecasting: From crystal ball to computer.* New York: John Wiley & Sons.

Armstrong, J.S. (1991). Prediction of consumer behavior by experts and novices. *Journal of Consumer Research, 18*(2), 251(6).

Artle, R., & Averous, C. (1973). The telephone system as a public good: Static and dynamic aspects. *Bell Journal of Economics & Management Science, 4*, 89-100.

Ashton, M. C., Jackson, D. N., Paunonen, S. V., Helmes, E., & Rothstein, M. G. (1995). The criterion validity of broad factor scales versus specific facet scales. *Journal of Research in Personality, 29*, 432–442. doi:10.1006/jrpe.1995.1025

Asthana, A., Cravatts, M., & Krzyzanoowski, P. (1994). An indoor wireless system for personalized shopping assistance. In *IEEE Workshop on Mobile Computing Systems and Applications*, Santa Cruz, CA. IEEE Computer Society Press.

Atkins, D. (1995). Audio information services and the electronic media environment. *Information Society*, pp. 75-83.

Austin, J., & Mawhinney, T.C. (1999). Using concurrent verbal reports to examine data analyst verbal behavior.

Journal of Organizational Behavior Management, 18(4), 61–81.

Avgerou, C. (2000). IT and organizational change: An institutionalist perspective. *Information Technology and People, 13*(4), 234–262.

Azuma, R. T. (1997). A survey of augmented reality. *Presence: Teleoperators and Virtual Environments, 6*(4), 355-385.

Ba, S., & Pavlou, P. A. (2002). Evidence of the effect of trust building technology in electronic markets: Price premiums and buyer behavior. *MIS Quarterly, 26*(3), 243–268. doi:10.2307/4132332

Bagozzi, R. P., & Warshaw, P. R. (1990). Trying to consume. *Journal of Consumer Research, 17*(2), 127-140.

Bagozzi, R., & Yi, Y. (1988). On the evaluation of structural equation models. *Journal of the Academy of Marketing Science, 16*(1), 74–94.

Bailey, J.E., & Pearson, S.W. (1983). Development of a tool for measuring and analyzing computer user satisfaction. *Management Science, 29*(5), 530–545.

Bajaj, A. (2000). A study of senior information systems managers' decision models in adopting new computing architectures. *Journal of the Association of Information Systems, 1*(4).

Baker, S., & O'Sullivan, D. (2001). Positioning CORBA, J2EE, Web services and other middlewares. *Proceedings of the 3rd International Symposium on Distributed Objects and Applications* (pp. 359–360).

Bakos, Y. (1998). The emerging role of electronic marketplaces on the Internet. *Communications of the ACM, 41*, 35-42.

Ball, D., Coelho, P.S., & Machas, A. (2004). The role of communication and trust in explaining customer loyalty: An extension to the ECSI model. *European Journal of Marketing, 38*(9/10), 1272–1293.

Bandura, A. (1986). *Social foundations of thought and actions*. Englewood Cliffs, NJ: Prentice-Hall.

Bandura, A. (1997). Self-efficacy: The exercise of control. New York: W.H. Freeman and Company.

Banham, R. (2003). Period of adjustment. *Journal of Accountancy, 195*(2), 43(6).

Barclay, D., Thompson, R., & Higgins, C. (1995). The partial least squares (PLS) approach to causal modeling: Personal computer adoption and use as an illustration. *Technology Studies, 2*, 285–309.

Barnes, S.J., & Vigden, R.T. (2002). An integrative approach to the assessment of e-commerce quality. *Journal of Electronic Commerce Research, 3*(3), 114–127.

Barnhart, S., Marr, W., & Rosenstein, S. (1994). Firm performance and board composition: Some new evidence. *Managerial and Decision Economics, 15,* 329–340.

Barrick, M. R., & Mount, M. K. (1991). The big five personality dimensions and job performance: A meta-analysis. *Personnel Psychology, 44*, 1–26. doi:10.1111/j.1744-6570.1991.tb00688.x

Barrow, D.C. (2001). Sharing know-how at BP Amoco. *Research Technology Management, 44*(3), 18-25.

Batt, R., Doellgast, V., & Kwon, H. (2005). *U.S. call center industry report 2004 national benchmarking report strategy, HR practices & performance* (CAHRS Working Paper #05-06). Ithaca, NY: Cornell University, School of Industrial and Labor Relations, Center for Adv. Human Resource Studies. htttp://digitalcommons.ilr.cornell.edu/cahrswp/6

Baumann, K. (1999). Matrix evaluation method for planned usability improvements based on customer feedback. In H.J. Bullinger and J. Ziegler (Eds.), *Human-computer interaction: Ergonomics and user interfaces* (pp. 701-705). Mahwah, NJ: Lawrence Erlbaum Associates.

Baumgarten, S. (1975). The innovative communicator in the diffusion process. *JMR, Journal of Marketing Research, 22*(1), 12–18. doi:10.2307/3150653

Beath, C.M. (1991). Supporting the information technology champion. *MIS Quarterly, 15*(3), 355–372.

Becerra-Fernandez, I., & Sabherwal, R. (2001). Organizational knowledge management: A contingency perspective. *Journal of Management Information Systems, 18*(1), 23-55.

Behling, O. (1998). Employee selection: Will intelligence and conscientiousness do the job? *The Academy of Management Executive, 12*, 77–86.

Belch, G. E., & Belch, M. A. (2004). *Advertising and promotion: An integrated marketing communications perspective* (6th ed.). New York: McGraw-Hill.

Benbasat, I., Goldstein, D., & Mead, M. (1987). The case research strategy in studies of information systems. *MIS Quarterly, 11,* 369–386.

Bendixen, M., & Mitchell, C. (2004). *Vodacom Customer Care*. Case Wits Business School, University of the Witwatersrand, South Africa.

Bentler, P.M. (1990). Comparative fit indexes in structural models. *Psychological Bulletin, 107*(2), 238–246.

Bentler, P.M., & Bonett, D.G. (1980). Significance tests and goodness of fit in the analysis of covariance structures. *Psychological Bulletin, 88,* 588–606.

Bentler, P.M., & Long, J.S. (1993). *Testing structural equation models.* Newbury Park, CA: Sage.

Bergeron, F., & Berube, C. (1988). The management of the end-user computing environment: An empirical investigation. *Information and Management, 14*(3), 107–113.

Berghel, H. (2005). The two sides of ROI: Return on investment vs. risk of incarceration. *Communications of the ACM, 48*(4), 15–20.

Berle, A., & Means, G. (1932). *The modern corporation and private property.* New York: Macmillan.

Bettenhausen, K. L. (1991). Five years of groups research: What we have learned and what needs to be addressed. *Journal of Management, 17,* 345–381. doi:10.1177/014920639101700205

Bettman, J., & Park, W. (1980). Effects of prior knowledge and experience and phase of the choice process on consumer: A protocol analysis. *The Journal of Consumer Research, 7*(3), 234–248. doi:10.1086/208812

Bienstock, C., Royne, M., Sherrell, D., & Stafford, T. (2008). An expanded model of logistics service quality: Incorporating logistics information technology. *International Journal of Production Economics, 113*(1), 203–222. doi:10.1016/j.ijpe.2007.03.023

Biren, B. (2000). *Xerox: Building a corporate focus on knowledge.* Fontainebleau: INSEAD.

Birkinshaw, J., & Sheehan, T. (2002). Managing the knowledge life cycle. *MIT Sloan Management Review, 44*(1), 75-84.

Biros, D. P., George, J. F., & Zmud, R. W. (2002). Inducing sensitivity to deception in order to improve decision making performance: A field study. *MIS Quarterly, 26,* 119–144. doi:10.2307/4132323

Bishop, G., Allen, B. D., & Welch, G. (2001). *Tracking: Beyond 15 minutes of thought.*

Blackler, F. (1995). Knowledge, knowledge work and organizations: An overview and interpretation. *Organization Studies, 16*(6), 1021-1043.

Blaikie, N. (2000). *Designing social research.* Oxford: Blackwell.

Bock, G.W., Zmud, R.W., Kim, Y.G., & Lee, J.N. (2005). Behavioral intention formation in knowledge sharing: Examining the roles of extrinsic motivators, social-psychological forces and organizational climate. *MIS Quarterly, 29*(1), 87-111.

Bollen, K. A., & Hoyle, R. H. (1990). Perceived cohesion: A conceptual and empirical examination. *Social Forces, 69,* 479–504. doi:10.2307/2579670

Bollen, K.A. (1989). *Structural equations with latent variables.* New York: John Wiley & Sons.

Bono, J. (2002). The role of personality in task and relationship conflict. *Journal of Personality, 70*(3), 311. doi:10.1111/1467-6494.05007

Bose, R., & Sugumaran, V.Application of knowledge management technology in customer relationship management. *Knowledge and Process Management, 10*(1), 3–17. doi:10.1002/kpm.163

Boster, J.S., & Johnson, J.C. (1989). Form or function: A comparison of expert and novice judgments of similarity among fish. *American Anthropologist, 91*(4), 866–889.

Boud, A. C., Haniff, D. J., Baber, C., & Steiner, S. J. (1999). Virtual reality and augmented reality as a training tool for assembly tasks. In *1999 International Conference on Information Visualisation*.

Bourquard, J. (2004). IT–Big investment, bigger returns. *State Legislatures, 30*(4), 18–22.

Boutin, P. (2004). Is e-voting safe? *PC World, 22*(6), 121-125.

Bouwman, M.J. (1984). Expert vs. novice decision making in accounting: A summary. *Accounting, Organizations and Society, 9*(3–4), 325–327.

Boyd, T., & Charlotte, M., H. (1999). The link between attractiveness of extrabrand attributes and the adoption of innovation. *Journal of the Academy of Marketing Science, 27*(3), 306–319. doi:10.1177/0092070399273002

Brajnik, G., Mizzaro, S., Tasso, C., & Venuti, F. (2002). Strategic help in user interfaces for information retrieval. *Journal of the American Society for Information Science and Technology, 53*, 343–358. doi:10.1002/asi.10035

Brancheau, J.C., Vogel, D.R., & Wetherbe, J.C. (1985). An investigation of the information center from the user's perspective. *Data Base, 17*(1), 4–17.

Brehmer, B. (1990). Strategies in real-time decision making. In R. Hogarth (Ed.), *Insights in decision making* (pp. 262–279). Chicago: University of Chicago Press.

Broniarzyk, S., Hutchinson, J., & Alba, J. (1992). What consumers 'really know' and what they know: investigations into the determinants of confidence and performance. *Advances in Consumer Research. Association for Consumer Research (U. S.), 19*, 191.

Brown, J.S., & Duguid, P. (1991). Organizational learning and communities-of-practice: Towards a unified view of working, learning and innovation. *Organization Science, 2*(1), 40-57.

Brown, J.S., & Duguid, P. (2001). Knowledge and organization: A social-practice perspective. *Organization Science, 12*(2), 198-213.

Brown, R.B., & Woodland, M.J. (1999). Managing knowledge wisely: A case study in organizational behavior. *Journal of Applied Management Studies, 8*(2), 175-198.

Browne, M.W., & Cudeck, R. (1993). Robustness of normal theory methods in the analysis of linear latent variant models. In K.A. Bollen & J.S. Long (Eds.), *Testing structural equation models* (pp. 136–162). Newbury Park, CA: Sage.

Burgess, D. (2005). What motivates employees to transfer knowledge outside their work unit? *Journal of Business Communication, 42*(4), 324-348.

Butler, T. (1998). Towards a hermeneutic method for interpretive research in information systems. *Journal of Information Technology, 13*(4), 285-300.

Cabrera, A., Cabrera, E.F., & Barajas, S. (2001). The key role of organizational culture in a multi-system view of technology-driven change. *International Journal of Information Management, 21*(3), 245-261.

Cabrera, A., Collins, W.C., & Salgado, J.F. (2006). Determinants of individual engagement in knowledge sharing. *International Journal of Human Resource Management, 17*(2), 245-264.

Cadbury, A. (1992). *The financial aspects of corporate governance.* Report of the Committee on the Financial Aspects of Corporate Governance, Gee and Co., London.

Cai, S., & Fun, M. (2003). Internet users' perceptions of online service quality: A comparison of online buyers and information searchers. *Managing Service Quality, 13*(6), 504–519.

Camerer, C.F., & Johnson, E.J. (1991). The process performance paradox in expert judgment: How can experts know so much and predict so badly? In K.A. Ericsson & J. Smith (Eds.), *Toward a general theory of expertise: Prospects and limits* (pp. 195–217). New York: Cambridge University Press.

Campbell, R.L., & Bello, L.D. (1996). Studying human expertise: Beyond the binary paradigm. *Journal of Experimental and Theoretical Artificial Intelligence, 8*(3–4), 277–291.

Carron, A. V., Widmeyer, W. N., & Brawley, L. R. (1988). Group cohesion and individual adherence to physical activity. *Journal of Sport & Exercise Psychology, 10*(2), 127–138.

Cartwright, D., & Zander, A. (1968). *Group dynamics.* New York: Harper Row.

Cavaye, A.L.M. (1996). Case study research: A multi-faceted research approach for IS. *Information Systems Journal, 6*(3), 227-242.

Chaiken, S., Liberman, A., & Eagly, A. H. (1989). Heuristic and systematic processing within and beyond the persuasion context. In J.S. Uleman & J.A. Bargh (Eds.), *Unintended thought* (pp. 212-252). New York: Guildford Press.

Champion, M. A., Medsker, G. J., & Higgs, A. C. (1993). Relations between work group characteristics and effectiveness: Implications for designing effective work groups. *Personnel Psychology, 46*, 823–850. doi:10.1111/j.1744-6570.1993.tb01571.x

Chan, C. W., Chen, L. L., & Geng, L. Q. (2000). Knowledge engineering for an intelligent case-based system for help desk operations. *Expert Systems with Applications, 18*(2), 125–132. doi:10.1016/S0957-4174(99)00058-5

Chan, S. (2004). Sarbanes-Oxley: The IT dimension. *The Internal Auditor,* (February), 31–33.

Chan, W. (2001). *Project Voyager: Building an Internet presence for people, places, and things.* Cambridge, MA: Massachusetts Institute of Technology.

Chang, J. O. (2005). Toward a unified view of customer relationship management. *The Journal of American Academy of Business*, March 2005, 32-38.

Charness, N. (1976). Memory for chess positions: Resistance to interference. *Journal of Experimental Psychology: Human Learning and Memory, 2,* 641–653.

Chase, W.G., & Simon, H.A. (1973). The mind's eye in chess. In W.G. Chase (Ed.), *Visual information processing.* New York: Academic Press.

Chatman, E. (1986). Diffusion theory: A review and test of a conceptual model in information diffusion. *Journal of the American Society for Information Science American Society for Information Science, 37*(6), 377–386.

Chatterjee, P. (2001). Online reviews: Do consumers use them? *Advances in Consumer Research. Association for Consumer Research (U. S.), 28*(1), 129–133.

Chau, P.Y.K., & Tam, K.Y. (1997). Factors affecting the adoption of open systems: An exploratory study. *MIS Quarterly,* (March), 1–23.

Chen, G., & Kotz, D. (2000). *A survey of context-aware mobile computing research.* Dartmouth College, Department of Computer Science.

Chen, G., Gully, S., & Eden, D. (2001). Validation of a new general self-efficacy scale. *Organizational Research Methods, 4*(1), 62–83. doi:10.1177/109442810141004

Chen, Z., & Dubinsky, A.J. (2003). A conceptual model of perceived customer value in e-commerce: A preliminary investigation. *Psychology & Marketing, 20*(4), 323–347.

Cheung, C. F., Lee, W. B., Wang, W. M., Chu, K. F., & To, S. (2003). A multi-perspective knowledge-based system for customer service management. *Expert Systems with Applications, 24*, 457–470. doi:10.1016/S0957-4174(02)00193-8

Chevalier, J., & Mayzlin, D. (2006). The effect of word of mouth on sales: Online book reviews. *JMR, Journal of Marketing Research, 43*(3), 345–354. doi:10.1509/jmkr.43.3.345

Chi, M.T.H. (1984). Knowledge derived categorization in young children. In D.R. Rogers & J.A. Sloboda (Eds.), *Acquisition of symbolic skills* (pp. 327–334). New York: Plenum.

Chi, M.T.H., Feltovich, P.J., & Glaser, R. (1981). Categorization and representation of physics problems by experts and novices. *Cognitive Science, 5,* 121–152.

Chi, M.T.N., Glaser, R., & Farr, M.J. (1988). *The nature of expertise.* Hillsdale, NJ.

Chienting, S., Jen-Hwa Hu, P., & Hsinchun, C. (2004). Technology implementation management in law enforcement. *Social Science Computer Review, 22*(1), 24–37. doi:10.1177/0894439303259881

Chin, W. (1998). Issues and opinion on structural equation modeling. *MIS Quarterly, 22*, vii–xvi.

Cho, K., Chung, T. R., King, W. R., & Shunn, C. (2008). Peer-based computer-supported knowledge refinement: An empirical investigation. *Communications of the ACM, 51*, 83–88. doi:10.1145/1325555.1325571

Cho, N., & Park, S. (2001). Development of electronic commerce user-consumer satisfaction index (ECUSI) for Internet shopping. *Industrial Management and Data Systems, 101*(8), 400–405.

Christianson, E.B., King, D.E., & Ahrensfeld, J.L. (1991). *Special libraries: A guide for management.* Washington: Special Libraries Association.

Chu, P. C., & Spires, E. E. (2000). The joint effects of effort and quality on decision strategy choice with computerized decision aids. *Decision Sciences, 31*, 259–292. doi:10.1111/j.1540-5915.2000.tb01624.x

Chua, P., & Hui, K. (1998). Identifying early adopters of new IT products: A case of Windows 95. *Information & Management, 33*(5), 225–230. doi:10.1016/S0378-7206(98)00031-7

Clarke, Y., & Soutar, G. (1982). Consumer acquisition patterns for durable goods: The Australian evidence. *The Journal of Consumer Research, 8*(4), 456–460. doi:10.1086/208887

COBIT. (1994). *Control objectives for information and related technology.* Rolling Meadows, IL: IT Governance Institute.

Coe, M.J. (2005). Trust services: A better way to evaluate IT controls. *Journal of Accountancy,* (March), 69–75.

Coffee, J.C. Jr. (2005). Internal controls: The scarlet letter. *Corporate Governance Advisor, 13*(1), 1–6.

Cohen, J., & Cohen, P. (1983). *Applied multiple regression: Correlation analysis for the behavioral sciences.* Hillsdale, NJ: Lawrence Erlbaum.

Cohen, W., & Levinthal, D. (1990). Absorptive capacity: A new perspective on learning and innovation. *Administrative Science Quarterly, 35*(1), 128-152.

Cole, C., & Gaeth, G. Chakraborty, & Levin, I. (1992). Exploring the relationship among self-reported knowledge, objective knowledge and consumer decision making. *Advances in Consumer Research. Association for Consumer Research (U. S.), 19*, 191.

Commission on Electronic Voting. (2005, June 20). Retrieved from http://www.cev.ie/htm/about/index.htm

Compeau, D. R., & Higgins, C. A. (1995). Computer self-efficacy: Development of a measure and initial test. *MIS Quarterly, 19*(2), 189–202. doi:10.2307/249688

Compeau, D. R., & Higgins, C. A. (1995). Application of social cognitive theory to training for computer skills. *Information Systems Research, 6*(2), 118–143. doi:10.1287/isre.6.2.118

Compeau, D., Higgins, C. A., & Huff, S. (1999). Social cognitive theory and individual reactions to computing technology: A longitudinal study. *MIS Quarterly, 23*(2), 145–158. doi:10.2307/249749

Compton, P. J., & Jansen, R. (1989). A philosophical basis for knowledge acquisition. *3rd European Knowledge Acquisition for KBS W/shop* (pp. 75-89).

Compton, P., Peters, L., Edwards, G., & Lavers, T. G. (2006). Experience with ripple-down rules. *Knowledge-Based System Journal, 19*(5), 289–380. doi:10.1016/j.knosys.2006.05.001

Computer loses 4,500 votes. (2004, November 4). Retrieved from http://www.wired.com/news/evote/0,2645,65601,00.html

Consortium for Service Innovation. (CSI, 2006). *The KCSsm Operational Model (Knowledge-Centered Support)* Version 3. Retrieved December 26, 2008 from http://www.serviceinnovation.org/included/docs/library/programs/KCS_OpModel_V3.7.pdf

Consortium for Service Innovation. (CSI, 2006). *Progress Software Application Support Services KCS at Work).* Retrieved December 26, 2008 from http://www.serviceinnovation.org/included/docs/library/programs/progress_casestudy.pdf

Constant, D., Kiesler, S., & Sproull, L. (1994). What's mine is ours, or is it? A study of attitudes about information sharing. *Information Systems Research, 5,* 400–421. doi:10.1287/isre.5.4.400

Constant, D., Sproull, L., & Kiesler, S. (1996). The kindness of strangers: The usefulness of electronic weak ties for technical advice. *Organization Science, 7*(2), 119–135. doi:10.1287/orsc.7.2.119

Cook, G. (1993). An empirical investigation of information search strategies with implications for decision support system design. *Decision Sciences, 24,* 683–697. doi:10.1111/j.1540-5915.1993.tb01298.x

Cooper, R. (1994). The inertial impact of culture on IT implementation. *Information Management, 27*(1), 17-31.

Cosley, D., Lam, S. K., Albert, I., Konstan, J. A., & Riedl, J. (2003). Is seeing believing? How recommender interfaces affect users' opinions. In *Proceedings for CHI 2003, 5, April 5-10, 2003* (pp. 585-592).

COSO. (1994). *Internal control—integrated framework.* Committee of Sponsoring Organizations of the Treadway Commission.

Costa, P. T., & McCrae, R. R. (1992). *NEO PI-R. The revised NEO personality inventory.* Odessa, FL: Psychological Assessment Resources.

Costa, P., & McCrae, R. (1987). Validation of the five-factor model of personality across instruments and observers. *Journal of Personality and Social Psychology, 52*(1), 81. doi:10.1037/0022-3514.52.1.81

Costigan, R. D., Ilter, S. S., & Berman, J. J. (1998). A multi-dimensional study of trust in organization. *Journal of Managerial Issues, 10*(3), 303-317.

Cotterman, W.W., & Kumar, K. (1989). User cube: A taxonomy of end users. *Communications of the ACM, 32*(11), 1313–1320.

Covaleski, M.A., & Dirsmith, M.W. (1988). An institutional perspective on the rise. Social transformation, and fall of a university budget category. *Administrative Science Quarterly, 33*(4), 562–587.

Cowan, D.A. (1986). Developing a process model of problem recognition. *Academy of Management Review, 11,* 763–776.

Cramton, C. D. (2001). The mutual knowledge problem and the consequences for dispersed collaboration. *Organization Science, 12,* 346–371. doi:10.1287/orsc.12.3.346.10098

Crowston, K., & Myers, M.D. (2004). Information technology and the transformation of industries: Three research perspectives. *Journal of Strategic Information Systems, 13,* 5–28.

Cutler, N. E., & Danowski, J. A. (1980). Process gratification in aging cohorts. *Journalism Quarterly, 57,* 269-277.

Cyert, J., & March, J.G. (1963). *A behavior theory of the firm.* Englewood Cliffs, NJ: Prentice-Hall.

Dahl, M. S., & Pedersen, O. R. (2005). Social networks in the R&D process: The case of the wireless communication industry around Aalborg, Denmark. *Journal of Engineering and Technology Management, 22*(1-2), 75-92.

Daily, C.M., Dalton, D.R., & Canella, A.A. Jr. (2003). Corporate governance: Decades of dialogue and data. *Academy of Management Review, 28*(3), 371–382.

Dalton, D.R., & Dalton, C.M. (2005). Sarbanes-Oxley legislation and the private company: If not for marriage then certainly engagement. *Journal of Business Strategy, 26*(2), 7–8.

Dalton, D.R., Daily, C.M., Certo, C., & Roengpitya, T. (2003). Meta-analyses of financial performance and equity: Fusion or confusion? *Academy of Management Journal, 46,* 13–26.

Dalton, D.R., Daily, C.M., Ellstrand, A.E., & Johnson, J.L. (1998). Meta-analystic reviews of board composition, leadership structure, and financial performance. *Strategic Management Journal, 19,* 269–290.

Damianides, M. (2005). Sarbanes-Oxley and IT governance: New guidance on IT control and compliance. *Information Systems Management,* (Winter), 77–85.

Das, A. (2003). Knowledge and productivity in technical support work. *Management Science*, *49*(4), 416–431. doi:10.1287/mnsc.49.4.416.14419

Datta, P. (2007). An agent-mediated knowledge-in-motion model. *Journal of the Association for Information Systems*, *8*, 287–311.

Davenport, E. (2002). Mundane knowledge management and micro level organizational learning: An ethological approach. *Journal of the American Society for Information Science and Technology, 53*(12), 1038-1046.

Davenport, T., & Beck, J. (2001). *The attention economy: Understanding the new currency of business*. Boston, MA: Harvard Business School Publishing.

Davenport, T.H. (1997). *Information ecology.* Oxford: Oxford University Press.

Davenport, T.H., & Hansen, M.T. (1999). Knowledge management at Andersen Consulting. Harvard Business School Case (9-499-032), July 7, 1999.

Davenport, T.H., & Prusak, L. (1998). *Working knowledge: How organizations manage what they know.* Boston: Harvard Business School Press.

Davenport, T.H., De Long, D.W., & Beers, M.C. (1998). Successful knowledge management projects. *Sloan Management Review, 39*(2), 43-57.

Davenport, T.H., Long, D.W.D., & Beers, M.C. (1998). Successful knowledge management projects. *Sloan Management Review, 39*(2), 43-57.

Davis, A., & Khazanchi, D. (2008). An empirical study of online word of mouth as a predictor for multi-product category e-commerce sales. *Electronic Markets*, *18*(2), 130–141. doi:10.1080/10196780802044776

Davis, F. D. (1989). Perceived usefulness, perceived ease of use, and user acceptance of information technology. *MIS Quarterly, 13*(3), 319-340.

Davis, G.B. (1982). *Caution: User developed systems can be dangerous to your organization.* MISRC-WP-82-04, MIS Research Center, University of Minnesota, USA.

Davis, S.A., & Bostrom, R.P. (1993). Training end users: An experimental investigation of the roles of the computer interface and training methods. *MIS Quarterly, 17*(1), 61–85.

Day, D.V., & Lord, R.G. (1992). Expertise and problem categorization: The role of expert processing in organizational sense making. *Journal of Management Studies, 29*(1), 35–47.

Day, G.S., & Nedungadi, P. (1994). Managerial representations of competitive advantage. *Journal of Marketing, 58*(April), 31–44.

De Long, D., & Fahey, L. (2000). Diagnosing cultural barriers to knowledge management. *The Academy of Management Executive, 14*(4), 113-127.

Dearstyne, B.W. (1993). *The archival enterprise: Modern archival principles, practices and management technique.* Chicago: American Library Association.

Dehning, B., & Richardson, V. (2002). Returns on investments in information technology: A research synthesis. *Journal of Information Systems*, *16*(1), 7–31. doi:10.2308/jis.2002.16.1.7

deHolan, P.M., Phillips, N., & Lawrence, T.B. (2004). Managing organizational forgetting. *MIT Sloan Management Review, 45*(2), 45-54.

Dellarocas, C. (2003). The digitization of word of mouth: Promise and challenges of online feedback mechanisms. *Management Science*, *49*(10), 1407–1425. doi:10.1287/mnsc.49.10.1407.17308

Dellarocas, C. (2006). How often should reputation mechanisms update a trader's reputation profile? *Information Systems Research*, *17*(3), 271–285. doi:10.1287/isre.1060.0092

Dellarocas, C. (2006). Strategic manipulation of internet opinion forums: Implications for consumers and firms. *Management Science, 52*(10), 1577–1593. doi:10.1287/mnsc.1060.0567

Dellarocas, C., & Wood, C. A. (2008). The sound of silence in online feedback: Estimating trading risks in the presence of reporting bias. *Management Science, 54*(3), 460–476. doi:10.1287/mnsc.1070.0747

DeLone, W.H., & McLean, E.R. (1992). Information systems success: The quest for the dependent variable. *Information Systems Research, 3*(1), 60–95.

DeLone, W.H., & McLean, E.R. (2003). The DeLone and McLean model of information systems success: A ten-year update. *Journal of Management Information Systems, 19*(4), 9-30.

Deng, P. (2008). Applying a market-based approach to the development of a sharing-enabled KM model for knowledge-intensive small firms. *Information Systems Management, 25*, 174–187. doi:10.1080/10580530801941389

Dennis, A. R., & Taylor, N. J. (2006). Information foraging on the web: The effects of "Acceptable" Internet delays on multi-page information search behavior. *Decision Support Systems, 42*, 810–824. doi:10.1016/j.dss.2005.05.032

DePaulo, P. J., & DePaulo, B. M. (1989). Can deception by salespersons and customers be detected through nonverbal behavioral cues? *Journal of Applied Social Psychology, 19*, 1552–1577. doi:10.1111/j.1559-1816.1989.tb01463.x

Desouza, K., Yamakawa, S., & Awazu, Y. (2003, September/October). Pricing organizational knowledge: An imperative. *Ivey Business Journal*, 1-5.

Desouza, K.C. (2003). Barriers to effective use of knowledge management systems in software engineering. *Communications of the ACM, 46*(1), 99-101.

Desouza, K.C. (2003). Barriers to effective knowledge management: Why the technology imperative seldom works. *Business Horizons, 46*(1), 25-29.

Desouza, K.C., & Awazu, Y. (2003). Constructing internal knowledge markets: Considerations from mini-cases. *International Journal of Information Management, 23*(4), 345-353.

Desouza, K.C., Awazu, Y., Yamakawa, S., & Umezawa, M. (2005). Facilitating knowledge management through market mechanism. *Knowledge and Process Management, 12*(2), 99-107.

Devaraj, S., Fan, M., & Kohli, R. (2002). Antecedents of B2C channel satisfaction and preference: Validation e-commerce metrics. *Information Systems Research, 13*(3), 316–333.

Dewally, M., & Ederington, L. (2006). Reputation, certification, warranties, and information as remedies for seller-buyer information asymmetries: Lessons from the online comic book market. *The Journal of Business, 79*(2), 693–729. doi:10.1086/499169

Dewing, I.P., & Russell. (2003). Post-Enron developments in UK audit and corporate governance regulation. *Journal of Financial Regulation and Compliance, 11*(4), 309–322.

Diamantopoulos, A., & Siguaw, J. (2000). *Introducing LISREL*. Thousand Oaks, CA: Sage.

Dickinson, J., & Kirzner, E. (1986). Priority patterns of acquisition of financial assets. *Journal of the Academy of Marketing Science, 14*(1), 43–49. doi:10.1007/BF02722156

Digman, J. M. (1990). Personality structure: Emergence of the five-factor model. *Annual Review of Psychology, 41*, 417–440.

Dill, D. L., Mercuri, R., Neumann, P. G., & Wallach, D. S. (2004, September 10). *Frequently asked questions about DRE voting systems*. Retrieved from http://www.verifiedvoting.org/ drefaq.asp#s1q1

Dill, D. L., Schneier, B., & Simons, B. (2003). Voting and technology: Who gets to count your vote? *Communications of the ACM, 46*(8), 29-31.

DiMaggio, P.J., & Powell, W.W. (1983). The iron cage revisited: Institutional isomorphism and collective rationality in organizational fields. *American Sociological Review, 48*(2), 147–160.

DiMaggio, P.J., & Powell, W.W. (1991). Introduction. In W.W. Powell & P.J. DiMaggio (Eds.), *The new institutionalism in organization analysis* (pp. 1–38). Chicago: University of Chicago Press.

Dodds, W.B., Monroe, K.B., & Grewal, D. (1991). Effect of price, brand, and store information on buyers' product evaluations. *Journal of Marketing Research, 28*(3), 307–319.

Doll, W.J., & Torkzadeh, G. (1988). The measurement of end-user computing satisfaction. *MIS Quarterly, 12*(2), 259–274.

Doll, W.J., & Xia, W. (1997). A confirmatory factor analysis of the end-user computing satisfaction instrument: A replication. *Journal of End User Computing, 9*(2), 24–31.

Doll, W.J., Deng, X., Raghunathan, T.S., Torkzadeh, G., & Xia, W. (2004). The meaning and measurement of user satisfaction: A multigroup invariance analysis of the end-user computing satisfaction instrument. *Journal of Management Information Systems, 21*(1), 227–262.

Doll, W.J., Xia, W., & Torkzadeh, G. (1994). A confirmatory factor analysis of the end-user computing satisfaction instrument. *MIS Quarterly, 18*(4), 453–461.

Dordick, H. S. (1993). America calling: A social history of the telephone to 1940. *Telecommunications Policy, 17*, 397-398.

Downey, J. (2006). Measuring general computer self-efficacy: A surprising comparison of three instruments in predicting performance, attitudes and usage. In *Proceedings of the Thirty-Ninth Annual Hawaii International Conference on System Sciences.*

Drennan, J., Mort, G. S., & Previte, J. (2006). Privacy, risk perception, and expert online behavior: An exploratory study of household end-users. *Journal of Organizational and End User Computing, 18*(1), 1–22.

Dreyfus, H.L., & Dreyfus, S.E. (1986). *Mind over machine: The power of human intuition and expertise in the era of the computer.* New York: The Free Press.

Drèze, X., & Zufryden, F. (1997). Testing Web site design and promotional content. *Journal of Advertising Research, 37*, 77-91.

Duffy, M.N. (2004). Section 404 opens a door. *Journal of Accountancy, 197*, 8.

Dutton, J.E., & Jackson, S.E. (1987). The categorization of strategic issues by decision makers and its links to organizational action. *Academy of Management Review, 12*, 76–90.

Dyer, J., & Nobeoka, K. (2000). Creating and managing a high performance knowledge-sharing network: The Toyota case. *Strategic Management Journal, 21*(3), 345-367.

Ebersole, S. E. (2000). *Adolescents' use of the World Wide Web in ten public schools: A uses and gratifications approach.* Unpublished doctoral dissertation, Regent University, Virginia Beach, VA.

Eden, D., & Kinnar, J. (1991). Modeling Galatea: Boosting self-efficacy to increase volunteering. *The Journal of Applied Psychology, 76*(6), 770–780. doi:10.1037/0021-9010.76.6.770

Edwards, G., Compton, P., Malor, R., Srinivasan, A., & Lazarus, L. (1993). PEIRS: A pathologist maintained expert system for the interpretation of chemical pathology reports. *Pathology, 25*, 27–34. doi:10.3109/00313029309068898

Edwards, J.S., Shaw, D., & Collier, P.M. (2005). Knowledge management systems: Finding a way with technology. *Journal of Knowledge Management, 9*(1), 113-125.

eGain (2004). Knowledge management for customer service: Ingredients for success. eGain Communications Corporation. http://www.egain.com.

Eighmey, J., & McCord, L. (1998). Adding value in the information age: Uses and gratifications of sites on the World Wide Web. *Journal of Business Research, 41*, 187-194.

Einhorn, H., & Hogarth, R. (1981). Behavioral decision theory: Processes of judgment and choice. *Annual*

Review of Psychology, 32, 53–88. doi:10.1146/annurev.ps.32.020181.000413

Eisenhardt, K.M. (1989). Agency theory: An assessment and review. *Academy of Management Review, 14*, 57–74.

Eisenhardt, K.M. (1989). Building theories from case study research. *Academy of Management Review, 14*(4), 532–550.

Ekstrom, M., Garcia, A. C. B., & Bjornsson, H. (2005). Rewarding honest ratings through personalized recommendations in electronic commerce. *International Journal of Electronic Business, 3*(3/4), 392–410. doi:10.1504/IJEB.2005.007280

Election Commission of India. (2005, June 28). *Electronic voting machine*. Retrieved from http://www.eci.gov.in/EVM/ index.htm

Elliott, M.T., & Speck, P.S. (2005). Factors that affect attitude toward a retail Web site. *Journal of Marketing Theory and Practice, 13*(1), 40–51.

Emmannouildes, C., & Hammond, K. (2000). Internet usage: Predictors of active users and frequency of use. *Journal of Interactive Marketing, 14*, 17-32.

Emmons, R. A., & Diener, E. (1986). Influence of impulsivity and sociability on subjective well-being. *Journal of Personality and Social Psychology, 50*(6). doi:10.1037/0022-3514.50.6.1211

Engell, J.F., Blackwell, R.D., & Kollat, D.T. (1978). *Consumer behavior*. Hillsdale, IL: Dryden.

Englis, B. G., & Solomon, M. R. (1996). Using consumption constellations to develop integrated marketing communications. *Journal of Business Research, 37*(3), 183-191.

Ericson, K. A., & Simon, H. A. (1980). Verbal reports as data. *Psychological Review, 87*, 215-251.

Espinosa, J. A., Slaughter, S. A., Kraut, R. E., & Et, A. (2007). Team knowledge and coordination in geographically distributed software development. *Journal of Management Information Systems, 24*, 135–169. doi:10.2753/MIS0742-1222240104

Evans, S., & Dion, K. (1991). Group cohesion and performance – A metaanalysis. *Small Group Research, 22*, 175–186. doi:10.1177/1046496491222002

E-voting problems reported as election gets under way. (2004, November 2). Retrieved from http://www.itworld.com/ Tech/2987/041102evoteprobs/

Fahey, L., & Prusak, L. (1998). The eleven deadliest sins of knowledge management. *California Management Review, 40*(3), 265-276.

Falconer, J. (1999). Implementing a dynamic corpus management system within a global consulting practice. *International Journal of Technology Management, 18*, 520–534. doi:10.1504/IJTM.1999.002784

Fama, E.F. (1980). Agency problems and the theory of the firm. *Journal of Political Economy, 88*(21), 288–307.

Fama, E.F., & Jensen, M.C. (1983). Separation of ownership and control. *Journal of Law and Economics, 26*, 301–325.

Fang, X. (2000). A hierarchical search history for web searching. *International Journal of Human-Computer Interaction, 12*, 73–88. doi:10.1207/S15327590IJHC1201_3

Farhoomand, A. F., & Drury, D. H. (2002). Managerial information overload. *Communications of the ACM, 45*, 127–131. doi:10.1145/570907.570909

Fawkes, J., & Gregory, A. (2000). Applying communication theories to the Internet. *Journal of Communication Management, 5*, 109-124.

Fenech, T., & O'Cass, A. (2001). Internet users' adoption of Web retailing: User and product dimensions. *Journal of Product & Brand Management, 10*(6), 361–381.

Ferrell, O.C. (2004). Business ethics and customer stakeholders. *Academy of Management Executive, 18*(2), 126–129.

Festinger, L. (1957). *A theory of cognitive dissonance*. Stanford, CA: Stanford University Press.

Festinger, L., Schachter, S., & Back, K. (1950). *Social pressures in informal groups*. Stanford, CA: Stanford University Press.

Fink, J. S., Cunningham, G. B., & Kinsicki, L. J. (2004). Using athletes as endorsers to sell women's sport: Attractiveness vs. expertise. *Journal of Sport Management*, *18*(1), 350–367.

Fischer, E. A. (2003, November 4). *Election reform and electronic voting systems (DREs): Analysis of security issues.* Retrieved from http://www.notablesoftware.com/papers/ RL32139.pdf

Fishbein, M., & Ajzen, I. (1975). *Belief, attitude, intention and behavior: An introduction to theory and research.* Reading, MA: Addison-Wesley.

Fisher, C. W., Chengalur-Smith, I., & Ballou, D. P. (2003). The impact of experience and time on the use of data quality information in decision making. *Information Systems Research*, *14*, 170–188. doi:10.1287/isre.14.2.170.16017

Flynn, L., Goldsmith, R., & Eastman, J. (1996). Opinion leaders and opinion seekers: Two new measurement scales. *Journal of the Academy of Marketing Science*, *24*(2), 137–147. doi:10.1177/0092070396242004

Flynn, R., & Preston, P. (1999). The long-run diffusion and techno-economic performance of national telephone networks: A case study of Ireland, 1922-1998. *Telecommunications Policy, 23*, 437-457.

Fogg, B. J., & Tseng, H. (1999). The elements of computer credibility. In *Proceedings of the CHI 1999, May 15-20, 1999* (pp. 80-87).

Folcher, V. (2003). Appropriating artifacts as instruments: When design-for-use meets design-inuse. *Interacting with Computers*, *15*(5), 647–663. doi:10.1016/S0953-5438(03)00057-2

Forman, C., Ghose, A., & Wiesenfeld, B. (2008). Examining the relationship between reviews and sales: The role of reviewer identity disclosure in electronic markets. *Information Systems Research*, *19*(3), 291–313. doi:10.1287/isre.1080.0193

Forman, H., & Lippert, S. K. (2005) Toward the development of an integrated model of technology internalization within the supply chain context. *International Journal of Logistics Management, 16*(1), 4-26.

Fornell, C., & Bookstein, F. (1982). Two structural equation models: LISREL and PLS applied to consumer exit-voice theory. *JMR, Journal of Marketing Research*, *19*, 440–452. doi:10.2307/3151718

Fornell, C., & Larcker, D. F. (1981). Evaluating structural equation models with unobservable variables and measurement error. *JMR, Journal of Marketing Research*, *18*(1), 29–50. doi:10.2307/3151312

Forsyth, D. (1999). *Group dynamics* (3rd ed.). Pacific Grove, CA: Brook/Cole Publishing.

Foucault, B. E., & Scheufele, D. A. (2002). Web vs. campus store? Why students buy textbooks online. *Journal of Consumer Marketing, 19*, 409-423.

Foxall, G. (1995). Cognitive styles of consumer initiators. *Technovation*, *15*(5), 269–288. doi:10.1016/0166-4972(95)96600-X

Foxall, G., & Seema, B. (1993). Cognitive style and use-innovativeness for applications software in home computing: Implications for new product strategy. *Technovation*, *13*(5), 311–323. doi:10.1016/0166-4972(93)90004-F

Foxall, G.R. (1983). *Consumer choice.* New York: St. Martin's Press.

Frank, J. D. (1997). Some determinants, manifestations, and effects on cohesiveness in therapy groups. *The Journal of Psychotherapy Practice and Research*, *6*(1), 59–70.

Frederico, P.-A. (1995). Expert and novice recognition of similar situations. *Human Factors, 37*(1), 105(18).

Fuller, M. A., Serva, M. A., & Benamati, J. (2007). Seeing is believing: The transitory influence of reputation information on e-commerce trust and decision making. *Decision Sciences*, *38*(4), 675–699.

Fulmer, W.E. (2003). Fulmer, William E., Buckman Laboratories (A). Boston: Harvard Business School Publishing.

Gagne, R. M. (1984). Learning outcomes and their effects: Useful categories of human performance. *The American Psychologist*, *39*, 377–385. doi:10.1037/0003-066X.39.4.377

Gallupe, R.B. (2001). Knowledge management systems: Surveying the landscape. *International Journal of Management Practices, 3*(1), 61-77.

Galunic, C., & Weeks, J. (1999). *Managing knowledge at Booz-Allen & Hamilton: Knowledge online and off.* Fontainebleau: INSEAD.

Garud, R., & Kumaraswamy, A. Vicious and virtuous cycles in the management of knowledge: The case of Infosys Technologies. *MIS Quarterly, 29*(1), 2005, 9-33.

Gatignon, H., & Robertson, T. S. (1985). A propositional inventory for new diffusion research. *The Journal of Consumer Research, 11*(4), 849–867. doi:10.1086/209021

Gebert, H., Geib, M., Kolbe, L., & Brenner, W. (2003). Knowledge-enabled customer relationship management: Integrating customer relationship management and knowledge management concepts. *Journal of Knowledge Management, 7*(5), 107–123. doi:10.1108/13673270310505421

Gefen, D., & Straub, D. W. (1997). Gender difference in the perception and use of e-mail: An extension to the technology acceptance model. *MIS Quarterly, 21*(4), 389–400. doi:10.2307/249720

Gefen, D., Karahanna, E., & Straub, D.W. (2003). Trust and TAM in online shopping: An integrated model. *MIS Quarterly, 27*(1), 51–90.

Gefen, D., Straub, D.W., & Boudreau, M.-C. (2000). Structural equation modeling and regression: Guidelines for research practice. *Communications of the AIS, 4*(7), 1–70.

Gelderman, M. (1998). The relation between user satisfaction, usage of information systems and performance. *Information & Management, 34*(1), 11–18.

Gerbing, D. W., & Anderson, J. C. (1988). An updated paradigm for scale development incorporating unidimensionality and its assessment. *Journal of Marketing Research, 25*, 186-192.

Gershuny, J., & Robinson, J. P. (1988). Historical changes in household division of labor. *Demography, 25*, 537-552.

Gerstiner, E., & Holthausen, D. (1986). Profitable pricing when market segments overlap. *Marketing Science, 5*(1), 55–69. doi:10.1287/mksc.5.1.55

Ghosh, B., & Scott, J. E. (2007). Effective knowledge management systems for a clinical nursing setting. *Information Systems Management, 24*, 73–84. doi:10.1080/10580530601038188

Gigerenzer, G., & Goldstein, D. G. (1996). Reasoning the fast and frugal way: Models of bounded rationality. *Psychological Review, 103*, 650–669. doi:10.1037/0033-295X.103.4.650

Gigerenzer, G., & Todd, P. M. (1999). Simple heuristics that make us smart. New York: Oxford University Press.

Girardi, A., Soutar, G., & Ward, S. (2003). Assessing price and ridgeway's use innovateness scale. In *Proceedings of the Australian and New Zealand Academy of Management Conference, Fremantle, Australia* (pp. 1-12).

Gist, M. E., & Mitchell, T. R. (1992). Self-efficacy: a theoretical analysis of its determinants and malleability. *Academy of Management Review, 17*(2), 183–211. doi:10.2307/258770

Glaser, R. (1989). Expertise and learning: How do we think about instructional processes, now that we have discovered knowledge structures? In D. Klahr & K. Kotovsky (Eds.), *Complex information processing: The impact of Herbert A. Simon* (pp. 269–282). Hillsdale, NJ: Lawrence Erlbaum.

Global/world income per capita/head 2004. (2004). Retrieved from http://www.finfacts.com/biz10/globalworldincomepercapita.htm

Gold, A.H., Malhotra, A., & Segars, A.H. (2001). Knowledge management: An organizational capabilities perspective. *Journal of Management Information Systems, 18*(1), 185-214.

Goldberg, L. R. (1999). A broad-bandwidth, public domain, personality inventory measuring the lower-level facets of several five-factor models. In I. Mervielde, I. Deary, F. De Fruyt, & F. Ostendorf (eds.), *Personality psychology in Europe, 7* (pp. 7-28). Tilburg, The Netherlands: Tilburg University Press.

Goldsmith, R. (1990). The validity of a scale to measure global innovativeness. *The Journal of Applied Business Research*, *7*(2), 89–97.

Goldsmith, R., & Hofacker, C. (1991). Measuring consumer innovativeness. *Journal of the Academy of Marketing Science*, *19*(3), 209–221. doi:10.1007/BF02726497

Goldsmith, R., Hofacker, C., & Eastman, J. (1995). The generality/specificity issue in consumer innovativeness research. *Technovation*, *15*(10), 601–612. doi:10.1016/0166-4972(95)99328-D

González, L. M., Giachetti, R. E., & Ramirez, G. (2005). Knowledge management-centric help desk: specification and performance evaluation. *Decision Support Systems*, *40*(2), 389–405. doi:10.1016/j.dss.2004.04.013

Goodhue, D.L., & Thompson, R.L. (1995). Task-technology fit and individual performance. *MIS Quarterly 19*(2), 213-236.

Goodman, P. S., Ravlin, E., & Argote, L. (1986). Current thinking about groups: Setting the stage for new ideas. In P.G.a. Associates (ed.), *Designing effective work groups* (pp. 1-33). San Francisco: Jossey-Bass, Inc.

Goodstein, J.D. (1994). Institutional pressures and strategic responsiveness: Employer involvement in work-family issues. *Academy of Management Journal, 37*(2), 350–382.

Goslar, M. (1987). Marketing and the adoption of microcomputers: An application of diffusion theory. *Journal of the Academy of Marketing Science*, *15*(2), 42–48. doi:10.1007/BF02723401

Gottschalk, P. (2006). Research propositions for knowledge management systems supporting it outsourcing relationships. *Journal of Computer Information Systems*, *46*, 110–116.

Govindarajulu, C. (2002). The status of help desk support: A survey. *Communications of the ACM, 45*(1), 97–100.

Govindarajulu, C., & Reithel, B.J. (1998). Beyond the information center: An instrument to measure end-user computing support from multiple sources. *Information & Management, 33*(5), 241–250.

Govindarajulu, C., Reithel, B.J., & Sethi, V. (2000). A model of end user attitudes and intentions toward alternative sources of support. *Information & Management, 37*(2), 77–86.

Grau, J. (2005). Asia-Pacific e-commerce: Spotlight on China, Japan and South Korea. *eMarketer.com*. http://www.emarketer.com/Report.aspx?ecom_asia_jul05

Gray, P. H., & Durcikova, A. (2005/2006). The role of knowledge repositories in technical support environments: Speed versus learning in user performance. *Journal of Management Information Systems*, *22*, 159–190. doi:10.2753/MIS0742-1222220306

Gray, P.H. (2000). The effects of knowledge management systems on emergent teams: Towards a research model. *Journal of Strategic Information Systems, 9*(2-3), 175-191.

Gray, P.H. (2001). The impact of knowledge repositories on power and control in the workplace. *Information Technology & People, 14*(4), 368-384.

Gray, P.H., & Meister, D.B. (2004). Knowledge sourcing effectiveness. *Management Science, 50*(6), 821-834.

Green, P.E., & Rao, V.R. (1971). Conjoint measurement for quantifying judgmental data. *Journal of Marketing Research, 8*(August), 355–363.

Greenacre, M. (1993). *Correspondence analysis in practice, Boca Raton, Fla.* London: Chapman & Hall/CRC.

Greenwood, R., & Hinings, C.R. (1996). Understanding radical organizational change: Bringing together the old and new institutionalism. *Academy of Management Review, 21*(4), 1022–1054.

Gregg, D. G., & Scott, J. E. (2006). The role of reputation systems in reducing on-line auction fraud. *International Journal of Electronic Commerce*, *10*(3), 95–120. doi:10.2753/JEC1086-4415100304

Grimard, J. (2004). Program evaluation and archives: Appraising archival work and achievements. *Archivaria, 58*(2), 69-88.

Grover, V., & Davenport, T.H. (2001). General perspectives on knowledge management: Fostering a research agenda. *Journal of Management Information Systems, 18*(1), 5-21.

Grundel, C., & Schneider-Hufschmidt, M. (1999). A direct manipulation user interface for the control of communication processes—Making call handling manageable. In H.J. Bullinger & Ziegler, J. (Eds.), *Human-computer interaction: Communication, cooperation, and application design* (pp. 8-13). Mahwah, NJ: Lawrence Erlbaum Associates.

Guimaraes, T. (1999). Empirically testing the relationship between end-user computing problems and information center success factors. *Decision Sciences, 30*(2), 393–413.

Gummerus, J., Liljander, V., Pura, M., & Van Riel, A. (2004). Customer loyalty to content-based Web sites: The case of an online health care service. *Journal of Services Marketing, 18*(3), 175–186.

Gummesson, E. (2000). *Qualitative methods in management research.* London: Sage Publication.

Gupta, A.K., & Govindarajan, V. (2000). Knowledge management's social dimension: Lessons from Nucor Steel. *Sloan Management Review, 42*(1), 71-80.

Guzzo, R. A., & Dickson, M. W. (1996). Teams in organizations: Recent research on performance and effectiveness. In J.T. Spence, J.M. Darley & D.F. Foss (eds.), *Annual Review of Psychology,* (pp. 307-338). Palo Alto, CA: Annual Reviews, Inc.

Haag, S., Cummings, M., & McCubbrey, D.J. (2003). *Management information systems for the information age.* New York: McGraw-Hill/Irwin.

Haas, M. R. (2006). Knowledge gathering, team capabilities, and project performance in challenging work environments. *Management Science, 52,* 1170–1184. doi:10.1287/mnsc.1060.0530

Hackman, J. R., & Morris, C. G. (1975). Group tasks, group interaction process, and group performance effectiveness: A review and proposed integration. In L. Berkowitz (ed.), *Advances in experimental social psychology* (pp. 45-99). New York: Academic Press.

Hackney, R.A., Burn, J., & Salazar, A. (2004). Strategies for value creation in e-markets: Towards a framework for managing evolutionary change. *Journal of Strategic Information Systems, 13*(3), 91–103.

Hair, J., Anderson, R., Tatham, R., & Black, W. (1998). *Multivariate data analysis* (5th ed.) Englewood Cliffs, NJ: Prentice Hall.

Hair, J.F. (1992). *Multivariate data analysis with readings.* New York: Macmillan.

Hair, J.T., Anderson, R.E., Tatham, R.L., & Black, W.C. (1998). Multivariate data analysis (5th ed.). Upper Saddle River, NJ: Prentice Hall.

Halverson, C. A., Erickson, T., & Ackerman, M. S. (2004). Behind the help desk: Evolution of a knowledge management system in a large organization. In *Proceedings of the 2004 ACM Conference on Computer Supported Cooperative Work* (pp. 304-313) (Chicago, Illinois, USA, November 06 - 10, 2004). CSCW '04. New York: ACM.

Hampe, J. F. (1999). Call center: technical and organizational challenges. Human-Computer Interaction: Ergonomics and User Interfaces. In *Proc. of 8th International Conference on Human-Computer Interaction (HCI International'99)* (pp. 1316-1320). Mahwah, NJ: Lawrence Erlbaum Associates.

Han, H., & Ocker, R.M. (2002). Is it worthwhile to target university students? *Decision Line,* (September/October), 18–20.

Hansen, M. T., Nohria, N., & Tierney, T. (1999). What's your strategy for managing knowledge? *Harvard Business Review, 77*(2), 106–116.

Hansen, M., & Haas, M. (2001). Competing for attention in knowledge markets: Electronic document dissemination in a management consulting company. *Administrative Science Quarterly, 46,* 1–28. doi:10.2307/2667123

Hansen, M.T. (2002). Knowledge networks: Explaining effective knowledge sharing in multiunit companies. *Organization Science*, *13*(3), 232-248.

Hansen, M.T., Nohria, N., & Tierney, T. (1999). What's your strategy for managing knowledge? *Harvard Business Review*, *77*(2), 106-116.

Harmon-Jones, E., & Mills, J. (1999). *Cognitive dissonance: Progress on a pivotal theory in social psychology*. Washington, DC: American Psychological Association.

Harr, R., & Wiberg, M. (2008). Lost in translation: Investigating the ambiguity of availability cues in an online media space. *Behaviour & Information Technology*, *27*(3), 243–262. doi:10.1080/01449290600874865

Harris, D. (2004, May). Your favorite icebreakers. *Training (New York, N.Y.)*, 23.

Harris, L.C., & Ogbonna, E. (2002). The unintended consequences of culture interventions: A study of unexpected outcomes. *British Journal of Management*, *13*(1), 31-50.

Harrison, A. W., & Rainer, R. K. (1992). The influence of individual differences on skill in end-user computing. *Journal of Management Information Systems*, *9*(1), 93–111. doi:10.1080/10580539208906858

Hasher, L., & Zacks, R. T. (1979). Automatic and effortful processes in memory. *Journal of Experimental Psychology: General*, *108*, 356-388.

Hasher, L., & Zacks, R. T. (1984). Automatic processing of fundamental information: The case of frequency of occurrence. *American Psychologist*, *39*, 1372-1388.

Hashim, J. (2008). Factors influencing the acceptance of web-based training in Malaysia: Applying the technology acceptance model. *International Journal of Training and Development*, *12*(4), 253–264. doi:10.1111/j.1468-2419.2008.00307.x

Hassebrock, F., Johnson, P.E., Bullemer, P., Fox, P.W., & Moller, J.H. (1993). When less is more: Representative and selective memory in expert problem solving. *American Journal of Psychology*, *106*(2), 155(35).

Hastie, T., Tibshirani, R., & Friedman, J. (2001). *The elements of statistical learning*. Springer-Verlag.

Haworth, D., & Pietron, L.R. (2006). Sarbanes-Oxley: Achieving compliance by starting with ISO 17799. *Information Systems Management*, *23*(1), 73–87.

Help America Vote Act of 2002, Public Law 107-252. (2002, October 29). Retrieved from http://www.electionline.org/site/docs/pdf/hr3295.pl107252.final.pdf

Hendrickson, A.R., Glorfeld, K., & Cronan, T.P. (1994). On the repeated test-retest reliability of the end-user computing satisfaction instrument: A comment. *Decision Sciences*, *25*(4), 655–667.

Hennig-Thurau, T., & Walsh, G. (2003). Electronic word-of-mouth: Motives for consequences of reading customer articulations on the Internet. *International Journal of Electronic Commerce*, *8*(2), 51–74.

Hennig-Thurau, T., Gwinner, K. P., Walsh, G., & Gremler, D. D. (2004). Electronic word-of mouth via consumer-opinion platforms: What motivates consumers to articulate themselves on the Internet? *Journal of Interactive Marketing*, *18*(1), 38–52. doi:10.1002/dir.10073

Hernandez, B., Jimenez, J., & Martin, J. (2008). Extending the technology acceptance model to include the IT decision maker: A study of business management software. *Technovation*, *28*(3), 112–121. doi:10.1016/j.technovation.2007.11.002

Hightower, J., & Borriello, G. (2001). *A survey and taxonomy of location systems for ubiquitous computing*. University of Washington, Department of Computer Science and Engineering.

Hinton, M., & Kaye, R. (1996). Investing in information technology: A lottery? *Management Accounting (London)*, *74*, 52.

Hirschman, E. (1980). Innovativeness, novelty seeking and consumer creativity. *The Journal of Consumer Research*, *7*(3), 283–295. doi:10.1086/208816

Hislop, D. (2002). Mission impossible? Communicating and sharing knowledge via information technology. *Journal of Information Technology*, *17*(3), 165-177.

Hockheiser, H., & Shneiderman, B. (2000). Performance benefits of simultaneous over sequential menus as task complexity increases. *International Journal of Human-Computer Interaction, 12*, 173–192. doi:10.1207/S15327590IJHC1202_2

Hodkinson, C., & Kiel, G. (2003). Understanding Web information search behavior: An exploratory model. *Journal of Organizational and End User Computing, 15*(4), 27–48.

Hoegl, M. G. (2001). Teamwork quality and the success of innovative projects: A theoretical concept and empirical evidence. *Organization Science, 12*(4), 435. doi:10.1287/orsc.12.4.435.10635

Hoffman, D. L., & Novak, T. P. (1996). Marketing in hypermedia computer-mediated environments: Conceptual foundations. *Journal of Marketing, 60*, 50-68.

Hoffman, L. J. (2004, September 15). *Internet voting: Will it spur or corrupt democracy?* Retrieved from http://www.cfp2000.org/papers/hoffman2.pdf

Hofstede, G. (1994). Management scientists are human. *Management Science, 40*(1), 4–13. doi:10.1287/mnsc.40.1.4

Holsapple, C.W., & Joshi, K.D. (2000). An investigation of the factors that influence the management of knowledge in organizations. *Journal of Strategic Information Systems, 9*(2-3), 235-261.

Holsapple, C.W., & Joshi, K.D. (2002). Knowledge management: A three-fold framework.. *The Information Society.*

Homburg, C., & Rudolph, B. (2001). Customer satisfaction in industrial markets: Dimensional and multiple role issues. *Journal of Business Research, 52*(1), 15–33.

Host, B. (2001). The impact on consumer behavior by virtual reality: Survey in the German furniture market. In *Proceedings of the 2001 Experiential E-Commerce Conference*, East Lansing, MI.

Hsu, L. L. (2006). The impact of industrial characteristics and organizational climate on KMS and BIP-Taiwan bioscience industry. *Journal of Computer Information Systems, 46*, 8–17.

Huang, M. J., Chen, M. Y., & Yieh, K. (2007). Comparing with your main competitor: The single most important task of knowledge management performance measurement. *Journal of Information Science, 33*, 416–434. doi:10.1177/0165551506076217

Huang, W., Wei, K., Watson, R. T., & Tan, B. (2003). Supporting virtual team-building with a GSS: An empirical investigation. *Decision Support Systems, 34*(4), 359. doi:10.1016/S0167-9236(02)00009-X

Huber, G. (1991). Organizational learning: The contributing processes and the literatures. *Organization Science, 2*(1), 88-115.

Hurtz, G., & Donovan, J. (2000). Personality and job performance: The Big Five revisited. *The Journal of Applied Psychology, 85*(6), 869. doi:10.1037/0021-9010.85.6.869

IDC. (2004). *U.S. consumer ISP market share.* Retrieved August 8, 2004, from http://www.idc.com/getdoc.jsp?containerId=30731

Implementing electronic voting in the UK. (n.d.). Retrieved from http:// www.odpm.gov.uk/ stellent/groups/odpm_localgov/documents/page/odpm_locgov_605188-01.hcsp#P50_1197)

India election 2004 statistics, facts and figures. (n.d.). Retrieved from http://www.neoncarrot.co.uk/h_aboutindia/india_election_stats.html

International Personality Item Pool. (2001). A scientific collaboratory for the development of advanced measures of personality traits and other individual differences. Retrieved December 12, 2004 from http://ipip.ori.org/

Internet usage and population in Oceania (South Pacific Islands, New Zealand, and Australia Internet users and population statistics). (n.d.). Retrieved from http://www.internetworld stats.com/stats6.htm

Internet usage for the Americas, Internet user statistics and population stats for 51 countries and regions: North America, Central America, South America and

the Caribbean. (n.d.). Retrieved from http://www.internetworldstats.com/stats2.htm

Internet usage in Asia (Internet users & population statistics for 35 countries and regions in Asia). (n.d.). Retrieved from http://www.internetworldstats.com/stats3.htm

Internet usage statistics: The big picture, world Internet users and population stats. (n.d.). Retrieved from http://www.internetworldstats.com/stats.htm

Internet world stats, usage and population statistics: European Union. (n.d.). Retrieved from http://www.internetworldstats.com/europa.htm#ie

ISWorld.net, qualitative research page, Section 7: Glossary. Quantitative, positivist research methods in information systems: Common method bias. (n.d.). Retrieved from http://dstraub.cis.gsu.edu/88/quant/7glossary.asp

Ivancevich, J.M., Duening, T.N., Gilbert, J.A., & Konopaske, R. (2003). Deterring white-collar crime. *Academy of Management Executive, 17*(2), 114–127.

Ives, B., Olson, M.H., & Baroudi, J.J. (1983). The measurement of user information satisfaction. *Communications of the ACM, 26*(10), 785–793.

Iyer, B., Shankaranarayanan, G., & Vvyner, G. (2006). Process coordination requirements: Implications for the design of knowledge management systems. *Journal of Computer Information Systems, 46*, 1–13.

Jacobs, J. A. (1998). Measuring time at work: Are self-reports accurate? *Monthly Labor Review, 121*, 42-53.

Jadad, A. R., & Gagliardi, A. (1998). Rating health information on the Internet: Navigating to knowledge or to Babel? *Journal of the American Medical Association, 279*, 611–614. doi:10.1001/jama.279.8.611

Jamal, A., & Goode, M.M.H. (2001). Consumers and brands: A study of the image of self-image congruence on brand preference and satisfaction. *Marketing Intelligence & Planning, 19*(7), 482–492.

Jarvenpaa, S. (1989). The effect of task and graphical format congruence on information processing strategies and decision making performance. *Management Science, 35*, 285–303. doi:10.1287/mnsc.35.3.285

Jarvenpaa, S.L., & Staples, D.S. (2001). Exploring perceptions of organizational ownership of information and expertise. *Journal of Management Information Systems, 18*(1), 151-183.

Jarvenpaa, S.L., & Todd, P.A. (1996-1997). Consumer reactions to electronic shopping on the World Wide Web. *International Journal of Electronic Commerce, 1*(2), 59–88.

Jarvenpaa, S.L., Dickson, G..W., & DeSanctis, G. (1985). Methodological issues in experimental IS research. *MIS Quarterly, 9*(2), 141–156.

Jasperson, J.S., Carte, T.A., Saunders, C.S., Butler, B.S., Croes, H.J.P., & Zheng, W. (2002). Review: Power and information technology research: A meta-triangulation review. *MIS Quarterly, 26*(4), 397–459.

Jasperson, J.S., Carter, P.E., & Zmud, R.W. (2005). A comprehensive conceptualization of post adoptive behaviors associated with information technology enabled work systems. *Management and Information Science Quarterly, 29*(3), 525-557.

Jennex, M. (2008). Exploring system use as a measure of knowledge management success. *Journal of Organizational and End User Computing, 20*(1), 50–63.

Jennex, M. E., & Olfman, L. (2006). A model of knowledge management success. *International*

Jennex, M.E. (2005). What is knowledge management? *International Journal of Knowledge Management, 1*(4), i-iv.

Jennex, M.E. (2006). Culture, context, and knowledge management. *International Journal of Knowledge Management, 2*(2), i-iv.

Jennex, M.E., & Olfman, L. (2002). Organizational memory/knowledge effects on productivity, a longitudinal study. In *Proceedings of the 35th Hawaii International Conference on System Sciences, HICSS35, IEEE Computer Society*.

Jennex, M.E., & Olfman, L. (2005). Assessing knowledge management success. *International Journal of Knowledge Management, 1*(2), 33-49.

Jennex, M.E., & Olfman, L. (2006). A model of knowledge management success. *International Journal of Knowledge Management, 2*(3), 51-68.

Jennex, M.E., Olfman, L., Pituma, P., & Yong-Tae, P. (1998). An organizational memory information systems success model: An extension of DeLone and McLean's I/S success model. In *Proceedings of the 31st Hawaii International Conference on System Sciences, January, IEEE Computer Society Press.*

Jennex, M.E., Smolnik, S., & Croasdell, D. (2007). Knowledge management success. *International Journal of Knowledge Management, 3*(2), i-iv.

Jensen, M.C. (1993). The modern industrial revolution, exit, and the failure of internal control systems. *Journal of Finance, 48,* 831–880.

Jepperson, R.L. (1991). Institutional effects, and institutionalism. In W.W. Powell & P.J. DiMaggio (Eds.), *The new institutionalism in organizational analysis* (pp. 143–163). Chicago: University of Chicago Press.

Johnson, E.J. (1988). Expertise and decision under uncertainty: performance and process. In M.T.H. Chi, R. Glaser, & M.J. Farr (Eds.), *The nature of expertise.* London: Lawrence Erlbaum.

Johnson, R. D., & Marakas, G. M. (2000). Research report: The role of behavioral modeling and computer skills acquisition-toward refinement of the model. *Information Systems Research, 11*(4), 402–417. doi:10.1287/isre.11.4.402.11869

Johnson, T. J., & Kaye, B. K. (2003). Around the World Wide Web in 80 ways. *Social Science Computer Review, 21,* 304-325.

Johnson-George, C., & Swap, W. C. (1982). Measurement of specific interpersonal trust-construction and validation of a scale to access trust in a specific other. *Journal of Personality and Social Psychology, 43*(12), 1306-1317.

Jones, B. (2000, January). *California Internet task force: A report on the feasibility of Internet voting.* Retrieved from http://www.ss.ca.gov/executive/ivote/final_ report.htm

Jones, M. C., & Price, R. L. (2004). Organizational knowledge sharing in ERP implementation: Lessons from industry. *Journal of Organizational and End User Computing, 16*(1), 21–40.

Jones, N. B., & Kochtanek, T. R. (2004). Success factors in the implementation of a collaborative technology and resulting productivity improvements in a small business: An exploratory study. *Journal of Organizational and End User Computing, 16*(1), 1–20.

Jones, S., Wilikens, M., Morris, P., & Masera, M. (2000). Trust requirements in e-business. *Communications of the ACM, 43*(12), 80-87.

Joreskog, K.G., & Sorbom, D. (1996). *Lisrel 8: User's reference guide.* Chicago: Scientific Software International.

Josang, A., Ismail, R., & Boyd, C. (2007). A survey of trust and reputation systems for online service provision. *Decision Support Systems, 43*(2), 618–644. doi:10.1016/j.dss.2005.05.019

Jurison, J. (2000). Perceived value and technology across four end users groups. *Journal of End User Computing, 12*(4), 21–28.

Kamis, A. (2006). Search strategies in shopping engines: An experimental investigation. *International Journal of Electronic Commerce, 11,* 63–84. doi:10.2753/JEC1086-4415110103

Kamis, A. A., & Stohr, E. A. (2006). Parametric search engines: What makes them effective when shopping online for differentiated products? *Information & Management, 43,* 904–918. doi:10.1016/j.im.2006.08.006

Kanfer, R., & Ackerman, P. L. (1989). Motivation and cognitive abilities: An integrative/aptitude-treatment interaction approach to skill acquisition. *The Journal of Applied Psychology, 74*(4), 657–690. doi:10.1037/0021-9010.74.4.657

Kang, B., Compton, P., & Preston, P. (1995). Multiple classification ripple down rules: evaluation and possibilities. In *Proc. 9th Banff Knowledge Acquisition for Knowledge Based Systems Workshop*. Banff. Feb 26 - March 3 1995, Vol 1: 17.1-17.20.

Kang, B., Yoshida, K., Motoda, H., Compton, P., & Iwayama, M. (1996). A help desk system with intelligent interface. In P. Compton, R. Mizoguchi, H. Motoda & T. Menzies (Eds.), *Pacific Rim Knowledge Acquisition Workshop, (PKAW'96)* (pp. 313-332). Sydney, School of Computer Science and Engineering, UNSW.

Kankanhalli, A., Tan, B.C.Y., & Wei, K.K. (2005). Understanding seeking from electronic knowledge repositories: An empirical study. *Journal of the American Society for Information Science and Technology, 56*(11), 1156-1166.

Kannan, P. K., Chang, A., & Whinston, A. B. (1998). Marketing information on the I-way. *Communications of the ACM, 41*, 35-40.

Kanungo, S., Sadavarti, S., & Srinivas, Y. (2001). Relating IT strategy and organizational culture: An empirical study of public sector units in India. *Journal of Strategic Information Systems, 10*(1), 29-57.

Karahanna, E., & Straub, D. W. (1999). The psychological origins of perceived usefulness and perceived ease-of-use. *Information & Management, 35*, 237-250.

Karau, S., & Hart, J. (1998). Group cohesiveness and social loafing: Effects of a social interaction manipulation on individual motivation within groups. *Group Dynamics, 2*, 185–191. doi:10.1037/1089-2699.2.3.185

Kaser, D.(2004). When all is nothing and something more. *Information Today, 21*(8), 16-17.

Kasper, G.M., & Cerveny, P.C. (1985). A laboratory study of user characteristics and decision-making performance in end-user computing. *Information and Management, 9*(2), 87–96.

Kasulis, J., Lusch, R., & Stafford, E. (1979). Consumer acquisition patterns for durable goods. *The Journal of Consumer Research, 6*(1), 47–55. doi:10.1086/208747

Katerattanakul, P. (2002). Framework of effective Web site design for business-to-consumer Internet commerce. *INFOR, 40*, 57-70.

Katz, E. (1959). Mass communication research and the study of popular culture: An editorial note on a possible future for this journal. *Studies in Public Communication, 2*, 1-6.

Kaye, B. K., & Johnson, T. J. (2002). Online and in the know: Uses and gratifications of the Web for political information. *Journal of Broadcasting & Electronic Media, 46*, 54-71.

Kelloway, E.K. (1998). *Using Lisrel for structural equation modeling: A researcher's guide*. Thousand Oaks, CA: Sage.

Kennes, J., & Schiff, A. (2007). Simple reputation systems. *The Scandinavian Journal of Economics, 109*(1), 71–91. doi:10.1111/j.1467-9442.2007.00481.x

Kerlinger, F. N. (1992). *Foundations of behavioral research*. Orlando, FL: Harcourt Brace & Company.

Kernan, M., & Howard, G. S. (1990). Computer anxiety and computer attitudes: an investigation of construct and predictive validity issues. *Educational and Psychological Measurement, 50*, 681–690. doi:10.1177/0013164490503026

Keser, C. (2003). Experimental games for the design of reputation management systems. *IBM Systems Journal, 42*(3), 498–506.

Khalil, O., & Elkordy, M. (1999). The relationship between user satisfaction and systems usage: Empirical evidence from Egypt. *Journal of End-User Computing, 11*(2), 21–28.

Kiel, G., & Layton, R. (1981). Dimensions of consumer information seeking. *JMR, Journal of Marketing Research, 18*(2), 233–239. doi:10.2307/3150957

Kim, K. (2001). Implications of user characteristics in information seeking on the World Wide Web. *International Journal of Human-Computer Interaction, 13*, 323–340. doi:10.1207/S15327590IJHC1303_3

Kim, M., & Compton, P. (2004). Evolutionary document management and retrieval for specialized domains on the web. *International Journal of Human-Computer Studies*, *60*, 201–241. doi:10.1016/j.ijhcs.2003.10.004

King, J.L. (1983). Centralized versus decentralized computing: Organizational considerations and management options. *Computing Surveys, 15*(4), 319–349.

King, J.L., Gurbaxani, V., Kraemer, K.L., McFarlan, F.W., Raman, K.S., & Yap, C.S. (1994). Institutional factors in information technology innovation. *Information Systems Research, 5*(2), 139–169.

King, W., & He, J. (2006). A meta-analysis of the technology acceptance model. *Information & Management*, *43*(6), 740–755. doi:10.1016/j.im.2006.05.003

Kirlik, A., Walker, N., Fisk, A.D., & Nagel, K. (1996). Supporting perception in the service of dynamic decision making. *Human Factors, 38*(2), 288(12).

Klapper, J. T. (1963). Mass communication research: An old road resurveyed. *Public Opinion Quarterly, 27*, 515-527.

Klein, H.K., & Myers, M.D. (1999). A set of principles for conducting and evaluating interpretive field studies in Information systems. *MIS Quarterly, 23*(1), 67-93.

Klein, K.J., & Sorra, J.S. (1996). The challenge of innovation implementation. *Academy of Management Review, 21*(4), 1055-1080.

Kleinmuntz, D. N., & Schkade, D. A. (1993). Knowledge displays and decision processes. *Psychological Science*, *4*, 221–227. doi:10.1111/j.1467-9280.1993.tb00265.x

Klenke, K. (1992). Construct measurement in management information systems: A review and critique of user satisfaction and user involvement instruments. *INFOR, 30*(4), 325–348.

Kling, R., & Iacono, S. (1984). The control of information systems development after implementation. *Communications of the ACM, 27*(12), 1218–1226.

Knight, M. B. (2005). *An empirical evaluation of groups and the use of technology to communicate*. Unpublished Dissertation.

Knight, M. B., & Pearson, J. M. (2004). Cohesion via technology: Information technology, individual personality and group cohesion. *Decision Science Institute conference* (pp. 5122-5126). Boston.

Knights, M., & Reed, K. (2004). UK PLC dealt Sarbox deadline. *Accountancy Age,* (3), 7–9.

Knowledge Storm. (2007). Search results for knowledge management systems. Retrieved September 4, 2007, from http://www.knowledgestorm.com/SearchServlet?ksAction=Search&col=kslive&rf=0&srchtype=key&stype=&bi=1&ei=0&oq=null&vf=null&tId=&sId=&sSeq=1&regId=&lsTime=null&type=key&kw=knowledge+management+systems&isAdv=false&x=0&y=0)

Kogut, B., & Zander, U. (1996). What do firms do? Coordination, identity, and learning. *Organization Science, 7*(5), 502-518.

Komiak, S.Y.X., Wang, W., & Benbasat, I. (2005). Trust building in virtual salespersons versus in human salespersons: Similarities and differences. *e-Services Journal*, 49-63.

Korgaonkar, P. K., & Wolin, L. D. (1999). A multivariate analysis of Web usage. *Journal of Advertising Research, 38*, 53-68.

Koufaris, M. (2002). Applying the technology acceptance model and flow theory to online consumer behavior. *Information Systems Research, 13*(2), 205–233.

Kourouthanassis, P., & Roussos, G. (2003). Developing consumer-friendly pervasive retail systems. *IEEE Pervasive Computing.*

Kraiger, K., Ford, J. K., & Salas, E. (1993). Application of cognitive, skill-based, and affective theories of learning outcomes to new methods of training evaluation. *The Journal of Applied Psychology, 78*(2), 311–328. doi:10.1037/0021-9010.78.2.311

Kraut, R., Mukhopadhyay, T., Szczypula, J., Kiesler, S., & Scherlis, B. (1999). Information and communication: Alternative uses of the Internet in households. *Information Systems Research, 10*, 287-303.

Krukow, K., Nielsen, M., & Sassone, V. (2008). A logical framework for history-based access control and reputation systems. *Journal of Computer Security, 16*(1), 63–101.

Kulkarni, U. R., Ravindran, S., & Freeze, R. (2006/2007). A knowledge management success model: Theoretical development and empirical validation. *Journal of Management Information Systems*, Winter.

Kumar, N., & Benbasat, I. (2006). The influence of recommendations and consumer reviews on evaluations of Websites. *Information Systems Research, 17*(4), 425–439. doi:10.1287/isre.1060.0107

Kurien, P., Rahman, W., & Purushottam. (2004). The case of re-examining IT effectiveness. *Journal of Business Strategy, 25*(2), 29–36.

Lai, V.S., & Li, H. (2005). Technology acceptance model for internet banking: An invariance analysis. *Information & Management, 42*(2), 373–386.

Langfred, C. W. (1998). Is group cohesiveness a double-edged sword? An investigation of the effects of cohesion on performance. *Small Group Research, 29*(1), 124. doi:10.1177/1046496498291005

Larkin, J.H., McDermott, J., Simon, D.P., & Simon, H.A. (1980). Expert and novice performance in solving physics problems. *Science, 208,* 1335–1342.

Larsen, R., & Ketelaar, T. (1991). Personality and susceptibility to positive and negative emotional states. *Journal of Personality and Social Psychology, 61*(1), 132. doi:10.1037/0022-3514.61.1.132

Lauw, H. W., Ee-Peng, L., & Ke, W. (2008). Bias and Controversy in Evaluation Systems. *IEEE Transactions on Knowledge and Data Engineering, 20*(11), 1490–1504. doi:10.1109/TKDE.2008.77

Lawler, E., Mohrman, S., & Ledford, G. (1992). *Employee involvement and total quality management: Practices and results in Fortune 1000 companies.* San Francisco: Jossey-Bass.

Lazar, J., & Norcio, A. (2003). Training novice users in developing strategies for responding to errors when browsing the web. *International Journal of Human-Computer Interaction, 15,* 361–377. doi:10.1207/S15327590IJHC1503_03

Lazarus, L. (2000). Clinical decision support systems: Background and role in clinical support. Retrieved from http://www.pks.com.au/CDSS_White_Paper_doc.pdf

Leavitt, J., & Walton, J. (1975). Development of a scale for innovativeness. *Advances in Consumer Research. Association for Consumer Research (U. S.), 2,* 545–554.

Leavitt, J., & Walton, J. (1988). *Openness of information processing as a moderator of message effects on behavior.* Working Paper, College of Business Administration, Ohio State University.

Lee, A.S. (1991). Integrating positivist and interpretivist approaches to organizational research. *Organization Science, 2*(4), 342-365.

Lee, C., & Bobko, P. (1994). Self-efficacy beliefs: Comparison of five measures. *The Journal of Applied Psychology, 79*(3), 364–369. doi:10.1037/0021-9010.79.3.364

Lee, C., & Chen, W.J. (2005). The effects of internal marketing and organizational culture on knowledge management in the information technology industry. *International Journal of Management, 22*(4), 661-672.

Lee, D., & Ahn, J. (2007). Reward systems for intra-organizational knowledge sharing. *European Journal of Operational Research, 180,* 938–956. doi:10.1016/j.ejor.2006.03.052

Lee, D.M.S. (1986). Usage patterns and sources of assistance for personal computer users. *MIS Quarterly, 10*(4), 313–325.

Lee, G.-G., & Lin, H.-F. (2005). Customer perceptions of e-service quality in online shopping. *International Journal of Retail & Distribution Management, 33*(2), 161–176.

Lefebvre, E., & Lefebvre, L. (1996). *Information and communication technologies: The impact of their adoption on small and medium-sized enterprises.* Retrieved from http://www.idrc.ca/

Legare, T.L. (1995). Minimizing resistance to technological change. *Information Systems Management, 12*(4), 59.

Leitheiser, R.L., & Wetherbe, J.C. (1986). Approaches to end-user computing: Service may spell success. *Journal of Information Systems Management, 3*(1), 9–14.

Leung, L. (2004). Net-generation attributes and seductive properties of the Internet as predictors of online activities and Internet addiction. *Cyberpsychology & Behavior, 7*(3), 333–348. doi:10.1089/1094931041291303

Levine, H.G., & Rossmoore, D. (1994). Politics and the function of power in a case study of IT implementation. *Journal of Management Information Systems, 11*(3), 115–133.

Levitt, B., & March, J.G. (1998). Organizational learning. *Annual Review of Sociology, 14*, 319-340.

Li, H., Daugherty, T., & Biocca, F. (2001). Characteristics of virtual experience in electronic commerce: A protocol analysis. *Journal of Interactive Marketing, 15*(3), 13-30.

Li, H., Daugherty, T., & Biocca, F. (2002). Impact of 3-D advertising on product knowledge, brand attitude, and purchase intention: The mediating role of presence. *Journal of Advertising, 31*(3), 43-57.

Li, Y., & Kettinger, W. J. (2006). An evolutionary information-processing theory of knowledge creation. *Journal of the Association for Information Systems, 7*, 593–617.

Li, Y., Qi, J., & Shu, H. (2008). Review of relationships among variables in TAM. *Tsinghua Science and Technology, 13*(3), 273–278. doi:10.1016/S1007-0214(08)70044-0

Liang, T., Lai, H., & Ku, Y. (2006/2007). Personalized content recommendation and user satisfaction: Theoretical synthesis and empirical findings. *Journal of Management Information Systems, 23*(3), 45–70. doi:10.2753/MIS0742-1222230303

Liao, Z., & Cheung, M.T. (2002). Internet-based e-banking and consumer attitude: An empirical study. *Information & Management, 39*(4), 283–295.

Liddle, R. J. (1998). Usability testing of a call center application: The importance and necessity of using scenario-driving scripts. In *Proc. of the Silicon Valley Ergonomics Conference and Exposition - ErgoCon '98* (pp. 31-32). Palo Alto, CA.

Lim, H., & Dubinsky, A.J. (2004). Consumers' perception of e-shopping characteristics: An expectancy-value approach. *Journal of Services Marketing, 18*(7), 550–513.

Lin, C. A. (1999). Online service adoption likelihood. *Journal of Advertising Research, 39*, 79-89.

Lindsey, K. (2002). Measuring knowledge management effectiveness: A task-contingent organizational capabilities perspective. In *Eighth Americas Conference on Information Systems* (pp. 2085-2090).

Lippert, S. K. (2001). *An exploratory study into the relevance of trust in the context of information systems technology.* Unpublished doctoral dissertation, George Washington University.

Liptak, A. (2004, November 7). *Voting problems in Ohio set off an alarm.* Retrieved from http://www.nytimes.com/2004/11/07/politics/campaign/07elect.html?ex=1117252800&en=21af6b0293e451c3&ei=5070)

Liu, J., & Issarny, V. (2007). An incentive compatible reputation mechanism for ubiquitous computing environments. *International Journal of Information Security, 6*(5), 297–311. doi:10.1007/s10207-007-0029-7

Liu, S.C., Olfman, L., & Ryan, T. (2005). Knowledge management success: Empirical assessment of a theoretical model. *International Journal of Knowledge Management, 1*(2), 68-87.

Lohse, G. L., & Spiller, P. (1998). Electronic shopping. *Communications of the ACM, 41*, 81-87.

Loiacono, E.T., Watson, R.T., & Goodhue, D.L. (2002). WebQual: A measure of Website quality. *Proceedings of the American Marketing Association: Winter Marketing Educators' Conference.* Austin, Texas, 432–438.

Loyd, B. H., & Gressard, C. (1984). Reliability and factorial validity of computer attitude scales. *Educational and Psychological Measurement*, *44*, 501–505. doi:10.1177/0013164484442033

Lu, M.T., & Yeung, W.L. (1998). A framework for effective commercial Web application development. *Internet Research: Electronic Networking Applications and Policy*, *8*(2), 166–173.

Lu, Y., Zhou, T., & Wang, B. (2009). Exploring Chinese users' acceptance of instant messaging using the theory of planned behaviour, the technology acceptance model, and the flow theory. *Computers in Human Behavior*, *25*(1), 29–39. doi:10.1016/j.chb.2008.06.002

Lucas, L.M., & Ogilvie, D. (2006). Things are not always what they seem: How reputations, culture, and incentives influence knowledge transfer. *The Learning Organization*, *13*(1), 7-24.

Luce, D.R., & Tukey, J.W. (1964). Simultaneous conjoint measurement: A new type of fundamental measurement. *Journal of Mathematical Psychology*, *1*(February), 1–27.

Lueg, J. E., Moore, R. S., & Warkentin, M. (2003). Patient health information search: An exploratory model of Web-based search behavior. *Journal of Organizational and End User Computing*, *15*(4), 49–61.

MacCormack, A., & Volpel, S. (2002). *Siemens ShareNet: Building a knowledge network*. Boston: Harvard Business School Publishing.

Macintosh, G., & Lockshin, L.S. (1997). Retail relationships and store loyalty: A multi-level perspective. *International Journal of Research in Marketing*, *14*(5), 487–497.

Mackay, J. M., & Elam, J. J. (1992). A comparative study of how experts and novices use a decision aid to solve problems in complex knowledge domains. *Information Systems Research*, *3*(2), 150–172. doi:10.1287/isre.3.2.150

Mackay, W. E. (1996). *Augmenting reality: A new paradigm for interacting with computers*. Orsay Cedex, France.

Maheswaran, D., Sternthal, B., & Gurhan, Z. (1996). Acquisition and impact of consumer expertise. *Journal of Consumer Psychology*, *5*(2), 115–133.

Maier, N. R. F., & Thurber, J. A. (1968). Accuracy of judgments of deception when an interview is watched, heard, and read. *Personnel Psychology*, *21*, 23–30. doi:10.1111/j.1744-6570.1968.tb02283.x

Maitland, A. (2004). BT chairman criticises US governance. *Financial Times*, *22*(1).

Mann, S., & Fung, J. (2001). VideoOrbits on eye tap devices for deliberately diminished reality or altering the visual perception of rigid planar patches of a real world scene. In *International Symposium on Mixed Reality (ISMR2001)*.

Mao, J., & Benbasat, I. (2000). The use of explanations in knowledge-based systems: Cognitive perspective and a process-tracing analysis. *Journal of Management Information Systems*, *17*, 153–180.

Marakas, G. M., Yi, M. Y., & Johnson, R. D. (1998). The multilevel and multifaceted character of computer self-efficacy: Toward clarification of the construct and an integrative framework for research. *Information Systems Research*, *9*(2), 126–163. doi:10.1287/isre.9.2.126

Marcolin, B. L., Compeau, D. R., Munro, M. C., & Huff, S. L. (2000). Assessing user competence; conceptualization and measurement. *Information Systems Research*, *11*(1), 37–60. doi:10.1287/isre.11.1.37.11782

Mark, K.M., & Darren. (2004). *Hill & Knowlton: Knowledge management*. London: Ivey Management Services.

Markus, L.M. (2001). Toward a theory of knowledge reuse: Types of knowledge reuse situations and factors in reuse success. *Journal of Management Information Systems*, *18*(1), 57-94.

Markus, M.L. (1983). Power, politics, and MIS implementation. *Communications of the ACM*, *26*(6), 430-444.

Markus, M.L., & Benjamin, R.I. (1996). Change agentry: The next IS frontier. *MIS Quarterly*, *20*(4), 385–407.

Markus, M.L., & Keil, M. (1994, summer). If we build it, they will come: Designing information systems that people want to use. *Sloan Management Review*, 11-25.

Marsh, H.W., & Hocevar, D. (1985). Application of confirmatory factory analysis to the study of self-concept: First-and higher-order factor models and their invariance across groups. *Psychological Bulletin, 97*(3), 562–582.

Marshall, D.P. (2002). Solving accounting problems: Differences between accounting experts and novices. *Journal of Education for Business, 77*(6), 325–329.

Massey, A.P., Montoya-Weiss, M.M., & O'Driscoll, T.M. (2002). Knowledge management in pursuit of performance: Insights from Nortel Networks. *MIS Quarterly, 26*(3), 269-289.

Matthews, D., & Schrum, L. (2003). High-speed Internet use and academic gratifications in the college residence. *The Internet and Higher Education, 6*, 125-144.

Mauri, C. (2003). Card loyalty: A new emerging issue in grocery retailing. *Journal of Retailing and Consumer Services, 10*(1), 13-25.

Mayer, A.F. (2003). Preparing for Basel II by optimizing Sarbanes-Oxley. *Journal of Bank Cost & Management Accounting, 16*(3), 27(7).

Mayer, R. N., Huh, J., & Cude, B. J. (2005). Cues of credibility and price performance of life insurance comparison Web sites. *The Journal of Consumer Affairs, 39*(1), 71–94.

McDermott, R. (1999). Why information technology inspired but cannot deliver knowledge management. *California Management Review, 41*(4), 103-117.

McDonald-Russell, D. E. (2002). *Profiling music consumers for viral marketing purposes: A test of the efficacy of combining uses and gratifications theory with the diffusion of innovation model.* Unpublished doctoral dissertation, University of Missouri, Columbia.

McFarlan, F.W., & McKenney, J.L. (1983). The information archipelago: Governing the new world. *Harvard Business Review, 61*(4), 91–99.

McGrath, G., & Schneider, A. (2000). Measuring intranet return on investment. Retrieved November 15, 2004 from http://intrack.com/intranet/ireturn.shtml

McGrath, J. (1964). *Social psychology: A brief introduction.* New York: Holt.

McGuire, W. J. (1974). Psychological motives and communication gratification. In J. Blumler & E. Katz (Eds.), *The uses of mass communications: Current perspectives on gratifications research.* Beverly Hills, CA: Sage Publications.

McHaney, R., & Cronan, T.P. (1998). Computer simulation success: On the use of the end-user computing satisfaction instrument: a comment. *Decision Sciences, 29*(2), 525–534.

McHaney, R., & Cronan, T.P. (2001). A comparison of surrogate success measures in on-going representational decision support systems: An extension to simulation technology. *Journal of End User Computing, 13*(2), 15–25.

McHaney, R., Hightower, R., & Pearson, J. (2002). A validation of the end-user computing satisfaction instrument in Taiwan. *Information & Management, 39*(6), 503–511.

McHaney, R., Hightower, R., & White, D. (1999). EUCS test-retest reliability in representational model decision support systems. *Information & Management, 36*(2), 109–119.

McInerney, C. (2002). Knowledge management and the dynamic nature of knowledge. *Journal of the American Society for Information Science and Technology, 53*(12), 1009-1018.

McKinney, V., Yoon, K., & Zahedi, F. (2002). The measurement of Web-customer satisfaction: An expectation and disconfirmation approach. *Information Systems Research, 13*(3), 296–315.

McLean, E.R. (1979). End users as application developers. *MIS Quarterly, 3*(4), 37–46.

McWhinney, W. (1992). *Paths of change: Strategic choices for organizations and society.* Newbury Park, CA: Sage.

Melling, W.P. (1994). Enterprise information architectures: They are finally changing. *Proceedings of ACM SIGMOD,* Minneapolis, MN.

Melnik, M. I., & Alm, J. (2002). Does a seller's e-commerce reputation matter? Evidence from eBay auctions. *The Journal of Industrial Economics, 50*(3), 337–349.

Mershon, B., & Gorsuch, R. L. (1988). Number of factors in the personality sphere: Does increase in factors increase predictability of real-life criteria? *Journal of Personality and Social Psychology, 55,* 675–680. doi:10.1037/0022-3514.55.4.675

Meyer, G. J., & Shack, J. R. (1989). Structural convergence of mood and personality: Evidence for old and new directions. *Journal of Personality and Social Psychology, 57*(4), 691. doi:10.1037/0022-3514.57.4.691

Meyer, J.W., & Rowan, B. (1977). Institutional organizations: Formal structures as myth and ceremony. *American Journal of Sociology, 83,* 340–363.

Michailova, S., & Husted, K. (2003). Knowledge-sharing hostility in Russian firms. *California Management Review, 45*(3), 59-77.

Microsoft Corporation. (2003). [On-line].http://office.microsoft.com/ marketplace/default.aspx?

Midgley, D. (1976). A simple mathematical theory of innovative behavior. *The Journal of Consumer Research, 3*(1), 31–41. doi:10.1086/208648

Midgley, D., & Dowling, G. (1978). Innovativeness: the concept and its measurement. *The Journal of Consumer Research, 4*(4), 229–242. doi:10.1086/208701

Midgley, D., & Dowling, G. (1993). A longitudinal study of product form innovation: The interaction between predispositions and social messages. *The Journal of Consumer Research, 19*(4), 611–625. doi:10.1086/209326

Miles, M. B., & Huberman, A. M. (1984). *Qualitative data analysis: A sourcebook of new methods.* Newbury Park, CA: Sage Publications.

Milgram, P., & Kishino, F. (1994). A taxonomy of mixed reality visual displays. *IEICE Transactions on Information Systems, E77-D*(12).

Miller, G. A. (1956). The magical number seven, plus or minus two: Some limits on our capacity of processing information. *Psychological Review, 63,* 81–97. doi:10.1037/h0043158

Mills, J. (2004). Faceted classification and logical division in information retrieval. *Library Trends, 52*(3), 541-571.

Mirani, R., & King, W.R. (1994). The development of a measure for end-user computing support. *Decision Sciences, 25*(4), 481–498.

Mitchell, W. S. (1999). *Social and psychological factors associated with Internet use in the home: A uses and gratifications study.* Unpublished doctoral dissertation, Bowling Green State University, Bowling Green, OH.

Mithas, S., Ramasubbu, N., Krishnan, M. S., & Fornell, C. (2007). Designing web sites for customer loyalty across business domains: A multilevel analysis. *Journal of Management Information Systems, 23*(3), 97–127. doi:10.2753/MIS0742-1222230305

Money, W., & Turner, A. (2005). Assessing knowledge management system user acceptance with the technology acceptance model. *International Journal of Knowledge Management, 1*(1), 8-26.

Moody, S. A. (2002). *Public radio on the Web: A uses and gratifications analysis.* Unpublished doctoral dissertation, University of Nevada, Reno.

Moran, T. P. (1994). Special issue on context in design. *Human-Computer Interaction, 9,* 1–149. doi:10.1207/s15327051hci0901_1

Mudd, S. (1990). The place of innovativeness in models of the adoption process: An integrative review. *Technovation, 10*(2), 119–136. doi:10.1016/0166-4972(90)90032-F

Mukund, A. (2002). CRM/KM Initiatives at 3M. Case. *ICFAI Center for Management Research (ICMR),* India.

Munro, M. C., Huff, S. L., Marcolin, B. L., & Compeau, D. R. (1997). Understanding and measuring user competence. *Information & Management, 33,* 45–57. doi:10.1016/S0378-7206(97)00035-9

Murch, R. (2001). *Project management: Best practice for IT professionals.* Upper Saddle River, NJ: Prentice Hall.

Murdack, G. (1989). Defining group cohesiveness: A legacy of confusion? *Small Group Behavior, 20,* 37–49. doi:10.1177/104649648902000103

Myers, M.D. (1994). A disaster for everyone to see: An interpretive analysis of a failed IS project. *Accounting, Management, and Information Technologies, 4*(4), 185-201.

National Science Foundation Internet voting workshop report. (2001, March). Retrieved from http://lorrie.cranor.org/voting/ipi-voting-report.pdf

Netemeyer, R. G., Bearden, W. O., & Sharma, S. (2003). *Scaling procedures: Issues and applications.* Thousand Oaks, CA: Sage Publications.

Neumann, P. G. (1990). Risks in computerized elections. *Communications of the ACM, 33*(11), 170.

Neumann, P. G. (2004). The problems and potentials of voting systems. *Communications of the ACM, 47*(10), 28-30.

Nevo, D., & Chan, Y. E. (2007). A Delphi study of knowledge management systems: Scope and requirements. *Information & Management, 44,* 583–597. doi:10.1016/j.im.2007.06.001

Nevo, D., Benbasat, I., & Wand, Y. (2003). Exploring meta-knowledge for knowledge management systems: A Delphi study. In *Proceedings of the International Conference on Information Systems (Seattle, Washington)* (pp. 439-449).

Newell, A., & Simon, H. A. (1972). Human problem solving. Englewood Cliffs, NJ: Prentice Hall.

Newell, S., Huang, J.C., Galliers, R.D., & Pan, S-L. (2003). Implementing enterprise resource planning and knowledge management systems in tandem: Fostering efficiency and innovation complimentarity. *Information and Organization, 13*(1), 25-52.

Newhagen, J., & Rafaeli, S. (1996). Why communication researchers should study the Internet: A dialogue. *Journal of Communication, 46,* 4-13.

Nezlek, G.S., Jain, H.K., & Nazareth, D.L. (1999). An integrated approach to enterprise computing environments. *Communications of the ACM, 42*(11), 82–90.

Nicholson, M., Clarke, I., & Blakemore, M. (2002). One brand, three ways to shop: Situational variables and multichannel consumer behavior. *International Review of Retail, Distribution and Consumer Research, 12*(2), 131–148.

Nieh, J., Yang, S.J., & Novik, N. (2000). *A comparison of thin client computing architectures.* CUCS-022-00, Columbia University, USA.

Nielsen, J. (1998). The reputation manager. Alertbox. Retrieved from http://www.useit.com/alertbox/980208.html.

Nielsen, J. (1999). Reputation managers are happening. Alertbox. Retrieved from http://www.useit.com/alertbox/990905.html.

Nieva, V., Fleishman, E., & Rieck, A. (1978). *Team dimensions: Their identity, their measurement, and their relationships* (Report No. DAHC19-78-C-0001). Washington, D.C: Advanced Research Resources Organizations.

Nikolaeva, R., & Sriram, S. (2006). The moderating role of consumer and product characteristics on the value of customized on-line recommendations. *International Journal of Electronic Commerce, 11*(2), 101–123. doi:10.2753/JEC1086-4415110205

Nisbett, R. E., & Wilson, T. D. (1977). Telling more than we can know: Verbal reports on mental processes. *Psychological Review, 84,* 231-259.

Nissen, M. E. (2005/2006). Dynamic knowledge patterns to inform design: A field study of knowledge stocks and flows in an extreme organization. *Journal of Management Information Systems, 22,* 225–263. doi:10.2753/MIS0742-1222220308

Nonaka, I., & Konno, N. (1998) The concept of "Ba": Building a foundation for knowledge creation. *California Management Review, 40*(3), 40-54.

Nonaka, I., & Takeuchi, H. (1995). *The knowledge-creating company.* New York: Oxford University Press.

Nord, G.D., & Nord, J.H. (1994). Perceptions and attitudes of end users on technology issues. *Journal of System Management, 45*(11), 12–15.

Nordheim, S., & Paivarinta, T. (2006). Implementing enterprise content management: From evolution through strategy to contradictions out-of-the-box. *European Journal of Information Systems, 15*, 648–662. doi:10.1057/palgrave.ejis.3000647

Nunnally, J.C. (1978). *Psychometric theory.* New York: McGraw-Hill.

Nunnally, J.C., & Bernstein, I.H. (1994). *Psychometric theory.* New York: McGraw-Hill.

O'Cass, A., & Fenech, T. (2003). Web retailing adoption: Exploring the nature of Internet users Web retailing behaviour. *Journal of Retailing and Consumer Services, 10*(2), 81–94.

Oliver, C. (1991). Strategic responses to institutional processes. *Academy of Management Review, 16*(1), 145–179.

Oliver, R.L. (1999). Whence customer loyalty? *Journal of Marketing, 63*(4), 33–44.

Olivera, F., Goodman, P. S., & Tan, S. S. L. (2008). Contribution behaviors in distributed environments. *MIS Quarterly, 32*, 23–42.

Ooms-Piepers, M., & Degens, R.M.I. (2004). SOX 404 business en tool alignment. *Compact KPMG, 31*(4), 26–33.

Oravec, J. A. (2005). Preventing e-voting hazards: The role of information professionals. *Journal of Organizational and End User Computing, 17*(4), i-iv.

Orlikowski, W. (2000). Using technology and constituting structures: A practice lens for studying technology in organizations. *Organization Science, 11*, 404–428. doi:10.1287/orsc.11.4.404.14600

Orlikowski, W.J. (1993). CASE tools as organizational change: Investigating incremental and radical changes in systems development. *MIS Quarterly, 17*(3), 309-340.

Orlikowski, W.J., & Baroudi, J.J. (1991). Studying information technology in organizations: Research approaches and assumptions. *Information Systems Research, 2*(1), 1–28.

Ornstein, N., & Schenkenberg, A. (1996). The promise and perils of cyber democracy. *The American Enterprise, 7*(2), 53.

Owen, C. B., Xiao, F., & Middlin, P. (2002). What is the best fiducial? In *The First IEEE International Augmented Reality Toolkit Workshop*, Darmstadt, Germany.

Owen, C. B., Zhou, J., Tang, K. H., & Xiao, F. (2003). Augmented imagery for digital video applications. In *CRC handbook of video databases.* CRC Press LLC.

Pajares, F. (1996). *Assessing self-efficacy beliefs and academic outcomes: The case for specificity and correspondence.* Paper presented at the annual meeting of the American Educational Research Association, New York.

Palanisamy, R. (2007). Organizational culture and knowledge management in ERP implementation: An empirical study. *Journal of Computer Information Systems, 48*, 100–120.

Palmer, J.W. (2002). Web site usability, design, and performance metrics. *Information Systems Research, 13*(2), 151–167.

Papacharissi, A., & Rubin, A. M. (2000). Predictors of Internet use. *Journal of Broadcasting & Electronic Media, 44*, 175-196.

Parasuram, A., & Grewal, D. (2000). The impact of technology on the quality-value-loyalty chain: A research agenda. *Journal of the Academy of Marketing Science, 28*(1), 168–175. doi:10.1177/0092070300281015

Parasuraman, A., Zeithaml, V., & Malhotra, A. (2005). E-S-QUAL: A multiple-item scale for assessing electronic service quality. *Journal of Services Research, 7*(3), 213–233.

Park, C.-H., & Kim, Y.-G. (2003). Identifying key factors affecting consumer purchase behavior in an online shopping context. *International Journal of Retail & Distribution Management, 31*(1), 16–29.

Park, J., & Kim, J. (2000). Contextual navigation aids for two World Wide Web systems. *International Journal of Human-Computer Interaction, 12*, 193–217. doi:10.1207/S15327590IJHC1202_3

Park, W., Feick, L., & Mothersbaugh, D. (1992). Consumer knowledge assessment: How product experience and knowledge of brands, attributes, and features affect what we think. *Advances in Consumer Research. Association for Consumer Research (U. S.), 19*, 193–198.

Parousch, J. (1965). The order of acquisition of consumer durables. *Econometrika, 33*(1), 225–234. doi:10.2307/1911897

Paul, D. L. (2006). Collaborative activities in virtual settings: A knowledge management perspective of telemedicine. *Journal of Management Information Systems, 22*, 143–176. doi:10.2753/MIS0742-1222220406

Pavlou, P. A., & Dimoka, A. (2006). The nature and role of feedback text comments in online marketplaces: Implications for trust building, price premiums, and seller differentiation. *Information Systems Research, 17*(4), 392–414. doi:10.1287/isre.1060.0106

Payne, J. E., Bettman, J. R., & Johnson, E. J. (1993). The adaptive decision maker. New York: Cambridge University Press.

Payne, J. W. (1982). Contingent decision behavior. *Psychological Bulletin, 92*, 382–402. doi:10.1037/0033-2909.92.2.382

Payne, J. W., Bettman, J. R., & Johnson, E. J. (1993). *The adaptive decision maker.* Cambridge, UK: Cambridge University Press.

Pentland, B.T. (1995). Information systems and organizational learning: The social epistemology of organizational knowledge systems. *Accounting, Management, and Information Technologies, 5*(1), 1-21.

Perry, M., & Bodkin, C. (2000). Content analysis of Fortune 100 company Web sites. *Corporate Communications, 5*(2), 87–96.

Perse, E.M., & Courtright, J.A. (1993). Normative images of communication media: Mass and interpersonal channels in the new media environment. *Human Communication Research, 19*(4), 485–503.

Pfeffer, J. (1981). *Power in organizations.* Marshfield, MA: Pitman.

Phillips, D. M., & Von Spakovsky, H. A. (2001). Gauging the risks of Internet elections. *Communications of the ACM, 44*(1), 73-85.

PITAC. (1999). *Information technology research: Investing in our future.* Retrieved November 15, 2004 from http://www.itrd.gov/pitac/report/

Polanyi, M. (1966). *The tacit dimension.* New York: Anchor Day Books.

Polyorat, K., & Alden, D. L. (2005). Self-construal and need-for-cognition effects on brand attitudes and purchase intentions in response to comparative advertising in Thailand and the United States. *Journal of Advertising, 34*(1), 37–48.

Poston, R. S., & Speier, C. (2005). Effective use of knowledge management systems: A process model of content ratings and credibility indicators. *MIS Quarterly, 29*(2), 221–244.

Poston, R., & Speier, C. (2008). Knowledge Management Systems Usage: Rating Scheme Validity and the Effort-Accuracy Trade-Off. *Journal of Organizational and End User Computing, 20*(1), 1–16.

Price, L., & Ridgway, N. (1983). Development of scale to measure use innovativeness. *Advances in Consumer Research. Association for Consumer Research (U. S.), 10*, 681–682.

Prieto, I. M., & Easterby, S. M. (2006). Dynamic capabilities and the role of organizational knowledge: An exploration. *European Journal of Information Systems, 15*, 500–510. doi:10.1057/palgrave.ejis.3000642

Quall, J.C. (2004). Implementing Section 404: A practical approach to the Sarbanes-Oxley Act. *CPA Journal, 74*(8), 52.

Raestrup, B. (2002). Call center agent network—A strategy against 'Cubicalization': A virtual community for call-center workers in the information industry. In H. Luczak, E. Cakir & G. Cakir (eds.), *Ergonomic Institut fur Arbeits- und Sozialforschung* (pp. 256-258). Forschungsgesellschaft mbH, Berlin.

Rafaeli, S. (1988). Interactivity: From new media to communication. In R. Hawkins, J. Wieman, & S. Pingree (Eds.), *Advancing communication science: Merging mass and interpersonal processes.* Newberry Park, CA: Sage Publications.

Rai, A., Lang, S., & Welker, R. (2002). Assessing the validity of IS success models: An empirical test and theoretical analysis. *Information Systems Research, 13*(1), 50-69.

Rai, A., Ravichandran, T., & Samaddar, S. (1998). How to anticipate the Internet's global diffusion. *Communications of the ACM, 41*, 97-106.

Rainer, K., & Carr, H. (1992). Are information centers responsive to user needs? *Information and Management, 22*(2), 113–121.

Rainer, R. K., & Harrison, A. W. (1993). Toward development of the end user computing construct in a university setting. *Decision Sciences, 24*(6), 1187–1202. doi:10.1111/j.1540-5915.1993.tb00510.x

Ram, S., & Jung, H. (1994). Innovativeness in product usage: A comparison of early adopters and early majority. *Psychology and Marketing, 11*(1), 57–67. doi:10.1002/mar.4220110107

Randel, J.M., & Pugh, H.L. (1996). Differences in expert and novice situation awareness in naturalistic decision making. *International Journal of Human Computer Studies, 45*, 579–597.

Ranganathan, C., & Ganapathy, S. (2002). Key dimensions of business-to-consumer Web sites. *Information & Management, 39*(6), 457–465.

Rao, A., & Monroe, K. (1988). The moderating effect of prior knowledge on cue utilization in product evaluations. *The Journal of Consumer Research, 15*(2), 253–264. doi:10.1086/209162

Rasmussen, H. S., & Haggerty, N. (2008). Knowledge appraisal and knowledge management systems: Judging what we know. *Journal of Organizational and End User Computing, 20*(1), 17–34.

Rauterberg, M., Mauch, T., & Stebler, R. (1996). The digital playing desk: A case study for augmented reality. In *Fifth IEEE International Workshop on Robot and Human Communication*, Tsukuba, Japan.

Ravishankar, M. N. (2008). Rewarding end-users for participating in organisational KM: A case study. *Journal of Organizational and End User Computing, 20*(1), 35–49.

Rekimoto, J., & Nagao, K. (1995). The world through the computer: Computer augmented interaction with real world environments. In *Symposium on User Interface Software and Technology (UIST'95).* ACM Press.

Rempel, M., & Fisher, R. (1997). Perceived threat, cohesion, and group problem solving in intergroup conflict. *The International Journal of Conflict Management, 8*(3), 216. doi:10.1108/eb022796

Resnick, M. L., & Montania, R. (2003). Perceptions of customer service, information privacy, and product quality from semiotic design features in an online web store. *International Journal of Human-Computer Interaction, 16*, 211–234. doi:10.1207/S15327590IJHC1602_05

Resnick, P., Zeckhauser, R., Friedman, E., & Kuwabara, K. (2000). Reputation systems. *Communications of the ACM, 43*(12), 45–48. doi:10.1145/355112.355122

Ribbink, D., van Riel, A.C.R., Liljander, V., & Streukens, S. (2004). Comfort your online customer: Quality, trust, and loyalty on the Internet. *Managing Service Quality, 14*(6), 446–456.

Rice, R., & Monkarsh, W. (1979). Time-phased interrelationships of group atmosphere, group performance, and leader style. *The Journal of Applied Psychology, 64*(4), 401. doi:10.1037/0021-9010.64.4.401

Richards, D. (2000). The reuse of knowledge: A user-centered approach. *International Journal of Human-Computer Studies, 52*(3), 553–579. doi:10.1006/ijhc.1999.0342

Richards, D., & Vazey, M. (2005). Closing the Gap Between Different Knowledge Sources and Types in the Call center. *Proc. Australian Conference in Information Systems (ACIS 2005)*, November 2005, Sydney, Australia.

Rivard, S., & Huff, S.L. (1984). User developed applications: Evaluation of success from the DP department perspective. *MIS Quarterly, 8*(1), 39–49.

Robey, D., & Boudreau, M.C. (1999). Accounting for the contradictory organizational consequences of information technology: Theoretical directions and methodological implications. *Information Systems Research, 10*(2), 167–185.

Robey, D., & Markus, M.L. (1984). Rituals in information system design. *MIS Quarterly, 8*(1), 5–15.

Robinson, T. T., & Carron, A. V. (1982). Personal and situational factors associated with dropping out versus maintaining participation in competitive sports. *Journal of Sport Psychology, 4*, 364–378.

Rockart, J.F., & Flannery, L.S. (1983). The management of end-user computing. *Communications of the ACM, 26*(10), 776–784.

Rodgers, E. (1958). Catgorizing the adopters of agricultural practices. *Rural Sociology, 23*(4), 346–354.

Rodgers, E. (1995). *Diffusion of innovations* (4th Ed.). New York: The Free Press.

Rogers, E. M., & Albritton, M. M. (1995). Interactive communication technologies in business organizations. *Journal of Business Communication, 32*, 177-195.

Romm, T., Pliskin, N., Weber, Y., & Lee, A. (1991). Identifying organizational culture clash in MIS implementation. *Information Management, 21*(2), 99-109.

Rone, J., & Berman, A. (2004). Musing on post-Enron reforms. *Journal of Accounting, Auditing and Finance, 19*(3), 331–342.

Rosenau, M. D. (1998). Successful project management: A step-by-step approach with practical examples. New York: John Wiley and Sons.

Rosenholtz, R., Li, Y., Mansfield, J., & Jin, Z. (2005). Feature congestion: A measure of display clutter. In *Proceedings of the SIGCHI Conference on Human Factors in Computing Systems*, Portland, OR.

Rubin, A. M. (1985). Uses and gratifications: Quasi-functional analysis. In J. Dominick & J. Fletcher (Eds.), *Broadcasting research methods.* Boston: Allyn & Bacon.

Ruggiero, T. E. (2000). Uses and gratifications theory in the 21st century. *Mass Communication & Society, 3*, 3-37.

Ruggles, R. (1998). The state of the notion: Knowledge management in practice. *California Management Review, 40*(3), 80-89.

Ruppel, C., & Harrington, S. (2001). Sharing knowledge through intranets. *IEEE Transactions on Professional Communication, 44*(1), 37-52.

Ruthven, I., Lalmas, M., & van Rijsbergen, K. (2003). Incorporating user search behavior into relevance feedback. *Journal of the American Society for Information Science and Technology, 54*, 529–539. doi:10.1002/asi.10240

Sabater, J. (2004). Evaluating the ReGreT system. *Applied Artificial Intelligence, 18*, 797–813. doi:10.1080/08839510490509027

Sabherwal, R., & Becerra-Fernandez, I. (2003). An empirical study of the effect of knowledge management processes at individual, group, and organizational levels. *Decision Sciences, 24*(2), 225-260.

Sabherwal, R., & King, W.R. (1992). Decision processes for developing strategic applications of information systems: A contingency approach. *Decision Sciences, 23*(4), 917–943.

Sacchi, S., & Burigo, M. (2008). Strategies in the information search process: Interaction among task structure, knowledge, and source. *The Journal of General Psychology, 135*, 252–270. doi:10.3200/GENP.135.3.252-270

Santos, J. (2003). E-service quality: A model of virtual service quality dimensions. *Managing Service Quality, 13*(3), 233–246.

Sarbaugh-Thompson, M., & Feldman, M. (1998). Electronic mail and organizational communication: Does saying "hi" really matter? *Organization Science*, *9*(6), 685–69. doi:10.1287/orsc.9.6.685

Sarvary, M. (1999). Knowledge management and competition in the consulting industry. *California Management Review, 41*(2), 95-107.

Saunders, C.S. (1981). Management information systems, communications, and departmental power: An integrative model. *Academy of Management Review, 6*(3), 431–442.

Savloainen, R. (1999). The role of the Internet in information seeking: Putting the networked services in context. *Information Processing & Management, 35*, 765-782.

Schaupp, L.C., & Belanger, F. (2005). A conjoint analysis of online consumer satisfaction. *Journal of Electronic Commerce Research, 6*(2), 95–111.

Schenk, K.D., Vitalri, N.P., & Davis, K.S. (1998). Differences between novice and expert systems analysts: What do we know and what do we do? *Journal of MIS, 15*(1), 9–50.

Schmidt, H. W., & Wegner, L. M. (2000). Shared XML documents in service centers of the future. In *Proc. of the 1st Int.l Conf. on Web Information Systems Engineering (Workshops)* (105-112). IEEE Comput. Soc, Los Alamitos, CA.

Schmitt, N. (1994). Method bias: The importance of theory and measurement. *Journal of Organizational Behavior, 15*(5), 393-398.

Schreier, M., Oberhauser, S., & Prügl, R. (2007). Lead users and the adoption and diffusion of new products: Insights from two extreme sports communities. *Marketing Letters, 18*(1-2), 15–30. doi:10.1007/s11002-006-9009-3

Schultze, U., & Boland Jr., R.J. (2000). Knowledge management technology and the reproduction of knowledge work practices. *Journal of Strategic Information Systems, 9*(2-3), 193-212.

Scott, W.R. (1987). The adolescence of institutional theory. *Administrative Science Quarterly, 32*(4), 493–511.

Seddon, P.B. (1997). A respecification and extension of the DeLone and McLean model of IS success. *Information Systems Research, 8*(3), 240-253.

Sengupta, J., Goodstein, R. C., & Boninger, D. S. (1997). All cues are not created equal: Obtaining attitude persistence under low-involvement conditions. *The Journal of Consumer Research*, *23*(1), 351–361. doi:10.1086/209488

Shanteau, J. (1988). Psychological characteristics and strategies of expert decision makers. *Acta Psychologica, 68*, 203–215.

Shanteau, J. (1992). Competence in experts: The role of task characteristics. *Organizational Behavior and Human Decision Processes, 53*, 252–266.

Shayo, C., Guthrie, R., & Igbaria, M. (1999). Exploring the measurement of end-user computing success. *Journal of End-User Computing, 11*(1), 5–14.

Shim, J.P., Shin, Y.B., & Nottingham, L. (2002). Retailer Web site influence on customer shopping: An exploratory study on key factors of customer satisfaction. *Journal of the Association for Information Systems, 3*, 53–76.

Shim, S., & Eastlick, M.A. (1998). The hierarchical influence of personal values on mall shopping attitude and behavior. *Journal of Retailing, 74*(1), 139–160.

Shiu, E.C.-C., & Dawson, J.A. (2002). Cross-national consumer segmentation of Internet shopping for Britain and Taiwan. *The Service Industries Journal, 22*(1), 147–166.

Shon, J., & Musen, M. A. (1999). The low availability of metadata elements for evaluating the quality of medical knowledge on the world wide web. In *Proceedings of American Medical Informatics Association Symposium* (pp. 945-949).

Shouhong, W. (2005). Business software specifications for consumers: Toward a standard format. *Journal of Organizational and End User Computing, 17*(1), 23–37.

Shuptrine, K. (1977). Identifying innovative behavior patterns using canonical analysis. *Journal of Business Research, 5*(3), 249–259. doi:10.1016/0148-2963(77)90014-5

Sigala, M. (2006). Culture: The software of e-customer relationship management. *Journal of Marketing Communications, 12*(3), 203–223. doi:10.1080/13527260600811787

Silvera, D. H., & Austad, B. (2004). Factors predicting the effectiveness of celebrity endorsement advertisements. *European Journal of Marketing, 38*(11/12), 1509–1526. doi:10.1108/03090560410560218

Smelcer, J., & Carmel, E. (1997). The effectiveness of different representations for managerial problem solving: Comparing maps and tables. *Decision Sciences, 28*(2), 391–420.

Smith, D., Menon, S., & Sivakumar, K. (2005). Online peer and editorial recommendations, trust, and choice in virtual markets. *Journal of Interactive Marketing, 19*(3), 15–37. doi:10.1002/dir.20041

Somers, T.M., Nelson, K., & Karimi, J. (2003). Confirmatory factor analysis of the end-user computing satisfaction instrument: Replication within an ERP domain. *Decision Sciences, 34*(3), 595–621.

Song, J., Jones, D., & Gudigantala, N. (2007). The effects of incorporating compensatory choice strategies in Web-based consumer decision support systems. *Decision Support Systems, 43*, 359–374. doi:10.1016/j.dss.2006.10.007

Soutar, G., & Cornish-Ward, S. (1997). Consumer acquisition patterns for durable goods and financial assets: A Rasch analysis. *Applied Economics, 29*(7), 903–911. doi:10.1080/000368497326561

Soutar, G., Bell, R., & Wallis, Y. (1990). Consumer acquisition patterns for durable goods: A Rasch analysis. *Asia Pacific International Journal of Marketing, 2*(1), 31–39. doi:10.1108/eb010212

Spector, P. E., & Brannick, M. T. (1995). The nature and effects of method variance in organizational research. In C. L. Cooper & I. T. Robertson (Eds.), *International review of industrial and organizational psychology* (pp. 249-274). Chichester, United Kingdom: Wiley.

Spence, M.T., & Brucks, M. (1997). The moderating effects of problem characteristics on experts' and novices' judgments. *Journal of Marketing Research, 34*, 233–247.

Spender, J.C. (1996). Making knowledge the basis of a dynamic theory of the firm. *Strategic Management Journal, 17*, 45-62.

Spiegler, I. (2000). Knowledge management: A new idea or a recycled concept? *Communications of the AIS, 3*(4), 2-26.

Spinellis, D. (1998). The computer's new clothes. *IEEE Software, 15*(6), 14–17.

Stafford, T. F. (2001). Measuring consumer motivations to use marketspace. In *ICIS Diffusion Interest Group in Information Technology (DIGIT) Proceedings*. Retrieved from http://mis.uah.edu/sigadit/workshops/files/DIGIT_2001_Stafford.pdf

Stafford, T. F. (2003). Differentiating between innovators and laggards in the uses and gratifications for Internet services. *IEEE Transactions on Engineering Management, 50*, 427-435.

Stafford, T. F., & Stafford, M. R. (1998). Uses and gratifications of the World Wide Web: A preliminary study. In *Proceedings of the 1998 American Academy of Advertising Conference*, Pullman, WA.

Stafford, T. F., & Stafford, M. R. (2001). Identifying motivations for the use of commercial Web sites. *Information Resources Management Journal, 14*, 22-30.

Stafford, T. F., Stafford, M. R., & Schkade, L. L. (2004). Determining uses and gratifications for the Internet. *Decision Sciences, 35*, 259-288.

Standifird, S. S. (2001). Reputation and e-commerce: eBay auctions and the asymmetrical impact of positive and negative ratings. *Journal of Management, 27*(1), 279–295. doi:10.1016/S0149-2063(01)00092-7

Standifird, S. S., & Weinstein, M. (2007). The transaction cost economics of market-based exchange: The impact of reputation and external verification agencies. *International Journal of the Economics of Business, 14*(3), 409–431. doi:10.1080/13571510701597510

Steel, P., & König, C.J. (2006). Integrating theories of motivation. *Academy of Management Review, 31*(4), 889-913.

Steenkamp, J., Hostede, F., & Wedel, M. (1999). A cross-national investigation into the individual and national cultural antecedents of consumer innovativeness. *Journal of Marketing, 63*(2), 55–69. doi:10.2307/1251945

Steiger, J.H. (1990. Structural model evaluation and modification: An internal estimation approach. *Multivariate Behavioral Research, 25,* 173–190.

Stein, E. W., & Zwass, V. (1995). Actualizing organizational memory with information systems. *Information Systems Research, 6*, 85–117. doi:10.1287/isre.6.2.85

Steiner, I. D. (1972). *Group processes and productivity.* New York: Academic Press.

Stenmark, D., & Lindgren, R. (2004). Integrating knowledge management systems with everyday work: Design principles leveraging user practice. In *Proceedings of the 37th Annual Hawaii International Conference* (pp. 9-18).

Sternberg, R. (1999). *Cognitive psychology.* Orlando, FL: Harcourt Brace & Company.

Stiff, J. B., & Mongeau, P. A. (2003). *Persuasive communications.* New York: The Guilford Press.

Stough, S., Eom, S., & Buckenmyer, J. (2000). Virtual teaming: A strategy for moving your organization into the new millennium. *Industrial Management & Data Systems, 100*(8), 370–378. doi:10.1108/02635570010353857

Straub, D.W. (1989). Validating instruments in MIS research. *MIS Quarterly, 13*(2). 147–169.

Suchman, M.C. (1995). Managing legitimacy: Strategic and institutional approaches. *Academy of Management Review, 20,* 571–610.

Suh, E., Diener, E., & Fujita, F. (1996). Events and subjective well-being: Only recent events matter. *Journal of Personality and Social Psychology, 70*(5), 1091–1092. doi:10.1037/0022-3514.70.5.1091

Sujan, M. (1985). Consumer knowledge: Effects on evaluation strategies mediating consumer judgments. *The Journal of Consumer Research, 12*(1), 31–46. doi:10.1086/209033

Svenson, O. (1979). Process descriptions of decision making. *Organizational Behavior and Human Performance, 23*, 86–112. doi:10.1016/0030-5073(79)90048-5

Swanson, E.B. (1994). Information systems innovation among organizations. *Management Science, 40*(9), 1069–1092.

Swartz, N. (2003). The cost of Sarbanes-Oxley. *Information Management Journal, 37*(5), 8.

Szymanski, D.M., & Hise, R.T. (2000). e-Satisfaction: An initial examination. *Journal of Retailing, 76*(3), 309–322.

Tabachnick, B., & Fidell, L. (1996). *Using multivariate statistics* (3rd Edition). New York: Harper and Collins Publishers.

Tan, K.C. (2001). A structural equation model of new product design and development. *Decision Sciences, 32*(2), 195–226.

Tang, A., Owen, C., Biocca, F., & Mou, W. (2002). Comparative effectiveness of augmented reality in object assembly. In *Proceedings of ACM CHI 2002*, Darmstadt, Germany.

Taylor, P., Hyman, J., Mulvey, G., & Bain, P. (2002). Work organization, control and the experience of work in call centers. *Work, Employment and Society, 16*(1), 133–150. doi:10.1177/09500170222119281

Teo, H.H., Wei, K.K., & Benbasat, I. (2003). Predicting intention to adopt interorganizational linkages: An institutional perspective. *MIS Quarterly, 27*(1), 19–49.

Thatcher, J., Strite, M., Stepina, L., & Liu, Y. (2003). Culture, overload and personal innovativeness with information technology: Expanding the nomological net. *Journal of Information Systems*, *44*(1), 74–81.

The Associated Press. (2007). China to surpass U.S. Internet users. *MSNBC.com*. Retrieved January 24, 2007, from http://www.msnbc.msn.com/id/16785918/

Thompson, R.L., Higgins, C.A., & Howell, J.M. (1991, March). Personal computing: Toward a conceptual model of utilization. *MIS Quarterly,* 125-143.

Till, B. D., & Busler, M. (2000). The match-up hypothesis: Physical attractiveness, expertise and the role of fit on brand attitude, purchase intent and brand beliefs. *Journal of Advertising*, *29*(3), 1–14.

Tractinsky, N., & Jarvenpaa, S.L. (1995). Information systems design decisions in a global versus domestic context. *MIS Quarterly, 19*(4), 507–534.

Treadwell, T., Ashcraft, D., & Kumar, V. K. (2001). *A pedagogy for collaborative on-line research and learning: The CORAL Model*. Retrieved August 13, 2004 from http://coral.wcupa.edu/about/pedagogy.doc

Treadwell, T., Lavertue, N., Kumar, V.K., & Veeraghavan, V. (2001). The group cohesion scale-revisited: Reliability and validity. *Action Methods 3*.

Tsang, A., & Zhou, N. (2005). Newsgroup participants as *opinion* leaders and seekers in online and offline communication environments. *Journal of Business Research*, *58*(9), 1186–1193. doi:10.1016/j.jbusres.2004.05.002

Tsoukas, H. (2001). What is organizational knowledge? *Journal of Management Studies*, *38*(7), 973-993.

Tsoukas, H., & Vladimirou, E. (2001). What is organizational knowledge? *Journal of Management Studies*, *38*(7), 973. doi:10.1111/1467-6486.00268

Tuceryan, M., Greer, D. S., Whitaker, R. T., Breen, D., Crampton, C., Rose, E., et al. (1995). Calibration requirements and procedures for a monitor-based augmented reality system. *IEEE Transactions on Visualization and Computer Graphics, 1*(3), 255-273.

Tuckman, B. W., & Jensen, M. A. C. (1997). Stages of small group development revisited. *Group & Organizational Studies*, *2*, 419–427. doi:10.1177/105960117700200404

Turban, E., Lee, J., King, D., & Chung, H. M. (2000). *Electronic commerce: A managerial perspective*. Upper Saddle River, NJ: Prentice Hall.

U.S. Census Bureau newsroom. (2005, July 6). Retrieved from http://www.census.gov/PressRelease/www/releases/archives/facts_for_features/001643.html

U.S. Census Bureau. (2001). *Unadjusted and adjusted estimates of monthly retail and food service sales by kinds of business*.

U.S. Federal Election Commission. (2004, September 13). Retrieved from http://www.fec.gov/pages/vssfinal/vss_implementation.html

U.S. home broadband penetration. (2004). *Broadband Business Report, 14*, 1.

van der Heijden, H. (2004). User acceptance of hedonic information systems. *MIS Quarterly, 28*(4), 695–704.

Van der Linden, D., Frese, M., & Sonnentag, S. (2003). The impact of mental fatigue on exploration in a complex computer task: Rigidity and loss of systematic strategies. *Human Factors . The Journal of the Human Factors and Ergonomics Society*, *45*, 483–494. doi:10.1518/hfes.45.3.483.27256

Van Scotter, J. R., & Motowidlo, S. J. (1996). Interpersonal facilitation and job dedication as separate facets of contextual performance. *The Journal of Applied Psychology*, *81*, 525–531. doi:10.1037/0021-9010.81.5.525

Vazey, M. (2007). *Case-driven collaborative classification*. Unpublished doctoral thesis, Macquarie University, Sydney, NSW.

Vazey, M., & Richards, D. (2004, August 9-13). Achieving rapid knowledge acquisition. In *Proc. Pacific Knowledge Acquisition W/shop (PKAW 2004)* (pp. 74-86). Auckland, New Zealand.

Vazey, M., & Richards, D. (2006, August 7-11). Evaluation of the FastFIX prototypes 5Cs CARD System. In

Proc. Pacific Knowledge Acquisition Workshop (PKAW 2004) (LNAI 4303, pp. 106-117). Guilin, China.

Venkatesh, V., & Davis, F. D. (2000). A theoretical extension of the technology acceptance model: Four longitudinal field studies. *Management Science, 46*, 86-204.

Venkatesh, V., & Morris, M. (2000). Why don't men ever stop to ask for directions? Gender, social influence, and their role in technology acceptance and usage behavior. *MIS Quarterly, 24*, 115–139. doi:10.2307/3250981

Venkatesh, V., Morris, M. G., & Ackerman, P. L. (2000). A longitudinal field investigation of gender differences individual technology adoption decision-making processes. *Organizational Behavior and Human Decision Processes, 83*(1), 33-60.

Venkatraman, M., & Price, L. (1990). Differentiating between cognitive and sensory innovativeness. *Journal of Business Research, 20*(4), 293–315. doi:10.1016/0148-2963(90)90008-2

Vessey, I. (1994). The effect of information presentation on decision making: A cost-benefit analysis. *Information & Management, 27*(2), 103–119.

Violino, B. (1998). ROI in the real world. *Information Week, 679*, 60–72.

Vishwanath, A. (2005). Impact of personality on technology adoption: An empirical model. *Journal of the American Society for Information Science and Technology, 58*(8), 803–811. doi:10.1002/asi.20169

Vlahakis, V., Ioannidis, N., Karigiannis, J., Tsotros, M., Gounaris, M., Stricker, D., et al. (2002). Archeoguide: An augmented reality guide for archaeological sites. *IEEE Computer Graphics and Applications, 22*(5), 38-50.

Von Krogh, G. (2002). The communal resource and information systems. *Journal of Strategic Information Systems, 11*(2), 85-107.

Von Krogh, G., Nonaka, I., & Aben, M. (2001). Making the most of your company's knowledge: A strategic framework. *Long Range Planning, 34*(4), 421-439.

Wakefield, R. L., & Whitten, D. (2006). Examining end-user perceptions of third-party organization credibility and trust in an e-retailer. *Journal of Organizational and End User Computing, 18*(2), 1–19.

Walsham, G. (1995). Interpretive case studies in IS research: Nature and method. *European Journal of Information Systems, 4*(2), 74-81.

Walsham, G. (1995).The emergence of interpretivism in IS research. *Information Systems Research, 6*(4), 376-394.

Walsham, G. (2001). Knowledge management: The benefits and limitations of computer Systems. *European Management Journal, 19*(6), 599-608.

Wang, E., Klein, G., & Jiang, J. J. (2007). IT support in manufacturing firms for a knowledge management dynamic capability link to performance. *International Journal of Production Research, 45*, 2419–2434. doi:10.1080/00207540601020437

Wang, R. Y., & Strong, D. M. (1996). Beyond accuracy: What data quality means to data consumers. *Journal of Management Information Systems, 12*, 5–34.

Wang, W., & Benbasat, I. (2008). Attributions of trust in decision support technologies: A study of recommendation agents for e-commerce. *Journal of Management Information Systems, 24*(4), 249–273. doi:10.2753/MIS0742-1222240410

Wang, Y., Lo, H.-P., & Yang, Y. (2004). An integrated framework for service quality, customer value, satisfaction: Evidence from China's telecommunication industry. *Information Systems Frontiers, 6*(4), 325–340.

Wang, Y.-S., & Tang, T.-I. (2004). A validation of the customer information satisfaction instrument for digital market context. *International Journal of Electronic Business, 2*(6), 567–582.

Wathen, C. N., & Burkell, J. (2002). Believe it or not: factors influencing credibility on the web. *Journal of the American Society for Knowledge Science and Technology, 53*, 134–144. doi:10.1002/asi.10016

Watson, A., & Cordonnier, V. (2001). *Information technology improves most of the democratic voting processes.* Retrieved from http://ieeexplore.ieee.org/

iel5/7561/20604/00953092.pdf?tp=&arnumber=953092&isnumber=20604

Watson, D., & Clark, L. (1992). Affect, personality, and social activity. *Journal of Personality and Social Psychology, 63*(6), 1011. doi:10.1037/0022-3514.63.6.1011

Watson, D., & Tellegen, A. (1999). The two general activation systems of affect: Structural findings, evolutionary considerations, and psychobiological evidence. *Journal of Personality and Social Psychology, 76*(5), 820–839. doi:10.1037/0022-3514.76.5.820

Wech, B., Mossholder, K., Steel, R., & Bennett, N. (1998). Does work group cohesiveness affect individuals? *Small Group Research, 29*(4), 472. doi:10.1177/1046496498294004

Weill, P., & Ross, J. (2005). A matrixed approach to designing IT governance. *MIT Sloan Management Review, 46*(2), 26–34.

Weiser, E. B. (2001). The functions of Internet use and their social and psychological consequence. *CyberPsychology & Behavior, 4*, 723-743.

Weiss, A. (2001). Click to vote. *Association for Computing Machinery: NetWorker, 5*(1), 18-24.

Wenger, E.C., & Snyder, W.M. (2000). Communities of practice: The organizational frontier. *Harvard Business Review, 78*(1), 139-145.

Wenhong, L., & Cook, D. P. (2007/2008). An empirical study of trust of third party rating services. *Journal of Computer Information Systems, 48*(2), 66–73.

Wheaton, B., Mutchen, B., Alwin, D.F., & Summers, G.F. (1977). Assessing reliability and stability in panel models. In D.R. Heise (Ed.), *Assessing reliability and stability in panel models* (pp. 84–136). San Francisco: Jossey-Bass.

White, R. W., Jose, J. M., & Ruthven, I. (2006). An implicit feedback approach for interactive information retrieval. *Information Processing & Management, 42*, 166–190. doi:10.1016/j.ipm.2004.08.010

Whitten, J. L., Bentley, L. D., & Dittman, K. C. (2000). Systems analysis and design methods. Boston, MA: McGraw-Hill Higher Education.

Wijnhoven, F. (1999). Development scenarios for organizational memory information systems. *Journal of Management Information Systems, 16*(1), 121-146.

Wijnhoven, F. (2003). Operation knowledge management: Identification of knowledge objects, operation methods and goals and means for the support function. *The Journal of the Operational Research Society, 54*(2), 194-202.

Wilkins, A.L., & Dyer Jr., W.B. (1988). Toward culturally sensitive theories of culture change. *Academy of Management Review, 13*(4), 522-533.

Willcocks, L., & Lester, S. (1991). Information systems investments: Evaluation of the feasibility stage of projects. *Technovation, 11*, 283–302. doi:10.1016/0166-4972(91)90027-2

Wolfinbarger, M., & Gilly, M. (2003). eTailQ: Dimensionalizing, measuring and predicting retail quality. *Journal of Retailing, 79*(3), 183–198.

Wonnacott, T.H., & Wonnacott, R.J. (1984). *Introductory statistics for business & economics.* New York: John Wiley & Sons.

Woo, K.-s., & Ennew, C.T. (2005). Measuring business-to-business professional service quality and its consequences. *Journal of Business Research, 58*, 1178–1185.

Wood, D., Kumar, V., Treadwell, T., & Leach, E. (1998). Perceived cohesiveness and sociometric choice in ongoing groups. *The International Journal of Action Methods, 51*(3), 122.

Woodrow, J. E. (1991). A comparison of four computer attitude scales. *Journal of Educational Computing Research, 7*(2), 165–187.

Wright, B. (1977). Solving measurement problems with the Rasch Model. *Journal of Educational Measurement, 14*(1), 97–116. doi:10.1111/j.1745-3984.1977.tb00031.x

Wu, J. H., & Wang, Y. M. (2006). Measuring KMS success: A respecification of the DeLone and McLean's model. *Information & Management, 43*, 728–739. doi:10.1016/j.im.2006.05.002

Xiao, B., & Benbasat, I. (2007). E-commerce product recommendation agents: Use, characteristics and impact. *MIS Quarterly, 31*(1), 137–209.

Xue, F., & Phelps, J. E. (2004). Internet-facilitated consumer-to-consumer communication: The moderating role of receiver characteristics. *International Journal of Internet Marketing and Advertising, 1*(2), 121–136. doi:10.1504/IJIMA.2004.004016

Yalom, I., & Rand, K. H. (1966). Compatibility and cohesiveness in therapy groups. *Archives of Gen. Psych, 15*, 267–275.

Yang, K. W., & Huh, S. Y. (2007). Intelligent search for experts using fuzzy abstraction hierarchy in knowledge management systems. *Journal of Database Management, 18*, 47–68.

Yang, X., Ahmed, Z.U., Ghingold, M., Boon, G.S., Mei, T.S., & Hwa, L.L. (2003). Consumer preferences for commercial Web site design: An Asia-Pacific perspective. *Journal of Consumer Marketing, 20*(1), 10–27.

Yang, Z., & Fang, X. (2004). Online service quality dimensions and their relationships with satisfaction: A content analysis of customer reviews of securities brokerage services. *International Journal of Service Industry Management, 15*(3/4), 302–326.

Yaniv, I. (2004). Receiving other people's advice: Influence and benefit. *Organizational Behavior and Human Decision Processes, 93*(1), 1–14. doi:10.1016/j.obhdp.2003.08.002

Yin, R.K. (1989). *Case study research: Design and methods* (revised ed.). Newbury Park, CA: Sage.

Zaccaro, S. J., & Lowe, C. A. (1988). Cohesiveness and performance on an additive task: Evidence for multidimensionality. *The Journal of Social Psychology, 128*, 547–558.

Zack, M.H. (1999). Developing a knowledge strategy. *California Management Review, 41*(3), 125-145.

Zeithaml, V., & Gilly, M. (1987). Characteristics affecting the acceptance of retailing technologies: A comparison of elderly and Non-elderly consumers. *Journal of Retailing, 63*(1), 49–68.

Zhang, P., & Dillon, A. (2003). HCI and MIS: Shared concerns. *International Journal of Human-Computer Studies, 59*, 397–402. doi:10.1016/S1071-5819(03)00109-5

Zhang, P., & von Dran, G.M. (2000). Satisfiers and dissatisfiers: A two-factor model for Website design and evaluation. *Journal of the American Society for Information Science, 51*(4), 1253–1268.

Zhang, S., Zhao, J., & Tan, W. (2008). Extending TAM for online learning systems: An intrinsic motivation perspective. *Tsinghua Science and Technology, 13*(3), 312–317. doi:10.1016/S1007-0214(08)70050-6

Zhao, X., Fang, F., & Whinston, A. B. (2006). Designing on-line mediation services for c2c markets. *International Journal of Electronic Commerce, 10*(3), 71–93. doi:10.2753/JEC1086-4415100303

Zhou, M., Dresner, M., & Windle, R. J. (2008). Online reputation systems: Design and strategic practices. *Decision Support Systems, 44*(4), 785–797. doi:10.1016/j.dss.2007.10.001

Zhu, W., Owen, C. B., Li, H., & Lee, J.-H. (2004). Personalized in-store e-commerce with the PromoPad: An augmented reality shopping assistant. *The Electronic Journal for E-Commerce Tools & Applications, 1*(3).

Zimmer, J. C., Henry, R. M., & Butler, B. S. (2007/2008). Determinants of the use of relational and nonrelational information sources. *Journal of Management Information Systems, 24*, 297–331. doi:10.2753/MIS0742-1222240310

Zokai, S., Esteve, J., Genc, Y., & Navab, N. (2003). Multiview paraperspective projection model for diminished reality. In *The Second IEEE and ACM International Symposium on Mixed and Augmented Reality (ISMAR '03)*, Tokyo.

Zucker, L. (1987). Institutional theories of organization. *Annual Review of Sociology, 13*, 443–464.

Zuckerman, A., & Chaiken, S. (1998). A heuristic-systematic processing analysis of the effectiveness of product warning labels. *Psychology and Marketing, 15*, 621–641. doi:10.1002/(SICI)1520-6793(199810)15:7<621::AID-MAR2>3.0.CO;2-H

Zviran, M., Glezer, C., & Avni, I. (2006). User satisfaction from commercial Web sites: The effect of design and use. *Information & Management, 43*(2), 157–178.

About the Contributors

Steve Clarke received a BSc in Economics from The University of Kingston Upon Hull, an MBA from the Putteridge Bury Management Centre, The University of Luton, and a PhD in human centred approaches to information systems development from Brunel University – all in the United Kingdom. He is Professor of Information Systems in the University of Hull Business School. Steve has extensive experience in management systems and information systems consultancy and research, focusing primarily on the identification and satisfaction of user needs and issues connected with knowledge management. His research interests include: social theory and information systems practice; strategic planning; and the impact of user involvement in the development of management systems. Major current research is focused on approaches informed by critical social theory.

* * *

Summer E. Bartczak is an assistant professor in the MIS Department in the College of Business at the University of Central Arkansas. She received her Ph.D. in Management Information Systems from Auburn University. She is a twenty-two year veteran of the United States Air Force and most recently taught in the Department of Engineering and Systems Management at the Air Force Institute of Technology. Published in several journals, her current research interests include information/information technology (IT) management, knowledge management (KM) and KM systems, IT/KM workforce issues, and IT/KM innovation, and organizational change.

James P. Downey is an assistant professor in the MIS Department in the College of Business at the University of Central Arkansas. He received his Ph.D. in Management Information Systems at Auburn University. He spent 25 years as an active duty Naval officer, including a tour at the U.S. Naval Academy, before leaving the Navy in November 2004. He has been published in many journals. His current research interests include human-computer interaction, project management, database management and data mining, and individual differences in the behavior of computing users.

D. Scott Hunsinger is an Assistant Professor in the Department of Computer Information Systems in the Walker College of Business. Before joining ASU, Scott served as Dean of Academic Affairs and Information Technology (2001-2004), System Administrator (1996-2000), and Instructor (1996-2004) at NCCATT, an institution in the NC Community College System. Scott has also taught in the Belk College of Business at UNC Charlotte and has worked for Microsoft Corporation and SouthTrust Bank. Scott is currently serving as a reviewer for the International Journal on Computers, Systems, and Signals, International Journal of Electronic Marketing and Retailing, Journal of Information Science and Technology, and for the ICIS, HICSS, ISECON, and San Diego International Systems conferences.

Michael B Knight is an assistant professor of professional programs in business at UWGB. Before joining UWGB, Michael held positions with Appalachian State University (2005-2008) as an Assistant Professor of Computer Information Systems and with Southern Illinois University (2001-2005) as instructor of Management and Information Systems. His current research interests include group dynamics and strategic IT adoption, end-user education & training, the use of IT for organizational/group communication, and qualitative managerial consulting. His work has been presented at conferences such as IRMA, AOM, AMCIS, and DSI; and can be found in the Journal of Organizational and End User Computing, and the Journal of Organizational Behavior. He has also received awards for teacher of the year 2004-2005, 2005-2006 and has been listed in the Who's Who of American Teachers twice (2003 & 2004). Michael is currently serving as a reviewer for the Journal of Organizational and End User Computing, Journal of Computer Information Systems, and for the IRMA, AMCIS, DSI and HICSS conferences as well as Co-chair of social issues in information technology for HICSS.

Robin S. Poston is a Systems Testing Research Fellow for the FedEx Institute of Technology at The University of Memphis and Assistant Professor of Management Information Systems at the Fogelman College of Business & Economics at The University of Memphis. She received her Ph.D. from Michigan State University. Dr. Poston's research focuses on understanding how individuals use credibility information in decision support systems, web-based knowledge management applications, recommender and feedback systems, internet-based dissemination of information, and systems testing management. She has published articles in publications such as MIS Quarterly, Decision Sciences, Communications of the ACM, Information Systems Management, Journal of Organizational and End User Computing, Journal of Information Systems, International Journal of Accounting Information Systems, and in major international conference proceedings. In 2007, she was awarded the Distinguished Teaching Award from The University of Memphis Alumni Association recognizing her excellence in teaching and has also won college research awards.

J. Michael Pearson is an Associate Professor of Information Systems at Southern Illinois University at Carbondale. Dr. Pearson currently serves as the editor for the Journal of Internet Commerce. Dr. Pearson has published over forty articles in journals such as the Communications of the ACM, Information & Management, Journal of Strategic Information Systems, Journal of Information Systems, Journal of Computer Information Systems, Decision Support Systems, Review of Business, Information Resources Management Journal and Public Administration Quarterly. His research interests are in the areas of technology adoption, e-commerce, management of quality, and IT project management.

R. Kelly Rainer, Jr. is the George Phillips Privett Professor in the Department of Management in the College of Business at Auburn University. He received his Ph.D. in MIS from the University of Georgia. He is a former Army officer and practicing dentist. The author of numerous articles and books, his current research interests are information security, psychometrics, and end user computing.

Debbie Richards is an Associate Professor in the Computing Department at Macquarie University. She joined academia after 20 years in industry resulting in a focus on research which can deliver practical outcomes and improvements often involving techniques from Artificial Intelligence and drawing on work in psychology and cognitive science. Her teaching covers software engineering; requirements, analysis and design, project and team management and object oriented programming. She enjoys running the capstone units for the department's degrees aimed at preparing graduates for their future careers in ICT. Research into collaborative learning, teaching and working draws her teaching and research interests together.

Marla B. Royne is professor and chair of the Department of Marketing & Supply Chain Management at the University of Memphis. She received her Ph.D. from the University of Georgia. Dr. Royne is currently the editor of the Journal of Advertising and is member of the Editorial Review Board for the Journal of the Academy of Marketing Science, the Journal of Current Issues & Research in Advertising, the Journal of Interactive Advertising and Marketing Theory. Her research has been published in such journals as Decision Sciences, International Journal of Production Economics, Journal of Retailing, Journal of Advertising, Journal of Advertising Research, Journal of Current Issues & Research in Advertising, Journal of Business Research and other publications. In 2005, she was named a Suzanne Downs Palmer Professor of Research in the Fogelman College of Business & Economics.

Cheri Speier is a Professor of Information Systems and Associate Dean for MBA/MS Programs at the Broad College of Business, Michigan State University. She received her Ph.D. from Indiana University in 1996 and has published articles in a breadth of disciplines including journals such as MIS Quarterly, Decision Sciences, Organizational Behavior and Human Decision Processes, Journal of Marketing, International Journal of Human and Computer Studies. Dr. Speier's research interests include the influence of work environments on decision making, acceptance and use of technology, and the effective use of information technology to support supply chain relationships. She is an Associate Editor at MIS Quarterly, Decision Sciences and IEEE and has been a member of research teams receiving funding from NSF and the Department of Homeland Security. Dr. Speier was awarded the MSU Teacher-Scholar award recognizing her excellence in teaching and research and has also won departmental research and teaching awards.

Geoff Soutar is a professor in marketing at the University of Western Australia. Professor Soutar has acted as consultant to a large number of private and public sector organisations in Australia and internationally and has been active in research across a wide area, publishing over 100 papers in journals across a wide range of management areas and presenting over 2000 papers at seminars and conferences. His present research interests include the marketing of services, especially educational services, the marketing of technology, the role of design in marketing, service quality measurement and management, marketing's role in the public sector, agribusiness marketing, union and organisational commitment, employees' technology experiences and the impact of technology on work attitudes and the impact of perceived export barriers on organisations' willingness to export. Geoff was made a Fellow of the Australian Marketing Institute in 1985, a life member of the Market Research Society in 1989, a Fellow of the Australian Institute of Management in 1994, a Fellow of the Marketing Institute of Singapore in 1996, an honorary Fellow of the Professional Sales and Marketing Institute in 1995 and a Fellow of the Australian and New Zealand Academy of Management in 1998 for his contributions to management, marketing, marketing research and education in Australia and the region. In 2008 Geoff was awarded the title of distinguished Fellow of the Australian New Zealand Academy of Marketing.

Steve Ward is a senior lecturer in marketing at Murdoch University. He has published46 refereed papers in leading international journals (including the The European Journal of Marketing, International Marketing Review, Journal of Marketing Theory and Practice andApplied Economics) books, and conferences. Steve has also worked as a market research consultant for bluechip companies such as Pacific-Dunlop, ANZ, Challenge Bank, BHP, Telstra, and Ford. His research interests include the effect of country-of-origin information on consumer judgements and choice; the development of consumer knowledge by children; consumer durable purchasing behaviour; service quality; marketing strategy and the environment; diffusion of innovations; marketing of pharmaceuticals and body image; global branding; wine marketing; and privacy research.

Index

I

K

L

M

N

O

P

Q

R

S

T

U